Postwar Japan
as History

EDITED BY
ANDREW GORDON

UNIVERSITY OF CALIFORNIA PRESS
Berkeley   Los Angeles   Oxford

University of California Press
Berkeley and Los Angeles, California

University of California Press, Ltd.
Oxford, England

© 1993 by
The Regents of the University of California

Library of Congress Cataloging-in-Publication Data

Postwar Japan as history / edited by Andrew Gordon.
    p. cm.
    Includes bibliographical references (p.) and index.
    ISBN 0-520-07474-2 (cloth : alk. paper). — ISBN 0-520-07475-0
(paper : alk. paper)
    1. Japan—History—1945-   I. Gordon, Andrew, 1952-   .
DS889.P63 1992
952.04—dc20   91-35737

Printed in the United States of America
9 8 7 6 5 4 3

CONTENTS

PART III • MASS CULTURE AND METROPOLITAN SOCIETY

PART IV • DEMOCRATIC PROMISE AND PRACTICE

Photographs follow page 216

ACKNOWLEDGMENTS

This project originated in a planning workshop in the spring of 1987 at Duke University. Participating were John Dower, Miles Fletcher, Sheldon Garon, Carol Gluck, Andrew Gordon, and Margaret McKean. This group organized a larger conference in April 1988 at which the contributors to this volume presented preliminary versions of the essays which follow. We then revised our essays and reconvened to discuss them in October 1989 at the University of California, San Diego. The composition of the group changed slightly over this span. At the 1988 meeting Don Roden presented a paper on gender roles and identity, but unfortunately he was unable to participate subsequently. Soon after the 1988 meeting the editor asked Sandra Buckley to contribute an essay on women in postwar history, and he invited Kathleen Uno to add her essay in the spring of 1990. Throughout the process the editor and organizers asked contributors to draw on their own research yet stretch beyond the bounds of their specialized expertise to offer broad interpretations. The responses naturally varied in the balance between monographic and "synthetic" inquiry, but all contributors speak to relatively broad issues in postwar history.

We are grateful to have had financial support from a wide variety of organizations. The conferences at Duke in 1987 and 1988 were funded by the Asian/Pacific Studies Institute, the Trent Foundation, and the Center for International Studies, all at Duke, as well as by the North Carolina Japan Center and the Social Science Research Council. The 1989 gathering at the University of California, San Diego, was supported by grants from the Japan Foundation and Social Science Research Council. Mavis Mayer and Gail Woods at Duke and Marta Vanlandingham at UCSD deserve special thanks for their energetic, effective administrative support. Miles Fletcher joined me in the earliest stages of the project as a co-organizer of the first planning workshop; he and Margaret McKean participated in both subsequent meetings as discussants and organizers. I want to thank them for their important role in conceiving this project and moving it forward.

INTRODUCTION

Andrew Gordon

The distance between 1945 and the present day, measured simply in years, now exceeds that between the turn of the century and the end of World War II. Yet for understandable reasons historians have ventured few systematic analyses of the postwar years. Perhaps most important, the absence of a "natural" boundary such as a revolution or a catastrophic war makes us slow to map the terrain of the recent past. In the late 1980s a belief that the time had come to attempt such analysis prompted the series of conferences that resulted in this book.

On a conceptual level the contributors shared a belief that the postwar era in some sense had ended as Japan became a dominant global economic power in the 1980s, although we recognized the difficulty of defining the condition called "postwar" Japan or declaring it to have ended. As early as 1955, as recently as 1990, and numerous times in between, Japan's postwar era has been deemed "finished," yet in this volume Bruce Cumings argues that Japan's subordinate position in a postwar international system had not ended even by 1990. One goal of this book is thus to clarify the varied senses in which people have defined the postwar era and marked its boundaries.

Our sense of urgency also stemmed in part from a practical motive. In teaching courses on modern Japanese history, society, and politics we were frustrated by the lack of historically focused English-language studies of the postwar decades for use in the classroom. Thus, we have sought to produce a coherent set of interpretive essays for students of modern Japan.

The essays in this book have two other major goals, reviewed in more detail in the conclusion. One is to delineate several contexts for consideration of postwar history. The volume seeks to place the history of postwar Japan in broader historical, international, and comparative contexts. We wish to locate the postwar experience in the broad sweep of the twentieth century, identifying longer trends that have shaped postwar changes, so most essays begin with consideration of the prewar and wartime years. We wish to place Japan in a global context of America's shifting but enduring hegemony, and a number of essays address this matter directly. Further, we have sought to compare Japan's postwar experience with those of the advanced capitalist societies of the West.

The second major goal is to explore three related themes of postwar history. First, in thinking of postwar Japan in historical terms we sought to understand the contingent, contested dimensions of the experience of the past five decades. At key historical moments advocates of alternative political programs or social ideologies came into sharp conflict. We wish to understand the process by which, and the context in which, some prevailed and others did not. In doing so, we hope to move beyond views of the era from 1945 to 1990 as a mere prelude to a fixed "present" or as an inevitable unfolding that justifies the present. We focus instead on an ongoing historical process marked by dramatic unexpected changes, such as Japan's extraordinary economic growth, as well as unanticipated continuities, such as the endurance of conservative rule.

Second, and closely related, is our effort to comprehend the conservative political and cultural hegemony of the postwar era. This hegemony was challenged and reformulated over the postwar decades, but it was not replaced or fundamentally disrupted. The third theme is the matter of "difference" in postwar Japan, which we approach from two directions. On the one hand, we describe the considerable extent to which the postwar decades have been characterized by heterogeneity of experience, of values, and of group interest. On the other hand, these essays describe the emergence and reproduction of a powerful ideology (and related policies) that denied difference and presented Japan as a harmonious, "middle-class" society.

From the start the contributors recognized a tension arising from our simultaneous pursuit of two potentially conflicting goals. We hoped our essays would serve as a text for study of the history of postwar Japan, but we wanted them to be broadly interpretive. We have dealt with this tension by promoting our interpretive goals at the expense of our "textbook" aspirations. That is, although we offer some balance and breadth in our coverage, our treatment is far from comprehensive, yet in some cases a single topic is treated from varied perspectives. We have tried to avoid the authoritative stance of a textbook. We explore an emerging field of study, identify points of controversy, try to make our own positions clear, and invite further debate.

Thus, readers will have to turn elsewhere for discussion of certain issues. In particular, this book devotes relatively little attention to three important topics: religion, education, and rural society. Sheldon Garon and Mike Mochizuki originally intended to study the relation of the New Religions and the state in their essay on social contracts but had to abandon this plan for reasons of time and space.[1] William W. Kelly and Sandra Buckley focus on education in relation to

1. The works of Helen Hardacre, *Kurozumikyo and the New Religions of Japan* (Princeton: Princeton University Press, 1986), and *Shinto and the State, 1868–1988* (Princeton: Princeton University Press, 1989), and James W. White, *The Soka Gakkai and Mass Society* (Stanford: Stanford University Press, 1970), offer points of entry for the study of religion in postwar Japan.

the lifeways of the middle class and the reproduction of gender role divisions, respectively, but the book does not treat education in postwar Japan in a separate chapter.[2] Kelly's essay also offers insight into the process by which rural Japan has been incorporated into what he calls a "metropolitan" culture in the postwar decades, but we do not present a sustained analysis of rural Japan.[3]

The volume begins with three essays that lay out a broad context for consideration of postwar history. John Dower analyzes the intimate ties between Japan's international and domestic politics as "central to the Japanese experience" of the postwar era. His broadly focused inquiry introduces a number of topics treated at length in other essays. Bruce Cumings then discusses Japan's position in the postwar world system, giving particular attention to the formative years of 1947–50. While recognizing the significant adjustments in Japan's position in the early 1970s and again in 1989–90, he stresses the basic continuity in Japan's position over the forty years from 1950 to the time of his writing. Carol Gluck analyzes how people in Japan have interpreted their own history during the postwar era. She both sheds light on the ideological diversity and contention that has characterized postwar Japan and sets forth a context of debate among Japanese historians in which readers can locate the essays to follow.

Japan's political economy is the subject of the next four essays. These essays are concerned principally with the nature of elite rule, the relations of the state with various social groups, and the costs of economic growth. Thus, they do not describe in depth the extraordinary growth of the economy or try to explain it. These subjects have been analyzed at length in numerous books and articles. The authors focus instead on how economic policies evolved. Laura Hein interprets key debates over economic policy, examining in particular how economic growth itself came to be inscribed as the primary measure of economic success in the postwar era. Gary Allinson then studies the nation's bureaucratic and business elites and describes the transformation of conservative rule across the postwar years. Both he and Sheldon Garon and Mike Mochizuki analyze the emergence of a pattern in which bureaucratic and political party elites negotiated with a variety of social interests. Garon and Mochizuki trace the evolution of "social contracts" between the state and both labor unions and small-business interests between the 1950s and 1980s. Koji Taira concludes this section with his interpre-

2. For more on education, see William Cummings, *Education and Equality in Japan* (Princeton: Princeton University Press, 1980); Thomas Rohlen, *Japan's High Schools* (Berkeley and Los Angeles: University of California Press, 1983); and Merry White, *The Japanese Educational Challenge: A Commitment to Children* (New York: Free Press, 1987). See also the translated work of an important Japanese critic of postwar education, Teruhisa Horio, *Educational Thought and Ideology in Modern Japan: State Authority and Intellectual Freedom* (Tokyo: Tokyo University Press, 1986).

3. For historical treatment of the Japanese countryside, see two books that examine the contrast between rural Japan of the 1950s and 1970s: Robert Smith, *Kurusu: The Price of Progress in a Japanese Village* (Stanford: Stanford University Press, 1978); and Ronald P. Dore, *Shinohata* (New York: Pantheon, 1980). See also Teruoka Shuzo, "Land Reform and Postwar Japanese Capitalism," in *Japanese Capitalism since 1945: Critical Perspectives*, ed. T. Morris-Suzuki and T. Sekiyama (Armonk, N.Y.: M. E. Sharpe, 1989).

tation of the "dialectics" of growth, state power, and distributive struggles. He describes the late 1960s and early 1970s as a time when a new "synthesis" enabled the conservative leadership to remain in control for the next twenty years.

Transformations and continuities in mass culture and society are the concern of the four essays in part 3. A variety of dramatic social changes unfolded over the postwar years. Education levels rose dramatically, the proportion of the population employed in agriculture fell sharply (from 45 percent in the 1940s to 8 percent by the mid-1980s), and levels of consumption increased tremendously. Despite such trends, which increased the realm of shared experience among Japanese people, the much-noted phenomenon of Japanese "homogeneity" was most salient at the level of ideology and rhetoric. William Kelly examines the diminution of some areas of difference (for example, working-class versus middle-class society, rural versus urban society) and the emergence of others. He identifies this process as a central social dynamic of postwar history and calls it the "transposition" of difference. Marilyn Ivy and Charles Horioka then offer two perspectives on the mass, consumer society that evolved in the postwar years. Ivy examines the nature of "cultural" production and consumption in postwar Japan, showing how the "mass culture" industry managed entertainment and advertising, exerting tremendous impact on the way Japanese imagined themselves and the world. Horioka analyzes changing patterns of material consumption over these same years. Kathleen S. Uno concludes this section with an essay on the shifting but durable ideology of the "good wife and wise mother." She shows how not only conservative male elites but also a broad range of women have understood or presented their role in terms of this ideology.

The final set of essays concerns the nature of democracy in postwar Japan. These essays recognize that democratic institutions, such as an elected, legally responsible parliament and a constitution that established popular sovereignty, have been in place since 1947. They address the more problematic matter of the ways in which democracy in practice has served Japanese citizens. Frank Upham explores the movements for social justice of outcastes (*Burakumin*), women, and pollution victims and analyzes how the bureaucracy and legal system have dealt with these challenges. Sandra Buckley looks in depth at the constraints on women in realms of work, reproduction, education, and politics. Andrew Gordon studies the relations of organized workers and managers primarily in large enterprises. J. Victor Koschmann traces the shifting stance of intellectuals as critics of the status quo. And James White touches on many of these groups by analyzing the broadly defined phenomenon of opposition movements. The Conclusion then reviews the book's objectives and returns to discuss the themes set out in the Introduction.

PART I

Contexts

CHAPTER ONE

Peace and Democracy in Two Systems

External Policy and Internal Conflict

John W. Dower

Ever since Japan's seclusion was ruptured by the Western nations in 1853, domestic and international politics have been interwoven for the Japanese. Slogans used to mobilize succeeding generations convey this interconnection. Thus, the forces that eventually overthrew the feudal regime in 1868 rallied around the cry "Revere the Emperor and Expel the Barbarians." The Meiji government (1868–1912) socialized citizens for Westernization, industrialization, and empire building under the slogan "Rich Country, Strong Military." Militant expansionists of the 1930s and early 1940s, equally concerned with renovation at home and autarky abroad, paired creation of a domestic "New Structure" with establishment of a "New Order" overseas. They saw the solution to domestic ills in the creation of a broader imperium in Asia, which they glossed with the rhetoric of "Coexistence and Coprosperity."

Although Japan ostensibly pursued a low posture diplomatically after World War II, the intimate relationship between international and domestic politics remained central. Again, catchphrases capture this. Immediately after the war, exhausted Japanese were rallied—and frequently inspired—by an idealistic agenda of "Demilitarization and Democratization." From the outset these ideals were recognized to be inseparable: destruction of the militarized state was essential to democratize Japan, and only the creation of a genuinely democratic nation could prevent the danger of future Japanese militarism. Once formal demilitarization had been accomplished, the enduring goal became to create and maintain "Peace and Democracy." Even exhortations such as the popular postsurrender slogan "Construction of a Nation of Culture" (*Bunka Kokka no Kensetsu*) were understood to be synonymous with the paired ideals of peace and democracy. For example, when Prime Minister Katayama Tetsu addressed the first Diet session held under the new postwar constitution in 1947, he concluded with an appeal to advance toward "the construction of a democratic nation of peace, a nation of culture" (*minshuteki na heiwa kokka, bunka kokka no kensetsu*).[1]

These key terms—*democracy, peace,* and *culture*—were subject to reinterpretation in the years that followed, and *culture,* by and large, was uncoupled from the other two. Throughout the postwar period, however, a large portion of political policy and contention continued to be contained, like a crackling electric current, within the polemical poles of *peace* and *democracy.* These are not rhetorical ideals peculiar to Japan, but they assumed a particular vitality there. *Peace* became the magnetic pole for both legitimization and criticism of external policy; *democracy* served the same function for highly contested domestic issues. And postwar controversies over military and international policy almost invariably became entangled with internal struggles concerning power, participation, national priorities, and competing visions of fairness, well-being, and social justice.

Where the actual structures of postwar power are concerned, two additional and uniquely Japanese phrases command attention. One is the "San Francisco System," which refers to the international posture Japan assumed formally when it signed a peace treaty with forty-eight nations in San Francisco in September 1951 and simultaneously aligned itself with the cold-war policy of the United States through the bilateral Treaty of Mutual Cooperation and Security. To the end of the Shōwa period, which effectively symbolized the end of the "postwar" era for Japan, the country continued to operate within the strategic parameters of the San Francisco System, although its global role and influence changed conspicuously after it emerged as an economic power in the 1970s. The second phrase, coined to designate the nature of domestic power relations, is the "1955 System." Here the reference is to a concatenation of political and socioeconomic developments in 1955, including the establishment of the Liberal Democratic Party (LDP) which governed Japan uninterruptedly over the ensuing decades. More generally, "1955 System" signifies a domestic political structure characterized by an internally competitive but nonetheless hegemonic conservative establishment and a marginalized but sometimes influential liberal and Marxist opposition.

Like all fashionable political phrases, "San Francisco System" and "1955 System" obscure as much as they reveal. Both Japan's incorporation into U.S. cold-war policy and the triumph of the conservative elites were evident from the late 1940s, when U.S. policy toward occupied Japan underwent a so-called reverse course, in which emphasis was shifted from demilitarization and democratization to economic reconstruction, rearmament, and integration into the U.S. anticommunist containment policy. The real genesis of both systems is thus much earlier than a literal reading of the popular labels would suggest. Moreover, the domestic as well as international milieu in which the Japanese operated changed

---

1. Hirano Kenichirō, "Sengo Nihon gaikō ni okeru 'bunka,' " in Watanabe Akio, ed., *Sengo Nihon no taigai seisaku* (Tokyo: Yūhikaku, 1985), 343–45.

constantly during the postwar period, and dramatically so after the early 1970s. From this perspective, it is argued, both "San Francisco System" and "1955 System" have an anachronistic ring when applied to the years after the mid-1970s or so. And, indeed, they do.[2]

Still, the two phrases remain highly suggestive for anyone who wishes to recreate postwar Japan as history. They reflect a worldview, looking both outward and inward, that was defined and described (and criticized) by the Japanese themselves. And, like all popular phrases that survive for more than a passing moment, they capture—certainly for Japanese analysts—a wealth of complicated and even contradictory associations. They are code words for the peculiar capitalist context, overseas and at home, in which postwar Japan developed. They are closely associated with the impressive international and domestic prosperity Japan attained between the 1950s and 1980s. At the same time, they evoke the internal schism and tension and even violence that accompanied Japan's attainment of wealth and power. For Japanese, "San Francisco System" and "1955 System" vividly symbolize the intense political conflicts over issues of peace and democracy that characterized Japan's emergence as a rich consumer society and powerful capitalist state.

Essentially, these conflicts pitted liberal and left-wing critics against the dominant conservative elites. At the peak of their influence in the 1950s and 1960s, these critics constituted an effective minority, capable of capturing popular imagination and influencing the national agenda. By the mid-1970s, though, the Left appeared spent as an intellectually compelling political force. Partly, the opposi-

2. I have discussed the "reverse course" in some detail in *Empire and Aftermath: Yoshida Shigeru and the Japanese Experience, 1878–1954* (Cambridge: Harvard Council on East Asian Studies, 1979), 305–68, and in "Occupied Japan and the Cold War in Asia," in Michael J. Lacey, ed., *The Truman Presidency* (Cambridge: Woodrow Wilson International Center for Scholars and Cambridge University Press, 1989), 366–409. For a criticism of the reverse-course argument by a former American participant in the occupation, see Justin Williams, Sr., "American Democratization Policy for Occupied Japan: Correcting the Revisionist Version," *Pacific Historical Review* 57, no. 2 (May 1988): 179–202, and rejoinders by John W. Dower (202–9) and Howard Schonberger (209–18).

The "1955 System" designation appears to have been introduced to intellectual circles in an article published by Masumi Junnosuke in the June 1964 issue of *Shisō*. See Masumi, *Postwar Politics in Japan, 1945–1955*, Japanese Research Monograph 6 (Berkeley: Institute of East Asian Studies, University of California, 1985), 329–42; see also Masumi, "The 1955 System in Japan and Its Subsequent Development," *Asian Survey* 28, no. 3 (Mar. 1988): 286–306. The rise and fall of the 1955 System was the subject of the 1977 annual publication of the Japanese Political Science Association: Nihon Seijigakkai, ed., "Gojūgo-nen taisei no keisei to hōkai," *Seijigaku nenpō 1977* (Tokyo: Nihon Seijigakkai, 1979). For a broad, annotated overview of Japanese academic analysis of the 1955 System, see Miyake Ichirō, Yamaguchi Yasushi, Muramatsu Michio, and Shindō Eiichi, " 'Gojūgo-nen taisei' no seiritsu to tenkai," in *Nihon seiji no zahyō: Sengo 40-nen no ayumi* (Tokyo: Yuhikaku, 1985), 83–116. Like any political or socioeconomic "system," the 1955 System was dynamic, and the so-called conservative hegemony from the outset was internally competitive and riven with tensions. For an analysis in English of the unraveling of the system, see T. J. Pempel, "The Unbundling of 'Japan, Inc.': The Changing Dynamics of Japanese Policy Formation," in Kenneth B. Pyle, ed., *The Trade Crisis: How Will Japan Respond?* (Seattle: University of Washington Society for Japanese Studies, 1987), 117–52.

tion simply had lost some of its most fundamental arguments: prosperity at home undermined the critique of capitalism, and economic superpower status abroad discredited the argument of subordination to the U.S. economy. Partly again, however, the antiestablishment critics had won some of their arguments or, more commonly, had seen their positions on social and geopolitical issues effectively co-opted by the conservatives. Despite polemics of the most vitriolic sort, postwar Japan never was split into completely unbridgeable ideological camps. The pro-American conservatives nursed many resentments against the United States, for example, while the liberal and leftist "internationalists" were susceptible to nationalist appeals. Schism in both camps, as well as accommodation between the camps, were thus persistent subtexts in the debates over peace and democracy. This ideological softness, as it were, helps explain the transition to the less polemical decades of the 1970s and 1980s. As the debates over peace and democracy receded, their place was taken by a rising tide of neonationalist thinking that stressed Japanese uniqueness and superiority. Although this late-Shōwa cult of exceptionalism had Japanese critics, it tapped a line of thought with strong left-wing as well as conservative roots.

Contention over global and domestic policies did not disappear in the last decades of Shōwa. Rather, it took different forms. Although Japan's emergence as an economic superpower resulted in undreamed-of influence, it also created unanticipated tensions—not only with the United States and the European community but also within Japan. At the elite level Japan's new capitalism spawned new contenders for power and influence within the conservative establishment. And at the popular level the almost catatonic fixation of the ruling groups on industrial productivity and economic nationalism stimulated citizens' protest movements that eschewed doctrinaire ideologies and focused on specific issues such as quality of life, environmental protection, community services, and the like. Less sweeping in vision than the earlier "peace and democracy" struggles, such extraparliamentary activities represented a new kind of grass-roots democracy.

In these various ways, it can be said that Japan entered a new stage in the early 1970s. Yet the old military and economic imbrication with the United States symbolized by the San Francisco System remained at the heart of Japan's external policy. The conservative hegemony—the bedrock of the 1955 System—continued to rule Japan, juggling more balls than in the past, bickering and backbiting within its own ranks, but in no real danger of being removed from center stage. And the great issues of peace and democracy, however muted by prosperity and national pride, remained just beneath the surface. Was the new superstate really democratic, really a constructive force for peace? In the 1970s and 1980s, as the old debates faded from the scene, these questions were asked from new perspectives by the world at large.

These broad areas of concern—the San Francisco System, the 1955 System, the conflicts within them and linkages between them, and the uncertain world that Japan stumbled into as an economic, financial, and technological superpower beginning in the 1970s—are addressed in the pages that follow.

THE SAN FRANCISCO SYSTEM

The intersection of "peace" and "democracy" in postwar Japan begins with the Allied occupation of 1945–52 and its evolution into the San Francisco System. Under the U.S.-dominated occupation, defeated Japan was initially demilitarized. The Imperial Army and Navy ministries were abolished. Former military officers were purged from public life, ostensibly "for all time." Under the famous Article 9 of the 1947 constitution, Japan pledged to "forever renounce war as a sovereign right of the nation and the threat or use of force as a means of settling international disputes." What this meant, it was explained at the time, was exactly what it seemed to mean. As Prime Minister Yoshida Shigeru put it, taking a colorful metaphor from the days of the samurai, under the new peace constitution the Japanese were prohibited from picking up even two swords in the name of self-defense.[3]

At this early stage Yoshida and his colleagues anticipated that for the foreseeable future Japan would fare best as an unarmed nation dedicated to restoring peaceful relations with the rest of the world, including China and the Soviet Union. Its security, the earliest scenarios went, might be guaranteed by the United Nations, or by a Great Power agreement, or if necessary by a bilateral agreement with the United States under which the main islands of Japan were protected by U.S. forces stationed elsewhere (possibly including Okinawa).[4] This was not to be. The peace treaty signed in San Francisco in 1951 was in fact generous and nonpunitive, including no provisions for future international oversight of Japan. Under the Security Treaty with the United States, however, Japan agreed to the retention of U.S. military bases throughout the country after restoration of sovereignty and was understood to have committed itself to rearmament. The United States retained de facto control of the Ryukyu Islands, including Okinawa, which by then had become its major nuclear base in Asia, while "residual sovereignty" was acknowledged to lie with Japan.

As anticipated, because of the military alignment with the United States, which Japan agreed to in order to regain its sovereignty, the Soviet Union refused to sign the peace treaty. Neither the People's Republic of China nor the Kuomintang regime on Taiwan were invited to the San Francisco conference, but subsequently, contrary to its hopes and expectations, the Yoshida government was placed under severe U.S. pressure to establish relations with the Kuomintang and join in the containment of China. In the terms of those times the peace settlement at San Francisco was thus a "separate peace." In the years that followed the

3. *Kanpō gōgai—shugiin,* 7th Diet sess., 28 Jan. 1950, 200; *Official Gazette Extra—House of Representatives,* 7th sess., 28 Jan. 1950, 15. For an extended treatment of Yoshida's interpretation of Article 9, see Dower, *Empire and Aftermath,* 378–82, 397–99.

4. The basic inside source on Japanese military and strategic projections between surrender and restoration of sovereignty is Nishimura Kumao, *San Furanshisuko heiwa jōyaku,* vol. 27 of *Nihon gaikō shi,* ed. Kajima Heiwa Kenkyūjo (Tokyo: Kajima Kenkyūjo, 1971). The Socialists, as represented in the Katayama Tetsu cabinet of May 1947 to March 1948, shared these views.

formal restoration of sovereignty to Japan in April 1952, these cold-war arrangements remained a central focus of opposition by domestic critics of the government and a source of friction within the U.S.-Japan partnership itself.[5]

At the time the Security Treaty was negotiated and came into effect, U.S. projections for a future Japanese military focused on ground forces and were exceedingly ambitious. The Japanese were told they should create an army of 325,000 to 350,000 men by 1954—a figure larger than the Imperial Army on the eve of the Manchurian Incident in 1931, and larger than ever actually was reached in the postwar period. It was assumed from the outset in U.S. circles that Japanese remilitarization should and would entail constitutional revision. This assumption emerged in secret U.S. projections in the late 1940s, before the Americans actually began rearming Japan, and was first publicly emphasized by Vice President Richard Nixon in November 1953. For many reasons—including not only fear of economic dislocation and social unrest in Japan but also fear that the zealots in Washington would go on to demand that Japan send this projected army to fight in the Korean War—Yoshida resisted these U.S. pressures and established a more modest pattern of incremental Japanese rearmament. Privately, he and his aides agreed with the Americans that constitutional revision would have to accompany any rapid and large-scale military build-up, and they argued that such revision was politically impossible at the time. After all, only five years or so earlier the Japanese had seen a war—and nuclear weapons—brought home to them. This, indeed, was and remained the critical card: because of popular support for the liberal 1947 "peace constitution," constitutional revision remained politically impossible in postwar Japan.[6]

As counterpoint to the permissive agreements on remilitarization reached between the U.S. and Japanese governments in the early 1950s, Article 9 thus survived as an ambiguous but critical element within the San Francisco System. It was reinterpreted cavalierly by the government to permit piecemeal Japanese rearmament, but at the same time it was effectively utilized to restrain the speed and scope of remilitarization. Successive Shōwa-era cabinets repeatedly evoked the constitution to resist U.S. pressure not merely for large troop increases but also for participation in collective security arrangements and overseas missions. As Prime Minister Satō Eisaku stated in 1970, "The provisions of the Constitution make overseas service impossible."[7] Because revision of Article 9 would open the door to conservative revision of other parts of the national charter as well, especially concerning guarantees of individual rights and possibly also the purely

5. Nishimura, *San Furanshisuko heiwa jōyaku*; Dower, *Empire and Aftermath*, 369–414; Frederick S. Dunn, *Peace-making and the Settlement with Japan* (Princeton: Princeton University Press, 1963); Michael Yoshitsu, *Japan and the San Francisco Peace Settlement* (New York: Columbia University Press, 1982).

6. I have summarized the official U.S. record in some detail in "Occupied Japan."

7. John Welfield, *An Empire in Eclipse: Japan in the Postwar American Alliance System* (London: Athlone Press, 1988), 250. This is the most detailed and useful source in English on Japan within the San Francisco System.

"symbolic" status of the emperor, debates over constitutional revision became the most dramatic single example of the intersection of postwar concerns about peace and democracy.

The text of the peace treaty was not made public until it was signed in September 1951, and details of the U.S.-Japan military relationship were worked out between the two governments only in the months that intervened between then and the end of the occupation in April 1952. Nonetheless, the general policy of incorporating Japan into U.S. cold-war policy was clear well before the outbreak of the Korean War in June 1950, and opposition within Japan mobilized accordingly. The political Left was factionalized in its analysis of these developments, but many of the basic principles that would underlie criticism of the San Francisco System in the years to follow were introduced by the left-wing parties and liberal and "progressive" (*kakushin*) intellectuals between 1949 and 1951. In December 1949 the Socialist Party adopted "Three Principles of Peace" for Japan: an overall peace settlement with all former enemies, opposition to bilateral military pacts or foreign military bases in Japan, and neutrality in the cold war. In 1951, after hard wrangling between the right and left wings of the party, the Socialists added, as a fourth peace principle, opposition to Japanese rearmament.

By far the most influential intellectual endorsement of these principles came from the Peace Problems Symposium (Heiwa Mondai Danwakai), a loose grouping of highly respected academics who first collaborated in November 1948 to issue a general statement on war, peace, and social justice signed by fifty-five scholars in the natural and social sciences. In a "Statement on the Peace Problem" released in January 1950 and signed by thirty-five intellectuals, the group elaborated on the three peace principles, warned that a separate peace could contribute to war, and emphasized the importance of avoiding dependency on the United States. The third Peace Problems Symposium statement, drafted largely by Maruyama Masao and Ukai Nobushige and published as usual in the monthly magazine *Sekai*, was issued in December 1950, after the outbreak of the Korean War and open commencement of Japanese rearmament. So great was the response that *Sekai* was said to have doubled its circulation.

The long third statement, signed by thirty-one intellectuals in the Tokyo chapter of the Peace Problems Symposium and twenty-one in the Kyoto chapter, dwelled on the flawed vision of those self-styled "realists" who adhered to a rigidly bipolar worldview and anticipated inevitable conflict between "liberal democracy" and "communism." The United States and Soviet Union both came under criticism, while the cold-war premise of the emerging U.S.-Japan military relationship—the argument that the Soviet Union was committed to fostering world communism through military means—was rejected. Japan, it was argued, could best contribute to peaceful coexistence by adopting a strict course of unarmed nonalignment under the United Nations. The final section of the statement was devoted explicitly to "the relationship between peace and the domestic structure" and argued that Japan's contribution to a world without war, as well as its best opportunity to attain economic independence, could be most effectively furthered by promoting social-democratic domestic reforms that were guided by neither Soviet ideology nor American-style cold-war objectives. The language was guarded here, referring in general and quite idealistic terms to fairness in the sharing of wealth and income, creation of a mature level of democracy, and supplementing the principles of a free economy (*jiyū keizai no genri*) with principles of planning (*keikaku genri*).[8]

These statements survived over the years as probably the best-known manifestoes of the Japanese peace movement. Neither then nor later was much attention given to undercurrents within them that seemed to run counter to a truly internationalistic and universalistic outlook. The famous third statement, for example, adopted terms faintly reminiscent of Japan's pan-Asian rhetoric in World War II by praising the neutrality espoused by India's Prime Minister Nehru as representing "the very essence of the Asian people's historic position and mission." At the same time, the statement introduced a subtle appeal to nationalism in arguing that neutrality represented "the only true position of self-reliance and independence for Japan." Most striking of all, however, was the attempt of the Peace Problems Symposium intellectuals to nurture antiwar sentiments in Japan by appealing directly to the suffering experienced by the Japanese in the recent war. "In view of the pitiful experience that our fatherland underwent during the war," the third statement declared, "it is only too clear to us what it can mean to sacrifice peace."[9] From the perspective of Japan's Asian victims, of course, such an appeal would seem shockingly parochial rather than internationalist. In the Japanese milieu, however, it tapped an almost instinctual strain of "victim consciousness" (*higaisha ishiki*) that cut across the political spectrum.

As the precise nature of the San Francisco System unfolded between 1951 and 1954, it became apparent to conservatives as well as the opposition that Japan had paid a considerable price for sovereignty. It now possessed a military of questionable legality and a bilateral security treaty that was unquestionably inequitable. "Preposterously unequal" was the phrase used by Foreign Minister Fujiyama Aiichi in 1958, and when treaty revision came on the agenda in 1960, U.S. officials agreed that the 1951 Security Treaty with Japan was the most inequitable bilateral agreement the United States had entered into after the war. It also became painfully clear to the Japanese that the price of peace was a divided country—indeed, a doubly divided country in the sense of both territorial and

---

8. "Sengo heiwaron no genryū: Heiwa Mondai Danwakai o chūshin ni," *Sekai,* July 1985, 150–51. This special issue commemorating the fortieth anniversary of the end of World War II contains the basic texts of the Heiwa Mondai Danwakai. A partial translation of the December 1950 statement appears in *Journal of Social and Political Ideas in Japan* 1, no. 1 (Apr. 1963): 13–19 (see also the critique of the progressive intellectuals by the editor, 2–13). For an overview of opinion on the original Security Treaty, see George R. Packard III, *Protest in Tokyo: The Security Treaty Crisis of 1960* (Princeton: Princeton University Press, 1966), 3–32.

9. *Journal of Social and Political Ideas in Japan* 1, no. 1 (Apr. 1963): 13.

spiritual division. The detachment of Okinawa from the rest of Japan turned Okinawan society and economy into a grotesque appendage to the U.S. nuclear strategy in Asia. Edwin Reischauer, ambassador to Japan in the early 1960s, later characterized Okinawa as "the only 'semi-colonial' territory created in Asia since the war," and the resentments generated by this territorial division persisted until the reversion of Okinawa to Japan in 1972, and even after. The spiritual division of the country was manifested in the political and ideological polarization caused in considerable part by the San Francisco System itself. As Yoshida put it, with another graphic military metaphor, this time from the Allied division of Korea at the end of World War II, the occupation and its cold-war settlement drew a "thirty-eighth parallel" through the very heart of the Japanese people.[10] This was hardly a trauma or tragedy comparable to the postwar divisions of Korea, China, Germany, or Vietnam. It suggests, nonetheless, the emotional and politically charged climate of the years that followed Japan's accommodation to American cold-war policy.

Most fundamentally, the San Francisco System subordinated Japan to the United States in psychological as well as structural ways and ate at Japanese pride, year after year, like a slow-working acid. In official U.S. circles it was acknowledged frankly, if confidentially, that the military relationship with Japan was double-edged: it integrated Japan into the anticommunist camp and simultaneously created a permanent structure of U.S. control over Japan. Even passionately anti-Soviet politicians like Yoshida did not regard the USSR as a direct threat to Japan and reluctantly accepted the continued presence of U.S. troops and bases as an unavoidable price for obtaining sovereignty along with assurances of U.S. protection. The primary mission of U.S. forces and bases in Japan including Okinawa was never to defend Japan directly but rather to project U.S. power in Asia and to "support our commitments elsewhere," as one high U.S. official later testified.[11] To many observers the argument that this U.S. presence also acted as a deterrent to external threats to Japan was less persuasive than its counterargument: that the external threat was negligible without the bases, but considerable with them. If war occurred between the United States and the Soviet Union, Japan inevitably would be drawn into it. At the same time, the U.S.

10. Fujiyama and Reischauer are quoted in Welfield, *Empire in Eclipse*, 147, 224. The American acknowledgment of the grossly inequitable nature of the 1951 treaty emerged strongly in later congressional hearings concerning revision; see U.S. Senate, Committee on Foreign Relations, *Treaty of Mutual Cooperation and Security with Japan*, 86th Cong., 2d sess., 7 June 1960. Yoshida's comments appear in Yoshida Shigeru, *Sekai to Nihon* (Tokyo: Bancho Shōbō, 1962), 186–87. Japan also was "divided" by Soviet acquisition of four small and virtually unpopulated islands north of Hokkaido, an emotional issue that remained unresolved when the Shōwa period ended.

11. Statement by Assistant Secretary of State U. Alexis Johnson, *U.S. Security Agreements and Commitments Abroad: Japan and Okinawa Hearings*, 91st Cong., 2d sess., pt. 5, 26–29 Jan. 1970, 1166; cited in Hideki Kan, "The Significance of the U.S.-Japan Security System to the United States: A Japanese Perspective," in Glenn D. Hook, ed., special Japan issue of *Peace and Change: A Journal of Peace Research* 12, nos. 3–4 (1987): 20.

military presence throughout the Japanese islands established an on-site deterrent against hostile remilitarization by Japan itself. Subordination of Japanese military planning to U.S. grand strategy was another and more subtle way of ensuring long-term U.S. control over Japan. So also was the technological integration of the U.S. and Japanese military forces—a process of institutionalized dependency that actually deepened after the mid-1950s, when priorities shifted from ground forces to the creation of a technologically sophisticated Japanese navy and air force.

Early critics of the San Francisco System characterized Japan's place within it as one of "subordinate independence" (*jūzokuteki dokuritsu*), including economic as well as diplomatic and military dependency. Although the phrase arose on the political Left, it was echoed throughout Japanese society—and at top levels in Washington and Tokyo as well. When U.S. planners in the Army, Navy, and State departments first turned serious attention to incorporating Japan into cold-war strategy in 1947, for example, they rejected not merely the premise that Japan could be neutral but also that it could ever regain an "independent identity." In this fiercely bipolar worldview, Japan realistically could be expected to "function only as an American or Soviet satellite." In November 1951, two months after the peace conference, Joseph Dodge, the key American adviser on economic policy toward Japan, bluntly told representatives of the Ministry of International Trade and Industry (MITI) that "Japan can be independent politically but dependent economically." When Japan was forced to participate in the economic containment of China and seek alternative markets elsewhere, especially in Southeast Asia, fear that Japan was doomed to an exceedingly precarious economic future was palpable throughout the country. At this stage almost no one anticipated that Japan had a serious future in the advanced markets of the West. Thus, as we learn from "Top Secret" records of the U.S. National Security Council, in September 1954 Secretary of State John Foster Dulles "told Yoshida frankly that Japan should not expect to find a big U.S. market because the Japanese don't make the things we want. Japan must find markets elsewhere for the goods they export."[12]

Such comments may be amusing in retrospect, but they remind us that Japan's emergence as a global economic power came late and abruptly and astonished almost everyone concerned. It involved a great deal of skill and hard work, to be sure, but also a large measure of good fortune. In the long run U.S. cold-war policies abetted Japanese economic growth at home and abroad in unanticipated ways. In return for acquiescing in the containment policy, for example, Japan received favored access to U.S. patents and licenses and technical expertise, as well as U.S. patronage in international economic organizations. At the same time, despite American rhetoric about free trade and an open international economic

12. See Michael Schaller, *The American Occupation of Japan* (New York: Oxford University Press, 1985), 104, on "independent identity"; see Dower, *Empire and Aftermath*, 420, on Dodge; see U.S. Department of State, *Foreign Relations of the United States, 1952–1954*, vol. 14, pt. 2, pp. 1724–25 (12 Sept. 1954), on Dulles; cf. ibid., p. 1693 (6 Aug. 1954).

order, these remained ultimate ideals rather than immediate practices. In the early postwar decades U.S. policy actually sanctioned import restrictions by the Western European allies as well as Japan to facilitate their recovery from the war, and these trade barriers were tolerated longer in Japan's case than they were in Europe. Also tolerated, until the early 1970s, was an undervalued yen exchange rate—that is, an overvalued dollar, which benefited Japanese export industries. Japan, more than Europe, also was permitted to retain tight restrictions on foreign exchange and capital investment that had been approved as "temporary" measures during the occupation. The closed Japanese domestic economy, which grew so rapidly in the late 1950s and 1960s and became a source of great friction between Japan and the United States and Europe by the end of the 1960s, reflected these protectionist policies sanctioned by the United States in the naive days when Japan was believed to have no serious future in Western markets—and when, by U.S. demand, Japan also was prohibited from establishing close economic ties with China. Although it is doubtful that the U.S. "nuclear umbrella" ever really protected Japan from a serious external threat, it is incontrovertible that the U.S. economic umbrella was an immense boon to Japanese capitalism.[13]

The Japanese economy also flourished within the San Francisco System in two additional unanticipated ways. Both the Korean War and the Vietnam War brought great profits and market breakthroughs to Japan. U.S. offshore procurements stimulated by the Korean War and thereafter routinized as "new special procurements" (*shin tokuju*) held Japan's balance of payments in line through the critical years of the 1950s. The Vietnam War boom, in turn, brought an estimated $1 billion a year to Japanese firms between 1966 and 1971—the period now identified as marking the opening stage of economic "maturity" for Japan and the beginning of the end of America's role as hegemon of the global capitalist system.[14]

At the same time, the constraints on Japanese remilitarization that stemmed from the early period of demilitarization and democratization and remained embodied in the constitution did more than merely buttress a general policy of go-slow rearmament. They also thwarted the emergence of a powerful defense lobby comparable to that in the United States. In the absence of a bona fide ministry of defense, the Ministry of Finance remained the major actor in shaping the postwar military budget. There was no Japanese counterpart to the Pentagon.

13. Cf. the concise summary "Economic Relations with the United States, 1945–1973" by Gary Saxonhouse in *Kodansha Encyclopedia of Japan* (Tokyo: Kōdansha, 1983) 8:161–64.

14. For the Korean War boom and "special procurements," see Takafusa Nakamura, *The Postwar Japanese Economy: Its Development and Structure* (Tokyo: University of Tokyo Press, 1981), 41–48; G. C. Allen, *Japan's Economic Recovery* (London: Oxford University Press), 19–22, 34–35, 166–69, 203. For the Vietnam War boom, see Thomas R. H. Havens, *Fire Across the Sea: The Vietnam War and Japan, 1965–1975* (Princeton: Princeton University Press, 1987), 96. This is a useful source on this period in general. Japan's entry into economic "maturity" is commonly dated from 1964, when the country was accorded full membership in the Organization for Economic Cooperation and Development (OECD) and "advanced country" status in the International Monetary Fund (IMF).

And despite a handful of large military contractors such as Mitsubishi Heavy Industries, there emerged no civilian defense sector remotely comparable to the military-industrial complex in the United States. Thus, contrary to the situation in America, the best scientists and engineers in postwar Japan turned their talents to the production of commodities for the civilian marketplace, rather than weapons of war. All this was critical to the economic take-off Japan experienced beginning in the late 1950s and the country's extraordinary competitiveness in ensuing decades. And all this also must be reckoned an integral part of the San Francisco System.

THE 1955 SYSTEM

Like the San Francisco System, the conservative hegemony later known as the 1955 System had its genesis in the occupation-period reverse course, when U.S. policymakers began to jettison many of their more radical democratic ideals and reforms. A general strike planned for 1 February 1947 was banned by General Douglas MacArthur. Prolabor legislation was watered down beginning in 1948. The immense power of the bureaucracy—augmented by a decade and a half of mobilization for "total war"—was never curtailed by the Occupation reformers (beyond abolition of the prewar Home Ministry), and the financial structure remained largely untouched despite initial proposals to democratize it. Fairly ambitious plans to promote economic democratization through industrial deconcentration were abandoned by 1949. Individuals purged from public life "for all time" because of their wartime activities or affiliations began to be depurged in 1950, and by the end of the occupation only a few hundred persons remained under the original purge designation. At the same time, between late 1949 and the end of 1950 U.S. authorities and the Japanese government collaborated in a "Red purge" in the public sector, and then the private sector, that eventually led to the firing of some twenty-two thousand individuals, mostly left-wing union activists. In July 1950, in the midst of this conspicuous turn to the right, the rearmament of Japan began.[15]

The San Francisco settlement thus took place in a setting of domestic turmoil, when both of the early ideals of "demilitarization" and "democratization" were under attack by the conservative elites and their new American partners. To critics, rearmament and the "Red purges," military bases and the gutting of the labor laws, the separate peace and resurrection of the old economic and political elites—all were part of a single reverse course that was simultaneously international and domestic in its ramifications. Japanese partisanship in the cold war

15. See Dower, *Empire and Aftermath*, and Masumi, *Postwar Politics in Japan*, for general political developments in the first postwar decade. The evolution of U.S. policy is closely documented by Howard Schonberger in *Aftermath of War: Americans and the Remaking of Japan, 1945–1952* (Kent: Kent State University Press, 1989). I have dealt at length with the extensive presurrender legacies to the postwar state and society in "The Useful War," *Daedalus*, Summer 1990, 49–70.

required the resurrection of the civilian old guard, and the old guard required the cold war to enlist U.S. support against domestic opponents.

With the exception of the brief Katayama interlude (May 1947 to March 1948), conservative leaders headed every Japanese cabinet of the postwar period, even before the reverse course was initiated. However, it was not until the third Yoshida cabinet, formed in January 1949, that the conservative leadership enjoyed a firm majority in the Diet. For Yoshida personally this proved to be an ephemeral peak of power and stability. The general elections of October 1952 saw the return to national politics of hundreds of formerly purged politicians, and by 1954 conservative ranks were severely factionalized. When Yoshida and his Liberal Party supporters were unceremoniously ousted from power in December 1954, it was not anticonservatives who did them in but rather a rival conservative coalition, the Democratic Party, headed by Hatoyama Ichirō. Hatoyama, who succeeded Yoshida as prime minister, was a former purgee with a record of support not only for Japanese aggression in the recent war but also for the suppression of dissent in the 1920s and 1930s. Also in the anti-Yoshida camp at this time was another future prime minister, Kishi Nobusuke, a brilliant technocrat who had been a leading economic planner in the puppet state of Manchukuo in the 1930s, a vice minister of munitions under Prime Minister Tōjō Hideki in 1943–44, and an inmate of Sugamo Prison from late 1945 to 1948, accused of class A war crimes but never brought to trial. The conservatives were unquestionably in the saddle, but so great was their internal fighting that they seemed capable of throwing each other out of it.

This turmoil set the stage for consolidation of the conservative parties a year later. In November 1955 Hatoyama's Democrats and Yoshida's Liberals merged to form the Liberal Democratic Party—which, like its predecessors, was neither liberal nor democratic and thus woefully misnamed. Over the ensuing decades the LDP retained uninterrupted control of the government, and this remarkable stability naturally became a central axis of the so-called 1955 System. The capacity for long-term planning that became so distinctive a feature of the postwar political economy was made possible in considerable part by this continuity of single-party domination. However, 1955 was a signal year in other ways as well, and it was this larger conjunction of political and economic developments that seemed to constitute the systematization and clarification of power and influence in postwar Japan—just one decade, as it happened, after Japan's surrender. These related developments took place in both the anticonservative and conservative camps.

It was, in fact, the Socialists and left-wing unionists who moved first. In January 1955 Sōhyō—the General Council of Trade Unions, which was closely affiliated with the left-wing Socialists—mobilized some eight hundred thousand workers in the first demonstration of what subsequently was institutionalized as the *shuntō* "spring wage offensive." From this year on, the *shuntō* became the basic vehicle for organizing enterprise unions in demanding industrywide "base up" wage increases on a regular—almost ritualized—basis. That same month the left-wing and right-wing factions of the Socialist Party, which had formally split in 1951 over whether to support the San Francisco settlement, agreed to reunite. Reunification was finalized in October, but well before then, in the general elections of February 1955, the two factions together won slightly more than one-third of the seats (156 of 453) in the critical House of Representatives. Significantly, this parliamentary representation gave them sufficient combined strength to block constitutional revision, which required a two-thirds vote of approval in the Diet.

The LDP merger in November was in considerable part a response to this specter of a reunified and purposeful left-wing opposition. At the same time, it also constituted the open wedding of big business with Japan's right-of-center politicians. Corporate Japan (the *zaikai*) not only played a decisive role in promoting the 1955 conservative merger but also mobilized the business community at this time as the major ongoing source of money for the LDP. The vehicle for assuring tight control of this political funding also was set up in those busy early months of 1955 in the form of an Economic Reconstruction Council (Keizai Saiken Kondankai) established in January and supported by all four major big-business organizations: the Japan Federation of Employers' Associations (Nikkeiren), Federation of Economic Organizations (Keidanren), Japan Committee for Economic Development (Keizai Dōyūkai), and Japan Chamber of Commerce (Nisshō). Although some big-business funds were made available to Socialists, the vast bulk of contributions funneled through the Economic Reconstruction Council (96 percent in 1960) went to the LDP. Reorganized as the Kokumin Kyōkai in 1961, this consortium provided over 90 percent of LDP funding through the 1960s and 1970s.[16] This consolidation and rationalization of the relationship between the *zaikai* and conservative politicians constituted two legs of the vaunted "tripod" on which conservative power rested over the ensuing decades. The third leg was the bureaucracy, which drafted most of the legislation introduced in the Diet and also provided a steady exodus of influential former officials into the LDP.

From a broader socioeconomic perspective 1955 also appeared to be, if not a watershed, at least a symbolic point at which lines of future development became clarified. Economically, the Korean War had wound down and as a consequence the previous year had been dismal for Japan, as conveyed in the catchphrase "1954 recession" (*nijūkyūnen fukyō*). Japanese missions to Washington in the waning years of Yoshida's premiership privately expressed deep and genuine pessimism about the future prospects of Japan's "shallow economy." Contrary to these gloomy prognostications, however, 1955 proved to be a turning point for the postwar economy, and the popular phrases of this year captured this turnabout as well: "postwar high" (*sengo saikō*) was one, "best year of the postwar economy" (*sengo keizai sairyō no toshi*)

---

16. Chitoshi Yanaga, *Big Business in Japanese Politics* (New Haven: Yale University Press, 1968), 83–87; Haruhiro Fukui, "Liberal Democratic Party," *Kodansha Encyclopedia of Japan* 4:385.

another. As it turned out, in 1955 the gross national product (GNP) surpassed the prewar peak for the first time, marking the symbolic end of postdefeat recovery. Indeed, the official *Economic White Paper* (Keizai Hakusho) published the next year heralded this accomplishment as signaling the end of the postwar period (*mohaya "sengo" de wa nai*). This upturn coincided, moreover, with the establishment of one of the most important of Japan's long-range industrial planning organizations, the Japan Productivity Center (Nihon Seisansei Honbu). Created on the basis of a U.S.-Japan agreement, with initial funding from both governments as well as Japanese business and financial circles, the center drew support from the ranks of labor as well as management and became the major postwar sponsor of technical missions sent abroad to study the most up-to-date methods of increasing industrial production. The formal wherewithal for exporting the products manufactured by these cutting-edge techniques also was obtained in 1955, when Japan was admitted to the General Agreement on Tariffs and Trade (GATT). It was also in 1955 that centralized planning was significantly advanced through creation of the Economic Planning Agency (in July) and the issuance (in December) of a Five-Year Plan for Economic Independence.[17]

By many reckonings the advent of mass consumer culture also dates from essentially this same moment in the mid-1950s. It was in 1955, for example, that MITI announced the inauguration of a "citizen's car project"; heretofore, the vehicle industry had concentrated on producing trucks (especially for U.S. use in the Korean War) and buses and taxis (including many for export to Southeast Asia). With MITI's plan as a springboard the "age of the citizen's car" (*kokumin jidōsha no jidai*) commenced with the appearance of the Datsun Bluebird four years later. The "age of the electrified household" (*katei denka no jidai*) is said to have materialized in 1955, when housewives dreamed of owning the "three divine appliances" (*sanshu no jingi*)—electric washing machines, refrigerators, and television—and magazines spoke of the seven ascending stages of household electrification: (7) electric lights, (6) radio and iron, (5) toaster and electric heater, (4) mixer, fan, and telephone, (3) washing machine, (2) refrigerator, and (1) television and vacuum cleaner. For whatever one may make of the fact, Godzilla made his debut in November 1954 and thus stepped into (or on) the popular consciousness in 1955. It was also at this time that book publishers began to cater more explicitly to mass tastes. Nicely befitting the advent of a new age of mass culture, another popular slogan of 1955 was "the age of neurosis" (*noirōse jidai*), a phrase sparked by several well-publicized suicides in midyear. As a popular weekly put it, claim-

---

17. For catchphrases, cf. Takahashi Nobuo, *Shōwa seso ryūkōgo jiten* (Tokyo: Ōbunsha, 1986), 142–43, 148–49. The "shallow economy" is discussed in Dower, *Empire and Aftermath*, 449–63. For the origins of the famous white paper phrase, see Nakano Yoshio, "Mohaya 'sengo' de wa nai," *Bungei shunjū*, Feb. 1956, reprinted in Bungei shunjū, ed., *"Bungei shunjū" ni miru Shōwa shi* (Tokyo: Bungei shunjū, 1988), 2:349–59; cf. Kōno Yasuko, " 'Sengo' no owari," in Watanabe, *Sengo Nihon no taigai seisaku*, 182. On the five-year plan, see Masumi, *Postwar Politics in Japan*, 237–39.

ing one was neurotic had now become an "accessory" (they used the English word) of modern people.[18]

That the consolidation of conservative power coincided with full recovery from the war and the onset of commercialized mass culture may help explain the staying power of the new conservative hegemony. This durability was not immediately apparent, however, and the decade and a half that followed witnessed a series of intense confrontations over basic issues of peace and democracy. The fundamental lines of political cleavage within the 1955 System have been summarized as pitting a conservative camp committed to revising the constitution and protecting the U.S.-Japan Security Treaty against a progressive (*kakushin*) opposition committed to doing just the opposite: defending the constitution and opposing the Security Treaty.[19] This summary is concise and clever, although it oversimplifies positions on both sides. The initial platform of the LDP did call for constitutional revision, and one of the first steps the new party took was to establish a Constitution Investigation Committee (Kempō Chōsakai) to prepare the ground for revision. At the same time, under Hatoyama and his successors the party also undertook to continue undoing "excesses" of the early democratic postsurrender reforms that lay outside the purview of the constitution—such as revision of the electoral system, abolition of elected school boards, imposition of restraints on political activity by teachers, promotion of "moral" and patriotic education, and strengthening of the police.

Concerning remilitarization, Hatoyama was more zealous than his predecessor Yoshida had been in supporting rearmament under the security treaty, but his reasons for doing so were by no means unambiguously pro-American. Rather, Hatoyama and his supporters desired accelerated rearmament of a more "autonomous" sort that in the long run would hasten Japan's escape from the American embrace. Just as the Security Treaty was a double-edged sword from the American perspective—simultaneously enlisting Japan as a cold-war ally and instituting U.S. controls over Japan—so also was advocacy of accelerated rearmament double-edged to the more ardent Japanese nationalists. On the surface, this policy accorded with U.S. demands for rapid Japanese rearmament, and the conservatives were indeed ideologically receptive to aligning with the Americans in their anticommunist crusade. At the same time, however, nationalists in the Hatoyama and Kishi line also endorsed accelerated remilitarization to reduce military subordination to their Pacific partner as quickly as possible. Here, in any case, their aspirations were frustrated, for popular support could not be marshaled in support

18. Konosuke Odaka, Keinosuke Ono, and Fumiko Adachi, *The Automobile Industry in Japan: A Study of Ancillary Firm Development* (Tokyo: Kinokuniya Company and Oxford University Press, 1988), 46, 102–5; Takahashi, 146, 149, 151; Sakakibara Shōji, *Shōwago* (Tokyo: Asahi Bunko, 1986), 124. On best-sellers, cf. Ueda Yasuo, *Gendai no shuppan: Kono miryoku aru katsuji sekai* (Tokyo: Risō Shuppansha, 1980), 162.

19. Miyake et al., " 'Gojūgo-nen taisei,' " 83, 88, citing Kamishima Jirō on the difference between the two camps.

of such a policy. The general public proved willing to accept slow rearmament in the mode established by Yoshida, with little concern about the sophistries of constitutional reinterpretation that this program required of the government's legal experts. As Hatoyama learned, however, just as other conservative leaders learned after him, to the very end of the Shōwa period, the public was not receptive to either rapid rearmament or frontal attacks on the constitution.

In attacking the conservatives the opposition essentially appropriated the slogan "peace and democracy" as its own, but exactly what this phrase meant was often contested among these critics themselves. As the intellectuals associated with the influential Peace Problems Symposium developed their "peace thesis" (*hei-waron*) in the late 1940s and early 1950s, it was argued that mobilization for peace must proceed through three levels: from the "human" (*ningen*) level, through the "system" (*seido*), and only on this basis to engagement in broad "international" (*kokusai*) peace issues. In the Japanese context this emphasis meant immersion in the "human" suffering of World War II (and, in actual practice, an outpouring of writings focusing on *Japanese* suffering in the battlefields abroad and under the air raids and atomic bombs at home). The Japanese "system" of overriding importance was to be found in the interlocking basic values enshrined in the new constitution, namely, people's rights, democracy, and pacifism. Finally, rooted in appreciation of these human and systemic values, the Japanese peace movement could move on to pursue basic goals conducive to the creation and maintenance of international peace. By the time the 1955 System was created, these goals usually were expressed as unarmed neutrality, backed by guarantees of support from the United Nations. In addition, inspired by two related events in 1954—the Bikini Incident, in which Japanese fishermen suffered radiation poisoning from the fallout of a U.S. hydrogen bomb test in the Pacific, and a spectacular grassroots petition drive against nuclear testing that was initiated by Japanese housewives and collected an astonishing twenty million signatures—by 1955 the Japanese peace movement also had come to focus especially keenly on the global abolition of nuclear weapons.[20]

Maintaining the constitution was of course the bridge that linked defense of peace and pacifist ideals to defense of democracy, but the latter cause extended beyond constitutional issues per se. Phrased softly, the opposition also was committed to protecting the livelihood (*seikatsu yōgo*) of the working class, which undeniably was being squeezed in the concerted quest for rapid industrial growth. In more doctrinaire terms, the overtly Marxist opposition wished to destroy monopoly capitalism and bring about a socialist revolution in Japan. The latter agenda predictably was endorsed by only a portion of the anticonservative opposition; and, predictably again, it caused the Left to splinter in self-destructive ways that did not happen on the Right, where factionalism was less ideological and

20. Takahashi Shin and Nakamura Kyūichi, "Sengo Nihon no heiwaron," *Sekai* 391 (June 1978): 202–25, esp. 202–7.

more personally oriented. Thus, while the 1955 System began with a Socialist merger and the anticipation, by some, that in time a genuinely two-party system might evolve in Japan, in actuality the Left failed to hold together or grow. As early as 1958 the political scientist Oka Yoshitake already had characterized the new political structure as a "one and one-half party system." Two years later a portion of the Socialist Party permanently hived off to form the less doctrinaire Democratic Socialist Party. By the end of the 1960s, after the quasi-religious Clean Government Party (Kōmeitō) also had emerged on the scene, it was common to speak of the political system as consisting of "one strong, four weak" (*ikkyō shijaku*) political parties.[21]

Before the opposition congealed as a permanent minority, however, it succeeded in mobilizing popular support in a series of massive protest movements that—like the earlier struggle against the occupation-period reverse course—dramatized the relationship between international and domestic politics. The first and most spectacular of these protests wedded opposition to revision and renewal of the Security Treaty (scheduled for 1960) to Kishi's assumption of the premiership in 1957. That Kishi, Tōjō's former vice minister of munitions, could assume the highest office in the country just twelve years after the war ended—and become, simultaneously, the symbol in Japan of the U.S.-Japan military relationship—graphically exemplified how far, and fast, Japan had moved away from the early ideals of demilitarization and democratization. In the end, the opposition drew millions of demonstrators into the streets and both lost and won its protest: the Security Treaty was retained and revised, but Kishi was forced to resign. In the process, a variety of concerned citizens were baptized in the theory and practice of extraparliamentary democratic expression.

This tumultuous campaign against the cold-war treaty and old-war politician overlapped, moreover, with the last great labor strike in modern Japanese history, which pitted workers at the Miike coal mine against an archetypical old-guard employer, the Mitsui Mining Company. The Miike struggle began in the spring of 1959 and in January 1960 turned into a lockout and strike that lasted 282 days and eventually involved hundreds of thousands of people. At Miike, the radical wing of organized labor confronted a broad united front of big business and the government, which correctly perceived the struggle as a decisive test for the future of state-led industrial "rationalization." And at Miike, labor lost. The defeat of the miners in late 1960 smoothed the path for the heralded "income doubling" policy of the new Ikeda Hayato cabinet, which assumed power when Kishi was forced to resign in June.

The interplay of domestic and international politics resurfaced dramatically in the late 1960s, when massive protests against Japan's complicity in the Vietnam War intersected with a wide range of domestic grievances. Indeed, in this struggle

---

21. Miyake et al., " 'Gojūgo-nen taisei,' " 83–84, 89–90, 117. The "four weak" parties were the Communists, Socialists, Democratic Socialists, and Kōmeitō.

the linkage of peace and democracy was recast in stunningly new ways. Under the influence of the New Left the anti–Vietnam War movement introduced a more radical anti-imperialist critique to the discourse on peace and democracy. Essentially, the late-1960s radicals argued that under the cold-war alliance Japan not only profited materially from the misery of other Asians but also contributed to the support of corrupt and authoritarian regimes outside Japan. Peace and prosperity for Japan, in short, were being purchased at the cost of war and the repression of democracy elsewhere. Vietnam and Korea were the great examples of this repressive profiteering for the protestors of the mid and late 1960s, especially after Japan normalized relations with the authoritarian South Korean government in 1965, under strong U.S. prodding—thereby contributing measurably to the ability of the Seoul regime to send troops to Vietnam in support of U.S. forces there. The radicalism of this critique lay in its attempt to think of democracy as well as peace in truly international and nonparochial terms, while situating the vaunted "income-doubling" policies of the 1960s in the specific context of the imbrication of Japanese bourgeois capitalism and U.S. imperialism. In the New Left critique, "peace and democracy" as the Old Left and liberals and ruling groups all imagined it was self-centered, self-serving, quintessentially bourgeois.

At the same time, the anti–Vietnam War movement intersected with highly charged domestic protests against the social and environmental costs of growth, the grasping hand of the state, and the autocratic governance of the universities. The latter, as the critics framed it, were turning into mere service organizations for the bureaucracy and big business. Antipollution movements centering on the mercury-poisoned community of Minamata and other tragic examples of environmental destruction peaked in the period between 1967 and the early 1970s. With them came a renewed appreciation of grass-roots democracy, exemplified in an impressive variety of "citizens' movements" (*shimin undō*), "residents' movements" (*jūmin undō*), and "victims' movements" (*higaisha undō*)—all legacies, each in its own way, of the 1959–60 street demonstrations and community protests against the Security Treaty and Kishi and in support of the Miike workers. The Sanrizuka struggle opposing forced sale of farmland to build the new Narita international airport was initiated by the farmers themselves in 1968. And the student struggles, which began with a five-month strike at Waseda University in 1965–66, reached a crescendo in 1968–69. At the peak of the student demonstrations more than 40 percent of the nation's 377 universities were affected by strikes, and most of these campuses were under occupation. Although many of the grievances voiced by student protesters were directed at university affairs, the student radicals—like many other citizens in the late 1960s, in Japan and in Europe and America as well—immersed themselves in the broad gamut of domestic and international issues. And at their ironic best they cleverly captured the interlock of internal and external developments. One of the slogans of student radicals at the University of Tokyo, for example, was "Dismantle the Tokyo Imperialistic University"—neatly meshing the notion of a revival of prewar autocracy (when the elite University of Tokyo had been named Tokyo Imperial University) with the argument that higher education in postwar Japan once again was serving primarily the purposes of an expansionist state.[22]

It is estimated that between 1967 and 1970 alone, more than eighteen million Japanese took to the streets to protest the war in Vietnam and demand the reversion of Okinawa to Japan. Uncounted others were involved in the university struggles and citizens' movements against the ravages of the growth-oriented state. As elsewhere, "people's power" entered the Japanese lexicon at this time as a legitimate and essential alternative to bourgeois parliamentary politics; and, as elsewhere, the theory and practice of "people's power" ranged from peaceful protest to wanton violence. By the mid-1970s the nationwide people's movement was moribund, but it left as legacies the memory and experience of grass-roots mobilization that could be evoked in more particularistic causes thereafter.

CONFLICT AND ACCOMMODATION TO THE EARLY 1970s

At the most conspicuous level the major controversies concerning military and international policy in postwar Japan involved left-wing criticism of the government's acquiescence in the San Francisco System. Almost all of the contentious issues of later years were encoded in the peace settlementthe separate peace, the Security Treaty and U.S. military bases in Japan, commitment to Japanese rearmament, detachment and semicolonization of Okinawa, entanglement in U.S. nuclear policy, and collusion in U.S. support of right-wing client regimes in the divided countries of Asia (China, Korea, and Vietnam). Inevitably, criticism of such government policies was inseparable from criticism of the United States. True to the early vision of the Peace Problems Symposium, the opposition position generally espoused an essentially nonaligned international role for Japan, although pro-Soviet and pro-Chinese allegiances also were conspicuous on the Left. At critical moments in the postwar debates opinion polls indicated that a large number of Japanese also supported the option of neutrality. Fifty percent of respondents to a survey in 1959 endorsed this option, for example, and at the height of the peace movement a decade later as many as 66 percent of Japanese questioned in one poll favored neutrality.[23]

It is misleading, however, to see the conservative and opposition positions on these issues as completely antithetical. Both sides were crisscrossed with schisms.

22. See Packard, *Protest in Tokyo,* for the 1960 struggle and Havens, *Fire Across the Sea,* for the anti-Vietnam War movement in Japan. The grass-roots movements are discussed in Margaret A. McKean, *Environmental Protest and Citizen Politics in Japan* (Berkeley and Los Angeles: University of California Press, 1981). On the university disturbances, see Henry D. Smith II, "University Upheavals of 1966–1969," in *Kodansha Encyclopedia of Japan* 8:171. I also have drawn on an as yet unpublished manuscript on the New Left by Mutō Ichio.

23. See Kan in Hook, *Peace and Change,* 27, for the 1959 NHK survey. Welfield, *Empire in Eclipse,* 197, cites a 1968 *Shūkan Asahi* poll showing 66 percent support for neutralism; an *Asahi shinbun* poll in 1969 showed 56 percent support.

At the same time, on many critical issues the two sides shared, if not common ground, at least comparable skepticism concerning the wisdom of U.S. policies. Beyond the usual factionalism endemic to the Left, the unity of the opposition was undercut by all the familiar postwar traumas of the international communist and socialist movements—the repression in Hungary and critique of Stalin in 1956, the Sino-Soviet split that followed soon after, the Cultural Revolution in China and Soviet invasion of Czechoslovakia, the communist concerns with "Trotskyist" deviations that accompanied the rise of the New Left in the 1960s, and the acrimonious debates over "capitalist and imperialist" nuclear weapons as opposed to "socialist and defensive" ones (which came to a head in Japan in 1963, when the Left split on whether to support the Partial Nuclear Test-Ban Treaty). The conservatives, too, although relatively cohesive in their anticommunism, nonetheless bifurcated into so-called Asianist and pro-American camps. This split was openly signaled in December 1964 and January 1965, when LDP members coalesced around either the staunchly pro-American Asian Problems Study Association (Ajia Mondai Kenkyūkai) or the more Asia-oriented Afro-Asian Problems Study Association (Ajia-Afurika Mondai Kenkyūkai).[24]

Even the most obsequious supporters of the pro-American position, however—such as Satō Eisaku, who succeeded Ikeda in 1964 and held the premiership until 1972—never planted both feet entirely in the American camp. From the earliest moments of the San Francisco System a fault line of disagreement and mistrust ran between Tokyo and Washington. While the conservative hegemony disagreed internally on a variety of critical policy issues beyond the appropriate speed and scope of remilitarization—including what policy to adopt toward China, Korea, Vietnam, and a nuclearized Okinawa—from the time of the Yoshida cabinets there was general conservative agreement that the U.S. vision of a bipolar world was inflexible and obsessively militaristic. As a consequence, in tactical if not fundamental ways there often occurred a convergence in the positions of the political Left and Right vis-à-vis the United States. One of the more amusing early examples of this convergence occurred in the very midst of the creation of the San Francisco System, when Yoshida—the great Red-baiter and bête noire of the Left—secretly encouraged the Socialists to organize antirearmament demonstrations while John Foster Dulles was in Tokyo. For Yoshida and his conservative successors as well, the specter of popular opposition to U.S. policies was an effective, and indeed desired, bargaining chip.[25]

As a general rule, Japanese of every political persuasion desired greater autonomy and more genuine sovereignty for their country. They differed on whether

24. Welfield points out conservative disagreements on international policy throughout *Empire in Eclipse;* see esp. 210–14. On internal LDP debates on China policy, see Haruhiro Fukui, *Party in Power: The Japanese Liberal Democrats and Policy-making* (Berkeley and Los Angeles: University of California Press, 1970), 227–62.

25. Takeshi Igarashi, "Peace-making and Party Politics: The Formation of the Domestic Foreign-Policy System in Postwar Japan," *Journal of Japanese Studies* 11, no. 2 (1985): 323–56.

this goal was better attained within the Security Treaty or outside it; and thus, in great confrontations such as the 1959–60 crisis over whether to revise the mutual security pact, there was indeed no common ground where policy was concerned. Both sides felt humiliation at the unequal nature of the original treaty. Whereas the conservative mainstream focused on the removal of inequality, however, the opposition argued that a more equitable treaty simply meant that Japan was committing itself to a larger military role. Nevertheless, the nationalist sentiments shared by participants on both sides of this struggle help explain the disintegration of the opposition over the ensuing years. Nationalism was a bridge on which leftists could sooner or later cross to join the LDP or even the extreme right-wing advocates of an independent Japanese military capability. The well-known critic Shimizu Ikutarō, who moved from being one of the most prominent intellectuals in the Peace Problems Symposium and 1960 protests to being an advocate of a nuclear-armed autonomous Japanese state a decade later, was but the most conspicuous example of this exodus of former radicals into the conservative camp. Even where dissidents of the 1950s and 1960s did not cross over to the other side, moreover, in later years many turned their focus of opposition further inward to concentrate on essentially domestic concerns.[26]

On a wide range of other contested issues the partial convergence in viewpoint of the conservative leaders and their critics was more straightforward. Despite their anticommunism, for example, many conservatives desired closer relations with the two communist giants, or at least with China. Similarly, the large number of U.S. troops and military bases that remained in Japan after the occupation, and after the Korean armistice in 1953, aggravated almost everyone. On a related issue, although the conservatives and their critics were in fundamental disagreement over whether Japan should rearm, conservative politicians, bureaucrats, and businessmen as a whole (with the exception of certain vigorous defense industry lobbies) gave relatively low priority to defense spending into the 1980s. As a percentage of the total general accounts budget, military spending peaked in 1954. As a percentage of the gross national product, defense spending as commonly calculated was less than 1 percent for a full decade before Prime Minister Miki Takeo grandly proclaimed a "One Percent of GNP" guideline in 1976.[27]

Such points of partial convergence in the outlook of the conservatives and opposition are easily extended. There was no fundamental disagreement on the desirability of the reversion of Okinawa to full Japanese sovereignty, for example, and eventually little disagreement on an early basic issue of contention: that Okinawa should be returned nuclear free. Neither the government nor opposition welcomed U.S. nuclear weapons on Japanese soil, and apart from a few conservative advocates of a Gaullist-style nuclear *force de frappe*, there was general agree-

---

26. For an extended critique of the conceptual shortcomings of the opposition as reflected in the 1960 struggle, see Takabatake Toshimichi, " 'Rokujū-nen anpo' no seishin shi," in Najita Tetsuo, Maeda Ai, and Kamishima Jirō, eds., *Sengo Nihon no seishin shi* (Tokyo: Iwanami Shoten, 1989), 70–91.

27. Welfield, *Empire in Eclipse*, 364–68, 413; on Japan's military industries, see 434–41.

ment that Japan itself should remain nuclear free. In December 1967, in response to a question in the Diet, Prime Minister Satō clarified this position as the famous "Three Nonnuclear Principles," which held that Japan would not manufacture nuclear weapons, possess them, or permit them to enter the country. Also, although U.S. policy at the time of the peace settlement secretly had anticipated Japan emerging as a major supplier of war-related material to the anticommunist camp, weapons production was not emphasized in subsequent years. Earlier in 1967, when public criticism arose concerning military-related exports to Vietnam, the Satō government responded with the "Three Principles of Arms Exports" prohibiting weapons sales to communist countries, countries under arms embargo by the United Nations, and countries in or on the verge of armed conflict. Under the Miki cabinet (1974–76) the ban was extended to include all countries and cover parts used in military equipment.[28]

Although Left and Right remained in fundamental disagreement on the Security Treaty in general, until the end of the Shōwa period successive conservative governments took care to reiterate that Japanese self-defense forces were constitutionally prohibited from engaging in overseas missions or entering into collective security pacts. The latter position was explicitly meant to scotch any prospect of a NATO-type Northeast Asia treaty organization coupling Japan with the Republic of Korea and Republic of China. In addition, although LDP policy consistently called for constitutional revision, in actuality the conservative thrust in this direction tended to wither away beginning in the mid-1960s, after the Constitution Investigation Committee that had been created after the LDP was formed failed to come up with clear recommendations to revise the national charter. Although a majority of committee members did favor revision, it had become clear by 1964, when the group issued its report, that the public opposed this.[29]

These points of tactical convergence help clarify the low-posture external policies followed by conservative cabinets ever since Yoshida's time, as well as the sources of friction that always characterized relations between the Japanese and American managers of the San Francisco System. At the same time, they also help explain how, over the course of the 1950s and 1960s, the ruling groups succeeded in taking away much of the fire of the opposition. By the beginning of the 1970s many of the most contentious issues of external policy had been defused by a combination of policy changes and the effective use of symbolic rhetoric that

28. Kenneth B. Pyle, "Japan, the World, and the Twenty-First Century," in Takashi Inoguchi and Daniel I. Okimoto, eds., *The Political Economy of Japan*, vol. 2, *The Changing International Context* (Stanford: Stanford University Press, 1988), 455–56.

29. The committee was established in 1956, met from 1957 to 1964, and dissolved in 1965. Its final report made clear that a majority favored revision, but no recommendation was made and the cabinet did not forward the report to the Diet. The nadir of the movement to revise the constitution is commonly dated from this time. This situation changed drastically after the Gulf War of 1991, when U.S. and European criticism of Japan facilitated the conservatives in dispatching an overseas "Peacekeeping Force" under United Nations auspices and thereby invigorated the movement to revise the constitution.

associated the conservatives with restraint on issues of remilitarization. Complementary accommodations took place on the domestic front. The massive protests of the late 1960s against the environmental destruction caused by growth-at-all-costs economic policies, for example, were so successful that the 1970 Diet became known as the "Pollution Diet" because of the large number of environmental protection laws it passed. More generally, these developments coincided with Japan's emergence as a mature bourgeois society, increasingly preoccupied with consumerism within and great-power status abroad.

The key moments at which hitherto inflammatory peace issues began to be detached from the agenda of public debate are fairly easy to identify. The aggravating presence of U.S. bases and troops in Japan was dramatically diminished between 1955 and 1960, when the so-called New Look (or Radford Doctrine) of U.S. strategic planners dictated that reliance on nuclear weapons made many overseas bases obsolete. Between 1955 and 1957 U.S. forces in Japan were reduced from 210,000 to 77,000 men, and by 1960 the number had dropped to 48,000. Simultaneously, the United States retreated from its extraordinary proposals to create a huge Japanese army immediately and began instead to direct military aid to creation of less conspicuous but more technologically sophisticated Japanese naval and air forces.[30] Where the mutual security treaty itself was concerned, the failure of the mass protests of 1959–60 to block treaty renewal essentially marked the end of this as a meaningful issue. Attempts to remobilize protests against the next round of treaty renewal in 1970 were ineffective. After 1960 the Security Treaty remained a convenient target of rhetoric, but a practical fait accompli.

The antinuclear movement in Japan began not in 1945 but in 1954. Until the latter part of the occupation, reportage and public remembrance of Hiroshima and Nagasaki were forbidden. It was the irradiation of Japanese fishermen by an American nuclear test in the Bikini Incident of 1954, and the death of one of the crew, that precipitated the postwar movement against nuclear weapons—and, on the Left, against nuclear energy. Even while resting comfortably under the U.S. nuclear umbrella, the conservative government did not hesitate to associate itself with antinuclear policies. Thus, the Japan Council Against Atomic and Hydrogen Bombs (Gensuikyō), founded in 1955, initially was supported by the LDP as well as parties and organizations on the Left and fell under Communist Party control only in the 1960s. In 1961 the LDP aligned itself with a new antinuclear federation, the national Council for Peace and Against Nuclear Weapons (Kakkin Kaigi). And in December 1967 Prime Minister Satō's "Three Nonnuclear Principles" were effectively introduced to suggest that the government shared the ideals of the popular antinuclear movement. Along with Article 9, the prohibition on arms exports first announced in 1967, and the "One Percent of GNP" ceiling on defense expenditures proclaimed in 1976, the Three Nonnuclear Principles be-

30. Welfield, *Empire in Eclipse*, 109–13.

came popularly identified as one of the four "symbolic constraints" on Japanese remilitarization. The government's ability to partially co-opt the antinuclear movement was further enhanced by an insular strain in the movement itself. To many Japanese, Hiroshima and Nagasaki became emblematic of World War II and thus symbolic of the unique suffering of the Japanese in that conflict. They became, that is, a way of remembering Japanese suffering while forgetting the suffering that the Japanese caused others. Such "victim consciousness"—already noted in the earliest statements of the peace movement—meshed well with the emerging neonationalism of the ruling groups.

Okinawa and China, two of the most blatant symbols of subordinate independence, were detached from the peace agenda between 1969 and 1972. By the end of the 1960s the United States had become persuaded that reversion of the Ryukyus to Japan was both feasible and wise. The development of intercontinental missiles reduced Okinawa's importance as a forward nuclear base. Pressure for reversion within Okinawa and throughout all Japan was becoming irresistible. Perhaps most interesting, the discrepancy in living standards between Japan proper and semicolonized Okinawa was becoming so conspicuous as to pose a potential serious embarrassment for the United States.[31] Thus, in the Satō-Nixon communiqué of November 1969 the United States defused this issue by agreeing to return Okinawa to full Japanese sovereignty by 1972.

Where China was concerned, Washington's unexpected rapprochement with the People's Republic in 1971 embarrassed the Japanese government, which had long adhered reluctantly to the containment policy. Nonetheless, it paved the way for Japan's own restoration of relations with Beijing, thereby removing one of the most galling features of the San Francisco System. China, obsessed by its tensions with the Soviet Union, accompanied its embrace of the United States and Japan by renouncing its previous expressions of concern about Japanese rearmament and the U.S.-Japan military alliance. This Chinese volte-face was also a severe blow to the Japanese peace movement, which hitherto had argued that Japanese remilitarization under the Security Treaty was a destabilizing factor in Asia. Moreover, the agony and madness of China's Cultural Revolution, which became apparent to the world a few years later, by indirection further discredited the Left.

By 1972 the Left thus had lost hold of many of its most evocative peace issues: U.S. bases in Japan, the Security Treaty, nuclear weapons, arms production, Okinawa, and China. A year later, with the armistice in Vietnam, the last great cause that had provided a modicum of common purpose among the opposition was removed. The average citizen turned inward, to bask in Japan's new international influence as an economic power and become consumed by material pursuits, exemplified in such mass-media slogans as "My Home−ism" and "My Car−ism." Concerned citizens redirected their "citizens' movements" or "residents' movements" toward particular grievances. The violent wing of the New

31. Kōno in Watanabe, *Sengo Nihon no taigai seisaku*, 192.

Left turned its fury as well as its tactics of armed confrontation (the so-called *geba*, from *gebaruto*, the Japanese rendering of the German word *Gewalt*, "force") inward to engage in theoretical disputes and self-destructive factional violence (*uchigeba*). Beheiren, the broad-based and charismatic People's Organization for Peace in Vietnam, which had effectively reconciled many of the Marxist and non-Marxist protest groups between 1965 and 1973, disbanded in January 1974. No comparable coalition—eclectic, populist, both humanitarian and radical, nonviolent, genuinely internationalistic and individualistic in outlook—ever took its place.

THE UNCERTAIN SUPERSTATE

In retrospect it is apparent that the early 1970s marked a major turning point in Japan's position within the international political economy. It is from this point that we can date Japan's emergence as a truly global power—and the corollary and irreversible decline of U.S. hegemony. At the time, however, this transformation of power was by no means clear. On the contrary, the 1970s were a traumatic decade for Japan's elites, marked by a succession of crises. Twenty years of slavish adherence to the U.S. containment policy were rudely rewarded by the "Nixon shock" of July 1971, when the American president unexpectedly announced U.S. rapprochement with China. One month later the Nixon shock was recharged with the "dollar shock," as two decades of low-posture Japanese neomercantilism seemed thrown into jeopardy by the unilateral U.S. decision to reevaluate the yen-dollar exchange rate. Already in the late 1960s the United States had begun to withdraw the economic umbrella that sheltered Japanese protectionism at home and economic expansion abroad. The 1971 dollar shock accelerated this process, and in 1973 the yen was allowed to float. This floating exchange rate coincided with the "oil shock" of October 1973, which brought an end to Japan's remarkable period of high growth rates and dropped the country into its most prolonged postwar recession. Production levels did not return to the 1973 level until 1978—just in time to be confronted with the "second oil shock" of January 1979. The scale of the 1979 shock was registered in a $25 billion shift in Japan's balance of payments from a $16 billion surplus in 1978 to an $8.6 billion deficit in 1979. Whereas the annual growth rate had been an extraordinary 10 to 11 percent between 1955 and 1970, in the 1970s it dropped to somewhat less than 5 percent. Concurrent with all these traumas, the country's quiet penetration of U.S. and European markets suddenly crackled into controversy, like a string of firecrackers that stretched through the 1970s and 1980s as well: over textiles in 1969–71; steel, television sets, and electronics beginning around 1977; automobiles from the turn of the decade; semiconductor chips and computers from the mid-1980s; purchase of U.S. properties from the late 1980s.[32]

Despite the stronger floating yen (which made Japanese manufactures more

---

32. For a general contemporary overview of the Japanese economy in the 1970s, see Daniel Okimoto, ed., *Japan's Economy: Coping with Change in the International Environment* (Boulder: Westview Press, 1982), especially the contributions by Gary Saxonhouse (123–48) and Hugh Patrick (149–96).

expensive abroad), Japan's penetration of foreign markets continued inexorably. And despite the end of abnormally high annual growth rates, the now-massive economy still grew enormously each year under the more normal rates. Still, it was only in 1979 that the exaggerated phrase "Japan as Number One" appeared on the scene, shocking Japanese and non-Japanese alike, albeit in very different ways. Japan was not number one. It was still a distant second to the United States in overall economic capacity, but every conventional index indicated the gap was closing rapidly. By the mid-1980s the United States had become the world's largest debtor country and Japan the world's great creditor. It was now a financial, not just "economic," superpower. In the closing years of the Shōwa period the "spin-on" military applications of Japan's advanced civilian technologies made it clear that, even without a military-industrial complex, Japan's technological accomplishments had made it a potentially significant military actor worldwide.[33] Neither structurally nor psychologically were the Japanese or anyone else in the world fully prepared to cope with such rapid, fundamental, and almost entirely unpredicted changes.

In this milieu, conflict over international issues was drastically transformed. Whereas controversy through the 1960s had focused primarily on military and peace issues, economic competition now dominated the scene, and nation-state tensions became far more engrossing than domestic confrontations. Neither in the 1970s nor in the 1980s, however, did the rise of Japan, growing economic strength of Europe, disintegration of Soviet power, and relative decline of a stumbling but still powerful America result in a clearly defined new global order. What existed, on the contrary, was closer to global disorder—and in this situation the most intense conflicts took place within the rickety old San Francisco System. The major disputes occurred, that is, among the capitalist powers and especially between Japan and the United States. Within Japan itself, policy-related conflict became increasingly detached from the public arena and more concentrated among the conservative elites, where expanding international involvement was accompanied by a proliferation of competing interests in both the corporate and bureaucratic sectors.[34] As internal conflict shifted to and expanded among these vested interests, it became less visible. The highly technical nature of international trade and finance—and, indeed, of many new military developments as well— also inhibited wide-ranging public debate. Specialists and insiders now controlled the terms of public discourse.

Isolated individuals and groups continued during this period to try to offer alternative visions beyond unbridled capitalist competition and (a new term for the 1980s) "technonationalism." They emphasized such global issues as the north-

<hr />

33. John W. Dower, "Japan's New Military Edge," *Nation*, 3 July 1989; Steven K. Vogel, *Japanese High Technology, Politics and Power*, Research Paper No. 2, Berkeley Roundtable on the International Economy, Mar. 1989.

34. See Pempel, "Unbundling of 'Japan, Inc.,' " for an analysis of this diversification among the ruling elites. This is generally seen as marking the end of the 1955 System. This same theme permeates many of the articles in Pyle, *Trade Crisis*.

south problem of growing disparity between rich and have-not nations, the social exploitation and distortions caused by multinational corporations in less developed countries, the depletion of global resources by economic powerhouses such as Japan and the other advanced industrialized countries, and the continuing intensification of the nuclear arms race. Where Japan itself was concerned, they pointed out that remilitarization was accelerating amidst all the hubbub about economics, which was entirely true. During the last decades of Shōwa the often-mentioned "symbolic restraints" on Japanese militarization all were violated in one way or another. Prime Minister Satō's famous Three Nonnuclear Principles, for example, were misleading from the start. Contrary to what they proclaimed, nuclear weapons apparently were brought in and out of Japan by the U.S. military as a matter of routine. Furthermore, the LDP coupled the Three Nonnuclear Principles with a less-publicized "Four Nuclear Principles," which included dependence on the U.S. nuclear "umbrella" and promotion of nuclear energy for peaceful use.

The critics also pointed out that the heralded "One Percent of GNP" restraint on defense spending was deceptive. In the first place, by NATO-style calculations, which include military retirement benefits and the like, Japanese military spending generally exceeded one percent of GNP. More important by far, 1 percent of a huge and constantly expanding economy was itself huge and constantly expanding. Thus, for most of the postwar period the rate of annual increase in Japan's *real* military expenditures was the highest in the world.[35] Moreover, in 1987 Prime Minister Nakasone Yasuhiro, an astute player with symbols, deliberately breached the one percent guideline. Four years earlier, at the urging of the U.S. government, Nakasone also had terminated another of the vaunted symbolic restraints on Japanese remilitarization by jettisoning the embargo on export of weapons and military-related manufactures. The United States desired to gain access to advanced Japanese technology in developing its "Star Wars" (Strategic Defense Initiative) dreams, and Nakasone's compliance opened the door to an absolutely uncertain future for Japanese activity in advanced weapons systems. Criticism of such developments by the remnants of serious opposition, however, made scarcely a ripple in popular consciousness.[36]

35. In 1976, the year the "1 percent of GNP" ceiling was first singled out as a formal guideline, Japan's military spending ranked seventh in the world—after the two superpowers, China, West Germany, France, and Great Britain. Its military budget was more than triple that of South Korea, far greater than that of any of the Warsaw Pact powers, and far greater than that of neutral powers such as India, Sweden, and Switzerland. Japan's 1976 military budget was almost 14 times that of 1954. For Britain over the same period the increase was 2.5 times, for France roughly 5 times, and for West Germany a little less than 7 times. Welfield, *Empire in Eclipse*, 366–69, includes useful tables of these expenditures.

36. Publishing houses such as Iwanami, which includes the monthly *Sekai* among its periodicals, continued to address these issues with a rigor reminiscent of the earlier period, and scholars such as Sakamoto Yoshikazu remained devoted to "peace research" in the broadest sense. See Sakamoto, *Shinpan: Gunshuku no seijigaku* (Tokyo: Iwanami Shinsho, 1988). For critical evaluations of the course of

The decline of intense public debate on such issues reflected an erosion of democratic ideals and practices at a time when Japan was, in fact, being called on internationally to offer a new vision of national goals and responsibilities commensurate with its new power. Indeed, there almost appeared to be a correlation between the rise to global eminence and decline of political idealism. Japan had become a prosperous superstate by mobilizing its population and resources resolutely behind productivity and economic nationalism, and its accomplishments drew understandable admiration and envy from throughout the world. The line between mobilization and regimentation is a fine one, however, and the Japanese state of the 1970s and 1980s also appeared to many observers, especially abroad, to have stepped over that line. In part, this perception reflected the partial success of the conservative hegemony in perpetuating the occupation-period "reverse course" and steadily undermining what were called the "excesses" of early postwar political idealism. Once "democratization" was replaced by economic development as the overriding objective, most Japanese had little choice but to become socialized to corporate and national goals. As time passed, such regimentation was sweetened by the material rewards of prosperity and hardened by nationalistic appeals. The emergence of a mass consumer society created an ethos of "middle-class" homogeneity and contributed immeasurably to depoliticization (or preoccupation with personal and local matters). Global eminence, in turn, nurtured not only legitimate feelings of national pride but also more ominous attitudes of exceptionalism and racial and cultural superiority.

In theory both Japan's emergence as a global power and the rapid growth of consumerism and middle-class ideologies should have stimulated an increasingly cosmopolitan outlook at all levels of society. In many respects, a broader supranational attitude did materialize: "internationalization" (*kokusaika*) was perhaps the most overworked catchword of the 1980s. The opposite, however, occurred as well. Insular, nationalistic fixations became stronger side by side with the intensification of international contacts. This apparent paradox is not difficult to account for, for the pride that Japanese felt at being called "number one" was compounded by fear and anger at the negative response of other countries to Japan's suddenly awesome competitive power. As foreign criticism of Japan's economic expansion mounted—emerging in accusations that the Japanese practiced "adversarial trade" or "neomercantilism" or "beggar-thy-neighbor" capture of markets, for example, or that domestic "nontariff barriers" and "structural impediments" made the Japanese market unfairly difficult for outsiders to penetrate—a defensiveness bordering on siege mentality developed in many circles. Mistrust and tension that had been latent within the old San Francisco System

democracy in postwar Japan, see Rokurō Hidaka, *The Price of Affluence: Dilemmas of Contemporary Japan* (Sydney: Penguin Books Australia, 1985); Gavan McCormack and Yoshio Sugimoto, eds., *Democracy in Contemporary Japan* (Sydney: Hale and Iremonger, 1986); and Takeshi Ishida and Ellis S. Krauss, eds., *Democracy in Japan* (Pittsburgh: University of Pittsburgh Press, 1989).

erupted openly. Strains of "victim consciousness" that had always existed across the political spectrum were drawn to the surface. War imagery became fashionable on all sides, albeit now in the post-cold-war context of "economic war" among the capitalist powers, especially the United States and Japan.[37]

In these circumstances, pride-inspiring and fear-inspiring at once, many Japanese began to turn inward and argue that the differences between the Japanese and other nations, races, and cultures were greater than the similarities and that Japan's contemporary accomplishments derived primarily from these unique characteristics—more so, that is, than from more general factors such as unanticipated historical opportunities (like war booms), global circumstances (such as the decline of the United States for reasons fundamentally having little to do with Japan), external patronage (notably the U.S. economic and military umbrella), transnational market mechanisms, rational (rather than cultural) policy structures and decisions, and, indeed, the consolidation of power in the hands of a competitive and diversified but still remarkably close-knit hegemony of business leaders, bureaucrats, and conservative politicians. Eventually this insular and usually narcissistic preoccupation with so-called traditional values took on a life of its own in the mass media—primarily in the runaway genre of writings and discussions devoted to the uniqueness of "being Japanese" (*Nihonjinron*)—but from the outset such introversion was promoted as a clearcut ideology by the conservative leadership.[38] In 1968, for example, the LDP showed its hand clearly in this regard when it attempted to turn centennial celebrations of the Meiji Restoration into an occasion for repudiating the most liberal ideals of the early postwar period. "We have forfeited the inherent form of the Japanese people," the party lamented in an important statement, and to rectify this loss it was desirable to reaffirm the great values of the Meiji era and bring about "the elevation of racial spirit and morality" (*minzoku seishin to dōgi no kōyō*).[39]

The conservatives never lost sight of this goal, and the closing decades of the postwar era saw them advance steadily toward it. They proved themselves masters of symbolic politics, and most of the controversial neonationalist developments of late Shōwa reflected this ideological fixation on recreating a traditionalistic "racial spirit" that would counterbalance the purportedly corrupting influences of excessive internationalization. In numerous ways the government assumed an increasingly active role in romanticizing the patriotic and public-spirited nature of

37. Kenneth Pyle has summarized the range of opinion on Japan's world role in two useful articles: see "Japan, the World" and "In Pursuit of a Grand Design: Nakasone Betwixt the Past and Present," in Pyle, *Trade Crisis*, 5–32.

38. For extended critical analyses of the *Nihonjinron* genre, see Ross E. Mouer and Yoshio Sugimoto, *Images of Japanese Society: A Study in the Structure of Social Reality* (London: KPI, 1986), and Peter N. Dale, *The Myth of Japanese Uniqueness* (New York: St. Martin's, 1986).

39. The full text appears in *Asahi shinbun*, 17 Jan. 1968, 2. The LDP also defined "the inherent form of the Japanese people" (*Nihon kokumin no honzen no sugata*) as consisting of "human love and public duty, love of the motherland and racial spirit, defense consciousness, etc." (*ningenai to kōtokushin, sokokuai to minzoku seishin, bōei ishiki nado*).

Japan's prewar imperial and imperialistic history. The corporate sector, on its part, made brilliant use of group pressures and "family" ideologies to reassert not merely the primacy of the group over the individual, but also the primacy of the family writ large (the corporation and the state) over the real nuclear family. Collectivist and consensual values were promoted as the antidote to individualistic democracy and the ideals of principled dissent.

The postwar period ended on this discordant clamor, with fanfare about "internationalization" mingling with paeans to "racial spirit" and "being Japanese." The juxtaposition of external and domestic concerns was familiar, but the contradictions between opening outward and turning inward, cosmopolitanism and exceptionalism, were unusually blatant. What this contradiction boded for the future was unpredictable. In every way, however, it seemed a far cry from the earlier and more visionary era when large notions of "peace" and "democracy" had defined the parameters of political consciousness.

CHAPTER TWO

Japan's Position in the World System

Bruce Cumings

What does Japan look like when it is viewed from without, as if it were a black box, as if little that happened within Japan was of great moment? In other words, what did Japan look like to the American architects of the postwar order? Dean Acheson, George Kennan, and John Foster Dulles—to take three of the most important planners—did not study Japan, nor did they know it; they wished to situate Japan structurally in a world system shaped by the United States so that Japan would do what it should without having to be told. In so doing they placed distinct outer limits on Japan's behavior, and these limits persist today.

From the standpoint of the world and the postwar settlement, Japan has not entered a "post-postwar" era, however much that may be true in the domestic sphere. Instead, the definition of Japan's place occurred in the period 1947 to 1950, to which I will pay greatest attention, and this definition still governs the situation today. In this period the tectonic plates of the substructure found their resting place after the earthquake of World War II; a strong aftershock came again in 1971, to account for Japan's increasing economic power, but in the early 1990s we remain in the system established in the late 1940s and modified in the early 1970s.

It is equally true that the dramatic events of 1989–90 in Europe and the Soviet Union have demolished part of the basis of the postwar settlement and the cold war. At this writing the "revolution of 1989" has had little impact on either the capitalist or the communist states of East Asia. But it is likely that it will, because Japan's postwar position is a regional expression of a war settlement that can be compared across the globe. So for the first time in forty years it appears that we have entered a period when Japan's position will be redefined. Merely to move from the passive to the active tense sends a chill up the American spine: we are in a period when Japan will redefine its position in the postwar world. But that is the subject of the future. Here we can turn to the subject of the past: postwar Japan's position in the world, considered as history.

THE GREAT CRESCENT AND THE KENNAN
RESTORATION, 1947–50

Caring little about the internal workings of a nation induces parsimony: stated succinctly, Japan in the postwar system has been an engine of the world economy, an American-defined "economic animal" shorn of its prewar military and political clout. This definition of Japan's place was hammered out in 1947, coterminous with (and as a result of) the cold war, and was deeply conditioned by Japan's benefits from America's wars in Korea and Vietnam. In this era, which ran from Truman through Johnson, Japan was a dutiful American partner, and the partner was tickled pink at Japan's economic success. As the American capacity unilaterally to manage the global system declined in the 1960s, however, a new duality afflicted the U.S.-Japan relationship: Japan should do well, yes . . . but not so well that it hurt American interests. American thinking about Japan remains firmly within that duality today, symbolized by the inability of elites to do more than oscillate between free trade and protectionism, between admiration for Japan's success and alarm at its new prowess. This ambivalence is, however, nothing new: industrial Japan has always inspired, in the world at large, surprise and awe, fear and loathing.

As I have argued elsewhere, when Japan is looked at from without, from the standpoint of the world, since 1868 two prime factors have accounted for much Japanese behavior and have imparted unique characteristics to the political economy: its position in the world system and the temporal dimension of its industrialization phases, that is, what is called "late" development.[1] Japan emerged as a modern state late in world time and in one of the few remaining interstices in the nineteenth century world system. Thus, Japan's industrialization, as well as its various pre-1945 colonial and aggressive ventures, have had a defensive, posthaste, even lathered aspect about them; no people has been more aware of the costs and benefits of sharp competition in the world system. The Western threat and Japan's relative backwardness concentrated the Japanese mind, just as Japanese success congealed in the Western mind two images of Japan, symbolized by England's Japanophilia and Germany's fear of "the yellow peril" at the turn of the century.[2]

With most of the good colonial territories already spoken for and with Western powers knocking at her door, Japan had little space to maneuver, apparently little choice but to colonize its contiguous neighbors. If Japan's reform and industrialization after 1868 were defensive, so it was with Japan's expansion: offensive to Taiwanese and Koreans, it looked defensive to Japanese planners in a predatory

1. See Cumings, *The Origins of the Korean War: Liberation and the Emergence of Separate Regimes, 1945–47* (Princeton: Princeton University Press, 1981), chaps. 1 and 2; but see also Cumings, "The Origins and Development of the Northeast Asian Political Economy: Product Cycles, Industrial Sectors and Political Consequences," *International Organization* 38, no. 1 (Winter 1984): 1–40.

2. Jean-Pierre Lehmann, *The Image of Japan: From Feudal Isolation to World Power, 1850–1905* (London: Allen and Unwin, 1978), 178.

world. Thus, unlike virtually any other imperial power, Japan colonized countries close to its borders. This strategy made a close, tight, integral linking of the colony to the metropole quite feasible. In the 1930s Japan—like all the other powers— withdrew from the world system and pursued with its colonies a self-reliant, go-it-alone path to development that not only generated remarkably high indus- trial growth rates but changed the face of Northeast Asia. In this decade what we might call the "natural economy" of the region was created; although it was not natural, its rational division of labor and developmental implants have skewed East Asian development ever since.

Japan's defeat in 1945 meant a quick collapse of this Northeast Asian system and foreign occupation of the homeland. The initial American policy was demili- tarization and democratization, assuming that the enemy and therefore the object of policy was Japan or, more particularly, Japanese militarism. This policy did not have much to say about postwar Japan's position in the world or the nearby region; indeed, the policy was predicated on the American relationship with the country thought likely to be the important power in East Asia, Nationalist China. The policy posited severe limits on Japanese industrial production and reparations procedures favoring not Japan but Japan's neighbors, all of which were to become independent of Japanese influence.

Japan was demilitarized and democratized during the early occupation years, if with less thoroughness than the proponents of the policy had hoped. But the regional and global implications of the early policy were exactly reversed in the "reverse course," as American planners came to look at Japan's near reaches to see what they could do for Japan, rather than what Japan could do for them. In retrospect it is thus proper to view the years 1945–47 as an exception to the general thrust of American policy toward Japan in the postwar period, a policy initially elaborated during the war years by Japanophiles in the State Department, who looked forward to reforms that would quickly restore Japan's position in the world economy and that would not penalize Japan's industrial leaders for their support of the war.[3]

By 1947 Japan had been replaced by a new American enemy, the Soviet Union, a point that will surprise no one. More important, it had also become apparent by 1947 that the hegemonic rules and systems enunciated at Bretton Woods in 1944 would not suffice to revive Europe and restore the world economy. The inherent multilateralism of the Bretton Woods arrangements would not work with prostrate European states, and England was too weak to make a real differ- ence; thus, the United States would have to take on a unilateral and expensive role if the nonsocialist industrial economies were to become engines of growth in the world economy.

From a world system perspective the United States was the one great power

3. Akira Iriye, *Power and Culture: The Japanese-American War, 1941–1945* (Cambridge: Harvard University Press, 1981), 149–54.

with the central economic, financial, and technical force to restore the health of the world economy. Although hegemony usually connotes "relative dominance" within the group of core states,[4] by 1947 it was apparent that the United States would have to exercise unilateral dominance for some time, given the gross asymmetry between the robustness of the American industrial system and the poverty of nearly all the others. This critical problem of industrial revival, spanning Western Europe and Japan, detonated basic shifts in 1947; the reverse course in Japan was thus *an outcome of global policy*—as William Borden has aptly demonstrated.[5] The new goal was the reconstitution and flourishing of the German and Japanese industrial economies as engines of world growth, now shorn of their former military and political force. But the revival of Axis industry also spelled out a new regional policy, as did the developing cold war.

Soviet-American conflict in central Europe had erected barriers to almost any exchange, a great divide known to Americans as the Iron Curtain. Both this and the subsequent "Bamboo Curtain" in East Asia sliced up marketing and exchange patterns that had underpinned important regional economies. The bulwarks dropped across the central front in Europe, and the developing cold war in Asia cut the Western European and Japanese economies off from peripheral and semiperipheral sources of food, raw materials, and labor: in Eastern Europe, grain from Poland and Hungary, meat and potatoes from Poland, oil and coal from Romania and Silesia; in East Asia, rice and minerals from Korea, sugar from Taiwan, coking coal from Manchuria, and tungsten from South China were all under threat. With the European recovery so sluggish, Japan still dormant, and communist parties threatening in Italy and France, China and Korea, this structural problem was newly perceived and demanded action in 1947. The East Asian expression of this policy had an elegant metaphor.

The foundation of containment in East Asia was a world-economy logic, captured by Dean Acheson's metaphor of a "great crescent" stretching from Japan through Southeast Asia and around India, ultimately to the oil fields of the Persian Gulf.[6] If Franklin Roosevelt was the architect of policy for a single, "one-world" system, when that conception failed Acheson and others devised a

4. Immanuel Wallerstein, *Historical Capitalism* (New York: Verso, 1983), 58.

5. William S. Borden, *The Pacific Alliance: United States Foreign Economic Policy and Japanese Trade Recovery, 1947–1955* (Madison: University of Wisconsin Press, 1984). See also Charles Maier, "The Politics of Productivity," in Peter Katzenstein, ed., *Power and Plenty* (Madison: University of Wisconsin Press, 1978), 45; and Joan Spero, *The Politics of International Economic Relations*, 2d ed. (New York: St. Martin's, 1981), 37–41.

6. William Borden and Michael Schaller have done original and pathbreaking work on the "Great Crescent" program (Acheson and the State Department used the term several times in 1949–50). See Borden, *Pacific Alliance*, and Michael Schaller, *The American Occupation of Japan: The Origins of the Cold War in Asia* (New York: Oxford University Press, 1985). I have set out my ideas here at greater length in *The Origins of the Korean War* (Princeton: Princeton University Press, 1990), vol. 2, chaps. 2 and 5; and in *Industrial Behemoth: The Northeast Asian Political Economy in the Twentieth Century* (Ithaca: Cornell University Press, forthcoming).

second-best strategy of regional concentrations of strength within the non-Communist "grand area" to forestall the greater catastrophe of further expansion by independent, socialist, state-controlled economies; they also were dead set against a less formidable type of political economy, the nationalist autarkies of the 1930s. Although containment was thought to be preeminently a security strategy against communist expansion, in East Asia the policy mingled power and plenty inextricably; Acheson's "defense perimeter" in Asia, which he articulated in January 1950, was a reference both to island defense positions and to the Great Crescent. Also, containment in Europe and Japan *always* meant two things: the overt goal of blocking communist expansion and the surreptitious goal of containing Germany and Japan (this is the interior logic of retaining American bases in Japan and seeking to keep reunified Germany as a part of NATO).

American planners thought the solution to the "dollar gap" and the sluggish European and Japanese recovery lay in lifting restrictions on heavy industry to make these economies self-supporting and in finding ways to combine Germany and Japan with their old providers of raw materials and markets. Borden wrote that Germany and Japan thus formed "the key to the balance of power" and shrewdly observed that whereas Germany was merely "the pivot" of the larger Marshall Plan program, "the Japanese recovery program formed the sole large-scale American effort in Asia."[7] Germany was divided and held by multiple foreign occupants and thus remained a pivot; unitary Japan under American unilateral dominance became the centerpiece of an Asian regional economy.

The Great Crescent fits nicely with a Wallersteinian world-system conception of multiple, overlapping tripartite hierarchies: if the United States was the dominant core economy in the world, Japan and Germany would underpin regional core systems and help reintegrate peripheral areas as exclusively held empires disintegrated. The "high-tech" industries of the 1940s, represented in world-competitive American firms such as Westinghouse, General Electric, IBM, General Motors, Ford, and the multinational oil firms, expressed America's "core" superiority; they had nothing to fear from Japan and Germany as long as the latter were kept on capital, technology, defense, and resource dependencies.

In East Asia, American planners envisioned a regional economy driven by revived Japanese industry, with assured continental access to markets and raw materials for its exports. This approach would achieve several ends: it would link together nations threatened by socialist state-controlled economies (containment), make Japan self-supporting (or continent), weave sinews of economic interdependence with Japan and the United States (plenty), and help draw down the European colonies by getting a Japanese and American foot in the door of the pound and franc blocs in Asia (power and plenty).

After the victory of the Chinese revolution the search for Japan's hinterland came to mean mostly Southeast Asia, but in 1947–48 Korea, Manchuria, and

7. Borden, *Pacific Alliance*, 15.

North China were all targets of potential reintegration with Japan. In a stunning intervention at the beginning of the famous "fifteen weeks," Secretary of State George Marshall himself scribbled a note to Acheson that said, "Please have plan drafted of policy to organize a definite government of So. Korea and *connect up* its economy with that of Japan" (Marshall's emphasis), a mouthful that captures with pith and foresight the direction of U.S. policy toward Korea from 1947 to the normalization with Japan in 1965.[8]

If Acheson was the architect of the Great Crescent and containment in East Asia, George Kennan was the engineer, accomplishing the reverse course in a number of deft strokes from early 1947 to early 1948, when he journeyed out to a momentous meeting with General Douglas MacArthur in Tokyo. The core of Kennan's containment vision was a parsimonious theory of industrial structure. Whereas Acheson shaped the grand area into which marched a bloc of American world-competitive industries, Kennan had a realpolitik conception of *national* industry: an advanced industrial base was essential to war-making capacity and great-power status. We had four such economies to their one, and things should be kept that way. That is, containment meant defending the United States, England, Western Europe, and Japan, but not worrying about every brushfire war or revolution in the pre-industrial underbelly, and especially not in what Kennan took to be distant and depraved Asia.[9]

Only Japan held Kennan's attentions in East Asia, and his new notoriety and strategic placement in 1947 made it possible for him to author the "reverse course," or what we may call the Kennan Restoration—even if he was helped along by Max Bishop and various others in the "Japan lobby."[10] If Acheson wanted Japan revived as an industrial power of the second rank and posted as an engine of world-economy accumulation, Kennan wanted it restored as a regional power of the second rank, hamstrung by the hegemonic power but free to dominate its historic territory. Kennan wanted Japanese power restored thus to butt up against the Soviets, to establish a balance of power like that at the turn of the century, and to save the needless spillage of American blood and treasure.

The operative document for the reverse course, developed in draft form under Kennan's aegis in September 1947, envisioned a Japan that would be "friendly to the United States," amenable to American leadership in foreign affairs, "industrially revived as a producer primarily of consumer's goods and secondarily of capital goods," and active in foreign trade; militarily it would be "reliant upon the U.S. for its security from external attack." The paper reserved to the United

8. Marshall's note to Acheson of 29 Jan. 1947, attached to Vincent to Acheson, 27 Jan. 1947, 740.0019 Control (Korea) file, box 3827, National Archives.

9. See especially his remarks in "Transcript of Roundtable Discussion on American Foreign Policy Toward China," U.S. State Department, 6–8 Oct. 1949 (Carrollton Press, 1977, item 316B).

10. On this lobby, see Howard Schonberger, "The Japan Lobby in American Diplomacy," *Pacific Historical Review* 46, no. 3 (Aug. 1977): 327–59; John G. Roberts, "The 'Japan Crowd' and the Zaibatsu Restoration," *Japan Interpreter* 12 (Summer 1979): 384–415.

States "a moral right to intervene" in Japan should "stooge groups" like the Japan Communist Party threaten stability. Leaving little to the imagination, it went on, "Recognizing that the former industrial and commercial leaders of Japan are the ablest leaders in the country, that they are the most stable element, that they have the strongest natural ties with the US, it should be US policy to remove obstacles to their finding their natural level in Japanese leadership."[11]

Thus, Kennan called for an end to the purge of war criminals and business groups who had supported them, a bilateral U.S.-Japan peace treaty to be "initiated in the immediate future," "minimum possible reparations," and, in general, an integration of Japan into the bipolar global structure. Later on Kennan did not shrink before etching out Japan's presumed need for an economic hinterland. In October 1949 he referred to "a terrible dilemma" for American policy:

> You have the terrific problem of how then the Japanese are going to get along unless they reopen some sort of Empire toward the South. Clearly we have got . . . to achieve opening up of trade possibilities, commercial possibilities for Japan on a scale very far greater than anything Japan knew before. It is a formidable task. On the other hand, it seems to me absolutely inevitable that we must keep completely the maritime and air controls as a means . . . of keeping control of the situation with respect to [the] Japanese in all eventualities . . . [it is] all the more imperative that we retain the ability to control their situation by controlling the overseas sources of supply and the naval power and air power without which it cannot become again aggressive.

As if the listener might mistake his intent, he went on, "If we really in the Western world could work out controls, I suppose, adept enough and foolproof enough and cleverly enough exercised really to have power over what Japan imports in the way of oil and such other things as she has got to get from overseas, we would have veto power on what she does need in the military and industrial field."[12] It was a masterful performance, elaborating in detail what the Japan Lobby figure Harry Kern meant when he said of the U.S.-Japan relationship, " 'Remote control' is best."[13]

Kennan went further than other officials were willing to go, however, in conjuring a military role for Japan. As he put it in September 1949,

11. "U.S. Policy Toward a Peace Settlement with Japan," 22 Sept. 1947, RG 59, Policy Planning Staff (PPS) file, box 32, National Archives (NA). This document was the basis for National Security Council (NSC) document 13/2 of October 1948, the instrument governing the reverse course. See NSC file, box 206, Harry S. Truman Library (HST).

12. "Transcript of Roundtable Discussion." For a fine account of Japan's postwar position in the world economy, see Jon Halliday, "The Specificity of Japan's Re-integration into the World Capitalist Economy after 1945: Notes on Some Myths and Misconceptions," *Rivista Internazionale di Scienze Economiche e Commerciali* 28, nos. 7–8 (July–Aug. 1981): 663–81.

13. Harry Kern, "American Policy Toward Japan," 1948, a privately circulated paper, in Pratt Papers, box 2, Naval War College, Newport, Rhode Island. "Remote control" was in Kern's quotation marks because it was George Sansom's term.

The day will come, and possibly sooner than we think, when realism will call upon us not to oppose the re-entry of Japanese influence and activity into Korea and Manchuria. This is, in fact, the only realistic prospect for countering and moderating Soviet influence in that area. . . . The concept of using such a balance of power is not a new one in U.S. foreign policy, and the [Policy Planning] Staff considers that we cannot return too soon, in the face of the present international situation, to a recognition of its validity.

This was a mere four years after Japan's defeat and the collapse of its empire in Korea and Manchuria. But Kennan was harking back forty years, to Theodore Roosevelt's role in justifying and supporting Japan's preeminent role on the Northeast Asian mainland.[14] That Koreans and Chinese might resist a reimposition of Japanese power was of little moment to Kennan; Korea and China were "black boxes," too, and a Japan that was America's junior partner was preferable to a Soviet Union that was not.

REGIONAL STRATEGY: CONTAINMENT AND ROLLBACK

Kennan's logic assumed a revival of Japan's regional military position, but what Acheson had in mind was a restoration of its economic role. The needs of the Japanese economy drove regional policy, just as the needs of the world economy drove Japan policy, as planners searched for a suitable Asian hinterland. Various plans to recover a hinterland bubbled up at the end of 1948, when it was obvious that the Nationalists had lost the civil war in China.

The CIA had issued new estimates in the light of the "fall" of China and the revival of Japan. Its estimate of "the strategic importance of Japan" in mid-1948 argued that the extension of Soviet control over North China, Manchuria, and "the whole of Korea" would result in "an incalculable loss of US prestige throughout the Far East"; it linked the revival of the Japanese economy to the need for a hinterland: "The key factor in postwar development of Japan is economic rehabilitation. As in the past, Japan, for normal economic functioning on an industrial basis, must have access to the Northeast Asiatic areas—notably North China, Manchuria, and Korea—now under direct, indirect, or potential control of the USSR." Southeast Asia might be able to compensate for the loss of Japan's old colonies, but there the Japanese would face European competition and indigenous anticolonial nationalism. Furthermore, Japan had to export and Southeast Asia would suffice only if native industry remained undeveloped there.

14. Kennan to Rusk and Jessup, 8 Sept. 1949, PPS file, box 13. Kennan went on to footnote Theodore Roosevelt's letter of 1905 to Senator Henry Cabot Lodge, saying that it is best that Russia "should be left face to face with Japan so that each may have a moderative effect on the other," and Tyler Dennett's judgment that "Japanese ascendancy in the peninsula" was preferable to "Korean misgovernment, Chinese interference, or Russian bureaucracy."

Thus, "geographical proximity and the character of its economic development make Northeast Asia [more] complementary to the economy of Japan," the CIA argued, mentioning markets and raw materials as the key elements; among them were Manchuria's iron ore and North Korea's ferrous alloys. An integration of these areas "could provide the largest industrial potential of any area in the Far East." But if Japan were "excluded from Northeast Asia" over a long term, this exclusion "would so drastically distort Japan's natural trade pattern that economic stability could be maintained only if the US were prepared to underwrite substantial trade deficits on a continuing basis." The report went on to say that the United States would also have to supply Japan with "many essential raw materials," such as lumber, pulp, and coking coal. Were the United States not to do this, Japan might "align itself with the USSR as the only means of returning to economic normality."[15]

The problem, of course, was that from mid-1948 onward Northeast China was under Communist control and a people's republic had been proclaimed in North Korea. The concern for recovering a peripheral hinterland for Japan thus began to move American policy beyond a passive containment and toward positive "rollback" by the beginning of 1949; rollback appeared not as a new policy but as an increasingly discussed alternative or contingency. Max Bishop, often thought to be a member of the State Department's "pro-Japan" contingent, was among the first to discern a new, postcontainment logic. As chief of the Division of Northeast Asian Affairs, he argued in December 1948 that the changed situation resulting from Mao's impending victory necessitated a careful review of policy: "Should communist domination of the entire Korean peninsula become an accomplished fact, the islands of Japan would be surrounded on three sides by an unbroken arc of communist territories. . . . [W]e would be confronted with increasing difficulties in attempting to hold Japan within the U.S. sphere." If South Korea should fall, the United States "would have lost its last friend on the continent"; failure to face this problem in Korea "could eventually destroy U.S. security in the Pacific." It was the ancient strategic logic of Hideyoshi and the Meiji *genrō:* Korea as a dagger at the heart of Japan.

Bishop suggested a "positive effort," in Truman Doctrine language, "to develop in non-Soviet northeast Asia a group of independent people . . . who, on an economically viable basis, are capable of successfully resisting communist expansion." Paraphrasing Kennan's logic, he noted that Northeast Asia constituted "one of the four or five significant power centers in the world." And so he asked the *containment* question: "whether communist expansion in northeast Asia had already reached the point at which the security interests of the U.S. required positive efforts to prevent further expansion." But then, he went on to ask a *rollback* question: "whether the communist power system, already brutally

15. CIA, "The Strategic Importance of Japan," ORE 43–48, 24 May 1948, Presidential Secretary's File (PSF), box 255, HST.

frank and outspoken in its hostility to the U.S., must be caused to draw back from its present extensive holdings."[16]

Perhaps the most stunning example of such thinking was written by an unnamed person in the liberal Economic Cooperation Agency (ECA). It identified Communist-controlled North China and Manchuria as the one area on the mainland "of vital importance to the U.S."; the Japanese had "proved it to be the key to control of China," and the United States ought to regard it in the same light. The region contained most of the heavy industry and "exploitable natural resources." Nearly 90 percent of China's coal came from there, and it also exported foodstuffs, especially soybeans. The nearest source of coking coal for Japan's steel mills would be West Virginia if Chinese resources were not available. Thus, "without the resources of this area, there would be literally no hope of achieving a viable economy in Japan." If the Soviet Union were to control this region, "Japan, Korea, and the rest of China would be doomed to military and industrial impotence except on Russian terms."

The author accordingly recommended a new, "limited" policy for the United States: "our first concern must be the liberation of Manchuria and North China from communist domination." This goal would require a "far-reaching commitment for American assistance" on the pattern of Greece, including the training and equipping of "a Chinese army capable of recovering and holding Manchuria and North China." Once the region were secured, the United States could pour in investment (it would not take so much, since the Japanese had earlier made the region "a going concern"); this investment should be accompanied by extensive reforms of land, tax, and credit arrangements. Here was not Curtis LeMay's hair-shirt rollback, but liberal rollback, "limited" rollback, and it was Japan-linked rollback: "The strategic and economic relationship of North China and Manchuria with Korea and Japan is especially clear." Acheson's reaction is not known, but a covering memo informed him that the document "has met with such approbation in a number of quarters that you might be interested in reading it."[17]

The principal planning for incorporating parts of Asia in Japan's regional sphere occurred in the summer and fall of 1949. From July through December the U.S. government conducted a wide-ranging review of Asia policy, culminating in National Security Council document 48, the new paper for Asia that made containment official policy in Asia, six months before the Korean War.[18] The most interesting and most important part of the NSC 48 process was the underly-

16. Bishop to Butterworth, *Foreign Relations of the United States* 6 (1948): 1337–41.

17. "U.S. Policy in China," 3 Nov. 1948, Acheson Papers, box 27, HST; this document was sent to Acheson by someone named "Joe" in the ECA, who was not necessarily the author. "Joe" was probably Joseph Jones, who at the same time proposed that the United States take the lead in "clearing China of communism on Japan's behalf," in Schaller's words; *American Occupation of Japan*, 142.

18. See Bruce Cumings, "Introduction," in Cumings, ed., *Child of Conflict: The Korean-American Relationship, 1943–1953* (Seattle: University of Washington Press, 1983); also Robert M. Blum, *Drawing the Line: The Origin of the American Containment Policy in East Asia* (New York: Norton, 1982).

ing economic conception that linked power and plenty and, more explicitly than the 1947 planning we discussed above, embodied a design for an Asian "grand area," a regional hierarchy of core, semiperiphery, and periphery in the broader world system. A revived industrial core in Japan came first; keeping South Korea, Taiwan, and Southeast Asia (including especially Indochina) in the world market came next; then there was the question of what other areas might be brought in if conditions permitted.

The vision behind the policy was the Smithian, internationalist creed of a world of interdependent free trade, encouraging the export of American plant and technology. The core thinking appeared first in a 31 August draft of NSC 48, unsigned and with no departmental identification, entitled "Asia, Economics Section."[19] It began by saying that American economic policy should be "measured against principles." What were the principles? First principle: "the economic life of the modern world is geared to expansion"; this expansion required "the establishment of conditions favorable to the export of technology and capital and to a liberal trade policy throughout the world." Second principle: "reciprocal exchange and mutual advantage." Third principle: "production and trade which truly reflect comparative advantage." Fourth principle: opposition to "general industrialization"—that is, Asian countries do indeed possess "special resources" and the like, "but none of them alone has adequate resources as a base for general industrialization." India, China, and Japan merely "approximate that condition." And then the injunction against mercantilism and self-reliance: "General industrialization in individual countries could be achieved only at a high cost as a result of sacrificing production in fields of comparative advantage." Fifth principle: certain parts of the world, such as Southeast Asia (but also parts of South America and Africa), are "natural sources of supply of strategic commodities and other basic materials," giving the United States "a special opportunity for leverage" as a "large and very welcome customer." Sixth principle: "in trade with countries under Soviet control or domination, the above principles are not applicable."

The paper went on to mention that Japan had obtained 80 percent of its coal from North and Northeast China and from northern Korea; that Japan's economy, to be viable, must quickly realize "an enlargement of foreign trade"; it should also revive steel production, but only to a level of four million tons or so, for domestic market needs; it should revive merchant shipping, but only to Asian countries; and it should find its markets in Asia, not elsewhere. (Japan, too, was unfit for comprehensive, world-class industrialization.)

Succeeding drafts embodied these ideas; a draft of 14 October elaborated on the virtues of a triangular, hierarchical structure, which "would involve the export from the US to Japan of such commodities as cotton, wheat, coal and possibly specialized industrial machinery; the export from Japan of such items as low-cost

19. In NSC 48 file, HST. The document has markings indicating it was coordinated with a CIA draft, if it was not itself drafted in the CIA; it also shows that Max Bishop, not an NSC member, checked it out on 15 September 1949.

agricultural and transportation equipment, textiles, and shipping services to Southeast Asia; and the export from the latter of tin, manganese, rubber, hard fibers, and possibly lead and zinc to the US."[20] A draft of 26 October referred to "certain advantages in production costs of various commodities" in the United States, Japan, and Southeast Asia, which "suggest the mutually beneficial character of trade of a triangular character between these three areas." In other words, this theory of comparative advantage and the product cycle elaborated a tripartite hierarchy of American core heavy industries, Japanese light industries and heavy industries revived to acceptable ceilings, and peripheral raw materials and markets.

If war had not broken out in Korea a few months after NSC 48 was approved, these plans might have been worth reading merely for their revealing assumptions. But the war made the ideas of Max Bishop and others appear prescient; and for a time the course of the fighting seemed to make feasible the implementation of a broader hinterland strategy.

PERILS OF PROPINQUITY: THE KOREAN WAR

John Foster Dulles joined the Truman administration in April 1950 as a roving ambassador responsible primarily for bringing about a peace treaty with Japan. This assignment brought Dulles to Tokyo in June 1950, a visit amid which the Korean War broke out. Dulles's internationalism had always placed him on the side of close U.S.-Japan ties and an easy peace. As Robert Murphy put it, "I always found him thoroughly for a close association with the Japanese—a great hope that this would become the focus of American influence and power in Asia." Dulles had "a very reasonable attitude on the question of war crimes," Murphy thought, and was "very affirmative . . . on the question of rearming Japan."[21] Like Acheson, Dulles represented a centrist, internationalist strain in American diplomacy that had long looked on Japan as a good junior partner of the United States and England, a history marred only by the aberration of Japanese militarism.

Dulles had crafted a noteworthy memorandum for Acheson before he left for his visit. Japan, he wrote on 7 June, could become a shining example in Asia of "the free way of life" and therefore aid the effort "to resist and throw back communism in this part of the world." But could Japan be saved, he wondered, if it were merely to adopt a defensive policy (i.e., containment)? As he put it, "If defense can only succeed as supplemented by offense, what are the practical offensive possibilities?" He suggested "some counter-offensives of a propaganda and covert character" to prevent communist consolidation of "recently-won areas." This was rollback, but it was rollback in the realm of rhetoric, rollback as "moral force." What Dulles, like Kennan, really wanted to do in regard to Japan

20. Unsigned draft of NSC 48 dated 14 Oct. 1949, NSC 48 file.

21. Robert D. Murphy Oral Interview, May and June 1965, J. F. Dulles Papers, Princeton University.

was to roll back the clock to an earlier conception of Japan's place in the world, before it went on the lamentable bender that ended with Pearl Harbor: an economic conception rather than one that would again loose a Japanese army on Asia.

Mingling power and plenty with the flair of an American Itō Hirobumi, Dulles declared that "physical propinquity" linked Japan to the mainland, yet Japan was now "closely encircled" by communism. He went on, "There is natural and historic economic interdependence between Japan and now communized parts of Asia. These are the natural sources of raw material for Japan." Japan ought to be able to build its own ships, export capital goods and not just consumer goods, and develop armed forces able to resist "indirect aggression" (i.e., an internal threat from the Left). He wondered if there were other places in Asia, outside the realm of communist control, where Japan might find raw materials and markets; he ended with the redundant observation that the peace treaty was "merely one aspect of the total problem."[22]

Propinquity is such a rare term that it could not but conjure the original context: Itō, first resident-general in Korea, authored a "perils of propinquity" statement about Korea as a dagger at the Japanese heart. Now the dagger was in communist hands, or very nearly so. Dulles's memorandum was penned after an extraordinary visit to Washington by Ikeda Hayato, Japan's finance minister, to deliver a personal message from Premier Yoshida. This was "so secret that Yoshida . . . did not inform his own officials of the aims of the mission." The main import was Yoshida's expression of apprehension about where and when the United States might choose to take a stand against communism in East Asia. Yoshida also put out a feeler suggesting that the Japanese might desire American military bases after the Occupation ended (which was not, however, anything new—he had said about the same in 1948).[23] Ikeda's meteoric rise from an obscure tax official to head of the finance ministry was the result of his close support from Japanese big business,[24] and he had additional concerns beyond those of Japan's security. In conferences with Joseph Dodge, Ikeda proposed measures to fund a big leap in Japanese exports to Asia. Dodge told Congress at the same time that "Washington must inevitably rely on Japan as a 'springboard' supplying 'the material goods required for American aid to the Far East.' "[25]

Shortly before Ikeda's arrival in Washington, Tracy Voorhees, also close to the

22. Dulles to Acheson, 7 June 1950, file 695.00 box 3006, National Archives.

23. Lowe, *Origins of the Korean War,* 86–90. Lowe writes that Yoshida had indicated to the British in October 1948 that Allied (i.e., American) troops would remain in Japan even after the treaty. According to John Dower, Yoshida "took the initiative in formally broaching the possibility of post-treaty bases." He did not confide his thoughts on this matter even to his closest associates and told Ikeda at the last minute; Dower, *Empire and Aftermath: Yoshida Shigeru and the Japanese Experience, 1878–1954* (Cambridge: Harvard Council on East Asian Studies, 1979), 374.

24. Chitoshi Yanaga, *Big Business in Japanese Politics* (New Haven: Yale University Press, 1968), 141–43.

25. Schaller, *American Occupation of Japan,* 229–31.

Japan Lobby, had returned from a Far Eastern survey to urge a revival of what was left of the Co-Prosperity Sphere. He backed a study by a member of his mission, Stanley Andrews, the director of Foreign Agricultural Relations, which urged the integration of production between Japan, South Korea, and Taiwan: "Japan is the biggest and most assured market for Korean rice in the same manner . . . [as it is of] Formosan sugar." As if to leave little to the imagination, the report referred to all this as "a restoration" that would "gradually provide a market of almost universal magnitude." He urged an integration of ECA, World Bank, Point Four, and Export-Import Bank financing to launch this program of restoration and growth. As the contents leaked, the British connected such thinking to the revival of prewar relationships, and the Soviets charged that the United States was trying to reestablish the Co-Prosperity Sphere. Ikeda's mission brought sharp attention in Japan, the press speculating about its purpose and its unprecedented secrecy.[26]

Dulles was a friend of Harry Kern, who was invited to fly with him to Tokyo. On 22 June 1950 Kern organized a dinner for Dulles at the home of Compton Pakenham, with "a few well informed Japanese." These included Marquis Matsudaira Yasumasa, related by marriage to the head of the Mitsui *zaibatsu* group and a former secretary to Count Kido Kōichi, Lord Keeper of the Privy Seal (the latter was convicted as a war criminal, but just before Pearl Harbor he and Matsudaira were part of an elite group opposed to a war policy). Matsudaira had "intimate contact with the court and access to the emperor." Present also were Sawada Renzō, related by marriage to the Mitsubishi group and reportedly connected to American intelligence; Kaihara Osamu, a man involved in the rural police and constabulary who later became secretary general of Japan's Defense Agency; and Watanabe Takeshi, a financial expert "close to the Chase Manhattan–World Bank group throughout the postwar period" and much later the chair of the Japan branch of the Trilateral Commission. The theme of the dinner was Japan's changing role in American strategy.[27] Dulles also met with Yoshida that day, urging on him Japan's rearmament. Yoshida responded with chuckles and parables and did not evince a desire to rearm his country before the Korean War.[28]

A few days after the dinner Matsudaira brought back a message for Dulles from the emperor, an unprecedented event in the postwar period made more remarkable by its circumventing the Supreme Command for Allied Powers (SCAP). Dulles told Kern that this was "the most important development" in

26. Stanley Andrews, with Robert R. West, "Coordination of American Economic Aid in South and Southeast Asia," in Voorhees to Pace, 4 Apr. 1950, RG 335, Secretary of the Army file, box 77, NA. Voorhees also sent this classified report to Herbert Hoover; Voorhees to Hoover, 4 Apr. 1950, PPI file, box 545, Hoover Presidential Library. See also *New Times*, 10 May 1950. This article refers to an American economic mission to Japan in April and quotes the *London Times* to the effect that what the United States hoped to do with Japan was reminiscent of prewar colonial relationships.

27. Kern to Pratt, 8 Sept. 1950, Pratt Papers, box 2; Roberts, " 'Japan Crowd,' " 401–2; Schonberger, "Japan Lobby," 352–54. See also Dower, *Empire and Aftermath*, 217.

28. Dower, *Empire and Aftermath*, 380–83.

U.S.-Japan relations during his visit. The content was less stunning, Hirohito calling for an advisory group of wise men who could bypass SCAP and its "irresponsible and unrepresentative advisors" in the interests of better relations. There is some question about the authenticity of the message, but Kern thought it was the first step in setting up "the machinery for reaching those who really hold the power in Japan." He urged both Dulles and Averell Harriman to pursue this opening "as vigorously as possible."[29] The main result of Dulles's visit in regard to Japan policy, and not necessarily his accomplishment, was MacArthur's well-known 23 June memorandum, in which he reversed his earlier position and urged that American forces be based in Japan.

I have come to see the Korean War as a North Korean and Chinese attempt to break the developing regional political economy that was the foundation of U.S. policy in the region by 1950, to break the Great Crescent. Stephen Krasner likes to say that nations can be divided into makers, breakers, and takers. The makers are in the core, the takers in the periphery. It is illustrative of Korea's middling position between core and periphery that it (or part of it) should have attempted to break the East Asian system in 1950. This is hardly the place to present an account of North Korea's motives for launching an assault on the South in June 1950.[30] But the one war motive for which the evidence is most abundant in early 1950 is the growing concern of the Democratic People's Republic of Korea (DPRK) with the revival of Japan and especially its economic and military relations with the Syngman Rhee regime.

In spite of their incessant denunciations of American imperialism, the North Koreans have always seen this as a disease of the skin, but Japanese imperialism as a disease of the heart (to borrow Chiang Kai-shek's metaphor). The North Korean regime was led by Manchurian guerrillas who had come of age in resisting Japanese imperialism. In 1950, so reams of verbiage in DPRK media had it, the United States was seeking to revive this system and reintroduce it in Korea.

In January 1950 Kim Il Sung remarked that "we still have not wiped out the Rhee country-sellers and we still have not liberated the people in the southern part." He then turned not to his accustomed subject, "the role of American imperialism in prolonging the deathbed-wriggle of the Rhee clique," but to Japanese imperialists, to whom Rhee had allegedly gone begging to save himself. He likened Rhee to the national traitor Yi Wan-yong, who aided and abetted the Japanese Annexation, in discussing Rhee's dispatch of Defense Minister Shin Sŭng-mo to Tokyo "to make secret arrangements with the Japanese bastards [*Ilbonnom*]."[31]

An emotional and utterly believable commentary remarked that Korean revo-

---

29. Kern to Pratt, 8 Sept. 1950, Pratt Papers, box 2; the message from the emperor is also in box 2. For more on this, and questions about its authenticity, see Roberts, " 'Japan Crowd,' " 402–3.

30. See Cumings, *Origins of the Korean War*, vol. 2, chaps. 9–11, 14, from which the following account is drawn.

31. *Nodong sinmun*, 20 Jan. 1950.

lutionaries had, to their great chagrin, failed to achieve their "sacred goal" of expelling the Japanese: "the faces of those who fell by the enemy's sword mortify us as they float up clearly in our remembrance." All the more reason, therefore, never again to allow this "sworn enemy" to "stretch its bloody hands to our territory again." Yet American policy, bankrupted by the Chinese victory, was now turning to the revival of Japanese militarism and collusion between Japan and the Republic of Korea (ROK). The Potsdam Declaration of demilitarization and democratization was being destroyed. "These facts cannot but pose a grave threat to the Korean people."

The article went on to cite the clause in the 1948 DPRK constitution stating that any country that aids and abets the reestablishment of Japanese imperialism threatens the independence of Korea and therefore becomes an enemy of Korea. Thus, the Korean people must unite ever more tightly around Kim Il Sung, "strengthen the alliance [*tan'gyŏl*] with the democratic countries led by the USSR, and with the Chinese people," and struggle ever more mercilessly to wipe out the Rhee clique.[32]

Internal DPRK materials show these same emphases in the spring of 1950. Topic number one in lectures for political officers of the Korean People's Army in June 1950 stated, "The basic policy of the American imperialists is newly to militarize Japan." They referred to, among other things, the revival of *zaibatsu* groups such as Mitsubishi, which previously owned many factories in northern Korea, American protection for biological warfare criminal General Ishii, a speech by General Robert Eichelberger urging a rearmed Japan, and American plans to keep bases at Yokusuka and Sasebo. This external aspect was, of course, linked to the continuance in South Korea of colonial social formations and bureaucracies and of pro-Japanese elements. Because Korea was Japan's first victim "above all other nations," it must monitor these activities, which constitute "a threat and menace to the Korean people."

Meanwhile, some Americans began to paraphrase Itō Hirobumi in depicting Korea's relationship to Japan. General William F. Roberts said of South Korea in March 1950, "This is a fat nation now with all its ECA goods, with warehouses bulging, with plenty rice [*sic*] from a good crop . . . an excellent prize of war; strategically it points right into the heart of Japan and in the hands of an enemy it weakens the Japanese bastion of Western defense." Now that the reader has dismissed this as the work of a military mind, let us listen to a *New York Times* lead editorial in late May, dealing with the Japanese peace treaty as the Dulles visit impended; it was titled "Japan's Perilous Position": "The Japanese since the time of Hideyoshi have called Korea the dagger pointed at Japan's heart. An abrupt American withdrawal [from Korea] . . . would mean the collapse of the free Korean state and the passage of the dagger once more into Russian hands.

32. Lead editorial, *Nodong sinmun*, 3 Mar. 1950. Ordinarily China would be included in "the democratic countries"; this is an extraordinary usage.

. . . What it comes down to is that if Japan is to be defended all of Japan has to be a base, militarily and economically."[33]

In June 1950 the Korean industrialist Pak Hŭng-sik showed up in Japan and gave an interview to the *Oriental Economist*, published the day before the war began. Described as an adviser to the Korean Economic Mission, he was also said to have "a circle of friends and acquaintances among the Japanese" (a bit of an understatement). In the years after liberation a lot of anti-Japanese feeling had welled up in Korea, Pak said, owing to the return of "numerous revolutionists and nationalists." Today, however, "there is hardly any trace of it." Instead, the ROK "is acting as a bulwark of peace" at the thirty-eighth parallel, and "the central figures in charge of national defense are mostly graduates of the former Military College of Japan." Korea and Japan "are destined to go hand in hand, to live and let live," and thus bad feelings should be "cast overboard."

The Japanese should buy Korean raw materials, he said, of which there was an "almost inexhaustible supply," including tungsten and graphite; the Koreans will then buy "as much as possible" of Japanese merchandise and machinery. They will also invite Japanese technical help with Korea's textile, glass, chemical, and machine industries. Pak himself owned a company that was an agent for Ford Motors: "we are scheduled to start producing cars jointly in Korea before long." The current problem, Pak said, was the unfortunate one that "an economic unity is lacking whereas in prewar days Japan, Manchuria, Korea and Formosa economically combined to make an organic whole."[34]

When the war broke out, the Truman administration (with Acheson in the lead) adopted a policy of containment—to restore the thirty-eighth parallel. Within a few weeks, however, pro-Japan figures like Dulles and Bishop, along with others who wanted to teach the communists a lesson, began pushing for a rollback into North Korea. The operative document for the march to the Yalu called for a "roll-back," and thus American forces steamed into North Korea in the fall of 1950. They met a regrouped North Korean Army and two hundred thousand Chinese "volunteers," destroying the calculus of rollback and, after much bloody fighting, reestablishing the status quo ante of June 1950.[35]

The irony of the pre–Korean War planning for a Japanese hinterland, of course, is that Japan never really developed markets or intimate core-periphery linkages in East and Southeast Asia until the 1960s. It was the Korean War and its manifold procurements, not the Great Crescent, that pushed Japan forward along its march toward world-beating industrial prowess (indeed, some have called the Korean procurements "Japan's Marshall Plan"). A war that killed three million Koreans was described by Yoshida as "a gift of the Gods,"[36] giving the

33. Roberts to Bolte, 8 Mar. 1950, G-3 Operations file, box 121, NA; *New York Times*, 27 May 1950. It remains for a logician to explain how Hideyoshi's twin aggressions, not to mention the annexation, constitute a Korean dagger pointed at the Japanese heart.

34. *Oriental Economist*, 24 June 1950, 636–39.

35. I cover this matter extensively in *Origins of the Korean War*, vol. 2, chaps. 20–22.

36. Dower, *Empire and Aftermath*, 316.

critical boost to Japan's economy. The Tokyo stock market fluctuated for three years according to "peace scares" in Korea. Yet the logic of an Asian hinterland persisted through the Korean War; it is remarkable to see how vexed the Eisenhower administration still was with "the restoration of Japan's lost colonial empire."[37] Ultimately this logic explains the deep reinvolvement of Japanese economic influence in Korea and Taiwan from the 1960s onward.

The Korean War also solidified the security structure in Northeast Asia, systematizing the boundaries of containment in the regional sphere (the Korean DMZ, the Taiwan straits) but also, as a consequence of the disastrous Sino-American war that burst out, eliminating rollback as a viable option. The Eisenhower administration abjured rollback except at the level of rhetoric and instead busied itself with noisy and, in retrospect, almost comic defenses of tiny places along the containment periphery, such as the islands of Quemoy and Matsu.

When the Korean War ended, both Taiwan and South Korea had absurdly swollen military machines—about six hundred thousand soldiers in each army, ranking among the highest military/civilian ratios in the world. Both were also authoritarian states with large security and intelligence bureaucracies. These big militaries served as a perimeter defense for the hegemonic "grand area," and their formidable policing power quieted labor and the Left. In this sense, these coercive facilities represent a completion of the Japanese state in the regional sphere, under American auspices. That is, Japan's state structure was shorn of its formerly powerful military and internal security apparatuses, but they were replicated where they were needed in the region and maintained at American expense. Without such military machines and expenditures Japan would have had to spend much more than 1 percent of its GNP on defense. With a wholly Red Korea, it is also questionable whether Japan's postwar democracy would have survived.

The Korean War proved definitive of the East Asian security system for a generation, but the Security Treaty concluded between Japan and the United States in 1953 remained a thorn in the Japanese body politic for a number of years thereafter. It resulted in a standing army of 180,000, euphemistically called the Japan Self-Defense Force, a network of American military bases throughout Japan, and a modest but steady buildup in Japan's military capabilities. Given the results of the Pacific War and widespread hatred for the militarists who took Japan into it, this outcome was controversial and went against the pacifist position taken in the postwar constitution. But Article 9—which expressed a consensual desire that Japan never again resort to aggression—remained in force.

37. At the 139th meeting of the NSC, 8 Apr. 1953, "The President expressed the belief that there was no future for Japan unless access were provided for it to the markets and raw materials of Manchuria and North China." Secretary of the Treasury George M. Humphrey wanted the United States to be "aggressive" in providing Japan and West Germany with a secure position where they could "thrive, and have scope for their virile populations. In some respects, it seemed to him, we had licked the two wrong nations in the last war." Whereupon, "Mr. Cutler [special assistant to the president] inquired whether the Council wished to go further than this and adopt a policy which would look to the restoration of Japan's lost colonial empire." Eisenhower said no, probably not. Eisenhower Papers (Whitman file), NSC Series, box 4, Eisenhower Library.

Although the ruling Liberal Democratic Party (LDP) always found a way to push security agreements with the United States through the Diet (frequently by violating or twisting parliamentary procedure), the opposition (in particular the Japan Socialist Party) noisily dissented from the postwar arrangements. This dissension came to a head in May 1960, when parliamentary brawling over the revised Security Treaty spawned massive demonstrations against President Eisenhower's impending visit, necessitating its cancelation. The Socialist Party's intransigence was supported by the major trade union federation, Sōhyō, and the militant student group Zengakuren.[38] This furor created a big breach in U.S.-Japan relations, necessitating a major demarche and reconciliation during the Kennedy period, for which the American ambassador, scholar Edwin Reischauer, deserves most of the credit.

"THE ROTATION OF THE EPICENTER"

In a remarkable speech in Seattle in 1951, General Douglas MacArthur said,

> To the early pioneer the Pacific Coast marked the end of his courageous westerly advance. To us it should mark but the beginning. To him it delineated our western frontier. To us that frontier has been moved across the Pacific horizon. . . . Our economic frontier now embraces the trade potentialities of Asia itself; for with the gradual rotation of the epicenter of world trade back to the Far East whence it started many centuries ago, the next thousand years will find the main problem the raising of the sub-normal standards of life of its more than a billion people.[39]

Behind the bipolar boundaries forged in 1950, Japan, South Korea, and Taiwan revived and today exercise a powerful gravity on their Communist neighbors. Call it the Great Crescent or the Pacific Rim, the Achesonian hegemony proved its staying power. In our time it now appears that the North Koreans and the Chinese (the Vietnamese, too, for that matter) merely succeeded in delaying for two decades the dynamism of this regional economy; they could contain military expansionism, but neither could contain the economic mechanisms of a potent regional capitalist sphere once it got going again in the mid-1960s. Instead, this political economy is lapping at their shores and threatening the heretofore impregnable bulwarks of the communist containment system. So perhaps it was the "natural economy" after all; perhaps here is a kind of "rollback" that works; perhaps this is how you achieve the "grand area" that was the midcentury goal of the internationalists.

However, as the capitalist mechanism became wedded to resurgent and resourceful East Asian civilizations, things have come full circle, long before MacAr-

38. See George R. Packard, *Protest in Tokyo* (Princeton: Princeton University Press, 1966).
39. Speech in Seattle, late 1951, quoted in Michael W. Miles, *The Odyssey of the American Right* (New York: Oxford University Press, 1990), 170.

thur's millennium: the rotation of the epicenter has put the American economy at risk in a way inconceivable in 1950. Capitalism moves forth in great cascades of creation and destruction,[40] waves of uneven development that distribute plenty here and poverty there; from the standpoint of the promise of 1950, the American political economy is now under permanent threat, with vast reaches of the old industrial heartland in varying states of decay and disintegration. The regions of high-tech industry exhibit a much more prosperous and progressive face, but for the first time since America began its industrialization, its leading industries, too, are under threat from Japan, Germany, and rapidly rising NICs (newly industrialized countries) such as South Korea.

Given this threat and the prevalence of wild charges that have become common in a growing "Japan-bashing" literature, it is important to emphasize that for much of the postwar period the United States has given every support to Japan and the other East Asian economies. If in the 1940s the United States structured a situation where Japanese industry could revive, in the 1960s the Kennedy administration placed strong pressures on Japan and its near neighbors (especially South Korea) to restore Japan's economic influence in the region. This pressure resulted in the normalization of relations between Korea and Japan in 1965 and a bundle of Japanese grants and loans that helped the ROK economy take off. The United States has also footed many bills for and given much help to the Japanese and Korean military organizations. The economic and military supports are by no means unilateral but have mutual benefits—not the least being continued American leverage over Japan and Korea on the pattern etched by Kennan in 1949.

During the Kennedy period W. W. Rostow—perhaps the major ideologue of modernization theory in the United States at the time with his influential book *The Stages of Economic Growth: A Non-Communist Manifesto*—was instrumental in this reinsertion of Japanese economic influence almost from his first day in office as an adviser to Kennedy in 1961.[41] Major figures in Japan studies chimed in, producing an influential literature arguing for Japan as a remarkable success story, even a miracle, of modernization.[42] It was also in the Kennedy period, however, when for the first time American leaders began criticizing Japan for its "free ride" in security affairs.[43] It is daunting to realize that this rhetoric now is

40. Joseph Schumpeter's point, of course.

41. See Jung-en Woo, *Race to the Swift: State Power and Finance in the Industrialization of Korea* (New York: Columbia University Press, 1990); W. W. Rostow, *The Stages of Economic Growth: A Non-Communist Manifesto* (Cambridge: Cambridge University Press, 1960).

42. See the Princeton University Press series of five books, including Marius Jansen, ed., *Changing Japanese Attitudes Toward Modernization* (Princeton: Princeton University Press, 1965), and Robert Ward, ed., *Political Development in Modern Japan*. For a cogent critique of this literature, see John Dower's introduction to the reissue of E. H. Norman, *Origins of the Modern Japanese State* (New York: Pantheon, 1974).

43. Senator Frank Church's speech of 22 April 1963 was probably the opening curtain in this long-running drama. See Makato Momoi, "Basic Trends in Japanese Security Policies," in Robert

entering its third decade, with Japan still spending about 1 percent of its GNP on defense, and with American politicians still complaining about it.

The mid and late 1960s were, of course, dominated by the escalating American war in Vietnam. As with the Korean War, Japan once again benefited greatly from offshore procurements; but now South Korea, too, found a periphery opening up in Vietnam, in warfare, construction contracts, and markets for its new exports. The war may have devastated Indochina and rent the fabric of consensus in the United States, but it was good business in Northeast Asia. The economic boom that proceeded in the 1960s and 1970s needs no elaboration here. The point is that in spite of that, we are not yet outside the confines and assumptions of the postwar settlement. When Ezra Vogel began a Harvard seminar on Japan by saying, "I am really very troubled when I think through the consequences of the rise of Japanese power," Samuel Huntington responded that Japan has "these really fundamental weaknesses—energy, food, and military security." It is, he thought, "an extraordinarily weak country." The paradox of the postwar Northeast Asian settlement is that they are both right, and we still live within the logic of that paradox.

The structure of U.S.-Japan relations has remained essentially the same since the early 1950s: the United States provides security, shapes the flow of resources to Japan (the dominating American role in the 1990–91 war in the Persian Gulf, from which Japan gets 60 to 70 percent of its oil, is a stunning recent example), and hopes that Japan will manufacture those products no longer produced efficiently in U.S. industries (textiles, autos, steel—at least until recently). The economic basis of the relationship is embedded in theories of comparative advantage and the product cycle: Japan moves from textiles and light-assembly industries in the 1950s, to cars and steel in the 1960s and 1970s, to electronics, computers, and "knowledge" industries in the 1980s. Although this international division of labor has been opposed in the United States by declining industries and protectionist interests, it has had the support of internationalists and free traders and of those high-technology industries that compete well in the world markets.

The contradictions in the relationship have multiplied, however, as the United States has sought increasingly to open the Japanese market and protect its own against Japan and as it has pushed Japan toward a burden-sharing defense role under the American hegemonic umbrella. At the turn of the century Roosevelt and Taft (and England, with which Japan was in alliance after 1902) were happy with a Japan strong enough to block the Russians militarily and economically weak enough to pose little threat to the United States or Great Britain. From the 1960s onward, however, American planners have wanted Japan to do well economically, but not so well as to hurt the American economy; they have wanted Japan to undertake a military role in the region, but only as an American

Scalapino, ed., *The Foreign Policy of Modern Japan* (Berkeley and Los Angeles: University of California Press, 1977), 353.

surrogate. No one expressed these contradictions better than that contradictory character, Richard Nixon.

THE NIXONIAN TRANSITION AND
THE REAGAN-BUSH CONTINUITY

Richard Nixon's strategy in regard to East Asia, briefly put, was to revive Dean Acheson's original position on China and to invoke for the first time the levers of power implicit in the settlement with Japan. The Nixon period was literally pivotal, being both continuous with previous policy and skewing policy toward the use of heretofore unmentionable means against American allies: especially the invocation of the outer limits of hegemony. The best example is his New Economic Policy, announced on V-J Day, 1971, when for the first time an American administration started sticking it to our erstwhile Japanese ally. For Japan this was the "Nixon *shokku*," but Nixon also reaped the rewards of the splitting of Moscow and Beijing, a split Acheson had projected and sought to bring about in 1949; and Nixon laid the foundations for the economic enmeshment of China with the United States and the world economy. Nixon did not so much change the rules of the game as remind us that the rules had powerful levers that could be invoked against Japan. He did the same with South Korea, where he withdrew a division of American troops and pressed the Koreans hard in textile trade negotiations. But Japan is the more important threat, and unease and foreboding have marked Japanese-American interactions ever since. We sense this attitude in the following simple statement by one Japanese commentator: "when Japan is weak and small, the United States is kind and generous . . . and when Japan becomes big and strong, the US gets annoyed and resorts to Japan-bashing."[44]

Nixon's engineer was not Kennan but Treasury Secretary John Connally. (Maybe *cheerleader* is the better metaphor.) His stock in trade was nasty comments about Japan ("Don't they remember who won the war?"); in 1979, during a failed campaign for the presidency, Connally was the first candidate to invoke the rhetoric of American nationalism and Japan bashing that is now so commonplace. If Japan did not abide by "fair trade," then "they could just sit in their Toyotas in Yokohama and watch their color TVs and leave us alone," so said Connally. For internationalists such as Zbigniew Brzezinski and David Rockefeller (and their brainchild, the Trilateral Commission), after the Nixon *shokku* the problem was how to shape the articulation of the new Japan with the world economy so that what Brzezinski called the "fragile blossom" did not turn into Tokyo Rose.[45] The early 1970s thus revealed an important split among American elites in regard to Japan: while most remained free traders interested in cooperation and interde-

44. Masahide Shibusawa, *Japan and the Asian Pacific Region: Profile of Change* (London: Croom Helm, 1984), 163.

45. See Zbigniew Brzezinski, *The Fragile Blossom: Crisis and Change in Japan* (New York: Harper and Row, 1972).

pendence (the Brookings Institution spilled oceans of ink arguing this position), others increasingly used neomercantilist measures to hold down competition from Japan.

Because of Japan's structural dependence growing out of the 1940s settlement, in the 1970s it was still subject not just to kicks in the shins but blows to the solar plexus. For example, the 1970s made clear that although the United States may be dependent on foreign oil, its relative vulnerability is so much less than Japan's that it can benefit from allied adversity. Many Japanese still believe the quadrupling of oil prices was abetted by Nixon and Kissinger to change the terms of trade to the American favor. But these important trends were overshadowed by dramatic changes in U.S.-China relations in the 1970s, under both Nixon and Carter, as the United States seemed to focus on the People's Republic as more important to American diplomacy than Japan was.

However, Japan reemerged as the centerpiece of American policy toward East Asia in the Reagan years (to the extent that the Reagan administration had an Asian policy). The essential idea was to place Japan first and link the rest of the region to that assumption and that connection. Judging Japan to be preeminent as a regional power because of its industrial prowess, the conception merged security and economics, pushing and prodding Japan toward filling out its economic capability with commensurate (or at least modestly appropriate) military power. Simultaneously the policy sought to enhance Japan's dependence on American high technology, most of it defense related. Defense Secretary Caspar Weinberger—who stayed in office for years and departed only when Reagan seemed to opt for Nixonian detente—was the author of the Japan-first tendency and pushed it from the inauguration onward.[46]

The security aspect of Reagan's Japan-first strategy was the Soviet development of a blue-ocean navy and the emergence of a powerful Pacific fleet, something begun in the 1960s but highly visible (if almost always exaggerated) by the late 1970s. Furthermore, the Carter Doctrine had drawn off American naval strength to the Indian Ocean and Persian Gulf, leaving the North Pacific with a reduced contingent of carriers and other ships.

Almost as soon as he took office, Weinberger began drawing up his five-year (1984–88) "Defense Guidance," which some later called "a revolution in military doctrine."[47] Whether it was that or not, various authors were certainly correct to focus on the plan's naval emphasis—or what some called "the Lehman Doctrine," after the brash secretary of the navy, John F. Lehman, Jr. The basis for a projected $200 billion, 600-ship navy, the doctrine had a strategic conception of the United States rather like that of Japan: the United States was akin to "an island nation," "vitally dependent on access to the sealanes for trade in peacetime

46. See Kiyofuku Chūma, "What Price the Defense of Japan?" *Japan Quarterly* 34, no. 3 (July–Sept. 1987): 251–58; Chūma cites Weinberger's continuous pressure to increase defense spending and commitments and notes how U.S. and Japanese defense hawks worked together in the 1980s.

47. Michael Klare, "The Reagan Doctrine," *Inquiry* (Mar.–Apr. 1984), 18–22.

and for reinforcement of allies in time of war." In 1981 Weinberger said that American dependence on such access was so great that "we must be able to defeat any military adversary who threatens such access." Michael Klare found the most significant innovation in the new naval policy to be "the concept of sending battle groups into 'high-threat' waters adjacent to the USSR in order to strike key Soviet facilities and to divert Soviet strength from the Central Front in Europe."[48]

Meanwhile, Americans seemed transfixed in the 1980s by the paradox of claiming to have launched Japanese development while wincing at the successes of this "offspring" in undermining American industries.[49] Lionel Olmer, Commerce Department under-secretary for foreign trade, argued that the United States had transferred $10 billion in advanced technology to Japan since 1950 in "the biggest fire sale in history"—but Japan had not reciprocated. What these Americans forget, of course, is precisely the Acheson-Kennan conception that deemed the revival of Japanese industry—requiring this transfer of technology—essential to the Great Crescent and the containment doctrine in the Far East. As we have seen, this "free ride" had a powerful corollary in making Japan dependent on the United States, giving the United States remarkable leverage over a competing economic power.

In January 1983 Prime Minister Nakasone Yasuhiro visited Washington, where he referred to the Japanese archipelago as "an unsinkable aircraft carrier putting up a tremendous bulwark of defense"; he also agreed to transfer a package of loans and credits totaling about $4 billion to South Korea—viewed by the Reagan people as a contribution to Korean, and therefore Japanese, security. Nakasone's Defense Minister, Sakarauchi Yoshio, stated at the same time that peace and security in Korea was "vital" to Japan and acknowledged that the United States and Japan were jointly studying mutual responses to "contingencies in the Far East area extending outside Japan."[50]

Before Nakasone came into office, Weinberger had called on Japan to develop the capacity to defend "the airspace and the sealanes up to a thousand miles from [Japan's] shoreline," something Japan committed itself to in 1981. In the 1980s Japan also began to participate in American naval exercises in the Pacific, such as the RIMPAC exercises off Hawaii. A new, domestically produced cruise missile, the SSM-1, was credited by some as giving Japan the capability to destroy Soviet surface ships in adjacent waters.[51]

Until the return to detente in the late Reagan years the Soviets kept up a steady drumbeat of attacks on American "collusion" with reviving Japanese militarism. The shooting down of KAL 007 in September 1983, of course, greatly intensified

---

48. Ibid.

49. Dean Acheson referred to Japan as "the West's obstreperous offspring" in his memoirs, *Present at the Creation: My Years in the State Department* (New York: Norton, 1969), 4.

50. *Business Week*, 14 Mar. 1983.

51. John J. O'Connell, "Strategic Implications of the Japanese SSM-1 Cruise Missile," *Journal of Northeast Asian Studies* 6, no. 2 (Summer 1987): 53–66.

security concerns for both powers in the region near Japan while demonstrating how extensive was American-Japanese cooperation in intelligence gathering. In July 1986, however, Mikhail Gorbachev gave an important speech on Soviet East Asian policy in Vladivostok; he called attention to U.S.-Japan cooperation in military exercises and the like, but also signaled a willingness to warm up relations with Japan and end the Soviet fixation, begun by Stalin and sustained for decades by Foreign Minister Andrei Gromyko, with a revanchist Japan.

Although this shift has not yet borne fruit, it would not be surprising if Russia's supple diplomacy in other regions eventually attains success in East Asia as well. Gorbachev held an unprecedented meeting with ROK President Roh Tae Woo in June 1990 and then normalized relations with the ROK in September 1990, perhaps seeking a way to influence Japan through Korea. Furthermore, the Reagan-Bush-Gorbachev summitry of the late 1980s and early 1990s, with various arms reduction agreements concluded or in the offing, severely undercut a prime rationale for pressing Japan on security issues: the Soviet threat in general, and the positioning of SS-20 missiles in the Soviet Far East in particular, which are now being dismantled. These changes may provide an important opening for Russia and Japan to improve a relationship that has been frozen for decades.

Washington's policy in the 1980s had another goal besides that of pushing and prodding Japan toward greater regional security efforts. A cover article in *Business Week* in 1983 argued that "if the Pentagon had its way, Japan would shoulder responsibility for bottling up the entire Soviet Pacific fleet within the Sea of Japan." But Washington's real goal, according to the article, was "to offer Japan a limited range of weapons, making Tokyo dependent on the U.S. for most of its military needs"; tying Japan to American military programs would in turn give the United States access to advanced Japanese technology in semiconductors, fiber optics, robotics, and ceramics. A key Defense Department official remarked that the United States, by contrast, did not intend to give Japan access "to any of our high technology."[52]

The technological conflict is particularly sharp in aerospace, where Americans worry about Japan's move into the industry—one of the few in which the United States still has a clear and commanding lead. Japan's Ministry of International Trade and Industry (MITI) has targeted aerospace for development and hopes that soon Japan will compete with Boeing and McDonnell-Douglas. In the meantime, Japan has set up joint ventures with Boeing to coproduce new commercial jets. American firms worry that Japan will produce its own commercial planes in the 1990s.[53]

It is uncertain whether technological dependencies can be sustained in computer hardware, where Japan is rivaling the United States in building the supercomputers essential to high-technology defenses and providing most of the semiconductor chips needed in all American computers. But Japan still lags far behind

52. "Rearming Japan," *Business Week*, 14 Mar. 1983.
53. Ibid.

in the requisite software and in systems engineering. Most of the software Japan uses for its air and sea defenses and for its electronic warfare systems comes from the United States. The United States may be a declining economic power, but it still does know how to do some things—like hemorrhage money into defense systems. The Star Wars project is the best example, of course, and is among other things a cloak for a state-led program to develop supercomputers and the requisite software—"industrial policy," national-security style.

Japan is unlikely to hold still for attempts to maintain technological dependencies, and it is by no means fully compliant with American wishes. Japan decided in January 1987 to breach the famed 1 percent of GNP for defense expenditures; a small incremental move, it was nonetheless a symbolic leap forward. But by 1990 it was back hovering at 1 percent, and its capacity to implement air and sea-lane defenses around Japan is at least a decade off and unlikely to gain speed with the retreat of Soviet power. A perfect illustration of the nature of the U.S.-Japan conflict here is Japan's refusal in 1991 to purchase Boeing AWACS planes. On the one hand, these electronic-battlefield planes are essential to Japan's commitment to police its air and sea lanes; the more Japan has, the more it can implement its thousand-mile pledge. On the other hand, Japan has its own electronic warfare technology and wishes to develop it further rather than rely on purchasing turnkey planes from Boeing (no doubt with some critical American technologies held back).[54]

The Japanese public is still hostile to a big defense buildup, in spite of reports of rising Japanese nationalism.[55] Even mild revisions of textbook accounts of Japan's prewar aggression in Asia have prompted frothy outrage at home and in neighboring countries; it may be that planners in the economic ministries were happy to see the revisions and the predictable response, which they can then point to as reasons to go slow on defense spending. Japanese pacifism, bred by the trauma of defeat in war, is deep and, in this writer's view, admirable and worthy of emulation by Americans. It remains a salutary brake on Japan's rearmament.

The other great issue between the United States and Japan in the 1980s has been trade conflict. This conflict expresses itself in continuous pressure for Japan to open its market to American goods and to sit still while our central bankers, like Paul Volcker and his successor Alan Greenspan, seek through the policies of the Federal Reserve to pass onto Japan and other nations the costs of American economic infirmity. The latter effort has induced a sort of "bankers' *shokku*" as one book after another appears in Japan claiming that American bankers, or Jews, or both, are involved in a conspiracy to keep Japan in its place.[56] A more substantive response came from Maekawa Haruo, former governor of the Bank of Japan, who

54. This dispute was discussed in a long article in the *New York Times*, 10 Feb. 1991.

55. An *Asahi shinbun* poll in March 1987 showed that only 15 percent of Japanese approved lifting the 1 percent of GNP limit on defense spending, and 61 percent were opposed. See Chūma, "What Price."

56. See, for example, *If You Can Understand the Jews You'll be Able to Understand the Japanese* (Tokyo: n.p., 1986).

issued a report in March 1986 calling for structural reform in the Japanese economy; the Foreign Ministry endorsed this reform in its "Blue Book" in July and called for a "second opening of the country," analogous to the Meiji Restoration.

For the next five years Japan took important measures to open its markets, although the beneficiaries were more likely to be the Asian NICs than American exporters. Japan's trade greatly deepened with Korea, Taiwan, Thailand, and other Asian states; in the period 1985–89 Japan's manufactured imports from Asia more than doubled, its direct investment in Asian economies grew sixfold, and its trade with Taiwan tripled; increasingly nations in the West Pacific (comprising East Asia, the ASEAN region, and Australia) trade more with each other than with the West. The West Pacific region will have as many consumers as the post-1992 European Economic Community (EEC) and a higher GNP than the EEC by the year 2000.[57] Instead of gearing up to compete in this dynamic region, Americans are more likely to complain about trade restrictions that other nations manage to get around.

It is clear that Reagan-Bush planning has continued the structure of the "reverse course" settlement—permitting Japanese industry or rearmament to grow, yes, but as a boon to American interests, not necessarily to Japanese interests, and only to the extent that it does not threaten American positions. The power-political elements of the postwar settlement have come increasingly to be used against Japan as the American capacity for producing economic growth and for invoking the old dependencies has declined. The original conception was that military and political means would be used to fashion the limits of the "grand area" but would give way to a glue provided by manifold economic relationships. But with Japan—and increasingly South Korea and Taiwan—besting America in economic competition, the United States seems reduced to mimicking previous empires in decline, flexing political and military muscles to get its way economically. This flexing usually takes the form of demands that Japan play a bigger role in Pacific security. Were Japan rapidly to fulfill this agenda and become a regional military power, who would benefit? It cannot be done without giving unwonted reinforcement to the Japanese Right and to a stirring Japanese nationalism, which would in turn stimulate even more anti-Japanese sentiment in the United States. This result can be readily appreciated in the debate over Japan's role in the 1990–91 Gulf War: while American politicians widely castigated Japan for doing nothing more than anteing up several billion dollars for the allied effort (and even that was almost aborted by domestic politics in Japan), one can imagine their reaction if this headline had appeared in the newspapers: "Japanese Fleet Steams for Persian Gulf." It is still, fortunately, an impossible headline.

Emphasizing the security elements of U.S.-Japan relations—with the assumption that Japan follows the American lead—will probably only hasten American

57. *Far Eastern Economic Review*, 21 July, 9 Aug., 30 Aug. 1990.

economic decline vis-à-vis Japan. Americans might better adopt a position of openness, if not humility, toward the lessons of Japanese industrial success—and follow their path of investing in wealth and human talent rather than weapons.

CONCLUSION: NO "POST-POSTWAR" YET; OR, WELCOME TO "AMERIPPON"

Robert Scalapino recently remarked, "Since U.S.-Japan relations rest fundamentally upon economic interdependence and strategic dependence, they will survive current and future storms."[58] This bland formula and rosy prediction nonetheless disclose, perhaps inadvertently, the essence of the relationship: economic interdependence (cum rivalry) and security dependency. The prediction makes sense only if we alter the statement to read that the relationship "will survive current and future storms" only if economic interdependence and strategic dependence continue.

Japan still prefers that the United States be the hegemon, providing the single world authority that guarantees the larger structure within which Japan exists and competes. But this task should be performed as it was until 1971, with Japan's growth understood to be salutary for the whole system, not detrimental to it. In other words, the United States should look after the whole, and let Japan look after the parts. The problem of our time, of course, is that the United States can no longer look after the whole.

In the 1940s and 1950s American military and political power etched the boundaries of the East Asian system, but slowly the element of power receded to the background as economic interchange increased—a definition of a mature hegemonic system. But the heyday of system maturity was remarkably brief: all too quickly economic competition between the United States and Japan revived, all too soon American planners looked askance at the unintended consequences of their own handiwork. Japan was the linchpin of U.S. strategy in the late 1940s and remains so today. But Japan's economic prowess came too soon for the system's health, from the standpoint of American interests; the growth of Japan's heavy industries was too closely hinged to the decline of American steel, automobiles, and electronics.

Since Nakasone left office, his successors have quietly sought to distance Japan from the bold commitments of the Nakasone years by reviving the "good neighbor" policy of showering aid on distant Southeast Asian countries, rather than bolstering the security of near neighbors like South Korea. The goal, it would seem, is to maximize the economic possibilities of the mature Northeast Asian regional system and soft-pedal the elements of power and security. But the 1947–50 settlement still defines the U.S.-Japan relationship: and so from outside Japan looking in, we have not yet reached the post-postwar epoch.

58. Robert A. Scalapino, "Asia's Future," *Foreign Affairs* 66, no. 2 (Fall 1987): 106.

Hanging in the balance is the future direction of American policy in the region. Centrist national security elites in the United States are sure they know which direction the U.S.-Japan relationship should take: deepened collaboration, pointing toward a joint condominium, in which Japan will continue to play second fiddle; that is, we will have the 1940s in the 1990s. Zbigniew Brzezinski qualifies as a centrist, I suppose, in that as a Democrat he helped to implement the basics of the Reagan foreign policy program in the latter part of the Carter administration. Ever since 1971 he and others in the internationalist elites have worried mightily about any sign of U.S.-Japan estrangement. In a recent article Brzezinski coined the term *Amerippon* to signify this joint condominium, a term redolent of the American internationalist position as the 1990s dawn:

> A greatly revitalized America can be nurtured by policies that exploit the special complementarity of American and Japanese interests, while also providing Japan with the safest route to continued growth. . . . The strengths of one compensate for the weaknesses of the other. . . . Working together ever more closely, they can assure for themselves unrivaled global economic, financial and technological leadership, while reinforcing the protective umbrella of American global military power.
>
> America needs Japanese capital to finance its industrial renovation and techno-logical innovation. . . . Japan needs American security protection for its homeland; it needs open access to the American market for its continued economic well-being. . . .
>
> Japan for many years to come will be heavily dependent on American security protection. . . . [H]ence the Japanese stake in a globally engaged America will remain great. With America heavily indebted, the American stake in a productive and prosperous Japanese partner will also grow.[59]

Brzezinski goes on to argue that for Japan "incalculable considerations . . . quite literally a matter of life or death" in its relationship to the United States mean that "Japan would simply not be—nor would it remain—what it is without the American connection." He therefore recommends "the deliberate fostering of a more cooperative, politically more intimate, economically more organic part-nership."[60]

I am not quite sure what to make of all this Ameripponia, but I think I hear a little voice between the lines saying, I surely hope so: I hope that "incalculable considerations" will convince the Japanese to remain under our "protective umbrella" lest Japan cease to be what it has been, a dutiful second-string partner in American global hegemony. I hope that the Japanese do need us, in spite of their financial and technical wizardry. I hope that the 1940s settlement will prevail in spite of the changed terms of U.S.-Japan relations. I hope . . .

The world of the 1990s is much more likely to be a virgin terrain in which one after another of the seeming certainties of the postwar settlement will come

59. "America's New Geostrategy," *Foreign Affairs* 66, no. 4 (Spring 1988): 695–96.
60. Ibid., 696–97.

unstuck. Russia now refuses to play the role of enemy, let alone "evil empire." Western Europe deepens by the day its moves toward a true common market, a potent regional political economy with burgeoning ties to Eastern Europe. Japan may not sit still for a dependent relationship on American military power and may also pose a regional option for its neighbors. Indeed, as we have seen, there is considerable evidence since the mid-1980s that Japan has deepened its regional influence; as the Asian "Berlin walls" crumble, Japan will be poised to pursue a German option, that is, to deepen its market position in socialist China, Korea, and Vietnam. In other words, the twenty-first century may well be one driven by Germany and Japan, an ironic tribute to their prowess and to the shortsightedness of American strategy in 1947.

The American people, however, do not yet understand the crises and challenges that face them. In a sense the internationalist vision has won: it has demonstrated on a world scale the superior ability of capitalism to deliver goods and services and enhance people's livelihood. But that does not mean that the American people have won. The dynamism of the Pacific Rim has its ineluctable counterpart in lost jobs, hollowed-out industrial cities, declining middle and working classes (with the contemporary absorption in "the drug problem" being a metaphor and an outcome of this decay). The internationalists were exporters not just of goods but of capital equipment and technology to make goods. The latter has now been married to a region that is accustomed to the rigors of hard work, that emphasizes educational prowess, and that has strong cultural and national pride. This marriage now presages a fundamental shift in the world economy.

But all this has little to do with the rhetoric of renewal, nostalgia, and a recaptured American dream with which Americans coasted through the Reagan era and which led them to support a "New World Order" under George Bush that, with the Gulf War, looked suspiciously like business as usual. If Japan is still caught within the confines of the postwar settlement, so is American thinking about Japan, oscillating between the dual discourse of Japan as miracle and menace, docile and aggressive, fragile blossom and Tokyo Rose. Only this contradictory discourse can explain why Japan rose on the American radar screen just as the Soviet Union receded. Thus, the United States confronts a new century, unlikely to be an American century, and a new but utterly undefined relationship with Japan, as the postwar settlement increasingly comes unstuck.

CHAPTER THREE

The Past in the Present

Carol Gluck

A VERY PRESENT PAST

The end of the war was also a beginning. Noon, August 15, 1945—the time of the surrender broadcast was inscribed in Japanese memory as the fictive moment when the past ended and the present began. Willing time to be broken and history severed, Japan turned toward the future, with the result that the past became more present than before. This was because the New Japan, as so many called it, was conceived as an inversion of the old. The prewar past, to be obliterated, had first to be retold. Thus, in the wake of an unjust and catastrophic war, history became a character in the postwar script to reenact Japan in a different mode. The past has since played many parts, but seldom in the course of nearly fifty years has it been allowed to exit the national stage.

First there was the prewar past or, more precisely, the issue of the war and "what had gone wrong" to cause it. But because people saw the war as a judgment on a longer history, the question immediately became the nature of Japan's modernity, and also of the premodern that preceded and was responsible for it. These two linked narratives, one of the war, the other of the modern, comprised the main historical agenda, newly construed from the vantage point of 1945. And the authenticity of "the postwar," or *sengo* (which in Japanese is a noun and suggests substance), depended on situating it both after the war and along the course of the modern. The eventual result was a third linked narrative that told the story of the postwar itself around the new theme of peace and prosperity.

In Japan, as in Germany, the postulation of a sharp break at the end of the war made continuity a troubling concern. What changed and what did not change across the alleged great divide of 1945—the year zero, the Germans named it—became a central question. Indeed, the postwar contestations over history had much to do with different views of how free the present could, or should, be of the past.

This is the realm of national history and public memory, where the past is collectively constructed, disputed, and perpetuated. Some, including Japanese scholars, refer to it as popular historical consciousness, while American and European historians speak of collective or public memory. By that they mean the various versions of national history created by historians, officials, schools, mass media, filmmakers, museums and monuments, public ceremonies, personal recollections, and the like. Diverse and often self-appointed, these custodians of the past produce different interpretations of the way things were, and why. They represent their own interests and view events from their own perspectives. They therefore do not agree, nor is there a collective product that constitutes a singular "thing" called public memory at any given time. No one group, whether the academic historians, the schools, or the mass media, possesses proprietary control over an Orwellian memory hole. Following one scholar's suggestion that such collectively negotiated memory is "more like an endless conversation," one can think of it as vernacular history.[1]

But the conversation is more contentious than congenial, and it does add up. National history is never neutral, and in postwar Japan, as elsewhere, the past was contested terrain on which other, larger battles over politics, society, and culture were being fought. In overdrawn strokes: the progressive critics of the emerging status quo judged modern history harshly as they sought to promote what they considered a more authentic democracy. Officiants and celebrants of the developing conservative consensus searched the same past for its brighter moments in support of their view of postwar economic and national goals. Popular culture purveyed other variants, affecting and refracting those of both critics and celebrants. Ordinary Japanese, as they are so often called, were also their own "historians," combining public versions with their own personal experience of the recent past.

Since national history is also ideology—a past imagined in the context of national identity—public memory is hegemonic, even if it is not singular. There is a weight to it. And as postwar Japanese constantly reconstituted the past in the light of the present, the weight of public memory changed. In the course of the postwar period, and closely related to the economic phenomenon now enshrined in collective memory as high growth (*kōdo seichō*), the dominant sense of the past shifted toward the conservative social and national center.[2]

Here the charge is to follow the traces of historical consciousness from the initial postwar moment in 1945–47 to the post-Shōwa seizure of public memory in 1989–90. This task includes identifying the main custodians of the past and examining their narratives of war, modernity, and postwar. It also means suggest-

---

1. David Thelen, "Memory and American History," *Journal of American History* 75, no. 4 (Mar. 1989): 1127. For Japan, see Kano Masanao, *"Torishima" wa haitte iru ka: Rekishi ishiki no genzai to rekishigaku* (Tokyo: Iwanami Shoten, 1988).

2. This is the counterpart in historical consciousness of the conservative consensus portrayed in the essays by Kelly, Koschmann, Ivy, Gordon, and others in this volume.

ing the interpretive templates that they used to understand history and evoking two ever-present "ghosts at the historical feast": the emperor and the United States. Finally, it entails describing what I call "the long postwar," the distinctive phenomenon that had Japan still calling and thinking of itself as postwar after nearly half a century. This long postwar was one consequence of the original *sengo* consciousness that wished and hoped for—although not necessarily believed in or lived—a history that could begin again at noon, August 15, 1945.

SEVERED HISTORY: THE BEGINNING
OF "THE POSTWAR," 1945–47

Defeated, liberated, and occupied all at once, in the autumn of 1945 the Japanese were suddenly both free and unfree to confront their past. After the defeat, many were ready to speak of the enormities of recent years; with liberation, they were free to do so; under foreign occupation, they were required to begin right away.

The Americans immediately forbade "false history," ordering children to ink out passages about sacred emperors and sacrificing samurai from their textbooks. They suspended historical instruction in the schools and began their censorship of the press. Having halted one history, the occupation restarted another, using what it called guidance to "re-interpret Japanese history objectively in the light of ascertained facts and without bias or hero-worship."[3] In the "true history" as General MacArthur saw it, the prewar past was "feudalistic," now to be utterly renounced in the name of what the occupation regarded as its historical opposite, democracy.

The Allies also put history on trial in the War Crimes Tribunal, reconstructing in massive evidential detail the record of expansionist "conspiracy" in the seventeen years between 1928 and 1945, during which the prosecution found that "every event was coldly calculated, planned for, and put into execution." The main conspirators were hanged, an unequivocal assignment of criminal responsibility to the leaders in the docket.[4] Victors' justice though it was, the stark narrative of the war produced by the trial was accepted by most Japanese of the time. Identifiable villains, a culpable because conspiratorial history, and a strong story line with a clear ending—this view of the war suited a country that so much wanted to break with its past.

But the occupation's attention to Japanese history was nonetheless an invasion of one country's national history by another. And when it came to the emperor,

3. From materials for a "Radio History of the Japanese People" (1946), in Tanikawa Takeshi, "Amerika no tainichi hōsō seisaku kenkyū: 'Rajio ni yoru Nihon jinmin no rekishi' no bunseki," Chūō Daigaku Hōgakubu, 1985 (mimeograph). On texts, see John Caiger, "Ienaga Saburō and the First Postwar Japanese History Textbook," *Modern Asian Studies* 3, no. 1 (1969): 1–16.

4. Richard H. Minear, *Victors' Justice: The Tokyo War Crimes Trial* (Princeton: Princeton University Press, 1971), 125–34; Hosoya Chihiro, Andō Nisuke, Ōnuma Yasuaki, and Richard H. Minear, eds., *The Tokyo War Crimes Trial: An International Symposium* (Tokyo: Kodansha International, 1986), 79–87.

the Americans applied historical thinking with ironic inconsistency. Having declared discontinuity with the feudal, militaristic past, they nonetheless chose not
to try the emperor as a war criminal, arguing that he provided a continuity useful
to postwar reform. The American drafters then wrote the imperial institution into
the new Japanese constitution. They transformed the emperor from sovereign to
symbol, but retained both the office and the person, Hirohito. This act evoked a
different sort of continuity—connected not to reform but to the prewar period—
which postwar public memory had to wrestle with. Over the years the war crimes
trial, the constitution, and the emperor each became the center of considerable
controversy, as Japanese urged that "occupied history" be rewritten in order to
be reclaimed.

In 1945, however, "liberated history" was far more strongly felt, as intellectuals, freed from both wartime suppression and chauvinistic imperial history (kōkoku-
shi), erupted into print with analyses of the recent past. Progressive historians
joined together across sectarian lines to dissect the emperor system, which they
censured, and to delineate "feudal" elements, whose historical opposite they
defined as the authenticity of the modern.[5] Their own premises were not new but
represented the Marxist and left-liberal thought of the 1920s, which had been
suppressed but not extinguished by the prewar government. Theirs was thus an
interrupted, not a discontinuous, discourse, and now that it had resumed they
believed that "true modernity" or the "democratic revolution" was at long last at
hand. This belief was one source of the surge of optimism they felt amidst the
hunger and privation of 1945–46. The other was what the historian Fujita Shōzō
described as the brightness (akarusa), the delight, at the downfall of the state, a
feeling so different, he said, from the hopes that had attended its establishment
after the Meiji Restoration. In Fujita's view the betrayal of those hopes by the
prewar emperor system had set the postwar historiographical agenda for himself
and his generation.[6]

The progressive intellectuals met their agenda by taking the long view and
tracing the roots of the prewar system deep into the premodern past. They
considered Japan's unmodernity to have been fundamental. Fascism and war were
no accident of demonic leadership or response to world conditions, but part of the
very social, political, and ideological structure of the nation. Like the Allies, they
also found Japanese history culpable, but in such a profound dimension that it
could not be put in the dock and hanged. It had instead to be thoroughly cleansed,
altered, and redirected. Believing that such fundamental change was possible,
they emerged from the war as "late moderns," wholly committed to realizing,

5. For the "progressive historians" (shinpoteki rekishika), see Inoue Kiyoshi, "Sengo rekishigaku no
hansei to tōmen suru kadai: shippai kara manabu itteian," Rekishigaku kenkyū 230 (June 1959): 3–4;
Arai Shin'ichi, "Rekken gojūshūnen ni yosete," Rekishigaku kenkyū 511 (Dec. 1982): 2–3. For general
intellectual comment, see the periodicals Chūō kōron, Sekai, Tenbō, 1946.

6. Fujita Shōzō, "Sengo no giron no zentei: Keiken ni tsuite," Seishinshiteki kōsatsu: Ikutsuka no danmen
ni sokushite (Tokyo: Heibonsha, 1982), 230.

finally, the world-historical visions of democracy or revolution. Far from a post-Hegelian "end of history" of the French sort, they believed that the "true history" of Japan's modernity had only now begun.[7]

In official utterance, the postwar beginning was expressed at first with the fastidious reticence understandable in bureaucrats who had remained in their posts while the national premises changed around them. With the controversy in 1946 over the first postwar history textbook, *Kuni no ayumi*, the long tug-of-war between education officials and progressive historians commenced, this time with the intervention of the occupation. The issue was the appearance of the Sun Goddess as the imperial ancestress, dutifully renamed a "myth" but still present at the beginning of Japanese schoolbook history.[8] On the recent past, however, official history was laconic to a fault:

> Our country was defeated. The people suffered very much during the long war. The military oppressed the people, waged an unreasonable war, and caused this misfortune.[9]

Simple enough, but whether the misfortune was the defeat, the war, or the suffering remained ambiguous.

The public speeches of the politicians emphasized transformation. Yoshida Shigeru, the architect of postwar conservatism, proclaimed the complete eradication of extreme militarism and nationalism. Never would Japan repeat the wrong-headed errors of those who had warped the popular will in the name of the emperor and brought the nation to ruin. Katayama Tetsu, Japan's only Socialist prime minister, spoke of the militarism and feudal bureaucratic system having been swept away, with the result that "the character of our country was completely transformed."[10] The new Japan, they chorused, was driving out the old.

The government leaders also practiced a kind of "transliterated history." The words changed, as if they were writing the past in another script. The Great Empire of Japan vanished from utterance, even in negative mention. Unlike postimperial Europe, Japanese public discourse admitted no attachment or loss, no ruefulness or remorse. It was a feat of contrary prestidigitation, suddenly to make nothing out of something, rhetorically to regret the war and forget the empire.

At the same time officials transposed their speech into what may have seemed safely demilitarized words: *minzoku*, the ethnic people (not *kokumin*, the statish people); *bunka*, culture; and *seikatsu*, livelihood or standard of living. Repeated in

7. For contrast, see chaps. 4–6 on Alexandre Kojève in Michael S. Roth, *Knowing and History: Appropriations of Hegel in Twentieth-Century France* (Ithaca: Cornell University Press, 1988).

8. Tōyama Shigeki, *Sengo rekishigaku to rekishi ishiki* (Tokyo: Iwanami Shoten, 1968), 65–72.

9. *Kuni no ayumi* (1946), in Kaigo Tokiomi, *Nihon kyōkasho taikei*, vol. 20, *Rekishi* 3 (Tokyo: Kōdansha, 1962), 463.

10. For Yoshida (June 1946): see pp. 357, 359; for Katayama (July 1947): see p. 369; in *Rekidai naikaku to sōri daijin* (Naikaku Shiryō Hensankai, 1975).

varying combinations, these words described the future in terms of "the rebirth of the people," a guaranteed "cultural livelihood" in a "cultural nation" (*bunka kokka*) or a "national culture" (*minzoku bunka*)—all phrases reminiscent of wartime ideology but now couched in the postwar terms of democracy and peace. The litany of culture worked both to displace politics and to create pride in a long cultural tradition, precisely the role the prewar imperial institution had played. Indeed, the new constitution was promulgated on the Meiji emperor's birthday in 1947, which was reinstated in 1948 as a national holiday called—Culture Day.[11]

The great majority of the Japanese were concerned less with culture than with livelihood in the immediate postwar years. Best-selling historical fiction was uncharacteristically absent just after the war. Swords and topknots, the standard iconography of popular history, were discouraged by the occupation, which forbade samurai themes of loyalty and revenge as feudal and even briefly banished the forty-seven *rōnin* from the kabuki stage. But contemporary history sold extraordinarily well, especially individual and reportorial accounts of prewar and wartime experiences. A journalistic compilation of two decades of the "uncensored inside history of Shōwa" sold out one hundred thousand copies within a week in December 1945. And together with a second volume published the following February, the book sold nearly eight hundred thousand copies, even in that winter of terrible hardship.[12] Yet the emphasis in movies, songs, radio, and the erotic "dregs magazines" that reached their peak in 1948 lay not in the soiled public past but in the present and the beginnings of a new and newly private life.

Despite the extremity of their daily lives, many marked August 15 as a great relief, a release from war and from the state. And while most Japanese lived their lives in continuity, they fastened on the thought of change. They all remembered then—and still remember now—their whereabouts and feelings at the noontime of surrender. The voluminous literature of reminiscence, part oral history, part diary, part reconstruction, perpetuated the frozen moment that separated the past from the present in personal memory.

Between 1945 and 1947, the Japanese (and the Americans) actively and in many cases consciously addressed the task of reconceiving recent Japanese history. Three tenets were established almost immediately: first, that history could begin as if anew, just as Japan could be, as it was said, "reborn"; second, that the war was the subject of a heroic narrative in which villains and victims were clearly

---

11. The Meiji constitution had been promulgated on *kigensetsu* in 1889, the holiday commemorating the legendary founding of the empire by Emperor Jinmu. Thus, the legitimating of new history by old repeated itself in 1947, this time with the reaffirmation of Emperor Meiji as the founding figure of modern Japan.

12. Mori Shōzō, ed., *Senpū nijūnen: Kaikin Shōwa rimenshi*, 2 vols. (Tokyo: Masu Shobō, 1945–46). The top best-seller in both years, this compilation was conceived independently of the occupation and proved far more popular than similar efforts by GHQ to tell the "truth" about Shōwa. See Asahi Shinbunsha, ed., *Besutoserā a monogatari* (Tokyo: Asahi Shinbunsha, 1978) 1:3–11.

identifiable and, once identified, would enable the Japanese to put the past behind them; third, that Japan's modernity had gone badly awry but could now be set right. Severed history, radical discontinuity, a new beginning—such were the fictions of *sengo* that emerged from cataclysmic war.

CUSTODIANS OF THE PAST

The realities of the next several decades were experienced by different "historians" in different ways, producing different chronologies of the postwar and different histories that vied with one another for legitimation and dominance. Of the many participants in public memory, four main custodians of the past may be identified here.

First are the progressive intellectuals, who remained active, articulate, and influential in postwar discourse. In the universities, in the newspapers and magazines, on television, in political debate and social movements, they possessed a prominence unimaginable in the United States, though closer perhaps to that of the intellectuals in France. This presence is all the more striking in light of their critical stance, which often diverged from the views of their countrymen, who nonetheless accorded them a hearing in the print and broadcast media. In the academy, the term *postwar historiography* was virtually synonymous with Marxist history-writing. So, too, among the so-called public intellectuals (*hyōronka*) whose forum is the media, the progressives were long identified as the consciousness and conscience of *sengo*.

They formed no single group or even a community, for they disagreed mightily among themselves. Think of them rather as portmanteau progressives, associated only by their tenacious commitment to preserve the promise of the original postwar reforms against what they called the rising "forces of reaction." In politics, they ranged themselves against the state, or in the larger sense, against the political and economic establishment. Indeed, in a country without an effective opposition party, one might say that the portmanteau progressives long functioned as a surrogate opposition. On any given issue, from the San Francisco peace treaty to the Persian Gulf War, they aligned themselves against the grain of the conservatives in power.

In public memory, too, they practiced "history as opposition." They particularly opposed any incursions of the prewar past into postwar education and national life. For decades Ienaga Saburō and other historians waged a battle against nationalistic textbooks in the courts.[13] Progressives protested the revival of imperial ideology—from the reestablishment of February 11 as a national holiday celebrating the mythical founding of the country, which took place in 1967 after twenty years of debate, to the ceremonial conduct of the state funeral of Hirohito

---

13. For a retrospective of the Ienaga trial at a quarter century, see "Tokushū: Kyōkasho saiban 25-nen," *Rekishi hyōron* 487 (Nov. 1990): 1–61.

in 1989 and the enthronement rites of the present emperor in 1990, which threatened the postwar constitutional separation of religion and the state. As critics of the modern, they located social politics at the center of history, seeking the basis for a more genuine democracy in postwar Japan, whether defined in revolutionary, populist, or social-democratic terms. They had high hopes, which were repeatedly disappointed by postwar history.

Because theirs was a chronology of protest, the progressives located the peak of their postwar experience in early *sengo*, from 1945 to 1947, when radical reform had seemed possible. They saw renewed prospects of a modern democratic politics in the Security Treaty protests of 1960 and some reduced residual hopes for participatory democracy in the citizens' movements of the late 1960s and early 1970s. But these hopes, too, disappeared entirely in the "conservatization" of the post-high-growth 1970s, and the progressives' long prominence waned with it. By the 1980s they felt that the brightness of the original *sengo* was now in full eclipse, the initial promise of the postwar betrayed by the bureaucratic state and conservative middle-mass society. They remained in opposition to the intrusions and revisions of the prewar past, but their place in the sun—and the television forum—was increasingly taken by conservative intellectuals who supported rather than opposed the postwar status quo.

These conservative intellectuals belonged to the second category of vernacular historians, who constructed what might be called status quo or establishment history. This includes all official forms of national history, whether produced by the government, the educational bureaucracy, politicians invoking history as they saw fit, or public ceremony. But it also includes intellectuals and others who shared similar views about the present and therefore about the past. In terms of hegemonic weight, this custodial group wielded the greatest institutional power. The progressives may have been preeminent in the academy and intellectual discourse, but the status quo view dominated official public memory. Like the Liberal Democratic Party (LDP), it was conservative, but it was not imperial history of the wartime sort. That mantle was inherited by a phalanx of the right wing, which produced latter-day emperorist history that sometimes interacted with, but did not prevail in, official memory. The establishment instead produced a moderated form of conservative consensus history.

The official postwar agenda set the twin goals of domestic reconstruction and recovery of international stature, or "regaining the trust of the world." But the recovery of a positive past figured importantly from the first. Whereas the progressives were critics who yearned for change, official speakers were celebrants who sought continuity. This they immediately found in the modernizing achievements of Meiji, upon which postwar Japan could build. Several months after independence, in September 1952, Prime Minister Yoshida made a speech to his party calling for education in Japan's "peerless history" as the basis for strengthening patriotism in preparation for rearmament. In the next few weeks he glossed this claim with a rendering of modern Japan that began with "the extraordinary progress made within a half century after the Meiji Restoration, when Japan had become one of the five great powers." But then the military, parties, and intellectuals had abused political power and embarked on a "reckless war" (the standard phrase) that was neither militarily wise nor in accordance with the intentions of Emperor Meiji.[14] Here the prewar past, the focus of the progressives, was effaced, and Meiji, which had ended in 1912, was stitched directly to the postwar.

The postwar chronology of establishment history traced an ever rising national trajectory from destruction to prosperity, from international humiliation to the status of economic superpower. Where the progressives clung to the original *sengo*, official history identified with "high growth." It defined high-growth economics to include not only a world-class GNP, but also the myth of an entirely middle-class society and the triumph of a Japanese-style modern. As crests of the upward rise, the celebrants marked 1956, when the government first declared, on economic grounds, that "the postwar is over."[15] Next came the Tokyo Olympics of 1964, described by the prime minister as enabling "the nations of the world to engage in peaceful competition on our shores and observe the progress we have made in our society." 1968 brought the Nobel Prize in literature and the third highest GNP in the world ("second in the free world," which sounded even better). At Expo 70 Premier Satō invited foreign visitors to view Japan, "where we are building a new civilization on the foundations of an ancient tradition."[16]

At the end of the 1970s Prime Minister Ōhira spoke of a "new age transcending the age of modernization," when culture would take the place of economics and the "rationalistic urbanization and materialistic civilization" of Western-style modernization would be replaced by a "Japanese-style welfare state."[17] As physical indication of the newly leveled society of middle-mass strata, he spoke of the unlikely but seductive prospect of the Japanese all living in "garden cities." Ōhira here epitomized establishment history, which had doubly displaced politics, once by economics and once by culture. Superior national culture, recognized internationally, stood at the center of such history. In the 1980s Prime Minister Nakasone evoked a "robust culture" built on "two thousand years of tradition," around which Japanese should reestablish their distinctive identity and share it with the world. Like the International Center for the Study of Japanese Culture established by his government in 1988, Nakasone linked the common call for "internationalization" to the revival of a cultural nationalism unencumbered by remembrance of the wartime past.[18] In public memory this theme reached a celebratory cre-

---

14. "Bankoku ni kantaru rekishi" speech, *Asahi shinbun*, 1 Sept. 1952; history speech, *Asahi shinbun*, 25 Sept. 1952.

15. "Mohaya sengo de wa nai": Keizai kikakuchō, *Keizai hakusho*, 1956.

16. *Tōkyō shinbun*, 14 Mar. 1970.

17. *Asahi shinbun*, 25 Jan. 1979.

18. "Robust culture and welfare nation" (*takumashii bunka to fukushi no kuni*): see, e.g., 3 Dec. 1982, 25 Jan. 1985, in Naikaku Seido Hyakunenshi Hensan Iinkai, ed., *Rekidai naikaku sōri daijin enzetsu shū*

scendo at the imperial funeral of 1989 and the enthronement ceremonies of 1990. Establishment voices exulted at the world's coming to pay its respects to Japan's contemporary economic power at rituals honoring the imperial embodiment of Japan's cultural tradition.

The third category of custodians, the purveyors of the popular past, expressed a somewhat different historical vision, related to but not captive of the others. On television and stage, in fiction and comics, in films, newspapers, and maga-zines—in the entire media-saturated world of postwar Japan—the past was a perennial favorite; and it sold. So many "history booms" were declared since the end of the war that, in retrospect, they appear to have been continuous. Indeed, the twentieth-century tradition of what is called mass literature (*taishū bungaku*), which began in earnest in the mid-1920s, had always depended heavily on best-selling historical fiction, and the Japanese appeared to have a greater tolerance for and interest in their history than did readers in many other coun-tries.[19]

A counterpart to the institutional power of the establishment, the informational power of the media is as important to the collective construction of memory in advanced capitalist societies as the schools were once thought to be. Now we know that textbooks corner only a small part of the popular historical imagination, which constantly amends its image of the past in response to products of the mass culture industry. The popular past includes commodified history, which is for sale; self- or other-censored history, when it is, for example, broadcast by state-sponsored television; and self-produced or even amateur history, which can be oppositional and still go on the air. Media history thus defies any simple reading of its content or agenda.

But one point seems clear in regard to public memory. To view the media as entirely in cahoots with the establishment or utterly in control of the mass imagination is to both exaggerate and oversimplify their power. In fact, students of public memory do not understand very well how the media operate in the construction of vernacular history. But any study of postwar Japanese memory must at least confront the fact that for years the progressive critics of the status quo paraded their historical wares in NHK prime time and in national newspapers and

---

(Tokyo: Ōkurashō Insatsukyoku, 1985), 1064–65, 1106; "2000 years of tradition": 10 Sept. 1983, ibid., 1087. See also Nakasone Yasuhiro, "Toward a Nation of Dynamic Culture and Welfare," *Japan Echo* 10, no. 1 (1983): 12–18. Progressives criticized the new center (called *Nichibunken* for short) as "*kokusuika* (ultranationalizing) in the name of *kokusaika* (internationalizing)"; Rekishigaku Kenkyūkai, ed., *Minshū bunka to tennō* (Tokyo: Aoki Shoten, 1989), 3, 101–33.

19. In a 1971 survey of "matters of concern," Japanese history ranked 50th in a field of 202 items that ranged from traffic accidents to tennis. High prices and pollution ranked higher than history, but history was of greater concern than clothing, foreign policy, cameras, or sumo. NHK Sōgō Hōsō Bunka Kenkyūjo, Kanshin Ryōiki Chōsa Kenkyūkai, ed., *Nihonjin no kanshin ryōiki* (Tokyo: Shiseido, 1973), 110–14.

magazines.[20] Though the audience may have remained unmoved by its arguments, the opposition nonetheless played its part in making media history.

In much of the popular past, the historical center was neither the social politics pursued by the progressives nor the national culture celebrated in official oratory. Instead, individuals were what history was all about. There were the heroes who made history, or tried to, and the common people, who endured it, and tried, too. On NHK the heroes appeared on the opulently produced historical drama that ran every Sunday night for a year. The most favored heroic periods remained, as they had been since the 1920s, Sengoku and Bakumatsu, the sixteenth and the nineteenth centuries. Both represented periods of change, when upheaval and opportunity were the rule and before order descended in the form of the Tokugawa system or the Meiji state. These were the times when it seemed to their chroniclers that men (and an occasional woman) could indeed make history, when ability counted more than class, and when the structures of society and politics were pliant to the exercise of human will.[21] Hideyoshi, the sixteenth-century "peasant unifier" of the realm, and Sakamoto Ryōma, the lowly samurai of high restorationist spirit, typified the one-man heroes—"what matters is me, one guy, Ryōma" (*ningen ippiki Ryōma*).[22] There were some antiestablishment nihilist loners as well, while the forty-seven *rōnin* remained the perennially favorite collective protagonist.

Whatever the reasons for the appeal of this man-makes-history (*jinbutsushi*) assumption, there is no doubt about its emphatic avoidance of a heroic modern. The dramas set in the twentieth century were apt to be those of common people—those who suffered the travails of modernity and war—not those who helped inflict them. These were the figures who came on every morning in the long NHK serials of homely lives set against the backdrop of grand historical events that they could little hope to affect. All the larger-than-life protagonists strode the landscapes of earlier times, as if the advent of modernity had somehow shrunk the horizon of nobility to a size incommodious to heroes. When NHK experimented in the mid-1980s with full-blown Sunday night dramas set in the Shōwa period, the ratings proved that the too-modern past did not play well in heroic prime time.[23]

20. Similar to the BBC in Britain, NHK (Nihon Hōsō Kyōkai) is a publicly owned radio and television broadcasting agency, which means that it is simultaneously independent and yet linked to the government in a way that commercial broadcasters are not.

21. Ozaki Hotsuki, *Taishū bungakuron* (Tokyo: Keisō Shobō, 1965), 346–50; Kuwada Tadachika, *Hadaka Taikōki: Toyotomi Hideyoshi no ningenzō* (Tokyo: Kōdansha, 1961), 15.

22. From Shiba Ryōtarō, *Ryōma ga yuku*, serialized in *Sankei shinbun*, 1962–66; published by Bungei Shunjūsha, 5 vols, 1968; televised as NHK Sunday night drama, 1968.

23. The first Sunday night serial (*taiga dorama*) set in the Shōwa period was "Sanga moyu" (1984), a story of Japanese Americans during World War II, which for a number of reasons drew very low ratings. The second, "Inochi" (1986), did better, but the experiment with twentieth-century subjects had not been repeated as of 1992, when a quintessential Sengoku hero, Oda Nobunaga, was again the subject of the annual drama. In contrast, the daily morning "TV novel" (broadcast from 8:15 to

Although it is not quite true that historical works featuring samurai of ages past are "nothing but contemporary fiction with topknots on," the changing parade of historical depiction does express a chronology of postwar popular experience.[24] It is a chronology of *seikatsu*, a term perhaps best rendered as "standard of living" in the 1950s and as "life-style" by the 1970s. The general direction was upward, particularly in the high-growth sixties. The emblematic work of the previous decade, Yamaoka Sōhachi's *Tokugawa Ieyasu*, ran to twenty-six volumes between 1950 and 1967, selling an exceptional ten million copies by 1965. The early volumes focused on the achievement of the Pax Tokugawa, during the years when the postwar peace was a dramatic issue, with overtones of the cold war. By the 1960s the question had shifted from securing the peace to managing the realm and in the new managerial society (*kanri shakai*), Ieyasu became a model for postwar salarymen who were said to read the series as a handbook of successful management practices.[25]

The 1960s also brought the "optimism boom" exemplified by the works of Shiba Ryōtarō, whose heroes might be revolutionaries like Sakamoto Ryōma or bureaucrats like Katsu Kaishū but were alike in being creatures of prosperity. Shiba's extraordinarily popular heroes acted as embodiments not of public or national achievement but of what one critic called "the brightness of the pursuit of desire."[26] This pursuit represented both the income-doubling high-growth line of the government and the rising consumer culture of the "Shōwa Genroku," when consumers of the late 1960s moved from the convenient "three treasures" to the middle-class "three *C*'s" and began to dream of the luxurious "three *V*'s."[27] Or rather, so they were advertised to do, for Shiba was the popular avatar of the emerging middle-class myth promoted by politicians and capitalists alike.

But social reality was often vastly discrepant, and people's lives did not conform to the consuming images they saw in the commercials. As a result the popular chronology of *seikatsu* followed a different postwar course than that of official history, which claimed a continuous climb in national progress and international stature. First, popular surety was always fragile and never evenly shared, especially by the considerable number of people whose prospects lay well below the allegedly universal middle class. The recession, price rises, and pollution of the

---

8:30 A.M. and again at 12:45 P.M.) with one of the highest recorded ratings was "Oshin" (1983–84), with its quintessential Shōwa protagonist, a woman whom audiences praised for her ability to "endure" (*taeru*) whatever state and society demanded through the bad times and the good.

24. Tada Michitarō and Ozaki Hotsuki, *Taishū bungaku no kansei* (Tokyo: Kawade Shobō, 1971), 12.

25. In the cold-war theme, Japan, like the small province of Mikawa, was caught between the mutual destructiveness of the Soviet Union (Nobunaga) and the United States (Imagawa) and saved from both by Ieyasu's peace. Tada and Ozaki, *Taishū bungaku no kansei*, 267–68.

26. Saitō Takashi, "Sengo jidai shōsetsu no shisō," *Shisō no kagaku* 67 (Oct. 1976): 12.

27. The three treasures (1957): washing machine, vacuum cleaner, refrigerator; the three *C*'s (1966): cooler, car, color television; the three *V*'s (1973): villa, *vacansu*, and visit (vacation house, overseas travel, and guests for dinner).

1970s demonstrated both the fragility and the costs of growth, and the phrase "The Age of Uncertainty" became the watchword of the day.[28] Second, even when people shared the establishment's pride in national achievement, as they did by 1990, they felt deprived in their allotment of the touted goods, from housing to welfare—what is known as the "rich Japan, poor Japanese" phenomenon. In the living room of televised history, where it was not public politics but private lives that mattered, the postwar experience had moved from deprivation to prosperity, which was accompanied by deprivations of its own.

The fourth agent of public memory is not public at all: it is the individual memories, the life stories, the personal pasts of people whose lives were ineluctably intertwined with the events of history with a capital *H*. Students of memory describe how individuals construct and reconstruct their memories in much the same way as nations do their histories, creating what Borges called a "fictitious past" that they can live with.

In postwar Japan, for example, the premise of historical discontinuity in 1945 rested somewhat precariously in the individual psyche. For each person had to weave together the past and present out of autobiographical stuff that often displayed no clear inner difference before and after August 15. Schoolteachers stopped leading military drills, war widows spoke more openly of the bitterness of loss, and local officials worried what defeat and the Potsdam Declaration would mean in their bailiwick. But they were the same people, inhabiting the same self, status, and daily life, except that the frame of social meaning had been suddenly changed around them. How they remembered—and reconciled—their wartime and postwar experience became part of their personal narratives, the stories they told themselves and passed on to their children.

The abrupt national turn from imperial state to democracy engendered count-less individual conversions. People, especially those in public places, changed from imperial patriot to democrat as if overnight. In one 1946 cartoon, the intellectual who just yesterday rode the back of the militarists shouting "Down with liberalism!" now cried "Down with the emperor system!" from the shoulders of the working man.[29] Some of these people had turned before, from Taishō liberal to Shōwa fascist, some would turn again, and some never turned at all, but it was a season of turning, which personal memory would later confront. In this

---

28. John Kenneth Galbraith's *Fukakujitsusei no jidai* [The Age of Uncertainty], published by TBS Britannica, was a best-seller in 1978, but the phrase was far more widely known than the book.

29. The cartoon, by Katō Etsurō, was entitled "The so-called survival arts of the intellectuals" (*Iwayuru interi no shoseijutsu*) and was published in *Van*, May 1946. See Sodei Rinjirō, "Satire Under the Occupation: The Case of Political Cartoons," in Thomas W. Burkman, ed., *The Occupation of Japan: Arts and Culture* (Norfolk: General Douglas MacArthur Foundation, 1988), 96, 102. Sodei explains that the cartoonist, himself a "double convert," was caricaturing a famous colleague who had made the "180-degree turnabout" from militarism to democracy.

regard the major effort devoted to studying the conversion (*tenkō*) from Marxism to nationalism of the previous generation during the 1930s could scarcely have been an incidental choice for postwar intellectuals who had themselves experienced the wrenching redirection of 1945.[30]

The definition of a presentable personal past is socially constituted. As time passes and attitudes change, so does the definition of presentability. People "reremember" their life stories to accord with the changing perception of an undefiled past. In early postwar Europe many claimed to have participated in the resistance to fascism, recalling a role perhaps more active than the one they had actually played. When, in later years, even passive collaboration was called into moral question, some reedited their experience to cast apparent collaboration as passive resistance instead. History with a capital *H*, in the form of the state, had called forth their earlier wartime actions. Now History, in its postwar guise, was judging those actions by a different standard, sparking delicate adjustments in personal recollection.

The adjustments sometimes moved from silence to remembrance. Such was the case of the postwar personal memory of many Japanese who had responded to the imperial call to settle the "new world" in Manchuria in the 1930s and were repatriated after the war to a "homeland" in which they felt themselves to be, and were sometimes treated as, unwelcome strangers. Their traumatic personal experience under Soviet invasion in 1945 was occluded at home by the defeat and the mythic postwar new beginning. The nation, which had roused them to do the work of empire, now repudiated the entire endeavor, leaving their personal pasts beside the postwar point. Despite documentary and literary expression, it was not until the 1970s that individual Manchurian memoirs began to flood into public view, as it became possible for the self-styled "children of Asia" to add their voices to the swelling reminiscences of Shōwa.[31] Again the larger national context determined the timbre of the personal pasts, with their strong tones of Japanese suffering and their still-held silences on the terrible harm that empire had done to others.

Similarly, the standard of acceptable public utterance of personal memories altered, as it seemed to become possible to say things aloud that one had privately felt for years. Comparing the two sizable genres of personal accounts, the literature of "August 15" and the reminiscences of "My Shōwa Era," one sees that in the late 1980s people spoke volubly of their anger at the human losses the war had caused and of the emperor's war responsibility, two private thoughts that had not come readily to public utterance in the mid 1940s. On the other side was the seemingly long suppressed sense of personal loss that impelled Etō Jun in the late

30. The classic postwar study is Shisō no Kagaku Kenkyūkai, ed., *Kyōdō kenkyū: Tenkō*, rev. ed., 3 vols. (Tokyo: Heibonsha, 1978).

31. For a discussion of literary expression, see Kawamura Minato, *Ikyō no Shōwa bungaku: "Manshū" to kindai Nihon* (Tokyo: Iwanami Shinsho, 1990).

1970s to write *What We Have Forgotten and What We Were Made to Forget*, with its anger at the postwar reforms as an imposed, illegal, and culturally brutal attempt by the occupation to deprive Japan of its rightful *sengo*.[32]

No single postwar chronology can be produced by a summary of the infinite series of differently remembered personal pasts. There are too many variants of the way the "little history" of individuals connects with the "big history" of the nation-state.[33] But there are significant generational patterns, particularly of those born in the "Shōwa single-digit" years (from 1927 to 1934).[34] The voluminous accounts of their personal experience of the war (*sensō taiken*) and of early *sengo* established the conventional chronology of postwar memory. Because of what they had been through, this age group virtually captured the memory market in the postwar decades. Not only war experience but also postwar reforms like the "peace constitution" and, for women, opportunities for their daughters (more fortunate than "we were") to marry whom they pleased brought history into the heart of their autobiographies, as did the unexpected prosperity of the following decades.

Younger generations whose memories began with the 1964 Olympics had neither war nor early postwar experience to burden their inner retrospection. They identified their historical context instead with the student movement, the education and employment scramble, or environmental issues. Younger still were those born "post-high-growth," who were in their twenties at Shōwa's end. Unable to recollect a world before Walkmans, they characterized late Shōwa Japan as agreeably peaceful and prosperous, citing housing costs and traffic accidents as banes of their particular slice of history. The life stories of the younger generations are only now being told into public memory, and they are likely, at long last, to be tales of the post-postwar.

Each of the four chronologies generated by the different groups of "historians"—and by others, for there are more—represents a differently lived postwar experience, and none treats the past in just the same way. For the progressives, the past continually betrayed the present by erupting into it; for the establishment, the past explained the achievements of contemporary Japan; in popular history, the past was meant to be *different* from the present; and in personal memory, the past was absorbed and fictionalized in myriad ways. Perhaps because most of them began with the premise of a radical break in 1945, their stories frequently told of continuities of one kind or another, either welcome or unwelcome.

32. Etō Jun, "Sengo to watakushi" (1966), in *Shinpen Etō Jun bungaku shūsei* (Tokyo: Kawade Shobō, 1985) 5:321–35; *Wasureta koto to wasuresaserareta koto* (Tokyo: Bungei Shunjū, 1979), 251–69.

33. "The Idea of Showa," in Carol Gluck and Stephen Graubard, eds., *Showa: The Japan of Hirohito* (New York: Norton, 1992), 20–21.

34. Those born between Shōwa 1 (from the last week of December 1926) and Shōwa 9 (1934) have come to be known as the "Shōwa hitoketa" generation. See Kelly's essay in this volume.

Since no single version of national history stood alone, each interacted, contended, and overlapped with the others in a continual custodial struggle for the past. Sometimes they supplemented and reinforced one another, as did the media history and the establishment version in the 1960s. Sometimes they worked against one another, the way the progressive historians who wrote the textbooks and the schoolteachers who belonged to the left-wing teachers' union worked against the conservative history propagated by the Ministry of Education. As times changed and the force of their interactions shifted, the field of public memory was increasingly weighted away from the critical to the celebratory, from politics to livelihood, from public to private. And as the weight shifted, the master narratives of Japanese history were differently interpreted.

NARRATIVES OF MODERNITY AND WAR

Before and beneath the narrated pasts of modernity and war lay the metanarrative of progress. Perhaps the oldest modern story of them all, the belief in progress as the telos of history established itself early and deeply in Meiji Japan, as it did elsewhere. In the twentieth century, whether the forward momentum was thought to be linear or dialectical, successful or failed, the directionality of history was seldom doubted. To the question "progress of and toward what?" the answer since Meiji had been, tautologically, "the modern." This belief in directed (or misdirected, but still purposeful) change since the nineteenth century led Japanese to think of the postwar task as the redirection of a longer evolutionary historical process that had run off course; hence the common reference to the Meiji Restoration as what Maruyama Masao called a "double image" of the immediate postwar period, when reforms could set modernity in motion.[35] The alleged break in 1945 in fact posited a continuity not between prewar fascism and postwar democracy but between modernization in its first phase and the chance the second time to get the modern right.

The transition to the modern is usually told either as a tale of emancipation, as in France, where liberty was the idealized goal, or as a tale of development, as in most of the later modernizing countries, where economic, and then political, change was the objective. Japan had some of both, but in the main, development proved the stronger theme. The contending poles of evaluation remained the same in postwar Japan as earlier. Either it was a cautionary tale—a modernity that had failed, as the progressives saw it, first from the vantage point of fascism and war in 1945, and later from the perspective of rampant "economism" in the 1970s[36]—or it was an inspirational fable, as the establishment glossed it, a modernity that had begun well, then derailed in the 1930s, but was soon back on track,

35. Katō Shūichi, Kinoshita Junji, Maruyama Masao, Takeda Kiyoko, eds., *Nihon bunka no kakureta kata* (Tokyo: Iwanami Shobō, 1984), 97.

36. Hidaka Rokurō, *The Price of Affluence: Dilemmas of Contemporary Japan* (Tokyo: Kodansha International, 1984), 63–78.

moving ever faster until prosperity and power put the imprimatur of success on the entire run of Japan's modern history.

Since the Meiji Restoration, like the French Revolution in France, appears as the founding event of modern times, its shifting interpretations mirrored both the historical consciousness of the times and the people's attitude toward "the possibilities of social change," to borrow the words of a progressive historian.[37] In the early postwar custody of progressives, who saw such possibilities as revolutionary, the Restoration—and more central to the narrative, the imperial state that it established—received a drubbingly critical appraisal. It had produced capitalism without a proper bourgeois revolution (as Marxist historians of the prevailing *kōza-ha* view continued to argue in a rendering of the absolutist imperial state that had originated in the late 1920s). Or it had resulted in industrialization without democracy, a modern nation without a modern citizenry, and imperial ideology without responsible politics. Feudal and otherwise traditional elements survived the Restoration to blight the modern state, a state that crushed all opposition, liberal and left alike.

This notion of a deviant modernity distorted by traditional survivals corresponds closely to the postwar historical indictment in Germany of its "special route" (*Sonderweg*) toward modernization, which resulted in what German scholars also call an ultimately disastrous "divergence from the West." The two countries had not only fascism, aggression, and defeat in common but also the temporal proximity of their modernization and its perceived denouement in war.

Reaction against the progressives' strong-minded and widely prominent view appeared in the mid-1950s. Even as the end of the postwar was announced for the first (though by no means the last) time in 1956, Kuwabara Takeo, a scholar of French literature, wrote the first (but scarcely the last) "reappraisal of the Meiji Restoration." He praised it as the first stage toward a modern nation, "the bourgeois revolution of an underdeveloped country," which he emended decades later to "a cultural revolution born of nationalism."[38] This was well before American scholars brought the "modernization argument" (*kindaikaron*) to Japanese shores in 1960. For two decades after the American interpretation appeared, progressive historians attacked what they called the "Reischauer line" for its positive appraisal of Japan's modernization, its view of the Restoration as a peaceful, pragmatic, and nonrevolutionary "revolution from above," and its

37. Tanaka Akira, *Meiji ishinkan no kenkyū* (Sapporo: Hokkaidō Daigaku Tosho Kankōkai, 1987), 260.

38. Kuwabara Takeo, "Meiji ishin no saihyōka," *Asahi shinbun,* 1 Jan. 1956, reprinted in Kuwabara *Meiji ishin to kindaika: Gendai Nihon o umidashita mono* (Tokyo: Shōgakkan, 1984), 199–202; and "The Meiji Revolution and Nationalism," in Kuwabara, *Japan and Western Civilization* (Tokyo: University of Tokyo Press, 1983), 155–73. For the cultural revolution, see "Meiji ishin to kindaika" (1983), reprinted in *Meiji ishin to kindaika,* 203–15; and "The Meiji Revolution and Japan's Modernization," in Nagai Michio and Miguel Urrutia, eds., *Meiji ishin: Restoration and Revolution* (Tokyo: United Nations University, 1985), 20–28.

suggestion that Japan was a model for Asian development.[39] Against very similar progressive protests, the government celebrated the Meiji centennial in the GNP-year of 1968 as a story of modernization with a happy national ending. Facing economic and political difficulty in 1974, Prime Minister Miki took comfort in the way "our forebears so splendidly overcame great difficulty at the time of the Meiji Restoration and the defeat in the second world war," representing our "century of history as a modern nation in Asia."[40]

In popular culture a "Restoration boom" also occurred in the mid-1950s, the first time since the late 1920s. But the heroes were the "noble failures," loyalist men of spirit like Yoshida Shōin and Sakamoto Ryōma, who did not live to see Meiji, and the stalwart Shinsengumi who fought and lost against the imperial cause. The samurai oligarchs who made the modern Meiji state were conspicuous by their absence. In the 1970s, however, Katsu Kaishū and Ōmura Masujirō, who served both shogunal and Meiji governments, figured as protagonists of popular Restoration history. Shiba Ryōtarō described them as the "technicians" who, after the revolutionary changes had been sparked by visionaries like Yo-shida, appeared to make the laws, armies, and institutions of the Meiji state.[41] From visionary to technocrat, from revolution to administration, Restoration figures had made the transition to the bureaucratic society of post-high-growth Japan.

The general postwar periodization is reflected in this contended narrative. In their hopes for the reforms of early *sengo*, progressive critics damned the Meiji Restoration as a failed revolution. Entranced by the high-growth middle period of the 1960s, establishment celebrants praised the Restoration as the first success in Japan's centenary march toward the modern. As people lived out the realities of the so-called post-high-growth, new-middle-mass society since the 1970s, the Restoration of popular lore retained its high historical glory but lost some of its human gloss. All these Restorations, and more, shifted together in the kaleido-scope of national history. No one view entirely drove out all others to produce a monochrome of memory.

It is also important to note, since the pattern holds true for other narrated pasts, that often the same individuals were saying the same thing since the 1950s, when Japanese of all opinions began to speak their historical mind in public.

39. For a summary of the Hakone conference of 1960, which became famous for introducing what Japanese called the "modernization argument," particularly as it was embodied in six volumes published by Princeton University Press as "Studies in the Modernization of Japan," see John Whitney Hall, "Changing Conceptions of the Modernization of Japan," in Marius B. Jansen, ed., *Changing Japanese Attitudes Toward Modernization* (Princeton: Princeton University Press, 1965), 7–41. For a standard progressive critique, see Kinbara Samon, *"Nihon kindaika" ron no rekishizō* (Tokyo: Chūō Daigaku Shuppanbu, 1968).

40. *Rekidai naikaku sōri daijin enzetsu shū*, 892.

41. Shiba Ryōtarō, *Kashin* (Tokyo: Shinchōsha, 1972) 1:231. This novel about Ōmura became the NHK annual historical drama in 1977. The so-called Katsu Kaishū boom occurred in the early 1970s.

Kuwabara and the others who spoke proudly of the Japanese modern in 1956 were still speaking so in 1986, and the same was true of the progressives, who remained ever critical of modernity as it turned out. What had changed, however, was the collective ambience of the times, which increasingly favored the positive appraisal, just as postwar social, economic, and political developments moved the center of national value toward preservation, not alteration, of the status quo. Many (the progressives excluded) were pleased when in the decade following their government's invocation of the "four modernizations," Chinese historians began again to look toward the Restoration and the practical achievements of the early Meiji leaders as a model for China.[42] A harsh reevaluation of the sort that hit the French Revolution at the time of its bicentennial in 1989 would, in that same year of Shōwa's end, have been unthinkable for the Restoration in Japanese public memory. For the story of the modern with a happy ending, the Meiji Restoration had been resoundingly restored as the indispensable happy beginning.

For the "once upon a time," there was Edo. Since the definition of the modern required an inverse, an origin, a "premodern," the Tokugawa period was continually reinvented as "tradition." The historical rehabilitation from dark, feudal Edo through potentially populist Edo to "rose-colored" Edo, as it came to be called, exhibited the familiar chronicle of brightening. As modernity improved its image, so, too, did tradition, which was defined in its most proximate phase, the time immediately before the modern, from 1600 to 1868. Indeed, Edo history was often called upon to do the entire job, freezing centuries of "tradition" ahistorically in Tokugawa form. And as the postwar years progressed, that tradition looked better and better. "Probably never before in world history have so many people lived in peace for so long. There was, moreover, no decline, so that the vitality of the people was passed along to the next era, to Meiji and after."[43] A far cry from the progressives' view of the oppressive unmodern shogunal state and remote from the swashbuckling and nostalgic landscapes of popular history, the newly risen Edo was not only indigenously modern before the advent of the West but was also, in the conceit of the 1980s, culturally *postmodern* before anyone had thought to invent such a term.[44] When Shōwa ended, a nostalgic "Edo boom" was in full swing.[45]

In public memory the master narrative of the modern swerved toward the pole of "a good modernity," but the collective accounts of the prewar past did not

---

42. For a study linking the Taika Reform, the Meiji Restoration, and the postwar reforms in such terms, see Liu Tianchun, *Riben gaige shigang* (Changchun: Jilin Wenshi Chubanshe, 1988).

43. Ōishi Shinsaburō and Nakane Chie, eds., *Edo jidai to kindaika* (Tokyo: Chikuma Shobō, 1986), 4. For an English version, differently edited, see Nakane and Ōishi, eds., *Tokugawa Japan: The Social and Economic Antecedents of Modern Japan* (Tokyo: University of Tokyo Press, 1990).

44. E.g., Karatani Kōjin, "One Spirit, Two Nineteenth Centuries," in Masao Miyoshi and H. D. Harootunian, eds., *Postmodernism and Japan* (Durham: Duke University Press, 1989), 259–72.

45. This is a historical version of the nostalgia described by Kelly in this volume.

produce anything like "a good war." Here the contention lay rather between the view of an unjust war, put forward immediately after the defeat, and later efforts to recount, if not a just, then perhaps a justifiable war. As background for this contestation, two abiding characteristics of the public rendering of the war were important. First, the heroic narrative, or drama, of an unjust war with clearly identified villains and victims remained strikingly unrevised over the years:

> the Pacific War—a war of peculiar savagery which Japan could have avoided if only its armed forces had kept away from politics.[46]

This simple scenario, written in 1975, echoed official history, both Japanese and American, from the early postwar years.

If the villains were clear, so were the victims: not the victims of Japanese aggression but the Japanese people themselves, who, it was said, "were embroiled" in the war by their leaders. In textbooks the war was often narrated in just such a fashion, as if events "were caused" without the intervention of human agency. This was history pronounced in the passive voice, closely related to what is known as "victims' history." The stance was confirmed by both the popular past, in which the people appeared as helpless before the state, and by personal memory, which viscerally recalled helplessness and suffering. Thus, the stark narrative of culpability produced by the "War Crimes Trial view of history" in the immediate aftermath of war survived the nearly half-century since.

The second, and related, survival was the prominence of the Pacific War in the narrative. The war in China appeared rather as prologue to the main tragedy, which was the war from Pearl Harbor to the atomic bomb. Occupied history played a role in this scenario, since in 1945 the occupation decreed a change in name from the imperialistic Greater East Asian War to the Pacific War, the war that the Americans knew so well. For years progressive historians wrote insistently of the "Fifteen Year War," precisely to make the point that for Japan, World War II did not begin at Pearl Harbor. Yet in a book intended to counter this displacement of the China war by "the spectacular action scenes" of the war in the Pacific, Ienaga Saburō could choose no other title than *The Pacific War*, for, as he explained, it was the only generally accepted term.[47]

The aggression that began in Manchuria in 1931 and escalated into total war against China from 1937 to 1945 was seldom the main focus of historical or moral attention. Instead, a balanced moral calculus set the attack on Pearl Harbor against the atomic bombs, which in turn gave Japan its bona fides as the victim of nuclear war in a new postwar mission of preserving peace. On the Rape of Nanking, however, public memory at first suffered amnesia, and for years where the China War should have resounded there was a skimming silence. Considering

46. Mainichi Daily News, ed., *Fifty Years of Light and Dark: The Hirohito Era* (Tokyo: Mainichi Newspapers, 1975), 198.

47. Ienaga Saburō, *The Pacific War, 1931–1945* (1968; New York: Pantheon, 1978), xiii; for "action scenes," see Ienaga Saburō, "Sengo nijūgonen no jiten ni tatte," *Sekai*, Jan. 1971, 155.

the importance of the Japanese-American relationship in postwar Japanese foreign affairs, the persistence of the emphasis on the Pacific War predictably
replicated in national memory the focus of Japan's international geopolitics.

Against this background the attempts at revision of the received view concentrated less on justice than on justification. As with other contended interpretations, the revisionists emerged early, at least by the middle period of the late 1950s
and 1960s. Ueyama Shunpei "reconsidered" the war in 1961, and in 1963
Hayashi Fusao wrote his "Affirmation of the Greater East Asian War" as a
hundred-year war against Western colonialism.[48] But their nationalistic positions
did not win legitimacy, beaten back in part by the energy of the progressives. It
was not until the early 1980s that an outbreak of revision in official history
suggested that the public threshold of historical rhetoric might have lowered. In
1982 government-approved textbooks softened the language of Japan's "invasion" of China into an "advance." In 1986 the Education Minister did mention
the Rape of Nanking, only to suggest that in the context of comparative atrocities
it was no worse than those committed by other nations. Others denied that the
event had taken place at all. In 1988 a cabinet official pronounced the Marco Polo
Bridge Incident of 1937 an "accident" and argued again that Japan had waged
only a defensive war against colonizing white races. In 1989 Prime Minister
Takeshita deferred the question of whether Japan's had been an "aggressive war"
to "later generations of historians," despite the fact that more than fifty years had
already passed.

That these official revisions met with outrage was due no longer to the progressives, whose power had receded in the era of "post-high-growth," but to the
outcry in Asian capitals. The coincidence of such pronouncements with similar
revisions in Germany, Italy, France, and elsewhere suggests commonalities of
context: distance in years from the war, rising nationalism, uncertainties in international geopolitics, and the belated expression of a certain generational memory.
In Japan it was notable that the war the officials chose to revise was the China
War, not the Pacific War, which preserved its historical calculus intact. Never
having been enshrined in national remembrance, the China War suffered more
easily the attacks of public forgetting. A "Manchurian boom" occurred in the late
1980s, and the Japanese orphaned during the war returned from China to
tear-jerking televised encounters with the families they had never known. But this
transposition of the China war—and its Japanese victims—to home social soil did
not intend, nor did it provide, any confrontation with the wartime past.

In Japan the wartime past remained largely in its initial immediate postwar
redaction. In Germany similar seizures of public memory took place later, and the
debate opened since the 1960s did not cease until unification in 1990. As a result
of such early closure, there were few contingencies in the Japanese narrative of

48. Ueyama Shunpei, *Daitōa sensō no imi* (Tokyo: Chūō Kōronsha, 1964); Hayashi Fusao, *Daitōa
sensō kōteiron* (Tokyo: Banchō shobō, 1964). Each includes articles previously published in *Chūō kōron*
in 1961 and 1963, respectively.

the war, which still marched rather purposefully from the early 1930s toward its inevitable end. Also, where the Germans thought of the problematic past as "Nazism," most Japanese thought of it in terms of the "war" rather than of the fascism and imperialism that led to it. And while intellectuals discussed the definition and appropriateness of the term *fascism,* there was, especially in comparison with Europe, a lack of attention to the details of its social history. Nor was the German question "What did you do during the war, father?" asked of the personal memory of the older generation in Japan. It was as if the prewar past had been so aggressively and tidily addressed in 1945 that it resisted review, debate, and the moral complexities of historicization in subsequent postwar years.

The fiftieth anniversary of Pearl Harbor in 1991 was commemorated with predictable public din in the same year as the sixtieth anniversary of the Manchurian Incident was passed over in a nearly audible civic hush. Japan faced renewed criticism from abroad for embarking on the next half-century of its international history without having adequately remembered the way the whole postwar story had begun.

TEMPLATES OF HISTORY

The different narratives and the different "historians" had more than the past in common. They also shared interpretive premises, laying similar templates over the material of history to make their sense of it. Because such templates are basic, almost intrinsic, to a given national history, few of Japan's were new with the postwar but rather drew on older, almost perennial concerns. Some became more prominent after the war, others less.

The quest for the people, for example, appeared in all dialects of postwar public memory. *Jinmin, minshū, taishū, jōmin, shomin, jinbutsu, ningen,* or *hitobito*—proletariat, democratic or populist masses, folkish or commoner populace, heroic individuals of popular legend, human beings, or just people plain and simple—the variants were numerous, but their roles were often similar. They were invoked as the new protagonists of history, as if to replace the state that had recently been so powerful. This renewed search for agents of social and political change apart from the state characterized postwar historical consciousness in many countries responding to the mid-twentieth-century state, which had wrought such harm to its own people and those it colonized or subjugated.

The emphasis on the people was a revised template of the relationship between state and society. For the progressive opposition it represented the effort to define the possibility of politics in a democratic form, but outside institutional structures like the Diet, which was associated with the state. Thus, the progressives articulated a discourse of democracy as contestatory or participatory social behavior, epitomized by the 1960 Security Treaty protest and other popular movements. Establishment history, important parts of which represented state institutional structures, also effaced the state, but in a different way. Official discourse emphasized coequal social share and responsibility—democracy as the right to the middle class. Popular history measured democracy in terms of flourishing "private livelihood" (*shiseikatsu*), which included intangible liberation from the state in the early postwar period, the increasingly tangible well-being of consumption in the 1960s, and later, the combination of both material and social goods that would enhance the quality of private life.

Thus, the role played by the people in history was the equivalent of the postwar definition of democracy in social terms. The vernacular understanding of democracy emphasized expanded mass access to improved economic and social goods, rather than electoral or parliamentary process. Vernacular history did much the same. The politics it defined as possible lay outside the conventional political realm, where politicians and bureaucrats, not democrats, held sway. For all the tales of the people, however, most postwar versions of the past harbored the belief that the state—the politicians and the bureaucrats—had almost always been in control and remained so today. It was precisely for that reason that the historians persevered in their quest for the people.

The relationship between the internal and the external provided another prominent, and perennial, template laid over the past. This took various forms, of which the axes of East and West, of insularity and openness, of Japan and non-Japan were surely the most pervasive. Despite more than a century of hybridization within Japan, the East-West axis remained clear and distinct, in conceptualization if not in fact. Its long-standing correlatives, tradition and modernity, were once again correlated. In the initial postwar years they were again conflated into Western modernity and Eastern tradition. Only now the valuation of the war years was reversed, especially by progressives, so that instead of "overcoming" Western models of modernity, the goal was finally to achieve them. The conflated axis could also be flipped to celebrate an Eastern modernity, an inversion that became increasingly characteristic of conservative rhetoric.

In historical terms the East-West axis was related to the shift in models against which Japan chose to measure its past—and present. The Western alternatives were Euro-American modernization, which was dominant after the war, or Soviet social revolution, advocated by the Left in the initial postwar decade. In their application to Japanese history, both models emphasized Japan's deviation from the appointed course of historical change. The call to break the hold of the West in favor of Asian (*Ajiateki*) models came in the early 1950s, in the context of the progressives' hopes for alignment with Asian revolutionary nationalism as an alternative to the cold-war alliance with the United States. Because of Japanese imperialism, however, Asia was never an easy referent for the progressives.[49] And conservative interpretations used it in the opposite sense, making the Meiji Restoration a model for "change in Asia."

49. Shibahara Takuji, "Meiji ishin to Ajia no henkaku," *Chūō kōron*, May 1962, 270–78.

Disillusionment, first with Moscow and then with Mao, left the progressives in Japan, as in other places, without a revolutionary model, West or East. Some turned inward toward indigenous models, forsaking external referents for such internal sources of modernity as the social communitarianism of the Tokugawa village. In the late 1970s Japan was itself declared a model, not only for China but for "America as number two." Although this suggestion was unacceptable to progressives, it was welcomed by the establishment and in popular discourse. By the mid-1980s it was standard official rhetoric to speak politically of Japan's triangular obligations toward the West and toward Asia, and historically of Japan's "new civilization, which had fused the civilization of East and West" as a world power and leading Asian nation. To the Asians themselves, this all sounded ominously familiar.[50]

The relationship between internal and external also appeared as the oscillating metaphor of insularity and openness to the world, often expressed by the words *sakoku*, the seclusion of the Tokugawa period, and *kaikoku*, the opening of the country in the nineteenth century. In the immediate postwar period, itself referred to as "the second opening of the country," seclusion was considered to have been a "misfortune," a "tragedy," which had cut Tokugawa Japan off from liberalizing tendencies and stunted its modernization.[51] As Edo began to acquire the characteristics of the protomodern in the middle period of the late 1950s and 1960s, *sakoku* was accorded less importance, since Tokugawa Japan was said to have managed considerable change without open commerce with the wider world.[52] And with the view of rose-colored Edo in the late 1970s and 1980s, isolation was seen as a positive political move that had created the Pax Tokugawa and prevented colonization as well as aroused the manifold cultural creativity of Edo.[53]

The rehabilitation of the historical *sakoku* corresponded to the metaphorical use of the term in contemporary context. Those who used "seclusion" in a negative sense urged the importance of the world context for Japan, as did advocates of "internationalization," which had become the equivalent of *kaikoku* by the 1980s.[54] Those with kind words for the *sakoku* of the past stressed that Japan's present strengths lay at home and that national pride should not be sacrificed to "world trends." In 1990–91 Prime Minister Kaifu sought to sell the Gulf War to the Diet by arguing that if Japan did not contribute, "it would tread the path of

50. Nakasone Yasuhiro, 6 Feb. 1984, in *Rekidai naikaku sōri daijin enzetsu shū*, 1104. For China, see Allen S. Whiting, *China Eyes Japan* (Berkeley and Los Angeles: University of California Press, 1989).

51. From different perspectives, see Inoue Kiyoshi et al., "Itsuwaranu Nihonshi," *Chūō kōron* (Aug. 1952), 196–97; Watsuji Tetsurō, *Sakoku: Nihon no higeki* (Tokyo: Chikuma Shobō, 1950); and *Uzumoreta Nihon* (Tokyo: Shinchōsha, 1951).

52. Tsuji Tatsuya, "Tokugawa sanbyakunen no isan," *Chūō kōron*, Sept. 1964, 120–40.

53. Ōishi and Nakane, *Edo jidai to kindaika;* see, e.g., 448–50. Scholarly reevaluation of the extent of *sakoku* also occurred during the 1970s and was related to, but not identical with, the view of rose-colored Edo. See Hayami Akira, *Rekishi no naka no Edo jidai* (Tokyo: Tōkei Sensho, 1977), 85–114.

54. E.g., Takeuchi Hirotaka, "Jinteki sakoku taisei kara dappi seyo," *Chūō kōron*, Oct. 1987, 96–106.

international isolation."[55] The either/or of insularity or openness, though long outrun by global realities, remained lodged in Japanese historical consciousness.

The polarity between Japan and non-Japan also ran through every historical version, but in public memory it was most closely connected with the reassertion of national identity. The *minzoku*, the ethnic people, appeared everywhere, often twinned with *bunka*, culture, its embodiment in history. Marxist historians identi-fied the *minzoku* as Asian in the context of national liberation movements of the early 1950s; peoples' historians in the 1960s located the *minzoku* in the context of the ethnographic folk culture of Yanagita Kunio; and nationalist intellectuals swept up in the *Nihonjinron* (discourse on Japaneseness) in the 1970s celebrated the ethnic Japanese in terms of cultural exceptionalism. *Minzoku bunka*, national cul-ture, was again a prominent theme in official language in the 1980s. Conservative intellectuals provided analyses of Japanese history that purported to discover the secret of Japanese culture, whether in the *ie* (family) system or, if necessary, all the way back in prehistoric Jōmon, where Umehara Takeshi insisted the true indige-nous "soul" of Japan originated, unadulterated by any foreign influence.[56]

Important parts of the internal landscape, however, lay outside the templates. Collective national history tends to produce a canonical past that excludes variant voices. In postwar Japan not only was there a greater range of "historians" than have been mentioned here, but there were also other stories. The most striking perhaps was that of Okinawa, which provided one of the rare vantage points from which to relativize Japanese history from within. Public memory in postwar Okinawa was vigorous and vivid, and the tales it told followed a different chronol-ogy and constructed a history with a different political meaning. Subjugated by the Satsuma domain during Tokugawa, Okinawa's modernity began not with the Restoration but with absorption into the Meiji state in 1872. Its people were truly embroiled in war and made victims twice over, once of the Japanese imperial army, who massacred the allegedly inferior Okinawans as spies, and once of the fighting in one of the bloodiest battles of the Pacific War. Okinawa's postwar also began in 1945, but under direct American rule, which did not end until 1972, creating a "long postwar" in the literal sense of the phrase. And after its "return to the ancestral country" in that year, Okinawa saw less of high growth and more of the American military than did any other part of Japan. That Okinawans also felt more negatively toward the Shōwa emperor than did any other part of Japan was noted on the mainland but not absorbed into public memory there.[57]

---

55. Speech to the Lower House, 25 Jan. 1991, *Asahi shinbun*, 26 Jan. 1991.

56. For example (and there are many), see Umehara Takeshi, "Wasurerareta ichimannen," *Umehara Takeshi chosakushū* (Tokyo: Shūeisha, 1982) 15:488. For the *ie*, see Murakami Yasusuke, Kumon Shunpei, and Satō Seizaburō, *Bunmei toshite no ie shakai* (Tokyo: Chūō Kōronsha, 1979); also Murakami Yasusuke, "*Ie* Society as a Pattern of Civilization," *Journal of Japanese Studies* 10, no. 2 (Summer 1984): 281–364.

57. See Norma Field, *In the Realm of a Dying Emperor: A Portrait of Japan at Century's End* (New York: Pantheon, 1991), 33–104.

The Koreans and other minorities in Japan had similarly dissonant stories to tell, as did women, whose accounts of their postwar chronology often began with the constitution and other reforms that changed their lives more than the promise of political democracy did. Women were suddenly "allowed to speak," recalled members of the older generation, and peace and equality of the sexes were frequently mentioned along with the ubiquitous washing machines and refrigerators. Such differently experienced social pasts seldom appeared in the main narratives, revealing the sorts of exclusion and homogenization that operated in public memory exactly as they did in society.[58]

GHOSTS AT THE HISTORICAL FEAST

The same should be said of the emperor, who was almost a narrative unto himself, or at least a master code for the other narratives of the Japanese past. The medieval historian Amino Yoshihiko said it clearly when he entitled the first chapter of his booklet in a popular history series, "Japanese Society Cannot Be Discussed If the Existence of the Emperor Is Ignored."[59] The emperor system, or *tennōsei*, was indeed a special problem. It appeared as an extraordinarily influential presence in all postwar versions of Japanese history, yet it was not readily comprehensible within the standard historical frameworks. Marxism could not capture it, nor liberalism, nor even conservative consensus history. As concrete, even monumental, as it was in fact, it acted in historical rendering as a sometimes spectral explanation for why things turned out the way they did. It was impossible to discuss the past without coming up against the emperor system. Yet it admitted of no easy explicability. It was like a ghost at the historical feast, always in attendance, related to both the past and the present, but elusive and morally and politically charged. Other national histories have ghosts of their own. Although there is no comparison in content, in terms of the way they haunt contemporary history, the Holocaust in Germany, racism in the United States, and the postimperial syndrome in Britain are specters similarly difficult to reckon with.

It was of course the emperor system of the prewar imperial state that set the task so centrally. Conceived of as a spreading institutional and ideological presence, it appeared far broader than the definition of the state. In part because of the symbolic power that attached to the emperor and in part because of its extralegal, suprahistorical character, the imperial institution possessed a potency that was invoked in narrating every period since ancient times—from the keyhole tombs to the present—to interpret the course of national history. In addition, since it seemed to exist nowhere else in similar form and did not fit the categories of other historical traditions, it was a fulcrum of "difference," which was central to criticizing, celebrating, and explaining Japan.

58. See the essays by Upham, Uno, and Buckley in this volume.

59. Amino Yoshihiko, *Nihon shakai to tennōsei*, Iwanami Bukkuretto no. 108 (Tokyo: Iwanami Shoten, 1988), 2.

Immediately after the war, the occupation and the progressives set out to penetrate "the veil of myth" that surrounded the prewar emperor system.[60] The progressive analysis was partly continuous with Marxist interpretations of imperial absolutism from the early Shōwa period and partly new since the war, as in Maruyama's "system of irresponsibility" and "interfusion of ethics and power."[61] Against this political grasp of *tennōsei* in 1946 was ranged the view of the emperor as a cultural institution, a view associated then with Tsuda Sōkichi. These two interpretations remained in contention throughout the postwar period. The "new" institution, the symbolic emperor system established by the 1947 constitution, had come by the 1970s to be associated with the same interpretive spectrum. Progressives combated the revivals of prewar *tennōsei* practices, which they saw refurbishing postwar *tennōsei* with some of the ideological trappings of the old. The establishment view, especially the Right of the LDP and the rising conservative intellectuals, associated the "democratic emperor" with the transformed new Japan and enveloped the institution once again in the raiments of cultural identity. This institutional continuity violated the break between prewar and postwar for those who opposed the imperial system, while it provided an inviolable link to the longer past for those who supported it.

The post-Shōwa retrospectives presented two Hirohitos, sundering the prewar institution from the postwar, despite the obvious difficulty that both emperors were one and the same man. The issue of Hirohito's war responsibility occasioned open debate, and polls and letters made it clear that significant numbers of Japanese agreed that the emperor bore some responsibility for the war, although they had seldom before said so in public. It was also clear that more than 80 percent of the population supported the present symbolic emperor system, which the progressives and some others, their numbers and influence dwindling, still opposed. It was as if the Shōwa emperor might be held responsible for prewar history, but the imperial institution was a creature either of the incalculably ancient or reassuringly recent postwar past and therefore acceptable. Young people, it was equally clear, could not follow such strained logic. It seemed to them that their elders were "hung up" on the Shōwa emperor for some unfathomable reason of generational memory. They themselves had had such minimal instruction in the subject that they could not be accused of forgetting what they had never been adequately taught.

The contention between constitutional and cultural interpretations of the imperial institution continued in connection with the imperial ceremonies of 1989–90. To the question, What is an emperor doing in a late twentieth-century advanced capitalist democracy? Japanese history provided no easily suitable answers. Nor were there wholly workable contemporary analogies elsewhere. Thus, the emperor remained available as a master code for both the

60. "Nihonshi kentō no kadai," *Chōryū*, Feb. 1946, 1.

61. Maruyama Masao, *Nihon no shisō* (Tokyo: Iwanami Shinsho, 1961), 37–38; *Thought and Behavior in Modern Japanese Politics* (New York: Oxford University Press, 1963), 8–21.

critical and the celebratory narratives, and the imperial institution remained contested terrain.

A second ghost had grown perhaps paler with the years, but the United States had been a foreign intrusion in domestic Japanese history since the end of the war and was still a palpable presence in the precincts of public memory in 1990. The narratives of modernity and war were initially rewritten and the myths of *sengo* initiated, not only under, but partly by, the occupation. Americans wrote the Japanese constitution, whose translation had to be cumbersomely negotiated from English into Japanese.[62] It may be impossible to find an analogy here either, considering that Japan, a sovereign nation, is currently operating in its fifth decade under a constitution written by a foreign power. Of course, the constitution is entirely Japanese by virtue of practice, but the ghostwriters were American.

Postwar Japan felt an even more powerful presence in the dominance of the United States in Japan's foreign relations, first during the occupation and then in the cold-war framework of the American imperium. That most Japanese wanted America to be there did not make their feelings about the dependence any less complicated. The United States provided Japan's major market for several decades and, beginning in the late 1960s, became the major critic of Japanese trade practices. American pressure was said to be one of the main agents of political change in Japan. Indeed, only two countries as closely intertwined as Japan and the United States could have reached the exquisite extremes of mutual bashing that characterized the early 1990s. The relationship of postwar political asymmetry, in which America was indubitably dominant, was complicated by the more recent asymmetry in the two economies, whereby the United States and Japan traded places of debtor and creditor. The difficult adjustment on both sides provoked a spate of retrospectives on postwar "Japamerika" or "Amerinippon," on the one hand, and a stream of futurology in both countries that prophesied another war between them, on the other. But as concerned as the United States had become with Japan by 1990, Japan was still far more obsessed with the United States.

Not only foreign relations but also its influence over domestic development made America loom large in Japan's historical rendering of itself. America, if not the model, was often taken as the comparative case, despite the fact that the United States and Japan were in many respects polar extremes. Comparisons between Japanese and European political economy, for example, often made more sense but were seldom invoked. American-made modernization history engaged Japanese scholars for years, and books such as the one you are reading receive attention out of proportion to their importance. None of this focus on America was all-determining, since postwar Japan both made and conceived its

62. Kyoko Inoue, *MacArthur's Japanese Constitution: A Linguistic and Cultural Study of Its Making* (Chicago: University of Chicago Press, 1991).

history on its own. But the United States was spectrally present, arousing tangled responses, whether to the war or the constitution, and staying on in Japanese public memory even after the world situation that gave it such presence had undergone substantial change.

"THE LONG POSTWAR" AND THE END OF SHŌWA

When the Shōwa era ended in 1989, it was said that the postwar would finally end as well. After the emperor's death came the deluge of Shōwa retrospectives in every genre of public memory and private reminiscence. Any narrative of the period, which began in 1926 and lasted until 1989, necessarily confronted the alleged discontinuity of 1945. After the war, *sengo* had displaced Shōwa in historical consciousness so that the decades were marked in public memory as postwar 10 (1955), postwar 20 (1965), and so on. But now that the period had ended and would be recounted for the first time in its entirety, Shōwa consciousness ran high. Yet in the ubiquitous media histories, the story remained a tale of two Shōwas.

The prewar past was depicted largely in terms of national events and the road to war, with the state as the protagonist. On television this segment ended in 1945, as if to say that the dark old Japan was now behind and the bright new one would follow on the morrow. When it did, the postwar past appeared as the familiar chronicle of ever-improving *seikatsu,* the road to economic prosperity and international stature. The prewar images of Manchuria–the February 26th Incident– Pearl Harbor and the postwar iconography of MacArthur–the Olympics–the affluent consumer were connected only by contrast, not by history. No continuity appeared across the divide of 1945.

Yet a competing chronology was also apparent. The established prewar-postwar story line shared time with a longer Meiji-Taishō-Shōwa saga, in which Shōwa completed the work of modernization that Meiji had begun. "The long modern," familiar since the earliest postwar evocations of Meiji, now seemed likely to achieve canonical status, though in the name of three emperors instead of one. Here there was continuity aplenty, but of a highly selective sort. The two prewar decades of Shōwa disappeared in an elision, which preserved the break in 1945 at the same time that it ignored the prewar period that had been the reason for the break in the first place. The narrative of the war thus disappeared into the narrative of "the long modern," which left a lacuna of history where the prewar past should have been. The appeal of the long modern extended even to the critics who had no wish to elide the war. Since the Meiji Restoration was "the departure point of modern Japan," a leading progressive historian wrote in the newspaper, the Meiji Restoration and the postwar reforms must now be examined as a "set" in the narrative of the modern past.[63]

63. Nakamura Masanori, "Meiji ishin kenkyū no konnichiteki imi," *Asahi shinbun* (yūkan), 4 Apr. 1989.

What, then, of the postwar? In common parlance there were at least three *sengo*. The first was the *real* postwar, that is, the immediate postwar period of reform and recovery that had so animated progressive hopes. That postwar, everyone seemed to agree, was over, for better or for worse. Then there was the penumbral *sengo* of dramatic economic rise, whose demise had been announced regularly since 1956. That postwar, historians declared, had become history sometime in the 1970s, when "post-high-growth" began. And yet people still spoke of postwar Japan through the 1980s. Prime Minister Nakasone urged a "general reckoning with the postwar" (*sengo no sōkessan*) as part of his nationalistic call to lay the wartime past to rest. Prime Minister Kaifu's inaugural address in 1989 invoked the recent past in the now standard trope: "In the postwar, Japan has risen from the ashes to the point that it is considered the most affluent country."[64] And, he implied, the rise was not over yet.

Most countries ceased to speak of themselves as "postwar" in the domestic sense by the late 1950s and became instead "contemporary." Japan's "long postwar" was as distinctive as it was anachronistic. One might argue that the name continued out of habit, awaiting a momentous event to end it, as the death of the emperor had ended the Meiji and Shōwa eras. More likely, however, there was a reason that public memory clung to the postwar. The founding myth of the new Japan, the mythistorical beginning in 1945, was in part responsible. The present—democracy, peace, prosperity, and all—owed its origins and authenticity to *sengo*. Clinging to the postwar expressed contentment with the status quo. Something similar is true of the widespread support for the constitution, which had long made it politically impossible for the right wing to force revision. The majority of Japanese associated their "peace constitution" with prosperity and were content to remain nomenclaturally postwar. A compendium of popular views of the constitution contained the repeated sentiment *Genzai no mama de yoi*—things are fine the way they are.[65] And as Kaifu's remark incanted, the way they are is prosperous.

The experience of high growth was as much responsible for shifting the weight of public memory toward the conservative consensus as were the conservatives themselves. The anxiety felt by the establishment that it all might come undone— Japanese spirit and culture lost, the will to work receded, the homogeneity threatened—was shared in less perfervid form by many ordinary Japanese who did not feel or care about "the completion of the modern" but wanted to see the continuation, and improvement, of their present lot and feared that they might not. The middle class, though it was never as universal and homogenized as it imagined itself to be, had become "life-style conservatives" (*seikatsu hoshushugisha*).[66] Perhaps

---

64. *Asahi shinbun*, 3 Oct. 1989.

65. INO Kikaku, ed. *Warera ga kenpō: "Yonda yonda"* (Tokyo: Shōgakkan, 1982).

66. Yamaguchi Yasushi, "Sanin senkyo ga utsushidashita 'seikatsu hoshushugi' no kōzō," *Asahi jānaru*, 8 July 1983; quoted in Kinbara Samon, ed., *Sengoshi no shōten* (Tokyo: Yūhikaku Sensho, 1985), 340.

the postwar was amuletic; to jettison the name would throw the entire system open to question. In the early 1990s few vernacular historians were of such a mind.

The third *sengo*, the international postwar, presented the greatest problem, since after 1989 it, too, was finally ending. Japan was being called to strut and fret its hour upon the world stage, where it had not had great success in modern times. Despite the increasing rivulet of official apologies to Asian countries, Japan had still to confront its aggressive past in Asia and relate its own national history responsibly to the national histories of other countries. And despite the increasing stridency of rhetoric between Japan and the United States, neither country had yet to adjust to the end of America's dominance of the relationship and put the postwar past responsibly behind them.

The word *responsibility* nagged Japanese domestic memory as well, because habits of victims' history were so long entrenched that people who felt helpless before history felt helpless before the present as well. There would be a vast generational sea change when those who experienced the war and *sengo* finally ceded their long prominence to children who had vaguely heard of the oil shock when they were born but for whom that Shōwa "was the distant, distant past."[67] Only then would "the long postwar" end and the collective construction of post-postwar memory finally begin.

BETWEEN THE PAST AND THE FUTURE

There is no end to public memory, and national history is a blunt instrument. In times of uncertainty, when there is no sure vision of the future against which to tell the story of the past, the instrument becomes still blunter. At such moments national history tends to become more nationalistic, a trend that is apparent in Japan and around the world in the early 1990s.

In Japan the postwar moment applied a kind of torque to history that cast the postwar in terms of discontinuity in the larger context of war and modernity. But, as in other countries, the postwar apprehension of national history was part of a longer twentieth-century discourse, which was merely obscured by the insistence on the break in 1945. The myth of a new beginning, itself a radically ahistorical notion, not only prevented seeing the twentieth century whole, but it also elided the prewar and wartime and perpetuated the notion of a long postwar. Fifty years after World War II, it is not a matter of "postwar Japan as history": postwar Japan *is* history. And for Japanese public memory, there is the dilemma.

In a deeper quandary about the future, the Japanese, like many others, have responded with a greater pride in the national past, the one linked inextricably to the other. Japan is not unusual in finding it difficult to pose the question of

---

67. Asahi Shinbun Teema Danwashitsu, ed., *Tennō soshite Shōwa: Nihonjin no Tennōkan* (Tokyo: Asahi Shinbunsha, 1989), 131–32.

adjustment to an altered world. Nor will its answer come easily. The status quo so prized by the conservative consensus does not suffice as a guide to either policy or identity. Its time is up. The celebration of a glorious past is, in effect, the avoidance of a demanding present—a combination that blinds both historical memory and contemporary vision. An end must be put, at long last, to *sengo*. This means assuming responsibility for the twentieth-century past, which now includes the prewar, the war, *and* the postwar eras. It also means assuming responsibility for the present: the post-postwar future depends upon it.

PART II

Political Economy

CHAPTER FOUR

Growth Versus Success
Japan's Economic Policy in Historical Perspective

Laura E. Hein

Japan is internationally renowned for its stunning economic performance. This achievement excites foreign envy and Japanese pride, partly because it seems so painlessly achieved. Japan appears to offer a model for economic success without suffering, contention, or even much effort. Unfortunately, this is an illusion. Over the course of the postwar decades the Japanese struggled not only to devise a strategy for economic development but also to define their economic goals. Moreover, the strategies chosen have had significant costs to some Japanese. Elites and nonelites agreed on the importance of rebuilding the economy by 1946, but their economic policies evolved only slowly past that initial and hard-won consensus as new problems regularly emerged. The evolution of postwar Japanese history is a tale less of solutions than of debates, some of which began long before 1945 and some of which are unlikely ever to be resolved.

"ECONOMIC SUCCESS" AND "ECONOMIC GROWTH"

There has been very little exploration of economic debate in the many studies of the postwar Japanese economy or of the precise ways in which the postwar Japanese approached economic problems. Rather, this question has been obscured by a different one: how to explain Japan's unusually high rate of economic growth. This is not the logical place to begin an analysis of the postwar Japanese economy, but unveiling the mechanisms of growth has been in fact the problem that has engrossed most researchers. Finding the "secrets" of Japanese economic success has driven nearly all work done on the economy since the 1960s.

This focus has biased the analysis of postwar Japan in a number of specific ways. First, it has obscured all those aspects of Japanese economic history that have not directly contributed to Japanese success. Second, it has imparted false prescience to the Japanese, persistently giving the impression that successes were anticipated and planned, and so has minimized the extent to which luck and international developments outside of Japanese control were crucial to economic growth. Third, it has implanted the idea that there is a national "Japanese model" that is broadly characteristic of and accepted by all Japanese society, ignoring much conflict and tension.

It is not surprising that many outside observers of Japanese economic policy assume that these achievements were the result of a carefully planned, consistent national economic strategy, for Japanese leaders have not hesitated to take credit for them. This myth is both internationally constructed and "made in Japan." For example, Ojimi Yoshihisa, vice minister of the Ministry of International Trade and Industry (MITI), proclaimed in a 1970 speech that

> the Ministry of International Trade and Industry decided to establish in Japan industries which require intensive employment of capital and technology, . . . industries such as steel, oil refining, petro-chemicals, automobiles, aircraft, industrial machinery of all sorts, and electronics including electronic computers. . . . According to Napoleon and Clausewitz, the secret of a successful strategy is the concentration of fighting power on the main battle grounds; fortunately, owing to good luck and wisdom spawned by necessity, Japan has been able to concentrate its scant capital in strategic industries.[1]

This bureaucrat presented a glowing but incorrect description of the development of Japanese industrial policy. He falsely left the impression that postwar Japanese officials knew which were "strategic industries" and that they agreed on where lay the "main battle ground" of economic policy. He also lumped together industries that were targeted early (steel) with ones that were adopted only later (petrochemicals), while glossing over one of MITI's worst embarrassments, its failure to see promise in Sony's new product, the transistor. In what later proved to be the right decision, Sony ignored government suggestions that the company use its resources for other projects. The military analogy also misleadingly suggested that a unified Japan had a clear, external enemy against which it could deploy its biddable economic forces. Success has a way of creating its own illusions, even for individuals who were involved in decision making.

But perhaps the greatest problem is that this approach confuses economic growth and economic success. Probably, if pressed, most people would define economic success by combining some measure of economic growth together with some measure of economic justice. However, in practice, economic growth alone is often the proxy for economic success, although these are not the same. Economic growth certainly can make tasks such as raising the general standard of living easier, but it does not ensure that any such redistribution will take place. In fact, a number of years ago John W. Bennett and Solomon B. Levine argued that

1. Yoshihisa Ojimi, "Basic Philosophy and Objectives of Japanese Industrial Policy," in *The Industrial Policy of Japan,* ed. Organization for Economic Cooperation and Development (OECD) (Paris: OECD, 1972), 15.

industrialization inherently generates what they called "social deprivation." In their formulation, economic success in Japan, as everywhere else, not only does not mean an end to social problems but also itself creates new ones.[2] The experience of countries in other parts of the world has included examples of social problems *created* by new wealth. Cocaine profits in the Andean nations provide the most extreme recent example.

Undeniably, postsurrender Japan is fundamentally more democratic, peaceful, and egalitarian than it was before 1945, and income distribution is far more even, but it is not at all obvious, either theoretically or empirically, how this situation is related to economic growth. Studies of wealth inequality show that much of the redistribution took place in the first postwar years, particularly as a result of land reform: that is, redistribution occurred *before* economic growth began.[3] In fact, consistent with Bennett and Levine's argument, not only have inequities in the system not disappeared, but many have grown worse during the last thirty years. Systemic dilemmas include urban density and its consequences,[4] pollution of the environment,[5] and wealth inequality.[6] Japan is no closer than it was forty-five years ago to solving these problems. The inequality that has grown most startlingly in tandem with Japan's GNP is the effect of skyrocketing urban land prices. While the family income of workers' households increased about thirteen-fold between 1960 and 1990, urban land prices increased about twenty-eight-fold.[7]

2. John W. Bennett and Solomon B. Levine, "Industrialization and Social Deprivation: Welfare, Environment, and the Postindustrial Society in Japan," in *Japanese Industrialization and Its Social Consequences,* ed. Hugh Patrick (Berkeley and Los Angeles: University of California Press, 1976), 439–92. See also Solomon B. Levine, "Social Consequences of Industrialization in Japan," in *Productivity: A Concept in Political Economy Reconsidered,* ed. Michael Sherman (Madison: Wisconsin Humanities Committee, 1984).

3. Toshiyuki Mizoguchi and Noriyuki Takeyama attempt to quantify the level of postwar poverty in *Equity and Poverty under Rapid Economic Growth: The Japanese Experience* (Tokyo: Kinokuniya, 1984), but say data are lacking. For an earlier effort, see Akira Ono and Tsunehiko Watanabe, "Changes in Income Inequality in the Japanese Economy," in Patrick, *Japanese Industrialization,* 363–90. See also Margaret A. McKean, "Equality," in *Democracy in Japan,* ed. Takeshi Ishida and Ellis S. Krauss (Pittsburgh: University of Pittsburgh Press, 1989), 201–24.

4. Problems of urban density include high land prices, cramped housing, miserable and long commutes, no place for children to play, and perennially congested roadways. This problem has become much more severe since the end of the war, particularly in the greater Tokyo area.

5. This category includes severe cases of pollution of the air, water, groundwater, land (both subsidence and heavy metals pollution), nuclear radiation potential, decommissioning of nuclear plants, direct poisoning of people, and noise pollution. See the essays by Upham and Taira in this volume for explicit ways in which these concerns have been subordinated to economic growth.

6. Taira's essay in this volume explores this issue in greater detail. Buckley demonstrates the growing participation of the female labor force in the postwar economy without equal compensation or opportunity. As in the United States, the middle-class ideal of supporting a family on one income is moving out of reach for more and more Japanese families.

7. Family income of urban worker households increased from an index of 11.7 in 1960 to 100 in 1980 and then jumped to 127.2 in 1985 and 149.2 in 1990. Meanwhile, the urban residential land price index has been calculated at 6.8 in 1960, with 100 pegged at March 1980. The disproportionate increase in land prices accelerated in the next decade, as the same index shot up to 137.7 in 1985 and

This development has made billionaires out of land holders and robbed middle-class Japanese who do not own property of the chance ever to do so. These issues are fundamental to any evaluation of economic success and call into question the ease with which we conflate economic growth and success.

Yet, rather than aiming for the complex and subjective goals of economic justice and economic success, many postwar Japanese (like postwar Americans and Europeans) accepted rapid GNP growth as a substitute. That such confusion was possible is in large part a tribute to the very real redistribution of wealth that did take place in postwar Japan and sets the postwar apart from economically undemocratic presurrender Japan. At the same time the removal of the economy (now presented as a technical problem of growth) from political debate was a profoundly political act—perhaps the most antidemocratic development of postwar Japanese history. As elsewhere in the technocratic world, decisions with major implications for Japanese society were recast as private, technical problems rather than occasions for public debate.

Nonetheless, this process of "political denaturing" was gradual and incomplete.[8] Various challenges have emerged throughout the postwar years, and the conflation of growth and success may not be sustainable. Tensions and contradictions over economic policy have continued to evolve in Japan at each stage of economic development. Some have been resolved, always through compromise, while others remain for the future. More and more, however, in recent years these tensions have been couched in terms of Japan's international relations rather than its domestic ones, obscuring the extent to which policy decisions stratify and divide Japanese from one another.

THE BIRTHRIGHT OF "POSTWAR JAPAN"

The postwar economy built on and broke with earlier Japanese history. Certainly 1945 presented a true rupture with the past for Japan both domestically and internationally. In the first few years after the war Japan suddenly became a fundamentally more egalitarian and democratic nation. Although this trend did not continue and gross inequities remained, as many of the essays in this volume demonstrate, the contrast to presurrender Japan was still stark. In the economic

---

continued its rapid climb to 189.5 in 1990. Land prices rose out of all proportion to other consumer prices in the same period. In 1987 alone, the consumer price index increased by 0.1 percent, but the cost of urban land (in the six largest cities) zoomed by 27 percent. For income and land figures, see Japanese Government Statistics Bureau Management and Coordination Agency, *Japan Statistical Yearbook* (Tokyo: Statistics Bureau Management and Coordination Agency, 1987), vol. 494:790; 1991, vol. 496:532; for comparison to consumer price index, see Japan Economic Institute Report No. 30A, 4 Aug. 1989, 5.

8. Carol Gluck coined this term in a pretechnocratic context; *Japan's Modern Myths: Ideology in the Late Meiji Period* (Princeton: Princeton University Press, 1985).

sphere this altered situation meant new attention to the desires of the general population for greater economic stability, higher wages, a better standard of living, and a larger role for nonelite groups in economic planning. This approach was a new postwar strategy, very different from the presurrender one. Moreover, early postwar Japanese debates on economic policy self-consciously addressed issues of justice, democracy, social responsibility, and political power. Without attention to these pressing matters—and resolution of some of the sharpest tensions in postwar society—rapid economic growth would have been impossible. As was unusually clear in the harsh environment of postsurrender Japan, economic decisions necessarily also shaped political and social choices.

Yet the postwar economy depended on powerful birthrights from both the prewar and wartime eras. Postwar Japan shared significant intellectual continuities with the prewar Japanese economy, as well as drawing on a strong presurrender economic base. Japanese in both presurrender and postwar Japan (and scholars today) debated the same central problems: how did their economic organization affect democracy, capitalism, war, and autonomy? For example, did the development of the economy foster or discourage economic and political democracy? Was a free market ideal for private enterprise, or should businesses cooperate rather than compete? What was the relationship between the Japanese economy and war? How much were Japan's economic and political choices constrained by international forces outside of its control? These questions suggest a continuity of debate, if not of strategies chosen, between pre- and postsurrender Japan. They also highlight the abiding problems of all advanced capitalist economies over the last century.[9]

This continuity of debate is visible in prewar writing about several specific areas of the economy. Throughout the reconstruction years the Japanese regularly drew on explanations of economic problems established before 1940, even when prewar practice was rejected. Experts on labor have attributed the develop-

---

9. Considerable Western literature attributes postwar growth to prewar factors. James Abegglen, *The Japanese Factory: Aspects of Its Social Organization* (Glencoe: Free Press, 1958), emphasizes traditional communal values. Johannes Hirschmeier and Tsunehiko Yui, *The Development of Japanese Business, 1600–1980*, 2d ed. (London: Allen and Unwin, 1981); Richard J. Samuels, *The Business of the Japanese State: Energy Markets in Comparative and Historical Perspective* (Ithaca: Cornell University Press, 1987); and Arthur E. Tiedemann, "Big Business and Politics in Prewar Japan," in *Dilemmas of Growth in Prewar Japan*, ed. James W. Morley (Princeton: Princeton University Press, 1971), 267–316, all stressed the pattern of business-government relations dating back to the Meiji era. W. W. Lockwood, *Economic Development of Japan* (Princeton: Princeton University Press, 1954); Kazushi Ohkawa and Henry Rosovsky, *Japanese Economic Growth: Trend Acceleration in the Twentieth Century* (Stanford: Stanford University Press, 1973); and G. C. Allen, *A Short Economic History of Modern Japan*, rev. ed. (London: Allen and Unwin, 1972), all focus on slow, rational modernization, while Kozo Yamamura, "Japan's Deus ex Machina: Western Technology in the 1920s," *Journal of Japanese Studies* 12, no. 1 (Winter 1986): 65–94, makes a case for the singular importance of technology transfer from abroad. Jon Halliday, *A Political History of Japanese Capitalism* (New York: Pantheon, 1975), and Jon Woronoff, *Inside Japan, Inc.* (Tokyo: Lotus Press, 1982), stress traditional forms of exploitation in the modern era.

ment of postwar Japanese economic institutions to compromise born out of conflict rather than to a straight progression of positive innovations.[10] Thus, the strong emphasis on seniority in the Japanese wage system, for example, represents a historic compromise between managers' desire to reward skill and workers' wish for an objective, rational basis for wage payments.[11] The seniority system was the culmination of a long battle over the criteria for wage payments, reaching back several decades by the 1950s.

Another example highlights a major difference between the United States and Japan. The ongoing debate through the first postwar decade between business leaders and bureaucrats about the proper role of the state in the economy revolved around the central prewar dilemma—maintaining stability. Although Japanese business leaders rejected the heavy-handed state interference in their firms that they had experienced during the war, they also feared a return to the chaotically competitive conditions of the 1920s. Managerial autonomy in a stable environment, rather than a free market, was their goal precisely because of their dual prewar and wartime experiences. Their search for stability meant that the business community cast the state as an ally as much as an ideological adversary; this was perhaps the most important prewar economic legacy to postwar Japan. Their prewar experience led Japanese government and business leaders after the war to resist American laissez-faire principles (though not technocratic ones), while the failures of the wartime economy soured the Japanese on strictly central-ized planning.[12] Presurrender experiences set the boundaries of debate over economic strategies since 1945. That is, postwar policies have operated within the intellectual framework established between 1920 and 1945—one of capitalism within certain policy limits. This diverse legacy, emphasizing long-term indicative planning, cooperation between private firms and government officials, and estab-lishment of common goals, rather than any specific solution, was Japan's heritage from the first forty-five years of the twentieth century.

Some of the most celebrated aspects of the postwar economy developed during World War II itself, which left Japan not only destroyed but also transformed. Total war required that the national economy be restructured to serve military needs. By August 1945 the Japanese economy could no longer provide consumer goods or even feed the Japanese population. Instead, it had been transformed, as best the Japanese knew how, into a huge military supply unit. These changes were structural and could not easily be reversed. They had significant implications for

10. Representative sources in English include Mikio Sumiya, "The Development of Japanese Labour Relations," *Developing Economies* 4 (1966): 499–515; Kazuo Okochi, Bernard Karsh, and Solomon B. Levine, eds., *Workers and Employers in Japan* (Tokyo: University of Tokyo Press; and Princeton: Princeton University Press; 1974); Andrew Gordon, *The Evolution of Labor Relations in Japan: Heavy Industry, 1853–1955*, East Asia Monograph Series (Cambridge: Harvard University Press, 1985).
11. Andrew Gordon, *Evolution of Labor Relations*, 380.
12. See William Miles Fletcher III, *The Japanese Business Community and National Trade Policy, 1920–1942* (Chapel Hill: University of North Carolina Press, 1989).

postwar development, including economic centralization through bureaucratic controls, standardization of production processes, and increased reliance on industrial policy—all changes dictated by the need to mobilize for total war. Often these policies and controls were militarily inadequate, but they did serve to legitimate the process of economic planning. In another important shift, the war encouraged a bias toward those goods used by the military, that is, heavy industrial products rather than textiles. These wartime economic transformations were not in themselves negative; indeed, some aspects clearly hastened later economic growth. For example, the war encouraged new developments in such areas as subcontracting, in-firm production techniques, product standardization, seniority-based wages, and technical training, all of which became key factors in Japan's postwar economic growth.[13] These features are attributable not to Japanese culture, not to a miracle, not to the slow, rational modernization of the prewar economy, but to military mobilization and the reorganization of much of Asia for the purpose of further military conquest.

There are many interesting features of this wartime bequest. One is the extent to which Japan's postwar success was based on its presurrender exploitation of the rest of Asia (and of Koreans brought to Japan). Bruce Cumings argues in this volume and in greater detail elsewhere that Japan's economic relations with East and Southeast Asian countries today reproduce a pattern of Japanese capital control and reliance on other countries for cheap labor that was developed by colonial bureaucrats in the presurrender years.[14] Another interesting and quite separate feature of the importance of military mobilization to postwar economic growth is that it mirrors the changes wrought by the war on the *American* economy. Although Japan's specific forms of subcontracting or the seniority wage system may be unmatched in other nations, the impact of total war mobilization on Japan closely resembles the effect on other industrialized, capitalist countries. Victor and vanquished were similarly transformed by the experience.[15]

Nonetheless, this analogy can be carried too far. Crucially, the Japanese experience also included losing the war. Defeat implied a discrediting of the Japanese military establishment and, more generally, a shift of social and political power within Japan. Surrender marked the failure of a national economic strategy that had relied on imperial expansion, oligopoly, and tight control at home. Domestically the Japanese elite could no longer enforce very low wages on the

13. For a longer discussion of the historiography of World War II and the postwar economy, see Laura E. Hein, "The Dark Valley Illuminated: Recent Trends in Studies of the Postwar Japanese Economy," *Bulletin of Concerned Asian Scholars* 16, no. 2 (1984): 56–58.

14. This postwar relationship between Japan and its former colonies is discussed in Bruce Cumings, "The Origins and Development of the Northeast Asian Political Economy: Industrial Sectors, Product Cycles, and Political Consequences," *International Organization* 38, no. 1 (Winter 1984): 1–40.

15. See Michael S. Sherry, *The Rise of American Air Power: The Creation of Armageddon* (New Haven: Yale University Press, 1987), and Charles Maier, "The Politics of Productivity: Foundations of American International Economic Policy after World War II," in *Between Power and Plenty*, ed. Peter Katzenstein (Madison: University of Wisconsin Press, 1978), 23–49.

urban population nor very high rents and taxes on the rural one.[16] All major industrialists and bureaucrats had based their economic plans on these assumptions. Thus, at micro- and macroeconomic levels, presurrender solutions to economic problems—indeed, much of the shape and direction of the presurrender economy—suddenly had become inappropriate to postwar conditions. These political power shifts triggered by defeat had enormous economic repercussions. The Japanese were forced to undertake a qualitative reordering of the political economy as much as a simple quantitative rebuilding.

The end of the war also meant that the Japanese economy now operated in a fundamentally different international context than did presurrender Japan. Probably the idea of a "Japanese economy" after World War II is misleading. Japan has not had a truly independent domestic economy at any point since 1945. Rather, the Japanese economy has been inextricably twined with the international one, and especially with the economies of the United States and, to a lesser extent, other Asian nations. It seems inappropriate to discuss the domestic aspects alone of such an export-oriented economy without considering Japan's position in the world as a fundamental part of the *definition* of Japan's economic growth.[17]

Without question, the most important international aspect of Japan's postwar economy was its connection to the United States. Although Japan's relationship with the United States is not now—and has never been—that of full ally, American patronage has been crucial to Japanese economic development. After the war this patronage more than compensated for disruptions and hostility to Japanese by other Asians, for the shrinking silk market, and for the loss of the imperial economy. It is hard to imagine what Japan would be like today in the absence of this patronage, particularly in the pivotal years of the early 1950s.

Moreover, the United States was not just the occupying power in Japan; it was also the hegemonic power of the postwar world. The international ethos of power changed after World War II, as did Japan's specific opportunities within the U.S.-dominated system. Although the Japanese consciously rejected some American approaches to organizing their economy, such as pitting firms against government regulators, they were deeply influenced by other economic concepts and practices exported from the United States. These included a faith in capitalist reconstruction to solve not only economic problems but also political ones, the belief that science and technology held the answer to social inequities, and the transformation of economic language from one that recognized the relevance of the economy to political and social issues to one that accommodated only admin-

16. See comparative presurrender and postwar data on household consumption presented by Horioka in this volume.

17. Integration into the world economy was always part of national economic planning, as is clear from the annual Japanese government white papers on the economy, which consistently have incorporated analyses of the interaction of the Japanese and the world economies for forty years. And, as Dower and Cumings stress in this volume, the Japanese economy was tied not only to American economic policy but also to U.S. global military policy.

istrative and technical problems. This constellation of beliefs, often called technocratic, was exported not only to postwar Japan but also to postwar Europe, sometimes by the very same American individuals.[18] Technology was an important intellectual *and* practical element in Japan's integration into the new hegemonic world order.[19]

In fact, Japan prospered within the U.S.-designed postwar world environment. This environment was predicated on the assumption that unfettered trade among noncommunist nations was the appropriate global economic structure. The United States and its brainchildren, the General Agreement on Tariffs and Trade (GATT) and the International Monetary Fund (IMF), maintained free trade and capital movement across national boundaries at a time when Japan was in no position to negotiate such privileges for itself. Moreover, the United States softened the impact of free trade policies for Japan with a number of specific policies, such as a generously high exchange rate for the yen between 1949 and 1971. These measures were designed to offset the fact that, although Japan had been a strong Asian power in the presurrender years (although weak vis-à-vis the West), it was much weaker in the immediate postwar era. Later, after the Japanese economy had grown at unprecedented rates, it became strong in relation not only to other Asian nations but also to the Western powers. This, too, was a new and unexpected development of the postwar era. United States global strategy to internationalize the capitalist economies provided a historic opportunity for Japan, although actual Japanese economic performance was completely unanticipated by the Americans, the Japanese, or anyone else. Nonetheless, Japanese economic growth ultimately rested on that particular international environment and was thus very much part of the global development of advanced capitalism in the twentieth century.[20]

Thus, postwar reconstruction required a new economic vision to accommodate international as well as domestic changes. This was the real challenge facing the Japanese in 1945. Somehow they had to create a social, political, and economic strategy that was appropriate to the new context of the postwar world. As

18. At the more specific level, this technocratic approach included exports of methods of product standardization, public relations strategies, and employee management theories. Volker Berghahn, author of *The Americanisation of West German Industry* (Cambridge and New York: Cambridge University Press, 1986), who commented on an earlier draft of this paper, noted that the economic debates and the phases of development described here for Japan exactly mirror developments in postwar West Germany.

19. See the essays in this volume by Allinson, Gluck, Gordon, and Koschmann and Ivy's comments on the way in which American television images of idealized middle-class life shaped the aspirations of Japanese who were just learning how to use consumer goods as their definition of success.

20. To some extent, economic growth rested on good timing and the sense to recognize an opportunity. The Japanese were able to seize the fleeting historic moment when free trade, an expanding international economy, a large technology gap, extensive American political and financial support, and cheap oil meant that economic growth was closest to the nation's grasp.

early as 1946 many Japanese understood that this vision necessarily had to include economic growth, a higher standard of living for the Japanese people, open international trade, and accommodation of U.S. policy in Asia. Many questions were still undecided, however, such as whether or not to nationalize major industries, what goods to export, where to sell them, how industry should be regulated, or who should make all of these decisions. The Japanese by no means had a clear blueprint for their economic future, nor did all of their efforts succeed. The postwar world presented new problems, and the Japanese disagreed among themselves over how to approach them or respond appropriately. Like economic policymakers everywhere, they were reduced to trial and error.[21]

CENTRAL ECONOMIC PLANKS: GROWTH AND TECHNOLOGY

Simply deciding whether or not to focus on the economy was the first major debate right after the war. In late 1946 the Japanese government under Yoshida Shigeru officially promised to maximize economic growth. The commitment to growth was a specific strategy chosen by the Yoshida cabinet, not an automatic development. Rather, this decision was made in order to reconcile or at least defuse deep political conflicts in postwar Japan. Like other postwar economic policies, it reveals contention rather than a natural consensus. From late 1946, with the adoption of the priority production policy, which concentrated all available resources in the coal and steel industries, the Japanese government strove not just for recovery or reconstruction but for growth and development in the direction of a sophisticated, high-wage economy. As such, it drew from a variety of constituencies, such as labor, business, academics, and bureaucrats, in part explaining how growth became the basis of a general postwar strategy. In other words, the acceptance of economic growth as a *primary goal* was itself a historical development during the postwar era.[22] This focus on economic growth was the first important feature of the economy to develop during the postwar era.

The Japanese had no clearly defined plan for economic development, but by 1949 the commitment to a high-valued-added economy with sophisticated export goods had also been added permanently to national economic policy. Their "rationalization" plan involved upgrading the quality of goods produced through infusions of technology in order to sell abroad. Again, this was a way of dealing with conflicting demands of different groups of Japanese, and economic policy development rested squarely on a historic compromise. This new policy, although

21. This was an enormous challenge for all nations after the war. Yet in some ways defeat freed the Japanese to jettison their old strategies, while victor nations, such as Britain, were far less willing to accept the new global environment. This psychological attitude is probably the kernel of reality within the commonly expressed fantasy that losing World War II was economically better than winning it.

22. See Laura E. Hein, *Fueling Growth: The Energy Revolution and Economic Policy in Postwar Japan,* East Asia Monograph Series (Cambridge: Harvard University Press, 1990).

frequently repressive in practice, contained promise for working-class Japanese. It inherently required the cooperation of industrial workers on a broad level and a literate, trained work force because the 1949 rationalization strategy depended on improving the *quality* of goods produced in order to win the essential export market. Elite Japanese took comfort from the widespread assumption that technology could enhance economic justice while avoiding redistribution of wealth. This dream of a technological fix for social problems was shared by the Americans in Japan and Americans at home.

Although developed as a proposal in 1949, rationalization was not easily accomplished. Conceptually, rationalization went through several stages and much debate. In its first incarnation it was designed to upgrade two basic industries: coal, and iron and steel. The coal half of this plan was a dismal failure, a fact rarely noted since attention has been riveted to the successful half, the iron and steel industry. Rationalization was later implemented in numerous other industries, but often in unanticipated ways. The blossoming of the oil refining industry, for example, surprised most Japanese planners. Its unexpected success created tension between the pro-coal and the pro-petroleum thinkers in Japan, a tension that took over a decade to resolve and has not fully disappeared more than thirty years later. Moreover, the Japanese were not at that time confident that the rationalization strategy was appropriate for their economy, nor was it fully developed. Fifteen years later they could present it as a unified theory, but it was still only one hopeful idea among many in 1950.[23]

The rationalization policy also required extensive American supplies of both capital and technology, involving complex interactions among American and Japanese government agencies and private groups, which all worked to upgrade the quality of Japanese goods. For example, in 1949 and 1950 occupation officials invited numerous American management training experts, industrial statisticians, and other specialists across the Pacific to advise the Japanese. The most famous of these, W. Edwards Deming, introduced the concept of quality control systems to Japan. He did so on his third trip to Japan, this time invited by the Japan Union of Scientists and Engineers, after approval from Supreme Command for Allied Powers (SCAP) officers. His ideas about quality control fit neatly with then-developing Japanese government rationalization policy and were officially encouraged. All parties agreed that Japan had to improve its ability to sell abroad if it was to survive economically and function as an effective economic and

---

23. See Hein, *Fueling Growth*. The fortunes of coal and iron and steel diverged so much that by 1960 they were rarely discussed together, in sharp contrast to almost all discussions of the economy until 1951. Interestingly, the two sectors are once again linked in recent discussions, this time as declining industries. For example, see Yoko Kitazawa, "Setting Up Shop/Shutting Up Shop," *Ampo: Japan-Asia Quarterly Review* 19, no. 1 (1987): 10–29. For works that credit rationalization policy for economic success, see Chalmers Johnson, *MITI and the Japanese Miracle: the Growth of Industrial Policy, 1925–1975* (Stanford: Stanford University Press, 1982); see also Hideichiro Nakamura, "Plotting a New Economic Course," *Japan Echo* 6 (special issue, "Economy in Transition"; 1979): 11–20.

strategic ally in the Pacific. Deming's approach to quality control provided a concrete strategy on which U.S. and Japanese business leaders and officials from both governments could cooperate.[24]

Even in that archetypal success story, iron and steel, the best efforts of Japanese rationalization-policy planners and effective application of Deming's ideas were not sufficient. Recovery was possible in 1950 and 1951 only because of the unusual demand created by the Korean War. Without the specific efforts of the American government to funnel dollar sales to Japan, it is not at all clear that the feeble economy of that era could have achieved industrial rationalization. The vital problem of export markets was not even partially solved until the Korean War, and its outbreak on 21 June 1950 was certainly more important to Japanese economic history than was the political milestone of independence in April 1952.[25]

The Korean War was a key moment for Japan's reintegration into the international economy after the long decades of autarky and war. American military orders were purposely placed with Japanese firms to provide them with precious "overseas" customers. This tactic allowed the Japanese companies to import American technology for more sophisticated future exports, a development encouraged by U.S. foreign policy makers. It was only after those last pieces of the puzzle of economic recovery—access to technology and markets—were in place that the Japanese could implement their own economic rationalization policy. In 1951, the first full year of the Korean War, the Japanese economy recovered to its pre–China War level. This lucrative relationship continued beyond the formal cease-fire in Korea. Between 1951 and 1956 U.S. military purchases in Japan paid for more than a quarter of Japanese imports. This rate of spending tapered off in the late 1950s, but then the Vietnam War jacked up U.S. military procurements again in the mid-1960s.[26]

Once again, the relationship of Japanese economic prosperity to war emerged as an issue. There was a moment just after World War II when this pattern had been criticized not just in Asia but also by the U.S. Pauley Commission on reparations, sent to Japan to redress the historic imbalance created by the Japanese military in the economic realm. The Pauley Commission's report wrestled

24. Mary Walton, *The Deming Management Method* (New York: Dodd, Mead, 1986), 10–15; W. Edwards Deming, *Out of the Crisis* (Cambridge: Center for Advanced Engineering Study, MIT, 1982), 2–6, 486–92.

25. To an unusual degree the periodizations generally used in discussions of postwar Japan are based on economic events, such as trade liberalization in 1960 and the oil shock in 1973–74. Considering that most historic turning points in any country are defined by political events, this economic periodization is eloquent testimony to the primacy of economics in discussions of postwar Japan. One exception is 1955, which Junnosuke Masumi and many others have used as a pivotal moment on the basis of political events. See Junnosuke Masumi, *Postwar Politics in Japan, 1945–1955* (Berkeley: Institute of East Asian Studies, University of California, 1985).

26. Thomas R. H. Havens, *Fire Across the Sea: The Vietnam War and Japan, 1965–1975* (Princeton: Princeton University Press, 1987), 92–97.

with the problem of global economic justice and Japan's historic and future
relationship with the rest of Asia, although it was soon superseded by American
policy calling for Japanese economic recovery.[27] But Asian memories are longer
on this point. Japan's former colonies have prospered since 1945 but have retained their subordinate relationship to Japan, perpetuating Asian tensions. The
complexity of these relationships harks back to the presurrender era and immediate postwar settlement and keeps alive the issue of economic and social justice on
an international scale.

Even after the occupation ended and the Japanese were freer to pursue their own
economic goals, how to achieve them remained a lively subject of debate. For
example, the Japanese debated through the 1950s whether they should emphasize
natural resource development within Japan or export industries. The first position
meant supporting the domestic coal and hydroelectricity industries whereas the
second implied an expansion of petroleum and coal imports. Men like Arisawa
Hiromi, Tsuru Shigeto, and the officials at the Economic Planning Agency within
the Japanese government argued that import minimization projects, like the
Tennessee Valley Authority in the United States, should have first priority. Worried about the expense and instability of overseas fuel supplies, they wanted less
vulnerability to changes in foreign political and economic climates. Undoubtedly,
Japan's prewar experience with autarky influenced their thinking. These men
believed that minimizing imports would protect them from overreliance on exports and that alternative development of hydroelectricity would help develop the
nation's sadly inadequate infrastructure. They also hoped that new technology
would yield previously undiscovered energy resources in Japan. This attention to
the foundations of the future economy—with its implicit acceptance of planning—continued to be an important element of Japanese economic policy.

Nonetheless, the other side of the debate carried the day. Nakayama Ichirō, the
primary spokesman, argued that the nation should focus first on expanding
exports because that was the *quickest* path to self-sufficiency. Nakayama argued
that Japanese economic conditions were very like those of nineteenth-century
Britain and that the limitations of a large population and few natural resources
were best resolved by embracing foreign trade rather than limiting it. Like the
British economy of a century earlier, the Japanese economy would be sustained
by processing imports and selling manufactured goods. Japan had no choice but
to trade in the world economy and thus had to accept vulnerability to events over
which it had no control, Nakayama argued. The debate was eventually resolved
in favor of Nakayama when the Japanese were forced to accept the physical limits

---

27. Edwin Pauley, "Pauley Interim Report to the President," 6 Dec. 1945, *Foreign Relations of the
United States, 1945* 6:1004–9. For a detailed history of reparations policy, see Ōkurashō Zaisei
Shishitsu (Ministry of Finance, Financial History Group), ed., *Sōsetsu: Baishō shūsen shori* (General
introduction: Reparations and termination of war measures), vol. 1 in *Shōwa zaisei shi: Shūsen kara kōwa
made* (Tokyo: Tōyō Keizai Shinpōsha, 1984).

of the domestic resource base. Even so, the Japanese were very reluctant to give up the psychological comfort of energy and food self-sufficiency. The Arisawa-Nakayama debate dragged on for nearly a decade, reflecting this discomfort. This and other debates on the fundamental nature of their economic policy reveal the many areas of continuing uncertainty over economic strategy well after the occupation years.[28]

During the 1950s the rate of GNP growth of the Japanese economy also began to increase. The period of "high-speed growth" began gradually since Japan still required economic recovery. With the population swollen by 25 percent over prewar figures, the Japanese economy had to grow simply to provide the same per capita output. When 11 percent annual growth arrived in the 1960s, it surprised most Japanese.[29]

THE FINAL KEY TO HIGH-SPEED GROWTH: DOMESTIC CONSUMPTION

High-speed growth was achieved only after at least two important changes in official economic strategy in 1959–60. Like earlier policies, both changes developed out of conflict, in response to political challenges to the dominance of growth and technology in Japanese economic strategy. Ironically, although these challenges forced official strategy to include some redistributive functions, the new compromises encouraged even faster growth, cementing Japan's commitment to higher GNP levels.

The first policy change was the transformation of the 1949 rationalization policy into a new concept—industrial structure policy. The recent collapse of the coal and textile industries had shown that rationalization was not equally possible in all sectors. Each had become a declining industry; that is, neither could be made internationally competitive through injections of technology. The success of rationalization policy had depended partly on world trade and technology markets, over which the Japanese had little control. Although the Japanese knew this, they had assumed originally that foreign technology existed to upgrade all industries. Recognition of the problems of declining industries required a new policy. By 1959 the Japanese had also learned to study the effects of rationalization itself, based on their experiences in such successful industries as electric power, oil

28. Nakayama Ichirō, "Nihon keizai no kao," *Hyōron*, Dec. 1949, 1–9. See also Economic Stabilization Board, "Stabilization as We See It," 1 Mar. 1949, 9; Arisawa Hiromi, "Nihon shihon shugi no unmei," *Hyōron*, Feb. 1950, 5–14. For comments on the influential nature of these articles, see the discussion in Tsuruta Toshimasa, *Sengo Nihon no sangyō seisaku* (Tokyo: Nihon Keizai Shinbunsha, 1982), 24–31.

29. For discussion in English, see Yutaka Kosai, *The Era of High-Speed Growth: Notes on the Postwar Japanese Economy* (Tokyo: University of Tokyo Press, 1986); Takafusa Nakamura, *The Postwar Japanese Economy: Its Development and Structure* (Tokyo: University of Tokyo Press, 1981); Tatsurō Uchino, *Japan's Postwar Economy: An Insider's View of Its History and Its Future* (Tokyo: Kodansha International, 1983). For GNP growth statistics, see Nakamura, *Postwar Japanese Economy*, 112.

refining, and machine tools. Rationalization of one industry could either help or hinder rationalization in another, and the Japanese were only beginning to understand how to manipulate these interindustry linkages in 1959. The problems of decline and linkage had to be addressed before the Japanese could transform their policy for economic reconstruction into one suitable for producing growth. Otherwise, some economic sectors would grow while others would falter.

The new "industrial structure" policy emerged out of MITI in late 1959. It used the metaphor of a biological life cycle to define and justify criteria for rationalization.[30] Industries at the beginning and end of their life cycle—like infant and aged humans—require more care than do mature sectors. From 1960 government assistance was increasingly targeted toward those two classes of industries. This was an important refinement of rationalization policy, which had previously emphasized basic industry. Although the two original declining industries were textiles and coal, the mature adult industries of one era are the pensioners of the next, as the oil refiners and petrochemical firms discovered in the 1970s. In fact, the policy implications of this analysis did not fully develop until these and other major industries began to suffer in the 1970s.[31]

Social welfare provisions were added to the policy after labor unions teased out a new economic justification for reincorporating social welfare and redistribution of wealth into discussions of the economy. Technology's inability to resolve all social ailments was laid bare by industrial structure analysis, and union members refused to shoulder the whole burden of their industries' reduced fortunes. The sharpest conflict occurred at the Miike coal mine, where the miners waged a six-month strike over job security and wages. All parties understood that this was not simply a debate between management and labor but intimately concerned government policy toward "sunset" industries. Labor's main accomplishment in that clash was to reintroduce debate on the relationship between economic justice and economic growth.[32] Recognizing that declining industries were part of the industrial life cycle eventually led to the development of a "soft landing" policy for workers in those areas. Those provisions both redeemed and tempered the technocratic approach.

In an equally important refinement, industrial structure, unlike rationalization, is a dynamic concept: appropriate policies for any given industry will change over time. This understanding of the dynamic quality of economies was a key policy contribution to Japan's subsequent high-speed growth. The first true energy policy was associated with this development, when the lengthy troubles of the coal

30. Tsūshō Sangyō Shō, Shōkō Seisaku Shi Kankōkai, ed. (Ministry of International Trade and Industry. Commission on the History of Trade and Industry Policy), *Sangyō gōrika (sengo)*, vol. 10 of *Shōkō seisaku shi* (Tokyo: Shōkō Seisaku Shi Kankōkai, 1972); see Johnson, *MITI and the Japanese Miracle*, 252–54, for a description of the development of this policy.

31. See Merton J. Peck, Richard C. Levin, and Akira Goto, "Picking Losers: Public Policy Toward Declining Industries in Japan," *Journal of Japanese Studies* 13, no. 1 (Winter 1987): 79–123.

32. On this episode, see also the essays by Garon and Mochizuki and Gordon in this volume.

mines led the Japanese to this conceptual breakthrough. Moreover, the effects of rationalization within one industry on development of another has become a standard aspect of study for industrial structure policy, providing an analytical framework for Japanese planners then and now. Industrial structure policy also assumed a permanent need for economic planning and government assistance to all industries at some stage of the life cycle. Like wartime and earlier postwar policies, it incorporated long-term planning into the Japanese economy. In theory as well as practice, economic planning repeatedly has been institutionalized in postwar Japan.

The second major economic initiative of 1960, the Ikeda administration's Income Doubling Plan, also championed redistribution of economic benefits within the context of a celebration of economic growth. The plan was designed explicitly to quiet political protest after mass demonstrations against the government's foreign policy. The Income Doubling Plan reaffirmed government responsibility for social welfare, vocational training, and education and increased spending considerably in these areas. It also sought to eliminate low-wage jobs and regional income disparities.

Yet the plan's greatest innovation was to redefine growth to include Japanese consumers as well as producers. Indeed, the government promised to double average household incomes within a decade, and, gratifyingly, the standard of living did jump dramatically in the next few years. Not only was the new wealth pleasant for consumers, but it also created a mass market that at last made high-speed growth possible.[33] This "consumption boom" was the final key to Japan's economic growth. In larger cultural terms, Ikeda and his allies transformed the image of consumer spending into a positive, officially sanctioned one. After decades (even centuries) of government exhortations to Japanese citizens to be thrifty and avoid ostentation, the invitation to spend meant an enormous shift in the ethics of economic behavior. In a suggestive correlation, mass consumer society, consumer consciousness, and consumer protest developed in Japan only after this point.[34] Most strikingly, although the official policies of 1960 were profoundly political responses to Ikeda's critics, 1960 marked the turning point in acceptance of technocratic thought and acceptance of growth as a goal in postwar Japan. High and continually expanding personal consumption satisfied most people.

Over the next decade the economy grew at an unprecedentedly high rate. Consumer goods proliferated and wages rose because of both the boom condi-

33. For the Income Doubling Plan, see Arisawa Hiromi and Inaba Hidezō, eds., *Keizai, Shiryō sengo 20-nen shi*, vol. 2 (Tokyo: Nihon Hyōronsha, 1966); Keizai Kikakuchō (Economic Planning Agency), *Gendai Nihon keizai no tenkai: Keizai kikakuchō 30-nen shi* (Tokyo: Ōkurashō Insatsukyoku, 1976); Nakamura, *Postwar Japanese Economy*, 83–89; Harry T. Oshima, "Reinterpreting Japan's Postwar Growth," *Economic Development and Cultural Change* 31, no. 1 (Oct. 1982): 1–43.

34. See the essays by Ivy, White, Taira, and Upham in this volume, especially on antipollution and citizens' movements.

tions and a growing labor shortage. Meanwhile, the ties between the Japanese and the international economies became increasingly complex, as various new trade and capital relationships developed. That period ended in 1973–74 with the OPEC oil embargo, which clearly signaled a new relationship between Japan and the rapidly changing world economy. The high-growth period ended then, and to a considerable extent "postwar Japan" ended with it.

The 1946 strategy had worked politically through 1973 to elevate economics as a central political theme of Japanese society. It also mediated political tension by taking elements proposed by various different groups and weaving them together. In so doing, this strategy also created the shape of the postwar settlement in Japan. By the early 1970s, after a decade of high-speed growth, the focus on economic administration and technology itself obscured the highly political dimension of postwar economic decisions—even when those decisions were the product of intense political debate. This economic strategy worked reasonably well as long as high-speed growth persisted. By the early 1970s clearly articulated, self-conscious opposition groups had begun to disappear from the Japanese economic debate.[35] Many of their most acute economic grievances had been redressed as wages, household goods, and social services all improved through the 1960s. Nonetheless, although those opposition voices subsided, statistical inequalities lingered, suggesting that the possibility for profound contention also still remained. That possibility took on new immediacy when economic growth dramatically slowed in the 1970s.

SLOW GROWTH: THE JAPANESE ECONOMY AND ITS PLACE IN THE WORLD AFTER 1973

A number of trends culminated in the early 1970s to bring an end to high-speed growth and, for a short time, stop economic growth altogether. One was that Japan had closed the technology gap that had powered high-speed growth for twenty years. For the first time, heavy manufacturing industries (such as aluminum and fertilizer production) were becoming *less* competitive internationally. Moreover, agriculture had shrunk so much that it could no longer provide a pool of low-productivity workers available for absorption into more high-productivity jobs. Another change was that American economic hegemony no longer rested on a firm foundation. The United States could no longer afford to prop up the international capitalist economy and act as the "free world's policeman." The

35. In this volume, Dower outlines some reasons why it grew harder to focus political debate after several major symbols rallying opposition groups lost their potency. Opposition groups include the worker/artisan culture described by Gordon, the anticapitalist intellectuals described by Koschmann, the critical historical visionaries described by Gluck, the independent producers of popular culture described by Ivy, and the peace activists who appear in Dower (all in this volume). See also Kelly and Taira on the developments of middle-class or middle-stream consciousness as distinct from achievement of middle-class status.

climate that had nurtured high-speed growth within Japan disappeared with those changes.

The Japanese, who had not thought much about the end to high-speed growth, were not intellectually prepared, nor did they have policies ready for this development. They were stunned when the United States acted unilaterally to change its economic relationship with Japan. These U.S. actions, known as "shocks" in Japan, forced the Japanese to reevaluate their place in the world political economy. First, in July 1971 the U.S. government recognized the People's Republic of China without alerting Tokyo to that major policy shift. In the next "shock," on 15 August 1971, the U.S. devalued its currency against the yen by 17 percent, again without consulting its Pacific ally. The Japanese were completely unprepared for the corresponding yen revaluation because they had continued to underestimate the real strength of their economy. As late as 1967–68 many Japanese officials were arguing for currency *devaluation*, even though the yen was almost certainly already too low.[36] Then in late 1972, after a poor harvest, the Americans embargoed exports of soybeans, threatening a traditional staple of the Japanese diet. Nor did the rest of the world look more hospitable. Just as the Japanese were adjusting to these changes, they confronted the biggest disruption of all—the OPEC oil embargo of 1973–74. Japanese leaders had not expected to be included in the embargo and, as with the "shocks," were thoroughly unprepared.

Thus, despite a decade or more of high-speed growth, most Japanese felt increasingly *insecure* about their place in the global economy. This sense of insecurity led to a new debate about Japan's place in the world, as the real consequences of Nakayama's economic strategy—a fundamental interdependence with the international economy—became vividly clear. A sense of vulnerability over vital imports of food and fuel swept the nation. Anxiety was equally strong over the postwar decision to follow the United States' lead, given that America's first priority clearly was America, not Japan. Even ostensibly faraway events, like the war between the Israelis and the Palestinians, had become central to Japan's economic health. Wealth without economic security suddenly seemed pointless.

Although nationalist rhetoric gained new legitimacy, renewed unease about Japan's place in the world economy and the terms of the U.S.-Japan partnership did not prompt Japanese leaders to radically change their foreign policy. They were reluctant to abandon the precedent established after the war by Prime Minister Yoshida Shigeru to accept American protection in return for prosperity, although Japanese trust in American benevolence decreased. Partly because the Japanese were so unprepared for changes in the international political economy, they had not (and still have not) found a viable alternative to life under the U.S. hegemon. Rather, these anxieties worked to obscure for most Japanese the fact

36. Uchino reports that Ministry of Finance officials secretly considered a yen *revaluation* in late 1969, but this move was vetoed for political reasons; *Japan's Postwar Economy*, 155. See also 175, 274–75.

that by 1973 Japan boasted one of the world's largest and most sophisticated economies. Few Japanese examined the effect of their economic actions on the rest of the world. Japan retained a curiously anachronistic insular quality. While alive to every pressure from overseas, most Japanese lacked a strong sense of reciprocal power.

Although Japanese foreign economic policy continued to be based on the fundamental assumptions of capitalist interdependence, open world markets, limited access to countries allied with the Soviet Union, and U.S. hegemony that were established in the early 1950s, anxieties over foreign economic pressures recast internal debates over political and economic problems into international ones. The pressures from overseas—to support one side or the other in the Mideast conflict, to open trade and capital markets, to maintain the embargo on certain goods to the Soviet Union and the Peoples' Republic of China[37]—served to defer domestic political debate just as economic growth had in the previous decades. Ironically, the growing fear of foreign domination occurred at a time when the Japanese economy was weathering realignments caused by the two oil embargoes better than most of the other major capitalist economies.

Fear of foreign economic power is not a new theme in Japan. On the contrary, it was a significant component in the prewar decisions to develop an empire and widen the war in 1941. Nonetheless, it had abated somewhat during the postwar era until the economic disruptions of the early 1970s gave anxieties about foreign domination of Japan renewed legitimacy and urgency. Those events brought home to the Japanese the inescapable relationship between economic diversification and increasingly complex ties to the global economy. At the same time, because those disruptions were interpreted widely as opportunities for foreigners to dominate Japan, they served to contain domestic political debate on economic strategy within a defensive, nationalistic framework.[38] Precisely because that transmutation of international tension into pressure for domestic unity echoed the prewar nationalistic strategies of mobilizing the population, the tendency to subsume divisions within Japan and focus on threats from abroad is disturbing. Such use of global economic friction to fend off domestic criticism can threaten democracy and peace.

The political uses of this conflation of foreign economic pressure and the need for domestic unity were obvious; they served to entrench the status quo, including the

37. The embargo on strategic goods to the USSR was a major international issue as late as 1987, when revelations that Toshiba Corporation had sold sophisticated military machinery to the Soviet Union touched off an international scandal.

38. These themes emerge in Yasuhiro Nakasone, "Toward a Nation of Dynamic Culture and Welfare," *Japan Echo* 10, no. 1 (Spring 1983): 12–18. In this volume, Kelly makes a similar point, as does Taira in his discussion of "Nipponists versus people." Note that Kelly and Ivy, who also argues that economic anxieties in the 1970s turned the Japanese culture introspective, both discuss the celebration of a new diversity within Japan in the 1980s, but both see it as fake, based on target markets and consumption patterns rather than any real distinction among the population. Indeed, these spurious differences serve to mask real divisions.

authority of existing government and business leaders. Yet few Japanese focused on
the conservative implications of this development, partly because their attention
was drawn to the diffuse nature of the boundaries between Japan's domestic
economy and the international one. Since Japan's prosperity depended on the
survival of the existing international order, Japanese inside and outside the government saw domestic and international problems as one and the same. Any changes
to the broad outlines of the postwar international economic order, because they
would profoundly affect the domestic economy, were potentially threatening.
Given the growing perception in other nations of Japan as a great economic success
during the 1970s, this was a surprisingly pessimistic evaluation.

In the case of Japanese officials, perhaps this pessimism developed in part
from the fact that they were losing control over the domestic economy. Not
only did their high-growth-era policies become inappropriate for the 1970s
economy, but the changes wrought by high-speed growth had themselves loos-
ened the government's grip on economic activities of Japanese firms. For example, one of the main methods the Japanese government had used to influence
Japanese businesses throughout the postwar era was strict control of foreign
exchange reserves. This technique was extremely effective while reserves were
scarce, but by the late 1970s Japanese export industries no longer needed to beg
for foreign exchange allocations. The growing level of offshore production by
Japanese firms also removed many activities from Japanese government scrutiny.[39] In these and other ways the inevitable global interdependence accompanying Japan's postwar economic strategy obscured real centers of Japanese
power at home and abroad.

Not only were government officials far more conscious of their loss of control
over the domestic economy than of their increase in influence over the international one, but they also were less aware that they shared this diminution of
control over transnational corporations with Western governments. Because of
this blind spot, nationalist political leaders inappropriately began to compare the
current configuration, in which all transnational corporations are becoming more
powerful and more independent of their home government, with the pre–World
War II system in which Japan—the state—was weak in comparison to Western
nations. The essentially domestic government-business conflict was redefined as
an anti-Japanese attack. The prewar analogy was eerily reflected by the West's
mirror image of Japan as a rogue economy (in which government and large
corporations are entirely undifferentiated) bent on world conquest, just as the
Japanese state was viewed as a rogue military force before 1945.[40]

---

39. T. J. Pempel, "The Unbundling of 'Japan, Inc.': The Changing Dynamics of Japanese Policy
Formation," *Journal of Japanese Studies* 13, no. 2 (Summer 1987): 288; Hugh Patrick and Henry
Rosovsky, "The Japanese Economy in Transition," in *Economic Policy and Development: New Perspectives,*
ed. Toshio Shishido and Ryuzo Sato (Dover, Mass., and London: Auburn House, 1985), 160.

40. For example, see *Japan Echo* 4, no. 3 (1977), especially Naohiro Amaya, "Cyclical Twenty-Five-
Year Periods in History and the Present Age," 16–28, and Toyoaki Ikuta, Nobuyuki Nakahara,

Japan's interdependence with the global economy accelerated in the mid-1980s with a massive yen revaluation and serious labor shortages. Deindustrialization, or the "hollowing" of the Japanese economy, took place at an unanticipated rate because of yen appreciation.[41] That is, Japanese manufacturers began moving to low-wage, pollution-tolerant sites in Asia. Other Japanese firms accelerated plans to build manufacturing plants in North America and Europe to fend off potential protectionist legislation, many rushing to enter Europe before the economic reorganization there in 1992. Meanwhile, the U.S. government, burdened with a swelling federal deficit, demanded greater economic concessions from the Japanese state.

Japan's new involvements coincided with a reemerging debate over Japan's proper stance in the global political economy, confirming the sense of vulnerability for some Japanese and dispelling it for others. The debate in Japan over this economic configuration centered on whether to evaluate it as a sign of Japanese strength or of Japanese weakness.[42] Some Japanese responded by worrying that the high value of the yen relative to other world currencies was as destabilizing as was the earlier era of economic weakness. Other, more self-confident individuals comforted themselves with the thought that U.S. economic decline was due to American laziness and ethnic diversity rather than any structural economic factors—factors shared by all capitalist economies. Meanwhile, economic muscle was increasingly attributed to the inherent superiority of Japanese culture and tradition. The focus shifted from Japanese perceptions of themselves as weak in the world to a self-definition of themselves as righteously strong but thwarted by malevolent outsiders. Japanese "subordinate independence" vis-à-vis the United States came under growing criticism. The runaway popularity in 1989 of *"No" to ieru Nihon*, which argued that Japan should say no to the United States, was graphic evidence that criticizing U.S. hegemony struck a responsive chord among millions of Japanese. Such criticism had emerged earlier from progressive critics of American cold-war and anticommunist policy, but it was now taken up by conservative elites, who were angered more by continued U.S. arrogance in the

Taichi Sakaiya, and Ken'ichi Kōyama, "The Day Japan Dies for Want of Oil," 78–85. For a more recent U.S. example of the many political statements on this theme, see the cartoon by Mike Luckovich of the *Atlanta Constitution*, depicting two identical newspapers, one dated 7 December 1941 and the other 7 December 1989; the two headlines are "Japan Bombs Pearl Harbor" and "Japan Buys Pearl Harbor." (This cartoon appeared in the *Chicago Tribune*, 13 Nov. 1989.)

41. The yen was pegged at 360 to one U.S. dollar from 1949 to 1971. It then rose gradually to about 238 to the dollar in 1984 and 1985. Late in 1985 the yen's value began to shoot up, averaging only 128 to the dollar in 1988. In 1989 it dropped slightly, for an annual average of 138 yen to the dollar, but rose again in late 1990 to 1985 levels. The 1991 average was 135 yen per dollar. See Japan Economic Institute, *JEI Report* no. 2B (12 Jan. 1990), 2, and no. 2B (17 Jan. 1992), 11.

42. Recent work by Western analysts also has concentrated specifically on this shift of the international economic environment, either gloomily suggesting that Japan will have difficulty responding to it or, in a more sanguine analysis, emphasizing Japan's capacity to adapt. For gloomy analyses, see the special issue of *Journal of Japanese Studies* 13, no. 2 (Summer 1987), especially Kozo Yamamura, "Shedding the Shackles of Success: Saving Less for Japan's Future," 429–56. In contrast, see Ronald Dore, *Flexible Rigidities* (Stanford: Stanford University Press, 1986), for a more hopeful analysis.

face of economic decline.[43] Nonetheless, Japanese leaders were still not ready to articulate a new bilateral relationship or a significantly new role in international affairs despite (or perhaps because of) the enormous shift in the international context caused by the collapse of the Soviet bloc and then the USSR itself between 1989 and 1992.

UNRESOLVED PROBLEMS

Despite this new level of confidence as Japan began the 1990s, several unsolved problems remained that had developed directly out of the economic strategy of the previous forty-five years: to achieve prosperity and political stability through economic growth, technology, and consumption. These problems included structural demands for ever-increasing cycles of investment, ecological destruction, and growing political estrangement between Japan and much of the rest of the world.

Japan was still locked into a dizzying cycle of new product development in the early 1990s. The Japanese high-growth system was based on the recognition that economic development is dynamic: new industries and processes must be introduced continuously to maintain growth within an international system. This was one of the great insights of the industrial structure policy of 1959. The strategy of constantly developing new products (including meaninglessly differentiated ones) was crucial to Japan's becoming an economic power and certainly contributed to the growing integration of the global economy. Yet that dynamic contained its own dangers. The rate at which industries matured and declined in Japan accelerated steadily—perhaps beyond the point where it should. This speed-up of the industrial life cycle has harmed communities, especially ones dependent on a single industry. Whole regions of Japan were depopulated as rapid shifts in industrial production rendered the plants and equipment there useless. Meanwhile, in the big cities negative effects included overbuilding, planned obsolescence, congestion, and the growing stress of urban life.[44] Too-rapid economic change stood in the way of full employment as worker training became obsolete at an increasingly rapid rate. The aging of the population made it harder to shift workers to new skills quickly, creating an atmosphere of human disposability with painful implications for both economic efficiency and personal satisfaction.[45]

43. The complaint is as much about America's loss of hegemony (without development of any new modesty) as about its perpetration; see *"No" to ieru Nihon,* by Morita Akio, chair of Sony Corporation, and Ishihara Shintarō, a prominent Diet member (Tokyo: Kōbunsha, 1989). The best-seller went through ten printings in 1989 alone.

44. Note Ivy's argument (in this volume) that the increased speed of consumption of cultural images serves to blur the line between reality and images, reducing the space available to recreate nonhegemonic images.

45. Yutaka Kōsai, "The Reasons That Unemployment Must Rise," *Japan Quarterly* 34, no. 3 (July–Sept. 1987): 234–40.

More generally, the implicit—and unsustainable—postwar assumption that rapid economic growth is normal and infinitely maintainable led to long-term neglect of the environment and of the quality of life. The continued emphasis on growth threatened the future standard of living in Japan and abroad. Even the newer, "knowledge-intensive" industries contributed to environmental degradation. The Japanese were very slow to appreciate the ecological effects of their industries on land, sea, and air. The government never threw its full weight behind pollution control or compensation to those poisoned by industrial waste. As late as 1990 the central government refused to negotiate compensation for some sufferers of Minamata disease.[46] Sadly, the natural beauty of Japan itself is nearly obliterated, while Japanese fishing, turtling, lumbering, and ivory-purchasing practices ravage the oceans, forests, and savannas of the world.[47]

The assumption that growth can last forever has also allowed the Japanese to indulge in a search for overseas scapegoats rather than accept the limits of the biosphere. For example, the common Japanese insistence that criticism of whaling is based on Western cultural taboos against eating whale rather than concern about decimation of the global whale population neatly illustrates the deflection of both domestic and international criticism of the official policy of maximizing economic growth. Prophecies of extinction—and thus the unavailability of whale meat to future generations of Japanese—have been transformed into racial criticism of Japanese custom. This mutation silences ecologically minded Japanese, particularly since foreign criticism often *does* include an element of disgust, reinforcing Japanese perceptions of themselves as buffeted by the outside world.

High-speed growth was possible because of the confluence of a specific set of international and domestic opportunities. But by the early 1990s the Japanese economy had grown so much that its sheer size alone profoundly affected the world economy—and made further high-speed growth much more difficult to attain. Attention to this fact, however, would demand a major debate about growth policy, something the Japanese have been unwilling to do. Rather, world events are still perceived as things that happen *to* Japan, all of which potentially threaten domestic prosperity. By ignoring Japan's growing role in shaping the global political economy, Japanese leaders deflected domestic dissent but also left themselves intellectually unprepared for new developments. Their conceptual myopia revealed itself in both general attitudes and responses to specific events. Japanese assumptions that their economic power derived from racial purity or

46. This decision occurred within the context of a legal suit for compensation by some people who wanted legal recognition as Minamata disease victims. Four separate courts recommended that the defendants in the long-running case accept mediation because the plaintiffs were beginning to die of old age. Two of the defendants, the prefectural government and the polluting corporation, agreed, but the central government preferred to pursue its case in court, adding several years before the matter could be resolved. Whereas the government had earlier tried to avoid the legal system, it was now to its advantage to embrace it. *Japan Times*, 19 Oct. and 30 Oct. 1990.

47. "The World's Eco-Outlaw? Critics Take Aim at Japan," *Newsweek*, 1 May 1989; "Environment: Putting the Heat on Japan," *Time*, 10 July 1989.

cultural superiority suggests an absence of intellectual tools to explain inevitable future problems (such as growing competition from the Republic of Korea). In a more concrete example, when Iraq invaded Kuwait in 1990, the Japanese government seemed surprised that its citizens were treated as political pawns along with Western nationals. Despite the long alliance with the United States and Japan's eager participation in the international petroleum market, few Japanese understood that their economic power largely determined the image Japan presented to the Arab world. This is disturbing: as long as the Japanese ignore the consequences of their own economic growth, their ability to meet future challenges will diminish.

CHAPTER FIVE

The Structure and Transformation of Conservative Rule

Gary D. Allinson

"Everyone is equal, but some are more equal than others." There may be a tinge of resentment hidden in this common observation about human equality, but it does reveal a general truth about conceptions of power. We all recognize that some people are more influential than others. In representative democracies elected officials in national governments are often the most powerful. They frequently join appointed bureaucrats in central ministries and the leaders of important interest groups to form one variant of what C. Wright Mills made famous as "the power elite."[1]

Japan's power elite in the postwar era provoked varying descriptions from a range of observers. Many asserted the importance of a ruling triad that included the bureaucracy, the conservative Liberal Democratic Party (LDP), and the big-business community.[2] Another group of scholars and pundits seemed intent on demonstrating an almost conspiratorial concentration of power. They attributed virtually untrammeled influence to bureaucrats, especially those in the economic ministries dealing with finance and international trade and industry.[3] Out of an interpretive dialectic with these two views emerged a third. Its adherents advocated a pluralist perspective in which elites either shared power with, or responded to the pressures of, organized societal interests.[4]

1. C. Wright Mills, *The Power Elite* (New York: Oxford University Press, 1956).

2. This view is articulated in Chitoshi Yanaga, *Big Business in Japanese Politics* (New Haven: Yale University Press, 1968), and summarized in T. J. Pempel, ed., *Policymaking in Contemporary Japan* (Ithaca: Cornell University Press, 1976).

3. The most important scholarly exposition of this perspective appears in Chalmers Johnson, *MITI and the Japanese Miracle* (Stanford: Stanford University Press, 1982). A number of journalists and former officials, such as James Fallows, Clyde Prestowitz, and Karel von Wolferen, began to propagate an almost paranoid version of this point of view in the late 1980s.

4. A brief analysis of some of the leading Japanese versions of these perspectives appears in Gary D. Allinson, "Politics in Contemporary Japan: Pluralist Scholarship in the Conservative Era—A Review Article," *Journal of Asian Studies* 48, no. 2 (May 1989): 324–32.

The ruling triad, bureaucracy-dominant, and pluralist models all help to explain some salient aspects of postwar politics. However, none of these models adequately characterizes the polity for the full forty-five years after 1945, and all of them fail to acknowledge the changes that occurred during a period that stretched for almost half a century. The ruling triad model, for example, approximates the power structure during one phase of the postwar era, but it does not adequately depict the early postwar period or the more complex events of the 1980s. Similarly, the bureaucracy-dominant model may identify the essence of one era, but it is too one-dimensional to capture the nuances of shifting power relations in other eras. Finally, the pluralist model is better suited to explaining events after the 1960s than before. We thus require fresh perspectives in order to achieve an adequate historical understanding of Japan's postwar elites.

This chapter illustrates how changing policy processes and outcomes were associated with structural transformations in the Japanese political elite between 1945 and 1990. My approach is based on two fundamental assumptions about elites and their behavior. One assumption is that elites are products of society and social institutions. Their lives are shaped by family conditions, educational institutions, economic circumstances, and occupational careers. The second assumption is that elites in parliamentary regimes exercise power under social constraints. The conduct of elites and their goals are shaped in some part by their own ties to society. In the case of elected politicians, for example, constituents and campaign contributors place restraints on their behavior. Even in the case of appointed bureaucrats, regulatory or policy clienteles impose limits on wholly arbitrary action. Power elites are thus not merely individuals animated by psychological attributes and political dispositions struggling among themselves for power and place. They are also social products whose political actions derive symbiotically from the context of the society in which they govern.

By adopting a perspective that links elite structures with policy processes, this chapter highlights how transformations among elites facilitated differing political outcomes. To trace the significance of structural transformations, I examine changing recruitment patterns among two groups. One consists of all postwar prime ministers and the ministers of finance, foreign affairs, and international trade and industry.[5] The other includes the chairs and vice chairs of Japan's major business association, Keidanren (Federation of Economic Organizations).[6] Recruitment patterns in the national bureaucracy are not detailed here because they have been well examined in other studies.[7]

---

5. These three ministerial portfolios are generally regarded as the most influential in postwar cabinets.

6. For a fuller discussion, see Gary D. Allinson, "Japan's Keidanren and Its New Leadership," *Pacific Affairs* 60, no. 3 (Fall 1987): 385–407.

7. See Akira Kubota, *Higher Civil Servants in Postwar Japan* (Princeton: Princeton University Press, 1969), and B. C. Koh, *Japan's Administrative Elite* (Berkeley and Los Angeles: University of California Press, 1989). Chalmers Johnson provides an important sketch of ancillary bureaucratic career patterns

In the forty-five years after 1945, changing recruitment patterns gave rise to three discernible phases of elite authority. Diffuse elites governed during the early postwar era. Their authority was identified by perduring dissension and overshadowed by the powers of Allied occupiers. Bureaucractic elites, who dominated key leadership groups for nearly two decades after the mid-1950s, pursued a politics of induced compliance. By the early 1970s, however, a third group of specialist elites emerged to replace the once-dominant bureaucrats. They were forced by circumstance to engage in a politics of competitive negotiation. These three phases of elite authority are discussed following a brief sketch of elites in Japan before 1945.

JAPAN'S PREWAR ELITES

The Meiji Restoration of 1868 was Japan's modern political revolution. The men who carried out the Restoration and exercised power in the new central government for nearly four decades thereafter were in most cases samurai from four domains in western Japan.[8] Although the rulers of the Meiji state were reformers who changed many old institutions and created even more new ones, they were in essence a hereditary elite. Their ancestors from Japan's military caste had governed the domains of the country for the preceding several centuries, and they had inherited this mantle of political authority. They relied on custom, force, and popular acquiescence to underpin their position. Their rule thus echoed the authoritarian traditions of the past while it exemplified the centralized authority of the modern nation-state, symbolized by the powers of the national bureaucracy through which they governed.

The hereditary elites who governed during the Meiji era (1868–1912) carried out a series of reforms that culminated in a new type of elite authority by the 1910s. The seedbed for the changes lay in such new institutions as modern universities, military academies, and an examination-based recruitment system for national civil servants. These institutions fostered the growth of several functionally specialized groups. The most prestigious imperial universities in Tokyo and Kyoto produced legal experts to compete for positions in a national bureaucracy. After the 1890s it recruited new members on the basis of merit rather than political affiliation.[9] Public universities and private colleges also produced lawyers,

in *Japan's Public Policy Companies* (Washington, D.C.: American Enterprise Institute, 1978).

8. Of the eighteen cabinets formed between 1885 and 1918, seventeen were led by men from Satsuma, Chōshū, Tosa, or Hizen, while 71 percent of the cabinet ministers who served during that era hailed from the three modern prefectures in which those four domains had been located. Nobuo Tomita, Hans Baerwald, and Akira Nakamura, "Prerequisites to Ministerial Careers in Japan, 1885–1980," *International Political Science Review* 2, no. 2 (1981): 237–39.

9. Robert Spaulding examines these developments in *Imperial Japan's Higher Civil Service Examinations* (Princeton: Princeton University Press, 1967).

engineers, journalists, educators, and businessmen who pursued lengthy careers in the private sector before entering public life. And the military academies trained an elite officer corps whose members frequently assumed political office before 1945.

When the oldest among the hereditary elites began to leave their positions in the 1910s, men who were products of these new institutions rose gradually to replace them. As powerholders during a new phase of elite authority, we can identify them as diffuse elites, in two senses. They were diffuse, first, with respect to their backgrounds. The hereditary elites had rather homogeneous traits by virtue of their former samurai status, but the diffuse elites rose from many occupational callings. They were nearly always well-educated graduates of the new public universities, private colleges, or military academies. Some were legal experts who had pursued careers in the national bureaucracy, others were wealthy businessmen, and still others were journalists, educators, or career military officers. A few were lifelong politicians.

These men were diffuse also with respect to the positions they occupied. In the fifty years before 1945 Japan operated under what we might think of as a multivocal constitutional order.[10] The opportunities for the exercise of power were themselves diffused among a variety of formal and informal institutions. Formal institutions included an elective national parliament, special advisory bodies such as the Privy Council, ministries of the central government, a relatively autonomous military establishment, and the imperial household. Informal institutions included the *genrō*, or oligarchs, and the *jūshin*, or senior statesmen.[11] Barriers to entering these institutions were quite permeable in most cases. Thus, a career military officer might join a political party and become the head of a civilian ministry. Or a successful businessman might be appointed to head the Ministry of Commerce and Industry (MCI), as often happened in the 1930s. Or, a far more likely occurrence, a talented bureaucrat might retire, win a Diet seat, become head of his former ministry, and end his career as a member of the Privy Council, or even as prime minister. The diffuse elites were men of varied talents and diverse careers who operated in a political system with multiple institutional voices.

During the phase of diffuse elites before 1945, power itself was more broadly dispersed than ever before. The dispersion of power among formal and informal institutions of state created formidable obstacles to political consensus to begin with. But dissension was further exacerbated by a profusion of nongovernmental groups that rose to play political roles in a society undergoing rapid, often disruptive change. In the midst of this volatile socioeconomic environment, elites had great difficulties in building durable bases of power and constructing enduring political alliances. Shifts of power among elites were frequent, sudden, and

10. One intriguing analysis of this system appears in Rob Steven, "Hybrid Constitutionalism in Prewar Japan," *Journal of Japanese Studies* 13, no. 1 (Winter 1987): 99–133.

11. Roger F. Hackett, "Political Modernization and the Meiji *Genro*," in Robert E. Ward, ed., *Political Development in Modern Japan* (Princeton: Princeton University Press, 1968), 65–97.

often significant in the quarter-century before 1945. It appeared momentarily during the 1920s that politicians leading party cabinets and working through an elective parliament might gain an upper hand.[12] But in the 1930s a coalition of bureaucrats and militarists, operating with the acquiescence of other elite groups, came to dominate the Japanese polity.[13] Their reckless policies and ill-advised aggression brought Japan to its knees in 1945, and their follies discredited many of Japan's prewar elites.

Elite recruitment practices embody their own limitations. Under the conditions of crisis that Japan faced in 1945, with much of its prewar elite discredited, there was only a restricted pool of elites available for national leadership and of course no hope of replenishing it from outside. There were other limitations as well. Prewar Japan had developed a preference for political elites who were well educated and successful in their occupational callings. They did not have to come from high-status families, although it must be acknowledged that members of the aristocracy enjoyed advantages if they wanted to exploit them. More generally, as long as men demonstrated their abilities during their adult careers, their successes often brought them wealth, enhanced their status, and heightened their prospects for recruitment and promotion into powerful positions. During the prewar era these elite recruitment biases worked more in favor of bureaucrats and military officers than other groups, although in comparison with the 1880s, business leaders and politicians also witnessed a rise in status before 1945.[14] But it was men of bureaucratic achievement who remained the elite favorites.[15] This accretion of bias, when coupled with occupation policies after the war, would have a powerful effect in shaping the transformation of elites during the postwar era.

JAPAN'S POSTWAR ELITES

The years between 1945 and 1990 coincided with three distinct phases of elite power. The initial phase represented a pattern of elite authority extending out of the prewar era. Diffuse elites first assumed power in the 1910s, and the salience of their pattern of authority continued into the 1950s. Bureaucratic elites provided leadership during a succeeding phase that began in the 1950s and lasted until the early 1970s. The third phase ensued when specialist elites emerged. Their appearance coincided quite closely with the epochal economic changes of 1973–74, and their authority seemed likely to extend well beyond 1990.

12. Peter Duus, *Party Rivalry and Political Change in Taisho Japan* (Cambridge: Harvard University Press, 1968).

13. Robert Spaulding, "The Bureaucracy as a Political Force, 1920–1945," in James W. Morley, ed., *Dilemmas of Growth in Prewar Japan* (Princeton: Princeton University Press, 1971), 33–80.

14. Between 1918 and 1945, 20 of 21 prime ministers and 129 of 188 cabinet ministers were former bureaucrats or military officers. Nakamura Akira and Takeshita Yuzuru, *Nihon no seisaku katei* (Tokyo: Azusa Shuppankai, 1984), 28.

15. Former bureaucrats comprised 45 percent of the cabinet ministers between 1918 and 1945; military officers comprised the next largest group at 24 percent. Tomita, "Prerequisites," 240.

Diffuse Elites

The diffuse elites who held power in Japan during the first postwar decade often operated in an environment of crisis politics, in three respects. First, the end of the war produced a crisis of sovereignty posed by the Allied occupation. A national legislature and a largely unreformed bureaucracy continued to function during the occupation, but their powers were often overshadowed by those of the Allied authorities, especially the Americans who dominated the Supreme Command for Allied Powers (SCAP). Second, war's end produced a crisis of reconstruction, necessitating quick action to restore social and economic security to the nation. Despite quixotic policies imposed by the occupiers, the Japanese managed by dint of hard work and some luck to restore the economy to its prewar peak by the mid-1950s. Third, defeat, occupation, and especially the purge created a crisis of political integration, seriously complicating problems of leadership recruitment and stability.

A crisis of integration was virtually inevitable owing to a defeat that discredited many prewar elites. Those most closely associated with the wartime effort—military leaders, aristocrats, some bureaucrats, and avid prowar politicians—would have faced opposition to continued leadership under the best of circumstances. The presence of a foreign occupying power assured their demise. An ambitious purge carried out after 1946 removed military officers as claimants to government office, and the postwar constitution stripped the military of its autonomous powers by subordinating it to civilian control. Politicians who had sat in the wartime Diet were purged from national life for as long as seven years. A few high-ranking bureaucrats directly implicated in the war effort were purged, but the large majority of national bureaucrats were allowed to pursue their calling. And aristocrats were dealt a severe blow when the aristocracy itself was eliminated and the assets of aristocratic families were seized. The purge thus cut a wide swath through surviving elites, leaving the nation to draw its early postwar leadership from the ranks of young and inexperienced politicians, former bureaucrats, or businessmen. In practice most elite positions fell to elderly prewar figures who had appeared to oppose the war and who could present themselves as men of moderate conservative stripe.

Among the six men who held the post of prime minister between 1945 and 1957, three were diplomats and three came from significantly different backgrounds. Shidehara Kijūrō, Yoshida Shigeru, and Ashida Hitoshi were all former career officials of the Ministry of Foreign Affairs. All of them had held distinguished official posts before the war. Yoshida, for example, had been Japan's ambassador to the Court of St. James, and Shidehara had served as minister of foreign affairs. The other three included an attorney and political activist (Katayama Tetsu), a career politician (Hatoyama Ichirō), and a former economic journalist (Ishibashi Tanzan). Katayama was the odd man out among all postwar prime ministers; a Socialist, he led the only Socialist coalition government before 1990. Like most influential politicians of his age, the career politician Hatoyama had been purged and could assume office only after he won his freedom in the early 1950s. Ishibashi was the editor of a respected economic publication whose English version, the *Oriental Economist,* was well known outside Japan. Elective politics was a second career for him, undertaken after the war when he was already in his sixties.

The varied nature of early postwar governmental leadership is more emphatically demonstrated by looking at the ministers at the Ministry of International Trade and Industry (MITI) and the Ministry of Finance (MOF) between 1945 and 1957. At both of these ministries it appears that there was either a constant tussle between politicians and former bureaucrats over who should hold office, or else there was a genuine difficulty in finding appointees with the right credentials, traits, and abilities. There was a strong tendency for elected politicians with prior experience in the business world to hold ministerial posts frequently and for lengthy tenures. In some cases businessmen without political experience were appointed. In other cases former bureaucrats were tapped to head the ministries they had previously served. The brief Socialist interregnum in 1947–48 certainly skewed the patterns in these two ministries. But even in its absence, governments were forced to draw ministerial leadership from a broad array of backgrounds in the first postwar decade, and the prewar pattern of diffuse elites therefore persisted.[16]

The Ministry of Foreign Affairs (MFA) represents an exception to this claim, however. For the first dozen years after Japan's defeat the government always called on former bureaucrats to head the foreign ministry. Yoshida Shigeru himself served nearly half of this period, holding the foreign ministry portfolio concurrently during his long tenure in the prime ministership. Among the other foreign ministers three were former old boys of the ministry itself, and one was an interloper from the prewar MCI. This pattern of appointment is undoubtedly explained by the need to coordinate Japanese foreign policy with the views of SCAP officials and American authorities, a task that former diplomats were skilled at conducting.

In the first postwar decade Japan's major business association, Keidanren, also drew its leaders from men of varied background. The diffuse character of its elite was personified by the chair during this period, Ishikawa Ichirō. The son of a prewar businessman, Ishikawa spent several years on the faculty of Tokyo Imperial University before entering his father's firm as a manager in the 1910s. He eventually rose to lead one of the largest chemical enterprises in the prewar era, Nissan Kagaku. In 1942 he left to become chair of his industry's control association (*tōseikai*), holding that quasi-governmental position until the end of the war.

---

16. Career backgrounds became even more diffuse after 1945. Whereas 45 percent of the cabinet ministers between 1918 and 1945 were former bureaucrats, only 30 percent of the ministers between 1945 and 1955 had backgrounds in government service. During this period, business leaders, journalists, and legislative aides, as well as some union officials, held cabinet posts more often than ever before or after. Tomita, "Prerequisites," 243.

For reasons not entirely clear, he escaped the purge, and when Keidanren was established in 1946 to replace its prewar predecessor, he became its first leader. He had been a respected but relatively minor figure before the war, and the vacuum of leadership created by the purge of business leaders certainly facilitated his rise to eminence after the war.[17]

The five men who served as vice chairmen during Ishikawa's tenure offer further testimony to the diffuse character of the early postwar elite even in the nation's principal business association. Three of them were lifelong private business leaders: Satō Kiichirō, the head of the Mitsui Bank, Sugi Michisuke, a trade company executive from the Osaka region, and Hori Bunpei, a longtime executive in the textile industry. The other two were former MCI bureaucrats, Watanabe Gisuke and Uemura Kōgorō. They held the vice chairmanship, however, by virtue of their postwar assignments: Watanabe was chair of Yawata Steel, and Uemura was, after 1952, executive director of Keidanren. Despite its role as a private-sector interest association, Keidanren thus possessed a visible bureaucratic component that reflected the continuation of a prewar bias for elites whose careers originated in the national bureaucracy.

These patterns of elite recruitment bespeak the problems of political integration noted above. The initially unknown, and eventually rather arbitrary, nature of the purge seriously complicated the ability of corporate groups, business associations, political parties, and the government itself to recruit and retain capable leaders. Once selected, individuals often held office for short tenures, and many of them did not possess the networks of personal relationship among government officials, party leaders, and business leaders that were to serve Japanese elites so well during the next phase of leadership. Add to these problems the difficulties of reconstruction and the shifting course of SCAP policy, and it is easy to understand the crisis atmosphere of early postwar politics. The obligatory recruitment of diffuse elites threw together individuals with incompatible life experiences and political outlooks and complicated the attainment of a workable political environment. Dissension was common because elite stability was lacking.

Dissension did not paralyze the policy-making machinery, nor did it prevent passage of laws and the enactment of policies that fundamentally altered Japanese life. But it was Allied occupiers acting through SCAP, not domestic political actors, who provided the impetus for most policy initiatives during the first five postwar years.[18] This was especially true of the major reforms in such areas as agriculture, education, labor, business concentration, and civil and constitutional law. These reforms could not have been implemented without the support of sympathetic associates in the Japanese bureaucracy. But this fact does not refute

17. Keizai Dantai Rengōkai, ed., *Ishikawa Ichirō tsuisoroku* (Tokyo: Kajima Kenkyūjo Shuppankai, 1971).

18. Two principal sources on the occupation are Kawai Kazuo, *Japan's American Interlude* (Chicago: University of Chicago Press, 1960), and Robert Ward and Yoshikazu Sakamoto, eds., *Democratizing Japan* (Honolulu: University of Hawaii Press, 1987).

the claim that SCAP set the agenda for, and determined the direction of, most policies between 1946 and the early 1950s.[19] However, as the major reforms came to fruition, enthusiasm within SCAP waned and many ardent reformers left Japan to resume their interrupted careers elsewhere.[20] These changes produced a vacuum that a more stable and assertive Japanese government began to fill.

The brief interregnum between the end of SCAP authority and the appearance of bureaucratic elites was marked by continuing dissension. Partisan conflict—among and within conservative parties and between conservative parties and their Socialist and Communist opposition—fostered high rates of elite turnover. Prime ministers and cabinet ministers held office for brief tenures, complicating the ability of elected officials to impose their stamp on the political process. Under such circumstances the bureaucracy enjoyed an extended moment of relative dominance. It had already been strengthened by SCAP's designation as the agent of Allied rule, and it was relatively stronger than the political parties because of its continuity in organization and personnel. Moreover, the bureaucracy benefited from the passage of many laws between 1952 and 1957 that diluted democratic reforms (in such areas as educational governance, local finance, and police administration) because such laws restored bureaucratic authority lost during the early years of the occupation. The powers that bureaucrats exercised from 1945 to 1957, owing in part to the unusual circumstances of the occupation, made them temporarily predominant figures in the domestic polity. Such powers also foreshadowed an era in Japanese history when bureaucrats—more specifically, former bureaucrats—capitalized on their momentary good fortune to assume positions of influence in many walks of life.

Bureaucratic Elites

During the mid-1950s former bureaucrats came overwhelmingly to dominate key elite positions in both the LDP and Keidanren. Bureaucrats were dominant during this era for many reasons. They were ambitious, talented, and well-connected individuals who enjoyed the esteem of their peers and elicited a possibly begrudging deference from the populace. But the unusual concentration of bureaucrats was probably attributable, as much as anything, to the purge in effect between 1946 and 1952. The purge intentionally drove older businessmen from the scene and opened new opportunities for younger businessmen and former bureaucrats. But it also, perhaps unintentionally, weakened political parties by

19. SCAP had influence over a host of lesser policies, too. For example, Hein (in this volume) notes how SCAP was able to override strong Japanese preferences for a centralized electrial industry and to force the creation of nine regional firms instead, while Garon and Mochizuki (also in this volume) illustrate how the politically important Small and Medium Enterprise Agency in MITI was created at SCAP initiative in the face of bureaucratic preferences for large enterprises.

20. A fuller discussion of the way in which declining enthusiasm and departing reformers affected SCAP endeavors appears in Gary D. Allinson, "Japan's Second Bureaucracy: Civil Service Reforms and the Allied Occupation," in Thomas W. Burkman, ed., *The Occupation of Japan: Educational and Social Reform* (Norfolk, Va.: MacArthur Memorial, 1982): 471–97.

stunting their ability to groom leaders. So many purged politicians were either too old or too ill suited to staging a comeback after 1952 that the parties in effect lost a cohort of potential elites. One should consider this problem in tandem with the weak position of politicians during the last dozen years of the prewar era as well. Overshadowed by other elites, career politicians were not taken altogether seriously as national leaders by 1945. Moreover, during the war they did not obtain the kind of ministerial experience that would have made them credible claimants to power after 1945 because wartime cabinets favored military officers, bureaucrats, aristocrats, and businessmen.

Therefore, in order to recruit men of intelligence, experience, and vision to positions of political and economic leadership, the nation was virtually obliged to turn to former bureaucrats. Young businessmen were an option, but they faced such economic challenges and enjoyed such career opportunities that politics must have seemed a risky, unappealing alternative. There was ample precedent for giving the nod to former bureaucrats, and they were not shy about accepting the offers. During the 1950s, therefore, each time a bureaucrat accepted a ministerial post, it meant one less opportunity for a career politician of that age or younger to gain the experience needed to lay claim to the prime ministership. Bureaucratic dominance of elite positions was thus not just a testimony to the talents and ambitions of the men who held power. It was also the unintended but inevitable consequence of attrition to recruitment among party politicians that began during the war and was exacerbated by the postwar purge. From a longer historical perspective, bureaucratic elites personified the residual effect of the bias toward bureaucrats that first appeared clearly with the hereditary elites of the Meiji era.

Between 1957 and 1972 all three men who served as prime minister were former high-ranking bureaucrats. They were Kishi Nobusuke (1957–60), Ikeda Hayato (1960–64), and Satō Eisaku (1964–72). Coincidentally, two of them, Kishi and Satō, were also brothers. They were descendants of a former samurai lineage from the Chōshū domain, but they were reared in different settings, pursued different courses through the bureaucracy, and belonged to different factions after entering politics. For our purposes it is the commonality of their bureaucratic backgrounds that is important. Kishi, Ikeda, and Satō had all achieved the highest position in the career civil service, the post of administrative vice minister (*jimu jikan*). Kishi had done so before the war in the MCI before becoming minister of commerce and industry in Tōjō's wartime cabinet. Ikeda had won his vice ministership at MOF and Satō at the Ministry of Communications (MOC). Entering politics after the completion of their bureaucratic careers, the latter two were protégés of Yoshida Shigeru. Under his patronage they rose quickly to assume important ministerial posts in the 1950s. All three of these men thus spent their formative and mature occupational years in bureaucratic settings. They were all about fifty years of age when they entered elective political life, and they won the top position in the LDP after only ten years of postwar parliamentary experience on average.

Kishi, Ikeda, and Satō all showed a preference for former bureaucrats when making appointments to the key ministerial posts at MOF, MFA, and MITI. Although men with bureaucratic backgrounds comprised only 25 percent of the LDP Diet contingent during this period, former bureaucrats comprised nearly 60 percent of the individuals chosen to head these three ministries between 1957 and 1972. At MITI, where former bureaucrats were relatively rare as ministerial appointees before and after this phase, former bureaucrats from MCI and MOF constituted half the appointees. At MOF 60 percent of the ministers were former officials from MOF, MCI, and MOC. And at MFA former bureaucrats shared time equally with two politicians and a former businessman.

Bureaucratic elites also played a central role at Keidanren during this phase of leadership because both chairs between 1956 and 1974 were former bureaucrats. It may be pressing the point to make this claim of Ishizaka Taizō, chair from 1956 to 1968. He had, after all, spent only four years at MOC in the 1910s before turning to the private sector. During the prewar era he had been a central figure at the Daiichi Insurance Company; in the postwar era he served as president and chair of Tōshiba. Far more symbolic of the bureaucratic presence at Keidanren was Uemura Kōgorō, executive director and vice chair from 1952 to 1968 and chair from 1968 to 1974.

Uemura was a quintessential former bureaucrat. He had entered the old Ministry of Agriculture and Commerce in 1919 with Kishi Nobusuke, fresh out of Tokyo Imperial University. They had both moved to MCI when it formed in 1925. After two years of service there, Uemura joined the new Resources Bureau in 1927. When it was absorbed by the new Cabinet Planning Board in 1937, he moved in as a department head and ended his bureaucratic career in 1940 as assistant director. He remained in a central position during the war as executive director of the control association for the coal industry. Like Kishi, Ikeda, and Satō, Uemura, too, was a man who had spent his formative and mature occupational years serving in high-level administrative positions within the central government bureaucracy.[21]

Under Ishizaka and Uemura fourteen different individuals served as vice chair. Nine were men who had spent their entire adult careers in the private sector. The other five were all former ministry or government bank officials. Three had begun their careers with MCI and had either remained there until retirement or moved into other governmental or quasi-governmental posts. Two had been employed by government banks. One joined Keidanren as executive director to succeed Uemura. The other was a former bank official called in to rescue the Nissan auto company. Thus, the bureaucratic coloration noted at Keidanren during the first postwar decade persisted into the 1970s, especially in the person of Uemura Kōgorō.

Uemura and his former MCI colleague Kishi Nobusuke personified the style

21. Uemura Kōgorō Denki Henshūshitsu / Sankei Shuppan, ed., *Ningen Uemura Kōgorō* (Tokyo: Sankei Shuppansha, 1979).

of politics that characterized this period of authority. Both were heirs to samurai lineages that emphasized service to the nation. Both came of age during a period when Japan was flexing its military muscle in East Asia and developing the industrial might to strengthen that muscle. Both spent the crucial part of their adult years in important staff or administrative positions where they influenced policy-making during the war. Victims of the purge, they had to step aside briefly in the late 1940s, but they both relished their return to power by the mid-1950s. Uemura and Kishi thus brought to their roles a large measure of common experience. It greatly facilitated the process of accommodating values, demands, and policies through a pattern of coordinated national policy-making that brought together the ruling party, the incumbent bureaucracy, and the big business community under the tutelage of senior former bureaucrats. These two individuals, and many others of their bureaucratic cohort, exploited their backgrounds, contacts, and aspirations to preside over national affairs during an extraordinary period in Japan's history.

The phase of bureaucratic elites coincided with an era of stable politics, rapid economic growth, and general social quiescence. The former Liberal and Democratic parties merged in 1955 to create a coalition entity called the Liberal Democratic Party. Through a combination of luck, astute electoral strategies, policy successes, and relatively widespread satisfaction, the LDP established a secure grip on power. A national consensus emphasized economic issues. The government pursued growth through policies that favored banks, large corporations, and exporters in the hope that material gains would eventually filter down to families and individuals. In due course they did, and many families experienced a pronounced increase in real incomes during this two-decade period. Not everyone benefited equally and satisfaction was by no means unanimous, as the chapters by Laura Hein and Koji Taira suggest. Moreover, political discontent and opposition remained energetic—if limited in scope. Student demonstrations in 1960, for example, contributed to the resignation of Prime Minister Kishi. But in retrospect, the threat to established institutions and to entrenched powers was much feebler than it appeared at the time. A majority of the Japanese citizenry, schooled to accept bureaucratic authority and numbed by the deprivations of a prolonged war, seemed to defer to leadership by bureaucratic elites while relishing the pleasures of a newfound affluence.

The Income Doubling Plan of the 1960s offers a vehicle for examining the policies that symbolized the era of bureaucratic elites. The man most responsible for articulating this policy was Ikeda Hayato. Ikeda began to develop his conceptions of the plan in early 1959. He drew on comments by Japanese economists, reports in English-language economic journals, and advice from such men as Shimomura Osamu, a bureaucratic loner whose views enjoyed little credibility among mainstream officials. Ikeda pieced together these many strands of advice, intent on formulating a comprehensive policy vision that would both help the nation improve its economic performance and help him improve his political prospects. A report from the Advisory Commission on Economics presented to the Kishi cabinet in December 1959 marked the official unveiling of the plan. As Kishi's minister of international trade and industry, Ikeda would have a key role to play in its implementation. But his role became even more central when the Kishi government fell shortly after, and Ikeda himself became prime minister. His cabinet formally approved the Income Doubling Plan in December 1960.[22]

From a purely economic perspective, the plan flew in the face of conventional wisdom at the time. It established what seemed to be highly ambitious goals for investment and employment levels, production increases, and export volumes. Its principal objective was to double incomes, both national (measured in GNP terms) and individual (presented in consumption terms). Japan's major economic journal, the *Nihon keizai shinbun,* responded originally with a skeptical view, and many economists and businessmen derided the estimates embodied in the plan.[23]

Far more than economic aims were at stake, however. From the outset Ikeda recognized the political promise inherent in the plan. He and the LDP were facing an electorate composed overwhelmingly of people who had suffered the deprivations of a war that stretched in some degree back to the early 1930s. Most voters had already experienced some improvements in their economic well-being by the late 1950s, but many were eager for even more. A satisfied electorate would aid the LDP in stabilizing the polity and in drawing to it a more secure base of materially contented voters. Government financial and investment policies would promote the interests of city banks, large enterprises, and some small firms, especially those engaged in the export trade. These efforts would solidify LDP ties to the corporate community. And public investment in social overhead capital, a major part of the plan, would lay the foundation for close relations with construction firms and construction laborers throughout the country, powerful bonds that eventually provided handsome benefits for all parties concerned.

Under the aegis of the Income Doubling Plan, Ikeda and his bureaucratic cohorts then dominating the LDP pursued what we can call a politics of "induced compliance." With the twin purpose of fostering rapid economic growth and building a majority political coalition, paternalistic guardians of the commonwealth set the agenda with a technocratic style. They emphasized planning and central guidance but eschewed excessive intervention in private markets. Men like Kishi and Ikeda were smart, haughty individuals who did not suffer fools easily, and they certainly had their own interests in mind. But they were also animated enough by a sense of public duty that they pursued policies with broad, national returns. In the case of doubling incomes, they struck on a program that met their political needs, served the national interest, and satisfied popular demands at the same time. The process through which the program was implemented relied on

22. This account relies on Shioguchi Kiichi, *Kikigaki: Ikeda Hayato* (Tokyo: Asahi Shinbunsha, 1975), and Itō Masaya, *Ikeda Hayato* (Tokyo: Jiji Tsūshinsha, 1985), esp. 141–50.

23. Nihon Keizai Shinbun, ed., *Sengo keizai no ayumi* (Tokyo: Nihon Keizai Shinbunsha, 1985), 184–87.

broad consultations. But it could also eventuate in directive persuasion, especially in the distinctive Japanese form of bureaucratic influence known as *gyōsei shidō* (administrative guidance). Critical constituents—banks, manufacturers, exporters, and potentially conservative workers—were drawn into the policy process through inducements of beneficial returns. Their co-optation legitimated the policy, strengthened the LDP's electoral base, and enhanced political stability simultaneously. In all these ways the Income Doubling Plan stands as an emblem of the authority of bureaucratic elites.

The Income Doubling Plan and its many ancillary laws, orders, edicts, and directives produced results that surpassed expectations. Targets for a ten-year period were often met in seven years or less. Incomes more than doubled, as did GNP, manufacturing output, and total exports. For nearly a decade the Japanese populace reaped the material gains—and the LDP the political rewards—of a policy whose time had clearly arrived. But by the late 1960s the costs of rapid growth had begun to outstrip its benefits in the eyes of many, and the groundwork for a new era in Japanese politics was laid.

Specialist Elites

Bureaucratic elites ushered in a prolonged period of stability and affluence. Paradoxically, their very achievements fostered a relative retreat of bureaucratic power and facilitated the advent of a new pattern of elite authority. Stability made it possible for the ruling party, private corporations, and many other organizations in Japanese society, including trade unions, to establish more routinized patterns of recruitment and promotion. The principal consequence of these practices was the emergence of separate channels of leadership recruitment that produced virtually closed professional hierarchies and a new pattern of elite empowerment.

One change in pattern occurred within the LDP. A prolonged period of stable majorities made it possible for the party to adopt more routinized patterns of promotion for its highest offices. During the 1950s and after, young entrants into party ranks were assigned to party research committees, legislative committees, and party offices at the advent of their parliamentary careers. As they won reelection, acquired experience, and proved their mettle, they rose to more challenging positions as chairs of party and parliamentary committees, as parliamentary vice ministers, and as ministers in low-status cabinet posts. Those who demonstrated their abilities in these posts went forward as occupants of still higher positions: chair of the party's general affairs or research council, secretary-general, or cabinet minister with jurisdiction over trade, foreign affairs, or finance. By the 1970s a clear ladder of promotion existed for those who wished to become party president, and therefore prime minister. Candidates were obliged to spend at least twenty-five years within the party, working their way step-by-step to the top. In this manner, seniority (often correlated with age), experience, and a factional leadership position became prerequisites for aspiring prime ministers. It is not surprising that such routinized, bureaucratic patterns of promotion were institutionalized during a period when former bureaucrats dominated the LDP.

Recurring assignments to committees and councils dealing with the same issues made it possible for individual Diet members to develop substantial policy expertise. Some LDP politicians commanded strong competence on agricultural matters, others on health and welfare issues, still others on educational reforms, and so on. Those who shared an interest and expertise in a given policy area became known as members of *seisaku zoku,* or policy tribes. *Zoku* members were actually specialists in their own right, men and women who understood how the LDP formulated policy in certain areas, negotiated its format with the bureaucracy, ushered bills through the legislature, and played a role in implementing laws. Many observers of Japanese politics during the 1970s and after felt that *zoku* members enabled the LDP to exercise a measure of power in its dealings with the standing bureaucracy that it had never before possessed, but it is difficult to affirm this claim with certainty.[24]

Routinized promotion within the LDP not only gave rise to the *zoku* phenomenon but also nurtured a strong reliance on familial relations as a criterion for recruitment to parliamentary candidacy. One observer found that in the late 1980s fully 45 percent of all LDP Diet members were second-generation politicians.[25] When the Kaifu cabinet was formed in August 1989, the three key cabinet positions all went to men whose fathers had served in the Diet before them. Whether this emphasis on family ties strengthened or weakened the LDP was a matter of controversy. Critics noted that such practices may have prevented talented outsiders from running, and they contended that, as with any hereditary aristocracy, such dependence on direct heirs would inevitably weaken abilities. Against these objections one can note that many of these second-generation politicians had impressive résumés of their own. Moreover, unlike members of a hereditary aristocracy they had to go before the voters periodically to reaffirm their positions. To win reelection they had to demonstrate their own abilities at providing service, raising funds for campaigns and staff support, delivering political payoffs to their districts, and participating in the legislative process. Firsthand knowledge of their fathers' political machines and their own prior service as private secretaries (Diet staff) to family relatives did favor them above others, but their continued electoral victories bespoke voter satisfaction with this aspect of democratic politics.

A process of internal grooming similar to that of the LDP also began to occur within the business enterprises whose leaders provided candidates for the top posts at Keidanren. Before 1945 leadership at Japanese business firms was unusually

24. Several contending views of this issue are discussed in Allinson, "Politics in Contemporary Japan."

25. This figure is cited in Uchida Kenzō, *Gendai Nihon no hoshu seiji* (Tokyo: Iwanami Shoten, 1989), 162. Uchida defines a second-generation politician as one who has had a grandfather, father, adoptive father, uncle, or older brother in the Diet.

volatile by comparison with patterns that emerged in the 1970s. It was common for men to move frequently among firms and for top executives to lead several firms in the course of a business career.[26] In the immediate postwar period this pattern continued. When large firms lost their leaders to the purge, they either had to promote young, inexperienced insiders to top posts or find men of stature, ability, and experience on the outside. During the early postwar era some former government officials responded to such calls; this situation explains in part the prominence of former bureaucrats at Keidanren during the 1960s and 1970s. But as reconstruction materialized and the economy embarked on its rapid expansion, companies began to rely far more on insiders who had risen through the ranks. Outsiders were called in less frequently, and the business community—like the ruling party—began to cultivate a new body of specialist elites.[27]

During the 1960s bureaucrats recognized these trends and understood their potential effects. Realizing that lucrative, influential positions in prestigious business firms were going to be less available than before, ministries began to create more external organizations that would serve as landing spots for bureaucrats "descending from heaven," or undergoing *amakudari* in Japanese parlance.[28] In due course such entities—some official, some quasi-official, many off-budget— served as important postretirement assignments for bureaucrats whose options in the private sector were shrinking.

Bureaucrats also recognized the implications of the changes taking place within the LDP. During the 1940s and 1950s the many bureaucrats who ran for Diet seats often waited until after they had assumed the two highest posts in the civil service, bureau chief (*kyoku-chō*) and administrative vice minister (*jimu jikan*). They were usually in their early fifties by then. At that time they could still expect to move quickly into cabinet positions and perhaps even lay claim to the prime minister's position by their early sixties, as Kishi, Ikeda, and Satō had done. However, during the 1960s experience within the LDP itself began to supersede the merits of an early bureaucratic career, putting pressure on politically ambitious bureaucrats to retire earlier and to enter the party at a younger age. Beginning in the 1960s bureaucrats who entered politics did in fact begin to leave office earlier, usually in their early forties. In this way they had time to move up the promotional ladder within the LDP to compete for top positions while they were still young enough to be viable candidates.[29]

26. These claims are based on data I have gathered in the course of my own unpublished research on business elites in twentieth-century Japan.

27. See Allinson, "Japan's Keidanren," and Kent E. Calder, "Elites in an Equalizing Role," *Comparative Politics* 21, no. 4 (July 1989): 379–403.

28. Such "special legal entities" rose in number from 65 in 1960 to 112 in 1974. Johnson, *Japan's Public Policy Companies*, 37.

29. Between 1946 and 1963, 62 percent of the former bureaucrats who won conservative seats in the Diet had risen to the post of bureau chief or higher. In contrast, that percentage dropped to only 36 between 1967 and 1984. Moreover, in testimony to the declining evidence of elective office among former bureaucrats, only 56 former bureaucrats won Diet seats in the LDP in the 17 years after 1967,

In a postwar constitutional order that emphasized the legitimacy of an elective legislature and thus bolstered the standing of political parties, party politicians were not to be counted out of the leadership picture indefinitely—especially when the bureaucrats leading the party adopted procedures to cultivate their successors from within party ranks. After 1972, therefore, career politicians returned with a vengeance to lead the LDP. Of the nine men who served as prime minister between 1972 and 1990, seven were lifelong politicians: Tanaku Kakuei, Miki Takeo, Suzuki Zenkō, Nakasone Yasuhiro, Takeshita Noboru, Uno Sōsuke, and Kaifu Toshiki. All of them were products of the postwar legislature except Miki Takeo, who entered the prewar Diet in 1937. All were groomed within party ranks for leadership positions, first by serving in a variety of minor party and governmental posts and later by winning ministerial appointments. On average they had over thirty years of parliamentary experience before assuming the prime ministership. Even "young" Kaifu had served for twenty-nine years in the Diet before he became prime minister at age fifty-eight in 1989. Seven of the men were also faction leaders. In this capacity they had demonstrated their talents for organization, leadership, and fund-raising and at the same time had proved their ability to integrate party operations with the opportunities, demands, and constraints of societal interests.

There were two former bureaucrats among the prime ministers between 1972 and 1990, Fukuda Takeo (1976–78) and Ōhira Masayoshi (1978–80). We could regard them as exceptions to the rule, or we could interpret their careers in a different light. Both Fukuda and Ōhira initiated bureaucratic careers in MOF. But in Ōhira's case, service as a private secretary to Ikeda Hayato opened a door to an elective political career long before he had risen to the top of the ministry. Fukuda left the ministry as only a bureau chief under a cloud of suspicion that probably would have prevented his ever becoming an administrative vice minister. Moreover, having entered elective political life in the early 1950s, he had to wait nearly twenty-five years before winning the post of prime minister. That is exactly how long the highest flier among postwar party specialists, Tanaka Kakuei, had to wait. Thus, we can view Fukuda and Ōhira both as a residuum of the era of bureaucratic elites and as precursors of the specialist elites. Their early careers as bureaucrats certainly conferred some advantages during the 1950s and 1960s, but they still had to pay their dues as party politicians before they won the top political prize rather late in life (at seventy-one in Fukuda's case, sixty-eight in Ōhira's).

Ministers at MOF, MFA, and MITI between 1972 and 1990 were drawn overwhelmingly from the ranks of career politicians. The preference was most pronounced at MITI, where career politicians served for virtually the entire period. (Party and factional fund-raising objectives undoubtedly played a role in

---

whereas 150 had won conservative seats in the 17 years before. Satō Seizaburō and Matsuzaki Tetsuhisa, *Jimintō seiken* (Tokyo: Chūō Kōronsha, 1986), 102, 233. See also Koh, *Japan's Administrative Elite*, 242–44, for evidence from the 1986 election that affirms the continuation of these tendencies.

such assignments.) MFA also fell frequently to politicians, perhaps to burnish the international credentials of prospective prime ministers. At MOF, however, which had always attracted a disproportionate share of former bureaucrats to the ministerial position, five former MOF officials served as minister. But we need to recognize that among key cabinet ministers during this period were several residual members of bureaucratic elites and precursors of specialist elites. In fact, Fukuda and Ōhira were two of them. A third was Miyazawa Kiichi, another former MOF official whose career paralleled Ōhira's very closely. All three of these men served frequently after 1972 in the three major ministerial positions. If they are treated as career politicians and specialist elites, then only a handful of former bureaucrats saw duty in these posts, and political dominance of major ministerial assignments became virtually complete. By the late 1980s career politicians were also more prominent in cabinets in general and bureaucrats commensurately less so. When Uno Sōsuke formed his government in mid-1989, only 5 of 21 ministers were former bureaucrats, and only 1 of the 5 was a former administrative vice-minister.

Chairs and vice chairs at Keidanren usually served three two-year terms, so the shift to a specialist elite in the business world took place in 1974, following Uemura's departure from Keidanren. Three men were chairmen after Uemura's tenure: Dokō Toshio, Inayama Yoshihiro, and Saitō Eishirō. Inayama followed to some extent in Uemura's footsteps. He began his career as a government bureaucrat in the prewar MCI, on assignment to the government-owned Yawata Steel firm. Inayama continued to be employed by Yawata and its wartime and postwar successors. He always stayed in the steel industry, but he always worked for a firm that was a kind of quasi-governmental enterprise enjoying a profoundly important position in Japan's steel industry. Saitō Eishirō was also a product of this enterprise, but he was young enough to have entered it as a business executive during its years as a private corporation. Dokō Toshio was a pure business manager. He started his career in a precursor to Ishikawajima-Harima Heavy Industries (IHI) and eventually rose to become president and chair of both IHI and the electrical manufacturer, Tōshiba. Dokō is best known for his outspoken, probusiness posture during his tenure at Keidanren and for his leadership of the administrative reform movements of the 1980s, an undertaking devised to impose private-sector business morality on what he felt was a profligate government and its bureaucrats.

Vice chairs at Keidanren were also drawn increasingly from among the ranks of pure business leaders after Uemura's departure. Twenty-five different individuals were vice chair between 1974 and 1990. Of that number only four were former bureaucrats. The remaining twenty-one were all private-sector business leaders who spent their entire careers in the corporate sector, usually with only one firm or enterprise group. They served over three-fourths of the total time devoted to high office at Keidanren during this era. Therefore, although some bureaucratic coloration still persisted at Keidanren, it, too, became an arena for a group of specialist elites who embodied distinctive career experiences and articulated political demands rooted in the environment of the corporate community.

The bureaucratic elites who presided over the dramatic expansion in the Japanese economy unwittingly and paradoxically contributed to their own demise in many ways. Rapid economic growth had the effect of promoting materialist, consumer values on a broad basis in the midst of an ebullient market economy. During the 1960s and after, the values and market orientations of the private sector endowed political relations themselves with the character of a massive, multifaceted exchange relationship.[30] More societal groups found themselves with the resources to organize and bargain politically.[31] Politicians in general and the ruling party in particular had to heed the appeals of such interests. Demanding grants, subsidies, contracts, and rewards of one kind or another, voters and interest groups traded their electoral support for government returns. In other cases they simply offered cash for favored treatment. By the late 1980s these practices had become so widespread that one advertising and real estate conglomerate known as Recruit tainted virtually every leader in the LDP through its bald contributions.

Endowing politics with the norms of the marketplace was just one consequence of the earlier experience of rule by bureaucratic elites. At least four other consequences were also important. First, Japan's extraordinary success as a manufacturer and exporter of high-quality consumer goods imposed a measure of dependence on the international economy that was unprecedented. As a result Japan became vulnerable to external events that sent occasional shock waves through society. High rates of inflation driven by international petroleum cartels and economic distress caused by exchange rate fluctuations were only two phenomena that seriously affected the economy between 1973 and 1990. Second, rapid economic growth dramatically altered the social configurations within Japan. Urban development provoked a host of problems within the cities at the same time it drew people off the farms and exacerbated the decline of rural society. Third, the affluence spawned by economic growth stimulated new political orientations. Private firms came to enjoy such financial autonomy that bureaucratic control over their decisions withered considerably. Families and individuals, women and youth, all of whom were enriched in many ways by the new affluence, found themselves harboring different political concerns. Fourth and finally, in the face of new social configurations and political concerns, politicians scrambled to sustain and renegotiate their alliances with constituents and supporters. Out of these changed circumstances emerged the social imperatives for the politics of competitive negotiation.

The competitive bargaining that characterized so much of Japanese politics

30. An important study that examines Japan's postwar politics from this perspective is Kent Calder's *Crisis and Compensation* (Princeton: Princeton University Press, 1989).

31. The authoritative study of postwar interest groups is Muramatsu Michio et al., *Sengo Nihon no atsuryoku dantai* (Tokyo: Tōyō Keisai Shinpōsha, 1986).

after the early 1970s perceptibly altered patterns of induced compliance on which bureaucratic elites had relied. To begin, specialist elites found it far more difficult to set the political agenda than their predecessors had. Bureaucratic elites were advantaged by a possibly unique moment in international history, and they had been able to create—and sustain, at least briefly—a national consensus on economic growth at a time when both domestic and international conditions were conducive to its pursuit. Specialist elites were obliged to deal with the demise of that salutary environment.

In fact, in another sense of the word the environment itself offered perhaps the first sign that elites could no longer set the agenda and plan policies with a technocratic style. Personal grievances, popular outrage, and organized opposition to environmental pollution beginning in the late 1960s forced a set of new issues onto the political agenda.[32] Others followed. Demographic changes associated with longer life expectancies made health and welfare issues more salient. Employee needs, technological change, and new values among younger generations fostered widespread concern with educational matters. Occasionally a strong political leader, such as Nakasone Yasuhiro, was able to grasp and promote an issue on his own initiative. But more often than not, politicians found themselves reacting to issues they had not anticipated. Even when a government did seem to have some grasp on a problem, corruption scandals or electoral reversals could force new issues on, or old issues off, the agenda.

Specialist elites also had to engage with a political process that was qualitatively different from that of their predecessors. The essay by Sheldon Garon and Mike Mochizuki (in this volume) eloquently affirms the importance of organized interests in Japanese politics as early as the prewar era.[33] By the 1960s, and certainly during the 1970s and 1980s, organized societal interests had become a far more influential political force than ever before. Higher levels of education throughout society, coupled with the expansion of technical and financial resources in both public and private hands, significantly increased the ability of societal interests to organize, develop expertise, conduct lobbying, and pursue their political objec-

32. In a polity where elites are selected according to age and seniority, the political modes that characterize a phase of elite authority actually precede the arrival of those elites in the very highest office. Thus, the politics of induced compliance were manifested in the late 1940s and early 1950s while the last diffuse elites still fought over the prime ministership. The politics of competitive negotiation were discernible during the 1960s before the first specialist politician, Tanaka Kakuei, became prime minister in 1972. In fact, although Tanaka had not been fully responsible for initiating that political mode, he had certainly been instrumental in exploiting, refining, and expanding the politics of competitive negotiation from the 1960s onward in his roles as cabinet minister and party secretary.

33. Although Garon and Mochizuki stress how early political bargaining arose, one can read their essay in a way that confirms the outlines of the case made in this chapter. LDP efforts to incorporate small business interests into its coalition after 1957 were directive and paternalistic. However, by the 1970s business had become more assertive and negotiations between small business organizations, the ministries, and the party had grown more intensely competitive.

tives. Politicians had to respond to such pressures out of a need for both electoral and financial support. Incumbent bureaucrats, too, found themselves increasingly hemmed in by organized interests.

A politics of competitive negotiation not only forced politicians and bureaucrats into a more defensive posture but also fostered a complex, shifting array of political allegiances and policy-making channels, as a brief glance at some critical issues illustrates. Both a national debt crisis and a more affluent society made financial issues salient political concerns after the early 1970s. Reliable studies suggest that private-sector interest groups, responding to domestic and international economic imperatives, were often able to maneuver MOF into adopting policies that it opposed. In other cases societal pressures brought to bear on politicians led to LDP intervention in interministerial disputes. In many instances, therefore, politicians or societal interests encroached on ministerial authority over financial policy and undercut bureaucratic dominance.[34] A similar diminution of ministerial authority was also occurring at MITI, which had presided over a set of highly successful industrial policies in the 1950s and 1960s. In a penetrating review of the subject one astute observer concluded that "in the 1980s Japanese industrial policy [was] characterized less by a protective government or government-inspired cooperation than by fierce and pugnacious competition among skilled, determined, and often aggressively independent firms."[35]

However, on other issues different patterns of influence pertained. Welfare became an important concern during the 1970s and 1980s because the costs of health care began to rise discernibly. One authoritative study indicates that bureaucrats managed to retain the initiative and to effectively challenge organized societal interests in this policy area.[36] Administrative reform (*gyōsei kaikaku*), one of the most conspicuous political movements of the 1980s, casts still different light on the policy process. In this instance a coalition of business leaders and LDP conservatives promoted significant institutional change that challenged both bureaucratic authority and the powers of organized labor. Finally, in the late 1980s the LDP confronted the need to adopt policies that seemed to renege on social contracts with two of its most important constituents, farmers and small retailers. In striving to respond to urban voters who might represent its base for the future, the LDP courted the risk of cutting itself off from its own successful past.

In sum, the balances of power and the lines of authority in Japanese political life became so blurred under the politics of competitive negotiation that casual

34. Two major studies of recent financial reforms are James Horne, *Japan's Financial Markets* (Boston: George Allen and Unwin, 1985), and Francis Rosenbluth, *Financial Politics in Contemporary Japan* (Ithaca: Cornell University Press, 1989).

35. Greg Noble, "The Japanese Industrial Policy Debate," in Stephen Haggard and Chung-in Moon, eds., *Pacific Dynamics: The International Politics of Industrial Change* (Boulder: Westview, 1989), 95.

36. See the essay by Takahashi Hideyuki in Nakano Minoru, ed., *Nihon-gata seisaku kettei no hen'yō* (Tokyo: Tōyō Keizai Shinpōsha, 1986), 237–66.

generalizations about ruling triads or dominant bureaucrats seem wholly inapt. More so than these two perspectives, the pluralist position does seem to capture some of the complexity of politics during the era of specialist elites. It is better able to account for the difficulties that elites experienced in setting the political agenda. It captures more of the dynamism underlying a political process in which many societal interests negotiated their political demands with politicians and bureaucrats. And a pluralist perspective conveys a better appreciation for the pervasive bargaining that undercut the capacity for technocratic biases in policy-making and shifted the ground of political action away from paternalistic inducements to compliance and toward competitive negotiation in the marketplace of political exchange.[37]

CONCLUSION

When patterns of elite recruitment and authority in Japan are compared with those in other advanced industrial countries, one feature stands out. Far more than in the United States, Britain, France, and West Germany, former bureaucrats played a conspicuous role among Japan's postwar elites. They held many important positions in the nation's peak business association, and into the early 1970s they held ministerial posts and occupied the prime ministership in disproportionately large numbers. Their preeminence was in part a legacy of the Meiji Restoration and the role that hereditary elites played after 1868. But their exceptional importance, especially during the two decades after the mid-1950s, was attributable as much to the consequences of war, defeat, occupation, and a political purge as it was to the talents, experience, and ambitions of former bureaucrats themselves.

Ironically, when bureaucratic elites did assume power, they adopted policies and practices that undermined future political prospects for most former bureaucrats who were younger than they were. They routinized bureaucratic norms of recruitment within the LDP that gave rise to politicians as specialist elites. They successfully cultivated a buoyant, materialist consumer society whose norms endowed political life itself with the character of a pervasive marketplace. And they pursued economic policies that significantly altered Japan's role in the international economy and dramatically restructured the configurations of domestic society. By the 1990s Japan's political elites confronted the severe challenge of integrating the demands of a fickle electorate with the capabilities of a state burdened by heavy debt, open to pervasive political contestation, and challenged by an unstable international environment. Like many other advanced industrial democracies, Japan, too, both nurtured and nervously tolerated increasingly sharp disparities in wealth, status, and power in a society where professional, conservative politicians held sway.

37. The brevity of this chapter and its principal focus on transformations in elite structures has permitted only tentative treatment of the associations between elite authority and policy processes and outcomes. Despite its shortcomings, if the discussion has suggested new lines of inquiry, then it has achieved one of the objectives for this volume.

CHAPTER SIX

Negotiating Social Contracts

Sheldon Garon and Mike Mochizuki

The historical study of relationships between the Japanese state and civil society since World War II is still in its infancy. Thanks to path-breaking work by Chalmers Johnson and Richard Samuels, we know a great deal about changing relations between the government and big business both before and after 1945.[1] Much less has been written historically about the postwar state's interaction with groups that represent millions of working-class and petit bourgeois Japanese. We have chosen to focus on two of these groups—organized labor and small-business associations.

Indeed, one cannot assess the meaning of democracy in postwar Japan without reference to the political significance of these popular organizations. To be sure, big business and elite bureaucrats, together with the Liberal Democratic Party (LDP) and its predecessors, constituted the core of the conservative coalition that ruled the nation continuously from 1948 through the 1980s, single-mindedly pursuing policies to enable Japanese industry to compete in world markets. However, it is equally true that from the dawn of the postwar era the conservatives had to reconcile their objectives for rapid, often wrenching economic growth with the tasks of maintaining social stability and a strong electoral base. In turn, influential segments of the labor movement and other secondary groups eagerly sought entry into the ruling coalition and the policy-making process. The result has been the appearance of several social contracts.

We define *social contract* as a political exchange relationship between the state and social groups that is mediated by interest organizations and that establishes public-policy parameters that endure over time. Typically the social groups use their market or political power to extract policy concessions from the state, while

1. Chalmers Johnson, *MITI and the Japanese Miracle: The Growth of Industrial Policy, 1925–1975* (Stanford: Stanford University Press, 1982); Richard J. Samuels, *The Business of the Japanese State: Energy Markets in Comparative and Historical Perspective* (Ithaca: Cornell University Press, 1987).

the state adopts such policies in exchange for their support. This support may take various forms ranging from direct electoral backing to restraints on collective action and a general acceptance of the socioeconomic order.[2] In the case of Japanese labor unions, organized workers exchanged their market power (the power to strike and disrupt production) for public employment and welfare programs, state recognition of a nationwide collective bargaining process, and participation in public-policy forums. Conversely, small-business associations exchanged their political power (the ability to mobilize voters) for governmental policies that would compensate for their weaknesses in the marketplace.

Although the Japanese state negotiated a series of social contracts over time, political accommodation was by no means the only possible outcome. The organizations that represent workers and small businesses might have continued to pursue militant strategies, as many had in the decade following World War II, by refusing to enter into cooperative relationships with the state or by seeking radical transformations of the socioeconomic order. For example, both the labor and small-business movements in France sustained nonaccommodative stances for significant periods.[3] Alternatively, workers and petty entrepreneurs might have forged a cross-class alliance, mobilizing to establish a social-democratic government. The formation of such a social coalition between workers and the urban and rural petite bourgeoisie explains in large part the political hegemony of the Social Democratic Party in Sweden.[4]

In Japan neither the French nor the Swedish alternatives emerged. The conservative political elites pursued an accommodative strategy that rewarded labor moderation and weakened those who adhered to a militant line. The governing coalition also responded to political pressures from small-business organizations to prevent them from defecting to the Left. Although the negotiated social contracts did not substantially deflect conservative governments from the basic course of economic developmentalism, they placed genuine constraints on the more ambitious plans of state officials and major industrialists.

Our historical perspective places the phenomenon of postwar democracy within the larger context of twentieth-century Japanese history. Several changes made the Japanese political system after 1945 significantly more democratic than were the prewar and wartime orders. In institutional terms the military was removed as a political force; sovereignty was transferred from the emperor to the

2. For a similar conceptualization of "social contract," see Alessandro Pizzorno, "Political Exchange and Collective Identity in Industrial Conflict," in *The Resurgence of Class Conflict in Western Europe since 1968,* vol. 2, *Comparative Analyses,* ed. Colin Crouch and Alessandro Pizzorno (New York: Holmes and Meier, 1968), 277–98.

3. Peter Lange, George Ross, and Maurizio Vannicelli, *Unions, Change, and Crisis: French and Italian Union Strategy and the Political Economy 1945–1980* (London: Allen and Unwin, 1982); Roger Eatwell, "Poujadism and Neo-Poujadism: From Revolt to Reconciliation," in *Social Movements and Protest in France,* ed. Philip G. Cerny (New York: St. Martin's, 1982), 70–93.

4. Gösta Esping-Andersen, *Politics Against Markets: The Social Democratic Road to Power* (Princeton: Princeton University Press, 1985).

people as exercised by the lower house of the Diet; and civil liberties were expanded. But in terms of state-society relations the central feature of postwar Japanese democracy may be that many social groups were able to negotiate social contracts and other agreements with the governing coalition, whereas in the prewar era they could not.

Before 1945 the state was reluctant to negotiate with interest groups, aside from big business, as autonomous entities. The establishment of the Imperial Diet in 1890—followed by the formation of national political parties and the brief era of party rule (1918–32)—provided some organizations, particularly small-business associations, with greater access to power. Nonetheless, beginning in the mid-1930s officials made a concerted effort to subordinate private interests to the state. In the relatively benign case of small business, the wartime government incorporated small and medium-sized firms into compulsory cartels dominated by large companies. When it came to organizations deemed threatening to social order, bureaucrats engineered the dissolution of the remaining labor unions in 1940 and brutally disbanded several burgeoning "new religions" that counted hundreds of thousands of adherents. The exclusion of the latter two sectors appears all the more extreme considering that the labor movement and the suppressed religions had enthusiastically endorsed Japan's war effort after 1931 and offered the regime excellent support bases among the working class and the petite bourgeoisie, respectively.[5]

The postwar political order has been more democratic in part because state officials learned from the mistakes of excluding cooperative groups. Other significant factors that stimulated alliances between the government and previously neglected sectors included the unambiguous institution of party government, the creation of new interest-oriented agencies, firmer guarantees of the right to organize labor unions, and, of course, the rapid growth of the labor movement and other popular associations after 1945.

By examining the evolution of social contracts throughout the postwar era itself, we also provide a historical explanation of recent political developments. It is well known that Japan's highly organized farmers became a pillar of the conservative parties during the early postwar years in exchange for generous protections.[6] In addition several students of contemporary politics have remarked on the efforts of the Liberal Democratic Party and the bureaucracy to negotiate with a broader array of organized interests, including labor unions and small-business associations, since the early 1970s. To most the conservatives' accommodative stance represents an unraveling of the 1955 System, a concept invoked by political scientists not only to refer to the year when the conservative parties

5. See Sheldon M. Garon, *The State and Labor in Modern Japan* (Berkeley and Los Angeles: University of California Press, 1987); Garon, "State and Religion in Imperial Japan, 1912–1945," *Journal of Japanese Studies* 12 (Summer 1986): 273–302.

6. Michael W. Donnelly, "Setting the Price of Rice," in *Policymaking in Contemporary Japan*, ed. T. J. Pempel (Ithaca: Cornell University Press, 1976), 102–200.

merged to form the LDP following the reunification of the Japan Socialist Party but also to convey that for the next fifteen years Japanese politics was polarized into "two major ideological camps" with little room for compromise.[7]

We argue instead that the process of negotiating social contracts dated back to the earliest days of the postwar era.[8] We also question whether there ever was a fully polarized 1955 System that had to erode during the 1970s, for many of the key social contracts that mark Japanese politics today were first negotiated between the mid-1950s and the early 1960s.

SMALL BUSINESS

The Small and Medium Enterprises Agency currently defines small and medium enterprises as having fewer than 300 employees and small-scale enterprises in commerce and services as employing fewer than 5 people. However, official definitions varied considerably over time and by the agency. In this essay *small business* refers primarily to commercial and manufacturing firms with fewer than 30 employees. Although the proportion of Japanese who own and work in these small enterprises has been declining in the postwar era, table 6.1 indicates that small establishments continued to employ more than half of the private sector's nonagricultural work force in 1986. Moreover, owners and family members working in enterprises with fewer than 30 employees accounted for an estimated one-quarter of the nonagricultural labor force in 1982.[9] The persistence of small family-run businesses was particularly striking in the retail and wholesale trades.

The small-business sector's relationships with the postwar ruling coalition were powerfully shaped by the political activism of its associations prior to World War II. To be sure, the state and big business placed serious constraints on the autonomy of small business before 1945. The nation's largest companies dominated the Japan Chamber of Commerce and Industry by the late 1920s, and economic bureaucrats repeatedly attempted to rationalize export-oriented production and curb cutthroat competition by organizing cartels or trade associations (*dōgyō kumiai*) of small and medium-sized businesses in similar product lines. As Japan's war with China demanded more resources after 1937, the government

7. T. J. Pempel, "The Unbundling of 'Japan, Inc.': The Changing Dynamics of Japanese Policy Formation," *Journal of Japanese Studies* 13 (Summer 1987): 255, 283, 293 n. 54; Michio Muramatsu and Ellis S. Krauss, "The Conservative Policy Line and the Development of Patterned Pluralism," in *The Political Economy of Japan*, vol. 1, *The Domestic Transformation*, ed. Kozo Yamamura and Yasukichi Yasuba (Stanford: Stanford University Press, 1987), 517, 532–34; see also T. J. Pempel and Keiichi Tsunekawa, "Corporatism Without Labor? The Japanese Anomaly," in *Trends Toward Corporatist Intermediation*, ed. Philippe C. Schmitter and Gerhard Lehmbruch (Beverly Hills: Sage, 1979), 231–70.

8. For a similar periodization, see Kent E. Calder, *Crisis and Compensation: Public Policy and Political Stability in Japan, 1949–1986* (Princeton: Princeton University Press, 1988).

9. Hugh T. Patrick and Thomas P. Rohlen, "Small-Scale Family Enterprises," in Yamamura and Yasuba, *Domestic Transformation*, 333, 626 n. 5.

TABLE 6.1.   Private Establishments and Persons Engaged (in thousands)

	1954		1986	
	Establishments	Persons Engaged	Establishments	Persons Engaged
Nonagricultural industries[a]	3,285	17,618	6,494	48,995
Employing 1–29	3,219 (98%)	10,787 (61%)	6,251 (96%)	27,834 (57%)
Retail and wholesale	1,605	4,921	3,046	15,673
Employing				
1–4	1,399 (87%)	2,703 (55%)	2,252 (74%)	5,019 (32%)
5–9	141 (9%)	894 (18%)	498 (16%)	3,163 (20%)

SOURCES: Sōrifū Tōkeikyoku, *Nihon tōkei nenkan, 1955–56* (Tokyo: Nihon Tōkei Kyōkai, 1957), 52–53; Sōmuchō Tōkeikyoku, *Nihon tōkei nenkan, 1989,* 120–21, 126–27.
[a]Excludes forestry and fisheries. Figures for 1954 include local publicly managed bodies.

sharply curtailed access to imported raw materials by small manufacturers, who were at the heart of the export sector. Small-business organizations were subsequently absorbed into the wartime state's "control associations."[10]

Nonetheless, in the three decades preceding World War II an autonomous small-business movement surfaced as a political force that the political parties and bureaucracy could not ignore. Shopkeepers and small-scale manufacturers first demonstrated their organizational clout in the thirty-year campaign to repeal the Business Tax Law of 1896. They objected to paying a fixed tax that was determined by such indirect criteria as a firm's capitalization and assessed real estate. Their neighborhood groups and trade associations increasingly united into citywide and regional federations, like the Tokyo Federation of Business Associations, which by 1930 counted 99,000 members. Impressed by the numbers and organization of small owners in their constituencies, the major parties and a party-led cabinet supported the repeal of the business tax in 1926, replacing it with a business earnings tax based on a firm's annual profits.[11]

Associations of urban shopkeepers mounted an equally vigorous drive to limit competition from the rapidly expanding department stores. Amidst the depression of the early 1930s, organizations representing tens of thousands of retailers demanded that the state enact a department store law. The proposed legislation would regulate hours of operations, further prohibiting the opening of new de-

10. Andō Yoshio, *Nihon no rekishi,* vol. 28, *Burujoajii no gunzō* (Tokyo: Shōgakkan, 1976), 233; Pempel and Tsunekawa, "Corporatism Without Labor?" 249–52; Johnson, *MITI and the Japanese Miracle,* 98–99, 160–61.

11. See Eguchi Keiichi, *Toshi shōburujoa undō shi no kenkyū* (Tokyo: Miraisha, 1976), chaps. 1–3.

partment stores and the expansion of existing stores. After the two major parties jointly sponsored a similar department store bill in 1936, officials of the Ministry of Commerce and Industry reluctantly offered their own bill. They did so both to appease the parties and to mollify the profound discontent of a sizable social sector. The government-sponsored Department Store Law of 1937 permitted the legally recognized association of department stores to regulate its own stores in many spheres, yet it also gave officials unprecedented powers to punish violations by suspending a store's operations, dismissing its executives, or revoking its authorization altogether.[12]

Given its prewar organizational advances, the small-business sector emerged from World War II with a strong desire to advance its collective interests in the political arena. Although the petite bourgeoisie had generally allied with the bourgeois parties before the war, it was not at all clear in the late 1940s that they would flock to the postwar bourgeois ruling parties. There was anger to spare over the wartime government's high-handed promotion of large firms at the expense of small producers. Furthermore, the early Liberal Party cabinets of Yoshida Shigeru appeared contemptuous of smaller enterprises. Under the Priority Production Plan of 1946 the government gave large firms preferential access to capital and materials. The third Yoshida cabinet's implementation of Joseph Dodge's recommendations for drastic retrenchment in 1949 was devastating for many small and medium-sized concerns, whereas many big companies received extraordinary loans from the large commercial banks.[13] In a telling remark to the Diet in 1952 Finance Minister Ikeda Hayato admitted that "it makes no difference to me if five or ten small businessmen are forced to commit suicide" because of the drive toward heavy industrialization.[14] Led by the All-Japan Small and Medium Industries Council (Zenchūkyō), small-business organizations demanded an end to the austerity program in 1949–50.[15]

So great was the small-business sector's displeasure with the Liberal Party that there existed the historical possibility of an alliance between the urban petite bourgeoisie and the Japan Socialist Party (JSP) from 1947 to 1950. The high point of the Socialists' appeal to small business came at the time of Katayama Tetsu's coalition cabinet (May 1947 to March 1948). For the first time in Japanese history a Socialist headed the government, and the JSP's coalition with two centrist bourgeois parties offered an unprecedented opportunity to construct a mass political base of workers and the lower middle classes. The left-center coalition continued in the cabinet led by the Democratic Party's Ashida Hitoshi (March–October 1948). In November 1947 the Katayama cabinet announced a

12. Tsūshō Sangyōshō, ed., *Shōkō seisaku shi* (Shōkō Seisaku Shi Kankōkai, 1980) 7:163–64, 168, 179–81, 205–12; Eguchi, *Toshi*, chap. 5.

13. Shinobu Seizaburō, *Sengo Nihon seiji shi* (Tokyo: Keisō Shobō, 1967) 3:999–1000.

14. Johnson, *MITI and the Japanese Miracle*, 202.

15. Higuchi Kenji, "Sengo chūshō kigyō undō no tenkai," in *Soshiki mondai to chūshō kigyō*, ed. Katō Seiichi, Mizuno Takeshi, and Kobayashi Yasuo (Tokyo: Dōyūkan, 1977), 236–39.

program to aid small firms suffering from the Priority Production Plan. At the initiative of American occupation authorities the centrist cabinets also tempered the economic bureaucracy's preference for large enterprises by creating the Small and Medium Enterprises Agency within the Ministry of Commerce and Industry (which became the Ministry of International Trade and Industry [MITI] in 1949). The succeeding Ashida cabinet sponsored the Small and Medium Enterprises Cooperative Unions Law (1948), which increased small firms' leverage in their dealings with large companies.[16]

The Socialists did not, however, succeed in consolidating a national base in the small-business sector. The JSP failed to capitalize on the political opportunity offered by austerity. In the wake of huge losses in the 1949 election, internecine struggles gave rise to separate Right Socialist and Left Socialist parties in 1951. A critical issue dividing the two wings concerned strategy toward the petite bourgeoisie. The right-wing Socialists called on the JSP to become a "national people's party" comprising all classes, including small proprietors and farmers, whereas the left wing insisted that the party remain a "class party" based on workers.[17] The left-wing strategy easily triumphed and dominated the Socialist camp until the mid-1980s. The Socialists' problems allowed the conservative parties to regain the initiative. Backbenchers in the ruling Liberal Party persuaded the Yoshida cabinet to reverse its retrenchment policies. With the upper house election of June 1950 in sight, the government negotiated with the United States to end Dodge's austerity program.[18] The militancy of small producers further eroded as American procurements for the Korean War revitalized the Japanese economy.

The stage was set for small business to negotiate a social contract with conservative politicians during the first half of the 1950s. This compact resulted in a steady stream of protectionist measures that were often enacted over the opposition of the market-oriented MITI bureaucrats and ruling party leaders. The prewar agenda of small business resurfaced in several campaigns. In 1953 and 1954 small-business associations persuaded MITI to intervene to check the expansion of large companies and to obstruct foreign investment in sectors in which small firms might be threatened. A broad coalition of retailers' groups again formed to block the growth of department stores, culminating in the enactment of a new Department Store Law in 1956. A national alliance to repeal commodity taxes emerged in 1952, and some 292 small-business organizations embarked on a drive to abolish enterprise taxes one year later. The latter effort resulted in a cut

16. Higuchi, "Sengo," 231–35; Nakamura Hideichirō et al., *Gendai chūshō kigyō shi* (Tokyo: Nihon Keizai Shinbunsha, 1981), 36–37.

17. Hara Nobito, "Shakaitō saiken taikai to Inamura-Morito ronsō," in *Sengo shakaishugi undō no saihensei*, ed. Kojima Tsunehisa and Tanaka Shin'ichirō (Tokyo: Kawade Shobō Shinsha, 1975), 89–99; Allan B. Cole, George O. Totten, and Cecil H. Uyehara, *Socialist Parties in Postwar Japan* (New Haven: Yale University Press, 1966), 27–28, 87–88.

18. Shinobu, *Sengo Nihon seiji shi* 3:1100–1103, 1130–31.

in the enterprise tax rate after these organizations formed the postwar era's first unified antitax league, the National Small and Medium Enterprises Tax System Reform Council (Zeikakukyō) in 1954.[19] Similar lobbying yielded the Small Business Finance Corporation (1953), through which the government lent money to smaller, though rarely the smallest, enterprises.[20] During the latter half of the 1950s small business secured increased tax deductions and low caps on local tax rates.[21] Most notable, in 1957 the Diet enacted the Small and Medium Enterprise Organization Law, which sanctioned the formation of commercial and industrial unions aimed at preventing excessive competition and infiltration by large firms. The initiative came not from MITI but from an intensive lobbying campaign by the newly formed Small and Medium Enterprise Political League (Chūseiren) and its five million members.[22]

The ruling party, for its part, reaped ample electoral benefits by responding to the demands of small business. The newly formed Liberal Democratic Party consolidated its mass base among farmers and the urban petite bourgeoisie during the latter half of the 1950s. Seeking to expand the party's organizational networks, the LDP supported passage of several laws that promoted the formation of small-business associations. In an effort to forestall the entry of a petit bourgeois party based on the new religion Sōka Gakkai, LDP politicians similarly backed the 1960 Commercial and Industrial Association Law, which encouraged the organization of small family businesses.[23]

Most important, the LDP established a small-business policy liaison council with representatives of the major small-business organizations in 1960. The following year the participating groups founded the postwar era's most inclusive peak association of small firms, the National General Federation of Small and Medium Enterprise Organizations (Sōrengō). The federation's platform pledged support for the government, the LDP, and a "liberal" economic system (i.e., antisocialist, not necessarily promarket) while calling on the government to cultivate small businesses as a force for social stability.[24] Sōrengō was neither as cohesive nor as hierarchically ordered as the farmers' association, Nōkyo (National Association of Agricultural Cooperatives). Nonetheless, small-business organizations formed several potent ad hoc coalitions to present shared demands to conservative politicians and bureaucrats.[25]

Although small business concluded its basic social contract with the state in the 1950s, the process of negotiating and renegotiating continued. The greatest threat

19. Higuchi, "Sengo," 239–43, 243–45.
20. Nakamura Kinji, *Chūshō kigyō seisaku kenkyū* (Tokyo: Kyōdō Shuppan, 1965), 288–92.
21. Higuchi, "Sengo," 249; Taguchi Fukuji, *Shakai shūdan no seiji kinō* (Tokyo: Miraisha, 1969), 215.
22. See Kobayashi Naoki, "Chūshō kigyō dantai soshiki hō no rippō katei," *Tōkyō daigaku kyōyō gakubu shakai kagakuka shakai kagaku kiyō* 7 (1957): 1–104.
23. Taguchi, *Shakai shūdan no seji kinō* 231–32; Takahara Masao, "Hoshutō no soshiki katsudō," *Shisō*, no. 420 (June 1959): 93.
24. Higuchi, "Sengo," 253–54.
25. Cf. Pempel and Tsunekawa, "Corporatism Without Labor?" 260–61, 268.

to the agreement occurred during the 1960s when the government retreated from the protectionist policies of the previous decade. In 1960 the LDP unveiled a "New Policy" with the support of the Small and Medium Enterprises Agency of MITI. New emphasis was placed on modernizing small businesses to enhance their international competitiveness in the face of trade and capital liberalization. In 1963 the Diet enacted both the Small and Medium Enterprises Basic Law and the Small and Medium Enterprises Modernization Law. By intent and in practice the legislation benefited the larger of the small and medium-sized enterprises, which received tax breaks and low-interest loans to modernize equipment and undertake mergers. MITI relied overwhelmingly on market forces, and bankruptcies and business failures increased dramatically after 1964.[26]

Yet the social contract essentially held despite the market-conforming modernization policy. Small-business associations had in fact played a central role in drafting and lobbying for the Small and Medium Enterprises Basic Law. Their support was based above all on the new opportunities for small entrepreneurs created by the booming economy. Keeping up their end of the bargain, the bureaucrats and politicians continued to provide several safety nets. The Ikeda and Satō cabinets took a very gradual approach toward the liberalization of capital and foreign trade for the purposes of protecting small business. Moreover, the LDP supported the passage of a series of laws to aid shopkeepers and others in small family firms. And on the tax front, to the consternation of the Ministry of Finance, the LDP maintained its electoral and social policy of lightly taxing small businesses and permitting widespread tax evasion. In 1968 the government significantly raised the deduction for wages paid to family members when calculating income.[27]

One would expect Japan's economic restructuring to have eroded the political clout of small business, but it did not. If anything, this social sector grew stronger politically, compelling the government to adopt a new set of protectionist programs during the 1970s. Small businesses were hit hard by the first oil shock and other economic dislocations of the early 1970s. At the same time the LDP sought to win over proprietors of minuscule family-run establishments, whom the Communist Party had been singularly successful in mobilizing since the late 1960s. Between 1976 and 1979 the government instituted a number of programs to aid ailing small businesses, assisting them to move into new trades. MITI endorsed these social measures because they did not obstruct the market-driven adjustment process itself.

No such consensus developed within the conservative coalition regarding two

26. Tatsumi Nobuharu and Yamamoto Jun'ichi, *Chūshō kigyō seisaku o minaosu* (Tokyo: Yūhikaku, 1983), 148–49; Nakamura Hideichirō, *Gendai chūshō kigyō shi*, 160–64, 179–80, 187–93.

27. Nakamura Kinji, *Chūshō kigyō seisaku kenkyū*, 329–30; Smaller Enterprise Agency, Ministry of International Trade and Industry, Government of Japan, *Outline of Policy for Smaller Enterprises: Japanese Experience* (Tokyo: Asian Productivity Organization, 1970), 135–38; Patrick and Rohlen, "Small-Scale Family Enterprises," 367–68.

other major policies. In the case of the 1977 domain regulation law, MITI, the Economic Planning Agency, Keidanren (the big-business federation), and Prime Minister Miki Takeo himself opposed legislation to inhibit big business from expanding into domains dominated by small firms. Nevertheless, a nationwide campaign by trade associations—backed by the opposition parties—induced more than 40 percent of the LDP's Diet members to join a parliamentary league in support of the legislation. A compromise bill passed, giving trade associations of small businesses considerable powers. In 1978 a similar coalition mobilized to strengthen the Large-scale Retail Stores Law of 1973, which had restricted the expansion of supermarkets and other large retailers.[28]

Developments in the late 1980s illustrated that, while under fire, the social contract of small business remained very much on the minds of those heading Japan's conservative coalition. The controversial question of tax reform was a case in point. Salaried employees and labor unions had long criticized the nation's income tax system for allowing farmers and small proprietors to pay taxes on only about half of their income whereas the paychecks of wage earners were subject to automatic withholding. In 1987 Prime Minister Nakasone Yasuhiro submitted a sweeping tax reform package that aimed in part at broadening his party's appeal among salaried employees and blue-collar workers. He proposed lower income-tax rates and, to make up for lost revenue, introduced a 5 percent value-added tax. Nakasone was forced to withdraw the measure in the face of vehement opposition from a strange coalition of organized labor, salaried employees' groups, *and* small-business associations. His successor, Takeshita Noboru, did push a reform program through the Diet in 1988, but only after granting major concessions to small businesses. His government opted for a 3 percent consumption tax that was based solely on the accounting records of firms, thus permitting blatant tax evasion by small businesses to continue. The package also exempted enterprises with annual revenues of less than 30 million yen from the tax and established a reduced rate for those with yearly sales of under 500 million yen.[29] The social contract of the 1950s was still very much alive.

When judged by comparative standards, it is clear that Japan's small businesses effectively gained and maintained a position within the ruling coalition. In the parallel case of Italy, a variety of policies, including favorable tax and labor legislation, contributed to making the small-business sector a dynamic factor in the economy and a pillar of social and political stability. Although the Communist Party managed to mobilize the petite bourgeoisie in some regions, this social group generally provided a firm electoral base for the ruling Christian Demo-

28. Hirose Michisada, *Hojokin to seikentō* (Tokyo: Asahi Shinbunsha, 1981), 40–50; Patrick and Rohlen, "Small-Scale Family Enterprises," 368–69; Mike M. Mochizuki, "Managing and Influencing the Japanese Legislative Process" (Ph.D. diss., Harvard University, 1982), 333–44; see also Nakamura Hideichirō, *Gendai chūshō kigyō shi*, 275–79, 309–16.

29. Shindō Muneyuki, *Zaisei hatan to zeisei kaikaku* (Tokyo: Iwanami Shoten, 1989), 195–228.

crats.[30] In the divergent case of postwar France, small-business movements were much more militant. They often employed violent tactics and called for fundamental social transformation rather than cooperation with the state. To be sure, the ruling Gaullist coalition adopted some piecemeal measures, such as regulating the expansion of supermarkets and relaxing tax collection efforts, but French small-business policy never approached the comprehensiveness of Japanese measures. Consequently the French conservatives failed to secure the political loyalty of small shopkeepers and artisans, many of whom helped to bring the Socialists to power in 1981.[31]

ORGANIZED LABOR

The process of negotiating a social contract between organized labor and the conservative establishment was more complex than in the case of small business. Several of the obstacles that stood in the way of compacts in the postwar era had their origins in the prewar and wartime experiences.[32] Japanese workers were less successful in political mobilization than were the urban petite bourgeoisie before 1945. Whereas most small-scale merchants and manufacturers affiliated with at least one business association, fewer than 8 percent of industrial workers belonged to unions at their peak in 1931. Second, differences in ideology and tactics fragmented the union movement throughout the prewar and most of the postwar periods. During the mid-1920s the labor movement broke into a social-democratic right wing, a left-center faction, and a pro-Communist left wing. Finally, organized workers suffered the stigma of social outsiders. The police readily suppressed workers who crossed the murky line between legitimate trade union activity and political radicalism. In contrast, small-business associations in the 1930s played on sentiments within the state and established parties that petty entrepreneurs constituted "the backbone of the nation" (*kokka no chūken*).

These factors did not prevent the emergence of accommodative sentiments within the labor movement, bureaucracy, and bourgeois parties during the interwar years, but they did impose serious constraints. When the Kenseikai (later the Minseitō) party and officials in the government's Social Bureau endeavored to enact a labor union law and other labor legislation during the 1920s, they were supported by self-styled "realists" in Sōdōmei (General Federation of Labor). However, a determined lobbying campaign by big and small businesses alike

30. Linda Weiss, "The Italian State and Small Business," *European Journal of Sociology* 25, no. 2 (1984): 214–41.

31. Eatwell, "Poujadism"; John T. S. Keeler, "Corporatist Decentralization and Commercial Modernization in France: The Royer Law's Impact on Shopkeepers, Supermarkets and the State," in *Socialism, the State and Public Policy in France*, ed. Philip G. Cerny and Martin A. Schain (New York: Methuen, 1985), 265–91.

32. See Garon, *State*, esp. 230–32.

defeated the Minseitō's union bill in 1931, bringing a halt to the party's interest in an alliance with the working class. Two years later the "realistic" leaders of the declining labor movement offered the government a nascent social compact whereby the unions would agree to the state arbitration of any labor dispute in exchange for the legal recognition of unions and the governmental regulation of employers.[33] It soon became apparent that state officials were not bargaining in good faith. The bureaucrats coaxed and coerced the unions into dissolving themselves between 1938 and 1940, reorganizing the nation's workers into a state-run labor front.

The fate of the prewar unions discredited the accommodative strategy in the eyes of many left-wing labor organizers after 1945. Reinvigorated by active support from American occupation authorities, the labor union movement organized nearly five million workers by December 1946. The Communist Party and left-wing Socialists dominated the largest federation, Sanbetsu (Japanese Congress of Industrial Organizations), and Sanbetsu's projected general strike for 1 February 1947 aimed at toppling the conservative Yoshida cabinet. However, General Douglas MacArthur foreclosed the possibility of Communist participation in the government by banning the strike.

MacArthur's actions strengthened the hand of the prewar "realists" in the right wing of the labor movement. Having reestablished Sōdōmei in 1945, they sought to form a centrist coalition government consisting of the Japan Socialist Party (JSP) and one or more of the bourgeois parties. Between 1946 and 1949 no one party commanded a parliamentary majority, and the conservative forces were divided among two major parties and several smaller groups. Although the bourgeois parties could have united to form a government, leaders from each of the two major parties made several attempts to forge coalitions with moderate Socialists and Sōdōmei officials. They did so not only to neutralize the rival bourgeois party but also to secure the cooperation of the labor movement in the painful process of reconstruction while isolating Communist influence within the unions.[34] In December 1946 Sōdōmei concluded an agreement with the Keizai Dōyūkai, a reformist business group with close ties to the bourgeois politicians who would participate in the coalition Katayama and Ashida cabinets. The labor federation pledged to support management's authority in the enterprise as well as the government's Priority Production Plan for economic reconstruction. In return the Dōyūkai committed itself to respecting organized labor's basic rights and the principle of "high wages" tied to both the cost of living and productivity increases.[35]

The opportunity for institutionalizing such a social contract with the government came in 1947 and 1948, when the JSP and prominent labor leaders entered

---

33. Ibid., 194.

34. Ibid., 243–44, 247.

35. Joe Moore, *Japanese Workers and the Struggle for Power, 1945–1947* (Madison: University of Wisconsin Press, 1983), 226–27.

the two coalition cabinets. Whereas the antilabor Yoshida government had suffered from unprecedented labor unrest, the Socialist-led Katayama cabinet initially enjoyed a period of industrial peace. Just as the centrist coalition created the Small and Medium Enterprises Agency for small business, the Katayama cabinet in 1947 established the Labor Ministry as a "service ministry for workers." The Labor Ministry instituted the Central Labor Standards Deliberative Council and the Central Employment Security Deliberative Council, and for the first time union representatives sat on important policy-making committees of the government in numbers equal to those of employers.[36]

By 1949, however, it was clear that labor's right wing had failed to win a viable social contract. Various developments had discredited the centrist experiment. The right-wing Socialists in the Katayama cabinet lacked control over the labor movement sufficient to implement various austerity measures over the protests of Sanbetsu and left-wing Socialists. Similarly, business interests within their coalition partner, the Democratic Party, vehemently opposed Katayama's proposal for the state management of the coal industry.[37] The generally antilabor Liberal Party won an overwhelming majority in the lower-house election of January 1949, accelerating the consolidation of the conservative forces.

The new Yoshida government proceeded to weaken many of the protections guaranteed by the 1945 Trade Union Law. Notably, the cabinet sponsored legislation that prevented workers in public enterprises from striking and that deprived civil servants of the rights both to strike and to bargain collectively. In the case of private enterprises the newly formed Nikkeiren (Japan Federation of Employers' Associations) coordinated a nationwide campaign to roll back the unions' gains of the early postwar years. Supported by the Americans, the Yoshida government carried out the Red purge in 1950, resulting in the dismissal of thousands of alleged Communists in the public and private sectors. Employers took advantage of the purge to encourage the formation of more cooperative "second unions."[38]

The conservative onslaught of 1949–50 temporarily slammed the door on any meaningful compromise between the state and organized labor. The discriminatory restrictions on the rights of public employees transformed the animosity between the ruling party and the radicalized public-sector unions into a long-lived feature of the postwar order. Occupation officials attempted in 1950 to create a moderate labor movement in the form of Sōhyō (General Council of Japanese Trade Unions), but left-wing Socialists quickly dominated the new labor organization.

Although most accounts highlight the acute polarization between the Liberal

---

36. Gyōsei Kanrichō, ed., *Shingikai sōran* (Tokyo: Ōkurashō Insatsukyoku, 1979), 394–97, 411–15.

37. Cole et al., *Socialist Parties in Postwar Japan*, 19–20; Shinobu, *Sengo Nihon seiji shi* 3:643–45.

38. Andrew Gordon, *The Evolution of Labor Relations in Modern Japan: Heavy Industry, 1853–1955* (Cambridge: Harvard Council on East Asian Studies, 1985), 337, 369–72; Garon, *State*, 239–40; see also Gordon's essay in this volume.

Democratic Party and the Japan Socialist Party after 1955, the middle to late 1950s also witnessed a second, more successful effort by the labor movement's right wing to negotiate a social contract. In 1954 Sōdōmei leaders cofounded Zenrō Kaigi (All-Japan Labor Union Congress) with several other unions that had earlier left Sōhyō in protest of the latter's emphasis on political strikes. While Sōhyō maintained its position as the largest national center, Zenrō made steady gains in Japan's expanding heavy industrial sector. Zenrō's share of organized labor grew from 9.8 percent to 13.3 percent between 1954 and 1961, whereas Sōhyō's declined from 49.4 percent to 47.5 percent.[39] In terms of the overall political system the appearance of Zenrō should be considered more seriously by those who speak of a polarized 1955 System. The Right and Left Socialist parties may have united in 1955, but Zenrō's refusal to merge with Sōhyō resulted in a growing centrist labor movement that stood between the LDP and the Left.

As moderate labor groups were emerging, the major business associations and the government embarked in 1954–55 on a drive to secure the cooperation of workers and labor unions in order to raise productivity and restrain inflationary wage increases. They sought to roll back Sōhyō's "base-up" demands for substantial wage hikes aimed at creating "living wages." In March 1955 MITI established the Japan Productivity Center as part of the new official policy. The founding businessmen and bureaucrats had not originally envisioned a major role for organized labor in the productivity center, yet they soon decided to invite the nation's labor groups to participate in the center alongside business representatives and academic experts. Sōhyō denounced the productivity drive as a stratagem to cut wages, dismiss workers, and reduce unions to the status of the wartime industrial patriotic associations.[40] In contrast, Sōdōmei and later Zenrō agreed to participate in the productivity center and the enterprise-level productivity drive, but only after stipulating a number of conditions.

Sōdōmei took a particularly contractual approach, insisting that the productivity center's directors recognize "eight principles." Sōdōmei pledged to support the campaign if increased productivity led to higher wages, better working conditions, expanded employment, lower prices, and the "independence of the Japanese economy and an improved standard of living for the people." Conversely, the labor federation vowed to resist employers' efforts to use the productivity drive to amass profits at the expense of exploiting labor, dismissing workers, and squeezing out small firms. Invoking what became the central slogan of its successor, Dōmei, in the 1960s, Sōdōmei called for "industrial democracy" in the process of boosting productivity. By this term it meant the formation of labor-management joint consultation committees at the enterprise, trade and industrial, and national levels. The labor organization further appealed to the government for programs to guarantee full employment and establish a minimum wage. Eager to involve

39. Kitagawa Ryūkichi et al., "Sōhyō to Zenrō," *Chūō kōron* 75 (Apr. 1960): 104–5.

40. Hyōdō Tsutomu, "Rōdō kumiai undō hatten," in *Iwanami kōza: Nihon rekishi* (Tokyo: Iwanami Shoten, 1977) 23:109–10, 113–15; see also Gordon's essay in this volume.

the labor moderates, the leaders of the Japan Productivity Center—with a representative of Nikkeiren looking on—signed an agreement with Sōdōmei's chairman accepting the "eight principles."[41]

Japanese labor scholars generally believe that Sōdōmei and Zenrō gave up the power to maintain adequate working conditions in many instances while failing to secure labor-management consultation in any real sense.[42] Yet as Sōdōmei predicted, sharp gains in productivity after 1955 did substantially raise real wages and expand employment. Moreover, the rapid spread of joint consultation bodies at the enterprise level significantly involved union leaders in the daily problems of companies.[43] According to one former Labor Ministry official, such Zenrō unions as the textile workers' federation (Zensen Dōmei) traded their support of the productivity drive for successful industrywide negotiations for a shorter working week in 1957. The Kishi government also sponsored the first minimum wage law in 1957, though it fell somewhat short of Zenrō's proposal.[44]

Whatever the judgment, the compact of 1955 was notable for its exclusion of Sōhyō and the public-sector unions. The Liberal Democratic Party's governments continued to isolate Sōhyō even as the latter abandoned its focus on Marxist political struggle in preference for economic unionism during the mid-1950s. The conservatives further refused to recognize Sōhyō's federations as negotiating agents in the annual spring offensives (*shuntō*), which Sōhyō first coordinated in 1955. The Kishi cabinet similarly resisted international and domestic calls to remove the provocative restrictions on public employees' right to strike.[45]

Developments in the early 1960s transformed the nascent social contract of 1955 into a pattern of interaction between the private-sector unions and the conservative coalition that essentially continued into the 1990s. In addition to employers and Labor Ministry officials the LDP took several steps to accommodate the labor movement. Ikeda Hayato's cabinet (1960–64) abandoned Prime Minister Kishi's confrontational tactics against the JSP and Sōhyō, which had culminated in the tumultuous events surrounding the revision of the U.S.-Japan Security Treaty in 1960. No event forced a change in the LDP's labor policy more than the heated labor dispute at Mitsui's Miike Coal Mine in 1959–60. As oil replaced coal as Japan's primary energy source, MITI and the mine owners formulated plans to reduce the labor force and rationalize production. The Sōhyō-backed miners' union at Miike resisted the massive dismissals, and management responded with a lockout in January 1960. In the most dramatic con-

41. Sōdōmei gojūnen shi kankō iinkai, ed., *Sōdōmei gojūnen shi* (Tokyo: Kōyōsha, 1968) 3:1053–60.

42. Hyōdō, "Rōdō kumiai undō hatten," 114.

43. Daniel M. Fuchs, "Labor Incorporation into the Japanese Political Economy" (senior thesis, Princeton University, 1987), chaps. 2–3; Ichirō Nakayama, *Industrialization and Labor-Management Relations in Japan* (Tokyo: Japan Institute of Labor, 1975), 184–85, 363–65, 372.

44. Motoi Hisashi, *Nihon rōdō undō shi* (Tokyo: Rōmu Gyōsei Kenkyūjo, 1983), 312, 338–39.

45. Ehud Harari, *The Politics of Labor Legislation in Japan* (Berkeley and Los Angeles: University of California Press, 1973), 84–89.

frontation in postwar Japanese labor history, twenty thousand Sōhyō activists joined the strikers to face ten thousand police in early July. At the initiative of the progressive labor minister Ishida Hirohide, the Central Labor Relations Commission mediated, and the dispute ended in September. The commission upheld the company's reductions in personnel, yet Mitsui was compelled to retract the discriminatory dismissals of militant unionists, to raise wages, and to guarantee adequate welfare for the workers.[46]

Although Japanese labor historians generally view the outcome of the Miike dispute as marking the death of a truly autonomous labor movement in the postwar era, the lessons of Miike prompted the government to play a much more active role in maintaining employment. The state assisted in retraining the laid-off miners, and in the words of Koji Taira and Solomon Levine, "The experience of Miike, although never repeated, remained a vivid reminder of the likelihood of forceful labor protest if significant changes were introduced without joint planning and consultation well in advance."[47] On the legislative front the Labor Ministry and the LDP cooperated to win the enactment of a number of laws designed to assist workers in moving into rapidly expanding sectors of the economy. The 1963 revision of the Unemployment Insurance Law granted financial support for training technical workers, subsidized housing to encourage workers to move to new jobs, and expanded employment programs for workers aged forty-five years or older.[48]

Electoral considerations also influenced the LDP's newly favorable attitudes toward labor issues and the labor movement. As chair of the Research Committee on the Organization of the LDP, the party's progressive Miki Takeo declared in 1963 that "a party that makes workers its enemy has no future." That same year Ishida Hirohide, who served four times as labor minister in the postwar years, warned that the LDP would lose its parliamentary majority as a result of rapid urbanization and industrialization unless the party appealed to wage earners.[49] In 1966 the LDP adopted Ishida's proposed "Labor Charter," which committed the ruling party to full employment, improved working conditions, and the promotion of social security.[50]

46. Rōsei Kenkyūkai, ed., *Ishida rōsei: Sono sokuseki to tenbō* (Tokyo: Rōmu Gyōsei Kenkyūjō, 1978), 147–63, 167–97; Shimizu Shinzō, "Miike sōgi shōron," in his *Sengo rōdō kumiai undō shiron* (Tokyo: Nihon Hyōronsha, 1982), 447–70.

47. Koji Taira and Solomon B. Levine, "Japan's Industrial Relations: A Social Compact Emerges," in *Industrial Relations in a Decade of Economic Change*, ed. Hervey Juris, Mark Thompson, and Wilbur Daniels (Madison: Industrial Relations Research Association, 1985), 259; for a different evaluation, see Gordon's essay in this volume.

48. Rōdōshō, ed., *Rōdōshō nijūgonen shi* (Tokyo: Rōdō Gyōsei Chōsa Kenkyūkai, 1973), 285–86, 401–13; Aramata Shigeo, Ogoshi Yanosuke, Nakahara Koji, and Mima Takato, *Shakai seisaku (1) Riron to rekishi* (Tokyo: Yūhikaku, 1979), 122–25, 187–88.

49. Miki Takeo, "Jimintō no kindaika o kō omou," *Seikai ōrai* 29 (Apr. 1963): 55–56; Ishida Hirohide, "Hoshutō no bijion," *Chūō kōron* 78 (Jan. 1963): 88–97.

50. Rōsei Kenkyūkai, *Ishida rōsei*, 289–331.

Far from a unilateral effort to co-opt the programs of the Left, the LDP's new labor policy relied heavily on negotiation with the labor unions and socialist parties. The government institutionalized several forums for tripartite deliberations on labor policy during the late 1950s and 1960s. Comprised of equal numbers of labor and employer representatives, the Labor Ministry's many deliberative and advisory councils proved crucial to devising the decade's employment programs and the important 1968 revision of the Minimum Wage Law.[51] Though occupying fewer seats than business representatives, four labor members also gained a voice in industrial policy on MITI's authoritative Industrial Council (established 1964). In 1970 the Labor Ministry sponsored the formation of the Industry and Labor Conference (Sangyō Rōdō Konwakai), consisting of influential labor leaders, employers, and government officials. The conference became the central forum for tripartite consultation on wage determination in the mid-1970s.[52]

The steady expansion of the moderate private-sector unions furthered labor's incorporation into the policy-making process. Politically Sōdōmei and Zenrō's hostility toward Sōhyō resulted in the second schism in the Socialist Party and the founding of the reformist Democratic Socialist Party in 1960. The DSP in turn encouraged the merger of Sōdōmei and Zenrō into Dōmei in 1964. Dōmei surpassed Sōhyō in members from private enterprises in 1967.[53] Although the DSP failed to overtake the JSP as the leading socialist party, it generally played a more active role in advancing labor and welfare legislation in the deliberative councils and parliamentary committees. In 1974 the DSP was primarily responsible for the enactment of the innovative Employment Insurance Law, by which the state subsidized employers to maintain workers.[54]

The government also adopted measures to accommodate Sōhyō as part of its new labor policy. Economic growth in the 1960s provided an excellent opportunity to blunt Sōhyō's militancy with sizable wage increases. In a historic meeting with Sōhyō's chair Ōta Kaoru in 1964, Prime Minister Ikeda agreed to raise the wages of public employees by an amount roughly equivalent to that negotiated by the private-sector unions in the spring offensive. The government recognized the spring offensive not so much because of Sōhyō's strength but because of the growing domination of the joint struggle by pragmatic private-sector unions, including Dōmei's affiliates. Leading private-sector unions from all four national labor centers founded the moderate International Metalworkers Federation-

51. In addition to the councils established under the Katayama cabinet, there were the Labor Problems Roundtable Conference (1955), Employment Deliberative Council (1957), Central Vocational Training Deliberative Council (1958), Central Minimum Wage Deliberative Council (1959), and Labor Problems Discussion Group (1961). Gyōsei Kanrichō, ed., *Shingikai sōran*, 290–94, 392–421; cf. Pempel and Tsunekawa, "Corporatism Without Labor?" 262.

52. Taira and Levine, "Japan's Industrial Relations," 259–60.

53. *Nihon kin-gendai shi jiten*, 1978 ed., s.v. "Zen Nihon Rōdō Sōdōmei," by Miyata Eijirō.

54. Mochizuki, "Managing and Influencing," 348–53; Fujinawa Masakatsu, *Nihon no saitei chingin* (Tokyo: Nikkan Rōdō Tsūshinsha, 1972), 162–73.

Japan Council (IMF-JC) in 1964. Led by Sōhyō's unusually accommodative steelworkers' federation (Tekkō Rōren), the IMF-JC unions emerged as the national pattern setters in the coordinated wage negotiations of the spring offensives of the latter half of the 1960s.[55]

During the early 1970s the evolving patterns of negotiation among government, business, and organized labor became explicit in response to a shared sense of economic crisis. The oil shock of 1973 followed the rapid appreciation of the yen and coincided with the Americans' growing demands for open Japanese markets in capital and foreign trade. In an effort to stay ahead of soaring inflation, the unions won an average wage increase of 32.9 percent in the 1974 spring offensive, prompting LDP leaders and bureaucrats to urge wage restraint to maintain Japanese competitiveness in world markets.

In what some have called the beginnings of a "Japanese-style incomes policy," Dōmei and the IMF-JC agreed to the government's call for lower wage demands. The chair of Dōmei, Amaike Seiji, announced in autumn 1974 that "if the government is sincere in its wish to stabilize prices and assist the socially disadvantaged, and management agrees to cooperate with such policies, labor is also willing to refrain from demanding the real wage increases to which workers are entitled as a result of economic growth."[56] The unions accepted a wage hike of only 13.1 percent, and the annual average wage increase fell thereafter, stabilizing at a low level during the 1980s.[57] Amaike, who as a young Sōdōmei official had attended the signing of the pact with the Japan Productivity Center in 1955, formally committed Dōmei to "social contractual methods" in January 1976. He proposed that labor, business, and government agree to expand the "system of participation for labor unions at the national, industrial, and enterprise levels" to pursue "full employment, price stability, improvements in the living standards and welfare of the people." Tekkō Rōren, the steelworkers' federation, called on the government to accept a similar "social contract" the following year.[58]

To what extent did each side benefit from the social contract of the mid-1970s? The gains for the conservative coalition were apparent. The government and business successfully reduced Japan's inflation rate to the lowest among advanced industrial nations by 1983. The conservatives also manipulated their alliances with the private-sector unions to hasten the decline of Sōhyō. Backed by the private-sector unions, the LDP government decimated Sōhyō's large public-sector unions through privatization.[59] The LDP's efforts since the early 1960s to expand its electoral base among workers, both unionized and unorganized, also paid off.

55. Shimizu Shinzō, "Sōhyō sanjūnen no baransu shiito" and "Sengo rōdō kumiai undō shi josetsu," in Shimizu, *Sengo rōdō kumiai undō shiron*, 20–22, 341.

56. *Japan Labor Bulletin* 11 (Nov. 1974): 3; Fuchs, "Labor Incorporation," 75.

57. For accounts of the 1975 spring offensive, see Taira and Levine, "Japan's Industrial Relations"; Shinkawa Toshimitsu, "1975 nen shuntō to keizai kiki kanri," in *Nihon seiji no sōten*, ed. Ōtake Hideo (Tokyo: San-ichi Shobō, 1984), 189–232.

58. Motoi, *Nihon rōdō undo shi*, 860–61.

59. See Fuchs, "Labor Incorporation," chap. 4.

According to one public opinion poll, support for the LDP among industrial workers rose from 20 percent in August 1965 to 50 percent in August 1986, while combined support for the JSP and DSP declined from 59 percent to 26 percent.[60]

Nonetheless, like the small-business sector, organized labor could claim a number of gains in forcing government and big business to consider the welfare of its members in the process of economic restructuring. The labor movement significantly expanded its role in policy-making and won some of the world's strongest employment-maintenance programs. In addition to the 1974 Employment Insurance Law the DSP provided the initiative in 1977 behind the enactment of both the Temporary Measures for Workers Displaced from Specific Depressed Areas and the Temporary Relief Law for Workers Displaced from Specific Depressed Industries. The latter law required employers in depressed industries to devise plans to help displaced workers find new jobs, and the employer was further "required to solicit the opinions of the representative labor unions and employee representatives on the proposed plan."[61] These laws institutionalized arrangements begun in the 1960s, when Dōmei and the IMF-JC unions established bodies for industrywide joint consultation to devise social policies for workers in depressed industries such as shipbuilding. The LDP government also came forth with increased social security benefits in 1973, and its achievement in reducing inflation unquestionably safeguarded many jobs and maintained real wages.[62]

Moreover, the social contract of the 1970s accelerated the unification of the private-sector unions into an increasingly active lobbying group for labor legislation and more favorable macroeconomic policies. In 1976 the IMF-JC unions founded the Trade Union Council for Policy Promotion, which began meeting regularly with LDP representatives and officials of the various ministries. The council expanded into the All-Japan Council of Private-Sector Labor Organizations (Zenmin Rōkyō) in 1982. Zenmin Rōkyō steadily regularized its meetings with the Labor Ministry, MITI, the Economic Planning Agency, and the LDP.[63] In November 1987 three of the four national centers—Dōmei, Chūritsu Rōren, and Shinsanbetsu—dissolved themselves, and their private-sector unions joined counterparts in Sōhyō to form the National Federation of Private-Sector Trade Unions (Rengō). When the public-sector unions entered Rengō two years later, the bulk of the Japanese labor movement became unified for the first time in its history. Some observers expected the new labor federation to play a pivotal role in forging a center-left political coalition as an alternative to conservative rule.

Relative to the successes of the small-business sector, however, labor's postwar

60. Asahi Shinbunsha Yoron Chōsashitsu, ed., *Nihonjin no seiji ishiki* (Tokyo: Asahi Shinbunsha, 1976), 122; Asahi Shinbunsha Yoron Chōsashitsu, ed., *Yoron chōsashitsuhō*, no. 16 (Jan. 1988): 5, 7, 11.

61. Kazutoshi Koshiro, "Job Security: Redundancy Arrangements and Practices in Japan," *Ekonomia* 89 (June 1986): 46.

62. Taira and Levine, "Japan's Industrial Relations," 252, 264.

63. Tsujinaka Yutaka, "Rōdōkai no saihen to hachijūroku nen taisei no imi," *Revaiasan* 1 (1987): 54–55.

social contracts have been woefully incomplete in their coverage. The major private-sector unions have done little since the occupation to protect the interests of women, temporary workers, and those employed in smaller firms. Moreover, total union membership plummeted from 55.8 percent of the labor force in 1947 to 24 percent in June 1992. It is hardly surprising that many Japanese accused the moderate unions of giving up too much for too little.[64]

Yet given the organizational weaknesses and ideological divisions of the Japanese labor movement, one must consider the viability and potential rewards of alternative strategies. A comparison with the French and Italian cases is instructive.[65] In both European nations organized labor similarly suffered from low rates of unionization and ideological conflict. But in postwar France the Communist-dominated labor movement rejected any cooperation with the state for the purposes of managing the national economy and negotiating a social contract. Moreover, in its hostility toward organized labor the state presented few opportunities for workers to advance economic and social reforms until François Mitterand's election as president in 1981. Although the Communists also emerged as a potent force in Italy, the unions gradually developed some autonomy from political parties to advance workers' interests. Consequently, like organized labor in Japan, Italian unions were willing to bargain with the state for favorable economic and social policies. The major difference between Italy and Japan lies at the level of party politics. In Italy labor's influence in policy-making was reinforced by center-left coalitions after 1963. In Japan the LDP formed ad hoc legislative coalitions with the Democratic Socialists and the Socialists to manage the Diet, yet the LDP's electoral power precluded the need to bring either labor-based party into the cabinet.

Unions in Japan were, of course, less able to shape public policies than were unions in such countries as Britain, West Germany, and Sweden, where organized labor was more united, unionization rates were higher, and social-democratic parties enjoyed lengthy periods in power.[66] Nevertheless, despite their organizational deficiencies and inability to forge a cross-class alliance necessary to establish a social-democratic government, Japanese unions used their market power to avoid political exclusion. As the spokespersons for long-term blue-collar workers, the labor movement's mainstream became increasingly effective from the mid-1950s through the 1980s.

CONCLUSION

By examining the cases of small business and the labor movement from a historical perspective, we seek to revise prevailing views that attribute the LDP's remark-

64. Shinkawa, "1975 nen shuntō," 223.

65. For a comparison of the Italian and French labor movements, see Lange, Ross, and Vannicelli, *Unions, Change, and Crisis.*

66. Peter Gourevitch et al., *Unions and Economic Crisis: Britain, West Germany, and Sweden* (London: Allen and Unwin, 1984).

able persistence to "creative conservatism"—that is, the seemingly unfailing ability of the ruling party, bureaucrats, and big business to promote popular policies from above, thus stealing the thunder of the opposition parties.[67] Instead, as we demonstrate, small-business assocations and labor organizations often advanced vigorous and autonomous demands that reshaped the programs of the conservative coalition.

This pattern of pressures *from below* prompting state responses had its roots in prewar Japan. Popular agitation from the early movements representing small businesses and, to a lesser extent, workers persuaded government officials to adopt some accommodative policies in order to preserve social order. The major difference between the prewar and postwar cases concerns the role of political parties. To be sure, various groups within the prewar bourgeois parties championed the interests of small businesses and advocated reformist measures for labor. During the 1930s, however, the decline of party power decisively shifted the locus of policy innovation to the state bureaucracy. In this context the exchanges negotiated between social groups and the state tended to be either fragile or skewed in favor of technocratic control.

The postwar constitutional reforms that established popular sovereignty and the primacy of the Diet and electoral politics altered this pattern of interest-group politics. Party politicians in the conservative camp demonstrated acute sensitivity to electoral trends in order to preserve their political dominance. Employing their parliamentary power, they compelled reluctant bureaucrats to accept compensatory measures for small businesses.[68] By the early 1960s the Liberal Democratic Party had consolidated its core social coalition of the self-employed (small-business proprietors and farmers). The party thereafter adapted its basic policies to sustain this coalition. Conservative politicians further collaborated with reform-minded bureaucrats in the Ministries of Labor and of Health and Welfare to make the private-sector labor movement a partner in the nation's economic strategy and to broaden the LDP's electoral base among wage earners.

The social contract became a central feature in the Japanese conception of democracy in the postwar era. That is, the public accepted the hegemony of the conservative coalition only as long as it seriously negotiated to accommodate the interests of various social organizations and as long as the pain of economic readjustments appeared to be shared equitably throughout society. This is not to say that the postwar social contracts were negotiated along lines inconsistent with the overall objectives of the conservative leadership. The subsidies, tax breaks, and protectionist regulations for small business did not undermine the role of big business in Japan's economic recovery and subsequent industrial development. Moreover, the preservation of a dynamic small-business sector provided the large firms with flexibility in adapting to economic changes. As for the unions, the

67. See T. J. Pempel, *Policy and Politics in Japan: Creative Conservatism* (Philadelphia: Temple University Press, 1982).

68. See Calder, *Crisis and Compensation*, 20–26.

conservatives unquestionably worked to divide organized labor and to foster a labor movement that supported a capitalist system geared toward higher levels of productivity and rapid growth. The postwar Japanese political order may be defined as democratic, but it nonetheless has been a highly managed form of democracy.

The grand social coalition of the self-employed and wage earners that was forged by the LDP appeared to be at a crossroads in 1990. Domestic and international developments served to exacerbate conflicts among elements in the coalition. Concerns about an impending fiscal crisis caused by the growing costs of welfare programs led the government to enact the highly unpopular consumption tax in 1988. The conservatives fell back on one of their oldest social contracts in granting remarkable concessions to small businesses, but at the cost of alienating supporters among consumers, workers, and salaried employees. Confronted by persistently large trade imbalances the United States intensified its efforts to open Japanese markets to foreign products. In response, the government liberalized the beef and citrus trade, although the move angered Japanese farmers. Under American pressure the conservatives further sought to streamline the distribution system and deregulate the retail sector, yet that policy, they feared, would also trigger protests from shopkeepers and wholesalers.

At the beginning of the 1990s the LDP faced two unattractive alternatives. It might jettison its social contract with the self-employed, definitively shifting its core social base away from farmers and small businesses to wage earners and consumers. Or the ruling party might opt for the risky strategy of ignoring international pressures in order to satisfy the terms of all of its social contracts. The LDP's difficulties gave the opposition parties an opportunity to construct a center-left coalition and defeat the conservatives after four decades of power. Whatever the outcome at the level of party politics, the realities of Japanese political economy seemed likely to demand a fundamental renegotiation of the postwar social contracts.

CHAPTER SEVEN

Dialectics of Economic Growth, National Power, and Distributive Struggles

Koji Taira

Long-term economic statistics suggest that somewhere in the early 1970s there was a turning point in postwar Japan's rate and style of economic growth.[1] The pre-1970s "miracle growth" at a rate exceeding 10 percent per annum turned into low growth at 5 percent or so in subsequent years.[2] In the late 1960s and early 1970s Japan experienced a variety of social protest movements: environmentalists, welfare rightists, citizens, workers, students, disadvantaged groups, and so on. International affairs (the Vietnam War, Nixon shocks, floating exchange rates, oil shocks) aggravated Japan's domestic problems. The ruling coalition of the business community, the LDP, and the state bureaucracy, frightened by the deepening crisis, made substantial concessions to some of the protest groups, with a lasting impact on the social distribution of national economic output.

All along, the ruling coalition demonstrated a surprising degree of political pragmatism and resilience. In the 1980s the newly consolidated Japan regained self-confidence and embarked on internationalization and Great Power diplomacy on the strength of its considerable economic weight in the world economy. In 1989–90 two new political developments appeared to hold back Japan's march

1. The most easily accessible general statistical source book is the bilingual *Statistical Yearbook of Japan* (*Nihon tōkei nenkan*), annually published by the Statistics Bureau of the Management and Coordination Agency (formerly the Prime Minister's Secretariat). A reduced form of this compendium is the annual *Nihon no tōkei* (Statistics of Japan) by the same office. The Statistics Bureau also publishes a handbook-style edition of economic statistics, *Keizai tōkei yōran* (Abstracts of economic statistics). For further information on statistical sources, see Horioka's essay in this volume.

2. In hindsight the decline in rates of economic growth in the 1970s was theoretically predictable within the framework of "long swings" and neoclassical economic analysis. In fact, before practically anyone was sure that the stage of "miracle growth" was over, a book published in 1973 predicted its end: see Kazushi Ohkawa and Henry Rosovsky, *Japanese Economic Growth* (Stanford: Stanford University Press, 1973).

toward world hegemony. The Recruit scandal revealed a moral hazard of the ruling coalition. As a result, the 1989 Upper House election deprived the LDP of its traditional majority, which demonstrated people's dissatisfaction with LDP leadership. The 1990 Lower House election allowed a substantial increase in the seats going to the Socialist Party, although the LDP still retained a majority. The ruling coalition had faced and overcome similar crises before, only to emerge stronger both domestically and internationally. Since 1990, although more moral, financial, and political scandals involving LDP politicians have broken out in a bewildering succession, the opposition parties have also failed to capitalize on their 1989–90 political gains or on the weaknesses of their foes.

Today Japan's aggregate economic statistics (the "fundamentals" of national power) are impressive.[3] Japan's per capita GNP surpasses that of the United States. Multiplied by a relatively large population, about one-half that of the United States, Japan's GNP accounts for more than 10 percent of the world's. Japan now is the biggest net creditor nation and the biggest donor nation of economic aid to less developed countries. Japan's comparative edge over the United States in growth performance will narrow the influence gap between the two countries in relation to the rest of the world.

The rise of Japan relative to the United States has generated an imaginative rhetoric: a Pax Nipponica replacing the Pax Americana, which had itself replaced the Pax Britannica. Historicist imagination in this vein has become intellectually popular on both sides of the Pacific.[4] Concerns over the fate of the United States have also spawned extensive reflections on the rise and fall of nations.[5] In these works, Japan is generally acknowledged as heir apparent to the United States. Even more audaciously, the rise of Japan is set in a grandiose Toynbeean framework of the rise and fall of civilizations, units of analysis larger than nation-states. Japan's rise is seen as a herald for Asia's rise in parallel to the decline of the West.

Some scholars probe the ethos underlying national competence; for example, Confucianism is seen as a foundation of the superior economic performance of Japan and some other Asian countries, again implying a conflict of civilizations between Confucian Asia and Christian West.[6] Some Japanese scholars more explicitly elevate Japan to the status of a civilization sui generis that can stand

---

3. For a quick international statistical comparison, see the annual *World Development Report* by the World Bank.

4. Shinohara Miyohei, *Keizai taikoku no seisui* (Tokyo: Tōyō Keizai Shinpōsha, 1982); Ezra Vogel, "Pax Nipponica?" *Foreign Affairs* 64, no. 4 (Spring 1986): 752–67.

5. Mancur Olson, *The Rise and Decline of Nations: Economic Growth, Stagflation, and Social Rigidities* (New Haven: Yale University Press, 1982); Paul Kennedy, *The Rise and Fall of the Great Powers: Economic Change and Military Conflict from 1500 to 2000* (New York: Random, 1987); Immanuel Wallerstein, *The Politics of the World Economy* (London: Cambridge University Press, 1984).

6. R. P. Dore, *Taking Japan Seriously* (Stanford: Stanford University Press, 1988); Morishima Michio, *Why Has Japan "Succeeded"?* (London: Cambridge University Press, 1982).

comparison with all of Western civilization, or with the entire world.[7] As "History" comes to an end, Japan rises to the position of America's number one adversary in the eyes of many Americans.[8]

These unending rhetorical excesses erode scholarly objectivity and neutrality and stimulate quarrels based on nationalistic preferences. "Japanese studies" ceases to be a field for scholarly endeavors and changes into a debating arena for "learn from Japan" advocates, post-cold-war strategists, conventional Japanophiles, and revisionist Japanophobes. This climate also discourages a critical examination of events and problems at subnational levels: that is, what has happened to ordinary people in the course of Japan's postwar economic growth and what may happen to them again as Japan continues to use economic growth as a major policy instrument for the glorification and hegemonization of Japan. A more modest level of analysis is called for.

When attention is focused on the anatomy of economic growth, one may see entirely different problems, and these problems may reduce much of the euphoria (or paranoia, as the case may be) about Japan's growth and its consequences. Indeed, during the period of the most miraculous growth, 1953–73, some aspects of economic activities can only be described as unjustified costs imposed on the general public, especially on its relatively defenseless members. Producers and the government evaded these costs, thus enabling themselves to concentrate resources in directly productive activities and to generate the miracle growth of GNP.

In this chapter I review some of the intertwining positive and negative aspects of Japan's postwar economic growth. At first there was the consensus that economic recovery and growth were the overriding national objective. Japan's success in the pursuit of this objective soon became a mixed blessing when it was realized that many desirable things—the environment, amenities of life, price stability, and care for the sick and disadvantaged—were extensively damaged or jeopardized. People reacted to the GNP-first policy with widespread, often violent protests. The clashes of the costs and benefits of rapid growth produced a solution that included new regulations for business, compensations for damages, and improved social security. Opinion leaders elaborated a superordinate ideology to eliminate conflict from Japanese society. The theme of the new ideology was that "we" are all equally middle-class and uniquely Japanese. In the meantime Japan became a world-class economic power, implying a new role in world affairs. The Japanese state's perception of its role in the world with signs of hegemonic aspirations induced dissent at home and misgivings abroad.

7. Murakami Yasusuke, "*Ie* Society as a Pattern of Civilization," *Journal of Japanese Studies* 10, no. 2 (Summer 1984): 301–50; Umesao Tadao, Harumi Befu, and Josef Kreiner, eds., *Japanese Civilization in the Modern World* (Osaka: National Museum of Ethnology, 1984).

8. Francis Fukuyama, "The End of History." *National Interest*, no. 16 (Summer 1989): 3–18; Chalmers Johnson, "Their Behavior, Our Policy," *National Interest*, no. 17 (Fall 1989): 17–27.

Thus, in the 1980s Japan began a new round of dialectic dynamics on a larger scale.

THE POINT OF DEPARTURE: GNP GROWTH AS A NATIONAL OBJECTIVE

The magic of GNP, first as a national policy instrument and then as a national objective, is eloquently pointed out by John Kenneth Galbraith, who reminisces that "in the United States it [GNP] came into prominence in the early nineteen-forties" and was used for the formulation of the "Victory Program for the production of aircraft and other armament." Galbraith believes that without that emphasis on GNP, resources would have been undermobilized for war and the U.S. success would have been less assured. Following World War II, GNP became "an index of the effectiveness of government, a measure of national vitality, the test of the economic system."[9]

Postwar Japan lost no time in adopting GNP as a strategic instrument in recovery plans. GNP soon became the most authoritative index of national economic achievements. Its rate of growth moved to the center of attention around which economic analysis and planning were organized. Economic growth largely meant the growth of the statistically measurable GNP. Japan's economic policy soon came to be known as "GNP-first" policy.

Among many economic plans, the most celebrated in Japanese memory is the Income Doubling Plan of Prime Minister Ikeda Hayato. The period covered by this plan was 1960–70, but the actual annual growth rate outstripped the planned rate fairly early, requiring a revised plan for the second half of the plan period. The revised Midterm Plan, announced early in 1965, described the outcome of economic growth: "The postwar economic growth of Japan has no parallel in the world. The postwar reconstruction phase came to an end in 1953. Between then and 1963, real GNP (at 1960 prices) grew at the annual average rate of 9.9%. The real GNP of 1963 was 3.2 times that of before the war (average for 1934–35)."[10]

Enthusiasm about GNP growth to the extent expressed in this document would have no parallel anywhere. GNP growth at an even higher rate continued throughout the 1960s. By 1970, however, the Japanese no longer thought that GNP growth was the great thing that they had once thought it. It was increasingly clear that GNP growth was obtained at a cost to the quality of life and the environment. In 1970 the *Asahi shinbun* ran a long series of reports and analyses entitled "Kutabare GNP!" (Down with GNP!).

Add the geographical dimension to the aggregate view of planned development. A special kind of national land-use plan concentrated industrial plants

9. John Kenneth Galbraith, "The GNP as Status Symbol and Success Story," in Asahi Shinbun Economic Department, ed., *Kutabare GNP* (Tokyo: Asahi Shinbunsha, 1970), iii.

10. Economic Planning Agency, *Chūki keizai keikaku* (Tokyo: Ministry of Finance Printing Office, 1965), 5.

along the "Pacific belt," which extended westward from Tokyo to Osaka, continued along the Inland Sea, and ended in northern Kyushu. On the seaboard, extensive reclamations were undertaken to accommodate gigantic complexes of heavy and chemical industrial plants. This location policy minimized the transportation costs for the bulky raw materials, fuels, and products that characterized these industries. But industrial and demographic concentrations intensified land and housing shortages. Incredible density of economic activities per square kilometer generated predictable disasters—traffic congestion, air and water pollution, water shortage, noise, odor, and other environmental problems.

The Japanese government also promoted a type of technology policy that was particularly harmful to the environment. The policy of "unbundling" complex technology allowed producers to set up the minimum technological core necessary for a quick, cheap start of operations. This policy meant that the heavy and chemical industrial plants, stripped of pollution control safeguards, simply dumped untreated smoke and waste into the environment. A polluters' paradise emerged, and as the scale of operation expanded, more pollutants entered the environment. Polluted air choked urban residents with respiratory difficulties, which were fatal in some areas. Water pollution wiped out coastal fishing along the industrial belt. Toxic wastes entered the food chain and produced unusual illnesses among people. In the cities exhaust from automobiles mixed with pollutants from smokestacks and produced toxic photochemical smog during the day. Injuries and fatalities from automobile accidents increased by leaps and bounds.

During the period of rapid GNP growth Japanese cities and industrial areas were virtual war zones. "Scrap and build" was the phrase the Japanese themselves used to describe the situation. The particular development strategy of government and business was reminiscent of the wartime strategy of resource mobilization. The preponderant role of the government in the nation's agenda regarding land use, international trade, technology choice, and credit allocation (now told extensively in many excellent studies of Japan's industrial policy) makes the Japanese economy of the GNP-first period appear to be an extension of the wartime economy.[11] The ethos was the same. During the war the Japanese were made to work selflessly in the attempt to win. After the war similar sacrifices were evidently expected in the interest of GNP growth.

War can be won, even though millions perish. Likewise, GNP can be increased, even though millions suffer. This is the most unfortunate aspect of the GNP accounting method. Suffering from pollution does not reduce GNP. Instead, the producers, free of the expenses for pollution prevention, can invest the financial resources saved through their neglect and produce more, adding to GNP. If the victims of pollution use equipment or services to relieve their suffering, they create demand for such equipment and services, which adds to GNP. If polluters are required to prevent pollution, an industry to produce pollution control devices

11. Chalmers Johnson, *MITI and the Japanese Miracle* (Stanford: Stanford University Press, 1982).

emerges and new investment opportunities open up. Destruction expands GNP. Nothing increases GNP faster than ravages of war, according to Milton Friedman. Repair of damages from natural disasters has also been a major component of Japan's annual capital formation, and GNP accounting generally does not distinguish disaster-mending investment from other investments. Thus, GNP gains are not necessarily welfare gains.

Thoughts of this kind made many scholars look for welfare indicators independent of GNP or as modifiers of the GNP figures. In the 1970s there was much talk about *net national welfare* (NNW), arrived at by subtracting estimates of damages to the quality of life from the usual GNP.[12] Researchers examined independent indicators, often called "social" indicators, based on a number of specific physical measures for amenities of life. No convincing measures emerged, however, to help assess how overall well-being changed over time. Unable to command consensus or respect, NNW soon faded out of popularity. GNP remained the only durable yardstick of economic performance and welfare.

SOCIAL COSTS OF MIRACLE GROWTH

Behind Japan's GNP is an accumulation of social costs not yet properly accounted for. However, the concept of social cost often defies economic valuation. John Bennett and Solomon Levine offer one definition of the concept: "In its broadest sense social cost refers to anything considered to be a loss borne by third persons resulting from productive activities—that is, not borne, directly at least, by the producers themselves. . . . Since social costs are dependent on someone perceiving them, the concept implies a sense of value, or social goals."[13]

Furthermore, even though victims perceive social costs that they are made to bear, there is no guarantee that the offenders will agree with them. During the period of miracle growth, Japanese producers vigorously resisted the idea of "internalizing" the social cost of their activities. In 1970 an economist observed: "Few countries that have reached the level of wealth that Japan has now reached, spend as small a proportion of their annual income on internalizing externalities."[14]

The well-known Minamata disease illustrates how business and government handled social costs and what obstacles the victims faced in seeking relief. The disease, which broke out in epidemic proportions for the first time in 1956, killed and maimed hundreds of people in the Minamata area of Kumamoto.

12. Maruo Naomi, *Datsu GNP jidai* (Tokyo: Daiyamondosha, 1971).

13. John W. Bennet and Solomon B. Levine, "Industrialization and Social Deprivation: Welfare, Environment, and the Postindustrial Society in Japan," in Hugh Patrick, ed., *Japanese Industrialization and Its Social Consequences* (Berkeley and Los Angeles: University of California Press, 1976), 446.

14. Albert Breton, "The Non-internalization of Externalities," *ASTE Bulletin* 13, no. 1 (Spring 1971): 31.

The cause was methyl mercury poisoning that originated in the industrial wastes released into Minamata Bay by the Japan Nitrogen Company (Nihon Chisso).[15]

What is noteworthy about this case is the extent of the business and government conspiracy to mislead the public and to cover up a "criminal" business action. On the role of the MITI and the LDP in relation to Minamata, Donald Thurston comments: "Operating under a high economic growth policy which sought a rapid increase in the wealth of the Japanese *nation* with almost no regard for the possible adverse effects on the Japanese *people,* the LDP and MITI, in apparent collusion with Chisso, squelched investigations of the disease and did nothing to bring Chisso to account" (emphasis in original).[16] The *nation* prospers but the *people* perish! This is a remarkable formulation of the state-society relationship during the period of Japan's miracle growth.

In the second half of the 1960s antipollution citizens' movements, as well as individual grievances, multiplied and spread throughout Japan. In this increasingly hostile climate a series of baffling publications was put out by various ministries. Three white papers published in 1969 devoted considerable space to environmental issues and openly criticized the government's GNP-first policy at the expense of the quality of life and the environment.

The most prestigious *Economic White Paper* (published in July 1969), subtitled *Challenge to Affluence,* bewailed the "anguish of a growing economy," pointing to economic and social imbalances that had developed because of the particular type of growth pursued by Japan.[17] The environmental issues demonstrated that anguish most vividly.

The *Welfare White Paper* of the Ministry of Welfare, as if to atone its past ineptness in relation to Minamata, offered a correct, concise analysis of causes and measures for pollution. Subtitled *Basic Conditions for Prosperity,* this white paper

---

15. Breton, "Non-internalization of Externalities"; Margaret A. McKean, *Environmental Protest and Citizen Politics in Japan* (Berkeley and Los Angeles: University of California Press, 1981); Donald R. Thurston, "Aftermath in Minamata," *Japan Interpreter* 9, no. 1 (Spring 1974): 25–42; Ui Jun, ed., *Gijutsu to sangyō kōgai* (Tokyo: United Nations University, 1984).

16. Thurston, "Aftermath in Minamata," 37.

17. Economic Planning Agency, *Keizai hakusho* (Tokyo: Ministry of Finance Printing Office, 1969), 174–258.

Parenthetically, it might be pointed out that the white paper's phrase "challenge *to* affluence"— *yutakasa* eno *chōsen*—kept many readers puzzling for some time. If it meant that "we challenge affluence," it implied "we don't like it," "we don't believe in it," or "we denounce it." Clearly, however, these were not the intended implications. The phrase then appeared to be saying "we should live it up"—enjoy a rich life-style appropriate to a big GNP. Subtitles of government white papers are chosen to set the tone or direction of policy to guide the popular sentiments in desired directions. The apparent ambiguity of "challenge to affluence" may have reflected the government's vacillation between "GNP first" and the quality of life as a policy priority. For an illuminating review of contents and sentiments of the series of economic white papers, see Sawa Takamitsu, *Kōdō seichō: "Rinen" to seisaku no dōjidaishi* (Tokyo: NHK, 1984).

declared: "Pollution is a bastard of economic growth and urban expansion."[18] The paper characterized the means of Japan's economic growth as "forced accumulation." The agglomerations of gigantic industrial plants at selected sites and the concentration of the population in major cities were seen to be the major causes of the pollution problem. The white paper then emphasized that the ultimate antipollution measures required an "*internalization* of pollution prevention as a *value objective* in all productive activities and life styles liable to generate pollution [my emphasis]."[19]

A most unusual incident in 1969 was that the Cabinet of the Ministers of State refused to approve the *National Life White Paper* submitted by the Economic Planning Agency, which also wrote the previously mentioned *Economic White Paper*. The fault of the *National Life White Paper* was that it quantified Japan's lag in standards of living behind other advanced countries, and some ministers felt insulted by the unfavorable comparison. A recalculation was ordered, but the document was eventually made official after some minor cosmetic changes.

This incident occurred against the backdrop of a general euphoria that Japan, in terms of aggregate GNP, had just surpassed West Germany and become number two, next to the United States, in the free world. Already as early as 1965 Kanamori Hisao had titled a book *Great Economic Power: Nippon*.[20] In this climate the ministers can be forgiven for assuming that Japan should also be shown to be a rich country when compared for living standards. To their chagrin, both the *Economic White Paper* and the *National Life White Paper* pointed out that in terms of per capita GNP, Japan ranked twenty-second among the free world countries. The implication was: the country was GNP-rich, but the people were poor.

Since the end in the early 1970s of the "miracle growth" of GNP, a great many changes have taken place. The deceleration of GNP growth to annual rates around 5 percent and the retrenchment of the smokestack industries, together with the expansion of the information industry, have contributed to the abatement of pollution. Laws have been enacted to define environmental standards. The Environmental Agency was established in 1971 to monitor the environmental conditions. The Japanese government used its diplomatic influence on the Organization for Economic Cooperation and Development and refurbished Japan's international image as a country united against pollution.[21] Certain indicators of air pollution show substantial improvement over the years. But progress in the control of water pollution in lakes, rivers, and seas has been negligible. Amenities of life in cities are far from what one would infer from Japan's GNP power. In 1979 Europeans crystallized the issue by calling Japanese workaholics living in "rabbit hutches." This remark induced confusing emotional reactions,

18. Ministry of Welfare, *Kōsei hakusho* (Tokyo: Ministry of Finance Printing Office, 1969), 141.
19. Ibid.
20. Kanamori Hisao, *Keizai taikoku: "Nippon"* (Tokyo: Nihon Keizai Shinbunsha, 1965).
21. Organization for Economic Cooperation and Development, *Environmental Pollution in Japan* (Paris: OECD, 1977).

mixtures of surprise, anger, agony, resentment, remorse, and so on. The white paper of 1981 denounced it as a misunderstanding born of a prejudice against Japan.[22] Nevertheless, in the 1980s inadequate housing became a new symbol of Japan's lag behind the West.

NEGLECT OF THE POOR

GNPism exalts a person's contribution to the growth of GNP as a condition for the level of living that he or she deserves. This proposition is often better known in inverted form: the actual level of living enjoyed or suffered by a person reflects his or her level of contribution to production. A conceptual issue here is how GNP growth in a market economy is related to social welfare and security. At the minimum, economic growth increases the income of the average person and his or her ability to save for rainy days. To this extent, economic welfare and security should increase with increasing GNP. On this ground, policymakers may see no need for special intervention in the economic process to promote welfare and security beyond what the market mechanism brings about. The naïveté of this view of economic growth was exposed by the vast negative externalities of growth.

Further, despite best intentions people sometimes can make wrong choices or moves, falling into temporary conditions of need. Risks of accidents and illnesses also exist. The young grow old and lose earnings from work. But GNPism regards care for the needy as a waste of resources. During the period of rapid growth it was in Japan's interest to neglect such care.

Article Twenty-five of Japan's postwar constitution stipulates that "all people shall have the right to maintain the minimum standards of wholesome and cultured living" and that "in all spheres of life, the State shall use its endeavors for the promotion and extension of social welfare and security, and of public health." Just as the state failed to ensure environmental safety during the period of miracle growth, so too did it fail to honor all people's "right to maintain the minimum standards of wholesome and cultured living" through "the promotion and extension of social welfare and security."

An illuminating constitutional case, known as *Asahi soshō* (Asahi suit), arose during this period. In 1957 Asahi Shigeru, a medical indigent hospitalized for tuberculosis under the public assistance program, sued the Minister of Welfare for the inadequacy of assistance by standards implied in Article Twenty-five of the constitution and the Livelihood Protection Law (Seikatsu Hogohō). The suit was a consequence of the Welfare Ministry's failure to process Asahi's complaints properly. The suit technically centered on the question of the adequacy of care as implied by "the minimum standards of wholesome and cultured living." The true impetus for the plaintiff's action arose from one fundamental legal principle

22. Economic Planning Agency, *Keizai hakusho* (Tokyo: Ministry of Finance Printing Office, 1981), 243.

of Japanese public assistance that makes the care of the needy a primary responsibility of their kin. Asahi was angered by the manner in which the government looked up and ordered his brother to bear part of the cost of medical care he was receiving under the public assistance program.[23]

Under the authority of the Livelihood Protection Law the Ministry of Welfare fixes the monetary values of the standards of assistance for the cost of living, housing, medical care, schooling, and various deductibles. Fixing these standards implements the constitutional "minimum standards of wholesome and cultured living." But the government usually claims that these standards are subject to budgetary constraints; that is, they should not be so high as to make the number of the eligible indigents and their needs exceed the budgetary capability of the government. However, the general public and especially the recipients are sensitive to how the administrative standards compare with what they infer from the language of the constitution. If the practical standards fall significantly short of what may be reasonably considered "minimum standards of wholesome and cultured living," then the shortcoming may imply a violation of the constitution.

In October 1960 the Tokyo District Court judged the case in favor of the plaintiff Asahi and voided the welfare minister's rejection of the plaintiff's complaints. The minister appealed. The Tokyo Superior Court sided with the minister in its verdict delivered in November 1963. The case moved up to the Supreme Court. The plaintiff died in 1964, and the case was fought at the Supreme Court by his heirs. In May 1967 the Supreme Court decided that the legal merit of the case disappeared with the death of the plaintiff. By way of comments the court further observed that the law empowers the minister of welfare to fix public assistance standards and that although any particular standards adopted by the minister of welfare could be questioned as to their adequacy (relative to needs), they could not be questioned from the standpoint of constitutionality or legality insofar as the minister's judgment and action were in conformity with the spirit or purposes of the law.

Two parts of the public policy were designed to ensure that all citizens will have socially acceptable minimum standards of living: (1) insurance against the risk of the loss of income, and (2) assistance to the individuals who, for whatever reasons, already live at standards below the social minimum. In the 1950s Japan's social insurance schemes against the loss of income or health were extremely limited. In the absence of a safety net the dangers that people might fall straight into poverty were pervasive. This situation generated a large number of poor and strained the resources of the public assistance administration. The Asahi case arose when social security measures were grossly inadequate and the public assistance schemes alone bore the brunt of responsibility for the constitutional entitlement of people to the "minimum standards of wholesome and cultured living."

---

23. Matsuo Hitoshi, ed., *Shakai hoshō tokuhon* (Tokyo: Tōyō Keizai Shinpōsha, 1967); Takano Shirō, ed., *Gendai no hinkon to shakai hoshō* (Tokyo: Chōbunsha, 1970).

The Asahi case implies several questions of general significance. The stringency of the means test coupled with low assistance standards makes a mockery of the spirit of assistance and service. In almost all countries, eligibility for public assistance requires the exhaustion of all personal means of support. How thorough this "exhaustion" should be, how rigorously the welfare bureaucracy tests the applicant, and to what extent the kin are called on to support the applicant are factors that determine the degree of generosity or cruelty of the system. During the period 1953–57 the Ministry of Welfare audited local welfare offices with extreme rigor and turned up a large number of cases that it considered ineligible.[24] Suspensions of benefits and rejections of applications increased dramatically under new guidelines. Asahi's difficulties arose during this period, when the Ministry of Welfare tightened eligibility requirements in reaction to earlier generosity that had apparently strained the budget of the Japanese government.

The relationship between the state and Asahi's kin demonstrates a very important legal principle peculiar to Japan: the primacy of private support for the indigent and the secondary, supplemental role of public support. This principle, which is written into the Civil Code and the Livelihood Protection Law, derives from the old-style *ie* (family) system in which the *ie* was a corporate unit of legal action and security arrangements. There is no *ie* in law anymore. The household is now formed by the marriage of male and female based on their free choice and consent, yet kinship ties are still regarded as a network legally responsible for mutual care and support. The *ie* is still alive in this sense. With this authority of law, the Welfare Ministry was able to look up Asahi's brother and demand his legal obligation to contribute to Asahi's support. In recent years the kin group has been used for care of the aged. Coupled with the rapid increase in aged population, younger kin (especially women) are often compelled to abandon their careers for the care of the aged parents or in-laws.[25]

Although the government was harsh in the administration of public assistance, it also sought less onerous ways to help people. Social insurance was one of them. During the 1950s official plans to establish a full-fledged social security system were already in the works. By 1961 Japan had introduced a variety of measures that added up to income (pension) and health insurances of universal coverage (*kokumin kaihoken, kokumin kainenkin*). The "insurance" schemes required payments of premiums, although benefits were not forthcoming until reserve funds were built up. The insurance schemes matured and began to pay benefits in the early 1970s. In the meantime there was the problem of those who were already poor or whose incomes were too low to pay the social insurance premiums. These poor needed immediate assistance. Instead of getting them on conventional public assistance, the Japanese social security system set up ingenious transitional measures to entitle the aged poor (though not other kinds of poor) to a "welfare

24. Takechi Hideyuki, "Seikatsu hogo gyōsei to 'tekiseika' seisaku," parts 1 and 2, *Quarterly of Social Security Research* 24, no. 3 (Winter 1988): 335–53, 24, no. 4 (Spring 1989): 450–67.

25. Satō Susumu, *Kōreisha fuyō to shakai hoshō* (Tokyo: Ichiryūsha, 1983).

pension" without prior payments of premiums. Likewise, the national health insurance system exempted low-income individuals from premium payments without losing the insurance benefits. By these manipulations many individuals who were poor were spared the stigma of poverty that would have resulted from receiving public assistance benefits. Even so, some poor could not be helped by the social insurance system however elastically the concepts were manipulated. They had to be helped by public assistance.[26]

THE STATISTICAL EXTENT OF POVERTY

Income data from the *Employment Status Survey* indicated that in 1968, 14.5 percent of households or 8.7 percent of individuals were poor; that is, they had incomes below the public assistance standard, or the poverty line.[27] The number of the poor is estimated by applying the poverty line to the size distribution of personal or household income. Unfortunately data on income distribution are not reliable: different sources give different income data with variable coverages of population and income, resulting in different estimates of poverty. There are no comprehensive data on income distribution for the whole population and for all sources of income. Researchers must make their own adjustments to the available data to suit their purposes.[28]

26. It may be useful to distinguish "technical" poor and "social" poor. The former are the poor with incomes below the recognized poverty line. The income test alone is sufficient to classify them as poor. However, not all of the technically poor perceive themselves as poor for a variety of social and psychological reasons. Many technically poor camouflage themselves as nonpoor and would vigorously object to anyone calling them poor. The receipt of "public assistance" (becoming a ward of the state) is a public certificate that one is poor. The government also tries to avoid branding some low-income people as poor by affording them benefits that are technically "assistance" but that are not associated with the stigma of "public assistance." The complexity of the sociopsychological dimensions of poverty distorts not only statistics but laws and administrative practices.

27. Chūbachi Masayoshi and Kōji Taira, "Poverty in Modern Japan: Perceptions and Realities," in Hugh Patrick, ed., *Japanese Industrialization and Its Social Consequences* (Berkeley and Los Angeles: University of California Press, 1986), 430.

28. My usual source of data for the estimate of the poor as a percentage of the population is *The Employment Status Survey* (Prime Minister's Office, Statistics Bureau), which is based on large samples drawn from all households and considers all incomes including transfer incomes (pensions, social security benefits, and public assistance), but excluding realized capital gains. Thus, one may say that the coverage of the incomes of the poor is rather complete but that that of the rich is highly deficient. For this reason, the estimate of overall equality or inequality in income distribution by data from this source may overstate equality (or understate inequality). Tadao Ishizaki ("Is Japan's Income Distribution Equal? An International Comparison," *Japanese Economic Studies* 14, no. 2 [Winter 1985–86]) has examined statistical sources and found them wanting in the coverage of population and income sources. The size distribution of income for 1968–69, as adjusted by Ishizaki, shows substantially lower income shares for the lowest deciles of the population (32). Takayama Noriyuki (*Fubyōdō no keizai bunseki* [Tokyo: Tōyō Keizai Shinpōsha, 1980]) estimates the extent of poverty by a formula that weights the number of the poor as a percentage of the population by measures of the income gap required to be filled to move the poor to the poverty line (to make them barely "nonpoor"). The poor as a percentage of the population in his data fall from 11.9 for 1960 to 7.6 for 1975. But he says that some of the decrease may be due to the use of the constant poverty line for the whole period (67).

The most thorough poverty studies ever undertaken for Japan are those of Eguchi Eiichi and his associates. Using the Tokyo segment of the *Employment Status Survey* of 1968 and the Tokyo standard of public assistance, they estimated Tokyo's poor to be 20.5 percent of the Tokyo population.[29] This astonishing rate of poverty contrasts sharply with the Chūbachi-Taira estimate of the national poverty rate. More surprises arose from the studies of Eguchi and his associates. In 1972 they conducted an exhaustive survey of all households in one of the 23 *ku* (wards) of Tokyo, Nakano-ku, which was thought to be typical and representative of Tokyo wards. Using Tokyo's public assistance standard of the same year, Eguchi found that the incomes of 26.2 percent of the Nakano-ku households were at or below the assistance standard.[30]

For perspective, the *Employment Status Survey* of 1982 produces an estimate of the extent of poverty much lower than the same survey of 1968 previously mentioned.[31] By the same method used earlier, the percentage of poor households in 1982 was 8.2 percent as compared with 14.5 percent in 1968. The rate of poverty among individuals was 5.8 percent as compared with 8.7 percent earlier. These figures indicate that between 1968 and 1982 poverty decreased considerably. However, some of this decrease was caused by the decrease in the official poverty line relative to the median income. With the same relative poverty line (40 percent of the median), the 1982 poor accounted for 9.2 percent of households or 6.5 percent of individuals. These figures still indicate a significant decrease in the extent of poverty compared with 1968. One might suppose that income distribution became more favorable to lower-income people in the course of the 1970s.

WORKERS' STRUGGLE FOR A LARGER SHARE

Rapid economic growth requires a structure and process of resource allocation that denies resources to nonproductive uses and maximizes savings for capital formation. The contrived scarcity of resources for social purposes, pushed to the extremes during the period of miracle growth, produced considerable damage in the poorer and weaker strata of society. Up a few notches on the social pyramid, the ordinary Japanese also suffered under the growth policy. Aside from measures to encourage personal savings and diverting them to capital accumulation at very low, sometimes negative, real interest rates, rapid growth required a minimization of the share of output going to workers so that the largest possible share was retained and reinvested by business. The industrial structure and the syndrome of incentives that accompanied this share mechanism trace their roots to nonegalitarian Japanese values.

Ascriptive or conventional inequalities based on age, sex, education, ethnicity, and religion persist and are tolerated. The family structure and socialization

29. Eguchi Eiichi, *Gendai no "teishotokusō,"* 3 vols. (Tokyo: Miraisha, 1979), 1:88.

30. Ibid., 1: 57.

31. Prime Minister's Office. Statistics Bureau, *Employment Status Survey* (Tokyo: Prime Minister's Office, Statistics Bureau, 1982).

process make these inequalities acceptable to the Japanese in early stages of their life experiences. The Japanese firms structure and reward the work force by the family metaphor, replicating the familiar inequalities learned in the family by the individuals. This is a well-known story that has been told countless times in the literature on Japanese management. Critiques of the Japanese management system from the standpoint of egalitarian values can be found only in vastly outnumbered "radical" publications.[32]

The acceptance and use of inequalities also appear in pronounced form in relations among business firms—that is, a hierarchically organized subcontracting system with many layers of subcontractors. Subcontractors become smaller, weaker, and more numerous in proportion to the economic and social distance from the major firm ("parent") and the primary subcontractor (*moto-uke*, first-layer agent for the parent firm). At the bottom are masses of self-employed individuals and households as well as labor contractors who recruit casual labor and channel it into the subcontracting system. Urban ghettoes (*yoseba, doyagai*) develop by collecting dropouts and drifters.

The economics of the subcontracting system demonstrate how "efficient" it is for maximizing the share of the top firms and minimizing that of workers in the aggregate. The parent and *moto-uke* firms dictate terms of transactions to the "children" firms, which do the same to the "grandchildren" firms, which in turn dictate to "great-grandchildren" firms, and so on. Eventually, at the bottom of the system the least advantaged workers bear the brunt of cost-cutting pressures coming down on them from all the higher levels of the system. By historical accident and by the logic of organizational convenience, organized labor is concentrated in the larger firms at the higher notches of the subcontracting system, sharing in the monopoly profits of their employers. While organized labor, a minority of the labor force, gains relatively, the system as a whole depresses labor's share in national output. This result is of course desirable from the standpoint of maximum capital accumulation and economic growth.

Under this kind of system, how can labor's share ever be increased? This is a complex issue. For now, suffice it to note that at the minimum the unions' determined struggles for higher wages are indispensable, provided that these struggles are supported by a far more widespread demand for social justice and that union gains have extensive spillover effects on all kinds of wages and benefits. Labor disputes increased throughout the period of rapid growth and culminated in the "big bang" of the spring offensive (*kokumin shuntō*) of 1974, when about 10 percent of Japan's wage and salary earners were engaged in strikes.[33] This proportion was three times as high as its U.S. counterpart in 1974.

32. Patricia Tsurumi, ed., *The Other Japan* (Armonk, N.Y.: M. E. Sharpe, 1988); Gavan McCormack and Yoshio Sugimoto, eds., *Democracy in Contemporary Japan* (Sydney: Hale and Iremonger, 1986).

33. Solomon Levine and Koji Taira, "Interpreting Industrial Conflict: The Case of Japan," in Benjamin Martin and Everett M. Kassalow, eds., *Labor Relations in Advanced Industrial Societies* (Washington, D.C.: Carnegie Endowment for International Peace, 1980).

The outcome was a substantial negotiated wage increase, 10 percentage points higher than the rate of inflation, which was 22 percent. Real wage increases throughout Japan in fiscal year 1974 (April 1974–March 1975) averaged 4.3 percent. However, the year 1974 turned out to be a year of depression with unprecedented negative economic growth. This situation meant that workers gained real-wage increases while the economy lost output and the employers suffered losses. All this added up to a substantial increase in labor's share in national output. The historic significance of this "share revolution" can hardly be exaggerated, given its rarity in any society. The only other "share revolution" occurred during early postwar years under intense and more prolonged labor militancy.

In 1974, then, the Japanese came close to a "class struggle." The overriding problem was how to cope with inflation, which had been triggered by the energy price revolution of 1973 and aggravated by union militancy. How to appease the unions became a top priority for the government. At the same time, the problem of the business sector could not be neglected. A part of the problem was how to scrap the now uneconomical industrial structure built on cheap oil. Restructuring implied massive unemployment, which was unacceptable to the unions and workers. The general public also would not tolerate a deterioration of living standards through inflation. An imperative for the government, then, was a coherent program to prevent unemployment, to control inflation, and to restructure the industry. New subsidies were granted to enterprises hard hit by the recession, while benefits to unemployed workers were expanded. This approach induced deficit finance on the part of the government. Deficit finance would have been inflationary had it not been for a sharp increase in national savings and a success in the control of the cost-push aspect of inflation. For the latter purpose, labor leaders were brought into "partnership" for policy formulation along with government and business leaders. This policy required strengthening an arrangement that was already in place, Sanrōkon (Industry and Labor Conference) in the Ministry of Labor. Unions' increased role in national policy-making was an important part of the new synthesis born of the "class struggle" of 1974.

TOWARD A NONSTRATIFIED, CLASSLESS, AFFLUENT SOCIETY

A broader ideological innovation finally abolished all contradictions. Prime Minister Miki Takeo, who came to power in December 1974, gathered around himself some liberal intellectuals led by Murakami Yasusuke of Tokyo University. This group generated a new ideological definition of Japan as a "Middle Mass Society" that was individualistic, egalitarian, and free of conflict. The role of the government was to ensure full employment and economic security to meet the requirements of desirable life cycles (*shōgai sekkei*, or life-cycle planning).[34] A con-

34. Nihon Keizai Shinbunsha, *Fukushi ronsō* (Tokyo: Nihon Keizai Shinbunsha, 1975).

cerned government and self-reliant individuals together would ensure a high degree of social welfare (*fukushi*) and equity (*kōsei*). However, this ideological sleight of hand was more a wishful thinking than a serious empirical generalization, as controversy over the "middle mass" hypothesis subsequently demonstrated.

The Japanese government regularly polls public opinion about the standard of living. Assuming that standards of living may be described as upper, middle, and lower, the government asks the polled individuals where they find themselves. Earlier each stratum was further divided into upper and lower. But around 1970 the middle stratum alone was divided into three levels: upper, middle, and lower. By this classification, the percentage of people choosing the "middle" was as high as 90 percent, with the "middle-middle" alone accounting for 59 percent. These simple opinion polls were variously interpreted and even gave rise to farfetched generalizations about the nature of Japanese society as a society of "new middle mass" in which social strata or classes had lost relevance as sources of political dynamics.[35] The "middle" identified by the opinion poll was also popularly called "middle stream" (*chūryū*). Further, Japan's "middle stream" is claimed by some scholars to be analogous to the West's "middle class." These slippery metaphors and analogues have created ferocious controversy.

Critics were appalled by the dogmatic simplicity of the opinion poll and the exaggerated interpretation of its results by apologists for the regime. A technical weakness mentioned by the critics had undeniable merit: given the variability of standards of living in any community ranging from very high to very low, practically everybody would be in the middle, because one could always point to someone above and someone below oneself.[36] In this sense the sample was "rigged" to produce what the pollster, the Japanese government, wanted. But the illusion of a "middle-mass society" was useful for stabilizing social conditions and strengthening law and order.

Other disputes also arose concerning Japan's middle-mass society. By showing the hard data on occupation, income, property, life-style, and so on, associated with the middle class in the West, the critics could easily demonstrate how dismal Japan's "middle class" (if the "middle mass" was that) was compared with the West's. To this contention those who equated "middle mass" to "middle class" offered the usual rebuttal that objective data were not the issue; the important point was how people felt about themselves, and if an overwhelming majority of Japanese felt that they were in the middle, Japan deserved to be considered as a middle-class society by definition. There is a grain of truth in this argument, for it suggests that the aggregate feelings of a society are just as objective as hard

35. Murakami Yasusuke, "The Age of New Middle Mass Politics: The Case of Japan," *Journal of Japanese Studies* 8, no. 1 (Winter 1982): 29–72.

36. Aoki Shigeru, *"Chūryū" ni mirai wa aru ka* (Tokyo: Tōyō Keizai Shinpōsha, 1981); Kishimoto Shigenobu, *Chūryū no Gensō* (Tokyo: Kōdansha, 1978).

statistical data. Because the middle class in the West is considered a desirable class to join, it gratifies the Japanese that almost all of them have now joined a class coveted in the West.

This is an old story: mind over matter. In Japan, unlike the individualistic and pluralistic West, there is apparently a strong centripetal orientation of values and aspirations. Everyone intensely desires to converge at the center, which also means "middle" (*chūshin, chūō*). Thus, in Japan it is relatively easy to aggregate and standardize individual feelings. Likewise, the Japanese can mobilize the national spirit for specific ends with relative ease and speed.

In light of these centripetal forces of values and motivations, it is understandable that the Japanese strongly believe in their homogeneity. The "middle" that every Japanese wants to join may well be an alias for homogeneity.[37] As one probes the meaning of *chū* (middle, inside, center) in Japanese psychology, one discovers that it is not a structural concept derived from, or related to, an objective hierarchical stratification, as in the Western class concept, but a middle stretch of the stream of social mobility. The basic fluidity of social structure is assumed as given. Everything flows and floats. For all practical purposes, except for a small number of unfortunate people washed out into the sea and another small number, like the emperor and his entourage, who live upstream or even beyond the cloud-covered peaks of the mountains, virtually everybody is happily together in the middle stretch of a stream. The semantics of *chū* and *ryū* defy attempts to interpret Japanese society by Western sociology of stratification. In fact, the unbelievable semantic muddle that characterizes the discussion of the "middle" is an attempt to deny the applicability of Western concepts to Japan and to affirm Japan's uniqueness.[38]

In addition to the "stream" metaphor of society, spatial imagery dominates Japanese views of society. Borders, frontiers, fringes, peripheries—such images evoke only fear or contempt. This attitude is a legacy of Chinese influence: China is the "middle kingdom," and its peripheries are all "barbarian." A single center, the *miyako* (metropolis), is the source of pride for everyone. To partake in that pride by moving into the center is an incentive for effort. The singularity of the center is coupled with expectations that the center alone can offer everything people consider desirable. These expectations allow the concentration of resources at the center. The primacy of the center creates a primate city such as Tokyo. With unquestioned authority and prestige the center dictates the national goals and commands the national effort for their attainment. Denial of divisive Western concepts and acceptance of the traditional worldview strengthen the unity of Japan and overcome all contradictions that arise from misguided infatuation with Western paradigms.

37. Kishimoto, *Chūryū no Gensō*, 103.
38. Ibid., 104.

CONCLUSION

In Japan the decade of the 1950s was a period of recovery and initial growth. The 1960s saw "miracle growth." In the 1970s Japan faced a series of crises and worked out a new solution. The solution was put to an acid test by the second oil shock of 1979–80, which induced acute stagflation in Europe and the United States. Japan was an exception. The public, business, and labor calmly shared the cost of resource transfer to OPEC through the imposed change in the terms of trade and bided their time to resume economic growth. The opportunity for growth shortly came via Reaganomics and a strong dollar. When the United States complained and engineered the depreciation of the dollar and the appreciation of the yen in 1985, a short-lived economic crisis occurred in Japan. Japan then made a remarkable comeback to another round of growth via domestic demand expansion. Nonstratified, classless Japan, having solved all internal contradictions, appears to be moving toward a remodeling of the world by sharing its excess savings through foreign aid and investment as well as trade. A Pax Nipponica looms over the horizon.

The ruling conservative coalition of Japan has been in power since the end of World War II except for the brief interlude of a Socialist-led government of 1947–48. Conservatives have been in power so long not because Japan is problem-free but because the LDP, business community, state bureaucracy, and conservative intellectuals have been flexible enough to co-opt critics', opposition parties', and protesting groups' reform agenda for solving problems occasioned, from time to time, by the continued success of their main objective, economic growth. The ruling coalition's ability to face problems and embrace solutions from all sources still continues. It must then be conceded that the ruling coalition has managed the dialectics of production and distribution rather well. In the early 1990s one is hard put to detect a major cleavage in Japanese society that may tear apart the social fabric.

By straining one's eyes, one may perhaps see some signs of disarray in Japan under the impact of external pressures demanding a greater international role for the country. Different Japanese react differently to the nature and extent of Japan's role in the world. There are "Nipponists," expansionist nationalists who derive a large part of life's meaning from the sovereign glory of Japan and who take Japan's macroeconomic power at face value. But there are also those who pay more attention to living conditions and wonder why they do not feel rich despite all the talk about Japan's being a great economic power. They are concerned with the quality of life. There are apparent disagreements between Nipponists and those concerned with the quality of life regarding Japan's priorities in resource allocation. These disagreements derive from the discrepancy between nominal per capita GNP, which is world-class and exceeds that of the United States, and real per capita GNP, which in purchasing power stands 30 percent below that of the United States. Environmental factors that are not adequately priced would, if taken into account, further reduce the Japanese standard of living.

This, then, is the new dialectic in Japanese society: Nipponists versus people. It is no startling discovery; it mirrors the earlier conflict between "GNP first" and welfare. Nipponists are generally statists. Ikutaro Shimizu cries, "Nippon, be a State!"[39] Some Japanese already exhibit a morbid obsession with Japan's sovereignty. More recently, the politician Shintaro Ishihara and the business leader Akio Morita offered a new Nipponist slogan: "The Japan that can say no."[40] Japanese businesses operating abroad also hide behind sovereignty for their convenience. Although Nipponists cut across many classifications, they are more numerous among state bureaucrats, big-business leaders, LDP politicians, and socioeconomic groups that work with and benefit from the establishment.

Who are the people concerned with the quality of life? They are the ordinary citizens and the rank and file of Japan's labor force. Their concerns are expressed in various ways. They want a standard of living and a quality of life as good as the Americans' and Europeans'. They know that Japan's GNP is potentially adequate for that purpose. The problem is that economic and social distortions born of the past policy emphasing GNP growth prevent a rational use of resources for improving the quality of life. They want fair compensation for their efforts and a fair share in the GNP they help produce. To attain that distributive justice, they must have a voice in policy formation and decision making regarding economic structure and resource allocation. The new labor confederation Rengō champions the drive for a better quality of life.

However, distributive struggles today are not as fierce as they were in the 1970s. No burning issues compel groups to coalesce and rally. Diverse inequalities still remain and new ones are created by economic and technological changes. One of the recent inequalities born of the economic boom induced by the successful policy for domestic demand stimulation is the rise in the inequality of asset distribution, especially in land ownership. This inequality has been accompanied by a reconcentration of population and economic resources in metropolitan centers, especially the Tokyo area. For urban Japanese, the distance between home and workplace has grown, and commuting consumes a large proportion of time on top of working hours that remain at the highest level among advanced countries. Rapid technological changes require endless rounds of redeployment and retraining of the labor force, and a fraction of that force fails to keep pace, disappearing into the "other Japan." Increasing longevity and declining fertility conspire to expand the ranks of aging and aged Japanese to whom an increasing share of GNP must be allocated through social security.

While domestic needs are increasing, the world's demand for Japan's economic

39. Shimizu Ikutarō, "The Nuclear Option: Japan, Be a State!" *Japan Echo* 7, no. 3 (Fall 1980): 33–45.

40. Ishihara Shintarō and Morita Akio, *"No" to ieru Nippon* (Tokyo: Kōbunsha, 1989); Ishihara Shintarō, Watanabe Shoichi, and Ogawa Kazuhisa, *Soredemo "No" to ieru Nippon* (Tokyo: Kōbunsha, 1990).

assistance is also increasing, which affords the Nipponists an opportunity to demonstrate Japan's economic power. Japan's expanding role in the world requires more resources for international transfer. To generate them, the nationalist economic policy for the expansion of trade surpluses and foreign investment earnings appears to be a desideratum.[41] Such expansion would compete with the resource requirements for the improvement of the quality of life at home. The idea of larger international contributions that is popular within the ruling coalition would then ignite distributive struggles in Japan. At present, however, resources seem sufficient to give more to both domestic and international requirements. Forces of dialectics are in equilibrium for the time being.

41. Solomon B. Levine and Koji Taira, eds., "Japan's External Economic Relations: Japanese Perspectives," special issue of *Annals of the American Academy of Political and Social Science* 513 (Jan. 1991).

PART III

Mass Culture and Metropolitan Society

CHAPTER EIGHT

Finding a Place in Metropolitan Japan
Ideologies, Institutions, and Everyday Life

William W. Kelly

IDENTITY AND DIFFERENCE IN POSTWAR SOCIETY

One can draw statistical profiles and ethnographic portraits to evoke very different models of postwar Japanese society as increasingly homogenous or persistently diverse. The dramatic figures for industrial growth and agricultural stagnation, rural exodus and urban sprawl, rising longevity and declining infant mortality, smaller family size and new housing options, and the escalation of educational credentialing demonstrate how transformed and leveled is the social landscape of the postwar decades. Many argue from such figures that these changes have erased earlier distinctions: of countryside and city, of farmer and factory worker, of extended families and nuclear families, of the poor and the rich, of basic schooling for the masses and higher education for a small elite. More equitable opportunities and more egalitarian outcomes, they feel, have standardized lifeways across the population, which largely identifies itself as a national "middle class" of shared, metropolitan aspirations.

To be sure, wider access to avenues of advancement and broader distribution of power and positions have both improved the general standard of life and narrowed the extremes. However, other statistics would caution us against drawing too quickly a model of rising middle-class homogenization. Employment has shifted dramatically away from the primary sector and toward manufacturing and service sectors. Yet the majority of corporate employment is in medium and small companies, wage differentials remain stubbornly wide, and part-time and temporary employment plays a significant role in work-force profiles. Marriage age, family size, household nuclearization, and other characteristics of family formation have become standard across the population, but rising difficulties in housing and caring for elderly parents and relatives have, if anything, complicated family histories. A national ministry, a standard curriculum, and near-universal high school graduation have homogenized the educational experience at the elementary and secondary levels, but there is still much variation at the preelementary and postsecondary levels. Postwar decades have seen a dramatic equalization of family incomes, but it is now clear that disparities in family assets are widening. A national health insurance and biomedical care system is in place, but practitioners in alternative medical and psychotherapies thrive, and sectarian New Religions continue to attract large memberships, which may be taken as symptoms of disenchantment with mainstream therapies and values.

Over the same postwar decades anthropologists and sociologists have built a rich ethnographic record that fleshes out and reinforces such paradoxical statistical profiles. Ronald Dore's portrait of the Tokyo ward of Shitayama in 1951, for example, evokes many sharp contrasts of life during the immediate postwar years of personal loss, family dislocation, material deprivation, and institutional chaos.[1] He found the "T" family—wealthy from wartime profiteering and then from American blood plasma contracts—living in a well-appointed mansion complete with a dozen servants, two late-model American automobiles, a ballroom, and air-conditioned bedrooms. Just down the street was the "A" family, squeezed into an eight-mat room above the greengrocer's shop, without water and with only brazier for cooking and heat. Mr. A's life had spiraled downward from tailoring to occasional day laboring; his wife was retarded and his children sick and ill fed. Between these poles stretched the other three hundred residents of the ward, much more frequently impoverished than enriched by the physical destruction and social dislocations. Already, however, the institutions that Dore went on to describe—including the local elementary school and a growing municipal bureaucracy—were proving effective vehicles for policies to broaden participation and widen opportunity.

Ten years later Ezra Vogel and David Plath witnessed some of the convergences fostered by economic recovery and political reconstitution. In their study of family dynamics in Mamachi Town, just east of Tokyo, Vogel and his wife realized that a double displacement—of population and life-style—was occurring in Mamachi in the late 1950s.[2] As he titled his book, a "new middle class" of white-collar employees was emerging amid the shopkeepers, small businesspeople, and professionals of the old middle class, and these new residents were changing Mamachi from urban fringe town to metropolitan bedburb. At the same time, Plath was out in Nagano Prefecture, in the hinterlands of Matsumoto City; predominant among the region's diverse lifeways were those of the farmer, the shopkeeper, and the wage-earner.[3] His book is both an ethnography of those lifeways and also a demonstration of the growing attractiveness of the life and

1. Ronald P. Dore, *City Life in Japan* (Berkeley and Los Angeles: University of California Press, 1958).

2. Ezra Vogel, *Japan's New Middle Class* (Berkeley and Los Angeles: University of California Press, 1963).

3. David W. Plath, *The After Hours: Modern Japan and the Search for Enjoyment* (Berkeley and Los Angeles: University of California Press, 1964).

leisure of the *sararīman*. His comments echoed conclusions of Vogel about this career path as "a model of life which is modest enough to be within the range of realistic hopes and modern enough to be worthy of their highest aspirations."[4]

Thomas Rohlen's study of a regional bank and the longitudinal portraits of rural villages by Dore and Robert Smith were further testament to the degree to which lifestyles were becoming regularized, affluent, and ever closer to a "mainstream" (*chūryū*) norm.[5] However, recent ethnography can be read for very different lessons—about the limits of such aspirations and the persistence of variations. For example, studying a Mamachi-like city in metropolitan Tokyo in the mid-1970s, Anne Imamura found its residents in at least five very different housing situations, with increasing immobility. In 1979–81 research in a Shitayama-like Tokyo neighborhood, Theodore Bestor found that the shopkeeping and small business "old middle class" was still vibrant, controlling local power and setting the tone for neighborhood life. Dorinne Kondo's study of work in a family confectionery business in another Tokyo ward underscored the strength of artisanal identity in opposition to white-collar work ways. Jennifer Robertson found that much public life in the metropolitan city of Kodaira was framed by the ideological distinctions of "natives" and "newcomers." Kenneth Skinner and Paul Noguchi have contributed ethnographies about employees of large organizations shunted to personnel sidetracks. And Rohlen's comparison of five Kobe high schools—from elite Nada to the dead-end night school—demonstrates how wide the postwar educational pyramid remains.[6] In short, ethnographies of postwar life present us with the same paradox as statistics of postwar life: homogenization and enduring difference.

What are we to make of such discrepant versions of postwar change? Perhaps they might be explained in terms of the long-standing debate in the social science of Japanese society between the relative merits of consensual and conflict models. This debate has pitted, for example, those who characterize Japanese commitment to the group and the natural harmony of a homogenous society against those

4. Vogel, *Japan's New Middle Class*, 268; compare Plath, *After Hours*, 35–37.

5. Thomas P. Rohlen, *For Harmony and Strength: Japanese White-Collar Organization in Anthropological Perspective* (Berkeley and Los Angeles: University of California Press, 1974); Ronald P. Dore, *Shinohata: Portrait of a Japanese Village* (New York: Pantheon, 1978); and Robert J. Smith, Jr., *Kurusu: The Price of Progress in a Japanese Village, 1951–1975* (Stanford: Stanford University Press, 1978).

6. Anne E. Imamura, *Urban Japanese Housewives: At Home and in the Community* (Honolulu: University of Hawaii Press, 1987); Theodore C. Bestor, *Neighborhood Tokyo* (Stanford: Stanford University Press, 1989); Dorinne Kay Kondo, *Crafting Selves: Power, Gender, and Discourses of Identity in a Japanese Workplace* (Chicago: University of Chicago Press, 1990); Jennifer Ellen Robertson, "A Dialectic of Native and Newcomer: The Kodaira Citizens' Festival in Suburban Tokyo," *Anthropological Quarterly* 60, no. 3 (1987): 124–36, and "*Furusato* Japan: The Culture and Politics of Nostalgia," *Politics, Culture, and Society* 1, no. 4 (1988): 494–518; Kenneth A. Skinner, "Conflict and Command in a Public Corporation in Japan," *Journal of Japanese Studies* 6, no. 2 (1980): 301–29; Paul H. Noguchi, *Delayed Departures, Overdue Arrivals: Industrial Familism and the Japanese National Railways* (Honolulu: University of Hawaii Press, 1990); and Thomas P. Rohlen, *Japan's High Schools* (Berkeley and Los Angeles: University of California Press, 1983).

who insist on individual difference, opposition to the group, and structural inequalities.[7] If so, we must see these two views of postwar society as contradictory; we must choose, and allow our choice to reinforce one or the other view of the underpinnings of Japanese society.

In fact, I do not find the consensus-conflict polarization particularly helpful. It precludes appreciating how necessarily connected are the incorporating and differentiating effects of institutions and ideologies in postwar Japan. It is less homogenization than standardization that characterizes this period, enforced by certain policies and practices and reinforced by certain choices that people have made. Earlier differences—for example, between country and city, farm and factory, small firm and large company, young and old, male and female—have not been entirely erased; rather, they have been transposed to a new postwar key of differences and tensions. Our task is therefore to formulate analytically the transformations that have both standardized and differentiated postwar society. That is the aim of this chapter.

In what follows I argue that these postwar transformations must be traced on three closely related levels: that of ideological process, that of institutional patterning, and that of the everyday routines of individuals. I consider first the spread of certain public discourses that have proved, rhetorically, both incorporating and differentiating. Among these discourses have been those of Japanese *culture*, which stereotypes traits as national "character" but then by associating character and heritage, exacerbates the ideological dichotomies of modernity and tradition; discourses of *class*, which in fact have declassed and "massified" the debate about societal stratification; a discourse on *generations*, which takes the first Shōwa cohort (1926–34) as a moral standard of postwar adult role commitment; and a discourse on the *life cycle*, which aims to reconceptualize popular notions of the life course in an age of "mass longevity."[8]

Next I address the second dimension of this transformation: the reorganization and effective reach of institutional sectors of postwar society that have patterned lifeways in those decades—especially the sectors of work, family, and schooling. These institutions have both standardized opportunities and constraints but at the same time required differential rewards and variable outcomes (in work conditions, family form, and school success). And finally, a third dimension is the level of individual lives, the choices particular people have made within these ideological and institutional fields, which have produced both convergences and divergences in the routines of daily life. This is the subject of the section titled "Individual Lifeways," which introduces the lives of two sets of postwar siblings.

Each of these topics, of course, has been well treated in the recent social science

7. Examples of this debate about polarities include Harumi Befu, "The Group Model of Japanese Society and an Alternative," *Rice University Studies* 66, no. 1 (1980): 169–87; and Ross Mouer and Yoshio Sugimoto, *Images of Japanese Society* (London: Routledge and Kegan Paul, 1986).

8. The phrase is from David W. Plath, *Long Engagements: Maturity in Modern Japan* (Stanford: Stanford University Press, 1980).

of Japanese society. In a brief essay I can be only selective and illustrative rather than comprehensive and definitive. However, my premise is that only in juxtaposing and relating these several levels of the postwar experience can we begin to understand and represent the nature of a society that has been so extraordinarily transformed in the last half-century.

CULTURE, CLASS, COHORT, AND CYCLE: RHETORICS OF PUBLIC CULTURE IN POSTWAR JAPAN

Among other developments, mass public education, a national readership, and a national marketplace have created both an ideological space—a public culture— and a cultural apparatus of public ministries and private media that are at once concentrated in the metropolitan center and pervasive throughout the peripheral regions. In this space and through this apparatus have been conducted several prominent debates that together constitute a loose field of public commentary and discourse about the shape of postwar Japanese society.

Culture, Character, and Tradition

One of the primary themes of public discourse in postwar Japan has been the fervent fascination with national character, a "Who are we Japanese?" boom, which has spawned a vast literature on the alleged uniqueness of all aspects of Japan. The focus of this "introspection boom" has been a putative Japanese exceptionalism expressed in allegedly unique features of Japanese culture or national character and ranging from the serious to the outrageous.[9] The former include Nakane Chie's well-known notion of Japan as a "vertical society" and Doi Takeo's characterization of a unique Japanese psychology of "indulgence and dependence."[10] Other analysts have claimed for Japan a language of nuance and silent empathic communication, a climate of resignation, and a democracy of hierarchical factions. More fancifully, the Japanese palate, the Japanese brain, and even Japanese bees and primates have been found to exhibit distinctive traits that cannot be fully grasped by the non-Japanese observer.[11] Newspapers and opinion journals are filled with articles such as those of prominent former government minister Amaya Naohiro, who has argued that strict antimonopoly laws are unnecessary and undesirable in a society like Japan, whose elemental unit is the harmonious group, not the competitive individual.[12]

Postwar ideologies of exceptionalism are hardly exceptional either in historical

9. Hiroshi Minami, "The Introspection Boom," *Japan Interpreter* 8, no. 2 (1973): 159–73; see also Koschmann's essay in this volume.

10. Chie Nakane, *Japanese Society* (Berkeley and Los Angeles: University of California Press, 1970); Takeo Doi, *The Anatomy of Dependence* (Tokyo: Kōdansha, 1973).

11. For critical reviews, see Peter Dale, *The Myth of Japanese Uniqueness* (New York: St. Martin's, 1986), and William W. Kelly, "Japanology Bashing," *American Ethnologist* 15, no. 2 (1988): 172–76.

12. Naohiro Amaya, "Harmony and the Antimonopoly Law," *Japan Echo* 8, no. 1 (1981): 85–95.

or comparative terms; the prewar cultural nativism of the folklorist Yanagita Kunio and our own post-Depression fixation on the American Way remind us of that.[13] All such ideologies share the strategy of what Dale has felicitously labeled "cultural exorcism," by which internal tensions are projected onto an external and inauthentic Other.[14] Postwar versions tend to hypostatize Japanese culture by counterexample to the contentious, meat-eating, patrifocal, loquacious, alienated West. For a state that was aggressively militaristic and is now aggressively mercantilist, the political utility of such a mode of reasoning is obvious; valorizing interdependence, racial purity, silence, and obligation is an effective apologetic for national pride and self-repression. To frame these qualities in psychocultural terms is an inclusive appeal to national character.

However, culture in the postwar period has been an argument, not a consensus. There is a divisive tension in this discourse as well. Culture as national character attempted to be all-embracing, but culture also came to be closely linked to "tradition" (dentō). In early postwar debates among intellectuals, this tension was often phrased as an argument about alternative modernities. J. Victor Koschmann has demonstrated in an incisive recovery of these controversies that by the late 1950s there was a conceptual opposition of "critical modernism" and "nationalist particularism," or what one might term Westernization and an autochthonous modernity, based on Japan's unique cultural attributes.[15] However, by the 1960s Japaneseness was increasingly rooted in a putative traditional past, and the politics of heritage came to be set against the very modern condition in which most Japanese found themselves.

Through the 1960s and 1970s Japanese culture was associated with and frequently expressed as an exaltation of Japanese folklore and rural nostalgia. A feverish furusato būmu (home village boom) idealized country life and country folk as the true examplars of Japanese values and communal forms. This exaltation not only exposed a contradiction in the discourse about culture but also caught Japan's regions in an ideological bind. In contrast to the modern center, policy planners and popular media imagined them simultaneously as inaka (the "sticks") and furusato. That is, as the backward "boonies," they had to be assimilated into "modern" society, but as the nation's "folk," they had to be preserved as testimony to a moral society.[16]

13. See, for example, the work of Warren I. Susman, Culture as History: The Transformation of American Society in the Twentieth Century (New York: Pantheon, 1985).

14. Dale, Myth of Japanese Uniqueness, 40.

15. J. Victor Koschmann, "Nihonjinron in Postwar Japanese History" (paper delivered at the 1988 annual meeting, Association for Asian Studies).

16. William W. Kelly, "Rationalization and Nostalgia: Cultural Dynamics of New Middle Class Japan," American Ethnologist 13, no. 4 (1986): 603–18; and "Japanese No-Noh: The Crosstalk of Public Culture in a Rural Festivity," Public Culture 2, no. 2 (1990): 30–45. From a somewhat different perspective, Marilyn Ivy offers a provocative interpretation of the containment as "tradition" of marginal expressions of plebeian culture such as oral tales, spirit mediums, and urban popular the-

Class, from Mass to Micromass

The long-standing belief in the efficacy of the three sacred imperial regalia (mirror, sword, and jewel) has been playfully commercialized by postwar mass media into a variety of slogans of consumer desires, such as the three *S*'s of the late 1950s and early 1960s, the three *C*'s of the mid-1960s, and the three *J*'s of the early 1970s.[17] Similarly, it is clear that the three statistical jewels of the postwar state have been the GNP, population mortality, and class identification. The last of these has meant the declaration of Japan as a "90 percent middle-class" society, which is itself an interpretation of the Survey on the People's Life-Style (*Kokumin seikatsu chōsa*), a well-known public opinion survey conducted annually for more than twenty years by the prime minister's office.[18]

Many commentators (myself included) have characterized postwar conceptions of class in such "new middle class" terms. However, it better problematizes the homogenizing thrust of the claim to see class, like culture, as a shifting field of discourse rather than as an ideological constant of the postwar decades. That is, there have been three broad rubrics in the recent historical trajectory of class. In the two decades of recovery and catch-up, 1945–65, much of the debate focused on the character of an emerging "mass society" (*taishū shakai*), together with speculations about a new middlebrow culture (*taishū bunka*), which Katō Hidetoshi and others argued was replacing earlier highbrow and then lowbrow phases as the dominant tone of public culture.[19]

By the mid-1960s the class debate was increasingly rendered by a new phrase, "the mass mainstream of 100 million people" (*ichiokunin sōchūryū*), who collectively now constituted a "new middle class." That is, middlebrow had become mainstream. Academically, the Social Stratification and Mobility (SSM) national surveys of Tominaga Ken'ichi and his colleagues gave credence to a widespread "white collarization" of the working population and such "status inconsistencies" among respondents as to undermine coherent class stratification. The theoretical economist Murakami Yasusuke proposed an alternative model of a homogenous

---

ater. Marilyn Ivy, "Discourses of the Vanishing in Contemporary Japan" (Ph.D. diss., Cornell University, 1988). For both Ivy and me, the discourse on "tradition" and the ambivalence toward the countryside have important prewar and early modern antecedents.

17. The 3 *S*'s were *senpūki*, *sentaku*, and *suihanki* (electric fan, washing machine, and electric rice cooker); the 3 *C*'s were *kaa*, *kūrā*, and *karā terebi* (car, air conditioner, and color television); and the 3 *J*'s were *jūeru*, *jetto*, and *jūtaku* (jewels, overseas vacation, and a house).

18. For English-language debate on this poll and its interpretations, see Shigeru Aoki, "Debunking the 90%-Middle-Class Myth," *Japan Echo* 6, no. 2 (1979): 29–33; Kōji Taira, "The Middle Class in Japan and the United States," *Japan Echo* 6, no. 2 (1979): 18–28; and Yasusuke Murakami, "The Age of New Middle Mass Politics: The Case of Japan," *Journal of Japanese Studies* 8, no. 1 (1982): 29–72.

19. Hidetoshi Katō, "Middle-brow Culture," *Journal of Social and Political Ideas in Japan* 11, no. 1 (1964): 70–74, a translation of his influential 1957 article. See also Koschmann's essay in this volume. On the mass society debates, see Hidaka Rokurō and Takahashi Akira, *Taishū shakai*, vol. 5 of *Kōza shakaigaku* (Tokyo: Tokyo Daigaku Shuppankai, 1957).

New Middle Mass, which nonetheless emphasized the blurring of class bounda-ries.[20] More popularly, the Prime Minister's Office surveys, begun in 1967, were read as evidence of a largely classless class consciousness. Wittingly or not, estab-lishment interests were well served by this rhetoric of mandarin planners and commentators. Economically, such an image both promoted and responded to new patterns of savings and spending.[21] Politically, it restated societal consensus at a time of student unrest, environmental protest, "oil shocks," "Nixon shocks," and other perturbations of the social order.

The nature and significance of middle-class consciousness (as *chūryū ishiki* was often glossed) remained the major focus in class/mass debates through the 1970s. By the early 1980s, however, this discourse took a new turn toward what some have called a "consumer culture" debate (*shōhi bunka ron*).[22] The preferred class commentators of the 1980s were not the social scientists but advertising executives such as Fujioka Wakao and consumer market researchers such as Ozawa Masako and Sekizawa Hidehiko, who introduced the terms *fragmented masses* (*bunshū*) and *micromasses* (*shōshū*).[23] A uniform middle class with standard needs, they claim, has given way to a "diversified middle class" with multiple preferences; Fujioka's micromass theory, for example, makes much of intuition, "cute" and "mismatch" aesthetics, and grasshopper consumers. Advertising's vision of Japanese society discovers or creates new trendsetters and big spenders, including, most famously, the "neo-homo sapiens" or the "new breed" (*shinjinrui*), a chimera of youth counterculture created as a magazine slogan in the mid-1980s.[24]

In short, class as a topic of public concern in the postwar decades was curiously shorn of its antagonistic rhetorical potential—despite a serious and substantial

20. Tominaga Ken'ichi, ed., *Nihon no kaisō kōzō* (Tokyo: Tokyo Daigaku Shuppankai, 1979); Murakami, "Age of New Middle Mass Politics." Ishida Hiroshi's test, using the 1975 SSM data, of these and two other competing models, is quite valuable; see his "Class Structure and Status Hierar-chies in Contemporary Japan," *European Sociological Review* 5, no. 1 (1989): 65–80.

21. See Horioka's essay in this volume.

22. For critiques of the "mainstream consciousness," see Ishikawa Akihiro, Umezawa Tadashi, Takahashi Yūetsu, and Miyajima Takashi, *Misekake no chūryū kaikyū* (Tokyo: Yūhikaku, 1982); and Kishimoto Shigenobu, *"Chūryū" no gensō* (Tokyo: Kōdansha, 1985). On the "consumer culture" debate, see Saitō Seiichirō, Hoshino Katsumi, Kurimoto Shinichirō, Ozawa Masako, Sekizawa Hidehiko, and Tanaka Yasuo, "Shōhi, kaikyū, soshite yutakasa," *Voice*, Mar. 1986, 88–113.

23. Fujioka Wakao, *Sayonara taishū* (Tokyo: PHP Institute, 1984), and *Sayonara sengo* (Tokyo: PHP Institute, 1987); for Ozawa and Sekizawa, see Hakuhodo Institute of Life and Living, *"Bunshū" no tanjō* (Tokyo: Nihon Keizai Shinbunsha, 1985).

24. See especially Nakano Osamu, *Wakamono bunka no kigōron* (Tokyo: PHP Institute, 1985), and Tetsuya Chikushi, "Young People as a New Human Race," *Japan Quarterly* 33, no. 3 (1986): 291–94. Also targeted are the career women, who were formerly dismissed as "Old Misses" but are now flattered as the "New Misses" and whose tastes are avidly courted through such product development strategies as LED (Ladies' Eye Development) teams. The government has given official sanction to this view in its annual *White Paper on National Livelihood*. See especially the 1985 edition (Tokyo: Economic Planning Agency, Prime Minister's Office, 1985) and the commentary on it in Hikaru Hayashi, "Lifestyle in the 1980s," *Kodansha Encyclopedia of Japan Supplement* (New York: Kodansha International, 1987), 28–30.

Marxist academic literature and despite continuing leftist political opposition.[25] It successfully imputed a bland homogenization to the population, but the horizontal typologies of high, middle, and low, the vertical sectoring of consumer groups, and even the reported status inconsistencies of Tominaga's new middle-class concept nonetheless remained as a constant counterpoint of differentiation.

Generational Cohorts, from Shōwa Hitoketa to Shinjinrui

Yet a third ideological theme of postwar public debate has been a typologizing of "generations" (*sedai*). Cohort distinctiveness and stereotyping has been a popular public passion since at least the Meiji period, but it has had particularly wide currency in the postwar years. The first postwar "generation" controversy was about responsibility in and for the war, particularly about differences between those of the Meiji/Taishō generation with experience before the fifteen-year period of war (1931–45) and the generation that knew no other kind of society than that after the invasion of Manchuria. The debate was sparked by Honda Shūgo's tripartite model, published in 1945 in *Kindai bungaku*. His was an effort to distinguish those whose experiences extended from Meiji "nationalism" through Taishō democracy to the militaristic nationalism of Shōwa; those whose experience extended from Taishō democracy through Shōwa nationalism to the postwar democracy of the American occupation; and those whose lives began under Shōwa nationalism and now extend well into the postwar democracy.

Very soon after that, however, the focal point of commentary shifted to Honda's third group, the so-called *Shōwa hitoketa* generation of those born in the single-digit years of Shōwa (1926–34). This was the generation whose childhood and youth spanned the "dark valley" (*kurai tanima*) of the depression and the war, the generation that was old enough to have suffered but young enough not to have inflicted suffering. They had managed the psychological divide and social chaos that was the transition to peacetime to become the bedrock of postwar recovery and boom. They became, in the popular imagination, the workaholic companymen (*mōretsu shaiin*) and the education mamas (*kyōiku-mama*), whose selfless efforts on behalf of company and children insured present and future prosperity.

The *Shōwa hitoketa* have been a departure and measure for much of the subsequent generational talk, even more definitively than their rough equivalents, "the children of the Depression," have defined postwar American age-grades.[26] For

---

25. See the Gordon and Dower essays in this volume. Recent sociological analysis has made much of the concerns about growing "class disparities" (*kaisō kakusa*) in the EPA's 1988 *White Paper on National Life*. An important article by Nishimura Yoshio traces growing income differentials in Japan to the structural changes in the economy during the mid-1970s, especially those introduced under the rubric of Japan as the "information society" par excellence of the future. See his "Jōhōshakai wa kaisōka suru," *Aestion* 15 (Fall): 60–83. Tessa Morris-Suzuki's renaming (and reanalysis) of "information society" as "information capitalism" is helpful; see her *Beyond Computopia: Information, Automation, and Democracy in Japan* (London: Kegan Paul International, 1988).

26. Glen H. Elder, Jr., *Children of the Great Depression: Social Change in Life Experience* (Chicago: University of Chicago Press, 1974). In several respects, my argument about the shape that this

example, judgments of the postwar population are often cohort-stratified by weakening social commitment and rising personal indulgence, although declining parochialism and growing internationalization is another continuum along which they have also been arrayed. The second decade of Shōwa produced the "double digits," or *Shōwa futaketa* (despite its literal meaning, the term usually refers only to those born from the mid-1930s to the mid-1940s). Reaching middle age in the late 1960s and early 1970s, they have been to many commentators the *mai hōmu–gata*, home-oriented types, who nonetheless retain a commitment to the workplace, if only to secure the status and resources to enable a prosperous home. Of more dubious commitment are the "new family types" (*nyū famirī-gata*), that is, the postwar baby boomers (especially those of the so-called *dankai sedai* of 1947– 51),[27] who are believed to be primarily concerned about a personal life-style and who lack any direct experience of the hardships prior to the high growth decades. To some commentators and analysts the decline continued unabated with the children of the 1960s and 1970s (including the second "baby boomlet" of 1971– 74). Much was made of the *shirake sedai*, the "reactionless" youth of the 1970s, who, it was despaired, lacked enthusiasm for everything, work and home. More recently the *shinjinrui*, the "new breed" youth of the 1980s, have been alternately feted and feared for their misplaced, though voracious, consumer appetites.

Thus, much of the "generation" talk also has an ideological effect of divide-and-unify. That is, it rhetorically age-grades the postwar experience, but in stratifying the population into such horizontal cohorts along a moral cline, it also reinforces a single scale of commitment to societal roles and responsibilities.

Life Cycles and Life Course, from the Fifty-Year to the Eighty-Year Lifetime

Yet a fourth construct that has framed public debate in the postwar decades with both an ideological force and sociological significance is the "life cycle" (*raifu saikuru*) or "life course" (*raifu kōsu*). These terms gained currency somewhat later than the other three, but since the mid-1970s "life course" has come to both reinforce and crosscut cohort imagery. "Life course studies" are now a thriving branch of academic research.[28] More important, it has become an influential rubric in several areas of political-economic policy as an instrument for regularizing people's thinking about normal behavior and decisions about life planning.

The widespread notion of an "appropriate age" (*tekireiki*) for marriage is one such example, but the banking industry was among the earliest to mobilize this

---

generation—or rather the discourse about this generation—has given to the postwar period is similar to Carol Gluck's discussion (in this volume) of private histories, public events, and collective memory.

27. *Dankai sedai*, the "clump generation," was a tag drawn from the title of the novel *Dankai no sedai* by Sakaiya Taichi (Tokyo: Bungei Shunka, 1980). See also Hitoshi Katō, "Japan's First Postwar Generation," *Japan Echo* 10, no. 1 (1983): 79–84.

28. For a useful review of this Japanese scholarship and its Western referents, see Susan Orpett Long, *Family Change and the Life Course in Japan,* East Asia Papers No. 44 (Ithaca: Cornell University China-Japan Program, 1984).

construct in exhorting customers about prudent household savings and spending practices.[29] David Plath, for example, has discussed a 1972 savings and loan advertisement, "For an Unhurried Life Plan" (figure 8.1). In effect, the bank was urging its customers to match a "timetable for family obligations" with a standard schedule for their financial planning.[30]

Of course, such self-interested advice is hardly foreign to any bank customer in Europe and the United States. The difference here is that this life-cycle talk has also proved useful to worker interests, though in ways that drew them ever more into the organizational fold, as illustrated by Rokurō Hidaka's recent reminiscence:

> During the term of the Miki cabinet in the mid seventies, theories about life cycles proliferated. At that time, I had occasion to read one life cycle schedule that had been drawn up by a large labor union in the private sector. The plan saw workers thru graduation from high school and the search for employment to retirement. It included such items as what durable consumer goods were necessary, when to purchase a house (on loan, of course), when to marry, how many children to raise, how many years of schooling these children should be given, and how to secure one's living after retirement. . . . But what is the aim of it all? It is this: that even shop-floor workers should be able to enjoy living standards comparable with section managers.[31]

A major reason for the state attention to the "life cycle" by the mid-1970s was its new vision of Japan as an aging society (*kōreika shakai*) and its nightmare of escalating public entitlements. State ministries began increasingly to refer to the "life cycle," as in the white paper on national livelihood. In particular, the official discussions came to identify an "eighty-year life span" (*jinsei hachi-jū-nen*) as a generalized schema for the population. This phrase has recently been popularized as a contemporary counterpart to the retrospectively labeled prewar "fifty-year life span" (*jinsei go-jū-nen*).[32]

For Japanese, like the populations of the rest of the industrialized world, living into one's fourth quarter of a century is now the statistical expectation, and much state concern focuses on how to (re)organize the third quarter—as in fact the *Shōwa hitoketa* generation leads the society toward "mass longevity." As has been noted for the United States, an earlier population pyramid is becoming an upright rectangle (figure 8.2). Thus, the rhetoric of the "eighty-year lifetime" also aims to reformulate one's later years as part of national planning for an "aging society."

29. The Prime Minister's Statistical Office conveniently collects public opinion on the proper age for marriage and reports in its *Yoron chōsa nenkan*. For the late 1970s, it was 22–25 for women and 26–30 for men. See Walter Edwards, *Modern Japan Through Its Weddings: Gender, Person, and Society in Ritual Portrayal* (Stanford: Stanford University Press, 1989), 63–64.

30. Plath, *Long Engagements*, 87–90.

31. Rokurō Hidaka, *The Price of Affluence* (Tokyo: Kōdansha, 1984), 70–71.

32. Again, the life cycle has been discussed cogently by David Plath, "The Eighty-Year System: Japan's Debate over Lifetime Employment in an Aging Society," *The World & I*, May 1988, 464–71.

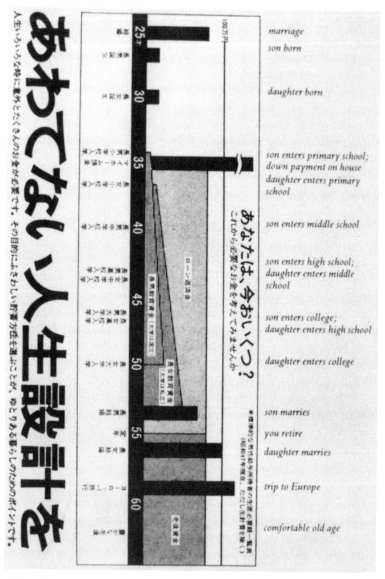

Figure 8.1. "For an Unhurried Life Plan": a 1972 savings and loan association advertisement. SOURCE: David W. Plath, *Long Engagements: Maturity in Modern Japan* (Stanford: Stanford University Press, 1980). Reprinted with permission.

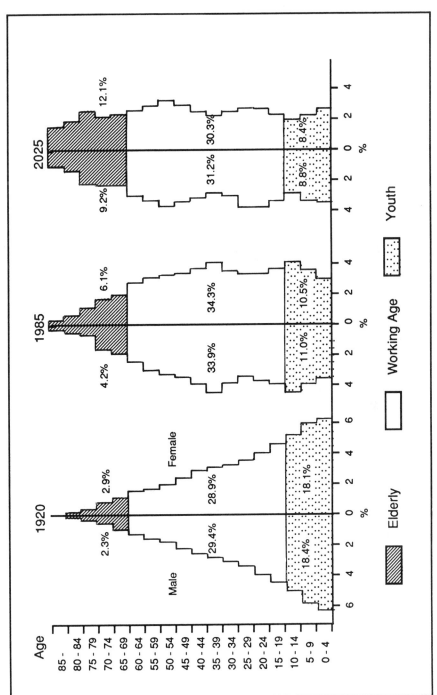

Figure 8.2. The population pyramid of Japan. SOURCE: Population censuses, Prime Minister's Office.

Government policy initiatives have been designed to encourage a more active and independent old age (e.g., "self-care" programs, Silver Volunteers, etc.) and, for the disabled and most senior elderly, to promote "home care" and continued privatization of caretaking responsibilities.[33]

For late Shōwa Japan this has been a preemptive rhetoric. Its population profile during the 1970s and 1980s was among the youngest of the countries in the Organization for Economic Cooperation and Development. However, it is rapidly aging, and by 2000, with 16 percent of the population over sixty-five, it will have one of the oldest profiles. Anticipation of this situation has heightened the urgency and frequency of appeals to the "eighty-year life span." Private industry and government planners now use it, for example, in legitimating a shift in the retirement policies of major corporations—as in the calls for raising the common mandatory retirement age from fifty-five to sixty. Recognition of an expanding "life cycle" also underlies the many policies and programs of "lifelong education" that have proliferated in late Shōwa to inculcate a longer-term attitude toward cultural recreation and vocational (re)training.[34]

A unique Japanese culture, a new middle class, the *Shōwa hitoketa* generation and its offspring, and a new eighty-year life-cycle norm are among the most potent and characteristic ideologies of postwar Japan. There are certainly others that both reinforce and counterbalance these four. As Kathleen S. Uno discusses elsewhere in this volume, there is a ubiquitous gender ideology of persistent male prerogative and, in the postwar valorization of the nuclear family, of what Edwards has labeled the complementary incompetence of the husband-wife couple. A Confucian idiom of relational hierarchy and performative obligation has proved to be a durable idiom of social conduct. And despite the reticulations that draw the population into a single metropolitan society, a renewed discourse of locality reinforces the antipodes of center and region, town and country.[35]

However, I wish to emphasize that the ideological themes selected here have complex, even contradictory effects. As students, readers, consumers, and viewers,

33. David W. Plath, "The Age of Silver: Aging in Modern Japan," *The World & I*, Mar. 1988, 505–13.

34. On the "age-sixty retirement system" (*rokujū-sai teinensei*), see Plath, "Eighty-Year System." Lifelong education programs include the culture center movements of local governments and private companies (especially department stores, broadcasting companies, and newspaper companies). Imamura's mid-1970s research in a western Tokyo suburb was located in part in the city's first culture center (*Urban Japanese Housewives*); see also Takeshi Moriya, "The History of Japanese Civilization Through Aesthetic Pursuits," *Senri Ethnological Studies* 16 (1984): 105–16.

35. See Edwards, *Modern Japan Through Its Weddings*, 116. On the Confucian idiom, see especially Thomas P. Rohlen, "Order in Japanese Society: Attachment, Authority, and Routine," *Journal of Japanese Studies* 15 no. 1 (1989): 5–40; Ronald P. Dore, *Taking Japan Seriously: A Confucian Perspective on Leading Economic Issues* (Stanford: Stanford University Press, 1987); and Robert J. Smith, *Japanese Society: Tradition, Self, and the Social Order* (Cambridge: Cambridge University Press, 1983). On locality, see Kelly, "Rationalization and Nostalgia," and Robertson, "Dialectic."

postwar Japanese have been drawn into a powerful field of public culture through books, advertisements, white papers, programs, columns, speeches. The dominant yet shifting constructs of culture, class, cohort, and cycle—their pervasiveness and "publicity"—offer new and unifying frames of experience. At the same time, however, they also construct new categories of distinction, and this double effect lies behind my characterization of a postwar transposition of difference to a register of standardization.

INSTITUTIONAL PATTERNING

The rhythms of life experiences in postwar Japanese society have been both idealized and routinized by three broad institutional arenas—the workplace, the household, and the school. Early postwar actions substantially reshaped each of these institutions—for instance, the reorganization of businesses and labor force during the early economic recovery, the new Civil Code, and the Allied occupation's revision of the educational system. On the one hand, powerful typifications of these institutions have narrowed the preferred meanings of support in family, success in school, and security in work. That is, both official policy and public opinion came to idealize career employment in large organizations, meritocratic educational credentialing, and a nuclear household division of labor between the working husband and the nurturing wife. The ideological effect of valorizing serious students, diligent corporate workers, and paired householders has been to define standards of achievement, images of the desirable, and limits of the feasible.

On the other hand, employment in large organizations, success in competitive college examinations, and a lifelong nuclear household have remained statistical minorities throughout the postwar period. The actual compositions of workplaces, schools, and families are far more diverse. That is, these ideals remain compelling and consequential even as they fly in the face of life's realities for many Japanese. Indeed, put differently, these institutional arenas have channeled postwar ambitions but have produced, indeed required, multiple outcomes. This managed differentiation contributes to the larger paradox of identity and difference in the construction of postwar society.

Work and Workplaces

The last four decades have seen a dramatic shift in the labor force. The decline of agricultural employment has been precipitous. In 1949 nearly half of employment was in agriculture; in 1986 that figure was 7 percent. In 1950 only 40 percent of all workers were employed outside of family businesses; another quarter were owners of independent enterprises, while a third of the labor force were family workers. By 1985 family workers were a mere 9 percent and independent owners but 15 percent of the labor force, while fully 76 percent were now employed workers. Paid work in postwar Japan has become overwhelmingly a matter of corporate or public organizational work.

The year 1955 was a widely recognized turning point in the postwar economy. Many levels of economic performance had finally returned to their prewar highs; mechanization was beginning to release labor in agriculture for industrial employment; and the economy was in an expansionary growth period (the so-called Jinmu Boom). Both the government and media commentators were announcing the "end of the postwar period." During the same year the American James Abegglen was working out a model of the Japanese large firm that was to have enormous influence within and outside of Japan. He identified as characteristically Japanese features those of lifetime employment, pay and promotion by seniority, entry from the bottom, and enterprise unionism.[36] His model was intriguing to foreign observers even though they were puzzled that "traditional" features could still serve efficient functions. It was precisely this theme of cultural legacy that initially discomforted many Japanese, who interpreted it as a measure of backwardness; they later embraced the description as flattering evidence of exceptionalism.

Abegglen's model has proved a tenacious image of work organization and conditions, but for at least three reasons it is also a seriously misleading one. First, as Andrew Gordon, Thomas Smith, and others have demonstrated, much of what he implied to be timeless, traditional, and "Japanese" was of recent, mixed, and negotiated origin.[37] Second, subsequent ethnographic studies have shown that even those large work organizations that appear to fit the model are more complexly and tensely structured. For instance, Rohlen shows in his study of Ueda Bank that the bank's promotion of both competitive drive and a cooperative ethic was not always easy for employees. Indeed, as with the bank's "spiritual training" programs, they are possibly contradictory: training to make one invulnerable and yet vulnerable, to simultaneously toughen and soften one's motivations and spirit, was held to be mutually reinforcing but could as easily be incompatible.

But getting ahead and getting along are not always reconcilable. At Ueda Bank as elsewhere, a stock motif of New Years' cards arranged a section's personnel in a circle of harmony (*wa*) around the section chief and his assistants.[38] In fact, the geometric rendering of such large companies is more like an overlay of circle, rectangle, and triangle. The centripetal force of company membership is crosscut by the rectangular stacking of entry-year cohorts into an age-grade hierarchy. It is further threatened by the inevitable, sanctioned competition among a cohort for the fewer and fewer positions of central responsibility and higher status, creating a pyramidal organizational chart. In sum, even the contemporary ideal of large

36. James Abegglen, *The Japanese Factory: Aspects of Its Social Organization* (Glencoe: Free Press, 1958).

37. Andrew Gordon, *The Evolution of Labor Relations in Japan: Heavy Industry, 1853–1955,* Harvard East Asia Monographs No. 117 (Cambridge: Harvard University Press, 1985); and Thomas C. Smith, "The Right to Benevolence in Japan: Dignity and Japanese Workers, 1890–1920," *Comparative Studies in Society and History* 26 (1984): 587–613.

38. See Rohlen, *For Harmony and Strength,* 140–41 (interleaf), for an example.

organization *sararīman* employment masks a field of opposing and often not easily balanced structural imperatives.[39]

Third, and perhaps most seriously, the large organization model is misleading because it fails to describe—or account for—the vast majority of postwar workplaces and careers, whose very presence is necessary for the existence of the large organizations. The postwar variant of "Confucian capitalism" is the uneasy articulation of a small core of full-time, lifetime, trained male employees and a peripheral cushion that includes female part-timers, second-career retirees, seasonal rural labor, and small regional subcontractors. These distinctions between the privileged and the peripheral are maintained both within large corporations and ministries and in their linkages to extensive subcontracting networks and subordinate agencies. Skinner vividly described, for example, the ways in which the pseudonymous JKII, a satellite public agency of a national ministry, was used both as a training ground for the ministry's elite track younger managers and as a dumping ground for its older, less talented executives. Within JKII, turnover at the top and permanently blocked avenues of advancement for its own employees had devastating consequences on morale and productivity.[40]

The subcontracting sector is one of medium and small firms, the so-called *chūsho kigyō* sector. These firms predominate in rural areas and depend heavily on seasonal male labor and "part-time" female workers.[41] However, it is crucial to realize that this sector cannot be characterized simply by subcontracting. About three-quarters of the Japanese work force is employed in companies with three hundred or fewer employees, and these figures have not changed appreciably in thirty years. There is enormous range in company autonomy, job mobility, technological innovation, career ladders, and authority structures. In fact, a number of recent studies are forcing a fundamental reappraisal of the distinctiveness and centrality of small enterprise to the postwar economy.[42] And as Sheldon Garon and Mike Mochizuki's chapter shows, the medium-to-small sector has agitated continually to improve its political position in the ruling conservative coalition.

In sum, despite corporate ideology, postwar patterns of work have been char-

39. See Gordon's essay in this volume for a different but complementary perspective on managerial and worker cultures within large companies.

40. Skinner, "Conflict and Command."

41. Kent E. Calder, *Crisis and Compensation: Public Policy and Political Stability in Japan, 1949–1986* (Princeton: Princeton University Press, 1989); David Friedman, *The Misunderstood Miracle: Industrial Development and Political Change in Japan* (Ithaca: Cornell University Press, 1988); and William W. Kelly, "Regional Japan: The Price of Prosperity and the Benefits of Dependency," *Daedalus* 119, no. 3 (1990): 209–27.

42. In addition to the books by Calder, Friedman, and Kondo, see the important essay by Hugh T. Patrick and Thomas P. Rohlen, "Small-Scale Family Enterprises," in Kozo Yamamura and Yasukichi Yasuba, eds., *The Political Economy of Japan*, vol. 1, *The Domestic Transformation* (Stanford: Stanford University Press, 1987), 331–84.

acterized by structural tensions within large organizations and uneasy and varied ties to the penumbra of medium-small firms. This description echoes those of other chapters in this volume—not only Garon and Mochizuki's essay but also Andrew Gordon's account of struggles between management and workers. Given this differentiated workplace patterning, adversarial work cultures, and political activity, one might properly wonder why moments of radical challenge were so few.

Kent Calder has noted two intersecting trends important for understanding these postwar class dynamics—the absence of sustained conflict over work and workplace organization despite the varieties and disparities. On the one hand, the near disappearance of agriculture and agricultural employment did not precipitate residential dislocation and regional unemployment in large part because many of the manufacturing jobs remained in the countryside. On the other hand, the role of organized labor has declined sharply, especially since the mid-1970s. The unionization ratio in 1949 was about 50 percent; in 1986 it was 28.2 percent (and days lost to labor disputes was less than one-tenth of 1949 figures). As Calder argues: "Private-sector labor, under the pressure of technological change and the growing export reliance of Japanese industry after the 1973 oil shock, forged closer ties with both management and the ruling Liberal Democratic party to protect its economic position; more militant public-sector labor was destroyed as a political force by the mid-1980s through extensive privatization."[43]

These developments suggest the ways by which difference has been both reproduced and contained. Nonetheless, the result has been not a docile and compliant work force but one that has actively shaped its workplaces. The structural imperatives of large organizations insure that the discipline and commitment achieved are at best contingent. Some of the medium-small sector provides the necessary and vulnerable flexibility for large organizations, but much of it remains dynamic and autonomous.

Schools and Schooling

Allied occupation authorities oversaw a thorough redesign of early postwar education: the multiple tracks of the prewar system were amalgamated into a single six-three-three progression; control was localized in district school boards; and curricular content was depoliticized by eliminating offensive moral teaching. Dore witnessed in 1950 Shitayama the residents' and teachers' enthusiasm for innovations like PTAs and "social studies." Although neither was well understood, the prospects of democratizing the process and widening the opportunities for educational advancement were powerful motivations behind the sharp drop in the birthrates in the 1950s.[44]

Within the next few years, however, many of the organizational trends were

43. Calder, *Crisis and Compensation*, 462.
44. Kozo Yamamura and Susan B. Hanley, "*Ichi hime, ni Tarō:* Educational Aspirations and the Decline of Fertility in Post-war Japan," *Journal of Japanese Studies* 2, no. 1 (1975): 83–125.

reversed. The national Ministry of Education succeeded in reasserting crucial control over budgetary, personnel, and curricular affairs, the entrance exam system was strengthened to determine admissions at the high school and university levels, and an underfunded and poorly regulated higher education system was allowed to proliferate. Its actions in turn fed an emerging image of postwar education as rigidly egalitarian, offering broad and uniform basic education but measuring ability by an absolutely discriminating exam yardstick, which selected those who could achieve impressively in a narrow range of factual knowledge. The commonality of the learning experience and the objectivity of the standard are held to legitimate the fairness of the outcome, whose credentialing sorts the population into adult roles.

Nonetheless, as in the arena of work, this stereotype conveys a false uniformity about the postwar education experience. It focuses attention at one level—that of academic secondary education—of a multitiered institution whose other levels we now understand to be organized along often different principles. A fuller account of schooling would consider the contrasts and links between early and elementary education; junior high and secondary levels; the junior colleges and universities; and childhood schooling and adult in-company training. Lois Peak, Catherine Lewis, and Joseph Tobin, for example, have drawn compelling pictures of early education as both strikingly different and clearly preparatory to later pedagogy and patterns: the deemphasis on academic skills, the teachers' marked preference not to impose order, solutions, and discipline, and the mobilization of small groups for those purposes.[45]

Even within the level of high school education, Rohlen has pointed to the tensions in the education system, in the political and procedural disputes between the teachers' union and the Ministry of Education, in the individual nature of test taking and the small-group initiative in social problem solving, in the muting of achievement and aptitude within a school, and in the highly visible tracking among schools in terms of public reputation.[46] Even for those successfully climbing the steep educational pyramid, after-hours cram schools for academic preparation have dichotomized the schooling experience into a daytime pedagogy that stresses conformity and uniformity and an evening pedagogy that aggressively hones individual competitive skills and spirit.

Drawing out the divisions within schooling highlights the parallels and points of articulation with the workplace. There is a close fit, for example, between core and periphery of work opportunities and the pinnacle and base of the education

45. Catherine C. Lewis, "From Indulgence to Internalization: Social Control in the Early School Years," *Journal of Japanese Studies* 15, no. 1 (1989): 139–57; Lois Peak, "Learning to Become Part of the Group: The Japanese Child's Transition to Preschool Life," *Journal of Japanese Studies* 15, no. 1 (1989): 93–123; and Joseph J. Tobin, David Y. H. Wu, and Dana H. Davidson, *Preschool in Three Cultures: Japan, China, and the United States* (New Haven: Yale University Press, 1989).

46. Rohlen, *Japan's High Schools*, and Rohlen, "The Juku Phenomenon: An Exploratory Essay," *Journal of Japanese Studies* 6, no. 1 (1980): 207–42.

pyramid. There are also instructive similarities between the organizational reliance on delegated responsibilities to the small work group, to the school homeroom, and to the preschool "squad." And Rohlen's observations about how the closely bounded high schools in his Kobe sample stifled student counterculture may have parallels with the ways in which enveloping corporations can co-opt autonomous worker organization.[47]

Families and Family Life

Certain developments, especially legal and demographic, have precipitated major changes in family form since 1945. In particular, the postwar Civil Code eliminated the mandate to continue family lines and primogeniture rules for succession and inheritance. Better health and nutrition rapidly extended life expectancy and the life course; a large proportion of the population is now living up to a third of their lives as grandparents.

Samuel Coleman has demonstrated both the standardization and the shifts in key elements of family formation that have resulted, including a later age of marriage, tight timing of first birth, the bunched birth of a second child, negligible premarital childbirth, and low divorce rates.[48] There is now a strong, age-specific association of marriage and fertility (figure 8.3). New middle-class ideology further legitimizes these patterns by stressing the full-time commitment of the *sararīman* husband to provide secure household income, the full-time commitment of the "professional housewife" to manage household expenditures and nurture the children, and equal commitment by the children to apply themselves to school success.

However, in many respects family form and marital experience remain diverse. The frequency of working married women belies broad salience of new middle-class norms of domesticity. In cultural terms one can see other ambiguities of family form in the changes in the marriage ceremony itself, which Walter Edwards has recently described. He shows that although much commentary on marriage change has posited a postwar shift from arranged to "love" marriages, such a view masks the still common experience that often combines some introductions and some initiative by the two individuals, some concern for objective characteristics and some importance to the "feelings" of the couple. In fact, the less noticed but much clearer shift has been the commercialization of postwar marriage. It would appear from Edwards's figures that about 75–85 percent of all marriage ceremonies and receptions are now conducted at professional wedding halls or hotels with similar services.[49] What is fascinating about his accounts of the ceremonies is their dramatic juxtaposition of themes of romance and responsibility, of dependence on and independence from a network of family and associates,

47. See Gordon's essay in this volume.

48. Samuel Coleman, "The Tempo of Family Formation," in David W. Plath, ed., *Work and Lifecourse in Japan* (Albany: SUNY Press, 1983), 183–214.

49. Edwards, *Modern Japan Through Its Weddings*, 50–51.

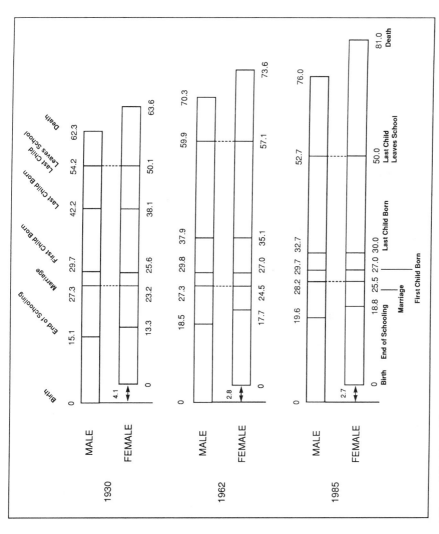

Figure 8.3. Mean life trajectories of Japanese males and females born in 1930, 1962, and 1985. SOURCE: Economic Planning Agency White Paper for 1985.

and the interdependence of the "complementarily incompetent" householder pair.

Indeed, a constructive ambiguity surrounds contemporary society's measure of full maturity. When is one considered adult? When do young people "enter society"? At the "ceremony of adulthood" at age twenty? With employment, in this age of nearly universal wage work after graduation? At marriage? Or with the birth of the first child, that is, at parenthood? To many, it would seem, the marital ideal is a household of *parents,* not newlyweds, thus lending an air of anticipation and incompleteness to the wedding itself.

It is curious that the proportion of nuclear families has remained roughly constant through the postwar decades (figure 8.4). Other circumstances, it appears, have slowed further nuclearization. Among them are state policies that have dealt ambivalently with the family in the last four decades. On the one hand, promotion of the nuclear family has facilitated greater mobility of the work force and has multiplied family units of consumption. On the other hand, there have been strong reservations about possible escalating calls on public resources for children (in the provision of day care), adults (in the provision of expanded housing stock), and the elderly (in the provision of health care). Thus, while characteristics of the *ie* "system" were disparaged in favor of the *katei* (household) or *kazoku* (family), in many respects a new opposition was introduced between the *sansedai kazoku* (the three-generation family) and the *kakukazoku* (the nuclear family). As a residential unit rather than patriarchal line, the three-generation family is promoted in a number of ways, including recent programs of two-generation mortgages. This is a low-interest housing loan offered to those who build *sansedai jūtaku,* designed with multiple bathrooms and kitchens to provide living space for elderly parents.

In short, despite the valorization of the conjugal couple and the nuclear household, it is likely that family experience for much of the population has and will continue to include phases of nuclear and extended household living. Inadequate day care compounded by the difficulties and expense of housing offer some advantages to remaining with parents. Later in life, the limitations of elderly hospitalization policy (which increasingly stresses "home care," *hōmu kea*) create pressures for generations to reassemble in some joint living arrangements. These and other circumstances contravene the homogenizing effects of legal and demographic change and insure a continued diversity of family form.

INDIVIDUAL LIFEWAYS: CONVERGENCES AND DIVERGENCES IN EVERYDAY LIFE

Still, neither homogenizing institutions nor hegemonic ideologies work inexorably. It is only through a close reading of individual lives as they embody and animate social forces that we can understand both the strength of these ideologies and institutions and their variable and imperfect manifestations in social patterns.

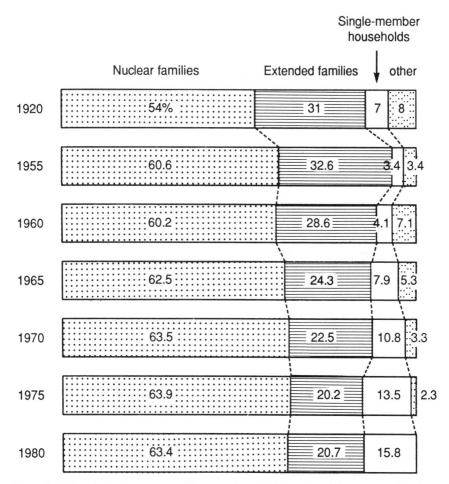

Figure 8.4. Trends in the structure of Japanese household membership. SOURCE: Population censuses, Prime Minister's Office.

In concluding this essay, I wish to briefly illustrate this dialectic of embodiment and animation with profiles of two sets of postwar siblings, the Itōs from a rural region in the northeast, and the Kimuras from a suburb of Kyoto. In their details the six life trajectories are widely diverse, yet in the regularization of their transitions and in their encounters with institutional demands, they are all recognizably and representatively postwar.[50]

The three Kimura siblings were all born in the first postwar decade in a town

50. This material comes from my own ongoing research. All names are pseudonyms, and details necessary to preserve anonymity have been changed. The Itōs figure briefly in Kelly, "Rationalization and Nostalgia," and in Kelly, "Japanese Farmers," *Wilson Quarterly* 14, no. 4 (1990): 34–41, from which I have borrowed several paragraphs.

on Kyoto's western border, which was then being suburbanized as was the Vogels' research site of Mamachi. Their father had been born in 1920 to a Kyoto merchant; he graduated from Kyoto University and served in the military in southern China for several years before exaggerating an injury and being returned to Kyoto. In 1945, through a family relative, he was introduced to and married the daughter (born in 1925) of a farmer whose land on the western edge of Kyoto was beginning to appreciate. With a gift of a land parcel from her father, they built a comfortable middle-class home. The father went to work for a large private railroad company in the region and rose through assignments in four of its various subsidiaries. He was a diffident company man who eschewed much of the normally obligatory after-hours socializing. His final position as labor relations specialist in one of the company's hotels suggested to him a postretirement "second career" as a labor consultant to small businesses in the Kansai area. He now has the requisite license and plans to practice as long as his health permits. His wife, having recently borne the burden of caring for her senile parents in their final five years, is supportive and insistent on his working. Her own efforts, however, to stay "busy" between visits to her children are limited to foreign language classes in the private Culture Center in her neighborhood.

The oldest child, the daughter Rumi, was born in 1946; her father encouraged her to pursue her education at a private university. In 1972, at twenty-six, she married a Swedish academic scientist whom she met while working as a tour guide for foreigners. They soon moved to Sweden, where they continue to live. She gives both piano and Japanese language lessons at home, as their three children approach adolescence.

The second child, the son Tetsuya, was born in 1947. He majored in engineering at a local private university; on graduation, with his advisor's recommendation, he was selected for a highly competitive position in the research institute of a major construction company on the outskirts of Tokyo. He met his wife through an introduction by one of his university professors and married in 1975 at age twenty-eight. They moved into a rental apartment in Tama New Town and in 1983, at odds of seven hundred to one, won a lottery drawing for a house site in a new development adjacent to their apartment complex. With company mortgage money and a two-generation bank loan, they had a modest $600,000 house built by 1988. His wife had quit her clerical job at marriage to raise two children; they are now entering high school, and she has returned to school to study bookkeeping. She has a part-time accounting job and hopes to free-lance, both for her children's school expenses and for the new house.

The second daughter, Mariko, was born in 1950. She followed her older sister to private university and then a master's degree in English literature. She stayed at home through several brief jobs teaching in private high schools. These years coincided with the period during which her mother's bedridden parents moved in. After several struggles with her parents over boyfriends and job frustrations, she sought refuge with her sister in Sweden, where she studied Swedish sufficiently to secure a job at the embassy in Tokyo. In 1982, at age thirty-two, she met and married Akira, a Japanese executive of a Swedish company. His father had just died, and they inherited his condominium in the center of Tokyo. Akira's mother divides her time between her son and daughter-in-law and her daughter in Kanazawa, the family's original home. Mariko adamantly resists Akira's occasional expressions of a desire for children.

For the moment the parents are among the healthy and active "young old," but the recent experience with the mother's parents has led to some discussion across the generations about future arrangements. Despite the parents' fond hopes that one of their children will return to Kyoto, careers clearly prevent that. In their own ways all three siblings have thought contingently about assuming a share of the caretaking, but there are no joint plans.

The three Itō siblings are rough contemporaries of the Kimuras from a rural region in the northeast. The oldest of the three, Noboru, was born to *Shōwa hitoketa* parents in 1949, just as the postwar land reform gave his grandfather clear title to the two hectares of rice paddy that the household had tenanted. His grandfather and his parents farmed this land through the 1950s and early 1960s while encouraging the three children to continue through high school.

Noboru's younger brother, Shōji (born 1950), graduated from the regional technical high school and went to work in a Yokohama auto parts factory. After holding a series of machine shop jobs in the Kanto area, he has settled into employment with a small pollution-control company in Yokohama. He now lives in a public rental apartment with his wife, who works part-time, and their two middle school children. The youngest sibling, the daughter Yumiko (born 1953), graduated from the regional commercial high school and immediately left for Tokyo to find work as a buyer for a Tokyo department store. After living with her boyfriend for a year, they were married in 1982 in an expensive ceremony at the Imperial Hotel in downtown Tokyo. She joined her husband in his family's small women's-clothing business; together they purchased a modest condominium in eastern Tokyo. The business went bankrupt, however, in the mid-1980s; the Itōs have complained since that Yumiko's husband had foolishly overextended himself. Yumiko and her husband were forced to rent out the condominium and live in a modest apartment with his mother while operating a small pet shop. His mother has provided day care for their one child, who will soon be in kindergarten.

Noboru's own decision to go to the agricultural high school was a difficult one, but he has stuck with farming long after nearly all of the young men of the settlement have given up. Noboru now handles three hectares of paddyland by himself, with only a bit of help at transplanting and harvest. In addition, he grows and pickles organic vegetables under a contract with a consumer cooperative in Tama New Town. He holds the contract with two acquaintances from nearby villages; each of them grows and processes independently, but they market under a common label. For his business he seasonally hires several older men and women of the village, including his own mother.

Noboru and Keiko, a year younger, were married in 1973 after introductions through mutual friends of their parents and a very brief courtship. She had agreed with the explicit stipulation that she could continue as a full-time salesperson at what was then the only department store on the plain. After nearly twenty years with the store, she remains on the sales floor; any advancement would have required assignments away from the region. In the 1960s the Itōs had been one of the first in the settlement to rebuild their house with tile roofing, full electrical wiring, and modern kitchen appliances. In the mid-1970s his parents built Noboru and Keiko a small, second-story addition to the house where the young couple have a bedroom and living room. Noboru and Keiko now look enviously on the layouts of more recent houses in the settlement that divide even more discretely the living and eating spaces of the adult generations.

Noboru's father now involves himself with local "good causes"—particularly school programs and senior citizen activities. He is a four-term town councillor, generally supporting the district's Socialist Dietman, and makes a little money as a school crossing guard. In the years since her own contributions to the paddy fields became unnecessary, Noboru's mother Fusae has risen most mornings at five o'clock to earn a bit of money doing piecework at home. For several years she did soldering for an electric-parts factory; recently she has been doing finish work for girls' clothing at 200 yen ($1.90) per piece. At six-thirty she stretches her sore back with the radio exercise program, and then she and Keiko prepare breakfast. While the children are at school, she tends the family's large vegetable garden and continues her piecework. She has been generally happy to assume much of the burden of raising her three grandchildren. As a young bride she had to return to the fields immediately after giving birth to her own three children, who were looked after by her mother-in-law. She enjoys this long-delayed chance to be a mother.

Keiko and Noboru's three children all moved up the educational ladder in 1990. The oldest, a daughter, passed a highly competitive exam to enter the region's preeminent high school; the second, a son and putative household successor, entered the town's junior high school, while the youngest, a second son, began elementary school. The Itōs' present educational concerns focus on the older two. Unlike students in other high schools, students in the daughter's high school are expected to go on to college, but the region's best school is still far from the top of the national pyramid. Personal ambitions and adult expectations push the students to aspirations for which even its regular, fast-paced curriculum cannot prepare them. In 1990 fully 120 of the 220 graduating seniors chose to take an extra year for intensive exam preparation, either by themselves (as so-called *rōnin*) or at special prep academies. As high school graduates Keiko and Noboru improved on their parents' elementary education, and they would undoubtedly be pleased with a college degree by their daughter. Yet they already recognize how bittersweet would be the satisfaction, not only because of her short-term pressures, but also because of the long-term probability that a college degree will take her, like many of the better educated, out of the region for work and marriage.

This prospect only heightens their anxieties about the older son. Given the three-year junior high system, they have eighteen months before they must decide which high school's entrance exam he will sit for. Is there a future in the family's farming? Is he interested? Should he be encouraged? How strongly should they encourage him? Noboru has a newfound enthusiasm for farming and the experience to develop a farming business partially independent of the cooperative network, but he still lacks confidence in the long-term future for local agriculture. Like virtually every other parent in the area, he will probably counsel his son toward other work.

In even this most cursory sketch of the basic life circumstances of this now middle-aged cohort, one can find ample evidence of how the ideologies and institutions of the postwar decades have shaped both the convergences and divergences of their lifeways. The three Itōs and the three Kimuras were born to parents attempting the common transitions of the immediate postwar: from tenancy to modern mechanized agriculture, from an old middle-class commercial background to new middle-class corporate employment. For all of the children schooling was crucial in their own development and emerging identity; it both synchronized their life transitions and sorted the opportunities available to them. Those opportunities led to a variety of jobs and careers, but what most shared, even Itō Noboru's farming and food processing, was a division of work and household and a high value on the security of the conditions and professionalism of the work.

In material circumstances and household income there are visible but not yawning differences among the six families. They have all been buffeted by the crosscurrents of saving and spending that simultaneously encourage thrifty households and spendthrift consumers. However, it is less in income than in assets that the gaps are wide and widening, through the good fortune and inheritance of the three Kimuras and Itō Noboru. As families, all six reflect the primacy of nuclear units (in physical space and social disposition) and persisting norms of organic solidarity (that is, the mutually exclusive spheres and complementary contributions of spouses). For both the Kimuras and Itōs the demands of career and attractions of work in metropolitan Tokyo have undermined connections to parents. Getting ahead and staying put are not easily reconciled. Nonetheless, there are important links across the adult generations, and it is likely that, despite the difficulties, several of the Kimuras will feel compelled to provide home care for their elderly parents later in the life cycle.

CONCLUSION

This essay has characterized postwar society by the wider subscription to ideological and institutional standards *and* the perpetuation of significant, antagonizing differences. How is one to resolve such an apparent paradox? What is the nature of the postwar societal order and what is the potential for disruption and societal disorder? As other chapters have suggested, these have certainly been matters of sustained debate. Controversies about the shape and significance of the postwar political economy, for instance, frequently turn on different interpretations about how managed or how negotiated is the social order. Some analysts, either critically or admiringly, have found Japan a paragon (or prison) of administered efficiency, the ultimate "managed society" (*kanri shakai*). Other, quite different models locate its special nature in the reverse: in the *absence* of a strong center. Action—and order—are the products of negotiations among pluralist interest groups or between state ministries and political parties.

However, neither elite coercion nor negotiated consensus most appropriately characterizes the social order of middle and late Shōwa. Its order is better described as co-optive, complicit, and contested. Postwar society is a co-optive order in the sense that predominant ideologies and institutions have been remarkably inclusive, embracing much of the population and regularizing their lifeways. It is a complicit order in that the inclusiveness of these ideologies and institutions has defused much potential conflict and infused widespread commitment. And it is a contested order in that public rhetorics and institutions shape and constrain ordinary lives in ways that are neither direct nor mechanical nor complete. There are no ideologies of sameness masking a reality of differences, with coercion and false consciousness preserving the former while masking the latter. Ideologies of culture, class, cohort, and life cycle have themselves been fields of argument rather than consensual tenets. The tensions that have strained workplaces, schools, and families in the postwar decades render institutional hegemony a problematical and not inevitable achievement.[51] Within and between these arguments and tensions, the people of middle and late Shōwa have acted, effectively and creatively, to construct and "lead" their lives.

Yet it would be misleading to exaggerate their field of choices. Much has worked against questioning and toward acceptance. Like ideologies and institutions everywhere, those of postwar Japan "normalize" in two senses. Ideological representation both generalizes and naturalizes, claiming for specific interests a natural universality. And the power of institutions is the power to normalize in the twin senses of idealizing and routinizing certain patterns of conduct. The terms of the rhetorical and institutional embrace around the people of postwar Japan have entailed distinctions that have reproduced and legitimated social differences, albeit in new forms.

51. Another version of these final paragraphs concludes William W. Kelly, "Directions in the Anthropology of Contemporary Japan," *Annual Review of Anthropology* 20 (1991): 395–431. That article also gives fuller treatment to issues of gender and marginalized populations than I have been able to here.

Political Economy

1. Having just renounced all claims to divine status the previous month, the newly "human" emperor (wearing hat and overcoat) visits female factory workers at the Shōwa Denkō factory in Kawasaki on 19 February 1946. This was the first of numerous such public excursions for the emperor. (Courtesy of *Asahi shinbun*.)

2. The emperor and empress wave to the crowd at the official celebration of the promulgation of the new constitution on 3 November 1946 in Tokyo. The emperor's appearance in front of a crowd of 100,000 people in front of the imperial palace contrasted to the promulgation of the Meiji constitution by Hirohito's grandfather in 1889 at a ceremony restricted to foreign dignitaries and top government officials. In both cases, however, the emperor was at the center of the event. (Courtesy of *Mainichi shinbun*.)

3. Portrait of the political elite of the high-growth era: Tanaka Kakuei's first cabinet, 7 July 1972. Four present or future prime ministers served in this cabinet. From left to right in the front row, they are Nakasone Yasuhiro (1982–87), Miki Takeo (1974–76), Tanaka Kakuei (1972–74), and Ōhira Masayoshi (1978–80). (Courtesy of *Mainichi shinbun.*)

4. Mammoth oil tanker waiting in Yokohama Bay to unload a cargo of crude oil in the 1960s. (Courtesy of *Mainichi shinbun.*)

5. Billboards and neon signs for Japanese products dominate the cityscape in Times Square, New York, in the 1980s. (Courtesy of Kyōdō Tsūshin Photo Service.)

6. Robots at work assembling robots in the Fanuc Corporation factory in Yamanashi Prefecture in 1990. (Courtesy of Fanuc Corporation.)

8. Another typical image of survival in 1945 and 1946 was that of city dwellers boarding trains for the countryside, to buy or barter with farmers for food. (Courtesy of Kyōdō Tsūshin Photo Service.)

Mass Culture and Society

7. Living among the rubble in Tokyo, fall 1945. Scenes such as this were common in major cities, and the experience of literally rebuilding from the ruins remained a vivid part of popular memory for decades. (Courtesy of Kyōdō Tsūshin Photo Service.)

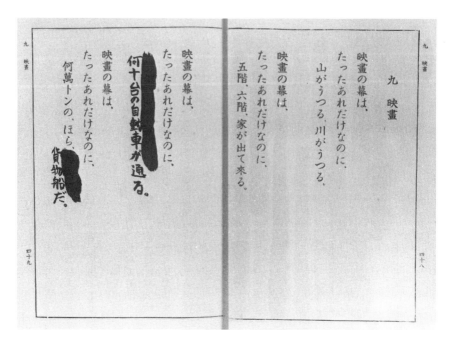

9. A hastily censored elementary reading textbook used immediately after the war. In this case, the line "several dozen tanks" has been replaced by "several dozen bicycles" and "battleship" has been blacked out in favor of "cargo ship." (Courtesy of *Mainichi shinbun*.)

11. Early postwar "picture-card show" (*kamishibai*). This form of popular entertainment was extremely popular in the late 1940s and 1950s, before being overwhelmed by television. Many comic-book artists began their careers by illustrating for this theater. This scene is from Shizuoka City in 1952. The original caption read, "A great revolution in *kamishibai*: electric lights and loudspeakers." (Courtesy of *Mainichi shinbun*.)

10. Early postwar "rental bookstore" (*kashi honya*) in Nagasaki, December 1953. The photographer recalls that "due to the shortage of paper and books, the sight of children reading in these shops was common. Once in a while the owner would chase them out, but they'd soon return. I was impressed at the vitality of these children." (Courtesy of Ōkubo Nobunari.)

12. Women at work carrying logs on Sado Island off the shore of Niigata Prefecture in September 1954. (Courtesy of Yoshioka Senzō.)

13. A counsellor employed by the Ministry of Welfare makes the rounds of farm villages in April 1952, explaining and promoting birth control and family planning. Soaring birth rates and abortion rates prompted this government program. (Courtesy of Kageyama Kōyō.)

14. The change in lifestyles of the high-growth era included a revolution in kitchen design revealed by these two photographs. In the first (above), a typical, poorly lit rural kitchen of about 1953, a hibachi is used to boil water and cook rice. In the second (opposite), from 1965, the "bright" new kitchen of a newlywed urban couple boasts an electric rice cooker, refrigerator, toaster, and gas range. (Courtesy of Kageyama Kōyō.)

15. Television culture, 1956. The entire family gathers around an early black-and-white television, reverently positioned next to the family's Shintō altar (*kamidana*). By 1959 2 million households had televisions; by 1962 the number had reached 10 million. (Courtesy of Kyōdō Tsūshin Photo Service.)

16. *Mai kā* (my car) is the Japanese expression for the family car, which became a symbol of the emerging consumer society in the 1960s. In this photograph from 1960 the parents and children together wash the family Subaru. (Courtesy of Kyōdō Tsūshin Photo Service.)

17. Young couples on a Saturday evening in August 1964 on the Wadakura bridge in the heart of Tokyo. As women and men increasingly sought marriage partners on their own, rather than through formal introductions, the expression *deito* (date) and the practice of dating became popular in the late 1950s and early 1960s. (Courtesy of Tomiyama Haruo.)

18. Family on a pedestrian mall in Tokyo, 1985. Beginning with the Ginza district of Tokyo in August 1970, municipal governments began closing major shopping streets to traffic on Sunday and holiday afternoons. Strolling along these so-called pedestrian heavens (*hokōsha tengoku*) remains an extremely popular family activity. (Courtesy of *Mainichi shinbun*.)

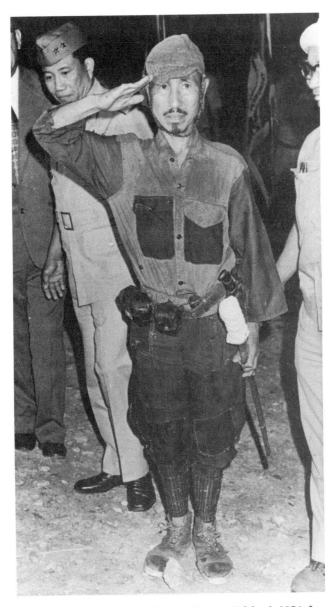

19. The last soldier returns: Onoda Hiro on 10 March 1974. Just as the two decades of high economic growth were coming to an end, the discovery and repatriation of two Japanese soldiers still in hiding on the island of Guam (Yokoi Shōichi, 1972) and in the mountains of the Philippine island of Lubang (Onoda) prompted many Japanese to focus once more on the experience of war and surrender. (Courtesy of *Mainichi shinbun*.)

Democratic Promise and Practice

20. Cover of the inaugural issue of the journal *Democracy* in
January 1946, one of numerous new publications concerned
with the promotion of democracy in postwar Japan. (Courtesy of Ōtsuki Shoten.)

21. The Omi labor dispute, 1954. Women silk workers carried out this strike against what they called "premodern" working conditions. Principal demands were for recognition of their union, freedom from forced participation in religious ceremonies, an end to company inspection of mail and personal belongings, freedom to leave company dormitories, and freedom to marry. The strikers received broad popular support and won all their demands. (Courtesy of Kyōdō Tsūshin Photo Service.)

22. Security Treaty crisis inside and outside the Diet. Chaos reigned within the Diet (20 May 1960) as the LDP forcibly ratified the U.S.-Japan Security Treaty (above). In response, thousands took to the streets in massive protests against the renewal of the treaty (opposite). The demonstration outside the Diet took place on 18 June 1960. (Courtesy of *Asahi shinbun.*)

23. Contemporary with the treaty protests (July 1960), coal miners at Mitsui Company's largest mine, in Miike on Kyushu Island, were engaged in the longest strike in postwar history. The strike lasted from December 1959 through all of 1960, ending in defeat for the miners. (Courtesy of Ohara Institute for Social Research.)

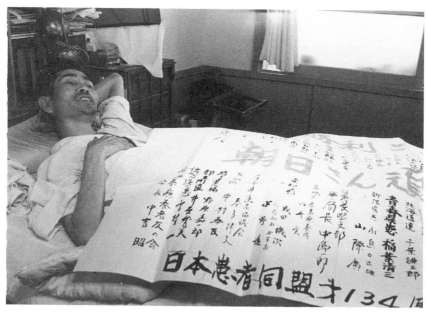

24. Plaintiff Asahi Shigeru of the Asahi welfare suit is shown here on his hospital bed, covered with a poster signed by supporters (1959). In this pioneering lawsuit Asahi sought to use the constitutional guarantee of a "right to a livelihood" to argue that the government's social welfare payments were unconstitutionally low. (Courtesy of Tanaka Machirō.)

25. A Minamata victim turns twenty. This is considered the age of adulthood in Japan, and young women who turn twenty in a given year dress in bright, formal kimono for a coming-of-age ceremony every January 15. Here the family of one victim of Minamata mercury poisoning gathers to celebrate their daughter's adulthood in 1977. (Courtesy of Kuwabara Shisei.)

26. New laws to regulate and prevent air and water pollution were passed in the early 1970s and have had some effect. But this 1987 photograph of Tokyo enshrouded in smog reveals that pollution remains a problem. (Courtesy of *Asahi shinbun*.)

CHAPTER NINE

Formations of Mass Culture

Marilyn Ivy

Although often peripheralized, the question of mass culture is really never far from the center of debates about the transformations of postwar Japan. Technologies of mass dissemination have unified the world—not necessarily in the benign image of Marshall McLuhan's global village but in a dispensation that has marginalized cultural differences at the same time that it has amplified disparities in wealth and power. Japan is arguably the most advanced mass society within this dispensation, with nearly universal literacy (and color television ownership), a nationwide educational curriculum, an enormous publishing industry (fifth in the world in the number of books published), and the largest per capita circulation of newspapers in the world.[1] An analysis of mass culture in postwar Japan is thus crucial not only for understanding the domestic interrelationship of capitalism, aesthetics, and technology but also for grasping the global implications of Japan's "economic miracle."

Critics today often use mass culture interchangeably with *consumer society, popular culture, commodity culture, culture industry,* and other related terms. I wish to make clear, however, that I do not use the term *mass culture* to suggest a spontaneously arising, communally based culture of the "masses"—something akin to what many term *popular culture*. Some critics no longer use the term *mass culture* at all because, in Theodor Adorno's words, they want "to exclude from the outset the interpretation agreeable to its advocates: that it is a matter of something like a culture that arises spontaneously from the masses themselves, the contemporary form of popular art."[2] They thus use terms such as *culture industry* to express a significant difference from so-called popular culture.[3] I also tend to follow these

1. The Tsuneta Yano Memorial Society, ed., *Nippon: A Charted Survey of Japan, 1990/1991* (Tokyo: Kokuseisha, 1990), 282–86.

2. Theodor Adorno, "Culture Industry Reconsidered," *New German Critique* 6 (Fall 1975): 12.

3. See Max Horkheimer and Theodor W. Adorno, "The Culture Industry: Enlightenment as Mass Deception," in Horkheimer and Adorno, *Dialectic of Enlightenment* (New York: Seabury, 1972).

critics in defining mass culture as administered, commodified culture pretargeted and produced for large numbers of consumers. Mass culture in this general sense arose together with industrial capitalism itself, for its very possibility is predicated on those technologies of both material and social production that emerged with the development of capitalism. It is thus intimately entwined with the large-scale production, dissemination, and consumption of commodities; in the postwar period the ascendancy of the electronic media, particularly television, has added new dimensions to this dynamic. I do not deny that specific social groups can resist or reappropriate mass-produced images and artifacts for their own ends and thus create popular subcultures. In this essay, however, I am primarily concerned with tracing a critical genealogy of postwar mass cultural formations; space does not permit a detailed analysis of thematic content, practices of resistance, or modes of consumption.[4]

Like *mass culture, masses* emerges as a problematic term in both Western and Japanese history. As Raymond Williams has shown, the English words *mass* and *masses* have a long history of overlapping and sometimes contradictory uses. He contends, however, that "the problems of large societies and of collective action and reaction to which, usually confusingly, [*mass*] and its derivatives and associates are addressed, are real enough and have to be continually spoken about."[5] In Japanese as well the delineation of the *taishū* is a complicated yet crucial task. *Taishū* is often translated as "the masses," particularly when it refers to a consumption category: the aggregate of consumers targeted by large-scale marketing. But it also has a more common referent: "the people" or the "populace." A *taishū shokudō* is a "people's restaurant"; *taishū bungaku* is "popular literature." Of course, the implicit comparison here is with elite or "high" restaurants or literature, and in that sense it reproduces one of the usages of *mass* in English: the popular, widely disseminated, lowbrow, and cheap as opposed to the elite, restricted, highbrow, and expensive. This opposition of high and low is constitutive for any consideration of mass culture. For example, Adorno contrasts mass culture with a realm of autonomous artistic production: mass culture as the degraded half of high modernism. Yet both mass culture and modernism appeared only with the advent of "modernization" itself.[6]

4. Most studies of mass culture tend to locate their object in the aesthetic or expressive realm—art, texts, theater, performances, events, movies. This sense has tended to dominate discussions of the culture industry—and not surprisingly, since the notion arose in conjunction with modernism in the arts. Yet another, broader perspective takes *culture* in an almost anthropological sense—culture as the entire nexus of meaning in a specific society. This second sense of *culture* comes closer to what I wish to consider, although I will at times be lingering on the production of the cultural in terms of the aesthetic.

5. Raymond Williams, *Keywords* (New York: Oxford University Press, 1976), 163.

6. As in the West, Japanese modernism arose in response to modernization and mass cultural phenomena. The critical difference here, of course, is that the "modern" emanated from the West; modernism, in its very essence, was associated with the domination of the West and thus had to be purged; consider, for example, the discourse on "overcoming the modern" (*kindai no chōkoku*) in 1942 and after. Until recently there had been very little research (even in Japanese) on mass culture or

As the media critic Kogawa Tetsuo has pointed out, however, *minshū bunka* is also an accepted translation for "popular culture" and in fact is closer to the idea of "people's culture" than is the term *taishū bunka*—yet *taishū bunka* is the dominant term. This sort of semiotic displacement—from *minshū* to *taishū*—prompts Kogawa to speculate that in Japan today popular culture is conceivable only as produced and disseminated by the mass media; popular culture is reproducible only as mass culture.[7]

The other Japanese word that refers to mass phenomena is the English loanword *masu* (mass); its most common use is *masu komi*, an abbreviated translation of "mass communication." *Masu mejia* (mass media) and *masu puro* (mass production) also appear regularly. *Taishū* makes at least latent reference to the "people," particularly the general laboring classes; *masu* does not evoke this populist dimension but rather refers directly to standardized, large-scale forces and structures precisely linked to the decline of any communally based, local (and thereby potentially "popular") culture.

In both senses, then, but particularly in the second one that *masu* elicits, "mass" phenomena in Japan (as in the West) have led to a leveling of consciously apprehended class distinctions. The decline of the *taishū* defined as the laboring classes is thus a partial result of the ascendancy of the culture industry. With the high growth of the 1960s and explosive expansion of the media the Japanese population came to be incorporated into a series of strikingly uniform and standardized taste groupings. These groupings were appropriately differentiated in terms of gender and generation but much less so in terms of class or regional affiliation: company president, company janitor, and farmer alike came to read the same magazines, watch the same television shows, and own the same basic array of electric appliances. The dissemination of this standardly differentiated culture to all sectors of Japanese society in conjunction with rising affluence has led most people (90 percent or more) to think of themselves as in the "middle"[8] —inspiring many analysts to question the viability of class as a category for analyzing Japanese society. Instead, concepts such as the "new middle-mass society" (*shin chūkan taishū shakai*) or the "new middle-stratum society" (*shin chūkansō shakai*)—along with simply "mass society"—have problematically emerged to replace the terms of class analysis.[9]

---

modernism in prewar Japan; the last few years, however, have witnessed a small boom in studies on the city, entertainment, and gender in the 1920s. See, for example, Minami Hiroshi, ed., *Nihon no modanizumu no kenkyū: Shisō, seikatsu, bunka* (Tokyo: Burēn Shuppan, 1982).

7. Tetsuo Kogawa, "New Trends in Japanese Popular Culture," in *The Japanese Trajectory: Modernization and Beyond*, ed. Gavan McCormack and Yoshio Sugimoto (Cambridge: Cambridge University Press, 1988), 54–55.

8. The term that corresponds to "middle class" in various surveys is instructive. In the Economic Planning Agency's surveys the term is *chūryū*, which can refer to a wider notion of the "middle" than the more specific phrase for the "middle class," equivalent to the classic bourgeoisie of Marxism, the *chūsan kaikyū*.

9. According to Inoguchi Kuniko, when Japanese are asked about their *kurashimuki* (circumstances, standard of living), more than 90 percent say they're in the "middle" (*chū*); when asked directly what

The actual objects and forms of consumption (comic books, television, movies); their production by what Adorno and Horkheimer termed the *culture industry*, which comprises the interrelated forces of industrial production, mass communications, and advertising; and the discourse on the "masses" (*taishū*), "mass culture" (*taishū bunka*), and "mass communication" (*masu komi*) sustained both by Japanese intellectuals as well as by the media—these form three terms of what we might call the *mass culture formation* in postwar Japanese history. In Japan, perhaps more so than in other advanced industrial nations, these three vectors have increasingly tended to coincide; for example, the critical discourse on mass culture, in the form of mass-marketed books, has become a profitable part of the culture industry itself. A central concern of this essay will be to trace the trajectory toward an increasingly comprehensive mass culture formation in postwar Japan.

PREWAR PRECEDENTS OF POSTWAR MASS CULTURE

The development of a national mass culture was initiated simultaneously with the advent of the Meiji period, when many of the apparatuses of modernity were established. An extraordinarily vibrant popular culture flourished in Edo and Osaka during the Tokugawa period (1603–1868), and we can find many thematic and formal precedents of later popular culture in the productions of the urban bourgeoisie of that period. But the *mass* culture I wish to address is linked with the rise of industrial capitalism; in that sense the Meiji period marked a break with earlier forms. The creation of a large-scale consumption society as early as the 1910s and 1920s paralleled developments in the United States, as much of an emergent global culture of consumption was patterned on American developments (indeed, America was the prime exporter not only of industrial production techniques and goods but also of technologies of desire and consumption, mass-marketing techniques, and forms of display).[10]

In many respects Japan was a full-blown mass society at least by the mid-1920s. Newspaper circulation had reached 6.3 million by 1924, and the magazine *Taiyō* had a monthly circulation of 300,000 as early as 1900.[11] The advertising industry (based on American models) paralleled the development of the print media, with Japan's largest ad agency (Dentsū) already in business by 1907. Narrative comic strips found thousands of eager young (mostly urban) readers. (Tsurumi Shunsuke notes that Japan's first indigenous comic strip, *Shōchan and the Squirrel*, was popular enough to generate spin-off products, such as caps modeled on the one worn by

class they're in, however, only about 25 percent say that they are "middle class" (*chūsan kaikyū*). Inoguchi Kuniko, "Chūryū to wa shōhi no kategorī datta no ka," *Chūō kōron*, July 1985, 86.

10. Victoria de Grazia discusses the impact of American commercial culture on modes of advertising, particularly the poster, in interwar Italy in her "The Arts of Purchase: How American Publicity Subverted the European Poster, 1920–1940," in *Remaking History*, ed. Barbara Kruger and Phil Mariani (Seattle: Bay Press, 1989), 221–57.

11. "Advertising," *Kodansha Encyclopedia of Japan* (Tokyo: Kōdansha, 1983), 16–17.

the strip's protagonist. He finds in such occurrences ample evidence for the existence of a bona fide mass society in the Japan of the 1920s.)[12] The Tokyo Broadcasting Station (a public utility corporation) began radio broadcasting on 22 March 1925, with corporations in Osaka and Nagoya soon following suit. Listeners had to apply for receivers' contracts (for a fee); even so, within one year there were 258,507 contracts. NHK (Nippon Hōsō Kyōkai) was formed as a merger of the three public corporations in 1926; by 1928 receivers' contracts had topped 500,000.[13] Department stores such as Shirokiya and Mitsukoshi flourished in the cities, shaping new styles of retailing, consumption, and leisure.[14] Theater, both cosmopolitan ones (*shingeki*) and ones based on elaborations of indigenous forms (*shinkokugeki*), flourished alongside "Asakusa opera," vaudeville, and films. In 1925 there were 813 movie theaters in Japan with 155 million spectators; in 1935 this figure had risen to 202 million.[15] Gender bending in the forms of the "modern girl" (*moga*) and "modern boy" (*mobo*), Marxism and modernism, labor unrest and state repression, mass culture and the avant-garde made their Japanese debuts, grounded in the urban matrix of modernity.[16] Rail transportation and a newly conceived "tourism" ensured the circulation of signs, goods, and people, both domestically and internationally (Japan's first round-the-world package tour commenced in 1908 under the auspices of Thomas Cook's branch office in Yokohama).[17]

Much of this emergent culture of modernity remained confined, of course, to the urban centers. The majority of Japanese lived in rural areas although they were increasingly incorporated as patriotic, literate, and consuming "citizens" (*kokumin*, "people of the nation"). The increasing militarization of Japan during the 1930s marked the decline of the consuming citizen, but with no lessening—rather, with an elaboration—of the techniques of social control we associate with mass societies. *Tennōsei* (the emperor system) enfolded all Japanese within an elaborate interlocking institutional structure of army, school, and patriotic, women's, and neighborhood associations. The media were more important than

12. Shunsuke Tsurumi, *A Cultural History of Postwar Japan, 1945–1980* (London and New York: Kegan Paul International, 1987), 29–30.

13. Masami Ito, *Broadcasting in Japan* (London and Boston: Routledge and Kegan Paul in association with the International Institute of Communications, 1978), 11–12.

14. According to Richard Sennett, the department store operates as a paradigm for the new experience of "publicness" generated by large-scale industrialization. Miriam Silverberg discusses the implications of Sennett's work in her own consideration of department stores within a larger analysis of the meaning of modernity in Taishō Japan's urban culture. See her "Living on the Urban Edge: Culture and Subculture in Taishō Japan" (paper presented at the 1986 Annual Meeting of the Association for Asian Studies, Chicago, 21–23 Mar. 1986).

15. Joseph L. Anderson, "Second and Third Thoughts about the Japanese Film," in *The Japanese Film: Art and Industry*, ed. Joseph L. Anderson and Donald Richie (Princeton: Princeton University Press, 1982), 455–56.

16. See Miriam Silverberg's acute analysis of the relationship of Marxism and modernity in prewar Japan in her *Changing Song* (Princeton: Princeton University Press, 1990).

17. Nakagawa Kōichi, *Kankō no bunkashi* (Tokyo: Chikuma Shobō, 1985), 12.

ever, as much for their negative role as a visible site for state intervention through censorship as for their positive role of dispensing "information," entertainment, and propaganda.[18] Thomas Havens states that "wartime Japan happily escaped the nightmare of a rootless mass society enslaved by huge centralized institutions." He finds instead that policies were implemented via descending layers of authority: community councils, neighborhood associations, and families.[19]

I question whether Japan escaped the classic nightmare of fascism; there is no doubt that the centralized wartime appropriation and consolidation of the machinery of the media formed the structure on which nationwide postwar mass cultural formations were built. Yet it would be facile to imagine a continuous trajectory from the 1920s to the present, for contemporary Japan as a nation-state is constructed against the discontinuity that the trauma of the war presents. The postwar advent of radically different technologies of dissemination, logics of production, patterns of consumption, and circuits of control—all made possible because of late capitalist developments in computerization and electronic media—has made possible this construction. To many observers these advances indicate the foreclosure of many of the liberating possibilities contained in earlier Japanese communal forms as they irrevocably displace any sustained possibility of the "popular." To other critics electronic mass culture contains numerous possibilities akin to the utopian moments in older "popular" cultures. Yet all agree that Japan's mass cultural formations are among the most powerful in the advanced industrial nations of the world.

THE EARLY POSTWAR

On August 15, 1945, the Japanese people heard the emperor's voice, most for the first time: on the radio, announcing their defeat. Those who heard that broadcast invariably speak of their shock at the emperor's reedy voice, disembodied, speaking an impossibly archaic language. The very moment that marked the end of the war for the Japanese people was a mass-mediated instance in which both voice and language were as unrecognizable as the unprecedented news that they announced. The later knowledge that the emperor was not speaking live, but that the imperial voice had emanated from a tape recorder, adds a strange twist to the moment, as if hearing the divine voice of the emperor for the first time could have

18. Thomas Havens details the repression of the late 1930s, when hundreds of newspapers were forced to stop publishing and the number of periodicals declined from 11,400 (1936) to 7,700 (late 1939). Radio increasingly became the main instrument for the dissemination of national propaganda (although in 1938 Japan still had only one-fourth the number of radios per capita as did the United States), but movies remained relatively free of strict government control until 1940. Havens, *Valley of Darkness: The Japanese People and World War Two* (New York: Norton, 1978), 21–22. Gregory J. Kasza documents the control of the mass media by the military-bureaucratic establishment in *The State and the Mass Media in Japan, 1918–1945* (Berkeley and Los Angeles: University of California Press, 1988).
19. Havens, *Valley of Darkness*, 89.

occurred only through layers of mediation.[20] In retrospect this mediation seems to portend the later powers of electronic reproduction that have come to pervade postwar Japan.

Radio, then, was the official media outlet for immediate information in the early postwar; until the start of commercial radio broadcasts in 1951 there was only one network, Japan's public broadcasting network NHK. NHK has continued throughout the entire postwar period to play a central part in the culture industry, and in the immediate aftermath of the war (and soon after under the control of the occupying forces) it disseminated both directives and "light" entertainment to the Japanese population. The American forces tightly controlled NHK, and even its programming featured jazz, thitherto unknown station breaks, and disk jockeys.

The historical accident that the United States, the original and prototypical mass culture, was the dominant occupying power determined the structures that later Japanese culture industries were to assume. The controlling and censorious American presence was of course pervasive in the early postwar period; all cultural productions had to receive official approval. The "Americanization" of Japanese life guaranteed the gradual reproduction of many of the commodity forms and products found in the United States.

In the immediate postwar years—from 1945 to 1950—the struggle for survival created an intensely fragmented, individualized sense of consciousness, which tended to preclude the formation of a "mass" sensibility. This individual consciousness partly explains why many writers identify a striking "subjectivity" (*shutaisei*) present after the war, an autonomy and individualistic consciousness that is often said to be missing in Japan's collectivist ethos.[21]

More than half of Japan's movie theaters had been destroyed during the war, yet most studios survived unscathed. Several films were released soon after surrender, with the Shōchiku Company's *Breeze (Soyokaze)* the first real postwar hit.[22] There was a boom in "general opinion magazines" (*sōgō zasshi*) in 1947, with dozens of new titles variously proclaiming the virtues of democracy and freedom; there were also short-lived pulp magazines (*kasutori zasshi*) based on American models.[23] In general, however, cultural production moved down to the local levels; these levels recreated more communal and unmediated modes of communication. In the dire immediate postwar period certain earlier forms

20. Not only was the language unintelligible, but severe static because of "technical difficulties" made much of the broadcast inaudible. See Nippon Hōsō Kyōkai, ed., *Fifty Years of Broadcasting* (Tokyo: NHK, 1977), 131.

21. For a consideration of *shutaisei* in postwar Japanese thought, see Koschmann's essay in this volume.

22. See Anderson and Richie, *Japanese Film*, 159.

23. Matsuura Sōzō, *Sengo jānarizumu shi ron* (Tokyo: Shuppan Nyūsusha, 1975), 54. *Kasutori* refers to low-grade spirits made from the lees of *sake;* by extension, *kasutori zasshi* indicates crude, low-quality magazines.

of *taishū bunka* (here used in its more populist sense) experienced a resurgence after a long wartime hiatus. Tsurumi Shunsuke has written of the revival of "picture card shows" (*kamishibai*) in which a narrator would tell stories to children while portraying the developments with large illustrated cards. Although this street entertainment itself was free, the storyteller made a living by selling candy to the assembled children after the performance. *Kamishibai* had flourished in the 1930s as an option for unemployed men (including out-of-work silent film narrators, or *benshi*), yet it declined during the war because most men were engaged in war-related work.[24] The presence of the *kamishibai* narrator—the *kamishibai ojisan*—riding a bicycle around his neighborhood beat became a tangible sign of a locally based popular culture. This form declined with the reconstruction of the movie industry and the advent of television in the mid-1950s, yet the artists who drew the illustrations for *kamishibai* shows went on to become the creators of "comics" (*manga*), the mainstay of the Japanese publishing industry.

Some earlier forms also flourished because they were able to evade occupation censorship more effectively than could centrally based forms such as kabuki and film. One such form was small-scale itinerant popular theater (*taishū engeki*), which presented plays replete with sword fights and valorizations of feudal loyalty—strictly taboo under the occupation.[25] The small scale and itinerancy of the troupes allowed them to elude the censors, particularly in provincial areas such as Kyushu, and they were wildly successful. They performed in makeshift theaters, often no more than roofless shacks without seats; if it rained, audience members would watch while holding umbrellas.

The return of these popular forms was closely linked with poverty and scarcity. A barter economy and the black market created the milieu for direct exchanges in a sort of primitive capitalist economy. Essential material objects attained a weight and profundity because of scarcity; *taishū engeki* actors, for instance, were often paid in rice and cigarettes, two valuable commodities.

The efforts at reconstruction by Japanese government and business were thus directed toward supplying the bare necessities of life; culture was detached from mass consumption, although there was still a vast (and growing) audience for radio, newspapers, magazines, and movies. But the lack of even basic commodities threw many back on their own resources or on their local communities, which became the scenes for a resurgence of small-scale popular forms and practices.

24. Tsurumi Shunsuke, *Sengo Nihon no taishū bunka shi, 1945–1980 nen* (Tokyo: Iwanami Shoten, 1984), 59–60.

25. *Taishū engeki* is a term that refers most generally to light, popular theater. The small-scale troupes to which I am referring have taken over this designation within the last ten years or so; previously they were referred to as "barnstorming" (*dosa mawari*) or "third-rate kabuki" (*sanryū kabuki*) troupes. Their repertoire comes from the genre of "period drama" or *jidaigeki* as it was codified in *shinkokugeki* ("new national theater") during the prewar period.

FORMATION AND EFFLORESCENCE
OF THE MASSES, 1955–70: ELECTRIC APPLIANCES,
PRIVATISM, AND TELEVISION

Many Japanese scholars agree in pinpointing 1955 as the dividing line between the postwar and the post-postwar, the year that ushered in the rapid transformations of all areas of Japanese life.[26] According to Kurihara Akira, 1955 is also the year that marks the true advent of "mass culture" as a particular historical formation associated with advanced industrial societies. He finds that the accelerated "technical innovations" of Japan's high-growth period led to a great inversion of the entire prewar social formation.[27] The cultivation of high-level consumer desires via innovations in production and marketing went forward on the basis of a newly acceptable "privatism," "productionism," and "modernism," values fully entrenched by the more affluent late 1960s and 1970s.

Thus in 1956, in a now famous statement, the government proclaimed in one of its ubiquitous white papers that the postwar period was over. This proclamation revealed an awareness that basic wants had been met; now high-level production and consumption were the goals. The late 1950s and early 1960s witnessed the gearing up of high growth and the formation of mass consumption.

People had crowded into the urban centers in search of work, and the appearance of vast hordes on the trains, at movie theaters, and in the stores prompted contemporary writers to speak of the "masses" and "crowding." Japan's enormous and elaborate department stores held special appeal during this time, even when luxuries were beyond the reach of most. Yet the establishment of Japan's first supermarket (Daiei) in 1957 pointed the way for the "distribution revolution" of the 1960s and 1970s, when chain and convenience stores gradually started to challenge the dominance of older consumer outlets.

There was a tremendous upsurge in publishing activity, with new weekly magazines (*shūkanshi*) dominating the market.[28] Many of the most popular and widely circulated current magazines in Japan today had their origins in the mid-1950s; they were particularly influential in the period before television. These new mass-market magazines and (later) television, along with the older media of radio and newspapers, showed the consumers what they should be, what they should aspire to, what they should consume in order to confirm their middle-class status.

Comics provide a point of continuity with prewar forms, although large-format

26. See Tatsurō Uchino, *Japan's Postwar Economy* (Tokyo: Kodansha International, 1983), 83–108.

27. Kurihara Akira, *Kanri shakai to minshū risei: Nichijō ishiki no seiji shakaigaku* (Tokyo: Shin'yōsha, 1982), 123–41.

28. The earliest weekly magazines were connected with the Sunday editions of newspapers. The magazine that became the *Shūkan asahi* was the first of these (1922). In 1956 *Shūkan shinchō* became the first weekly magazine to appear without direct connections to a newspaper. See "Weekly Magazines: Keys to an Information Society," *Japan Update*, Spring 1988, 9–10.

comic books were not widespread until after the war.[29] Many out-of-work artists started creating *manga* for shops that loaned out books for a fee.[30] *Gekiga*, referring to dramatic, "realistic," narrative comics, was a term born in 1957, and it indicated a shift away from prewar forms.[31] There was a veritable "*manga* boom" in 1965, which had tapered off somewhat by the early 1970s. Yet in 1974 there were still more than seventy-five types of specialized *manga* magazines with a total circulation of more than twenty million per month.[32]

Manga also became a point of critique of mass culture in the 1960s in the aftermath of the demonstrations against the U.S.-Japan Security Treaty as intellectuals turned away from the established Communist Party. There was a reconsideration of the idea of the *taishū* as a replacement for the seemingly elusive proletariat. The immense popularity of *manga*—their continuing appeal in the midst of high growth and an ever-burgeoning electronic media industry—prompted a series of debates over the nature of mass versus popular culture and over the possibilities of popular resistance contained within mass forms. This debate preoccupied scholars such as Tsurumi Shunsuke, with his tripartite division between "pure" arts made and appreciated by professionals; *taishū* arts, made by professionals and appreciated by amateurs; and the arts occupying the border between the two, where art is made and enjoyed by amateurs. By the late 1960s *manga* were produced and consumed within each of Tsurumi's three categories.[33]

Television, of course, rapidly came to be the medium that circumscribed the limits of debate on mass culture. The introduction of television in 1953 radically changed the nature of advertising and consumption, partly because televisions themselves became one of the most desired objects to consume. The national telecast of the crown prince's wedding in 1959 feverishly spurred television sales (royal weddings seem to operate as universal consumer stimulants). When television broadcasts began in 1953, few people could afford a television at fifteen thousand yen a set; yet from 1956 to 1960 the percentage of Japanese families owning televisions rose from less than 1 percent to almost 50 percent.[34] Within a few years television was vying with Japan's mass-circulation newspapers as the major mass medium. Television soon outstripped the movies as the prime source

29. Kure Tomofusa, *Gendai manga no zentaizō* (Tokyo: Century Press, 1986), 23.

30. Tsurumi pinpoints three factors important in shaping postwar Japanese comics: *kamishibai*, the lending bookstore, and women cartoonists. Tsurumi, *Cultural History*, 28–45.

31. Ishiko Junzō, the well-known scholar of *manga*, distinguishes between *manga* as written with Chinese characters, *manga* written in *katakana*, and *gekiga*. *Manga* in *katakana* is the most inclusive form; written in Chinese characters, *manga* signifies older, prewar forms. By contrast, *gekiga* (or *sutorii manga*, as Osamu Tezuka calls them) emphasize the longer, narrative forms popular after the war. These comics have connecting frames, have an "authentic" or "realistic" feel, are not usually humorous, and are aimed primarily at young male readers. Ishiko, *Sengo manga shi nōto* (Tokyo: Kinokuniya Shoten, 1980), 11–13.

32. Ishiko, *Sengo manga shi nōto*, 5.

33. See Kure, *Gendai manga no zentaizō*, 24.

34. Uchino, *Japan's Postwar Economy*, 105.

of entertainment for Japanese; 1964, the year of the Tokyo Olympics, was a turning point in media history, when it became clear that television—partly by incorporating the "period drama" (*jidai geki,* usually referring to so-called samurai drama) genre from film—had overtaken film in popularity.[35] Yet movies (including imported, particularly American, movies) retained their power to create stars and to stimulate trends.[36]

An important aspect of television at this stage was its broadcasting of entertainment, particularly American serials such as "I Love Lucy" and "Father Knows Best." These depictions of "typical" American families surrounded by consumer luxuries and electric appliances such as refrigerators, vacuum cleaners, and washing machines—and with the family car parked in the driveway—had a powerful impact on the Japanese psyche. The middle-class "American way of life" became the utopian goal and the dream of many Japanese in the 1950s, a goal tied to unflagging hard work as the basis for commodity acquisition. American television shows became the basis for the new middle-class image—particularly what objects, what possessions constituted the middle class—portrayed in Japanese television serials and in the movies as well. During this period Japanese came to equate the middle class with a life-style that included a telephone, a refrigerator, and a Japanese-style bath; those people who had acquired those things were, purely and simply, the middle class.[37] And television quickly became the primary means for the codification and dissemination of this conception of the middle class as a consumption category.

With the Ikeda cabinet's Income Doubling Plan of 1960 the full-scale heyday of the masses was assured; according to many accounts, 1960 (rather than 1955) thus marked the critical take-off point for high economic growth, which peaked in the early 1970s. Consumer demand rose during this time as most households began to afford the electric appliances of their dreams (it is almost as if one could write a postwar history of Japan according to electric appliances). Electric appliances fueled the consumer revolution of the 1960s; as we have seen, they became the objects of desire, the signs of middle-class inclusion, the unparalleled commodity fetishes for the Japanese in the 1950s and 1960s. Electric appliance manufacturers were the leading advertisers. Electric appliances standardized the image of the average household and what the average housewife should possess. Not only did they become the standard for middle-class status, but their presence and placement within Japanese dwellings (standardized in the form of housing projects, or *danchi*) also homogenized Japanese domestic space, which became a "concretized metaphorical scene" of social equality: if every household contained the same electric appliances in similarly constricted domestic spaces, then house-

35. Anderson, "Second and Third Thoughts," 453.

36. Movie viewing peaked in the period 1955–60, thereafter declining; Hakuhōdō Seikatsu Sōgō Kenkyūjo, ed., *Bunshū no tanjō* (Tokyo: Nihon Keizai Shinbunsha, 1985), 21.

37. Nakai Michiko, "Kaisō ishiki to kaikyū ishiki," in *Nihon no kaisō kōzō,* ed. Tominaga Ken'ichi (Tokyo: Tōkyō Daigaku Shuppankai, 1979); quoted in *Bunshū no tanjō,* 21.

holds were democratically equalized.[38] Rather than equalization, however, some view this process as one of homogenization, an elimination of differences as nuclear familial units constructed themselves as "micro-utopias" sealed off from external conflict;[39] or as privatization, a dangerous shrinking of social networks and forms of association into the modular confines of "my home" (*mai hōmu*). The contradiction of privatization lies in this: the more one thinks that a secure private sphere has been constructed—using the home, family, and consumer goods as the basis—the more the bureaucratized, technocratic public sphere has succeeded in consolidating its control.[40]

Advertising was a powerful means by which culture industries intervened to shape and construct the emerging mass consumer society. Status consumption increased as everyone anxiously tried to keep up with the rising stimulation of demand. Ads appealed directly to this anxiety: Nissan's ad campaigns boasted, "Our car is the most spacious. It makes your next-door neighbor's look small."[41] The age of standardized consumption, if only modestly conspicuous, had begun. By a peculiar, yet familiar, mass-mediated logic, everyone became an "other" as desire was deflected from the sphere of "needs"; one knew what one wanted only by being told what others had. Not limited to the urban areas, this pattern of rising consumption extended to the countryside, too, effecting perhaps the most profound transformation in postwar Japanese society: the assimilation of rural Japan into a national metropolitan culture.[42]

The 1960s witnessed the incorporation and assimilation of the viewer into television. No longer content to broadcast news, ads, and entertainment, television now featured hypothetical viewers through their representatives, the studio audience or participants in game shows. The now securely codified Japanese institution of the amateur song show burgeoned in the 1960s. Television had an unprecedented influence on language, creating and diffusing popular slang and neologisms at a breakneck clip.

Television also brought to the screen Vietnam and the demonstrations against the U.S.-Japan Security Treaty. Underground theater, sexual and musical experiments, and the "new wave" of Japanese cinema provided serious critiques of the dominant consumption society, while regional and issue-specific citizens' move-

38. "Concretized metaphorical scene" is Kashiwagi Hiroshi's phrase: *gutaika shita metafuorikku na fūkei;* see Kashiwagi, "Kōdo seichō ga motarashita mono: Mikuro yūtopia to shite no kakukazoku," *Sekai,* Dec. 1985, 79.

39. Kashiwagi sees this process determined by the logic of capitalism in postwar Japan; the high-growth period of the 1960s prepared the way for the atomization of the 1970s and 1980s, in which a further "micro-ization" of the nuclear family into constituent monads (individuals) has already occurred.

40. See Tada Michitarō, "The Glory and Misery of 'My Home,' " in *Authority and the Individual in Japan,* ed. J. Victor Koschmann (Tokyo: University of Tokyo Press, 1978), 207–17.

41. *Bunshū no tanjō,* 28.

42. See William Kelly's essay in this volume.

ments contested pollution and social injustice. Yet all these forms of resistance were increasingly framed within the logics of the mass media and what would come to be called the "managed society" (*kanri shakai*).[43] The late 1960s, in fact, witnessed the first coherent policy studies of the "information society" (*jōhō shakai*), in which various government and government-allied think tanks outlined their plans for the coming shift toward information industries—computers, robotics, new media networks, automated production systems. The rhetoric of these statements announced a technocratic utopia in which manual labor would be reduced, creativity would flower, and "information" would claim a greater and greater share of the value of commodities.[44] This rhetoric—and its implementation—would intensify through the 1970s and 1980s, paralleling similar developments in other advanced industrial societies.

THE 1970S: "DISCOVER JAPAN," THE MANAGED SOCIETY, AND INFORMATION CAPITALISM

By the early 1970s there was a growing suspicion about the fruits of the high-growth period, including the impact of mass media. Pollution scandals and urban congestion had become foci of citizen's protest movements, and student protests and demonstrations against Japan's collusion with the United States during the Vietnam War were widespread in the late 1960s. Yet it was the "Nixon shock" of 1971 and the "oil shock" of 1973 that decisively revealed the fragility of the Japanese economy and that further spurred a retrenchment and retrospective movement in Japan. Self-reflection on the nature of Japaneseness intensified, turning into a genre in itself.

Television continued to consolidate its share of the mass media market; in 1975 television overtook newspapers as the prime medium for advertising.[45] The decline of movie attendance (and the decline of older forms of theatergoing) directly paralleled this rise of televisual medium.

More than sixty million Japanese attended Expo '70, the grand international exhibition that symbolically consolidated Japan's powerful position in the world economic community. Japan's national railways, compelled to stimulate consumer demand after the exposition, hired Dentsū (Japan's largest advertising agency and one of the world's largest purveyors of mass culture) to create an ad campaign to lure new consumers into the travel market. The result was "Discover Japan," probably the largest and longest-running ad campaign in Japanese his-

43. A term translated directly from the Frankfurt School's notion of the "administered society."

44. Tessa Morris-Suzuki unravels and critiques the ideologies of the information society in her excellent book *Beyond Computopia: Information, Automation, and Democracy in Japan* (London and New York: Kegan Paul International, 1988). The term *information society* itself was coined in Japan by Hayashi Yūjirō; Morris-Suzuki, *Beyond Computopia*, 7.

45. Ito, *Broadcasting in Japan*, 10.

tory, which reorganized the entire cultural topography of Japan according to a continuum of "tradition" and "modernity."[46]

"Discover Japan" targeted Japanese desires for a simpler rural past, yet its recuperation of that past indicated all the more clearly the difficulty of escaping the managed society of the 1970s. In Kurihara Akira's analysis, the "managed society" is the form that mass society has taken in Japan; it eclipses the former boundaries between the masses and the elites, surrounding all in its comprehensive grasp. The managed society is a reorganization of mass society according to the technical rules of industrialization, in which internal management becomes naturalized and everyone "voluntarily submits" to the power of what is. Yet Kurihara sees the possibility of resistance in certain kinds of mass culture, which he divides into three ascending strata in terms of their distance from specific social groups and their lives. His *taishū bunka I* operates as a lost horizon of communal forms and convivial everyday life; in *taishū bunka II*—the "typical" mass culture of movies, newspapers, pop songs, and baseball—he finds the possibility of resistance, of "ample room for the projection of desires and needs and for the exercise of the imagination."[47] Although these forms of mass culture are of course produced by specialists in the culture industry, he finds that they are counterhegemonic in relation to the more all-encompassing managed society.[48] It is only in *taishū bunka III* that the possibility of resistance is thoroughly preempted; dominated by television and video, commercials, office automation, and surveillance, this stratum of mass culture differs from stratum II because of its higher level of dissemination and consumption. Even more so, however, it differs because it "embodies the technical rationality of industry, while it acts in a rule-governed, standard, and integrated way."[49] Managed mass culture is intimately linked with the rise of the service industries in the 1970s and after. Culture tends to be passively received in the form of "services" as this systematized, heteronomous production of values becomes normalized within everyday life.

According to Tessa Morris-Suzuki, the increasing emphasis on information industries in the 1970s (and their attendant powers of surveillance) was not purely a natural outcome determined by a sort of inherent teleology of technology itself. Instead, she finds the "information society" concept to be a planned policy

46. The creator of "Discover Japan" has written a book about the ad campaign. See Fujioka Wakao, *Kareinaru shuppatsu: Jisukabā Japan* (Tokyo: Mainichi Shinbunsha, 1972). It is ironic that the title of this campaign urging Japanese to rediscover authentic origins is a direct transfer from the well-known American tourism campaign, "Discover America." This same Dentsū executive has led the charge in proclaiming the death of the consuming masses and the advent of a new "age of feeling" (*kansei jidai*) with its "micromasses" (*shōshū*), a term he coined. I have written on the "Discover Japan" campaign and its relationship to the later "Exotic Japan" campaign in "Tradition and Difference in the Japanese Mass Media," *Public Culture* 1 (Fall 1988): 21–29.

47. Kurihara, *Kanri shakai to minshu risei*, 30; translation mine.

48. Fredric Jameson has noted the utopian dimensions of mass cultural products in "Reification and Utopia in Mass Culture," *Social Text* 1 (Winter 1979): 130–48.

49. Kurihara, *Kanri shakai to minshu risei*, 130; translation mine.

response to the crises in Japanese capitalism of the late 1960s and early 1970s (particularly after the Nixon and oil shocks).[50] New ideologies and directions were needed in the aftermath of high economic growth and the declining possibilities of mass production. What emerged was not only the high-tech solution in all its seeming apolitical purity but also a single-minded drive to maintain the profitability of corporate enterprises. There was a need to create diversified markets for the products of new, information-based industries. Rather than the neutral *information society*, then, she prefers the more explicit *information capitalism* to describe the transformation of the Japanese economy in the 1970s and through the 1980s.

Although Kurihara, Morris-Suzuki, and a diverse range of social critics decry the dominance of the *jōhō/kanri shakai*, seeing in it a foreclosing not only of the possibilities of individuality but also of popular forms of culture, another group of critics, economists, marketing specialists, and advertisers—by putting the accent on desire and consumption—see instead the emergence of a new, feeling-based individual sensibility in the 1980s. They have in fact proclaimed the "death of the masses" and the birth of the "fragmented masses" (*bunshū*), according to one text; the "metamasses" (*chōtaishū*), according to another; and the "micromasses" (*shōshū*), according to yet another.[51] This affirmative consumer-culture theory argues that the masses no longer exist as they did in the 1960s and 1970s and that the shift in consumption can be explained by the diversification and differentiation of consumer "masses" (the notion of "differentiation" [*saika*] has become a key term not only in consumer culture theory but also in Japanese academic discourse), a shift away from economies of scale and massive "hit" products, and a wider range of goods.[52]

THE 1980S AND 1990S: MICROMASSES, DIFFERENTIATION, "EXOTIC JAPAN," AND NEONOSTALGIA

According to the new consumer-culture theorists, groups with varying value orientations have replaced the undifferentiated masses. People now think more specifically about what they want; they no longer buy simply in accordance with others. No longer do booms occur on the scale they once did, and no longer do hit products garner the mass market they once did. Since everyone has the same basic array of consumer goods already, what exceeds that array signifies the individual's specific desires. The rise of service industries, the increased buying of

50. Morris-Suzuki claims that the end of high growth was already in sight as early as 1968 or 1969—precisely when the *jōhō shakai* concept began to be bandied about; *Beyond Computopia*, 50. Gordon, in his essay in this volume, describes a parallel ascendancy of "managerial culture" during this period.

51. For the "micromasses," see Fujioka Wakao, *Sayonara, taishū: Kansei jidai o dō yomu ka* (Tokyo: PHP Kenkyūjo, 1984); for the "metamasses," see Gekkan Akurosu Henshūshitsu, ed., *Ima, chōtaishū no jidai* (Tokyo: Parco Shuppan, 1985); and for the "fragmented masses," see *Bunshū no tanjō*.

52. These trends are, of course, evident in the United States and European countries as well.

luxury products, and ever-so-subtle advertising appeals to "feelings" and "sensibilities" mark the 1980s and 1990s.[53]

What consumer-culture theorists take as their point of departure is the scaling down of consumption levels after the period of high growth. To stimulate consumer demand, producers have been compelled to appeal to (and create) highly targeted, diversified, and nuanced types of consumer desire. The presentation and dissemination of information has become paramount. Consumers demand more information in order to make well-considered choices about objects of consumption, including a greater selection of cultural commodities. Alongside the widely circulated mass magazines a new sort of "catalogue information magazine" (*katarogu jōhō zasshi*) has developed, with serial displays and comparisons of goods and services. New computer technologies and the "new media" have stimulated the publication of local "town papers" and small publications. What all these media and new forms have in common is a "softening," a more local, direct, and useful connection with a more specifically targeted and limited consumer. According to the texts that proclaim the end of mass culture, those who use the media this specifically cannot be considered the "masses." Now people can make choices according to their own tastes; a wealth of information allows an individualized selection not previously possible. Discriminating consumption is all the more necessary for the so-called new rich and new poor who have upset the cultural patterns of the monolithic middle class/mass.

Ozawa Masako has analyzed this differentiation of the masses and the new consumer individualization, and she has found that the value of a consumer's assets has the greatest effect on consumption (two other crucial factors are the size of the city in which the consumer resides and income). Since the period of high growth there has been an increasing widening of asset differentials; more recently, income differentials have increased also. She finds these widening differentials leading to greater gaps among consumers' purchasing power. She concludes—not surprisingly—that consumer demand is fragmenting in two ways, through "diversification of preference and stratification of purchasing power."[54] Again the regnant concept of information provides the way out of capitalism's impasse, as she proclaims that "information is taking the place of scale as the key factor in corporate competition. . . . The merits of scale are being replaced by the merits of knowledge as the era of mass consumption gives way to the age of stratified consumption."[55]

Critics of these new consumer theories do not dispute the facts on which they are based: no one can deny the proliferation of goods and services, the stratification of consumers, or the differentiating powers of advertising and the media in

53. Much of my analysis here comes from marketing texts that purport to give producers and advertisers the scoop on socioeconomic trends in Japan. See the three texts mentioned above, as well as Gekkan Akurosu Henshūshitsu, ed., *Jidai wa pawā o ushinatta no ka* (Tokyo: Parco Shuppan, 1983).

54. Masako Ozawa, "Consumption in the Age of Stratification," *Japan Echo* 12, no. 3 (1985): 53.

55. Ozawa, "Consumption," 53.

contemporary Japan. Rather, these critics dispute the positive values attributed to the current shifts: instead of the budding of a "flexible" individuality they find an even more complete solidification and mystification of the populace.[56] To these critics discussions of the metamasses and the fragmented masses indicate only how powerfully entrenched the ideologies of the managed society are. Thus, even though consumers are "fragmented," consumption as a general norm has not declined. And as Morris-Suzuki has shown, the strategies of consumer targeting are intimately linked to the crisis in Japanese capitalism and the rise of information as a solution to this crisis. And, of course, an even more radical perspective sees all such discussion of the masses and their differentiation as merely a repression of the problem of class in Japan today.[57]

It is striking that some of Japan's most prominent intellectuals—for example, Yoshimoto Takaaki, Ueno Chizuko, and Asada Akira—agree with the marketing experts (albeit in a nuanced fashion) that the new patterns in consumption indicate a liberation of desire and subjectivity.[58] Many of them find in television commercials an ironic, metatextual commentary on current consumer capitalism; they hold up copywriters as today's version of the avant-garde. Asada Akira has pointed out that the differences between products are no longer as important as the differences between ads themselves; ads have thus become a pleasurable utopia of "difference" and play. His analysis goes even further, however, in claiming that "the difference generated by advertisements is also nothing more than a means for . . . getting ahead of the competition"; "the world of advertisement is nothing more than a space where the enjoyment of differentiation and the drive for accumulation meet."[59]

This discourse on consumption, advertising, and information also enfolds a related one about the status and power of media images in Japan today. The dominion of television (challenged recently by video) has increasingly blurred the line between a stable, external "reality" and an imaged one, in Japan as well as in other advanced industrial societies. These developments have led many to speak of Japan as thoroughly postmodern in its cultural forms, since one of the

56. One of the most persistent critics is Nishibe Susumu. See his "Denunciation of Mass Society and Its Apologists," *Japan Echo* 13, no. 1 (1986): 39–43; see also "Japan as a Highly Developed Mass Society: An Appraisal," *Journal of Japanese Studies* 8, no. 1 (Winter 1982): 73–96. The reference to "flexible" individuality comes from Yamazaki Masakazu, *Yawarakai kojinshugi no tanjō* (Tokyo: Chūō Kōronsha, 1984).

57. This would be the critique that a number of Western analysts of the media would make, seeing in the sort of affirmative mass-media theory as it has developed in the West a denial of class and popular struggle. One scathing example of Marxist media criticism is Armand Mattelart's introduction to *Communication and Class Struggle*, Vol. 1, *Capitalism and Imperialism*, ed. Armand Mattelart and Seth Siegelaub (New York: International General, 1979).

58. A number of these intellectuals themselves have become mass-media stars, and their books, best-sellers.

59. Asada Akira, "Saika no paranoia," in his *Tōsōron* (Tokyo: Chikuma Shobō, 1984), 13; translation mine. Asada's analysis echoes Jean Baudrillard's thinking on the political economy of the sign; Baudrillard, *For a Critique of the Political Economy of the Sign* (St. Louis: Telos Press, 1981).

hallmarks of the postmodern is the dominance of images and the impossibility of thinking about a social reality without considering the powers of the media.[60]

The social imaginary as revealed in current touristic rhetoric, for example, discloses an increasing blurring of boundaries, here in the sense of historical and cultural ones. "Discover Japan" signified the desire to return to authentic yet unknown origins. In the 1980s its successor "Exotic Japan" depicted global cultures as a series of internally foreign travel destinations. The "Exotic Japan" campaign, which started in 1984, encouraged Japanese to look at Japan with the eyes of the foreign other; it tried originally to appeal to the Japanese fascination with the Silk Road by reemphasizing its eastern terminus, Japan itself. Japan was seen as part of the exotic cultural ensemble traversed by the Silk Road, "Asia" in its most comprehensive sense. To this end the campaign highlighted this larger Asia within Japan. "Exotic Japan" in its expanded sense, however, implied not only the foreign within the native but also the native as foreign: Japan itself as exotic.

It is therefore not surprising that "Exotic Japan" should coincide with a boom in nostalgia products (*nosutarujī shōhin*), and nostalgia advertisements (*nosutarujī kōkoku*). These products and ads focused particularly on the 1920s and 1930s, but their primary targets were not people who grew up in the 1920s but rather young people who know nothing of prewar Japan, which thus became another frontier of the "exotic."[61]

As the debates on consumption and advertising reveal, however, it is possible to construe these 1980s developments in radically divergent ways. These debates parallel those in other advanced industrial societies about the status of postmodernity—debates that show the degree of contestation inherent in any attempt to characterize technological and social change. Although it is clear that current forms of information and media representation indicate a shift in the way society can be imagined—and thus potentially indicate new political possibilities—I would argue (as do Nishibe, Kurihara, and Morris-Suzuki) that ultimately the overall trend toward the management of persons has intensified with the ongoing consolidation of power within large enterprises.

Throughout the postwar period, particularly the 1970s and 1980s, Japanese developments have paralleled those in other advanced capitalist sectors of the global economy, albeit with their own timing and trajectory. For example, in America of the late 1950s there was much talk about the end of class society and the advent of the first truly "middle class" (or, alternatively, "classless") social order.[62] The rhetoric of late twentieth-century Japan uncannily echoes

60. I analyze the linkages between mass media, discourse, and postmodernism in "Critical Texts, Mass Artifacts: The Consumption of Knowledge in Postmodern Japan," in *Postmodernism and Japan*, ed. Masao Miyoshi and H. D. Harootunian (Durham: Duke University Press, 1989).

61. Fredric Jameson examines this sort of nostalgia in "Postmodernism; or, The Cultural Logic of Late Capitalism," *New Left Review* no. 146 (Sept.–Oct. 1984): 53–92.

62. Vance Packard demystified this type of thinking in *The Status Seekers* (New York: McKay, 1959), arguing instead that certain kinds of class distinction were becoming even more marked, as consumers

those Eisenhower-era pronouncements, perhaps with more justification. The United States with its Pax Americana has undoubtedly been the primary point of origin for innovations in the techniques of the culture industries (advertising, marketing, distribution, media), cultural forms (pop music, movies, television and radio programming, video culture), technologies (television and radio receivers, cable television, electric appliances, musical equipment), and many oppositional social movements and their idioms (feminism, ecology). Yet as the global balance of economic power has shifted, so has the role of the United States. Japan is now the leader in the production and exportation of the electronic "hardware" of global culture industries: tape recorders, Walkmen, VCRs, CD players, tapes. It is also a massive exporter of the products of industrial culture (fashion, pop music, films) to East and Southeast Asia, but it has not yet attained global prominence in this area, leaving much of the market share to the as yet undisputed leadership of American culture.[63] Video games (particularly Nintendo), robot toys, animated films, and translated *manga* are some of the areas in which Japan is now actively exporting cultural products to the West. Correspondingly, Japan is a voracious and seemingly insatiable consumer of American cultural forms as well as an attentive observer of American trends and techniques of marketing and advertising.

This division of mass cultural labor between the United States and Japan has been sharply threatened, however, with the acquisition in September 1989 of Columbia Pictures by Sony and by Matsushita's purchase in November 1990 of MCA (which includes Universal Pictures). The purchase by Japanese companies of major producers of a quintessentially American aesthetic form—film—brought into the open fears about the connections between national power and cultural industries. This unprecedented merger of enormous cultural hardware and software companies into transnational megacorporations has spurred critics to ask whether Japanese intervention in such an area as vital as the film industry might not stifle criticism of Japan within the movies. Throughout the various editorials and articles ran a persistent thematic thread: that film is a powerful medium for shaping and molding people's perceptions and thus has tremendous political and national import. The potential loss of internal control of a culture industry provoked, then, a whole array of assertions about the strategic importance of the media, which in turn revealed continuing American fears about Japanese economic dominance.

The question of difference and resistance is crucial within the framework of information-saturated mass cultural formations. In the early 1980s, for example, *taishū engeki*, which had been driven to the point of extinction by television,

sought to elevate their status. See Kimindo Kusaka, "What Is the Japanese Middle Class?" *Japan Echo* 12 (1985): 41.

63. Bernard Miège, in his valuable *The Capitalization of Cultural Production*, notes Patrice Flichy's observation that "Japan's hegemony in the field of mass-produced equipment goes well with America's domination of audiovisual programs and professional electronics." Miège also points out that the Japanese are becoming more and more active in the production of "new images" worldwide; *Capitalization of Cultural Production* (New York: International General, 1989), 47.

experienced a resurgence. Some of its most popular actors became lionized by the media as it attracted a new audience from among the urban young. The ambivalence of this kind of recuperation is not easily resolved: *taishū engeki* players, long used to reduced circumstances, welcomed the additional attention and money, yet they realized the fragility of the resurgence and the paradoxes of being framed within an NHK-inspired vision of "popular" or "folk" culture. Postwar Japan has had its share of protest movements, minority literatures, rich oppositional theater and music, feminist groups, cooperative social arrangements, avant-garde writing, and small-press (*mini komi*) publications. There has been a range of small-scale forms of resistance, from the "free radio" movement to the truly microlevel oppositional practices that must traverse any social order. Yet the continued precarious status of these forms and practices, both in Japan and in a global order where the massive capitalization and consolidation of culture proceeds unabated, is at once both the sign and the guarantee of the powers of the mass cultural industries of the late twentieth century.

CHAPTER TEN

Consuming and Saving

Charles Yuji Horioka

It is well known that the postwar Japanese economy provided the world with its first example of sustained double-digit growth in real GNP and that this phenomenal growth performance enabled Japan to recover from the devastation of World War II and join the ranks of the developed countries within just a few decades. However, it is perhaps less well known outside of Japan, although certainly not surprising, that this extraordinary economic expansion dramatically altered the texture of the Japanese people's lives, especially their consumption and saving patterns.

In this essay I analyze trends in the level and composition of consumption and saving in Japan during the past century and show how dramatically they changed as a result of the rapid economic growth during the postwar period. My analysis clearly shows that the emergence of a mass consumption society is a postwar phenomenon, as are the high levels of household saving. The latter finding is especially significant because it suggests that, contrary to popular belief, the high savings rates are *not* due primarily to cultural factors and that they are a temporary phenomenon.

THE LEVEL AND GROWTH OF CONSUMPTION

The level of per capita real consumption in Japan has shown a long-term upward trend during the past 110-odd years (figure 10.1). It increased from 286 1975 U.S.

The author is grateful to Ronald Dore, Andrew Gordon, Takeo Hoshi, Kōji Taira, Edward Tower, and other participants of the two "Postwar Japan as History" conferences and to Tuvia Blumenthal, Atsushi Maki, David Merriman, and two anonymous referees for their valuable comments.

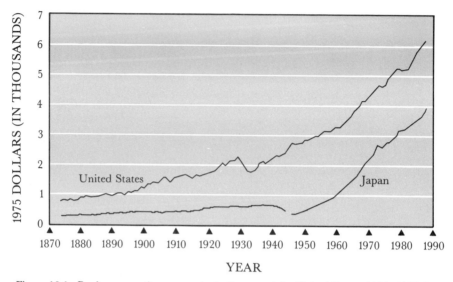

Figure 10.1. Real consumption per capita in Japan and the United States, 1874–1988 (in thousands of 1975 U.S. dollars).

NOTE: The figures shown here and in figure 10.2 include the consumption of households, private unincorporated nonfinancial enterprises, and private nonprofit institutions serving households but exclude government consumption. The Japanese figures were first converted to 1975 yen and then to 1975 U.S. dollars using the 1975 consumer goods purchasing power equivalent of 278.4 yen per dollar calculated by Irving B. Kravis and associates. The 1945 figure for Japan is not available.

SOURCES: The data for figures 10.1 and 10.2 were taken from Alan H. Gleason, "The Level of Living in Japan and the United States: A Long-Term International Comparison," *Economic Development and Cultural Change* 37 (Jan. 1989): 266–67, but were updated by the author (the 1985 figures were revised and the figures for 1986–88 were newly calculated). See Gleason for detailed information concerning data sources, calculation method, etc. Gleason uses the Long-Term Economic Statistics for pre-1940 Japanese data, Thomas S. Berry's estimates for 1874–88 U.S. data, John W. Kendrick's estimates for 1889–1928 U.S. data, and national income accounts data for more recent years. The 1985–88 figures for Japan were calculated from data in Economic Planning Agency, ed., *Annual Report on National Accounts*, 1990 edition (Tokyo: Ministry of Finance Printing Bureau, 1990), 120–21. The 1985–88 figures for the United States were calculated from data in the *Survey of Current Business* (U.S. Department of Commerce, Bureau of Economic Analysis) 70 (July 1990): 98.

dollars in 1874 to 3,957 1975 U.S. dollars in 1988, which corresponds to a more than 13.8-fold increase and to an average annual growth rate of 2.33 percent.[1] (The only period during which real per capita consumption showed a sustained decline was the wartime period from 1937 to 1946.) By contrast, the level of per capita real consumption in the United States increased only 7.9-fold during the

1. These and all of the figures in this section were taken from Alan H. Gleason, "The Level of Living in Japan and the United States: A Long-Term International Comparison," *Economic Development*

same period, which corresponds to an average annual growth rate of only 1.83 percent.

However, the rate of growth of real per capita consumption in Japan has shown considerable trend discontinuity: it averaged 1.42 percent per year during the prewar period (1874–1937), −6.58 percent per year during the war years (1937–46), 7.53 percent per year during the early postwar period (1946–73), and 2.61 percent per year during the post-oil-crisis period (1973–88).

If we focus on the high-growth period (1955–73), the growth rate of real per capita consumption averaged 7.51 percent per year.[2] This growth rate is high in both absolute and relative terms, but is it commensurate with the double-digit rates of economic growth recorded during this period? In other words, were consumers able to reap the full benefits of rapid economic growth? If we examine the evidence, the growth rate of real gross national product averaged 9.44 percent per year during the 1955–73 period, which is 1.93 percentage points higher than the average growth rate of real per capita consumption during the same period. Of this difference, 1.12 percentage points are due to population growth, and most of the remaining 0.81 percentage points are due to increases in corporate and household saving. With respect to the latter, it is true that a more rapid growth of real per capita consumption would have been possible if corporate and household saving had not increased,[3] but it must be borne in mind that saving also confers utility on consumers because it represents protection against unexpected emergencies as well as resources for future consumption. In fact, assuming saving was done voluntarily, Japanese consumers presumably allocated their income between consumption and saving so as to maximize their utility. Thus, we cannot conclude that Japanese consumers did not reap the full benefits of economic growth simply because the growth of consumption levels lagged behind the growth of GNP as a result of increases in saving.[4] The level of household dispos-

---

and Cultural Change 37 (Jan. 1989): 261–84, but were updated by the author. The reader should refer to Gleason and the notes to figure 10.1 for information concerning sources, calculation method, and so on, but an important point to note is that the figures for both countries are denominated in 1975 U.S. dollars and that the Japanese figures were converted to U.S. dollars using purchasing power parities, which is preferable to using market exchange rates for the reasons discussed in Martin Bronfenbrenner and Yasukichi Yasuba, "Economic Welfare," in *The Political Economy of Japan*, vol. 1, *The Domestic Transformation*, ed. Kōzō Yamamura and Yasukichi Yasuba (Stanford: Stanford University Press, 1987), 96–97. These and all of the national income accounts data for Japan reported in this essay do not incorporate the October 1990 benchmark revision based on 1985 prices, the data from which were not yet available at the time of this writing.

2. This figure was calculated by the author from national income accounts data. It differs slightly from the 7.30 percent figure implied by Gleason's data, presumably because I use a later revision of the data.

3. (Net) corporate saving consists of the retained earnings (undistributed profits) of corporations, but it ultimately accrues to individuals—in particular, to individual stockholders—via capital gains on their stockholdings.

4. The same point is made by Bronfenbrenner and Yasuba, "Economic Welfare," 100–101. It should be noted, however, that although saving was done voluntarily during the postwar period,

able income or of private national income is perhaps a more meaningful measure of consumer welfare than the level of consumption is, and the real growth rates of both income concepts were roughly equal to that of GNP during the high-growth period.[5] Thus, I tentatively conclude that Japanese consumers *were* able to reap the full benefits of rapid economic growth.

An international comparison of growth rates of real per capita consumption shows that Japan's prewar growth rate was somewhat lower than those of the United States and Sweden, about equal to those of Germany and Canada, considerably higher than those of the United Kingdom, Italy, and Norway, and thus approximately equal to the average of the Western developed countries.[6] By contrast, the postwar growth rate was much higher than those of the other developed countries during the high-growth period and somewhat higher even during the post-oil-crisis period.[7]

By the early Meiji period Japan's real per capita consumption was already more than one-third that of the United States, even though "Japan had just emerged from a prolonged period of feudalism and economic isolation" (figure 10.2).[8] However, the ratio improved little during the remainder of the prewar period. It increased briefly to 40 percent in 1894 but fell to 25 percent in 1906 and was no higher at the end of the prewar period than it was in the early Meiji period (it was 36–37 percent in both 1874–75 and 1934). Moreover, it declined sharply after 1934 because of Japan's involvement in the Pacific War, falling to less than 14 percent by 1946. During the postwar period, by contrast, the Japan/U.S. ratio improved dramatically, increasing to nearly 64 percent by 1982. However, its rate of improvement slowed after 1973, and it declined slightly between 1982 and 1986 even though it maintained a level in excess of 60 percent.

Thus, as in the case of the absolute level of Japan's real per capita consumption, the Japan/U.S. ratio showed considerable trend discontinuity both at the time of the Pacific War and at the time of the first oil crisis. Moreover, the rapid improvement in both absolute consumption levels and the Japan/U.S. ratio during the early postwar period was not merely a process of recovery from the war

---

consumer decisions were distorted by various government policies and institutions, many of which were explicitly designed to promote saving. I am indebted to David Merriman for this point.

5. Household disposable income is defined as the sum of household consumption and household saving, while private national income is defined as the sum of household consumption, household saving, and corporate saving.

6. Ryōshin Minami, *The Economic Development of Japan: A Quantitative Study*, trans. Ralph Thompson, Ryōshin Minami, and David Merriman (Basingstoke and London: Macmillan, 1986), 396.

7. Charles Yuji Horioka, "Shōhi/chochiku no kokusai hikaku: Nihonjin no seikatsu wa hontō ni yutaka ka?" *Nihon keizai kenkyū* (Japan Center for Economic Research Economic Journal) 20 (May 1990): 47–48. English version forthcoming in *Economic Development and Cultural Change*.

8. Gleason, "Level of Living," 268.

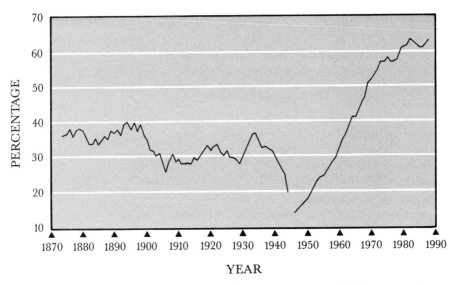

Figure 10.2. Real consumption per capita in Japan, as a percentage of U.S. consumption, 1874–1988.

SOURCES: See figure 10.1.

inasmuch as it continued long after consumption had recovered to its prewar level (the level of real per capita consumption and the Japan/U.S. ratio surpassed their prewar peak levels in 1954 and 1964, respectively).

A final point to note is that Japan's level of real per capita consumption still lags far behind that of the United States despite the dramatic improvements therein. In fact, Alan Gleason estimates on the basis of current trends that Japanese consumption levels will not catch up to those of the United States until the middle of the next century.[9] Moreover, Japan also lagged behind Canada, Iceland, Switzerland, Luxembourg, Norway, France, and the United Kingdom as of 1987 even though she had surpassed Italy, West Germany, and the remaining developed countries.[10] Thus, Japan has come a long way in terms of consumption levels but still has a long way to go.

Moreover, the data on consumption levels discussed thus far are an imperfect measure of consumer welfare, as noted by Gleason.[11] For example, pollution, urban congestion, leisure time, and social infrastructure such as parks and roads are not taken into account. The earlier conclusion that Japanese consumers were able to reap the full benefits of rapid economic growth would have to be modified,

9. Ibid., 275.
10. Horioka, "Shōhi/chochiku," 47–48; see also Gleason, "Level of Living," 276.
11. Gleason, "Level of Living," 262.

and Japan would lag even further behind the United States and the other developed countries if such factors were taken into account.[12]

I have thus far tried to place consumption levels in postwar Japan in historical and international perspective, but other standards of comparison are possible. For example, one could ask the counterfactual question of what consumption levels would have been if Japan had pursued a strategy different from the growth strategy actually pursued (such as one that placed more emphasis on consumer welfare). It would be difficult to predict the outcomes of strategies not actually pursued, but if such an analysis could be done, it would be very meaningful.[13]

THE COMPOSITION OF CONSUMPTION

The dramatic improvements in consumption levels documented in the previous section were accompanied by equally profound changes in the composition of consumption, with a pronounced shift occurring from necessities and traditional products to luxuries and Western products. This section analyzes trends over time in the composition of consumption by category (commodity group), while the following section analyzes the Westernization over time of consumption patterns.

Tables 10.1 through 10.4 present data on the composition of consumption by category. Tables 10.1 and 10.3 show the actual budget shares of each consumption category, while tables 10.2 and 10.4 show what the budget shares would have been if relative prices had remained constant at 1934–36 levels (in the case of table 10.2) and 1980 levels (in the case of table 10.4). The data in tables 10.1 and 10.3 reflect changes in both prices and quantities, while the data in tables 10.2 and 10.4 allow us to focus on changes in quantities.

We would expect the budget shares of necessities such as food, clothing, and shelter to decline and the budget shares of luxuries to increase in response to increases in household incomes, and this pattern is, in general, what we observe in the case of Japan. For example, the budget share of food, the most basic necessity (referred to as the Engel coefficient), declined sharply during the prewar period, from about two-thirds in 1875 to less than one-half in 1940 in the case of both the current-price and constant-price data. It increased temporarily during the immediate postwar period (to 70 percent in the case of the current-price data and to 56 percent in the case of the constant-price data) because of the poverty of that period, but it then resumed its decline, falling back down to 1940 levels

12. However, other omitted factors such as crime rates and health would *narrow* the gap between Japan and the other developed countries. The concept of net national welfare (NNW) takes account of many of these factors, and Miyohei Shinohara and Hisao Kanamori have estimated NNW for Japan; unfortunately, comparable data are not available for most other countries. See Bronfenbrenner and Yasuba, "Economic Welfare," 98–99, and also Taira's essay in this volume.

13. I am grateful to Takeo Hoshi and Lawrence Krause for this point. See also the Hein and Taira essays in this volume.

by the mid-1950s. Moreover, it continued its decline thereafter as well, falling to about one-fifth by 1988 in the case of both types of data.

The budget share of clothing, another necessity, increased until 1973 except for a sharp drop following the war, but it has shown a downward trend since then.[14] The budget share of housing (rent), also a necessity, has shown an upward trend throughout in the case of the current-price data (except for the same prewar/postwar discontinuity), but it has, if anything, shown a downward trend in the case of the constant-price data (except during the 1915–40 and 1973–81 periods). This discrepancy between trends in the current-price data and those in the constant-price data suggests that the increases in the current-price budget share are due to increases in the relative price of housing rather than to increases in the quantity consumed. The budget share of fuel and light, which is shown separately from that of housing only in the pre-1955 data, declined until about 1900, increased during the remainder of the prewar period, and declined again during the early postwar period.

The budget share of furniture, household goods, and so on, data for which are available only for the period since 1955, increased until the middle to late 1960s but has been declining since then (except for an upturn in the constant-price data since 1981). In addition, the budget share of social expenses, data for which are available only for the prewar period, showed a downward trend after 1900 in the case of the current-price data and a downward trend throughout in the case of the constant-price data.

By contrast, the budget shares of luxury goods and services such as medical expenses, transportation, communication, recreation, leisure, education, cultural services, and miscellaneous have generally shown upward trends over time (except for medical expenses during the 1885–1910 period).[15]

In sum, the budget shares of necessities have generally been declining, at least after a point, while the budget shares of luxuries have generally been increasing. This is precisely the compositional shift we would have expected in response to the dramatic improvements in the standard of living that occurred. Moreover, the temporary reversal in long-term trends that occurred in response to the sharp declines in income during and after World War II is also generally consistent with our expectations.

The evidence suggests that income growth has been the primary determinant

14. The pre-1955 data and the post-1955 data are not strictly comparable. The significant differences in the 1955 figures from the two sources, especially in the case of clothing, are presumably due to differences in coverage.

15. The Family Income and Expenditure Survey conducted by the Statistics Bureau of the Management and Coordination Agency (formerly the Statistics Bureau of the Prime Minister's Office) provides a more detailed breakdown of the composition of consumption. Data from this survey will not be analyzed in detail, but they show that expenditures on automobiles, automotive maintenance, communication, recreational goods and services, pocket money (the detailed uses of which are not known), and social expenses (gifts, entertaining expenses, and membership fees) have increased the most sharply.

TABLE 10.1. Composition of Consumption Based on Current-Price Data, 1875–1955
(in percentages)[a]

Year	Food	Clothing	Housing	Fuel and Light	Medical and Personal Care	Transportation	Communication	Social Expenses	Education, Recreation, and Miscellaneous
1875	65.9	7.3	8.4	5.9	3.3	0.2	0.0	5.3	3.8
1880	68.7	8.3	5.8	4.0	3.2	0.2	0.1	6.0	3.8
1885	64.1	6.9	8.8	4.3	5.1	0.2	0.1	6.3	4.2
1890	66.3	7.2	8.8	3.3	4.4	0.6	0.1	5.2	4.0
1895	62.3	10.6	8.3	3.2	4.4	0.9	0.2	6.1	4.0
1900	61.7	10.0	7.9	3.1	4.1	1.2	0.3	7.6	4.1
1905	63.5	8.0	8.2	3.2	3.5	1.5	0.4	7.5	4.2
1910	61.3	9.3	9.7	3.5	2.6	1.8	0.4	7.1	4.3
1915	59.9	9.2	10.0	4.2	3.8	2.2	0.5	5.2	5.0
1920	61.8	12.5	6.4	4.6	3.3	2.4	0.4	3.2	5.5
1925	59.1	10.2	10.7	3.8	3.6	2.9	0.5	3.4	5.9
1930	53.5	9.7	13.7	4.4	4.3	3.4	0.6	3.3	7.1
1935	50.3	12.8	11.7	4.3	6.6	3.2	0.7	2.6	7.8
1940	48.9	11.0	13.0	4.5	5.7	4.1	0.6	3.6	8.5
1946	70.2	6.9	6.4	5.6			10.9		
1947	66.3	8.8	5.3	5.6			13.9		
1948	62.3	8.3	8.4	4.9			16.1		
1949	63.1	8.8	7.9	5.0			15.1		
1950	59.6	11.4	8.9	5.1			15.1		
1951	56.3	15.1	8.3	4.9			15.4		
1952	54.0	15.7	9.0	4.9			16.4		
1953	52.5	15.0	10.1	4.7			17.8		
1954	52.4	13.9	10.2	4.5			19.0		
1955	51.1	13.5	10.9	4.3			20.3		

SOURCES: Kazushi Ohkawa and Miyohei Shinohara, eds., *Patterns of Japanese Economic Development: A Quantitative Appraisal* (New Haven: Yale University Press, 1979), 338–41.
[a]The totals may not equal 100 because of rounding error.

TABLE 10.2. Composition of Consumption Based on Constant-Price Data, 1875–1955
(in percentages)[a]

Year	Food	Clothing	Housing	Fuel and Light	Medical and Personal Care	Transportation	Communication	Social Expenses	Education, Recreation, and Miscellaneous
1875	64.5	2.7	13.1	2.7	2.2	0.1	0.0	11.8	2.8
1880	65.7	3.6	11.8	2.4	2.5	0.2	0.1	10.3	3.4
1885	65.8	3.2	12.6	2.8	3.7	0.2	0.1	8.8	2.8
1890	62.8	4.1	11.1	2.5	3.5	0.4	0.1	8.9	6.5
1895	61.3	6.4	10.2	2.3	3.3	0.8	0.2	9.6	6.0
1900	59.8	6.7	10.3	2.3	3.4	1.3	0.2	9.7	6.3
1905	59.1	6.0	11.7	2.7	2.9	1.9	0.3	9.7	5.7
1910	60.0	6.8	12.3	2.7	2.3	1.1	0.3	9.2	5.3
1915	62.7	7.2	8.8	3.6	3.6	1.5	0.3	6.7	5.5
1920	59.9	8.9	10.4	4.0	3.0	2.3	0.4	3.9	7.1
1925	56.9	7.7	13.0	4.1	3.3	2.9	0.4	3.8	7.8
1930	54.2	9.8	12.5	4.5	4.2	3.2	0.6	3.4	7.7
1935	50.0	12.9	11.6	4.3	6.7	3.2	0.7	2.6	8.0
1940	47.4	7.7	14.5	4.7	6.1	6.1	0.7	4.5	8.3
1946	55.9	5.2	10.9	8.5	19.4				
1947	56.5	5.3	11.2	8.2	18.8				
1948	55.9	5.0	12.4	7.8	18.9				
1949	55.9	5.0	12.0	7.6	19.5				
1950	53.7	6.8	11.4	7.4	20.7				
1951	51.8	9.2	10.8	6.8	21.4				
1952	49.5	11.8	11.9	6.2	20.5				
1953	48.7	12.1	11.6	5.8	21.8				
1954	47.7	11.8	11.8	5.6	23.1				
1955	47.4	11.7	11.7	5.2	24.0				

SOURCE: Ohkawa and Shinohara, *Patterns of Japanese Economic Development*, 342–45.
[a]The figures are based on data denominated in 1934–36 prices; totals may not equal 100 because of rounding error.

TABLE 10.3. Composition of Consumption Based on Current-Price Data, 1955–88
(in percentages)[a]

Year	Food, Beverages, Tobacco	Clothing, Footwear	Rent, Utilities	Furniture, Household Goods, Miscellaneous Household Expenses	Medical, Health	Transportation, Communication	Recreation, Leisure, Education, Cultural Services	Miscellaneous
1955	50.1	6.4	12.0	6.4	5.5	4.8	5.7	9.1
1956	47.4	6.9	12.8	7.0	5.4	5.0	6.0	9.5
1957	46.5	6.9	13.4	7.0	5.4	5.2	6.1	9.5
1958	44.4	6.9	14.0	6.9	5.6	5.4	6.4	10.3
1959	43.0	6.7	14.6	7.3	5.6	5.5	6.9	10.5
1960	41.7	7.0	14.9	7.7	5.6	5.5	7.0	10.6
1961	40.1	7.2	15.1	8.0	5.9	5.5	7.2	11.0
1962	38.5	7.7	15.1	8.1	6.3	5.5	7.3	11.5
1963	37.1	8.2	15.2	8.6	6.5	5.6	7.4	11.5
1964	35.4	8.1	15.8	8.7	7.2	5.7	7.6	11.7
1965	35.2	8.1	16.5	8.4	7.5	5.7	7.1	11.5
1966	34.2	8.2	16.7	8.3	7.4	6.2	7.3	11.7
1967	33.3	7.9	16.6	8.0	7.5	6.6	7.8	12.1
1968	32.2	7.8	16.3	8.1	7.7	6.9	8.4	12.6
1969	31.2	7.7	16.2	8.0	7.7	7.3	9.1	12.8

1970	30.4	7.7	16.2	7.7	7.9	7.8	9.2	13.1
1971	29.3	8.0	16.7	7.3	7.8	8.0	9.4	13.5
1972	28.3	8.0	16.6	7.5	8.0	8.1	9.7	13.9
1973	27.6	8.8	16.1	7.9	7.8	8.6	9.2	14.1
1974	28.3	8.4	15.5	7.6	8.4	9.1	9.0	13.9
1975	28.4	8.1	15.6	6.3	9.0	9.6	8.8	14.2
1976	28.1	8.2	16.1	6.4	9.0	9.6	9.0	13.6
1977	27.5	7.7	16.7	6.1	9.2	10.0	8.9	14.0
1978	26.2	7.5	17.1	5.8	9.6	10.0	8.9	14.8
1979	24.8	7.5	17.1	6.2	9.8	10.2	8.8	15.7
1980	24.6	7.3	18.1	5.9	9.9	10.2	8.8	15.3
1981	24.5	6.9	18.7	5.5	10.1	10.1	8.8	15.4
1982	23.7	6.9	18.5	5.5	10.3	10.1	9.1	15.8
1983	23.4	6.6	18.7	5.5	10.4	10.1	9.1	16.0
1984	23.0	6.5	18.9	5.5	10.3	9.8	9.4	16.6
1985	22.5	6.4	18.9	5.5	10.3	9.5	9.6	17.3
1986	21.9	6.3	18.7	5.4	10.6	9.5	10.0	17.7
1987	21.0	6.2	18.8	5.6	10.8	9.4	10.2	18.0
1988	20.4	6.1	18.9	5.6	10.9	9.8	10.3	18.1

SOURCES: The data for 1955–70 were taken from *National Economic Accounts Quarterly* 78, no. 1 (1988): 138–47. The data for 1971–81 were taken from Economic Planning Agency, *Report on Revised National Accounts on the Basis of 1980* (Tokyo: Ministry of Finance Printing Bureau, 1986) 2:168–69. The data for 1982 were taken from Economic Planning Agency, *Annual Report on National Accounts* (Tokyo: Ministry of Finance Printing Bureau, 1989), 246–47. The data for 1983–88 were taken from Economic Planning Agency, *Annual Report on National Accounts* (Tokyo: Ministry of Finance Printing Bureau, 1990), 244–45.
aTotals may not equal 100 because of rounding error.

TABLE 10.4. Composition of Consumption Based on Constant-Price Data, 1955–88
(in percentages)[a]

Year	Food, Beverages, Tobacco	Clothing, Footwear	Rent, Utilities	Furniture, Household Goods, Miscellaneous Household Expenses	Medical, Health	Transportation, Communication	Recreation, Leisure, Education, Cultural Services	Miscellaneous
1955	45.4	5.3	18.8	4.6	4.1	4.4	7.2	10.6
1956	44.5	5.6	18.4	4.9	4.1	4.6	7.2	11.3
1957	43.8	5.7	18.1	5.0	4.2	4.6	7.5	11.5
1958	42.6	5.9	18.0	5.0	4.4	4.8	7.4	12.5
1959	42.0	6.0	17.8	5.5	3.9	4.9	7.6	13.0
1960	41.4	6.3	17.4	5.8	4.1	5.0	7.6	13.3
1961	40.2	6.7	17.2	6.1	4.3	5.1	7.4	13.7
1962	38.7	7.3	17.3	6.3	4.4	5.2	7.3	14.3
1963	36.9	7.8	17.3	6.9	4.9	5.4	7.1	14.0
1964	35.9	7.7	16.8	7.1	5.7	5.6	7.3	14.0
1965	35.4	8.0	17.1	7.1	5.9	5.9	6.8	13.8
1966	35.0	8.1	16.6	7.2	6.0	6.2	7.0	13.8
1967	34.0	7.9	16.1	7.0	6.3	6.8	7.5	14.3
1968	32.6	7.9	16.0	7.3	6.2	7.4	8.0	14.7
1969	31.3	7.9	15.5	7.3	6.5	8.0	8.6	14.8
1970	30.2	7.9	15.5	7.1	6.7	8.5	9.1	15.0

1971	29.3	8.0	15.8	6.8	7.1	8.8	9.2	15.1
1972	29.0	8.0	15.4	7.0	7.0	8.7	9.4	15.5
1973	27.9	8.1	15.4	7.2	7.4	9.3	9.3	15.3
1974	27.5	7.6	16.4	6.4	8.3	10.0	9.1	14.7
1975	27.6	7.6	16.7	5.7	8.9	10.5	8.5	14.6
1976	27.0	7.9	17.1	6.1	8.8	10.3	8.7	14.0
1977	26.7	7.4	17.4	5.9	9.3	10.3	8.8	14.2
1978	25.8	7.4	17.6	5.8	9.0	10.6	8.7	15.2
1979	24.9	7.3	17.3	6.2	9.2	10.5	8.6	16.0
1980	24.6	7.3	18.1	5.9	9.9	10.2	8.8	15.3
1981	24.3	6.9	18.5	5.5	10.3	10.1	8.7	15.6
1982	23.8	7.0	18.1	5.7	10.6	9.8	9.1	15.9
1983	23.3	6.7	18.1	5.8	10.9	10.0	9.3	16.1
1984	22.5	6.6	18.2	5.9	10.7	9.9	9.7	16.6
1985	22.2	6.5	18.2	6.0	10.1	9.6	9.9	17.5
1986	21.7	6.3	17.9	6.0	10.2	9.8	10.2	18.0
1987	21.1	6.1	17.7	6.2	10.3	9.8	10.6	18.2
1988	20.4	5.9	17.7	6.2	10.4	10.2	11.0	18.2

SOURCES: The data for 1955–70 were taken from *National Economic Accounts Quarterly* 78, no. 1 (1988): 138–47. The data for 1971–81 were taken from Economic Planning Agency, *Report on Revised National Accounts on the Basis of 1980* (Tokyo: Ministry of Finance Printing Bureau, 1986) 2:168–69. The data for 1982 were taken from Economic Planning Agency, *Annual Report on National Accounts* (Tokyo: Ministry of Finance Printing Bureau, 1989), 246–47. The data for 1983–88 were taken from Economic Planning Agency, *Annual Report on National Accounts* (Tokyo: Ministry of Finance Printing Bureau, 1990), 244–45. The figures are based on data denominated in 1980 prices. Totals may not equal 100 because of rounding.

[a] The figures are based on data denominated in 1980 prices. Totals may not equal 100 because of rounding.

of trends over time in the composition of consumption, and econometric analysis confirms this finding for the case of the budget share of food.[16] It is possible that changes in relative prices also influenced trends in the composition of consumption, but the fact that trends over time were generally similar in the cases of both current-price and constant-price budget shares suggests that changes in relative prices were of relatively little importance. The only major exceptions are clothing and housing. The constant-price budget share of clothing increased much more sharply than did its current-price budget share during the prewar period because of the fall in the relative price of clothing, which in turn was the result of the domestic revolution in textile technology.[17] By contrast, the current-price budget share of housing has shown an upward trend despite the relative stability of its constant-price budget share because of the increase in the relative price of housing, which in turn has been largely the result of the sharp increase in land prices.[18]

An additional point to note is that, as in the case of the level of consumption, there was considerable trend discontinuity at the time of World War II and at the time of the first oil crisis. For example, the current-price (constant-price) budget share of food declined at an average rate of 0.26 (0.26) percentage points per year during the 1875–1940 period, *increased* at an average rate of 3.55 (1.42) points per year during the 1940–46 period, and declined at an average rate of 2.12 (0.95) points per year during the 1946–55 period, 1.25 (0.97) points per year during the 1955–73 period, and 0.49 (0.49) points per year during the 1973–88 period.[19] Thus, as in the case of the level of consumption, change was the most rapid during the early postwar period, less rapid during the post-oil-crisis period, and least rapid during the prewar period. However, despite differences in the *speed* of change, the *direction* of change was generally the same throughout, and in that sense there was a basic continuity.[20]

Almost all countries have shown similar trends over time in the composition

16. Horioka, "Shōhi/chochiku," 52.

17. Minami, *Economic Development of Japan*, 399.

18. The sharp increase in land prices was caused in large part by the rapid urbanization of the population. Atsushi Maki conducts a more rigorous analysis of the determinants of trends over time in the composition of consumption during the 1960–70 period and corroborates my finding that the impact of income growth was greater than the impact of price changes. He also examines the impact of habit persistence and household size and finds both to be important. Maki, *Shōhi senkō to juyō sokutei* (Tokyo: Yūhikaku, 1983), 120–24.

19. The 1946–73 period was broken up into two subperiods partly because the pre-1955 data and the post-1955 data are not strictly comparable and partly because I wanted to show that change was rapid even after the recovery from the war had been completed.

20. The Family Income and Expenditure Survey is informative because it provides breakdowns of the data by various household characteristics. For example, it provides breakdowns by income quintiles, and these breakdowns reveal considerable variation in the composition of consumption by income. For example, the budget share of food in the highest income quintile has consistently been 4 to 7 percentage points lower than the overall average during the postwar period. Put another way, trends in the budget share of food in the highest income quintile have led trends in the overall average by about ten years. For example, the budget share of food in the highest income quintile in 1960 was roughly equal to the overall average in 1973, thirteen years later.

of consumption (for example, the budget share of food has fallen not only in Japan but in all countries), but the rate of change has been far more rapid in the case of Japan during both the prewar and postwar periods.[21] Despite the more rapid rate of change, however, the composition of consumption in Japan is still somewhat "backward" compared to that of the most highly developed countries. For example, as of 1987 the budget share of food in Japan was still more than 1.5 times that of the United States and was also higher than those of Canada, New Zealand, the Netherlands, the United Kingdom, and France even though it had fallen below those of West Germany, Italy, and the remaining developed countries.[22] Thus, Japan has not yet caught up with the United States and the other most highly developed countries with respect to either the level or the composition of consumption despite dramatic improvements in both.

THE WESTERNIZATION OF CONSUMPTION PATTERNS

The dramatic changes in the level and composition of consumption in Japan have been accompanied by an equally dramatic Westernization of consumption patterns (what might be called an "international demonstration effect").[23] For example, the share of rice and *mochi* (rice cakes) in total cereal consumption has shown a long-term downward trend, falling from 96.0 percent in 1926 to 59.1 percent in 1989 (table 10.5).[24] Moreover, not only has the share of rice declined, but the quantity consumed has also fallen. For example, the average annual consumption per household of nonglutinous rice in 1989 was only 30 percent of what it was in 1960 (128.40 kilograms versus 430.45 kilograms). By contrast, the shares of bread and noodles have generally shown upward trends during the postwar period: the share of bread increased 11.9-fold from 1.9 percent in 1947 to 22.7 percent in 1989, while the share of noodles increased 4.7-fold from 3.5 percent in 1947 to 16.4 percent in 1989.

Thus, there has been a dramatic shift away from traditional cereal products toward Western cereal products since at least 1925. However, it should be noted that rice is still by far the dominant cereal product and that the shift toward Western cereal products has slowed somewhat in recent years (the budget share of rice declined by 11.3 percentage points between 1969 and 1979 but by only 8.7 percentage points between 1979 and 1989).

21. Horioka, "Shōhi/chochiku," 50–52, and Minami, *Economic Development of Japan,* 397–98.

22. Horioka, "Shōhi/chochiku," 48–52. Bronfenbrenner and Yasuba, "Economic Welfare," 103, suggest that the budget share of food has remained relatively high in Japan because of the relatively high price of food (especially the government-supported price of rice), combined with a relatively low price elasticity of demand for food, but Horioka, "Shōhi/chochiku," 52, finds that Japan's relatively low level of per capita real consumption is the primary explanation.

23. Bronfenbrenner and Yasuba, "Economic Welfare," 103–4, also discuss this phenomenon.

24. The share of rice increased between 1949 and 1960, but this increase occurred because rice consumption was temporarily depressed during the war years and the early postwar years owing to the shortage of rice and the substitution of barley and other inferior grains for rice (note the bulge in the "other" category between 1939 and 1955, especially 1947–50).

TABLE 10.5 Composition of Cereal Consumption, 1926–89
(in percentages)

Year	Rice and mochi (rice cakes)[a]	Bread	Noodles	Other[b]
1926	96.0		4.0	
1931	91.4		8.6	
1932	92.7		7.3	
1933	93.0		7.0	
1934	93.3		6.7	
1935	93.5		6.5	
1936	93.0		7.0	
1937	93.3		6.7	
1938	93.8		6.2	
1939	90.9		9.1	
1940	87.3		12.7	
1947	62.6	1.9	3.5	32.0
1948	62.1	5.0	5.9	27.0
1949	60.3	6.4	5.5	27.7
1950	60.7	9.0	6.3	24.1
1951	70.8	10.3	6.7	12.2
1952	74.8	8.5	5.7	11.0
1953	77.0	7.5	5.4	10.1
1954	76.1	9.0	5.4	9.5
1955	76.4	8.7	5.0	10.0
1956	81.5	6.9	4.2	7.4
1957	83.2	6.9	3.8	6.0
1958	83.5	7.2	3.9	5.4
1959	83.8	7.6	4.0	4.6
1960	83.9	7.9	4.4	3.7
1961	82.6	8.8	5.4	3.2
1962	81.2	9.7	6.1	2.9
1963	82.3	8.4	6.8	2.6
1964	80.4	8.9	8.3	2.3
1965	80.5	8.9	8.6	2.1
1966	79.8	9.3	9.0	2.0
1967	80.1	9.1	9.0	1.8
1968	80.5	9.2	8.7	1.7
1969	79.1	10.1	9.2	1.5
1970	78.1	10.7	9.7	1.5
1971	76.6	11.3	10.6	1.5
1972	75.5	12.0	11.0	1.5
1973	72.9	12.9	12.6	1.6
1974	67.2	15.7	15.3	1.8
1975	68.9	15.2	14.2	1.7
1976	69.2	15.8	13.3	1.7

TABLE 10.5 (*continued*)

Year	Rice and mochi (rice cakes)[a]	Bread	Noodles	Other[b]
1977	69.1	16.4	13.0	1.6
1978	68.4	16.9	13.2	1.5
1979	67.8	17.0	13.7	1.5
1980	65.6	18.7	14.1	1.6
1981	65.2	19.2	14.0	1.6
1982	65.0	19.3	14.1	1.6
1983	64.1	19.6	14.7	1.6
1984	64.1	19.4	14.8	1.6
1985	64.2	19.3	14.9	1.6
1986	63.6	19.8	15.0	1.6
1987	62.5	20.4	15.3	1.8
1988	60.4	21.7	16.1	1.8
1989	59.1	22.7	16.4	1.8

SOURCES: The data for 1926–40 were taken from Tōyō Keizai Shinpōsha, ed., *Shōwa Tōkei Sōran* (Tokyo: Tōyō Keizai Shinpōsha, 1980) 2: 360. The data for 1947–86 were taken from Management and Coordination Agency, Statistics Bureau, ed., *Comprehensive Time Series Report on the Family Income and Expenditure Survey, 1947–1986* (Tokyo: Japan Statistical Association, 1988), 86–89, 618–21. The data for 1987–89 were taken from Management and Coordination Agency, Statistics Bureau, ed., *Annual Report on the Family Income and Expenditure Survey*, 1989 edition (Tokyo: Japan Statistical Association, 1990), 246–50.

NOTE: The figures for 1926–40 refer to worker households living in all cities; the figures for 1947–62 refer to all households living in cities with populations of 50,000 or more; and the figures for 1963 and later refer to all households nationwide. Totals may not equal 100 because of rounding error. Data for 1927–30 and 1941–46 are not available.

[a] The figures for 1926–50 exclude expenditures on *mochi* (rice cakes) because data are not available.

[b] The category "other" includes barley and other cereals, flour, and (for the years 1950–62) processing charges.

The proportion of Western products has shown an upward trend in other consumption categories as well (table 10.6). For example, expenditures on Western-style fresh cakes as a proportion of total expenditures on fresh cakes increased from 23.6 percent in 1958 (the first year for which data are available) to 57.2 percent in 1982 (a 2.4-fold increase) before leveling off.

Similarly, Western (black) tea consumption as a proportion of total tea consumption increased from 3.0 percent in 1951 (the first year for which data are available) to 18.0 percent in 1987 (a sixfold increase) before leveling off. There was a corresponding decline in the share of Japanese (green) tea, and in fact there was a decline not only in the share but also in the quantity consumed: the average annual consumption per household of Japanese tea in 1989 was only 50 percent of what it was in 1956 (1,291 grams versus 2,595 grams).

As another example, the consumption of the major Western alcoholic beverages (beer and whiskey) as a proportion of the consumption of all major alcoholic

TABLE 10.6. Consumption of Western Products as a Proportion of Total
Consumption in Each Category, 1947–89
(in percentages)

Year	Fresh Cakes[a]	Tea[b]	Alcoholic Beverages[c]	Clothing (outerwear)[d]
1947	—	—	44.8	—
1948	—	—	37.7	—
1949	—	—	25.9	—
1950	—	—	17.1	—
1951	—	3.0	17.6	89.1
1952	—	2.9	17.6	89.0
1953	—	3.3	20.7	88.6
1954	—	4.7	19.2	89.0
1955	—	3.3	19.7	87.4
1956	—	3.8	24.1	85.6
1957	—	4.3	26.0	84.3
1958	23.6	5.6	30.7	80.3
1959	27.6	5.7	33.1	80.5
1960	31.2	6.2	35.9	79.6
1961	34.8	6.1	43.2	76.9
1962	37.0	5.3	45.8	76.8
1963	39.0	5.2	46.1	75.0
1964	41.3	6.1	49.4	76.1
1965	43.4	6.7	50.1	74.8
1966	46.4	7.8	48.8	73.4
1967	46.8	7.8	51.9	73.8
1968	47.4	7.9	51.4	72.6
1969	48.2	8.6	55.0	72.9
1970	49.0	8.2	56.5	72.4
1971	48.9	8.2	57.8	72.6
1972	50.0	7.5	61.1	75.1
1973	51.7	7.6	63.0	75.0
1974	49.8	8.0	62.1	76.9
1975	51.5	7.9	63.9	78.1
1976	53.4	7.4	64.3	78.6
1977	54.6	7.3	66.1	79.0
1978	55.8	7.4	69.0	79.8
1979	56.8	7.3	70.3	80.5
1980	56.9	10.0	70.5	80.2
1981	56.4	10.1	70.5	80.6
1982	57.2	9.1	71.4	79.4
1983	56.9	10.4	72.2	82.4
1984	56.1	12.2	69.7	82.2
1985	55.1	16.3	68.0	83.1
1986	53.8	17.5	69.1	83.5

TABLE 10.6 *(continued)*

Year	Fresh Cakes[a]	Tea[b]	Alcoholic Beverages[c]	Clothing (outerwear)[d]
1987	53.0	18.0	70.6	83.0
1988	53.5	17.3	71.8	84.8
1989	53.9	17.0	73.1	84.8

SOURCES: The data for 1947–86 were taken from Management and Coordination Agency, Statistics Bureau, *Comprehensive Time Series Report*, 101–3, 106, 638–43, 648–49. The data for 1987–89 were taken from Management and Coordination Agency, *Annual Report on the Family Income and Expenditure Survey*, 1989 edition, 284, 287–91, 302–3.

The figures for 1947–62 refer to all households living in cities with populations of 50,000 or more; the figures for 1963 and later refer to all households nationwide.

[a] The figures represent expenditures on Western-style fresh cakes such as *kasutera* (sponge cakes), cakes, etc., as a percentage of total expenditures on fresh cakes, where total expenditures on fresh cakes include expenditures on both Western-style fresh cakes and Japanese-style fresh cakes such as *yōkan* (sweet bean jelly), *manjū* (bean-jam cakes), etc.

[b] The figures represent the quantity consumed of Western (black) tea as a percentage of total tea consumption, where total tea consumption includes the consumption of both Western tea and Japanese (green) tea.

[c] The figures represent the quantity consumed of the major Western alcoholic beverages (beer and whiskey) as a percentage of the total consumption of the major alcoholic beverages (*sake, shōchū*, beer, and whiskey). However, the figures for 1947–50 exclude whiskey consumption because data are not available.

[d] The figures represent expenditures on Western-style outerwear (men's suits, jackets, slacks, overcoats, raincoats, etc.; women's dresses, skirts, slacks, overcoats, raincoats, etc.; school uniforms for boys and girls; and children's and babies' clothing) as a percentage of total expenditures on outerwear, where total expenditures on outerwear include expenditures on both Western-style outerwear and Japanese-style outerwear such as men's, women's, and children's *kimono*. Western-style outerwear excludes shirts, blouses, and sweaters.

beverages was temporarily high in 1947–49, but if this period is disregarded, this portion showed a strong upward trend, increasing from 17.1 percent in 1950 to 73.1 percent in 1989 (a more than 4.3-fold increase). There was a corresponding decline in the share of the major traditional alcoholic beverages (sake and *shōchū*), and in fact, in the case of sake, there was a decline not only in the share but also in the quantity consumed: the average annual consumption per household of sake in 1989 was only 61 percent of what it was in 1974 (13,880 milliliters versus 22,843 milliliters).[25]

In the case of clothing, expenditures on Western outerwear as a proportion of total expenditures on outerwear were already high (89.1 percent) by 1951 (the first year for which data are available), and moreover, this proportion declined during the subsequent two decades, falling to 72.4 percent in 1970. However, it has been increasing anew since 1970, attaining a level of 84.8 percent in 1988–89.

Thus, the conclusion is the same as in the case of cereal consumption: the share of Western products has generally shown an upward trend but in many cases has

25. In the case of *shōchū*, there was a sharp decline in the quantity consumed between 1953 and 1972 but an equally strong resurgence between 1972 and 1985; it resumed its decline in 1986.

leveled off in recent years. Moreover, the share of traditional products was still high as recently as 1989: 59 percent in the case of cereals, 46 percent in the case of fresh cakes, 83 percent in the case of tea, 27 percent in the case of alcoholic beverages, and 15 percent in the case of clothing (outerwear). These figures show that there is considerable variation among consumption categories in the degree of Westernization but that there is no category in which traditional products have been displaced entirely.[26]

Henry Rosovsky and Kazushi Ohkawa, in a more comprehensive analysis, find that as of 1955 the consumption of indigenous commodities was still prevalent, accounting for approximately one-half of total consumption expenditures, and that in the same year approximately one-half of household assets consisted of indigenous goods. However, they find evidence of a decline over time in the importance of indigenous consumption: as of 1955 81 percent of household assets purchased prior to 1941 consisted of indigenous goods, whereas the corresponding percentages for goods purchased between 1941 and 1945 and between 1946 and 1955 were 76 and 46 percent, respectively.[27] All of these results corroborate my own findings.

As for why the consumption of indigenous commodities has declined relative to the consumption of Western commodities, Rosovsky and Ohkawa suggest that the reason lies in the fact that expenditure elasticities tend to be much higher in the case of Western commodities than in the case of indigenous commodities. In other words, Western commodities tend to be luxuries whose consumption increases more than proportionately in response to increases in income, whereas indigenous commodities tend to be necessities whose consumption increases less than proportionately or even declines in response to increases in income. Given this tendency, the budget share of Western commodities will increase and that of indigenous commodities will decline in response to increases in income.

Another possible cause of the increasing share of Western commodities is changes in the relative prices of traditional and Western commodities. Data from the Family Income and Expenditure Survey indicate that this explanation applies in the case of some commodities but not in the case of others.[28] For example, the

26. Maki, *Shōhi senkō to juyō sokutei*, 120–24, finds fairly strong evidence of a habit persistence effect, which retards the shifting of tastes from traditional products to modern products. For example, he finds that habit persistence has exerted upward pressure on the budget share of Japanese-style clothing and downward pressure on the budget share of Western-style clothing. Tuvia Blumenthal suggests that the demonstration effect was weak in the case of nondurable goods such as food but strong in the case of durable goods such as televisions, refrigerators, and washing machines; see Blumenthal, *Saving in Postwar Japan*, Harvard East Asian Monographs No. 35 (Cambridge: East Asian Research Center, Harvard University/Harvard University Press, 1970), 69–75.

27. Henry Rosovsky and Kazushi Ohkawa, "The Indigenous Components in the Modern Japanese Economy," *Economic Development and Cultural Change* 9 (Apr. 1961): 476–501.

28. All of the statements in this paragraph are based on an analysis of data on prices and on physical quantities consumed. Changes in expenditures will mirror changes in physical quantities consumed only if demand is price elastic, but this condition was apparently met in all of the cases

fact that the price of Western tea increased much more slowly than the price of Japanese tea during the 1951–87 period can help explain the Westernization of tea consumption during this period, and similarly, the fact that the price of Western-style clothing increased much more slowly than the price of Japanese-style clothing during the 1970–89 period can help explain the Westernization of clothing consumption during this period. By contrast, the fact that the price of Western cereal products increased more rapidly than that of rice during the 1960–89 period cannot explain the Westernization of cereal consumption during this period, and similarly, the fact that the relative prices of the major alcoholic beverages were roughly unchanged during the 1950–83 period cannot explain the Westernization of alcohol consumption during this period.[29]

A third possible reason for the Westernization of consumption patterns in Japan is that the tastes of Japanese consumers have changed as a result of increased exposure to foreign commodities and life-styles. Martin Bronfenbrenner and Yasukichi Yasuba feel, and I agree, that this factor was probably more important than changes in income levels or in relative prices.[30]

Thus, convergence toward Western patterns has occurred not only with respect to the level and composition of consumption but also with respect to the consumption of products of Western origin. However, the degree of convergence has been far from complete in all three respects. Moreover, the reasons for the three types of convergence are somewhat different. The convergence with respect to the level and composition of consumption reflect increases in household incomes and—to a lesser extent—changes in relative prices, while the increase in the consumption of products of Western origin reflects these same factors as well as changes in consumer tastes.

THE RISE OF A MASS-CONSUMPTION CONSCIOUSNESS

The dramatic changes in the consumption patterns of the Japanese people that I have documented were accompanied by an equally dramatic change in their consciousness—namely, the emergence of a mass-consumption consciousness or, to borrow Rokurō Hidaka's term, a *standardization of values*.[31] As Hidaka wrote in 1980,

---

considered. In the cases of rice and clothing, data on prices and quantities consumed were not available for broad commodity groups, and thus the analysis had to be done at a more disaggregated level; by contrast, in the case of fresh cakes, data on prices and quantities consumed were not available at any level of aggregation.

29. The price of whiskey increased the fastest, that of beer the slowest, and that of the traditional alcoholic beverages (sake and *shōchū*) at an intermediate rate, but the differences were relatively small.

30. Bronfenbrenner and Yasuba, "Economic Welfare," 103.

31. Rokurō Hidada, *The Price of Affluence: Dilemmas of Contemporary Japan* (Tokyo: Kōdansha International, 1984). (A Japanese-language edition was published by Iwanami Shoten in 1980 under the title *Sengo shisō o kangaeru.*)

A qualitative change in the consciousness of the Japanese is taking place at a level much more profound than philosophical and ideological debate. Most Japanese now desire to maintain and expand their present modes of life generated by high economic growth. While many contend that the Japanese value system has diversified, the range of choices affecting style of life are limited. They are limited, for instance, to the question of whether to use one's bonus for the down payment on a family car, for an overseas trip, or for savings. In the sense that there is a determination to maintain and expand existing standards of living and life styles, values have been standardized, not diversified, and these standardized values have penetrated into the depths of our consciousness.[32]

Hidaka then offers the example of a labor union's ideal for a "lifetime consumption plan" and concludes:[33] "The first impulse may be to laugh, but I find nothing funny about this labor union version of life cycle planning. It shows how deeply the desire for a comfortable life has penetrated into our psyche."[34]

As I see it, this change in consumer values functioned as both cause and effect of the dramatic changes in consumption patterns. In other words, changes in the objective behavior and subjective values of Japanese consumers were mutually reinforcing.

THE LEVEL OF SAVING

The consumption data considered thus far reveal the emergence of an unprecedented consumer society in postwar Japan (albeit one that was restrained in comparison to the United States and the other most highly developed countries), but the data on household saving are even more striking. They reveal the emergence in the mid-1950s of household saving rates whose levels are virtually without precedent in either historical or comparative contexts.

As table 10.7 shows, Japan's household saving rate was extremely volatile and not necessarily very high during the prewar period.[35] One regularity that can be discerned, however, is that it was much higher during wartime. For example, it was 11 percent in 1906, just after the Russo-Japanese War of 1904–5, ranged from 5 to 19 percent during World War I and the two years following, and

32. Hidaka, *Price of Affluence*, 70.

33. Ibid., 70–71; quoted in Kelly's essay in this volume.

34. Hidaka, *Price of Affluence*, 71. Hidaka regards the emergence of this new consciousness as one manifestation of the shift from "sacrifice of the self in service to the state" or "we will do without until we win" to "indulgence of the self, neglect of the public" and of the emergence of the age of "economism."

35. I focus throughout on the household saving rate. Similar patterns can be observed in broader saving rate concepts such as the private and national saving rates, but there are some differences. For example, national saving was not as high as household or private saving during World War II because of heavy government borrowing (dissaving), and the private and national saving rates peaked in 1970, several years earlier than the household saving rate. See Charles Yuji Horioka, "The Determinants of Japan's Saving Rate: The Impact of the Age Structure of the Population and Other Factors," *Economic Studies Quarterly* 42 (September 1991): 237–53.

increased from 6–11 percent in 1934 to an incredible 44 percent in 1944 as Japan's involvement in the Pacific War deepened.

The reasons for the higher household saving rates during wartime periods differ from case to case. During the Russo-Japanese and Pacific wars, resources were diverted from consumer goods production to military-related production, which in turn led to reduced consumption and increased saving. During the Russo-Japanese War this diversion was accomplished through consumption-restricting increases in rural and urban land taxes and the sale of war bonds to households,[36] whereas during the Pacific War it was accomplished through rationing, other direct controls,[37] and saving promotion measures. With respect to the latter, a national savings movement was launched by cabinet decision in 1938 and energetically promoted by the government.

> The competent ministry was the Ministry of Finance where the National Savings Promotion Bureau (the vice minister assumed the director-generalship) was set up, and officials solely in charge of savings promotion were stationed in local governments and in relevant Japanese Government offices overseas. In addition, the National Savings Promotion Committee with its members comprising competent figures in all sectors was formed to give necessary advice to the Minister of Finance for deciding on a savings promotion policy and a target for the increase in savings. [The formation of savings associations, covering various districts, professions and all lines of business was accelerated,] and the government, under the National Savings Association Law, gave preferential treatment to savings handled by the associations. With this movement acting as a springboard, and by mobilizing people's organizations such as women's societies, youth associations, and religious groups, the government prepared a system to encourage savings in every possible manner.[38]

In the case of World War I, in which Japan participated only peripherally, the mechanism was completely different. Japanese exports expanded rapidly during the war years partly because Japan became a major supplier of munitions and shipping services to the Allies and partly because she took over Asian export markets that were cut off from Europe,[39] and because exports expanded so rapidly, internal demand, especially consumption, had to be sacrificed. Moreover, wealth disparities widened during the war years because high corporate profit rates increased the real incomes of merchants and industrialists,[40] and because the wealthy tend to save a higher proportion of their income, the widening of wealth disparities may also have contributed to the higher household saving rates.

Thus, the high household saving rates during these periods were to a large

36. Gleason, "Level of Living," 269.

37. See, for example, Takafusa Nakamura, *Economic Growth in Prewar Japan,* trans. Robert A. Feldman (New Haven: Yale University Press, 1983), chap. 10.

38. Central Council for Savings Promotion, *Savings and Savings Promotion Movement in Japan* (Tokyo: Central Council for Savings Promotion, 1981), 27.

39. Gleason, "Level of Living," 269.

40. Nakamura, *Economic Growth in Prewar Japan,* 145–47.

TABLE 10.7. Household Saving Rate, 1906–88

Year	Long-term Economic Statistics	Old System of National Accounts[a]	New System of National Accounts
1906	11.0		
1907	4.0		
1908	− 0.2		
1909	0.7		
1910	0.3		
1911	3.3		
1912	− 1.1		
1913	− 2.5		
1914	− 0.4		
1915	4.8		
1916	11.0		
1917	15.9		
1918	18.7		
1919	11.1		
1920	9.2		
1921	2.2		
1922	0.8		
1923	− 4.9		
1924	− 4.6		
1925	− 3.0		
1926	− 1.4		
1927	2.4		
1928	1.7		
1929	3.5		
1930	4.8	6.1	
1931	6.3	10.0	
1932	7.0	11.7	
1933	7.4	12.1	
1934	6.3	11.2	
1935	9.1	17.5	
1936	8.4	18.7	
1937	6.2	18.8	
1938	17.5	21.4	
1939	23.5	26.7	
1940	23.0	28.2	
1941		32.9	
1942		32.5	

TABLE 10.7 (*continued*)

Year	Long-term Economic Statistics	Old System of National Accounts[a]	New System of National Accounts
1943		35.5	
1944		43.8	
1945		—	
1946		2.3	
1947		− 4.6	
1948		− 0.5	
1949		− 1.9	
1950		14.7	
1951		12.8	
1952		10.3	
1953		7.8	
1954		9.6	
1955		13.4	12.2
1956		13.7	13.1
1957		15.6	12.7
1958		15.0	12.7
1959		16.7	14.0
1960		17.4	14.6
1961		19.2	15.9
1962		18.6	15.5
1963		18.0	14.8
1964		16.4	15.3
1965		17.7	15.6
1966		17.4	14.8
1967		19.0	13.9
1968		19.7	16.6
1969		19.2	16.8
1970		20.4	17.6
1971		20.7	17.8
1972		21.7	18.2
1973		25.1	20.5
1974		25.7	23.2
1975		25.1	22.9
1976		24.3	23.2
1977			21.8
1978			21.0
1979			18.3
1980			18.0
1981			18.4
1982			16.6

TABLE 10.7 *(continued)*

Year	Long-term Economic Statistics	Old System of National Accounts[a]	New System of National Accounts
1983			16.3
1984			16.0
1985			15.9
1986			16.3
1987			15.0
1988			14.7

SOURCES: The figures in columns 1 (all years) and 2 (1930–50) are based on Ohkawa and Shinohara, *Patterns of Japanese Economic Development*, 261–70. Household saving was calculated as private saving minus corporate saving. The 1951–76 figures in column 2 are based on Economic Planning Agency, ed., *Yearbook of National Income Statistics* (Tokyo: Ministry of Finance Printing Bureau, 1978), 76–79. The figures in column 3 are based on data taken from Economic Planning Agency, ed., *Report on National Accounts from 1955 to 1969* (Tokyo: Ministry of Finance Printing Bureau, 1988), 88–91; Economic Planning Agency, *Report on Revised National Accounts on the Basis of 1980*, 108–10; and Economic Planning Agency, *Annual Report on National Accounts*, 1990 edition, 88–91.

NOTE: The household (personal) saving rate is defined as household saving as a percentage of household disposable income, where the household sector is defined to include households, private unincorporated nonfinancial enterprises, and private nonprofit institutions serving households. All figures are on a calendar year basis except for the 1946–50 figures in column 2, which are on a fiscal year (April 1–March 31) basis. Data for 1945 are not available.

[a]The 1930–50 figures are not consistent with the 1951–76 figures.

extent the result of forced or compulsory saving under extraordinary circumstances and thus do not support the view that the Japanese have always been thrifty and that their high propensity to save has its origins in the prewar period.[41] If wartime periods are excluded, Japan's household saving rate was not unusually high during the prewar years. In fact, it was very low and often negative. The range of variation during the 1906–44 period was from − 5 to 12 percent, and the maximum value prior to 1930 was only 4 percent if the years 1906, 1915–20, and 1935–44 are excluded.

Moreover, Japan's household saving rate was not unusually high during the early postwar years either. It ranged from − 5 to 2 percent during the 1946–49 period and was high (10–15 percent) during the 1950–52 period only because of the Korean War.

The impact of the Korean War was similar to that of World War I. Although Japan was not directly involved in the war, the Special Procurements (*tokuju*) of the

41. It is possible that Japanese households became accustomed to saving a high proportion of their incomes as a result of being forced to do so for extended periods of time, and in that sense the high household saving rates during certain periods of the prewar and war years may have laid the foundation for the high household saving rates observed during the postwar period. However, high saving rates during wartime periods have not led to increased saving rates in later years in other countries. For example, the U.S. saving rate has been low during the postwar period despite the high saving rates (19–25 percent) recorded during the war years (1942–45). Thus, proponents of this view need to explain why it applies in the case of Japan but not in the case of the United States and other countries.

UN forces in Korea and the UN troops, primarily American, stationed in Japan yielded an unexpected bonanza to the Japanese economy. They were, however, a mixed blessing because they caused a revival of inflation, a diversion of resources away from consumer goods production, and a widening of income disparities,[42] which in turn caused consumption to stagnate and household saving rates to increase.

If the period of the Korean War is excluded, Japan's household saving rate did not make it into the double digits until 1955, a full ten years into the postwar period. After 1955, however, Japan's household saving rate not only remained in the double digits but also showed a long-term upward trend (except during the early 1960s), peaking in 1974–76 at a level of 23–26 percent. Since then it has shown a moderate decline, falling to less than 15 percent by 1988, but it has remained high by international standards. Thus, as in the case of the level and composition of consumption, the household saving rate showed trend discontinuity around the time of the first oil crisis.

By comparison, the personal saving rate of the United States (the equivalent of Japan's household saving rate) has fluctuated between 3 and 9 percent during the postwar period. It was thus only one-half to one-third of the Japanese rate, sometimes even less. The household saving rates of most of the other developed countries have been higher than that of the United States but lower than that of Japan.[43] In other words, Japan and the United States have been at opposite extremes in terms of the level of their household saving rates.[44] Italy, Singapore, and Taiwan are among the few countries showing higher household saving rates than Japan.

Thus, Japan's household saving rate is one of the highest in the world, but high household saving rates are primarily a postwar phenomenon—in fact a post-1955

42. Yutaka Kōsai, *The Era of High-Speed Growth: Notes on the Postwar Japanese Economy*, trans. Jacqueline Kaminski (Tokyo: University of Tokyo Press, 1986), 70–76.

43. Horioka, "Shōhi/chochiku," 52–55, and Charles Yuji Horioka, "Future Trends in Japan's Saving Rate and the Implications Thereof for Japan's External Imbalance," *Japan and the World Economy* 3 (1992): 307–30.

44. Hayashi has pointed out that there are a number of conceptual differences between the official saving figures for Japan and the United States and that adjusting for these differences causes the U.S.-Japan gap to narrow considerably; see Fumio Hayashi, "Why Is Japan's Saving Rate So Apparently High?" in *NBER Macroeconomics Annual 1986*, ed. Stanley Fischer (Cambridge: MIT Press, 1986), 1:147–210. Similarly, Derek Blades and Peter H. Sturm have found that making a number of conceptual improvements in the data causes the differences between the saving rates for Japan and the other member countries of the Organisation for Economic Cooperation and Development (OECD) to narrow as well; see Derek Blades, "Alternative Measures of Saving," *OECD Economic Outlook Occasional Studies*, June 1983, 66–84; Derek Blades, "Household Saving Ratios for Japan and Other OECD Countries" (mimeograph, OECD, 1988); and Derek W. Blades and Peter H. Sturm, "The Concept and Measurement of Saving: The United States and Other Industrialized Countries," in *Saving and Government Policy*, ed. Federal Reserve Bank of Boston (Boston: Federal Reserve Bank of Boston, 1982), 1–30. However, in both cases a substantial difference remains even after all adjustments have been made. Thus, conceptual differences and deficiencies are not the entire explanation for saving rate differences.

phenomenon. We can reject the view that Japan's high saving rate is the result
of cultural factors such as national character or Confucian and Buddhist teachings
because Japan's saving rate should have always been high and should have shown
a downward trend rather than an upward trend if this view were correct (the latter
because cultural influences presumably weaken over time in response to increased
exposure to foreign influences).[45]

What, then, are the factors responsible for Japan's high household saving
rate?[46] Since Japan's high household saving rate is primarily a postwar phenomenon, we should rely on factors unique to the postwar period to explain it. Two
that come to mind are (1) the rapid growth rate of income and (2) the low level
of household assets resulting partly from the wartime destruction of housing and
other physical capital and partly from the decline in the real value of financial
assets caused by the postwar hyperinflation.

With respect to (1), rapid income growth will lead to a higher household saving
rate if, for example, (a) households believe that the increase in income is temporary and therefore save most of the increase (the permanent income hypothesis)
or (b) households are not able to adjust their consumption patterns in pace with
increases in income (the consumption lag or habit persistence hypothesis).[47]

With respect to (2), the argument is that Japanese households saved in an attempt
to restore their asset holdings to desired levels. This hypothesis is discussed by
Lawrence Christiano and Fumio Hayashi, who refer to it as the "reconstruction
hypothesis," as well as by Ryūtarō Komiya and Miyohei Shinohara.[48]

In my opinion, these two factors were primarily responsible for the high
household saving rate during the high-growth period. Note, moreover, that since
both factors became inapplicable after the first oil crisis (income growth slowed
dramatically and household asset holdings had attained a high level by then) they

45. Kanamori Hisao and Miyohei Shinohara are two eminent economists who espouse the view
that culture is an important influence on saving behavior; see Kanamori, "Nihon no chochiku-ritsu
wa naze takai ka," *Keizai geppō*, 30 Oct. 1961, 89–96; and Shinohara, *Industrial Growth, Trade, and
Dynamic Patterns in the Japanese Economy* (Tokyo: University of Tokyo Press, 1982), 160. By contrast,
Ryūtarō Komiya, an equally eminent economist, strongly criticizes this view; see Komiya, "The
Supply of Personal Savings," in *Postwar Economic Growth in Japan*, ed. Ryūtarō Komiya, trans. Robert
S. Ozaki (Berkeley and Los Angeles: University of California Press, 1966), 157–86. See Charles Yuji
Horioka, "Why Is Japan's Household Saving Rate So High? A Literature Survey," *Journal of the
Japanese and International Economies* 4 (Mar. 1990): 54–56, for a detailed discussion of the impact of
culture on saving behavior.

46. The causes of Japan's high household saving rate are discussed in detail in Hayashi, "Why Is
Japan's Saving Rate So Apparently High?"; Horioka, "Japan's Household Saving Rate"; Komiya,
"Supply of Personal Savings"; Kazuo Satō, "Saving and Investment," in Yamamura and Yasuba,
Political Economy of Japan 1:137–85; Shinohara, *Industrial Growth*; and elsewhere. Hence these causes will
be discussed only briefly here.

47. See Horioka, "Japan's Household Saving Rate," and Satō, "Saving and Investment," for a
number of alternative explanations.

48. See Lawrence J. Christiano, "Understanding Japan's Saving Rate: The Reconstruction Hy-
pothesis," *Quarterly Review* (Federal Reserve Bank of Minneapolis) 13 (Spring 1989): 10–25; Fumio
Hayashi, "Is Japan's Saving Rate High?" *Quarterly Review* (Federal Reserve Bank of Minneapolis) 13
(Spring 1989): 3–9; Komiya, "Supply of Personal Savings," 177; and Shinohara, *Industrial Growth*, 158.

can also explain the decline in the household saving rate since the first oil crisis.

Moreover, a number of secondary factors—such as the low level of social security benefits, the relative unavailability of consumer credit, and the low proportion of the aged in the total population—can also help to explain the high level of Japan's household saving rate during the high-growth period, and they can also help to explain the post-oil-crisis decline inasmuch as they have become increasingly inapplicable during this period.[49]

Finally, a number of factors—such as the bonus system and the various tax breaks for saving—were applicable throughout most of the postwar period and can therefore help explain not only why the household saving rate was high during the high-growth period but also why it maintained a relatively high level even after the first oil crisis despite showing a moderate downward trend.

Thus, the high level of Japan's household saving rate during the postwar period is the result not of cultural factors but of economic, institutional, and demographic factors, many of which are only temporary.[50] In fact, the household saving rate has already begun to decline, presumably as a result of the slowdown in economic growth, the increase in household asset holdings, improvements in social security benefits, and the increasing availability of consumer credit. Moreover, the rapid aging of the population and possibly also the abolition of most tax breaks for saving on 1 April 1988 can be expected to cause the decline in the household saving rate to accelerate in future years.[51] Thus, Japan's high household saving rate is not only a relatively recent phenomenon but also one that will probably not continue indefinitely into the future.

GENDER DIFFERENCES

There is unfortunately little information available on male-female differences in consumption and saving patterns, but the little information that is available

49. The unavailability of consumer credit was in large part the result of government policies designed to channel virtually all available funds to the business sector for the purpose of financing investment in plant and equipment, and these policies in turn reflected the government's bias toward production, investment, saving, and growth at the expense of consumption. The fact that consumers turned to *sarakin* (loan sharks) charging exorbitant interest rates when they could not obtain loans from banks and other conventional financial institutions shows how strong their desire to consume was and supports my argument that the high household saving rates were the result of structural rather than cultural factors. See Horioka, "Japan's Household Saving Rate," 68–69, for a discussion of the impact of the availability of consumer credit on saving and Hiroshi Iwadare, "Sarakin," in *Kōdansha Encyclopedia of Japan: Supplement* (Tokyo: Kōdansha, 1986), 46–47, for a discussion of *sarakin* and the *sarakin* crisis of the late 1970s and early 1980s.

50. It is, however, possible that culture has an indirect effect on the level of the saving rate by influencing institutions and policies that affect saving behavior. I am indebted to Tuvia Blumenthal for this point.

51. See Charles Yuji Horioka, "Why Is Japan's Private Saving Rate So High?" in *Developments in Japanese Economics*, ed. Ryūzō Satō and Takashi Negishi (Tokyo: Academic Press/Harcourt Brace Jovanovich Japan, 1989), 145–78; Horioka, "Determinants of Japan's Saving Rate"; and Horioka, "Future Trends."

suggests some interesting differences. In the case of young single persons, women seem to be, if anything, *more* consumption-oriented than men are. For example, single working women in their early twenties are more than twice as likely to travel abroad for pleasure than are single working men in the same age group, and young women (those in high school or college and those in their early twenties who are single and working) have fewer qualms about spending time and money on recreation than do young men in the same categories.[52] Young women also spend large amounts on clothing and accessories, especially brand-name goods; in fact, a public opinion survey found that young women have a strong preference for luxury (high-class) goods and services, whereas older people regard such items as being unaffordable and as having a negative image.[53]

Moreover, these gender differences are becoming increasingly pronounced over time: between 1984 and 1989 the consumption expenditures of single women of all ages increased 13.0 percent in real terms and those of single women under the age of 30 increased 15.8 percent, whereas the corresponding figures for single males were 1.2 percent and 2.0 percent, respectively. The rate of increase in spending by category also varied considerably by sex, with sports, hobbies, and lessons (cooking, English conversation, etc.) showing the biggest increases in the case of single women and accessories such as watches and handbags and nonalcoholic beverages showing the biggest increases in the case of single men.[54] Thus, the tendency to spend more, especially on leisure and recreation, is far more pronounced in the case of single women than in the case of single men.

At the same time, however, young working women ("office ladies") manage to save a considerable proportion of their income (31.0 percent in the case of those living in Osaka and 21.4 percent in the case of those living in Tokyo),[55] with the most common motives for saving being marriage and travel.[56] As a result, single women have 1.9 times as much savings as single men have (7,520,000 yen versus 3,920,000 yen) and far less debt (440,000 yen versus 770,000 yen).[57] The apparent contradiction can be explained by the fact that in Japan young unmarried women (as well as men) typically live with their parents and contribute only a nominal amount toward food expenses.[58] Thus, they are able to spend considerable amounts on overseas travel, recreation, brand-name clothing and accessories, and so on, and still have enough left over to save 20 to 30 percent of their income.

52. *Nihon keizai shinbun*, 11 Sept. 1989, 53, and 11 Sept. 1990, 34. One reason for this difference may be that working hours are shorter for women as a result of the types of jobs to which they are relegated.

53. *Nihon keizai shinbun*, 12 Oct. 1988, 11.

54. *Nihon keizai shinbun*, 5 Sept. 1990, 34; *Mainichi Daily News*, 5 Sept. 1990, 1.

55. *Nihon keizai shinbun*, 2 Feb. 1990, evening ed., 13.

56. *Nihon keizai shinbun*, 29 Jan. 1990, 53.

57. *Nihon keizai shinbun*, 5 Sept. 1990, 34; *Mainichi Daily News*, 5 Sept. 1990, 1. The data pertain to 1989.

58. *Nihon keizai shinbun*, 12 Oct. 1988, 11; *Mainichi Daily News*, 27 Sept. 1990, 1.

After marriage, however, the behavior of Japanese women changes abruptly. They usually control the family budget but do so with an iron hand, economizing wherever possible and sacrificing their own needs and desires for those of their husbands and children. For example, husbands receive generous allowances (an average of 45,900 yen per month in 1989 and 47,500 yen per month in 1990),[59] and children also receive allowances, but wives themselves have little discretionary income of their own. Only 35.1 percent of wives had their own allowances in 1990, and moreover, the average amount was only 27,700 yen per month, or 58.3 percent of the average amount received by husbands.[60] It is thus not surprising that, whereas men find that life becomes easier after marriage, women find that it becomes harder.[61] In fact, perhaps it is precisely because Japanese women know how hard their lives will become after marriage that they allow themselves a few excesses during their single years.

In any case, about the only similarity between the behavior of single women and married women is their high saving rate. The reasons for the high saving rates of the two groups are quite different, as discussed above, but it is true nonetheless that both groups contribute toward Japan's high household saving rate. In fact, it has been suggested (but not verified empirically) that Japan's household saving rate is so high partly because women hold the purse strings.

CONCLUSION

In this essay I have shown how dramatically consumption and saving patterns changed during the postwar period, especially during the high-growth period, and how these changes enabled Japan to become a mass-consumption *and* "mass saving" society within a few short decades.

If we look at Japan's postwar experience in historical perspective, the *direction of change* of both the level and composition of consumption was the same during the prewar and postwar periods: the level of real per capita consumption increased, and the composition of consumption shifted from food and other necessities to luxuries and from traditional products to Western products. Thus, if the temporary setback at the time of the Pacific War is disregarded, there has been a basic continuity in consumption trends during the past century.

However, trends in the *rate of change* of the level and composition of consumption exhibited trend discontinuity at the time of the Pacific War and also at the time of the first oil crisis of 1973–74: both the level and composition of consumption changed the most rapidly during the early postwar period, less rapidly during the post-oil-crisis period, and least rapidly during the prewar period. Moreover, the ratio of real per capita consumption in Japan to that in the United States and

59. *Nihon keizai shinbun*, 29 Aug. 1989, 34, and 11 Apr. 1990, 7.
60. *Nihon keizai shinbun*, 11 Apr. 1990, 7.
61. *Nihon keizai shinbun*, 16 Sept. 1989, 34.

Japan's household saving rate showed the same discontinuities: the former showed little improvement during the prewar period, increased rapidly during the early postwar period, and has continued to increase but at a slower rate during the post-oil-crisis period, while the latter remained at a low level during the prewar years (except during wartime periods), increased to double-digit levels during the early postwar period, and has shown a downward trend (but has remained relatively high) during the post-oil-crisis period.[62] Thus, we must not deny the basic continuity of trends during the past century, but neither must we exaggerate them.

An international comparison showed that both the level and composition of consumption have improved more rapidly in Japan than in the United States and the other developed countries but that despite the rapid improvement Japan still lags considerably behind the most highly developed countries in both respects. Similarly, Japanese consumption patterns have become increasingly Westernized over time, but they still show a substantial traditional component, and moreover, the trend toward Westernization has slowed in recent years. Thus, we must not belittle the speed and magnitude of change in Japan during the past century, especially during the high-growth period, but neither must we exaggerate them. The convergence toward the other developed countries is far from complete.

One reason why Japan's consumption levels have not yet caught up with those of the most highly developed countries is her high and rising levels of household and corporate saving. As noted earlier, however, high saving rates will not necessarily have an adverse impact on consumer welfare because saving also confers utility on consumers. Moreover, Japan's saving rate can be expected to fall sharply in future years as the population ages and as other temporary factors that have increased Japan's saving rate in the past become less applicable. Thus, per capita consumption can be expected to attain a level more commensurate with income levels.

However, this factor alone will not be enough to eliminate the gap between consumption levels in Japan and the other developed countries. For example, Gleason calculates that lowering Japan's household saving rate to U.S. levels

---

62. An analysis of the causes of the discontinuities in consumption and saving trends is beyond the scope of this essay, but they are presumably caused in large part by discontinuities in the rate of economic growth. With respect to the acceleration of economic growth after World War II, Kazushi Ohkawa and Henry Rosovsky characterize it as "trend acceleration" rather than trend discontinuity and attribute it to Japan's rising social capability to import technological progress, which they in turn attribute to a growing capital formation proportion, rising income, learning by doing, and institutional innovation; see Ohkawa and Rosovsky, *Japanese Economic Growth: Trend Acceleration in the Twentieth Century* (Stanford: Stanford University Press, 1973). By contrast, Minami criticizes the Ohkawa-Rosovsky thesis, arguing that "much of the post-war growth rate cannot be explained simply as a continuation of the pre-war trend" and that "it was the result of factors peculiar to the post-war period"; Minami, *Economic Development of Japan,* 52.

would have reduced the gap between real per capita consumption levels in the two countries in 1985 by only about 20 percent.[63]

A far more important reason for the gap in consumption levels is that income levels in Japan still lag considerably behind those of the other developed countries if the conversion to a common currency is done using purchasing power parities (even though income levels are roughly comparable if the conversion is done using market exchange rates). This discrepancy suggests that a major cause of the gap in consumption levels is the high level of consumer prices in Japan. High consumer prices are, in turn, due largely to import restrictions on food and other consumer products,[64] and in my opinion, removing such restrictions would be the most effective way to improve consumer welfare in Japan. Moreover, such a policy would also appease Japan's trading partners and thus would kill two birds with one stone.

A secondary cause of the high level of consumer prices in Japan is the inefficient distribution system, which in turn is due in large part to government restrictions on large-scale retail establishments. Removing such restrictions would be another way of enhancing consumer welfare and, at the same time, appeasing Japan's trading partners, who believe that Japan's inefficient distribution system is one factor making it difficult for imports to penetrate the Japanese market.

Finally, government regulation of the prices of many products (such as certain food products, gas, and electricity) and the high price of land, which in turn is due in large part government restrictions on land use and land tax policies, are also said to have contributed to the high level of consumer prices in Japan. Thus, price deregulation and policies to encourage more efficient land use would also help to lower consumer prices. What is needed, in short, is the abolition of all government policies and regulations that impede the unfettered operation of the market mechanism and artificially elevate prices.

Finally, additional ways of enhancing the welfare of Japanese consumers become apparent if we define consumer welfare broadly to include pollution, social infrastructure, and leisure time: stricter pollution standards, increased investment in social infrastructure such as parks, roads, and sewers, and shorter working hours.

In my opinion, these policies would, if implemented, lead to substantial improvements in the welfare of Japanese consumers even without further increases in income levels, and moreover, many of them would simultaneously ease frictions between Japan and her trading partners, as noted earlier. The Japanese govern-

---

63. Gleason, "Level of Living," 276.

64. As a result of such restrictions, the cost of living in Japan is 1.5 times higher than the U.S. level and 1.2 times higher than the West German level. The gap is attributable primarily to the high cost of food, which, as we saw earlier, accounts for about one-fifth of the household budget. Food prices in Japan are on average 2.5 times higher than U.S. levels and 1.3 times higher than West German levels; see Heizō Takenaka, "We *Want* to Pay More," *Look Japan* 34 (July 1988): 18.

ment was unable to implement these policies in the past because farmers, small shopkeepers, and other groups that would be adversely affected by them were the very groups with the most political power, but the government has finally begun to overcome their opposition, in large part because of escalating pressure from abroad.[65] It is indeed fortunate that policies that ease frictions with other countries will at the same time enable Japanese consumers to enjoy a standard of living commensurate with Japan's economic strength.

65. The best example of this is the U.S.-Japan Structural Impediments Initiative (SII) of 1989–90, as part of which Japan agreed, among other things, (1) to ease restrictions on large-scale retail establishments, (2) to deregulate prices and adopt steps to reduce price differentials relative to other countries, (3) to reform land tax policies and adopt other measures to ensure more efficient land use, and (4) to boost investments in social infrastructure.

CHAPTER ELEVEN

The Death of "Good Wife, Wise Mother"?

Kathleen S. Uno

A definition of Japanese woman as "good wife, wise mother" (*ryōsai kenbo*) emerged in Japan at the end of the nineteenth century.[1] In the aftermath of the Sino-

Unlike the other essays in this volume, this one evolved not from the two conferences described in the Preface but from a paper of the same title that I presented at the Association for Asian Studies annual meeting on 8 April 1990. I had planned for the paper to be the germ of a book that I would write over a decade; instead, I produced an essay for publication within ten weeks of its initial presentation. Consequently, I regret that time and space limitations prevented more thorough research and treatment of some organizations and aspects of postwar women's movements. I dedicate this essay to sisters whom I met at the Shinjuku Ribu Sentā during my first visit to Japan nearly twenty years ago — especially Tanaka Mitsu, Wakabayashi Taeko, Ishikawa Michiko, "Ōyama," and "Nakyama" — in the spirit of a common cause, though they may disagree with my analysis. And I would like to express my appreciation to Christine Gailey, Andrew Gordon, Peter Gran, Laura Hein, Dorinne Kondo, Bob Moeller, Barbara Molony, Tanaka Kazuko, and Stephen Vlastos for their encouragement and perceptive comments on earlier versions of this chapter.

1. The germinal work in Japanese on *ryōsai kenbo* is Fukaya Masashi, *Ryōsai kenboshugi no kyōiku*, 2d ed. (Nagoya: Reimei Shobo, 1977). Among many other works on prewar *ryōsai kenbo*, see Komano Yōko, "Ryōsai kenboshugi no seiritsu to sono naiyō," in Tanaka Sumiko, ed., *Josei kaihō no shisō to kōdō, senzen hen* (Tokyo: Jiji Tsūshinsha, 1975) 1:142–43; Katano Misako, "Ryōsai kenboshugi no genryū," in Kindai Joseishi Kenkyūkai, ed., *Onnatachi no kindai* (Tokyo: Aki Shobō, 1978), 32–57; Nakajima Kuni, "Boseiron no keifu," *Rekishi kōron*, no. 49 (Dec. 1979): 61–68; Nakajima Kuni, "Ryōsai kenbo kyōiku no seiritsu," *Joshi kyōiku mondai*, no. 2 (Winter 1980): 140–52; Koyama Shizuko, "Kindaiteki joseikan toshite no ryōsai kenbo shisō: Shimoda Jirō no joshi kyōiku shisō ni miru tenkei," *Joseigaku nenpō*, no. 3 (Nov. 1982): 1–8; Nagahara Kazuko, "Ryōsai kenboshugi kyōiku ni okeru 'ie' to shokugyō," in Joseishi Sōgō Kenkyūkai, ed., *Nihon joseishi* (Tokyo: Tōkyō Daigaku Shuppankai, 1982), 149–84; Tachi Kaoru, "Ryōsai kenbo," in Joseigaku Kenkyūkai, ed., *Onna no imēji, Kōza joseigaku 1* (Tokyo: Keisō Shobō, 1984), 184–209; Mitsuda Kyōko, "Kindaiteki boseikan no juyō to tenkei," in Wakita Haruko, ed., *Bosei o tou* (Kyoto: Jinbun Shoin, 1985) 2:121–29. In English, see Sharon Sievers, *Flowers in Salt: The Beginnings of Feminist Consciousness in Meiji Japan* (Stanford: Stanford University Press, 1983), esp. 22–24; Kathleen S. Uno, "Good Wives and Wise Mothers in Early Twentieth-Century Japan" (paper presented at a joint meeting of the Pacific Coast Branch of the American Historical Association and the Western Conference of Women Historians, 21 Aug. 1988); Martha Tocco, "Before Ryōsai Kenbo: Women's Educational Traditions in the Early Meiji Period" (paper presented

Japanese War of 1894–95, prominent men, especially officials in the Ministry of Education (Monbushō), began to champion "good wife, wise mother" as woman's[2] proper role in imperial Japan. As the term suggests, *ryōsai kenbo* defined women as managers of domestic affairs in households and nurturers of children. From the late 1890s until the end of World War II, "good wife, wise mother" increasingly pervaded the mass media and the higher levels of public and private girls' higher schools, institutions that influenced the upper ranks of society, and came to constitute the official discourse on women in Japan. Although it was a clearly articulated part of state ideology, *ryōsai kenbo* failed to become a hegemonic ideology, partly because it did not match the life experiences of many women and partly because despite government repression, the critical voices of educators, leftists, and feminists spread dissonant visions of womanhood through their writings, protests, and alternative institutions. After 1945 association with the discredited ideology of the prewar imperial state tarnished "good wife, wise mother" as a shining ideal of Japanese womanhood.

Yet following a half-century of official promulgation, the influence of *ryōsai kenbo* did not immediately evaporate in the postwar era. Thus, one may ask, to what extent did "good wife, wise mother," the official prewar ideal of womanhood, continue to influence discussions of femininity in post–World War II Japan? Exploring answers to this question sheds light on changes in Japanese conceptions of womanhood over time, which in turn illuminates Japanese ideas of gender. Such investigations also contribute to the new efforts by historians to explore continuities and discontinuities between prewar and postwar Japan and the character of Japanese society and state since 1945.

In this essay I trace the influence of *ryōsai kenbo* in postwar state policies and society, locating post-1945 trends in a context of ideological and social changes taking place since the late nineteenth century.[3] I argue that although overt attempts by the state to dictate womanhood have decreased in intensity since

---

at the Eighth Berkshire Conference of Women Historians, 8 June 1990); Tocco, "An Ever-Widening Gyre: Women's Higher Education in Japan, 1850–1912" (Ph.D. diss., Stanford University, in progress).

2. For a discussion of the term *woman*, see works such as Joan Scott, *Gender and the Politics of History* (New York: Columbia University Press, 1988); Linda Alcoff, "Cultural Feminism Versus Poststructuralism: The Identity Crisis in Feminist Theory," *Signs: Journal of Women in Culture and Society* 13, no. 3 (Spring 1988): 407–35; Mary Poovey, "Feminism and Deconstruction," *Feminist Studies* 14, no. 1 (Spring 1988): 51–65. Although I have not abandoned this term in my analysis, I find their questioning of the unity of "women" and "womanhood" compelling. For this reason I refer to "women's movements" rather than "the women's movement" and try to avoid monolithic references to "the Japanese woman" and "Japanese women" in this chapter.

3. It is difficult to speak of civil society in prewar Japan, as universal suffrage was not in effect until 1928, and even after that, repressive laws regarding freedom of speech, press, and assembly greatly limited the possibilities for political opposition and social criticism.

Other studies of postwar transformations of concepts and social patterns include the essays in this volume by Dower, Hein, Kelly, and Gordon.

1945, a transmuted vision of women that often emphasized their difference from men as homebound wives and mothers continued to influence state policies toward welfare, education, employment, sexuality, and reproduction at least until the late 1980s. Beyond the state, transmuted forms of *ryōsai kenbo* shaped the employment policies of corporations and stimulated women themselves to participate in consumer, day-care, anti-military-base, antinuclear, environmental, and other social movements in order to protect children and family life in the early (1945–60) and high (1960–75) postwar periods.[4] But by the 1970s a second wave of female activists rejected earlier transformations of *ryōsai kenbo*. At first they demanded greater autonomy from male control in domestic and public life, and later they requested greater male participation in home life.

In examining the historical trajectories of wifehood and motherhood over nearly a century, I seek to contribute to the growing literature exploring gender issues in modern and postwar Japan, for in 1991 Western historians had not yet written works discussing the postwar period.[5] Here, because of space limitations, I treat *ryōsai kenbo* and its components, wifehood and motherhood, as ideas validating social policies and action rather than as day-to-day activities in households.[6] I argue that motherhood eclipsed wifehood as the more important compo-

4. Two works that explore culture as resistance are Ann Walthall, "Peripheries," *Monumenta Nipponica* 39, no. 4 (Winter 1984): 371–92, and Christine Gailey, "Culture Wars: Resistance to State Formation," in Christine Gailey and Thomas Patterson, eds., *Power Relations and State Formation* (Washington, D.C.: American Anthropological Association, 1987), 35–56.

5. The early modern (or Tokugawa era) lasted from 1600 to 1867; the modern (or prewar) era is usually defined as the years between 1868 and 1937. Full-length works by Western historians treating pre–World War II womanhood include Sievers, *Flowers in Salt;* Dorothy Robins-Mowry, *The Hidden Sun: Women in Modern Japan* (Boulder: Westview Press, 1983); Mikiso Hane, *Reflections on the Way to the Gallows* (Berkeley and Los Angeles: University of California Press, 1988; New York: Pantheon, 1990); E. Patricia Tsurumi, *Factory Girls: Women in the Thread Mills of Meiji Japan* (Princeton: Princeton University Press, 1990); Gail Lee Bernstein, ed., *Recreating Japanese Women, 1600–1945* (Berkeley and Los Angeles: University of California Press, 1991). Similar works on postwar womanhood include Joy Paulson and Elizabeth Powers, eds., *Women in Changing Japan* (Stanford: Stanford University Press, 1976), and Gail Lee Bernstein, *Haruko's World* (Stanford: Stanford University Press, 1983). Regarding prewar manhood, see Henry D. Smith III, *Japan's First Student Radicals* (Cambridge: Harvard University Press, 1976); Donald Roden, *Schooldays in Imperial Japan: A Study in the Culture of a New Elite* (Berkeley and Los Angeles: University of California Press, 1980); and Earl Kinmonth, *The Self-Made Man in Meiji Japanese Thought* (Berkeley and Los Angeles: University of California Press, 1981). At present, there are no works by historians on gender or postwar manhood; for one sketch of terrains of gender by an anthropologist, see Theodore Bestor, "Gendered Domains: A Commentary on Research in Japanese Studies," *Journal of Japanese Studies* 11, no. 1 (Winter 1985): 284–89. In Japanese, a few basic works in women's history include *Fujin mondai shiryō shūsei* (Tokyo: Domesu Shuppan, 1977–78); Mitsui Reiko, *Gendai fujin undōshi nenpyō* (Tokyo: San'ichi Shobō, 1974); Joseishi Sōgō Kenkyūkai, ed., *Nihon joseishi kenkyū bunken mokuroku* (Tokyo: Tōkyō Daigaku Shuppankai, 1983); Joseishi Sōgō Kenkyūkai, ed., *Nihon josei shi*, 5 vols. (Tokyo: Tōkyō Daigaku Shuppankai, 1982), esp. vol. 4, *Kindai*, and vol. 5, *Gendai;* and Wakita Haruko, ed., *Bosei o tou*, 2 vols. (Kyoto: Jinbun Shoin, 1985).

6. Regarding actual practices of wives and mothers in prewar Japan, see Takie Lebra, *Japanese Women: Constraint and Fulfillment* (Honolulu: University of Hawaii Press, 1984), esp. 158–216; Mikiso Hane, *Rebels, Peasants, and Outcastes* (New York: Pantheon, 1982), esp. 79–101; Kathleen S. Uno,

nent of "good wife, wise mother" during the 1930s and has become increasingly dominant in the postwar era, a theme that is also an assertion of the historicity (or social construction) of Japanese wifehood.[7]

Many of the themes explored in this chapter resonate with significant debates beyond the field of Japanese studies. Prewar and postwar contests over definitions of womanhood carried out by officials, educators, and social critics on the one hand, and by female activists on the other, involved the issues of women's "difference" from men and equal rights or "equity" issues;[8] analysis of these Japanese discourses contributes to important, ongoing discussions of these concepts in gender studies, social history, and present-day women's movements. Currently historians of women and gender are also wrangling over the nature of feminism. Can feminism and women's movements best be categorized by dichotomies? If so, which ones? Or should dualisms be avoided and multiplicities embraced? The perspective on Japanese women's movements spanning the prewar and postwar eras in this chapter suggests that the arguments, issues, and organizations of Japanese female activists can provide rich material to advance these discussions of "equity" versus "difference" and the characterization of women's movements and feminisms.

RYŌSAI KENBO IN PREWAR STATE AND SOCIETY

Modern Japanese nationalism produced "good wife, wise mother" along with compulsory education, industrialization, military modernization, and constitu-

---

"Women and Changes in the Household Division of Labor: Toward Explanation," in Bernstein, *Recreating Japanese Women*, 17–41. See also Shidzue Ishimoto, *Facing Two Ways* (1935; reprint Stanford: Stanford University Press, 1984); Etsu Sugimoto, *A Daughter of the Samurai* (New York: Doubleday, 1935); and Robert J. Smith and Ella Lury Wiswell, *The Women of Suye Mura* (Chicago: University of Chicago Press, 1984). For postwar Japan, see Takie Lebra, *Patterns of Japanese Behavior* (Honolulu: University of Hawaii Press, 1976), 137–55; Gail Lee Bernstein, *Haruko's World* (Stanford: Stanford University Press, 1983); Carol Simon, "A Long-Distance Ticket to Life," *Smithsonian* 17, no. 2 (Mar. 1987): 44–56; Merry White, "The Virtue of Japanese Mothers: Cultural Definitions of Women's Lives," *Daedalus* 116, no. 3 (Summer 1987): 149–64; and Anne Imamura, *Urban Japanese Housewives: At Home and in the Community* (Honolulu: University of Hawaii Press, 1987), 19–23, 69–80.

7. Major English works treating prewar wifehood include Lebra, *Japanese Women;* Uno, "Women and Changes"; Ishimoto, *Facing Two Ways;* Sugimoto, *Daughter of the Samurai;* Smith and Wiswell, *Women of Suye Mura;* Kiyoko Segawa, "Japanese Women in the Last Century," in Barbara Molony and Merry White, eds., *Proceedings of the Tokyo Symposium on Women* (Tokyo: International Group for the Study of Women, 1978), 1–9; and Chizuko Ueno, "The Position of Japanese Women Reconsidered," *Current Anthropology* 28, no. 4 (Aug.–Oct. 1987): S77–S81. Regarding postwar wifehood, see Lebra, *Japanese Women;* Bernstein, *Recreating Japanese Women;* Imamura, *Urban Japanese Housewives;* Ueno, "Position of Japanese Women"; Suzanne Vogel, "Professional Housewife: The Career of Urban Middle Class Japanese Women," *Japan Interpreter* 12, no. 1 (Winter 1978): 16–43; and Robert J. Smith, "Gender Inequality in Contemporary Japan," *Journal of Japanese Studies* 13, no. 1 (Winter 1987): 1–25.

8. See, for example, Joan Scott, "Deconstructing Equality-Versus-Difference; Or, the Uses of Poststructuralist Theory for Feminism," *Feminist Studies* 14, no. 1 (Spring 1988): 33–50; and Hester Eisenstein and Alice Jardine, eds., *The Future of Difference* (1980; reprint New Brunswick: Rutgers University Press, 1985).

tionalism. In the early 1870s the government viewed development of the potential of individuals through education and broadened political participation as a means of strengthening the nation against the threat of Western imperialism. In the absence of gender restrictions a few bold young women enrolled in college preparatory courses, while others demanded popular constitutional government and woman suffrage at protest rallies in the 1880s.[9] But even before the institutionalization of *ryōsai kenbo*, the government began to limit women's public activities. After the mid-1880s the education ministry, citing women's "difference" from men, excluded girls from rigorous postelementary education.[10] Ideologues, bureaucrats, and politicians began to laud the family as the foundation of the state, to equate filial piety with loyalty to the emperor, and to exalt the emperor as the father of all Japanese subjects in the family-state (*kazoku kokka*). At the same time the fundamental purpose of education shifted from cultivation of the individual's talents to inculcation of state-approved moral virtues—diligence, frugality, filial piety, love of country, reverence for and obedience to the emperor, and zeal for national improvement.[11] But by 1890 the constitution and laws denied women both suffrage and participation in other political activities.[12] Thus, negative policies preceded positive ones; until after the Sino-Japanese War the state lacked a constructive plan to mobilize the female half of the population to contribute to national development.

Ryōsai kenbo defined women's contribution to the good of the nation to be their labor as "good wives" and "wise mothers" in the private world of the home. Ideally the "good wife" carefully managed the affairs of the household and advanced the well-being of its adult members, while the "wise mother" devoted herself to rearing her children to become loyal and obedient imperial subjects.[13] According to a former education minister, the domestic tasks of the *ryōsai kenbo* complemented those of her husband. Each worked in different ways for the sake of the nation:

9. Nakajima Kuni, "Meiji shoki no joshi kyōiku," *Joshi kyōiku mondai*, no. 1 (Fall 1979): 169–77; Sievers, *Flowers in Salt*, 26–53.

10. Nakajima, "Meiji shoki," 174.

11. See Kenneth Pyle, "The Technology of Nationalism: The Local Improvement Movement," *Journal of Asian Studies* 33 (1973): 51–60; Carol Gluck, *Japan's Modern Myths* (Princeton: Princeton University Press, 1985). To compare these modern values with those cultivated by the early modern state, see Ronald Dore, *Education in Tokugawa Japan* (Berkeley and Los Angeles: University of California Press, 1964), chaps. 2, 6–9.

12. Sievers, *Flowers in Salt*, 51–54.

13. Late nineteenth-century liberals often referred to *kokumin*, often translated as "citizen" but more accurately translated as "person," "national" (in its nominative sense), and even as "subject" in prewar Japan; however, increasingly in the twentieth century, influential political tracts discussed the obligations of *shinmin* (imperial subjects). For example, see Atsuko Hirai, "The State and Ideology in Meiji Japan: A Review Article," *Journal of Asian Studies* 46, no. 1 (Feb. 1987): 88–103, esp. 93–97. The emperor, his advisers, and top bureaucrats determined policy; the role of the masses increasingly became that of "subjects"—executors of the imperial will embodied in directives handed down from above—rather than "citizens" entitled to participate in political decision making.

The man goes outside to work to earn his living, to fulfill his duties to the State; it is the wife's part to help him, for the common interests of the house, and as her share of duty to the State, by sympathy and encouragement, by relieving him of his anxieties at home, managing household affairs, and above all, tending the old people and bringing up the children in a fit and proper manner.[14]

Yet *ryōsai kenbo* was not a rigid construct; expectations for women's performance as *ryōsai kenbo* differed by class. A model wife helped with the household enterprise if necessary, as this 1939 elementary school ethics lesson illustrates: "She helped her husband . . . by cultivating the rice and vegetable fields or by picking up firewood in the mountains. She also served her mother-in-law industriously, and did sewing, washing, and all the other household tasks by herself. She even did the chore of feeding the horses."[15]

However, women of the privileged classes did not need to contribute to the family income, and their servants did the household chores. Instead, the state asked elite women to devote themselves to educating their children, the future leaders of the nation. Although official exhortations to *ryōsai kenbo* excluded women from direct participation in politics, they did not prohibit economic activities, for women's work was essential to many small farming, fishing, retailing, and manufacturing enterprises.[16]

Ryōsai kenbo *and the Prewar State*

In the decades after 1899 the state made *ryōsai kenbo* the cornerstone of women's education, first in the public higher girls' schools, then in the coeducational elementary schools and private mission schools for girls.[17] In 1906 Education Minister Makino Nobuaki considered the creation of good wives and wise mothers to be the fundamental purpose of education, grounding his arguments for distinct goals and subject matter in girls' higher education in conceptions of women's difference.

As the male and female sexes differ, so too do their duties (*honbun*) differ. The purpose of girls' education is to make *ryōsai kenbo*. Recently some girls have received specialized education and wish to engage in vocations, but they are exceptional. In

14. Dairoku Kikuchi, *Japanese Education* (London: John Murray, 1909), 266, cited in Robert J. Smith, "Gender Inequality in Contemporary Japan," *Journal of Japanese Studies* 13, no. 1 (Winter 1987): 8. Three successive education ministers—Kikuchi, Makino Nobuaki, and Komatsubara Eitarō—were the architects of "good wife, wise mother" educational policies.

15. R. K. Hall, *Shūshin* (New York: Bureau of Publications, Teachers College, Columbia University, 1949), 135–36.

16. Fukaya, *Ryōsai kenboshugi no kyōiku*, 155; Uno, "Women and Changes."

17. Komano, "Ryōsai kenboshugi," 142–43. In the early modern period, household management including helping with production took precedence over mothering. Thus, the emphasis on mothers as natural and effective educators of children was by and large a post-1868 innovation. In English, see Sievers, *Flowers in Salt*, 4; Uno, "Good Wives and Wise Mothers"; Kathleen S. Uno, "Childhood, Motherhood, and State in Early Twentieth-Century Japan" (manuscript). For a contrasting view, see Martha Tocco, "Before Ryōsai Kenbo."

the end, a girl's duty is to become someone's wife and someone's mother; to manage the household; and to educate children.[18]

Both sexes were to be dutiful, patriotic subjects; however, the Education Ministry stressed additional traits for women—submissiveness to parents, husband, and in-laws, modesty, and chastity.[19] After 1899 instilling of these virtues rather than academic training prepared young women to contribute to society and state through household management and child rearing rather than political, artistic, or economic activity in the public world.[20]

Late nineteenth-century laws also hampered women's full participation in the world outside the home. Severe restrictions on women's political participation predated the institutionalization of *ryōsai kenbo* in the educational system by a decade. Denial of the right to vote, to found political associations, or, before 1925, to attend or speak at political meetings reinforced the domestic destiny of women promoted by the educational system.[21] Furthermore, the 1898 Civil Code placed nearly all women under the authority of a male head of household who chose the family domicile, controlled the family assets, managed his wife's property, and approved marriages of women under twenty-five (and men under thirty) years of age. A woman could become household head only in absence of a male candidate, and then only if she were unmarried or widowed. Wives had much greater difficulty gaining divorces than husbands did. All in all, the Civil Code hampered women's ability to live outside a male-headed household.[22]

An important shift in *ryōsai kenbo* occurred in the context of rising militarism in the 1930s as a new emphasis on women as the bearers rather than the socializers of children superseded the initial stress on educating children and household management.[23] Concern over falling population growth rates and the poor phy-

18. Komano, "Ryōsai Kenboshugi," 141.

19. These qualities are nearly identical to early modern upper-class womanly virtues. In English, see Atsuharu Sakai, "Kaibara Ekiken and 'Onna-Daigaku,' " *Cultural Nippon* 7, no. 4 (Dec. 1939): 43–56, and Basil Hall Chamberlain, *Things Japanese: Being Notes on Various Subjects Connected with Japan* (London: Kegan, Paul, Trevich, Trebner, and Co., 1890), 67–76.

20. From the 1880s, public activity in the form of charitable and philanthropic work was acceptable for women. In English, see Sievers, *Flowers in Salt*, 93; Uno, "Childhood, Mothood, and State"; Sally Hastings, "From Heroine to Patriotic Volunteer: Women and Social Work in Japan," Women in International Development Working Paper No. 106, Nov. 1985.

21. Sievers, *Flowers in Salt*, 52–53, 206; Sharon Nolte, "Women, the State, and Repression in Imperial Japan," Women in International Development Working Paper No. 33, Sept. 1983.

22. Kurt Steiner, "Postwar Changes in the Japanese Civil Code," *Washington Law Review* 25, no. 3 (Aug. 1950): 291–93. See also J. E. de Becker, William Sebald, trans., *Principles and Practice of the Civil Code of Japan* (London: Butterworth, 1921), esp. 521–788.

23. Some scholars argue that this shift was so marked that it constituted a new paradigm of womanhood. See Nakajima Kuni, "Kokkateki bosei," in Joseigaku Kenkyūkai, ed., *Onna no imēji, Kōza joseigaku 1* (Tokyo: Keisō Shobō, 1984), 235–63, and Yoshiko Miyake, "Doubling Expectations: Woman's Factory Work and the Praise of Motherhood under State Management in Japan, 1937–45," in Bernstein, *Recreating Japanese Women*, 267–95. One treatment of wartime images of women is

siques of army conscripts spurred the government to adopt pronatalist policies; reproductive legislation promoted motherhood in order to serve state manpower needs. Repression of Japan's birth control movement in 1938, coupled with earlier bans on abortion, allowed women little choice but to carry pregnancies to term.[24] The National Eugenic Law (Kokumin Yūsei Hō, 1940) aimed to provide robust manpower for the empire by preventing handicapped births.[25] The slogan "Give birth and multiply" (*Umeyo, fuyaseyo*) and the Precious Children Battalion (Kodakara Butai), comprised of women commended by the government for extraordinary fertility, encouraged childbearing for state needs. And the 1938 Maternal and Child Protection Law (Boshi Hogo Hō) offered for the first time state assistance to needy mothers and their children.[26] Emphasis on motherhood from the mid-1930s made the Japanese state hestitate fully to mobilize women for factory work until the war was virtually over.[27] But as good wives (*ryōsai*) who managed household budgets and consumption, women were exhorted to frugality in order to conserve resources for military needs.[28]

Ryōsai kenbo *in Prewar Society*

In prewar society, *ryōsai kenbo* influenced company policies regarding the residence, wages, and education of female factory workers.[29] First, as young women

William Hauser, "Women and War: The Japanese Film Image," in Bernstein, *Recreating Japanese Women*, 296–313.

24. Abortion had been banned since 1880, but the government had not needed to emphasize women's childbearing role because of sufficiently high population growth rates; Moori Taneki, *Gendai Nihon shōni hoken shi* (Tokyo: Domesu Shuppan, 1972), 47–48.

25. Sandra Buckley, "Body Politics: Abortion Law Reform," in Gavan McCormack and Yoshio Sugimoto, eds., *The Japanese Trajectory: Modernization and Beyond* (Cambridge: Cambridge University Press, 1988), 208–9.

26. Buckley, "Body Politics," 209; Noriko Sano, "Japanese Women's Movements During World War II," *Feminist International*, no. 2 (1980): 78; Dee Ann Vavich, "The Japanese Women's Movement: Ichikawa Fusae, Pioneer in Women's Suffrage," *Monumenta Nipponica* 22, nos. 3–4 (1967): 421–22; Thomas Havens, "Women and War in Japan, 1937–45," *American Historical Review* 80, no. 4 (Oct. 1975): 927–30.

27. Miyake, "Doubling Expectations," 267–70, 281–95; Havens, "Women and War," 913–27; Thomas Havens, *Valley of Darkness* (New York: Norton, 1978), 106–13; Barbara Molony, "Women and Wartime Employment," *Feminist International*, no. 2 (1980): 79–82.

28. Havens, *Valley of Darkness*, 15–20; Sano, "Japanese Women's Movements," 78.

29. Regarding female factory workers' daily lives and resistance, see Sievers, *Flowers in Salt*, 64–86; Hane, *Rebels, Peasants*, 173–225; Janet Hunter, "Labour in the Japanese Silk Industry in the 1870s: The *Tomioka Nikki* of Wada Ei," in Gordon Daniels, ed., *Europe Interprets Japan* (Exeter, Eng.: European Association of Japanese Studies, 1984), 20–25; E. Patricia Tsurumi, "Female Textile Workers and the Failure of Early Trade Unionism in Japan," *History Workshop*, no. 18 (Fall 1984): 3–27; Gail Lee Bernstein, "Women in the Silk-Reeling Industry in Nineteenth-Century Japan," in Gail Lee Bernstein and Haruhiro Fukui, eds., *Japan and the World: Essays in Honour of Ishida Takeshi* (New York: St. Martin's, 1989), 54–77; E. Patricia Tsurumi, *Factory Girls: Women in the Thread Mills of Meiji Japan* (Princeton: Princeton University Press, 1990); Barbara Molony, "Activism among Women in the Taisho Cotton Textile Industry," in Bernstein, *Recreating Japanese Women*, 217–38. To compare the experiences of

rarely lived on their own, parents raised few objections to factory dormitories that facilitated exploitation of young, single female operatives. Second, because young women were not expected to be self-supporting, female employees did not necessarily receive a living wage. Companies deducted portions of workers' earnings to pay for living costs and fines and sometimes sent additional sums directly to their parents in the countryside. Third, company education slated women for the home. For example, a recruitment flyer for Tokyo Muslin boasted that the moral benefits of employment included "becoming a magnificent (*rippa na*) person." At the same time, in stating that "in addition to regular education, sewing, flower arranging, tea ceremony, etiquette, and manners were carefully taught to all," the leaflet declared the arena for women's achievements to be the home rather than the public realm.[30] In these ways business enterprises, too, upheld official models of womanhood and gender.

Notwithstanding the sustained efforts of the state and industrialists to shape female attitudes and behavior, resistance to *ryōsai kenbo* emerged in prewar Japan. Sharon Sievers has discussed early twentieth-century feminism, while Margit Nagy has treated debates over revision of the Civil Code before 1930. Miriam Silverberg has analyzed representations of the *moga* (modern girl; also *modan gāru*), the epitome of assertive young women who rejected chaste, submissive domesticity, and Yukiko Hanawa has asserted that rural women responded to urban conceptions of femininity, including *ryōsai kenbo*, by fashioning their own distinctive visions of womanhood.[31] Other studies have treated aspects of the prewar

---

female factory operatives with those in other employments, see Kathleen S. Uno, "One Day at at Time: Work and Domestic Life of Urban Lower-Class Women in Prewar Japan," in Janet Hunter, ed., *Japanese Women Working* (London: Routledge, 1993), and Miriam Silverberg, "Eroticizing the Japanese Cafe Waitress" (paper presented at the conference "Female and Male Role Sharing in Japan: Historical and Contemporary Constructions of Gender," University of Michigan, 20 Dec. 1991).

30. Hosoi Wakizō, *Jokō aishi* (1925; reprint Tokyo: Iwanami Shoten, 1954), 61–62. In addition, such education probably sought to ease the moral stigma that tainted the reputations of women working outside the home. Regarding attitudes toward such female workers, see Bernstein, "Women in the Silk-Reeling Industry," 68; B. Molony, "Activism," 228–29.

31. Sievers, *Flowers in Salt;* Margit Nagy, " 'How Shall We Live?' Social Change, the Family Institution, and Feminism in Prewar Japan," Ph.D. diss., University of Washington, 1981; Yukiko Hanawa, response to question at colloquium presentation "Voices from the Periphery: Imagining Rural Women," Harvard University, Japan Forum, 11 May 1990; Miriam Silverberg, "The Modern Girl as Militant," in Bernstein, *Recreating Japanese Women*, 239–66. See also Hane, *Reflections;* Diana Bethel, "Visions of a Humane Society: Feminist Thought in Taisho Japan," *Feminist International,* no. 2 (1980): 92–94; Laurel Rodd, "Yosano Akiko and the Taishō Debate over the 'New Woman'," in Bernstein, *Recreating Japanese Women*, 175–98; Masanao Kano, "Takamure Itsue: Pioneer in the Study of Women's History," *Feminist International,* no. 2 (1980): 67–69; Barbara Sato, "The *Moga* Sensation: The Intellectual Response to Early Showa Mass Culture" (unpublished paper); Hamiru Bābara (Barbara Hamel), "Modan gāru no jidaiteki imi," *Gendai no espuri,* no. 188 (1983): 84–85; Satō Bābara Hamiru (Barbara Hamel Satō), "Josei—Modanizumu to kenri ishiki," in Minami Hiroshi, ed., *Shōwa Bunka, 1925–1945* (Tokyo: Keisō Shobō, 1989), 198–231; Satō Bābara Hamiru, "Modan gāru no tōjō to chishikijin," *Rekishi hyōron,* no. 491 (Mar. 1991): 18–26.

women's suffrage movement, a challenge to the state's formulation of domestic activities as women's contribution to the national weal.[32] Furthermore, various social reform, labor, and proletarian organizations dissented from the state's ideology of womanhood in the 1920s and 1930s.[33]

In the great surge of nationalist sentiment following the Manchurian Incident (September 1931), feminism, including women's suffrage, was redefined as un-Japanese and unpatriotic. In this inhospitable intellectual climate women's suffrage organizations abandoned their quest for political rights equal to those of men. Instead, they sought to demonstrate women's capacity for responsible political participation by championing clean elections and passage of legislation to protect motherhood.[34] As two important sectors of the imperial state, the military and the bureaucracy, became preoccupied with reproduction of the nation's labor supply in the late 1930s and 1940s, female activists employed appeals to motherhood to raise public awareness of women's concerns and to increase their public authority. Their efforts assisted passage of the Maternal and Child Protection Law and encouraged appointment of women to positions of public influence. After 1938 the government appointed leaders of women's organizations such as Hani Motoko, Ōtsuma Kotaka, and Yoshioka Yayoi and prominent female educators such as Yamada Waka, Ichikawa Fusae, and Kawasaki Natsu to national war mobilization committees.[35] Arguments premised on women's difference from

32. Vavich, "Japanese Women's Movement"; Kathleen Molony, "One Woman Who Dared: Ichikawa Fusae and the Woman Suffrage Movement in Japan," Ph.D. diss., University of Michigan, 1980; Sharon Nolte, "Women's Rights and Society's Needs: Japan's 1931 Suffrage Bill," *Comparative Studies in Society and History* 28 (1986): 690–714; Barbara A. Molony and Kathleen Molony, *Ichikawa Fusae: A Political Biography* (Stanford: Stanford University Press, forthcoming).

33. George O. Totten, *The Social Democratic Movement in Prewar Japan* (Boston: Heath, 1965), 359–64; Hane, *Reflections;* Uno, "Childhood, Motherhood, and State," chap. 7.

34. Vavich, "Japanese Women's Movement," 420–21; Tetsu Katayama, *Women's Movement in Japan* (Tokyo: Foreign Affairs Association of Japan, 1938), 27–29; Junko Kuninobu, "The Development of Feminism in Modern Japan," *Feminist Issues* 4, no. 2 (Fall 1984): 5–10; Kathleen Molony, "A Feminist Approach to 'Election Purification': Ichikawa Fusae and the Women's Suffrage Movement," paper presented at the Association for Asian Studies Annual Meeting, Philadelphia, 22 Mar. 1985; Vera Mackie, "Feminist Politics in Japan," *New Left Review,* no. 167 (Jan.–Feb. 1988): 53–59; Gregory Pflugfelder, "Politics and the Kitchen: The Women's Suffrage Movement in Japan," paper presented at the Association for Asian Studies Annual Meeting, Chicago, 6 Apr. 1990; Sheldon Garon, "The Women's Movement and the Japanese State: Contending Approaches to Political Integration, 1890–1945," paper presented at the symposium "New Directions in the History of Gender in Modern Japan," Princeton University, 7 Dec. 1990.

35. Sano, "Japanese Women's Movements," 78. Miyake argues that after the state became more concerned with population growth, the labor supply, and the stability of the family system in the late 1930s, prominent women such as Mori Yasuko, an intellectual, and Tanino Setsu, a labor inspector, attempted to gain workplace concessions and greater public influence for women by asking the state and private sector to augment its protection of motherhood. Mori even argued that women's reproductive functions were grounded in their biological differences from men and that women deserved a more central role in the family because of the importance of these functions. Miyake, "Doubling Expectations," 275–77.

men, especially as mothers but also as wives, apparently produced the greatest gains for women in the prewar period but at the cost of organizational autonomy; independent women's associations became a casualty of the war when they dissolved in 1941.[36]

RYŌSAI KENBO IN POSTWAR STATE
AND SOCIETY

The extensive restructuring of Japanese state and society after 1945 affected conceptions of womanhood including *ryōsai kenbo*. The early American occupation nurtured democracy in Japan to prevent a resurgence of militarism. The new constitution and revised legal codes granted Japanese women unprecedented political, economic, and civil rights.[37] Moreover, the old ethics curriculum emphasizing "loyalty," "filial piety," the "family-state," and *ryōsai kenbo* vanished from school classrooms.

But these sudden, fairly drastic postwar changes did not relegate *ryōsai kenbo* to the dustbin. I concur with Japanese researchers that "good wife, wise mother" remained influential in Japan into the late 1980s.[38] The term *ryōsai kenbo* itself fell into disuse after 1945, but the conservative ruling party, (the Liberal Democratic Party [LDP]) and private companies continued to formulate policies which assumed that wifehood and motherhood came first for women. Nonetheless, in the postwar era conservatives could no longer silence women by locking them away in the home. Often activated by their own new interpretations of *ryōsai kenbo*, women on countless occasions organized at the local, regional, and national levels to express their views on matters of public policy ranging from national defense to working conditions, education, child care, consumption, sexual mores, pollution, and local development.[39]

Continuing a transformation begun in the prewar era, motherhood rather than wifehood became the dominant image of Japanese womanhood despite the fact

36. Sano, "Japanese Women's Movements," 78.

37. These included the rights to vote, to manage property while married, and to inherit part of their husband's estate; equality in employment, education, marriage, and divorce; and freedom of residence. See Buckley's essay in this volume for further details.

38. Fukaya, *Ryōsai kenboshugi no kyōiku*, 268–313. See S. Tanaka, *Josei kaihō*, vol. 2; Mackie, "Feminist Politics," 59–75; Kuninobu, "Development of Feminism," 11–21; Sandra Buckley and Vera Mackie, "Women in the New Japanese State," in Gavan McCormack and Yoshio Sugimoto, eds., *Democracy in Contemporary Japan* (Armonk, N.Y.: M. E. Sharpe, 1986), 176–85. In Japanese, see four essays in Joseigaku Kenkyūkai, ed., *Onnatachi no imēji*: Amano Masako, "Gendai Nihon no hahaoya zō," 74–101; Inoue Teruko, "Masukomi to josei no jidai," 42–73; Noguchi Masayo and Kimura Keiko, "Gakkō kyōiku to joseikan," 24–41; and Hirano Takako, "Gendai no joseikan," 1–23.

39. For other perspectives on women's postwar activism, see Buckley's and Upham's essays in this volume. Regarding the peace movement, see the Dower and Koschmann essays; regarding the labor movement, see Gordon's and Mochizuki and Garon's essays; regarding the antipollution movement, see Upham's essay.

that women existed as full-time or nonworking mothers only among the upper ranks of the urban new middle class, a small but influential segment of the population.[40] In the high and late postwar eras the images of the devoted mother and the pathological mother replaced the prewar image of the harried junior housewife dominated by her tyrannical mother-in-law.[41] Woman's image as mother also contrasted sharply with the high and late postwar image of the Japanese male—a man in a dark blue suit commuting by train to a company, an actor in the public world, rather than a father or husband in the private world of the home.[42]

I offer three reasons for the postwar ascendance of motherhood. First, mothers became more visible in postwar households, for long-term demographic changes and postwar democratic ideologies made it less likely that a young bride, the mother of a household's young children, would share the hearth with another adult woman (generally her husband's mother) as she did before World War II.[43] Second, the diffusion of vacuum cleaners, washers, refrigerators, gas ranges, indoor plumbing, and prepackaged foods eased somewhat a wife's burden of household chores, allowing her to devote more time to childrearing.[44] Third, the rise of employment for wages decreased the proportion of housewives working in family enterprises.[45] In sum, as wives' work in serving their in-laws, maintaining the household, and assisting in the family enterprise diminished, their nurturing activities as mothers became more apparent.

Ryōsai kenbo *and the Postwar State*

State policies regarding labor, education, reproduction, and welfare provided ample evidence that politicians and bureaucrats did not entirely abandon the prewar belief that "Women's place is in the home" (*Josei wa katei ni*). Neverthe-less, they modified their conception of female domesticity to fit postwar economic realities. After the mid-1960s the task of the "good wife, wise mother" evolved from the duty to do reproductive and productive work at home into the obligation

40. Regarding motherhood, wifehood, and work of lower class urban women, see Kondo, *Crafting Selves*, 274–85; Glenda Roberts, "Non-Trivial Pursuits: Japanese Blue Collar Women" (manuscript), esp. part 3. Regarding rural women, see Ronald Dore, *Shinohata* (New York: Pantheon, 1975); Robert J. Smith, *Kurusu* (Stanford: Stanford University Press, 1975); Bernstein, *Haruko's World*.

41. On the devoted mother, see Ian Buruma, *Behind the Mask* (New York: Pantheon, 1984), chap. 2; regarding the pathological mother, see, for example, Kawaii Hayao, *Bosei shakai Nihon no byōri* (Tokyo: Chūō Kōronsha, 1976); Yamamura Yoshiaki, *Nihonjin to haha* (Tokyo: Tōyōkan, 1971).

42. Bernard Eccleston, *State and Society in Postwar Japan* (New York: Blackwell/Polity Press, 1989), 171.

43. See data on changes in household composition over time in Buckley's essay in this volume. See also Tadashi Fukutake, *The Japanese Social Structure*, 2d ed. (Tokyo: University of Tokyo Press, 1989), 124.

44. Japan External Trade Organization, *Japan Handbook* (Tokyo: Japan External Trade Organiza-tion, 1985), 37–41; National Women's Education Centre, "Ratio of Households with Major Electric Appliances," *NWEC Newsletter* 6, no. 1 (May 1989): 11.

45. Buckley's essay in this volume describes postwar trends in female employment in greater detail.

to manage household affairs while if necessary engaging in paid work that did not prevent fulfillment of domestic responsibilities.

State employment policies (and corporate ones as well) demonstrated the postwar persistence of *ryōsai kenbo*, at least for the period before implementation of the Equal Employment Opportunity Law in 1986.[46] To cope with a growing shortage of workers in the mid-1960s, state labor policies promoted full-time work for unmarried women and part-time work for married women because of their "family responsibilities" (*katei sekinin*), especially their childrearing responsibilities (*ikuji sekinin*).[47] A 1963 report of the Economic Deliberative Council (Keizai Shingikai) stressed "reentry employment" and the "part-time system" for "women who worked before marriage and are returning to the labor force after having left during the childrearing years."[48] Furthermore, tax incentives discouraged married women from full-time entry into the labor force,[49] while the 1972 Working Women's Welfare Law emphasized the need to help women "harmonize" their home and work responsibilities, a problem that it assumed men did not face.[50] Thus, state labor policy from 1963 until 1986 or later encouraged women to enter the labor force without reducing their responsibilities for household management and child care.[51]

Despite new but reluctant encouragement of married women's work outside

46. Regarding post-1986 trends, see Barbara Molony, "The 1986 Equal Employment Opportunity Law and the Changing Discourse on Gender," and Martha Tocco, "Women, Employment and the Popular Press" (papers presented at the annual meeting of the Association for Asian Studies, 8 Apr. 1990).

For the sake of brevity I touch on corporate employment policies in this discussion of government labor policy; more detailed treatment can be found in Buckley's and Upham's essays. However, it is worth noting that the corporate world and the state disagreed over labor policy in the 1930s and in the postwar era, particularly when business interests resisted proposals for improvement of labor standards generated by the government in response to external pressure, such as the International Labor Organization.

47. In 1983 69 percent of female employees were married, compared to 45 percent in 1960; Amano, "Dēta ni miru josei no sengo yonjūnen," *Sekai*, no. 478 (Aug. 1985): 60. See also Buckley's essay in this volume.

48. "Kezai hatten ni okeru jinteki nōryoku kaihatsu no kadai to taisaku," 131–32, cited in Asakura Mutsuko, "Rōdōryoku seisaku to fujin rōdō," in Fukushima Masao, ed., *Kazoku: Seisaku to hō*, vol. 2, *Gendai Nihon no kazoku seisaku* (Tokyo: Tōkyō Daigaku Shuppankai, 1976), 299.

49. "As long as a wife earns less than 900,000 yen ($6,000) per year, her income is not taxed and her husband can still take advantage of the 570,000 yen ($3,800) spouse deduction allowance. If her earnings surpass the limit, she will have to earn a lot more in order to offset the tax increase." Kittredge Cherry, "Part-Time Jobs," *Womansword* (New York and Tokyo: Kodansha International, 1987), 104.

50. Molony, "Equal Employment Opportunity Law," 12. As Buckley and Shinotsuka note, women's home life affected their experiences in the paid labor force. Overall, their employment was characterized by full-time, "regular" employment until marriage, "retirement" to rear young children, and return to the work force on a part-time basis after their children enrolled in school. See Buckley's essay in this volume and Shinotsuka Eiko, "Keizai hendō to josei," in Joseigaku Kenkyūkai, ed. *Onnatachi no ima*, 31, 37–41.

51. In fact, welfare policies for a time increased women's home responsibilities, as women were expected to care for aged in place of social facilities; see Buckley's essay for details.

the home, a vision of women as bearers of the nation's manpower still informed important laws regulating reproduction. The provisions of the 1948 Eugenic Protection Law (Yūsei Hogo Hō) are, like those of the prewar National Eugenic Law (Kokumin Yūsei Hō), still "aimed at preserving the woman's role as mother [*bosei hogo*], rather than her health as an individual." And it is still "illegal to prescribe the birth control pill for contraceptive purposes."[52] That reproductive policies served national rather than women's needs was further suggested by the fact that laws against abortion were not erased from the statutes.[53] But in the postwar era, women's wombs were borrowed largely to meet the labor needs of industry rather than the needs of corporate households (*ie*) for successors or the state's need for colonists and military conscripts.

The Ministry of Education did not completely abandon its prewar mission, grounded in the assumption that women's difference or "special character" (*tokusei*) as wives and mothers slated them for the home.[54] Some educational historians argued that whereas before the war *ryōsai kenbo* education aimed to develop girls' special character (*tokusei kyōiku*), in the postwar era of high economic growth the same principle reemerged in a new guise as "Women's place is in the home."[55] Some degree of streaming by gender emerged in postwar secondary curricula, although schools themselves became coeducational. Although the 1976 curricular reforms in theory permitted junior high school boys and girls to choose freely either industrial arts or homemaking classes, in reality teachers' and textbooks' emphasis on the distinct male and female roles discouraged students from making nontraditional choices. In 1969 the ministry made homemaking courses mandatory for high school girls. Vigorous opposition to this change arose during the 1970s, but despite Japan's signing of the 1980 Convention to End All Forms of Discrimination Against Women, the ministry retained the homemaking requirement for girls until 1989.[56] Implementation of the Equal Employment Opportunity Law provided some impetus to curricular change, but in the junior colleges, the postsecondary institutions most commonly attended by girls, education suited to women's "special nature" still prevailed in the late 1980s.[57]

52. Buckley and Mackie, "Women," 178–79.

53. Ibid.

54. In fact, "special function" might be a more accurate description of women's difference stemming from their physiological capacity to bear children. And physiological "difference" was generally assumed to make women responsible for childrearing as well. One encounters few arguments linking wifehood to female physiology.

55. Kameda Atsuko and Tachi Kaoru, "Gakkō ni okeru sekushizumu to joseigaku kyōiku," in Joseigaku Kenkyūkai, ed., *Onna no me de miru, Kōza joseigaku* 4 (Tokyo: Keisō Shobō, 1987), 84.

56. Komano Yōko, "Kyōiku no ba ni miru seisabetsu," *Shisō no kagaku*, ser. 6, no. 127 (1981): 33–34; *NWEC Newsletter* 7, no. 1 (May 1990): 6. Compulsory education ends after junior high school, but 91.9 percent of girls in 1977 entered public high schools; Ann P. Brannen, Sheila J. Ramsey, Betsy J. Olsen, Barbara Wilt, "The Red Thread and the White Kimono: Japanese Women, Omote and Ura," *International Journal of Intercultural Relations* 3 (1979): 483.

57. Kameda and Tachi, "Gakkō ni okeru sekushizumu," 84; Keiko Fujimura-Fanselow, "Women's Participation in Higher Education in Japan," *Comparative Education Review* 19 (1985): 471–85, 476.

Ryōsai kenbo *in Postwar Society*

In the realm of civil society, examination of the goals and issues of women's social movements in postwar Japan reveals both transmutation and rejection of *ryōsai kenbo*.[58] Freed from prewar legal and ideological constraints on political activities, women quickly assumed public roles for themselves as the guardians of the home and formed associations, organized protests, and mounted petition campaigns in order to speak out on issues affecting family life.[59] Although groups and individuals sought varying degrees of economic and social changes, what can be called "wifeist" and "maternalist" ideas strongly informed the goals of most early postwar women's associations. Because they assumed that women would marry, manage households, and have children, many of their activities sought to extend wives' and mothers' influence in political and economic affairs beyond the home and to protect working mothers.[60]

Thus, early postwar associations such as the Housewives' Association, National Coordinating Council of Regional Women's Organizations, and Mothers' Congress coordinated tens of thousands, even millions, of members in nationwide crusades as wives, mothers, or both to improve home life. However, despite the prevalence of maternalist and wifeist logic, in the 1950s and 1960s women's organizations affiliated with labor unions and progressive political parties—such as the Housewives' Council of the Japan Coal Miners' Union, the Japan Women's Council, and the New Japan Women's Association—mixed equity (or equal rights) with wifeist and maternalist arguments in their quests for social reform.

Major national women's organizations founded in the early postwar era remained active into the 1990s,[61] but the 1970s seem to have been a watershed for the evolution of women's movements, as for many other antiestablishment groups.[62] At the end of the 1960s new women's groups emerged from the student

---

58. Analyses of the history of postwar women's movements in Western languages, especially treatments of the pre-1970 period, though few, include Wake Fujioka, ed. and trans., "Women's Movements in Postwar Japan" (Selected articles from Tsuji Seimei, ed., *Shiryō: Sengo nijūnen shi* [Tokyo: Nippon Hyōronsha, 1966]) (Honolulu: East-West Center, 1968); Kazuko Tanaka, *A Short History of the Women's Movement in Modern Japan* (n.p., 1977), 45–52; Molony and Molony, *Ichikawa Fusae*. Works treating primarily post-1970 developments include Mackie, "Feminist Politics"; Buckley and Mackie, "Women"; Buckley, "Body Politics."

59. The rescinding of Article 5 of the Peace Preservation Law in 1922 had allowed women to attend and participate in political meetings, but new restrictions on "dangerous thought" and a generally repressive political atmosphere discouraged women from taking full advantage of their newly won rights before the occupation. In the postwar era, the easing of controls on freedom of speech, press, and assembly as well as the general encouragement of political initiatives by new groups gave great impetus to women's movements as well as labor and rural tenant unions.

60. Protection of motherhood also included guarding the health of young, single, childless female workers who were regarded by unions, state, and employers as future mothers.

61. For example, the Housewives' Association, National Coordinating Council of Regional Women's Associations, and the Mothers' Congress. The Christian Women's Reform Society, founded in 1886, is also active today.

62. See the essays by Koschmann and Dower in this volume.

and anti–Vietnam War movements.[63] In the 1970s and 1980s members of the Fighting Women's Group, Tanaka Mitsu, Atsumi Ikuko, Ueno Chizuko, and others questioned the inevitability of women's domestic destiny and attacked key elements of the social structure—family, corporations, and state—as male-dominated institutions. Few in number, female activists of the high postwar era nonetheless sought to contribute actively to the death of prewar *ryōsai kenbo*.

The Logic of Early Postwar Movements I: Wife, Mother, and Guardian of the Home
The concerns of wives clearly shaped the goals of the Housewives' Association (Shufuren), founded in September 1948 by housewives seeking to defend their family budgets from increases in ration prices and food shortages.[64] Accordingly, this group focused on the concerns of women as wives and mothers who selected household goods for husbands, children, and themselves. In later postwar consumer movements, women pressured manufacturers to lower prices and to provide safer, higher quality goods. One housewife belonging to another consumer organization dominated by women, the Committee for Safe Foods, moved from apolitical study of consumer issues to public crusades for the banning of AF-2, a food preservative, during the 1970s.

> We are the generation which didn't have time to study. . . . We never imagined the group would come in this direction. We thought the country was preserving our interests. . . . I never imagined the corporations did anything wrong. . . . We heard about AF-2 and wondered why things like it are made. We wondered about the corporations and government who made them. We realized that there are things which cannot be solved by staying in the household. Since we had always been in the household we had never realized that. It's no longer possible to be a *ryōsai kenbo* while staying in the household.[65]

In other words, this activist housewife reinterpreted "good wife, wise mother" to justify her involvement in larger public issues that affected home life.

Women in the early postwar period also justified their public activities in terms of motherhood. As one might expect, the goals of the umbrella organization Mothers' Congress (Hahaoya Taikai, established June 1955) reflected a strong maternalist orientation;[66] however, the philosophies of its constituent organizations ranged from family-oriented organizations such as the Setagaya Family

63. K. Tanaka, *Short History*, 45–52; Tanaka Mitsu, *Inochi no onnatachi e* (Tokyo: Tabatake Shoten, 1972), 306–10; Inoue Teruko, "Ūman ribu no shisō," in Tanaka Sumiko, ed., *Josei kaihō no shisō to kōdō, sengo hen* (Jiji Tsūshinsha, 1975) 2:215–35.

64. K. Tanaka, *Short History*, 38. Tanaka called Shufuren the forerunner of later Japanese consumer movements; however, housewives also participated in prewar consumer movements. See, for example, Oku Mumeo, *Nobi akaaka to—Oku Mumeo jiden* (Tokyo: Domesu Shuppan, 1988), 91–94.

65. Catherine Lewis, "Women in the Consumer Movement," in Molony and White, *Proceedings*, 81–82.

66. The name "Hahaoya Taikai" has also been translated as Mothers' Meeting and Japanese Mothers' Rally; K. Tanaka, *Short History*, 40; Fujioka, "Women's Movements in Postwar Japan."

Association (Setagaya Kateikai) and the Japan Child Protection Association (Nihon Kodomo o Mamoru Kai) to the nonmaternalist Women's Democratic Club (treated below) and the equity and maternalist orientations of the Federation of Japanese Women's Associations (Nihon Fujin Dantai Rengōkai, or Fudanren) and the women's sections of national teachers' and public railway unions.[67] The venerable Christian Women's Reform Society (Kirisutokyō Fujin Kyōfūkai, established 1886) also supported the concern for human life and the pacifism of the Mothers' Congress. Its manifesto, accepted by all the sponsoring women's groups, vividly conveyed the participants' intentions:

> We mothers in Japan have come together from north and south with children on our backs . . . and we have spoken our words of prayer for world peace in our sincere desire to safeguard the happiness of our children. . . . [In the past,] mothers were forbidden even to mention this very natural feeling they had: that they neither liked nor wanted war. We mothers were not even allowed to shed tears as we sent our sons away to war; we had to bear this sadness only by gritting our teeth. . . . [And our war dragged] into the war countless other youths of foreign countries, causing their mothers to experience the same thing.
>
> We are confident that fathers and children will support and encourage . . . this great march begun by mothers.
>
> And only through their cooperation would we be able to participate in movements such as the Movement to Prohibit Nuclear Testing and the Movement for World Peace.
>
> We are no longer isolated individuals, scattered and weak.[68]

The organization initially passed a set of twenty-five resolutions premised on mothers' responsibility to guard the family and to preserve human life. Nine resolutions addressed the quality of children's education (mainly at school); five, mothers' medical, health, and welfare issues; and three, women's rights—the abolition of prostitution, protection of women workers' childbearing capacities, and opposition to revival of the prewar family system. Of the remainder, four concerned the protection of human life in general, including proposals to decrease traffic accidents, aid atomic bomb victims, and oppose military bases and nuclear weapons; one concerned aspects of national fiscal policy, and one opposed "unemployment and layoffs which threaten the livelihood of the family."[69]

The Logic of Early Postwar Women's Movements II: Domesticity and Equity
Reliance on arguments grounded both in women's domestic functions and in a more general sense of rights characterized the goals and issues of four major early postwar women's organizations—the National Coordinating Council of Regional Women's Associations, Japan's largest federation of women's organizations; the Housewives' Council of the Japan Coal Miners' Union; and two women's organi-

67. The Japanese Child Protection Association was headed by Hani Setsuko.
68. Fujioka, "Women's Movements in Postwar Japan," 80–81.
69. Ibid., 83.

zations affiliated with the Socialist and Communist parties, respectively, the Japan Women's Council and New Japan Women's Association.[70] In contrast, the concerns and assumptions of a fifth organization, All-Japan Women's Federation, whose members included LDP and other conservative women, more closely resembled *ryōsai kenbo* than those of any other postwar organizations.[71]

The early postwar goals of the Housewives' Council of the Japan Coal Miners' Union (Nihon Tankō Shufu Kyōgikai, or Tanfukyō) revealed aspirations rooted in women's role as guardian of the home as well as aspirations for women as individuals in their own right. Established on 11 September 1952, its initial membership rolls listed 104,000 members in 106 branches throughout the country. At that time its three objectives were (1) "to build a country of peace and culture"; (2) "to rationalize and better our lives and to safeguard the family by joining hands with labor unions"; and (3) "to elevate the social and economic status of the coal miners' housewives."[72] The second aim sprang from a wish to protect home life, but the first and third aims suggested a desire to improve the situation of women, as Japanese miners' wives but also as citizens of the nation and world. The sense of self-interest and the pacifism of these miners' wives were not in keeping with prewar official ideologies of womanhood.

The huge rural constituency of the National Coordinating Council of Regional Women's Associations (Zenkoku Chiiki Fujin Dantai Rengō Kyōgikai, or Chifuren, established 1952) also undermined *ryōsai kenbo* by taking up issues beyond those directly concerned with domestic affairs. To be sure, Chifuren engaged in national campaigns centering on women's existence as housewives and mothers, including demanding the abolition of legalized prostitution, opposing the use of stimulant drugs by youths, mounting efforts to rid towns and villages of mosquitoes and flies, and educating wives in sanitary food-handling practices. And some mid-1950s crusades for the improvement of home life—opposition to aboveground nuclear testing and blocking the revival of the prewar family system—challenged the political status quo. Yet crusading for clean elections and requesting government funds for continuing education classes reflected the participants' identity outside the household as citizens, students, and women rather than

70. In addition to housewives' auxiliaries of labor unions, there also existed women's sections of labor unions comprised of women workers.

Two other important groups, the Postwar Committee on Countermeasures for Women (Sengo Fujin Taisaku Iinkai, established August 1945) and the Federation of Japanese Women's Organizations (Nihon Fujin Dantai Rengōkai, or Fudanren, established 1948), also employed domestic and equity arguments in explaining their activities and objectives, but lack of space prevented their inclusion in this chapter. In English, regarding the former, see Fujioka, "Women's Movements in Postwar Japan," 1–4; regarding the latter, Robins-Mowry, *Hidden Sun*, 106–7, 215, 217; National Women's Education Centre, "Women's Groups in Japan," *NWEC Newsletter* 7, no. 1 (May 1990): 5–6.

71. It is common to regard the post-1970s organizations as the second wave of the postwar women's movement, but it may be that the latter three associations, all linked to political parties and established in the wake of the 1960 U.S.-Japan Security Treaty protests, may constitute the second wave of women's activism, which would make the high postwar groups the third wave of postwar women's movements.

72. Fujioka, "Women's Movements in Postwar Japan," 49–50.

their domestic roles as wives and mothers.[73] Thus, early postwar rural women, too, redefined domesticity in order to validate and to extend their activities in the public world, but they also felt entitled to make demands for social change as women and citizens.[74]

The initial statement of the Japan Women's Council (Nihon Fujin Kaigi, established April 1962), affiliated with the Japan Socialist Party, employed the language both of equity and universal rights and of defending the home. In protesting layoffs of women workers under the guise of "rationalization," the founding prospectus defended women's right to a place outside the home; however, it also strongly emphasized women's special interest in "peace," "unemployment," "our children's education," "medical care," and "old age," as had other postwar women's movements.[75] In common with these movements, the Japan Women's Council assumed that women rather than men were guardians of family life. Yet it asked women to broaden their understanding of the world beyond the home through study of politics and economics in order to "bring about a society, truly peaceful and democratic as stated in the Constitution, in which women and children can live in true happiness."[76] The basis for women's participation in public affairs was grounded in their domestic responsibilities (that is, their difference from men) and in their constitutional rights to the suffrage and equal employment.

The objectives of the New Japan Women's Association (Shin Nihon Fujin no Kai, established October 1962), affiliated with the Japan Communist Party (JCP), emphasized the maternalist concerns of protecting "women and children from the dangers of nuclear war" and "the happiness of children," as well as two nondomestic aims, "attainment of women's rights" and "betterment of life." The emphasis on domestic and nondomestic aims also characterized the JCP's December 1945 General Plan for Women's Activities (*Fujin kōdō kōryō*), which called for an end to discrimination in employment and education, general improvement of working conditions, and special measures to protect mothers—menstrual leave, maternity leave, prenatal care, nutritional improvement, and free day care, the latter three especially for working mothers. The 1945 plan in fact had adopted a more radical stance than that of the 1962 platform, boldly calling for "rationalization and mechanization of household chores such as laundry and cooking" in keeping with the Marxist aim of liberating women to participate fully in the world outside the home.[77]

In contrast, the concerns and underlying assumptions of the All-Japan

73. Yukiko Hanawa seems to advise against asserting too strongly the nondomestic identity of rural women; "Voices from the Periphery."

74. Fujioka, "Women's Movements in Postwar Japan," 32–39.

75. At the same time, it opened with a critique of the ruling conservative party's productivity first philosophy: "despite economic growth, economic problems remain. . . . [There is a] gap between the secure and insecure—day laborers, the unemployed, middle-aged and older people, especially middle-aged women"; ibid., 59–60.

76. Ibid.

77. Ibid., 17; see also 16, 18.

Women's Federation (Zen Nihon Fujin Renmei, established 2 November 1960) seemed rather unlike those of the other early postwar women's organizations. Its single mention of hopes for "eternal peace for all mankind" was overshadowed by its nationalism, as seen in its aspirations to "love our fellow countrymen and our country and our Japanese heritage"; "endeavor to safeguard . . . our culture of long tradition"; and "strive toward prosperity and happiness for our people."[78] However, statements such as "one still finds a confusion of ideas, warped education, and an increase in the number of juvenile delinquents" and "we aim to safeguard our families" suggested a strong streak of maternalism. Its willingness to call on men in defining its ultimate aims—six men initially served as advisers and consultants to the organization—seemed rooted in the prewar conception of *ryōsai kenbo,* which denied women's autonomy and moral authority.[79]

The Logic of High Postwar Movements: Beyond Ryōsai kenbo
The women's movements of the 1970s rejected new interpretations of *ryōsai kenbo* (that is, women's difference) as justification for activism, although such ideas had not been completely absent in the early postwar era. Here I touch on the views of the Women's Democratic Club, an early postwar organization, then turn to late postwar activism, treating the Fighting Women's Group (Gurūpu Tatakau Onna, established 1970); Tanaka Mitsu, one of its central figures; Atsumi Ikuko, a late 1970s activist; and the views of the five prominent women activists at the 1990 symposium "Japanese Women Speak Out: A Public Forum."[80] The influence of the ideas of the latest postwar wave of women's movements cannot be inferred simply from their numerical strength. Extensive media coverage of leading individuals and groups carried their views on womanhood and society and their proposals for change to a nationwide audience despite the small membership of these newest women's movements. In 1990, spurred no doubt by significant postwar demographic and economic changes of earlier years, the debates concerning the goals, issues, and justifications of women's activism had not yet ended.[81] Nevertheless, the muting of maternalist and wifeist arguments in the ideals of the Women's Democratic Club, founded during the occupation; the maternalist influence on the Fighting Women's Group's leader, Tanaka Mitsu; and the personal and organizational ties between first- and second-wave activists cautioned against assuming a great disjuncture between pre- and post-1970 women's movements.

78. Ibid., 56.
79. Ibid., 56–57.
80. In English, see also Buckley's essay in this volume; Chizuko Ueno, "Women's Labor under Patriarchal Capitalism in the Eighties," *Review of Japanese Culture and Society* 3, no. 1 (Dec. 1989): 1–9; Taeko Tomioka, Chizuko Ueno, Noriko Mizuta, Miriam M. Johnson, Myra Strober, and Miho Ogino, "Symposium, Women and the Family: Post-Family Alternatives," *Review of Japanese Culture and Society* 3, no. 1 (Dec. 1989): 79–96.
81. The impact of these changes on women's estate is also treated in Buckley's essay in this volume.

The absence of appeals to action as wives and mothers was striking in the aims of one very early organization, the Women's Democratic Club (Fujin Minshu Kurābu, established March 1946).[82] Its founding statement advocated "democratization of women so that never again could women be led to war blindly" and "to attain and safeguard peace—the great prerequisite to happiness," but it did not seek only women's, children's, or the family's well-being.[83] Yet the statement's warmth, feeling, and choice of words express an earnest appeal to the idealism of ordinary Japanese women:

> Every woman must bury her oppressive past and rise up with courage and prudence with the wisdom befitting a woman who devotes herself to the building of a bright and healthy Japan. . . . We must come to a [self-]realization of the life-potential that rests in women and of its importance in the building of a happy society. . . . We Japanese women who truly love life will spare no effort; we Japanese women who earnestly seek a guarantee of peace and happiness from society will endeavor to develop our abilities . . . by giving frank utterance to our true feelings about our aspirations . . . and by learning the means through which we can attain our wishes . . . [we are] about to sail forth on the ocean of goodwill of the millions of Japanese women whose future knows no limit.[84]

A quarter of a century later two hundred helmeted women marched in an October 1970 peace demonstration under banners reading "What is femininity?" and "Mother, is marriage really bliss?" heralding the emergence of a woman's movement explicitly rejecting domesticity as women's inevitable destiny. The hallmark of the post-1970 wave of the Japanese women's movement was its insistence that women should be free to choose *not* to become mothers and wives. Thus, many of the newer organizations struggled not simply to expand women's public influence as wives and mothers but to increase their domestic autonomy and open new avenues of participation outside the home. Their efforts ranged from maintaining access to abortion and improving access to the birth control pill to help free women from unwanted reproductive responsibilities to pushing for greater equity in the workplace to lessen women's economic dependence on men and to establishing female enterprises suited to the needs of women workers.[85]

"Why Sexual Liberation? A Prospectus on Women's Liberation" (10 October 1970), the first manifesto of the Fighting Women's Group (leaders of that October 1970 contingent), identified the postwar cult of productivity (*seisansei shijōshugi*) as the logic of men and asserted that the questioning of "production first" thinking that informed popular struggles against the Vietnam War and pollution at home also hoisted a standard for women's revolt. The Fighting Women's Group pro-

82. The founders included leading Communist and Socialist women such as Miyamoto Yuriko, Hani Setsuko, Sata Ineko, Matsuoka Yōko, Katō Shizue, Akamatsu Tsuneko.

83. Fujioka, "Women's Movements in Postwar Japan," 19.

84. Ibid., 21–22.

85. Inoue, "Ūman ribu"; "Japanese Women Speak Out: A Forum," Japan Society, New York City, 31 May 1990.

posed immediate action on only one issue, opposition to the criminal abortion law, although it later took part in the 1973 coalition opposing tightening of the Eugenic Protection Law. The manifesto offered an idealistic, rather individualistic approach to freedom: "the liberation of the female sex can in fact be attained as self-liberation from consciousness which denies sex in daily interactions with men and in struggles against authority."[86] Its leading figure, Tanaka Mitsu, criticized the Japanese family system (*ie seido*) as well as existing forms of marriage and domesticity although she displayed much concern for the emotional needs of children and mothers in *Inochi no onnatachi e,* the book that made her the best known of the group's members.[87] The fact "that Japanese weapons and trucks . . . were killing Vietnamese children" partially motivated Tanaka's new left activism, which in turn led her to discover women's issues.[88] Her criticism of the prewar family and capitalism and her desire to cherish human life have much in common with the logic of earlier women's movements. Yet as she hurled probing questions such as "Can a woman live as a wife, as a mother although she doesn't live as a woman?" and "What is it to live as a woman and what in the world is a woman?" Tanaka's rejection of domestic roles helped carry female critiques of existing society beyond earlier discourses.

Another new-wave thinker was Atsumi Ikuko, scholar, poet, and founder of the journal *Feminist (Feminisuto)*.[89] In 1980 Atsumi advocated broadening the range of life choices open to women (and to men as well).

> Generally men's role is the production of materials outside and women's role lies in the production of life at home. So, a big difference exists between men's and women's values. Japanese feminist theory considers that both are equally important. Men should be more involved in the production of life, and women, in the production of materials. . . . The current feminist movement aims at the kind of society in which a woman can not only be economically independent but also be free to choose the way she wants to live. In such a society, if she wants to be a housewife, it's all right, but a woman who wants to work can do so without being discriminated against. It seeks to change roles not only in the family but also in society.
>
> Consistency, logicality, responsibility, planning ability, and leadership are regarded as masculine values, while sensitivity, altruistic love, nurturing ability, and amiability are regarded as feminine values. I hope they will be indistinguishable in the twenty-first century.[90]

86. M. Tanaka, *Inochi no onnatachi.* Another anticapitalist, anti-imperialist feminist group is Asian Women's Liberation (Ajia Josei Kaihō), with well-known members such as Matsuoka Yōko and Matsui Yayori. In English, see Robins-Mowry, *Hidden Sun,* 224; Mackie, "Feminist Politics," 67–68, 84; Vera Mackie, "Multinational Sex in Asia," in McCormack and Sugimoto, *Japanese Trajectory,* 229.

87. Two of the four chapters, "Personal History" and "Female Child Murderers and Liberation," totaling about one-third of the body of the text, treat these issues; M. Tanaka, *Inochi no onnatachi,* 93–146, esp. 130, 173–218.

88. Ibid., 125.

89. Anonymous, "Interview with Atsumi Ikuko," *Feminist International,* no. 2 (1980): 89. Regarding other feminist publications, see Buckley's essay in this work.

90. Anonymous, "Interview with Atsumi," 89.

By refusing to claim that nurturing, love, and sensitivity are innate feminine values, Atsumi could seek for men and women to become more like one another rather than for women as wives and mothers to continue indefinitely as the more nurturing sex.

The views of the five well-known panelists in "Japanese Women Speak Out: A Public Forum" revealed influences from post-1970s women's movements. Although the participants agreed that motherhood was still important to Japanese women, they all sought ways to broaden women's participation in the work force. Takahashi Masumi, housewife, writer, and grass-roots activist with the national women's networking group Agora, described ways in which older married women could start businesses allowing them to combine homemaking, individual satisfaction, and income earning instead of working as marginal part-timers for existing enterprises. Sugahara Bando Mariko, a division chief in the Statistics Bureau of Japan's General Management Agency, spoke of government plans to fund elder-care assistance programs, which would help free women for careers or other pursuits outside the home. Wakita Naoe, president of Dentsū Eye, discussed the rise of women-owned businesses and the need for more women in management-level positions, although she also noted that conservatives still attempted to dissuade young women from working outside the home. Ueno Chizuko, sociologist and social critic, observed that women's experiences in the labor force ranged from part-timers to entrepreneurs and career-track employees but called for a "feminization of work" rather than a "masculinization of women." Shimomura Mitsuko, editor-in-chief of one of Japan's top weeklies, *Asahi Journal*, labeled "Japan, Inc." "a machine created for the purpose of improving productivity that keeps churning on" although the issue had become the "quality of life." As though acting on Ueno's recommendation, on assuming her position Shimomura commanded her five male deputy editors to take off at least four days a month. In the late postwar era, not only Ueno and Shimomura but also other individuals and groups encouraged men to cut back on their committments to work in order to increase male involvement in child care, elder care, daily chores, and leisure at home, which in turn would aid women's escape from domesticity. In 1991, although there were ample signs that some women sought increased participation in the public world, there were also indications that many were reluctant to abandon their "difference" from men, especially as mothers.

CONCLUSION

Postwar Transformations of Ryōsai kenbo *and Women's Movements*

It is hardly surprising that the aging male politicians, bureaucrats, and businessmen who crafted postwar state and corporate policies still expected women to center their lives around housekeeping, childrearing, and submissiveness to husband and officials, much like the *ryōsai kenbo* ideal of prewar years. But it is also important to note that even conservatives modified their vision of womanhood in the postwar era. For example, they have accepted greater participation of women in local affairs—as citizens and community officials concerned about local development, education, and pollution. They did not block the employment of married women outside the home, although they constantly warned working wives and mothers not to neglect their home responsibilities. Given the long working hours of men and the scarcity of labor at present, even staunch supporters of female domesticity condone, rather grudgingly, women's activities outside the home. The alternative would have been unfilled jobs and impoverished local community life, for there were low-level positions in the economy and polity that men were too busy to occupy.[91]

The vitality and diversity of postwar Japanese women's movements has been impressive. Initially eager to extend the influence of the "good wife and wise mother" beyond the home, they sought to sustain family life under the desperate, chaotic conditions of the early postwar years and to attain lasting peace and happiness for women and children through social reform. The early postwar women's movements contested major aspects of defense, employment, welfare, fiscal, legal, and educational policies as they struggled to reshape Japan's social environment to fit newly empowered wives' and mothers' visions of a healthy family, society, and world. Their struggles, grounded in assumptions of women's difference from men, won significant victories. These arguments have remained persuasive, and in 1991 many organizations founded in the early postwar years were still active.

In denying the inevitability of wifehood and motherhood and asserting a woman's right to choose to contribute to home life, public life, or both domains, post-1970s postwar women's movements chose to jettison rather than to reshape the conception of *ryōsai kenbo*. While accepting women's differences from men, they emphasized opening to individual women full participation in all aspects of the world beyond the home or drastically reconstructing the world more than pressing collectively to influence decisions made by male authorities. Thus, women's movements of the late postwar era tended to advocate choices for women beyond the home—that women be able to occupy positions of power in the polity and economy and that they be free not to marry or to have children. At times, the new wave of female activists has issued far-ranging critiques of the Japanese family, economy, state, and culture as institutions of male control. In 1991 it was difficult to fully assess the achievements and influence of these new women's movements. The mass base of post-1970s women's movements was small; the vast majority of women lacked the educational attainments or personality traits required for career-track employment and, rather than regarding the family as a source of oppression, viewed it as a wellspring of personal satisfaction. Yet many factors, including implementation of the Equal Employment Opportu-

91. Chizuko Ueno, "The Japanese Women's Movement: The Counter-Values to Industrialism," in McCormack and Sugimoto, *Japanese Trajectory,* 178–84. In 1990 articles regarding immigrant laborers appeared fairly frequently in the Japanese press (see for example *Sekai,* Jan. 1990); this was not the case when I was in Japan in summer 1987.

nity Act since 1986 and the rising proportion of women in the labor force, especially working mothers, may increase the appeal of the ideas of post-1970s women's movements, which tended to be grounded in arguments of equality to a greater extent than difference.[92]

The women's movements that rejected *ryōsai kenbo* may have had their genesis in the rising (though not universal) prosperity of the high postwar era, which encouraged a shift away from the early postwar emphasis on family survival and permitted consideration of possibilities for women beyond the home. During the early postwar era women took on the role of guardians of the household and nurturers of life and banded together under desperate conditions to try to achieve a minimal subsistence; acting as wives and mothers, they gained a measurable degree of influence in political and economic affairs. Later, with ample food, clothing, shelter, and fuel readily at hand, it became possible for women to aspire to an even greater range of activities and influence in society. The pursuit of wider options for women seemed consistent with late postwar trends in consumption—the shift from concern for meeting subsistence minima to improvement of the quality of life discussed in the essays by Kelly and Horioka.

The postwar women's movements clearly had prewar antecedents, but they differed in two important respects from their predecessors. In the 1930s and 1940s women also strove to expand their influence as wives and mothers beyond the home, and to some extent they succeeded.[93] However, there were clearly defined limits to what they could achieve. First, only those movements whose aims coincided with state goals were tolerated, which suggests that "success" was less a case of women influencing the state than the state using or co-opting women's initiatives. Second, the fact that *ryōsai kenbo* ideology extolled submissiveness as a female virtue and that the law denied women suffrage or the right to form political organizations stunted prewar organizational growth. After 1945 the early postwar ideology of "democracy" and rights granted by the new constitution provided legal protection and legitimacy to women's organizations, greatly increasing their capacity to recruit new members and to exert social and political influence.

Indeed, the achievements of postwar women's movements positively shaped Japanese society. The efforts of postwar women's organizations, at times in alliance with each other and with other mass movements, blocked the legal reinstatement of the prewar family system in 1954; abolished legalized prostitution in 1956; affected price, quality, and safety of consumer goods after 1960; sparked drives to obtain settlements for pollution victims and local communities threatened by environmental degradation after the mid-1960s; prevented tightening of the abortion law in 1973 and 1982; and after two decades of effort, removed the home economics requirement for high school girls. In other words, they

92. See Buckley's essay in this volume. See also Michiko Takahashi, "Working Mothers and Families," *Review of Japanese Culture and Society* 3, no. 1 (Dec. 1989): 21–30, esp. 23–24.

93. As I mentioned earlier, egalitarian arguments and proposals for increasing women's influence in society were eclipsed in this ultranationalist era.

helped shape the economic, political, and social contours of postwar Japanese society. Yet Japan in 1991 would have been a different world if all the campaigns of postwar women's movements had succeeded, for a number of important struggles that challenged the policies of the LDP and the business establishment did not achieve their objectives. These campaigns included opposition to layoffs of full-time female employees in the 1940s and 1950s; demands for equality in the workplace throughout the period; and protests against nuclear weapons and U.S. military bases, strongest before 1970.[94]

The Logic of Women's Movements

In postwar Japanese discourses on women, the prevalence of arguments concerning women's ability to bear children and their responsibility for childrearing and household management—in short, concerning some of women's differences from men—was striking. Such notions appeared in the thinking of a very wide range of women's organizations and in the views of the male-dominated conservative establishment as well. With the exception of the Democratic Women's Club, organizations questioning wifehood and motherhood as women's sole destiny emerged only in the latter half of the postwar era; furthermore, their membership was much smaller than that of early postwar associations, such as the Housewives' Association and the National Coordinating Council of Regional Women's Organizations, whose activism was strongly rooted in transformations of *ryōsai kenbo*.

Exploration of justifications for postwar women's movements in Japan, however, also resonates with the terms of an ongoing debate among historians of the Atlantic world concerning the nature of women's movements and feminism.[95]

94. Mackie, "Feminist Politics," 60–76; National Women's Education Centre, "Women's Groups in Japan," *NWEC Newsletter* 7, no. 1 (May 1990): 6; Yayori Matsui, "Protest and the Japanese Woman," *Japan Quarterly* 22, no. 1 (Jan.–Mar. 1975): 32–39. See also Upham's and Buckley's essays in this volume. Regarding the women's participation in the environmental movement, see Matsui, "Protest"; Robins-Mowry, *Hidden Sun*, 240; Etsuko Kaji, "Kawasaki Steel: The Giant at Home," *AMPO: Japan-Asia Quarterly Review* 9, no. 4 (Oct. 1978): 31–32; Kurt Steiner, Ellis S. Krauss, and Scott C. Flanagan, eds., *Political Opposition and Local Politics in Japan* (Princeton: Princeton University Press, 1980), chaps. 6–8; Margaret McKean, *Environmental Protest and Citizen Politics in Japan* (Berkeley and Los Angeles: University of California Press, 1981), esp. 83–88, 108–18, 127–28; and Jeffrey Broadbent, "Progress and Pollution: Industrial Growth Versus Environmental Protection in a Japanese Community" (manuscript), chap. 8. A rereading of these works, save Broadbent, suggests that additional studies more fully analyzing participation along gender lines will lead to new appreciation of women's activism in these movements. In Japanese, see S. Tanaka, *Josei kaihō* 2:41–63, 178–214; Maruoka Hideko, ed., *Nihon fujin mondai shiryō shūsei*, vols. 8–9; Itoya Toshio and Esashi Akiko, *Sengoshi to josei no kaihō* (Tokyo: Gōdō Shuppan, 1977); Kanamori Toshie, *Jinbutsu fujin undōshi* (Tokyo: Rōdō Kyōiku Sentā, 1980); Joseigaku kenkyūkai, ed., *Onna wa sekai o kaeru, Kōza joseigaku* 3 (Tokyo: Keisō Shobō, 1986), 1–135.

95. Karen Offen, "Defining Feminism: A Comparative Historical Approach," *Signs: A Journal of Women in Culture and Society* 14 (1988): 119–57; comments by Nancy Cott and Ellen Dubois, *Signs: A Journal of Women in Culture and Society* 15 (Autumn 1989): 195–209; Naomi Black, *Social Feminism* (Ithaca: Cornell University Press, 1989); Nancy Cott, *The Grounding of Modern Feminism* (New Haven: Yale University Press, 1987).

Karen Offen has found "two distinct modes of historical argumentation or discourse that have been used by women and their male allies on behalf of women's emancipation from male control in Western societies," the "relational" and the "individualist." Relational feminist arguments "proposed a gender-based but egalitarian vision of social organization" and "emphasized women's rights *as women* (defined principally by their child bearing and/or nurturing capacities in relation to men)"; by contrast, "individualist arguments posited the individual, irrespective of sex or gender, as the basic unit."[96] Naomi Black proposes "to identify two strands of feminism, which reach from the origins of the movement into the present and the future: equity feminism and social feminism." Equity feminism would "extend rights now enjoyed by other groups . . . to women"; social feminism "would fit into the category of role extension if such a term existed," for "its arguments extrapolate from the accepted domestic role of women."[97] Third, in contrasting a "woman movement" composed of three streams arising in the nineteenth century with "feminism," which developed after the second decade of the twentieth century, Nancy Cott avoids the dichotomies of Offen's relational-social feminisms or Black's individualist-equity feminisms, instead identifying an unresolved tension between arguments based on women's "difference" from men and those based on sex or gender equality in the earlier "woman movement."[98] Its successor, the feminist movement, felt no need for women to inhabit existing gender roles and in fact offered "a critique of gender hierarchy" embedded in "a critique of the social system," which "reactivated demands for women's rights."[99]

The prominent wifeist, maternalist, and guardian-of-the-home arguments in postwar Japanese women's movements might seem to fit Offen's or Black's categorization; however, like Cott, I prefer to avoid dichotomies altogether, for two reasons. First, along with others pursuing women's history and women's studies I question the tendency in Western academic reasoning to establish binary oppositions, which can obscure the richness and diversity of the object or phenomenon under investigation.[100] Linda Alcoff's warning about the need to "proceed with historical and sociological analysis without ever losing sight of the need to problematize key concepts" is relevant here.[101] The analyses of feminism by Josephine Donovan, Alison Jaggar, and Rosemary Tong, which posit multiple streams of feminism, also have much to offer those pursuing women's history and gender

---

96. Offen, "Defining Feminism," 134–35.

97. Black, *Social Feminism*, 28–29.

98. Cott, *Grounding of Modern Feminism*, 18–19, 20.

99. Ibid., 35, 37. Cf. "self-development as contrasted to self-sacrifice or submergence in the family"; ibid., 39.

100. Scott, *Gender*, 10–11, 25–27, 40–41; Kondo, *Crafting Selves*, 31–48; Uno, "Women and Changes"; and Nancy Hartsock, "The Feminist Standpoint: Developing the Ground for a Specifically Feminist Historical Materialism," in Sandra Harding and Merrill B. Hintikka, eds., *Discovering Reality* (Dordrecht: D. Reidel, 1983), 297.

101. Alcoff, "Cultural Feminism," 426.

studies.[102] Too much attention to a single opposition—whether it is maternal versus nonmaternal women's movements, relational versus individualistic feminism, or social versus equity feminism—obscures other issues such as the relationships between feminism and racism, materialism, or Orientalism.[103] Second, numerous postwar Japanese women's organizations and campaigns drew both on arguments grounded in the extension of *ryōsai kenbo* and on equity arguments of various types in validating their existence and concerns. That is, many women activists did not dichotomize social and equity (or relational and individualist) arguments and assumptions. Some pursued both sorts of reasoning; many formed coalitions with organizations holding views differing from their own on numerous occasions.[104]

And the Future?

Late postwar demands for the extension of workplace protection to men are worth noting. Instead of assuming a need to protect women because of their "difference" as childbearers and childrearers or pursuing equality with overworked male workers by eliminating regulations protecting female employees, some advocates for women asked that protection in the form of shorter working hours be extended to men to give them time to care for their children and elderly parents. Strikingly, one suburban Tokyo city government granted the request of its employees' union for equal childrearing leave for fathers. In 1991 it was still not clear whether this was an isolated event or the beginning of a new trend in Japanese employment policies.[105] Regardless of the outcome, these seemed to be demands for men's or human liberation rather than for the progress or advancement of women alone.

Despite these gains, "good wife, wise mother" still informed the policy propos-

102. Josephine Donovan, *Feminist Theory: The Intellectual Traditions of American Feminism* (New York: Ungar, 1986); Alison Jaggar, *Feminist Politics and Human Nature* (Totowa, N.J.: Rowman and Littlefield, 1983); and Rosemary Tong, *Feminist Thought: A Comprehensive Introduction* (Boulder, Colo.: Westview Press, 1989).

103. Alcoff, "Cultural Feminism"; Barbara Christian, "The Race for Theory," in *Feminist Studies* 14, no. 1 (Spring 1988): 67–79; Trinh T. Minh-ha, "Difference: A Special Third World Issue," *Discourse* 8 (Fall–Winter 1986–87): 11–38; Judith Williamson, "Woman Is an Island," in Tania Modleski, ed., *Studies in Entertainment: Critical Approaches to Mass Culture* (Bloomington: Indiana University Press, 1986), 99–118; Rema Hamami and Martina Rieker, "Feminist Orientalism and Orientalist Marxism," *New Left Review*, no. 170 (July–Aug. 1988): 93–109.

104. This group included the Mothers' Congress as well as coalitions opposing revival of the family system in 1954 and the tightening of the abortion law in 1973 and 1982.

105. Ueno, "Japanese Woman's Movement," 180. Further, passage of the May 1991 Childcare Leave Law, which allows male and female regular employees to stay home to care for children under age one, suggested that a new trend toward greater gender equality in home and workplace might indeed be emerging. However, the limitations of the law were significant, for it failed to mandate paid leave and excluded part-time and, until 1 April 1995, small-business employees (both of which include high proportions of women). Etuko Furuhashi, "The Childcare Leave Law," *NWEC Newsletter* 8, no. 2 (Nov. 1991): 7–11.

als of some conservative officials. At a private meeting of politicians in July 1990 Aizawa Hideyuki, director-general of the Economic Planning Agency, expressed a strong desire for Japanese women to place racial and national interests above personal gratification and to have larger families:

> There is a mood [in Japan] to enjoy life, rather than giving birth and suffering. . . . Many Japanese women have entered university and taken a job and that will lead them to marry late and have a shorter time for having babies. . . . At every wedding reception that I have attended, . . . I speak out and say that if this excellent Japanese tribe is on its way to becoming extinct, then I cannot die easily.[106]

And in an October 1990 address to the United Nations' (UN) Summit for Children, Prime Minister Kaifu Toshiki, a former education minister, advocated that "the education of girls be recognized, as they are the mothers of the future." The prime minister's thinking replicated prewar *ryōsai kenbo*—women in Japan, and elsewhere, too, should be educated to labor in private to serve state needs— although postwar state goals emphasized maintaining the productivity and prosperity and training upright citizens rather than expanding the monarch's realm. In contrast, Nafis Sadik, executive director of the UN Population Fund, declared that "education, health, and well-being of girls should be an end in itself."[107]

Yet in the late postwar era there were indications that significant numbers of Japanese women had aspirations beyond childbearing, childrearing, and household management. Survey results revealed that in Tokyo in 1981, 23 percent of female junior high graduates, 27 percent of female high school graduates, 30 percent of female junior college graduates, and 42 percent of women college graduates opposed the statement "Men should work outside and women should guard the home."[108] And men's views may have been shifting as well. Also in 1981, when Tokyo men and women replied to the question "Is the division of labor by sex irrational?" two-thirds of working women and full-time housewives (66 and 63 percent respectively) answered yes, while well over half (60 percent) of the husbands of working wives and nearly half (45 percent) of the husbands of full-time housewives also agreed.[109] An August 1987 survey of 5,000 men and women nationwide indicated that, although only 24.7 percent of the respondents felt that "it is all right for women not to get married," only about half (43 percent) agreed with the statement "Men work, women take care of the home." And a 1990 Prime Minister's Office survey found that only 34.7 percent of 1,655 male

106. Clayton Jones, "Japanese Leaders Lament Baby Deficit," *Christian Science Monitor*, 3 Aug. 1990, n.p. Many thanks to Kenneth Kusmer for calling my attention to this article.

107. Jocelyn Ford, "Kaifu Unveils Fund for Literacy in Asia," *Japan Times*, 1 Oct. 1990, 1. I am grateful to Andrew Gordon for calling my attention to this article. Buckley's chapter contains analysis of similar remarks made on 18 June 1990 by Finance Minister Hashimoto Ryūtarō.

108. Sodei Takako, "Kazoku no henka to josei no yakuwari," in Joseigaku Kenkyūkai, ed., *Onnatachi no ima*, 63.

109. Ibid.

and 25.1 percent of 2,096 female respondents (both sexes, 29.3 percent) agreed with that formulation of gender roles.[110] Nonetheless, the attitudes of young urban women hinted that the demise of "Women's place is in the home" loomed on the horizon in the future.

And what of the future of scholarship on "good wife, wise mother" and other issues in women's and gender history in postwar Japan? In tracing the postwar trajectory of *ryōsai kenbo*, this essay has pursued one of a myriad of questions scholars can ask about the history of women in Japan since 1945. Yet some of the issues and themes deserving further attention should be apparent. We need additional investigation of many aspects of postwar wifehood and motherhood, including class differences in norms and practices; further analysis of the ideologies, leaders, organizations, and activities of postwar women's movements; and much more study of postwar masculinity. Still there remain other unanswered questions. Although individual women may have had doubts and dissatisfactions, in the West the prevailing images of the postwar Japanese woman have been those of the contented housewife and devoted mother or the shy, submissive, exotic. Yet I contend that to investigate postwar womanhood, gender, and society, we need to comprehend the logic, membership, duration, and impact of postwar Japanese women's movements and to reconcile their characteristics with our image of women in postwar Japan. Moreover, the dynamism of women's movements suggests that without further consideration of the role of women and women's organizations in the labor, environmental, antinuclear, consumer, and other mass movements that shaped society and culture since 1945, we can achieve only a *partial* understanding of postwar Japan.

110. National Women's Education Centre, "Survey Results: Public Opinion Survey on Women," *NWEC Newsletter* 4, no. 2 (Nov. 1987): 4; Naikaku Soridaijin Kānbō Hōkoku Shitsu, *Josei ni kansuru seron chōsa* (Tokyo: Naikoku Soridaijin Kanbō Hōkoku Shitsu, 1991), 1, 27–28. Regarding results of 1972 and 1979 prime minister's office polls by age and sex, see Sodei, "Kazoku," 62.

PART IV

Democratic Promise and Practice

CHAPTER TWELVE

Unplaced Persons
and Movements for Place

Frank K. Upham

At the end of World War II Japan faced the necessity of developing its own form of democracy. Prewar development had been cut short by institutional weaknesses and political events, but defeat created a range of possibilities for political development that rivaled even those of the Meiji period. More than in any other time in history the Japanese people were free—indeed, were forced—to create their own vision of democracy and social justice. The legal and political reforms of the occupation established the initial context for political development within which a new constitution and revised legal system were to establish individual liberties and the rule of law as the cornerstones of Japan's new democracy. The goals of the Allies were consistent with the views of many progressive Japanese as well. In 1946 Maruyama Masao identified the failure of Japanese law to recognize and protect "the internal freedom of the individual" as a major cause of the failure of Japan's democracy.[1]

It should not surprise us, however, that the democracy and legal system that eventually evolved diverged in important ways from the reformers' initial expectations. The relationships among individuals and groups, the status of marginal groups within mainstream society, and the visions of justice that emerged were the product of the particular history and politics of postwar Japan, not the reflection of Western influence or progressive ideals. To discover this form of democracy and to gain insight into the role of law in Japanese society, we need to examine therefore not only the intentions and ideals behind the original institutions but also the history of the legal and political struggles for equality and justice that animated postwar Japan.

Women were particular beneficiaries of legal reform. Article 14 of the new

1. Masao Maruyama, *Thought and Behaviour in Modern Japanese Politics* (London: Oxford University Press, 1963), 1–24.

constitution guaranteed equality before the law for all Japanese and prohibited discrimination based on "race, creed, sex, social status, or family origin." Article 24 guaranteed individual freedom in choosing a spouse and the equality of the sexes within marriage, both principles directly contrary to earlier practice, and required that legislation concerning choice of spouse, property rights, inheritance, choice of domicile, divorce, and other matters pertaining to marriage and family should guarantee the "essential equality of the sexes." Accordingly, the family law provisions of the Civil Code were revised to eliminate preferential treatment for males, including provisions regulating parental power, child custody, mutual support, and divorce. In employment the Labor Standards Act of 1947 specifically prohibited wage discrimination based on sex and created a wide range of legal protections for women workers.

Another goal of legal reform was the elimination of discrimination against minorities. The largest ethnic minority consisted of Korean residents and Japanese nationals of Korean origin, but there were also significant numbers of Chinese residents and a smaller number of Ainu, the aboriginal inhabitants of northern Honshu and Hokkaido. All suffered from some degree of discrimination, but perhaps the best-known minority in Japan was racially and ethnically indistinguishable from other Japanese. The Burakumin were descendants of outcaste groups who followed occupations, such as grave digger or butcher, considered unclean in Tokugawa society and who were legally excluded from human society.[2] Despite titular emancipation in 1871 the Burakumin continued to suffer severe social discrimination throughout the prewar period, and the inclusion of "social status" in Article 14 and similar protections against discrimination in statutes like the Labor Standards Act were directed specifically at their liberation.

But eliminating discrimination against minorities and women was only part of an even more fundamental goal. The intent of the drafters of the constitution and other liberal legislation was to accomplish nothing less than the legal, political, and social emancipation of the Japanese individual. To do so, they had to overcome what Japan's leading postwar sociologist of law, Kawashima Takeyoshi, identified as the "weak legal consciousness" of Japanese: a tendency to forego the assertion of legal rights and to submit to the demands of the group and social superiors.[3] To Japanese intellectuals such as Maruyama and Kawashima true democracy demanded not only equality for women, Burakumin, and other groups but also ordinary citizens who were willing and able to enforce legal rights even when social pressure demanded conformity and submission.

This essay attempts an initial appraisal of the postwar history of constitutional

2. George deVos and Hiroshi Wagatsuma, *Japan's Invisible Race: Caste in Culture and Personality* (Berkeley and Los Angeles: University of California Press, 1966), although outdated, is still a valuable introduction to the origins and history of the Burakumin.

3. Takeyoshi Kawashima, "Dispute Resolution in Contemporary Japan," in Arthur Taylor von Mehren, ed., *Law in Japan: The Legal Order in a Changing Society* (Cambridge: Harvard University Press, 1963), 41–72.

rights and democratic practice by looking at persons who have historically been denied entry into the mainstream institutions of Japan and by asking whether they have been able to find a place within Japanese society. I have chosen Burakumin, women workers, and victims of industrial pollution. The condition of the first two groups will give us some idea of the degree of realization of the ideal of equality in the postwar period. The reaction of pollution victims and other ordinary citizens to severe industrial pollution will give us a sense of whether the traditional legal consciousness continued or whether the average Japanese became willing to pursue his or her individual rights despite social and political pressure.

THE BURAKUMIN

The postwar treatment of Burakumin and the government's attempt to eliminate Buraku discrimination contrasted sharply with the American approach to civil rights. The United States outlawed discrimination against minorities and encouraged their employment through affirmative action. The goal was the integration of minorities into mainstream economic and social life by prohibiting discrimination as they applied to schools, looked for work, or bought a house. Meanwhile, little direct assistance or attention was given to the condition of minorities as a group. As a result, individual African Americans and members of other minorities have been able to gain positions of economic, social, and political power in society while the general condition of minorities has improved little if at all after the 1960s.

The Japanese approach was quite different: individual Burakumin were given little help in entering the mainstream, but Burakumin as a group received large amounts of financial and material assistance in improving their standard of living. The result was the mirror image of the situation of African Americans. The ghettos where most Burakumin live were dramatically improved. New schools, community centers, and apartment blocks were built; roads were widened; sewage, electricity, and other utilities were installed or upgraded; and police and fire protection was enhanced. Similarly, and again in contrast to the situation for many African Americans, educational attainment improved, substantially narrowing the gap with majority Japanese. Although Buraku groups complained that much remained to be done, no one disputed that tremendous improvements were made or that Burakumin were better off than before the programs began.

Viewed from the perspective of the individual, however, the situation was less promising. Despite the constitutional prohibition against state discrimination, there was no law banning private Buraku discrimination. Aside from haphazard judicial developments and a few specific provisions in occupation-era statutes such as the Labor Standards Law, it remained perfectly legal, for example, for employers to refuse to hire Burakumin or for universities to reject Buraku applicants. And they did. The result was the almost total absence of acknowledged Burakumin in elite universities and in any but menial occupations. Available statistics were unreliable, but there were few of the "success stories" of Burakumin breaking into elite mainstream society as business leaders, politicians, or national bureaucrats that were relatively common for American minorities.

Efforts to Eliminate Buraku Discrimination

The reasons for this approach were historical as well as political and legal. Before the war the Buraku movement had been identified with leftist causes and had even managed to elect its leader, Matsumoto Jiichirō, to the Imperial Diet from a district with only a minority of Buraku voters. After Japan's defeat the newly formed Buraku Liberation League (BLL) renewed social and political efforts for equality and forged close ties to the Japanese Communist Party (JCP) and the Japanese Socialist Party (JSP). Throughout the 1950s and early 1960s the BLL's participation in a wide range of leftist causes helped gain wider recognition for the justice of their demands, and in the early 1960s the BLL successfully called on leftist support in organizing a series of mass demonstrations and protest marches.

Direct political action achieved considerable success. First, local governments in areas with large numbers of Burakumin initiated *dōwa* ("harmony" or "assimilation," a term often used as a euphemism for Buraku) programs to improve the ghettos' physical environment, enhance educational attainment, and educate the general population on the evils of discrimination. Second, in 1961 the central government created the Deliberative Council for Buraku Assimilation to study the situation and recommend possible action. The council's 1965 report put the Buraku issue onto the national agenda.[4] It emphatically denied both the widely held belief that Burakumin were racially or ethnically different from other Japanese and the standard Marxist interpretation that discrimination was merely a "feudal" remnant that would disappear as Japan approached the stage of advanced capitalism. On the contrary, the report argued that discrimination was deeply rooted in the psychology of Japanese society, a society where premodern concepts of social status, family background, and group orientation were still the basis of social order. The report concluded that the Burakumin's poor conditions were directly attributable to discrimination and recommended specific legislation to address their situation.

Despite the report's conclusion that group orientation was the basis of discrimination, the resulting 1969 statute, the Special Measures Law for *Dōwa* Projects (SML), ignored this fundamental question. It provided financial incentives for governments to aid Burakumin, but it created neither legal duties on the part of government nor any legal rights for individuals. Most important, although the SML urged all citizens to strive to overcome discrimination, it did not declare discrimination illegal. Unlike American civil rights statutes, it did not enable individual Burakumin to use the courts to pursue equality of treatment. Nor did

4. For an account of the formation and history of the Deliberative Council, see Prime Minister's Office, *Dōwa taisaku no genkyō* (Tokyo: Ministry of Finance Printing Bureau, 1977). The full text of the 1965 report is appended at 220–73.

it give the government the power to do it for them. Thus, while it became more difficult politically and socially to discriminate after 1969, it remained perfectly legal, and many employers and universities continued to investigate applicants' family background and to reject those suspected of being of Buraku origin.

The SML's legal limitations were of little concern to the BLL, however, because its leaders had always been skeptical of the value of civil rights litigation. They doubted the fairness of majority judges and were not eager to see individual lawsuits detract from the solidarity of the movement or from their leadership position. For, although the SML made little difference legally, it contributed to a political climate that had enabled the BLL to convince local governments to initiate programs that transferred a significant amount of wealth to the Buraku community. Besides physical improvements, many programs included a wide range of direct cash payments to Buraku families regardless of income. In the mid-1970s in Osaka, for example, every Buraku family received various grants, allowances, subsidies, and scholarships that could easily exceed 400,000 yen annually, not including indirect benefits such as subsidized rent, new apartment blocks reserved for Burakumin, favorable interest rates on certain loans, preferential entry into public day care, and convenient access to community facilities.[5]

There were significant political costs to these transfer payments. Limiting welfare programs and public housing to Burakumin, some of whom were financially well off, created resentment among majority Japanese, many of whom were poor and in need of housing. It also led to a bitter and irreconcilable break with the JCP, which vehemently opposed such programs as unnecessary and divisive. But perhaps the most telling criticism of these programs is not what they did but what they largely failed to do: eliminate Buraku discrimination and enable individual Burakumin to move into the mainstream of Japanese society.

Permanent employment with large corporations was the aspirational norm of most Japanese, and the apparent failure of the SML and affirmative action programs to enable Burakumin to get such jobs represented a strong counterweight to its success elsewhere. The most dramatic evidence of continued discrimination in employment was the series of books, known as Buraku lists, giving the names of Buraku ghettos. Because of the difficulty of determining who is of Buraku origin, persons or companies wishing to discriminate had long hired private detectives to check on the background of prospective employees or marriage partners. Until the 1970s detectives simply inspected an individual's family registry, which was open to the public and would indicate Buraku origin. In the mid-1970s, however, the Ministry of Justice responded to BLL pressure and restricted access to family registries, greatly complicating the detectives' job.

The first of the Buraku lists appeared shortly thereafter. With such a list, an educated guess could be made about a person's background by address alone.

5. For a description of the nature and scope of these programs in the 1970s, see Frank K. Upham, "Ten Years of Affirmative Action for Japanese Burakumin: A Preliminary Report on the Law on Special Measures for *Dōwa* Projects," *Law in Japan: An Annual* 13 (1980): 39.

The first list was quickly suppressed, its author roundly condemned, and his corporate customers given a formal reprimand by the Ministry of Justice. The reprimand termed the purchase an "exceedingly pernicious violation of human rights" and urged the purchasing firms to strive for a "fuller understanding of the Buraku problem."[6] Since no law had been broken, however, no legal action was possible and the first list was quickly followed by many others; by the late 1970s at least eight separate lists had appeared and been bought by thousands of companies, individuals, and at least one university. These books were useful for one purpose alone: discriminating against Burakumin. The persistence of the authors and their market was eloquent testimony to the continuing strength of Buraku prejudice in Japan.

Despite its obvious shortcomings the SML approach satisfied most of the major actors in Buraku policy until the 1980s. The clear improvements in physical environment, educational attainment, and other areas enabled the Liberal Democratic Party (LDP) and the relevant bureaucracies to point to significant results. Corporate Japan, by contrast, could operate as usual without having to face the question of its direct responsibility for continued discrimination. Individual Burakumin, who felt the impact of continued employment discrimination most acutely, were receiving significant benefits that might be lost if the status quo were altered to emphasize personal initiative. Their advocacy organization, the BLL, had gained a broker's role in the transfer payments and stood to lose considerable financial power if government policy shifted away from group advancement. In the 1980s, however, majority resentment and budgetary constraints combined to create a political consensus that a change in policy was necessary.

The scheduled expiration of the SML in 1982 provided a focus for the debate. Arguments against the SML's extension emphasized the impropriety of extravagant *dōwa* programs and criticized the BLL's aggressive tactics for attacking discrimination. The BLL countered that much work needed to be done and that the SML should be extended and strengthened to provide a comprehensive and permanent approach to Buraku discrimination. The eventual compromise temporarily extended the SML but narrowed its focus to improvements in the physical environment, insuring that little would be done to eliminate discrimination itself.

The BLL's response was to lobby for a "basic law" directed specifically at the Buraku problem. At the time Japan had eleven basic laws that served as symbols of a permanent national commitment to certain goals and that established a framework for government policy-making in a particular area. Besides ensuring the continuation of *dōwa* projects, the appeal of a basic law for the BLL was threefold. First, it would have permanently institutionalized the national commitment to the goals of the 1965 Deliberative Council report and established a legal

6. *Asahi shinbun,* 6 June 1976.

framework for a comprehensive approach to Buraku discrimination. Second, it would have obligated the government to take specific action in a broad range of areas beyond urban renewal. Third, it would have prohibited a wide range of discriminatory acts and provided the statutory basis for direct legal attacks on discrimination. The BLL draft contained a catchall provision against any wrongful discrimination on the basis of race, ethnicity, belief, sex, physical or mental handicap, or social origin or status and specifically prohibited discrimination in recruitment or hiring, discriminatory background checks, including investigations of prospective marriage partners, and public use of discriminatory language.

By the 1980s, therefore, the BLL was ready to acknowledge the potential role for law in combating discrimination. Other participants in antidiscrimination policy-making, however, argued that the Buraku problem was on the road to solution and strongly opposed any measures except continued urban renewal projects and "enlightenment" programs intended to educate majority Japanese to the evils of discrimination. The government's fundamental position was that making discrimination illegal would create more problems than it would solve: "To root out discrimination, it is necessary to reform the psychology that gives birth to it. This can be done by enlightenment. Not only can it not be done by punishment, . . . punishment will drive discriminatory consciousness underground and harden it."[7] Legislation also raised constitutional questions. The provisions against background checks and employment discrimination, for example, threatened the freedoms of marriage and contract recognized by the constitution. Critics also argued that sanctions would have limited deterrent effect and that proving that discrimination was the cause of any particular behavior would be extremely difficult.

Affirmative Action in a Group-Oriented Society

Although neither the government nor the BLL ever spelled out the goals of Buraku strategy beyond "eliminating discrimination," one can assume that *dōwa* policy was intended to raise the general level of income and educational attainment to a point where Burakumin would have been able to compete effectively in Japanese society. Once this goal had been achieved, individuals would have had the choice to enter mainstream society without disguising their origin.

If such was the goal, the strategy failed. One wonders, furthermore, whether it ever had a chance of success under the approach chosen. Although it raised economic and educational levels, it did nothing to capitalize on these advances and in fact seemed often to diminish the chances of integration. Given the tenacity of Buraku discrimination in Japan, it does not seem likely that even full economic parity, even had it been possible, would alone have meant acceptance by ordinary Japanese. Burakumin would still have had the worst jobs with the lowest status,

7. Chiiki kaizen taisaku kyōgikai, ed., *Kihonmondai kentō bukai hōkokusho,* 5 Aug. 1986, 31.

and their economic position would have remained tenuous and dependent. There was, in short, very little point in attempting to raise the status of the group without concomitant efforts to facilitate individual mobility.

This was true precisely because of, not despite, the importance of groups in Japanese society. As long as individuals were judged by group affiliation, one might suppose that the primary goal of *dōwa* policy would have been to enable Burakumin to enter mainstream groups. Only when the individual Burakumin had an affiliation with a respected group would he or she have been able to escape identification solely as a Burakumin. Entry into other social groups need not have meant the denial of Buraku origin or rejection of the Buraku community. Individuals are always members of many groups simultaneously, but for male Japanese and their families in the postwar period the primary one was the firm. And for the government to reject this avenue of integration while stressing programs that increased the isolation of Burakumin seems to have been at best shortsighted.

The proposed legal restrictions on Buraku discrimination would seem to have been a logical first step toward integration, but most Japanese seemed much more comfortable with giving Burakumin significant amounts of money than in trying to force employers to hire them. It is hardly surprising, for example, that the LDP refused to embrace a new initiative or abandon what had become in many ways an ideal position for it. The ringing language of official proclamations on the *dōwa* problem and the conspicuous urban renewal projects served as highly visible symbols of the government's commitment to social justice while simultaneously leaving the basic structure of discrimination untouched. The magnitude of *dōwa* programs may have been a financial burden on some localities, but the political return was substantial: the impression that justice was being served with no significant restriction on the social and employment discrimination that most large firms appear to have found congenial both to their economic needs and to their conception of the company family.

WOMEN WORKERS

The place of women within postwar society largely defied the egalitarian and individualistic rhetoric of the Occupation. The image of the three-generation household advocated by the government in the late 1970s exemplified both government ideology and the reality for most Japanese women: women entered the work force after graduation from high school or college, resigned after marriage to raise children, reentered the work force in their early thirties, and then again resigned to care for elderly parents or in-laws. Despite the centrality of women's rights in postwar reforms, government and business policies toward working women have stressed not equality or freedom of choice for women but their supporting role in the household and at the workplace.

Throughout most of the postwar period these policies were extremely successful in channeling women into roles that complemented those of men and that contributed greatly to Japan's economic success. By the mid-1980s, however, this very success had combined with political and legal forces to threaten the erosion of the gender-based social order of the previous forty years and raise the possibility of increased employment opportunities for women in a way that contrasted sharply with the evolution of the Burakumin's situation.

The "Traditional" Status of Working Women

The contribution of women to the Japanese economy has always been crucial. Before World War II, women were concentrated in agriculture and light manufacturing, and their role as low-wage laborers in these sectors remained crucial after the war. Women workers later became equally indispensable in the government and service sectors, especially the financial and distribution industries, where they constituted a huge pool of well educated, moderately skilled employees with little expectation of either employment security or high wages.

Although women entered companies as permanent employees, they either resigned or were forced out on marriage or childbirth and therefore rarely acquired sufficient seniority in their initial jobs to command high wages. When they returned to the work force after childrearing, companies refused to hire them except as "temporary" or "part-time" employees, legal categories that denied them full entry into the company family. They generally could not join the union, did not receive wage increases based on seniority, and had none of the employment security or fringe benefits of regular employees. As such, no matter how long they remained as "temporary" employees of the same company or how many hours a week they worked as "part-time" employees, their status, wages, and working conditions did not improve substantially.

It does not require sophisticated economic analysis to realize the value of these women to Japan's postwar growth. Not only did they historically receive less than half of average male salaries—a ratio that steadily *declined* through the 1970s and 1980s—but the older, married reentrants provided skilled and mature labor that was relatively easy to lay off in economic downturns. Meanwhile, companies reserved their managerial and supervisory positions for their permanent employees. Thus, by structuring its wage and promotion system to stress continuity as well as duration of tenure and by making a clear legal distinction between its permanent employees and part-time and temporary ones, the typical Japanese company was able to cut costs while avoiding direct gender-based wage discrimination, which had been prohibited by the Labor Standards Law in 1947.

But the contribution of working women to postwar Japan is only partly that of productive labor for low wages. The M-shaped pattern of female participation in the labor market—high rates of participation in their early twenties before marriage, low participation while raising children, and high participation in their late thirties through fifties—also meant that women were available to maintain the Japanese family and to realize the ideal of the three-generation family. The long hours and company loyalty of the typical Japanese *sararīman* are possible only so long as there is an equally diligent and loyal wife managing virtually every aspect of household life from childrearing to budgeting. The high levels of educational attainment and low levels of social welfare spending in the postwar period can be at least in part attributed to the presence of women in the home to attend to the children's education and the care of the elderly and infirm.

It is important to stress at this point that the clarity and completeness of role differentiation in Japanese society is not attributable solely to a voluntary choice by women to stay home and eschew participation in the mainstream labor market. On the contrary, it is attributable to a substantial extent to the effective denial of choice. Japanese government and business consciously created a role for women that—at least according to poll data—was satisfying for most women and highly valued, indeed celebrated, by the rest of society. But keeping women in their "place" depended not only on making their place as attractive as possible but also on making every effort possible in a free society to limit women's choice to decline the role established for them.

If one assumes a causal relationship between the postwar consensus that women belong in the home and the social fact that virtually all of them were there, it is not at all clear that the former caused the latter. Well into the 1950s Japanese women occupied high-wage, blue-collar jobs on the shop floors of most factories. That they had virtually disappeared by the 1960s was not because they had voluntarily resigned or because young women did not wish to enter those jobs; they disappeared because Japanese companies initiated policies forcing them to resign and then refused to assign newly hired women for anything but subordinate jobs. Not only did the government not oppose these measures in the private sector, where their legality was questionable, but it actively discriminated against women itself, a practice that, because it involved direct state action, was clearly unconstitutional. Private labor unions usually went along with the exclusion of women from regular employment, so that Japanese women had little choice but to submit to a vision of society designed by men.

As of the early 1980s, therefore, it would have been extremely difficult to argue that the occupation's legal reforms had succeeded in "democratizing" women's place in Japanese society in any but a formal sense. The extension of the vote to women, the elimination of the household (*ie*) system from family law, and legal provisions excluding women from certain types of dangerous or onerous work dramatically improved women's material situation and enhanced their bargaining position vis-à-vis the men in their lives, but they did little in terms of practical freedom of choice. On the contrary, many women who were part of the surge of democratic feeling of the 1950s later argued that popular attitudes toward the role of women in the family and the workplace actually became more "traditional" during the 1960s and 1970s. Instead of a willingness to treat women as individuals and to recognize "the internal freedom of the individual" woman to choose her own role within society, economic dependence on men and identification with socially determined gender roles were stronger than at any time since before the war.

The Passage of the Equal Employment Opportunity Law

Despite enormous difficulties, individual working women resisted discrimination throughout the postwar period. Since the other major institutions of Japanese society were hostile, women frequently turned to the courts for help, and the courts generally responded favorably.[8] The Sumitomo Cement case decided by the Tokyo District Court in 1966 is typical. Plaintiff Suzuki Setsuko went to work for Sumitomo Cement in July 1960, two years after Sumitomo had introduced new policies against hiring women with more than a high school education, limiting women to support jobs, and requiring them to resign on marriage or, if unmarried, at the age of thirty. Three years later Suzuki married but refused to resign. On 17 March 1964 she was fired.

The reasons cited by Sumitomo for its introduction of a marriage retirement system were simple. As long as the company followed the common pattern of compensation by seniority rather than merit or job classification, wages of unproductive regular employees in menial positions would rise almost as fast as everyone else's. Since women entered the company as regular employees just like men, they were paid the same and enjoyed basically the same step increases each year. Because they were relegated to jobs where their productivity could not rise, however, they were soon making more than they were worth. The perceived alternatives were simple: pay women less than men or force them to retire before their wages outgrew their productivity. The almost universal response was a form of early retirement system like Sumitomo's. To Japanese companies, sex discrimination was consistent with Japan's laws and customs and seemed a natural and fair solution to a genuine dilemma.

Beginning with the Sumitomo Cement case itself, Japanese courts took a different view of both law and custom. Over the following two decades, they struck down dozens of early retirement systems and other forms of gender discrimination, and they did so despite an initial consensus that such discrimination was perfectly legal. Because the equal rights provision of Article 14 of the constitution prohibited only government discrimination, the courts could not apply it directly to private employment discrimination. Instead they used Article 90 of the Civil Code, which prohibited acts in violation of "public order and good morals," and then defined these phrases in terms of the ideals of the constitution and Article 1-2 of the Civil Code, which required that the code be interpreted consistent with the essential equality of the sexes, to conclude that any unreasonable discrimination violated Article 90. To determine that policies like Sumitomo's were unreasonable, the courts needed only note that the wage squeeze that "forced" the

---

8. The cases are discussed in Frank K. Upham, *Law and Social Change in Postwar Japan* (Cambridge: Harvard University Press, 1987), 129–65.

company to choose early retirement was a product of its own personnel policy, not the fault of its female employees.

The Sumitomo Cement line of cases gave female employees important legal protection on the job, but it did little to get women good jobs. Since employers could no longer compel early retirement, many decided to hire only women likely to retire early voluntarily. As a consequence, many firms stopped hiring female graduates of four-year universities altogether in favor of high school or junior college graduates, who the companies assumed were less likely to stay on after marriage. The result was that by the late 1970s Japan was the only advanced nation where women's employment opportunities and wages relative to men were actually declining.

The 1980s, however, saw the appearance of several factors that combined to cause the passage in 1985 of the Equal Employment Opportunity Act (EEOA) and a substantial change in the nature of employment possibilities for Japanese women. The first was the likelihood that the continuing antidiscrimination litigation would expand beyond retirement issues and restrict employers' freedom in recruiting, hiring, tracking, and promotion policies. Since the mid-1960s each successive case won by the plaintiffs had implicated a slightly different form of discrimination, and although few had directly and explicitly restricted policies beyond termination, the trend was clear enough to convince many employers that some form of accommodation was desirable.

The second factor was increasing international pressure on Japan to end overt discrimination against women. In the mid-1970s, inspired by the International Women's Year of 1975 and the United Nations' declaration of 1976–85 as the Decade for Women, the Japanese government promised to eliminate discrimination by 1985. Then at the 1980 session of the UN General Assembly, Japan signed the Convention on the Elimination of All Forms of Discrimination Against Women, formally committing the government to provide equal employment opportunity to women by 1985.

It is unlikely, however, that these two factors would have been enough to cause significant change in women's situation without a gradual revision of personnel policies for regular employees in many firms away from the one-track, seniority-based system within which all employees entered the firm with the same legal status. Before the 1980s corporations had begun to assign entering employees to one of two career tracks: a general course for subordinate jobs and an elite management track. (Some firms added a third track for specialists such as computer programmers or switchboard operators.) In the context of this restructuring of employment patterns it was relatively easy to design ways to avoid the dilemma posed by female employees during the Sumitomo Cement era, and companies began in the late 1970s and early 1980s to announce a willingness to employ women in management-track positions for the first time.

This trend accelerated dramatically in response to the EEOA and the Ministry of Labor's implementation efforts. In a remarkable reversal of the trend of the

1970s the employment rate for female university graduates climbed steeply in the 1980s and by 1988 had reached 75.2 percent, the highest rate in thirty years and approaching the figure for males of 78.8 percent. Although the majority of these women entered the general or specialist track, the mid-1980s also witnessed a media boom about the new career women: reports of the first department head at such-and-such corporation, the first Japanese woman to be transferred overseas by so-and-so securities firm, and so on were evidence of substantial changes in corporate personnel policies. For the first time, Japanese women had at least the theoretical choice to compete with Japanese men on an equal basis.

Statistically, the movement of women into management-track programs remained small, however, and the EEOA's effect on the vast majority of women was at best ambiguous. Although it urged the equal treatment of women throughout the employment relationship, the EEOA did not legally prohibit many forms of discrimination. Instead, it established mediation machinery within the Ministry of Labor to handle potential disputes. The EEOA did, however, weaken the statutory protections for ordinary working women and enabled Japanese companies to demand more of their female employees, including increased overtime, inconvenient shift work, and sudden transfers. The EEOA also did nothing to hinder the trend toward increasing use of part-time employees, most of whom were female. Nor did it reverse the decline in women's relative wages. Whatever the fate of the few women with aspirations to the boardroom, therefore, most women continued to work for low wages in jobs with little or no security.

The additional opportunities of the EEOA brought additional uncertainties, a trade-off that many Japanese women had opposed at the time of the drafting of the EEOA and which many continued to resist. But however one may appraise the changes in employment conditions for Japanese women, the employment picture of the 1980s contrasted sharply with the strict segregation of the previous decades and with the continuing stagnation and absence of choice for Japanese Burakumin. Although the situation of the average female worker may have been only indirectly affected, the social acceptance of women entering the management track in major banks and corporations must be seen as a significant step toward liberating all Japanese from the communal and hierarchic social structure and consciousness that intellectuals like Maruyama and Kawashima saw as a major impediment to full democracy. To determine whether and how much that consciousness changed more generally, however, we need to examine how ordinary citizens defend their interests against holders of superior social and economic power.

POLLUTION VICTIMS

One group of ordinary Japanese who learned to defend themselves in the postwar period were those whose lives and communities were shattered by industrial pollution in the 1950s and 1960s. They often found themselves in a lonely and bitter struggle for survival against not only the polluting corporations but also the strongly held consensus that citizens should be willing to sacrifice private interests for the economic recovery of the country. To most Japanese and to many of the victims themselves, the appropriate behavior for persons harmed by industrialization was to suffer in silence. To stand up for one's rights, and especially to do so in the courts, was to be selfish and disloyal—to put one's own interests above those of Japan.

The Course of Pollution

One such group was the fishermen of Minamata, a small city on Kyushu, the southernmost of Japan's four main islands. The economy of the surrounding area depended largely on fishing and agriculture, but since 1908 Minamata City itself had been the site of a large chemical plant owned by the Chisso Corporation. Chisso was both an envied source of employment and a frequent source of conflict. Beginning in 1926 local fishermen periodically demanded and received compensation for pollution to their fisheries, but it was not until the 1950s that events proved pollution to be causing much more profound damage than a decline in the commercial fishing catch:

> By 1953, ominous evidence appeared in Minamata. Birds seemed to be losing their sense of coordination, often falling from their perches or flying into buildings and trees. Cats, too, were acting oddly. They walked with a strange rolling gait, frequently stumbling over their own legs. Many suddenly went mad, running in circles and foaming at the mouth until they fell—or were thrown—into the sea and drowned. Local fishermen called the derangement "the disease of dancing cats," and watched nervously as the animals' madness progressed.
>
> Inexorably, the dancing disease spread to humans. By the early '50's, a number of Minamata fishermen and their families were experiencing the disquieting symptoms of a previously unknown physical disorder. Robust men and women who had formerly enjoyed good health suddenly found their hands trembling so violently they could no longer strike a match. They soon had difficulty thinking clearly, and it became increasingly difficult for them to operate their boats. Numbness that began in the lips and limbs was followed by disturbances in vision, movement, and speech. As the disease progressed, control over all bodily functions diminished. The victims became bedridden, then fell into unconsciousness. Wild fits of thrashing and senseless shouting comprised a later stage, during which many victims' families, to keep the afflicted from injuring themselves or others, resorted to securing them with heavy rope. About forty percent of those stricken died.[9]

Because the symptoms were concentrated in poor fishing villages along Minamata Bay, the residents of more affluent areas assumed that they were caused by hygienic deficiencies and reacted by shunning the victims, their fami-

9. Norrie Huddle and Michael Reich, *Island of Dreams: Environmental Crisis in Japan* (New York: Autumn Press, 1975), 106–7. This book was reprinted with a new introduction by the authors by Schenkman Books, Cambridge, MA, in 1987.

lies, and their fellow villagers. As a result, victims were under extreme pressure to hide their condition or give a false address when seeking treatment. As the following dialogue between a leader of the Minamata patients and a mother of an afflicted child illustrates, this pressure reinforced a desire to avoid singling oneself out in any way and led to an underreporting of the disease even after causation had become clear:

> *Kawamoto:* At the end of December, if you are told it is not the Minamata disease, what will you do? Will you reapply [for official designation of your daughter as a victim]?
>
> *Mother:* Well, to apply after having two examinations already. . . .
>
> *Kawamoto:* But there are people who have had three, four examinations—or five in some extreme cases—and they've been designated, so you can't very clearly tell with just one or two examinations. There's no reason to give up just because she hasn't been designated the first time.
>
> This time, really, you see, this time you have to demand that you be told the name of the disease. Unless you do something like that, she'll never get designated, not with the way they're doing it now . . . or is it something about the neighbors you're worried about?
>
> *Mother:* Somehow it seems a bit forward to me.[10]

Since the symptoms of mercury poisoning included deformities and mental retardation, part of the reluctance to step forward was due to the general Japanese attitude of shame and fear toward physical or mental abnormalities. But the victims' reticence went deeper than shame alone. In other instances of industrial pollution where the damage did not involve any abnormal symptoms whatsoever, the reaction of victims and their neighbors was often identical to that of the fishermen of Minamata. Their reasons are explained by Katō Mitsukazu, a victim of air pollution from the village of Isotsu near Yokkaichi City, the site of severe air pollution:

> In Isotsu, as for the residents' way of thinking, everyone wants to do only what the others do. In whatever meeting, it's everyone together, following the group. So in the case of pollution damage, too, everyone must act together. If an antipollution suit is started, the whole group has to do it. This consciousness is very strong. Group unity forms very quickly, but it's a different story when it's a question of one of them stepping forward to take some positive action himself.[11]

Victims who contemplated legal action were threatened with ostracism and considered selfish and unpatriotic:

> Back in 1963, you'd wash something, hang it out to dry and it'd be black immediately. You'd wash it again and a third time . . . and yet we still shut up and took it, didn't we? "For the sake of the country, for the sake of industrial expansion

10. Noriaki Tsuchimoto, director, *Minamata: The Victims and Their World* (Tokyo: Higashi Productions, 1972).

11. "Yokkaichi kōgai ni okeru jūmin katsudō," 514 *Jurisuto* 134 (1974).

... there's nothing we can do." No one said anything. Even now you hear "[those plaintiffs] know there's something in it for themselves"—that kind of thinking still exists.[12]

But the reluctance to stand out and the submissiveness to social authority had limits. When not only individual but community survival was threatened, reticence became determination and the victims in Minamata, Yokkaichi, and elsewhere began to demand redress, first of the polluters themselves and later of the government. In 1959 the Minamata victims formed the Mutual Assistance Society to negotiate with Chisso and by the end of the year had reached an agreement with Chisso. The settlement served Chisso's purposes well. Not only were the amounts grossly inadequate—300,000 yen ($830) for deceased victims and 100,000 yen ($280) annually for the living—but the agreement specified that the payments were in the nature of sympathy payments (*mimaikin*) rather than compensation and explicitly left open the question of causation.

The agreement reestablished social harmony in the Minamata area and bought several years of quiescence for Chisso and its government supporters. Had events elsewhere not dramatically altered the balance of power in Minamata, redirected the attention of the national media to pollution, and brought the victims new political allies, the 1959 negotiations might have come to represent one more instance of successful Japanese informal dispute resolution. But even during this dormant period in Minamata the main actors were busy maintaining the 1959 settlement, and the events of this uneventful period illustrate what "harmony" can mean and what it can cost to maintain it.

Although it was not until 1968 that the government formally agreed that organic mercury was the causative agent, government research on Minamata disease had pointed to Chisso as early as 1958, when the Ministry of Health and Welfare (MHW) notified other government agencies that the disease was likely caused by eating fish and shellfish contaminated by Chisso effluents. This notification was kept secret, but a subsequent report by researchers from the Kumamoto University Medical School was published the next year. Although the report studiously avoided any mention of Chisso as the source of the contamination, the government disbanded the team, canceled its funding, and transferred the question of causation from the MHW to the Ministries of International Trade and Industry (MITI) and Agriculture and Forestry (MAF) for "reexamination." For the next eight years MITI and MAF continued to profess doubt as to the causation and source of the disease, and the Ministry of Justice repeatedly refused to investigate Chisso even after all three ministries had clear evidence of Chisso's role.

The see-no-evil attitude of the powerful government ministries and the continuing obstruction by Chisso reinforced the effect of the *mimaikin* agreement, and the victims and fishermen of Minamata had little choice but to suppress their frustrations and grievances. But the Minamata pollution was only the first mani-

12. Ibid.

festation of a national problem, and the local settlement was doomed when another "strange disease of unknown cause" was discovered in 1964 in Niigata Prefecture on the island of Honshu. The symptoms were similar to Minamata disease; the victims' diet was largely fish; and investigation quickly revealed the presence of a factory using exactly the same processes as Chisso. Japan's second case of mercury poisoning had been discovered.

Although the government used the same tactics that had worked to suppress information in Kyushu—even to the extent of canceling funding for the Niigata University Medical School research team—events in Niigata moved too quickly for the government to marshall effective countermeasures. The Niigata University researchers made their research public in April 1967, despite strong objections by senior officials, and the victims' attitude quickly radicalized. With the support of leftist lawyers who had moved to the area shortly after the initial discovery and a strong local support group partially organized by those lawyers, the victims filed suit in June. Three months later suit was filed in the Yokkaichi air pollution case, then in July 1968 in the Toyama cadmium poisoning case, and finally, in June 1969, against Chisso by one faction of Minamata disease patients. As these cases progressed over the next several years, they became known as the Big Four pollution cases.[13]

By 1969 it had been sixteen years since the disease first appeared and eleven years since the MHW had secretly identified Chisso as the probable cause. The reasons for this delay were complex. They included the low socioeconomic status of the victims, their dispersal in several fishing villages along Minamata Bay, the economic and political domination of the area by Chisso, lack of access to legal resources, and a disinclination on the part of many victims to challenge authority, particularly through litigation.

Before we can evaluate these factors, however, there are two less obvious factors of importance. The first is legal doctrine. Chisso's legal personnel carefully drafted the terms of the 1959 *mimaikin* agreement to maximize the company's legal and psychological leverage. Not only Chisso but also the government often referred to the Minamata problem as being privately settled by this agreement. Equally important were the doctrines of tort law—or at least the actors' perceptions of those doctrines—that would cover any litigation. The victims' opponents were quick to discount the possibility of winning a tort suit on the merits because of a lack of what was referred to as "scientific" proof of causation. The belittling of the possibility of litigation in this manner not only discouraged litigation itself but also had the important psychological effect of making any compensation a matter of grace rather than of right. This psychological leverage was at the heart of the use of the term *mimaikin* in the 1959 agreement and was reinforced constantly thereafter.

A second factor in the delay and one crucial to understanding the degree of

13. See Upham, *Law and Social Change*, 28–67, and Julian Gresser, Kōichirō Fujikura, and Akio Morishima, *Environmental Law in Japan* (Cambridge: MIT Press, 1981).

rights assertiveness in postwar Japan was the legal nature of the settlement process. Central to the creation of the 1959 agreement was the manipulation of the information made possible by the informality of mediation. Both Chisso and the government regularly suppressed information whenever it suited their interests. Not only did Chisso deny information requested by researchers, but it was revealed later that it had halted experiments conducted in 1959 by plant personnel that had re-created Minamata disease symptoms in cats by feeding them Chisso wastewater. The suppression of vital data was greatly facilitated by the informal methods of protest and dispute settlement used by the victims. Had the fishermen and patients relied on more formal channels, manipulation of information would have been more difficult. Under the informal process of mediation, however, both the production of data and the setting of the mediation agenda remained under the control of Chisso and its allies.

The Antipollution Movement and Response

By the late 1960s, when the decisions to sue Chisso and other polluters were made, popular attitudes toward industrialization and environmental protection had already changed. And by 1973, when the Minamata plaintiffs won the largest tort award in Japanese history, the antipollution movement ignited by the Big Four was being described as a radically new form of Japanese political action, one that challenged not only the closed and consensus-based style of traditional politics but also the self-image of the Japanese as preferring harmony to conflict. In addition to exposing latent social divisions, the experience of pollution victims showed that rights assertion and litigation could be valuable tools in achieving justice and protecting one's self-interest.

The Big Four and the activities accompanying them were the forerunners of the citizens' movements that dominated Japan's political landscape in the 1970s: politically mobilized grass-roots organizations focused on local or regional issues and employing a combination of litigation, symbolic violence, and electoral politics to achieve concrete, nonideological ends.[14] Citizens' movements developed and operated outside the historical channels of political action in Japan. Although supported by opposition parties, they were not captured by them or identified with them, and they avoided both the abstract ideologies of the leftist parties and the personalistic loyalties of the LDP. Their adroit use of the courts and the judges' sympathetic response gave them a national forum for their grievances. Even if ultimately unsuccessful legally, the very posing of social and political questions as legal issues meant that they would be debated in the mass media; that public positions on particular issues would have to be taken by the LDP and the bureaucracy; and that the informal and closed decision-making process of the Japanese government would be exposed to public scrutiny.

14. For a description of these movements, see Margaret McKean, *Environmental Protest and Citizen Politics in Japan* (Berkeley and Los Angeles: University of California Press, 1981).

To regain the political initiative, the LDP and its allies had to discredit or preempt this new model of social action, but before this end could be achieved, they had to eliminate the pollution that was driving the citizens' movement phenomenon. Once the pollution was under control, the government could right the moral imbalance created by its unconscionable negligence in places like Minamata and begin to rebuild trust in traditional authority.

Controlling pollution was expensive but relatively easy. Once forced to move, the government and its business allies acted quickly and effectively. In less than a decade Japan went from being clearly the most polluted of the major industrial countries to comparing favorably on those indexes of pollution related to human health. The government used basically the same legal tools used elsewhere, compulsory emission and effluent controls on both stationary sources and automobiles, but it was able to use them more effectively and vigorously than elsewhere because the degree of pollution had created a political consensus that made it very difficult to oppose antipollution measures openly.

Controlling the most acute forms of pollution did not necessarily mean that citizens' movements would disappear, however. For one thing, regulating current pollution would not compensate those whose health had already been injured by past pollution. Furthermore, by the early 1970s environmental activism had moved beyond the human disasters of Minamata and Yokkaichi to focus on quality-of-life issues such as noise pollution and highway siting. To divert this activism away from the courts and politics, the government had to find an alternative for tort suits to compensate pollution victims and a mechanism for anticipating and defusing local pollution issues before they developed into national disputes.

The government's answer was legislation to create bureaucratic machinery for both the compensation of existing victims and the resolution of current and future disputes. The government accomplished the former by certifying victims and distributing to them funds—more than 85 billion yen (approximately $425 million) by 1980—provided by polluting firms. Although ostensibly applicable to future pollution, compensation was in practice limited to victims who were already the focus of controversy in the 1970s, and by 1987 the scheme had been essentially dismantled. The government addressed the conflict resolution problem by establishing a bureaucratic scheme for the identification, investigation, and mediation of pollution-related disputes.

The stated purpose of both compensation and mediation was cheap and prompt relief for pollution victims, but the drafters' goals went beyond efficiency. Bureaucratic intervention in civil disputes was touted as consistent with Japanese tradition and responsive to the assumed Japanese preference for government paternalism and noncontentious conflict resolution. Before one assumes, however, that these measures were the result of the strength of traditional values—of the weak legal consciousness of Kawashima—it is necessary to note that the initial recommendations for responding to the pollution crisis had emphasized compensation through a tort system strengthened by the creation of strict liability for pollution injuries. This approach was successfully opposed by business groups and MITI, which emphasized the primacy of industrial development and urged the replacement of the tort system by a comprehensive system of extrajudicial dispute resolution by the bureaucracy.

The development of the mediation and compensation systems, therefore, was less the result of traditional values than of political will. And the end result—the replacement of the courts and citizens' movements with concerned bureaucrats in the management of environmental conflict—is quite consistent with an interpretation stressing the government's role in creating and maintaining the very values that intellectuals of the immediate postwar period such as Maruyama and Kawashima believed had stunted Japan's prewar democratic development.

CONCLUSION

A few comments on the fate of "unplaced persons" in postwar Japan are possible. First, very few people, no matter how despised, no matter how low their station, were left alone to perish. The Burakumin, despite their lack of success in eliminating discrimination in employment, were better off economically than they were before the war and as a group were much better taken care of than disadvantaged minorities in the United States. The vast majority of Japanese women, even those for whom the distant promise of the EEOA was a cruel joke, enjoyed a degree of economic and social security that a more mobile society might have denied them. Although women were for the most part relegated to an inferior role in the workplace, the stable family structure of Japan for most of this period ensured for them a role that was valued and dignified, if not equal to that of men in terms of social power. Even the story of pollution victims indicates that outsiders in postwar Japan—and the victims certainly became outsiders when they defied authority and turned to litigation—need not perish financially if they could unite to bring their plight to the attention of the nation.

Second, although one can argue about degrees of willingness to litigate versus other forms of dispute resolution, there is little evidence from the experiences of the Burakumin, women, and pollution victims that indicate timidity or an unusual reluctance to confront authority. It is certainly true that it took many years for the Minamata patients to sue, but it must be remembered that they were poor, relatively uneducated, without significant political power, and facing an antagonist that not only dominated the economics and politics of the region but also was blindly supported by the central government. The BLL may have chosen a strategy that led them away from litigation and that ultimately isolated them from other poor Japanese, but they did not do so because they were afraid to confront the government or their social superiors. On the contrary, their often excessive use of confrontational tactics eventually damaged their cause. And the dozens of women workers who sued their employers from the 1960s through the 1980s did so in the face of harsh criticism by their unions and the society in general. Although none of these episodes may demonstrate a "rights consciousness" in the narrow sense of legal rights or the rule of law, they certainly indicate that the gains made by these groups in the postwar period were fought for; they were not granted as a matter of paternalistic grace, however much the government or business might have tried to make it appear so.

Third, the foregoing notwithstanding, very little of what has happened to these groups in postwar Japan would lead one to conclude that the individualistically premised democracy of the occupation reformers or the internal freedom of the individual identified by Maruyama Masao was achieved or even desired by most Japanese. The gains that were realized generally came only by dint of disciplined group action that may in some instances have actually limited the options of individual group members. The Burakumin and pollution victims may have been financially secure relative to analogous groups elsewhere, but they remained outside the mainstream of Japanese society as a group and were frequently immobilized as individuals.

Fourth, the civil rights litigation of the women workers was an exception to this rule, however, and the subsequent EEOA increased opportunities for the few women fortunate and determined enough to compete with men on the men's terms. The changing role of women in the workplace and at home may eventually become the most important factor undermining the centrality of the group and conventional norms in the future, but the number of women able to act on the new opportunities remained so small that they had little short-term effect.

Fifth, one key to understanding why freedom of choice and individual social mobility remained relatively weak is the government's reaction to social change or conflict. At every juncture where it had a chance, the government took action to discourage individual action, particularly legal action, and to reward cooperation and dependence on the bureaucracy. The choice between strengthening the tort system to handle pollution disputes and compensate victims and establishing a system of government compensation and mediation was a particularly clear instance of a common practice. The refusal to make discrimination illegal or provide a legal right to either Burakumin or women may have been justified by reference to traditional values and the importance of voluntary cooperation, but it is equally well explained by a desire both to avoid losing control over social change and to reinforce these very values.

Sixth, what appears to have been at least an official disinclination to develop a legal system of the type envisioned by the original reformers did not mean that such a legal system would not develop despite government efforts to the contrary. Although the number of environmental suits dropped in the 1980s, women continued to bring discrimination actions to the courts and the BLL began pushing for legislation creating a private right against ethnic and status discrimination. It was possible, in other words, that the form of democracy envisioned in the immediate postwar period, a vision dominated almost entirely by the American model, would eventually be realized in Japan. What seemed more likely, however, was that Japan had developed its own form of democracy that reflected the particular history and politics of contemporary Japan.

CHAPTER THIRTEEN

Altered States

The Body Politics of "Being-Woman"

Sandra Buckley

Japanese and non-Japanese often cite the 1947 constitution as the turning point for women's rights in Japan. Paragraph one of Article 14 guarantees that "All of the people are equal under the law and there shall be no discrimination in political, economic or social relations because of race, creed, sex, social status or family origin."[1] One of the primary targets of the newly drafted constitution was the *ie* or household system. Before 1947 all family-related law was based on a system of primogeniture and patrilineal households. The new constitution stipulated that

> marriage shall be based only on the mutual consent of both sexes and it shall be maintained through mutual co-operation with the equal rights of the husband and wife as its basis.
>
> With regards to choice of spouse, property rights, inheritance, choice of domicile, divorce and other matters pertaining to marriage and the family, laws shall be enacted from the standpoint of individual dignity and the essential equality of the sexes.[2]

Indeed, the new constitution bodes well for women's rights in the postwar period; however, in this essay I argue that constitutional or legal reform is not half the story in the Japanese case. Gender-based discrimination operated across all levels of society throughout the postwar period. This essay is divided into three sections: "Women's Work: Production and Reproduction"; "Education: Engendering Difference"; and "The State and Body Politic(s)." It explores the interactive dynamics of these three basic dimensions of a woman's life as they both organize the identity of "being-woman" in Japan's postwar history and define Woman's relationship to the body politic—"being Japan."

1. As translated in Lois J. Naftulin, "Women's Status Under Japanese Law," *Feminist International* (Tokyo) 2 (1980): 13.
2. Ibid.

WOMEN'S WORK: PRODUCTION AND REPRODUCTION

In the three decades immediately following Japan's defeat the family unit underwent an extensive refiguration from the traditional production function of self-employed extended family households to the consumer function of nuclear wage-earning households. Between 1955 and 1988 the percentage of self-employed households in primary industry fell from 40 percent to 25 percent of total households while worker households increased from 49 percent to 64 percent. This same period saw a 50 percent increase in the total number of households in Japan and a significant drop in the average family size from 5.00—the average for the period 1925–55—to 3.19 in 1987, by which time nuclear households accounted for 60.5 percent of all households.[3] This restructuring of the basic social unit was accompanied by a parallel demographic migratory pattern out of rural areas into urban centers, particularly Tokyo and the surrounding industrial zones of the Kanto region. The consumerism of the new urban nuclear unit of the 1960s and 1970s depended on surplus disposable income or borrowing power (which required collateral or a credit rating), a constant supply of consumer goods, and "informed" (desiring) consumers. The need for surplus income in order to perform in accord with the mainstream norms of the newly defined consumer-oriented environment was one major influence in two closely related developments in women's lives over the 1960s and 1970s: the reduction of the number of births per household and the movement of women out of unpaid family work into the salaried work force. The new consumer function of the urban nuclear family is not the only explanation for either of these two trends, but it is a significant contributing factor in each case. I consider each of these trends more closely and analyze their multiple points of intersection.

Women's magazines and other popular publications of the Taishō period made frequent reference to the phenomenon of *shokugyō fujin* (working women). The term was generally used with a negative connotation. "O.L." (office lady) emerged as the comparable term in the postwar period. Despite the negative marking of the term *shokugyō fujin*, the requirement for increased female labor participation in the wartime industries together with the economic necessity of women's work to meet the hardships of the immediate postwar years led to a new public tolerance toward a female presence in the work force.[4] Although the flow of male labor out of the armed forces back into the domestic work force and the return of large numbers of repatriated Japanese from the colonized territories placed pressure on the number of available positions in the drastically reduced industrial base of the late 1940s and early 1950s, one survey showed that in 1948 as many as 54 percent of the women in the Tokyo area were working to support

3. *Statistical Handbook of Japan* (Tokyo: Statistics Bureau Management and Co-ordination Bureau, 1989), 22. Hereafter, editions of the *Statistical Handbook* will be cited by title and date.
4. Ichibangase K., *Sengo fujin mondaishi* (Tokyo: Domesu Shuppan, 1978). This work details the change in public attitude toward women's work during the postwar years.

or supplement family income.[5] Women's employment conditions were controlled by the Labor Standards Act, which followed a "separate but equal" strategy; that is, women were legally guaranteed equal access to employment opportunity and equal pay for equal work, but these guarantees were compromised by protective clauses that secured maternity and menstruation leave for all female employees and prohibited women from night shifts and certain forms of strenuous labor. The protective clauses were all directly related to values encoded in the eugenic protection policies of the war years. What was protected by law was the reproductive function of the female worker, not the worker herself. Employees were able to justify discriminatory employment practices on the grounds that women could not perform the same jobs or follow the same career paths as men. What resulted were distinct gender-differentiated entry tracks into the work force and separate male/female employment profiles even in the case of equally qualified male and female members of a recruitment cohort.

Throughout the occupation era the primary employment of the majority of women nationwide remained unpaid family work. Salaried employment was generally undertaken as a supplement to the family income—two obvious exceptions being widows and divorcees supporting single-parent households. Through the mid-1950s salaried employment for women was largely limited to the manufacturing and service industries, and the average age of women in the work force was 23.8 years (1948).[6] Another significant characteristic of female labor was the fact that the majority of women workers were unmarried (65.2 percent in 1955) and left the work force permanently either with marriage or the birth of the first child. Each of these trends in women's employment began to change significantly toward the late 1950s and early 1960s.[7]

The shift from unpaid family labor to salaried employment among women was rapid and had a major impact on the configuration of the Japanese work force. Between 1953 and 1980 the number of salaried female employees increased from 4 million to 13.5 million.[8] This dramatic shift was accompanied by several other trends, including delayed labor-force participation caused by increased participation of women in postsecondary education (thus delaying work-force entry), the emergence of an M-curve in women's employment statistics as more women returned to the work force after the birth of the last child, and a shift away from full-time to part-time employment. The most obvious consequence of all these factors was a substantial increase in the average age of women in the work force (from 23.8 in 1949 to 35.2 in 1983).[9] The trends toward reentry into the work

5. Dorothy Robins-Mowry, *The Hidden Sun: Women of Modern Japan* (Boulder: Westview, 1983), 167.

6. Ibid., 168.

7. Detailed profiles of women in the work force in the immediate postwar period are given in Ichibangase, *Sengo fujin mondaishi*, chaps. 2–3.

8. Robins-Mowry, *Hidden Sun*, 167.

9. T. Ikeda, *Facts and Figures of Japan* (Tokyo: Foreign Press Centre, 1985), 83. Hereafter, editions of *Facts and Figures* will be cited by title and date.

force after childbirth and the increase in part-time employment clearly intersected with shifts in government and industry priorities and the structure and function of the urban nuclear unit. Women's productive and reproductive functions come into direct play with one another with the coincidence of women's increased representation in salaried employment positions and the decline in the number of births per household. The site of this interplay is public policy.

Women's work, paid or unpaid, was often crucial to the survival of individual family households and their labor-force participation was clearly central to the reconstruction of Japan's postwar industrial base. As the Japanese economy moved beyond recovery into a period of rapid acceleration, however, a controversy developed around the continuing trend for women to work after marriage and even after childbirth. Japan's popular media became host to a discourse of the feminine that has continued, unresolved and ever evolving, what I refer to as the discourse of "being-woman." In its earliest form in the late 1950s and early 1960s it was known as the "housewife debate" (*shufu ronsō*). This debate was not without precedent in Japan. The issue of a woman's obligation or nonobligation to the function of *bosei* (motherhood or nurturing) was the central focus of Hiratsuka Raichō's public debates with the different approaches of both Yosano Akiko and Miyazaki Mitsuko during the 1910s and 1920s. It is not a coincidence that this debate also occurred at a time when women's representation in the work force was rapidly increasing during a period of economic growth and industrial expansion.[10]

The main vehicle of the debate in the late 1950s was the popular women's magazine *Fujin kōron*. The central point of contention was whether the primary role of women should be that of wife/mother or whether they should have the right to pursue a career, and if so, then whether or not the welfare function should be carried by the family or the State. What is most striking about this debate is the extent to which the general readership of *Fujin kōron* rejected arguments favoring women's rights to place career over family and sided with the proponents of a more conservative, neotraditionalist argument for the priority of motherhood. This trend is particularly interesting given that it represents the opposite of the emerging reality of women's changing employment choices at that time. The make-up of the readership may hold some explanation of this reality gap, but there is not sufficient space here to explore this discrepancy between the representations of popular discourse and the reality of employment statistics.

By the early 1960s the government and various joint government and industry commissions were also lending their voice to the "housewife debate." Government studies were predicting a serious imbalance between the unemployed per-

---

10. For detailed discussion of the significance of public debates around the family and the status of women, see Tanaka Sumiko, *Josei kaihō no shisō to kōdō: Sengohen* (Tokyo: Jiji Tsushinsha, 1975), chap. 2; Maruoka Hideko, *Fujin shisō keiseishi nōto*, vol. 2, chap. 3; and Ichibangase, *Sengo fujin mondaishi*, chap. 4.

sons ratio and active employment opening ratio. Although female participation had been an easy stop-gap measure for the immediate shortfall in the labor force during the first stage of Japan's postwar recovery, now, as all the indicators pointed to continued rapid economic acceleration, the government became increasingly concerned that this approach was contributing directly to the reduced level of the nation's birthrate—a phenomenon that created fears of a long-term decline in the available labor pool. A government white paper on child welfare published in 1963 stated that "a deficiency in the level of nurturing is creating a risk for the children of this generation." The same document referred to "the decline in child welfare in the wake of women's increased penetration of the workforce."[11] The question of reproduction and production fused into a single policy issue in Prime Minister Satō Eisaku's ill-fated public appeal, soon after his election in 1964, that Japanese women bear more children. The echo back to the rhetoric of the wartime eugenic policies created an immediate and heated reaction from women's groups.[12]

The immediate and organized response to a statement such as Satō's represented a new level of political sensitization and willingness to mobilize among women. The history of what is often referred to as the second wave of Japanese feminism (the first being the prewar suffragist movement) is not a simple one and requires far more attention than there is space for here. Others have covered this ground well enough already.[13] What is most significant about the 1960s and 1970s is the multiplicity of feminisms that emerged over these two decades. The forms of resistance to those policies of the body politic that sought to organ-ize women's individuated bodies, both in their reproductive and productive functions, were diverse and not infrequently conflictual. Japanese feminism remained highly fragmented into the 1980s and this fragmentation continues to be both a strength and weakness of the movement. Women's groups have come together at different junctures of policy reform to reject the state's power to define the condition of "being-woman" and to fight for women's right to self-determination.[14] Although the number of women actively involved in a continuous way in the women's movement is relatively low, the movement has a proven capacity to mobilize women in sufficient numbers around single-issue, limited-term campaigns to be

11. Ichibangase details both the debates and policy developments concerning motherhood and child welfare; *Sengo fujin mondaishi*, chap. 4. See also see Maruoka, *Fujin shisō keiseishi nōto*, vol. 2, chap. 8.

12. Robins-Mowry, *Hidden Sun*, 167.

13. Tanaka Mitsu's autobiographical *Inochi no onnatachi e* (Tokyo: Tabata Shoten, 1972) gives one of the most detailed and moving accounts of the period of rapid change during the 1960s. Further details in English are available in my collection of interviews with leading Japanese feminists over the summers of 1987 and 1988. The material has been compiled, together with selected translations, in the manuscript "The Broken Silence: Voices of Japanese Feminism."

14. For more detailed discussion in English of the major women's groups in Japan, see Vera Mackie, "Feminist Politics in Japan," *New Left Review*, no. 167 (Jan.–Feb. 1988): 53–59.

able to influence political currents. The fight against abortion law reform and the 1989 election campaign for the Upper House are two of the more obvious examples of this capacity.[15]

An impressive track record of political mobilization and resistance strategies notwithstanding, the reality gap between the strength of the neotraditionalist response to the housewife debate of the late 1950s and the continued increase in female employment patterns of that same period did not disappear in the 1960s and 1970s. At the same time that the *minikomi* (an extensive feminist alternative communications network) was developing across Japan in the mid-1960s to 1970s, women (often the same women who were involved in the *minikomi*) were consuming mass-produced images of the ideal housewife and home as a wave of *mai hōmu*-ism (my home-ism) swept Japan's domestic media and markets. As the economy strengthened, salaries continued to rise and disposable incomes grew in a climate of minimal unemployment and contained inflation. The content of both the articles and advertisements in women's magazines and daytime television reflected the new age of consumerism. Recipes for leftovers and articles for sewing low-budget wardrobes were gradually replaced by gourmet recipes calling for imported ingredients. Fashion shifted from utilitarian low-budget items to designer collections. Television advertising increasingly focused on a well-dressed (Western) and perfectly coiffured woman (also often Western or Japanese-American) standing in a spacious Western-style kitchen surrounded by state-of-the-art electric appliances. Women were drawn into a relationship of desire with this technologized, Westernized domestic interior. Luxury-item departments of major department stores moved away from an over-the-counter, closed-display approach to the open floorplan, demonstration model that had worked so well in the United States since the early 1960s. The luxury items of the 1950s were now the domestic right of every consumer/housewife of the 1960s, accessible in the department store and at home for a price. The representations of advertising and the popular media (magazines, television, and film) directed women's lives into the interior spaces of the urban nuclear unit, which was itself being physically restructured in the wave of high-density urban architecture (*danchi* and *manshon*) of the 1960s and 1970s.

Despite the intensity of the neotraditionalist reaction to the housewife debate of the late 1950s and the sheer weight of the media campaign constructed around images of the happy urban consumer/housewife through the 1960s and into the 1970s, the reality gap persisted. An increasing number of women remained in the work force after marriage. The birthrate continued to decline, and a strong new trend developed of more women opting to reenter the work force after the birth of the last child. The emergence of the new consumer culture is not enough to explain these patterns, but it is intimately related to each. *Mai hōmu*-ism and an

15. Details of this period are drawn from an interview with Saito Chiyo and an article "Nihon no feminizumu to wa nani ka?" *Agora,* no. 131 (1988): 115–37, which I have translated and transcribed in "Broken Silence."

acute shortage of public housing (only 7 percent of all residential units in Japan are government housing) led many young wives to remain in the work force past marriage in order to improve the chances of saving a down payment for a *danchi* (small high-rise apartment) or *manshon* (condominium).[16] The expense of furnishing and maintaining a high-tech household added to the financial burden of households before and after childbirth, leading more women to seek reentry to the work force after the birth of the last child as a means of protecting a desired standard of living. The future burden of educational costs was another factor in reentry choices. Improved access to contraception and abortion made birth control choices easier and guaranteed a high degree of self-determination for women in this regard. Family planning became an integral part of the financial management of the household for Japanese women through the 1960s and 1970s. Prime Minister Satō's call for women to bear more children missed the mark entirely, for it failed to identify the complexity of issues that were leading women into a dramatically new life cycle by the mid-1960s.

During the postwar period there have indeed been significant changes in the life cycle of women. These changes offer a site for the exploration of the relationship between the individuated female body and the body politic over this period. The statistical trend over the last two decades has been for an increase of approximately 1.5 years in women's life expectancy for every three years documented. Womens' life expectancy in 1978 was already high at 78.33 but had risen to 81.39 in 1987; the life expectancy of women born in the period 1935–36 was calculated in 1940 to be 49.63.[17] An increase of almost thirty-two years (1940–87) in the life expectancy of women cannot, on its own, account for recent shifts in the timing and duration of women's reproductive stage. It becomes a determining factor only when located in relation to parallel shifts in the Japanese economy.

The final year of the reproductive stage of a woman's life in 1940 was projected at 35.1 years. Since then, there has only been a slight shift in the age at which women have their first child (23.2 to 26.2), but there has been a major shift at the end of the reproductive stage. By 1987 the projected length of the reproductive stage had fallen to a mere 2.2 years. This dramatic shift in the life cycle of Japanese women is closely paralleled by a shift to a pattern of work-force reentry after the birth of the last child. The number of women participating in the work force is growing annually, but the dominant form of employment has changed from full-time to part-time.

According to government statistics, women constituted 40 percent of the total work force in 1988 (women's groups placed the figure as high as 48 percent).[18] However, the nature of women's work is undergoing a dramatic refiguration with the shift toward part-time employment. Since the mid-1970s the majority of women returning to the work force after childbirth have done so as part-timers.

16. Fuse Akiko, "Japanese Family in Transition," part 2, *Japan Foundation Newsletter,* Dec. 1984, 2.
17. *Statistical Handbook of Japan* (1987), 18.
18. "Population by Employment Status," in *Statistical Handbook of Japan.*

Women's withdrawal from the work force at childbirth is not voluntary. In a survey 77 percent of Japanese women employees stated that although their company had no written policy, it was expected that women would step down on marriage or the birth of the first child.[19] Opportunities for reentry into full-time employment are extremely limited. The number of women employed part-time increased approximately 80 percent between 1978 and 1988, when it reached a total of 4.46 million.[20] In Japan a part-time employee is officially defined as any employee who works less than thirty-five hours a week. Part-time female employees receive drastically reduced access to employee benefits, are frequently excluded from union membership, can be terminated on notice without compensation, and earn an average of 58 percent of the full-time male wage.[21] Only 29 percent of companies in Japan employed part-time labor in 1970 as compared with 53 percent in 1988; the trend toward part-time employment was strongest in companies of 1–29 employees, where the figure has risen to 51 percent.[22]

It should be noted that a recent feminist publication on part-time employment has argued that official statistics seriously underestimate the number of women employed in this category.[23] This underestimation in part reflects the difficulty of gathering accurate statistics for shadow employment.

It is not difficult to understand why employers have been attracted to the current shift toward part-time employment. The advantage of a large reserve labor pool that is cheap, educated, nonunionized and "disposable" is obvious, especially in the case of small to medium-sized companies. Why women have entered part-time employment in such large numbers is a more complex question. The swing became increasingly apparent over the 1970s. A 1983 survey of working women indicated that 28.9 percent were working to support their household, 54.6 percent were working to supplement household income, and 31.8 percent were working for savings.[24] The first figure represents the growing number of single mothers and divorcees. By the 1980s the divorce rate had reached 20 percent of new marriages, with the majority of divorces (74 percent) petitioned for by women. The two major grounds for divorce petitions from women were violence (37.6 percent) and extramarital affairs (35.7 percent).[25] In Japan alimony has usually been built into the divorce settlement when children are involved, but there remained no effective mechanism of enforcement throughout the 1980s. State benefits for single mothers and divorcees forced onto welfare remained insufficient to sustain an average-sized family above the poverty level throughout

19. *Statistics Relating to Women's Unemployment* (Tokyo: Employment Opportunities Centre, 1982).

20. "Female Aged Workers Needed but Get Paid Less, Paper Shows," *Japan Times Weekly Overseas Edition*, 5 Aug. 1989, 12.

21. "Hourly Wage Index for Females," in *Facts and Figures of Japan* (1985).

22. Ikeda T., "Naze onna wa pāto taimu o shitai no ka?" *Agora Monthly*, no. 133 (Sept. 1988): 10, 11.

23. Ibid., 10.

24. Fuse, "Japanese Family in Transition," 3.

25. Naftulin, "Women's Status under Japanese Law," 13.

this same period. Part-time, shadow employment continued to be an important source of essential additional income to women on welfare.

Another survey conducted in 1985 explored the reasons behind the choice of part-time rather than full-time employment. Of the women surveyed, 48.5 percent answered that the flexibility of working hours was best suited to their circumstances.[26] By the late 1980s the majority of working women were married, reversing the situation of the prewar and early postwar periods. In 1955 65.2 percent of working women were single; by 1982 the percentage of women workers who were married had risen to 58.8 percent.[27]

This shift was accompanied by a gradual increase in the average age of women in the workplace. Statistics for female part-time employees in the three sectors of manufacturing, wholesale and retail (including food service), and services show that the average age of women employees increased by five years during the period from 1970 to 1986.[28] The average age moved from the late thirties into the mid-forties, reflecting the rapidly increasing number of women returning to the workplace after childrearing. The desire for surplus disposable income, the need to save in anticipation of the constantly increasing cost of education, and the more long-term goal of saving for security in old age in a system not geared to geriatric welfare—all these factors encouraged women to return to employment as soon as possible after the birth of the last child. The standard pattern by the early 1990s was for women to reenter the work force in their late twenties, to begin to save for educational expenses in their early thirties, to transfer the focus of savings to the cost of childrens' weddings in the early forties, and to begin saving for retirement in their middle to late forties.[29] Although Japan boasted a high standard of living according to all the international indicators (with the notable exception of home ownership and living space), the quality of life was seldom maintained during concentrated periods of expenditure (postsecondary education, wedding ceremonies, etc.) without the supplemental income of the wife's part-time employment. The M-curve trend became increasingly marked over the late 1960s and 1970s, offering an almost perfect example of this employment model by the late 1970s. Over the 1980s, however, the right-hand side of the M-curve began to stretch out into a gentle slope rather than the steep decline of the model. This change reflected a gradual but constant increase in the number of women over the age of fifty who remained in the work force on a part-time basis.

26. *Facts and Figures of Japan*, 12.

27. The figure of 65.2 percent is cited in Robins-Mowry, *Hidden Sun*, 177, from a 1980 labor force survey, conducted by the the Prime Minister's Office; the 1982 figure is taken from *Facts and Figures of Japan* (1982).

28. "Female Part-timers, Age, and Regular Earnings per Hour by Industry and Type of Enterprise," in *Japan Statistical Yearbook, 1988* (Tokyo: Statistics Bureau and Management and Co-ordination Agency, 1988).

29. Fujiwara Mariko, *Japanese Women in Turmoil* (Tokyo: Hakuhādo Institute of Life and Living, 1984), 42.

The need to save for security in old age has been particularly acute in Japan throughout postwar history. The level of welfare benefits paid to the elderly has been insufficient to sustain a standard of living above the poverty line. People have saved intensely through the last two decades of their working lives to supplement their social security income. The elderly have been hard-pressed to depend on their children for financial support when the nuclear family unit was already under considerable financial pressure. From 1965 to 1985 there was a dramatic increase in the number of elderly households in relation to all other households. By 1985 one of every four Japanese aged sixty-five or older was living alone or only with a spouse. The number of elderly living alone doubled since 1960, and the number of elderly couples living alone has tripled over the same period.[30] The situation was most severe for women, who made up the majority of the elderly, and the number of women continuing to work, particularly in part-time employment, into their fifties and sixties increased in the 1980s. The male/female wage differential increased dramatically for workers aged fifty-five and older, which became a major factor motivating employers to actively seek out women in this age group.[31]

Some observers have argued that more married women returned to the work force because of the free time at their disposal in an age of high-tech domestic appliances; however, such arguments minimize the burden carried by women, who often work six to seven hours a day in addition to their unpaid labor as homeworker. "Choice" is a very controversial concept in the context of women's employment. The move from extended family households to nuclear families has shifted the burden of child care fully onto the mother in the absence of grandparents or external facilities. Of the 24,000 afterschool care centers considered necessary to meet present demand, only 4,739 were in operation in 1982; it was estimated that only one in five children who should be attending nurseries actually had access to the public system.[32] There were 15,115 kindergartens in operation in 1988, but only 41 percent of these were public.[33] Private kindergartens were expensive and had long waiting lists. Moreover, the majority would not accept children under twelve months of age. In addition to the general social pressure on mothers to stay at home for at least the first year after a birth were the added institutional obstacles of the twelve-month age limit at kindergartens and the heavily monitored public system of infant welfare centered around local motherhood clinics. Accounts of "educational" sessions for mothers at these clinics frequently described the emphasis placed on a full-time nurturing role. Some feminists have drawn parallels between the educational function of the clinics and the wartime rhetoric of eugenics.[34]

30. Fuse, "Japanese Family in Transition," part I, *Japanese Foundation Newsletter*, Oct. 1984, 9–10.
31. "Model Wages by Age and Academic Career (1987)," *Japan Statistical Yearbook, 1988*.
32. Fuse, "Japanese Family in Transition," part 2, 6.
33. "School Statistics, May 1988," *Japan State Yearbook, 1988*.
34. See Koga Akie, "Kanri sareru sei: Boshi hoken no jittai," *Shinchihei*, Aug. 1983, 88–92.

The 1984 survey of the motivation of part-time women employees quoted above assumed that the respondents had a genuine choice among a range of options. The very concept of choice needs to be problematized in this context. If women had not been required to resign "voluntarily" with the birth of their first child, if public attitude toward working mothers was less damning, if day-care facilities were adequate, if women had had the option after childbirth to return to the same corporation without a loss of wage or seniority—if all these factors had been different, is it possible that the number of women following the current M-curve of employment would have decreased? The use of the concept of choice or preference in a survey dealing with women's part-time employment obscures the complexity of the context within which women make such decisions.

Another major factor that affected the decision to enter part-time rather than full-time employment was the massive gender-based wage differential. A standard and predictable set of justifications for this differential developed in Japan during the UN Decade of Women when it was made a major issue of public debate by feminists seeking a government commitment to wage parity. According to this standard account, women and men entered the work force with wage parity, but as employers recognized that female employees were likely to marry and have children within the first ten years of employment, they were disinclined to place females in management-track positions. In non-career-track positions, annual salary increments were lower, and therefore women's salaries gradually fell behind those of the male members of the same cohort.[35] The situation was purportedly compounded by women's "preference" to return to the job market, during or after childrearing, as part-time employees. Women were also more likely to enter low-paying small to medium-sized companies both at the time of initial entry and at reentry into the work force.[36]

The statistics raise serious questions about this scenario. Although it is true that women have a lower average for years of continuous employment, the difference between males and females is not as great as might be expected. The figure for women is 6.3 as compared with 11.3 for men.[37] These figures for both men and women raise serious questions about the standard stereotype of Japanese lifetime employment practices. Unions have frequently cited the increase in female part-time workers as a direct threat to the security of male full-time employees and thus as a factor in reducing the average period of continuous employment for full-time male employees. Not surprisingly, the unions have generally not proven a source

35. Nakamura Kayako, *Pāto taimu Q & A* (Tokyo: Gakuyo Shoin, 1983). This work was one of the earliest comprehensive studies of the phenomenon of part-time employment. For statistical information, see Ikeda, "Naze onna," 10–13. See also Maruoka, *Fujin shisō keiseishi nōto,* chap. 5, for her analysis of the relationship between women's part-time employment and the period of rapid economic growth.

36. Salaries at a company of 5–29 employees will be 61 percent of salaries at a company employing 500; Fuse, "Japanese Family in Transition," part 2, 6.

37. "Average Age and Years of Continuous Employment of Workers (1983)," in *Facts and Figures of Japan* (1985).

of support for women's claims for equal opportunity and wage parity. That the period of continuous employment has been shorter for women in part reflects higher levels of attrition among females during periods of economic cutbacks, so the statistics should not be taken as a simple indicator of women's preferred pattern of employment. This view exaggerates women's self-determination in the work force and ignores the limiting effect of the contexts of women's employment.

Furthermore, where there are figures for a cohort of women and men employed full-time for extended periods of time within the same corporation—as in the case of women who are able to keep their position after childbirth or women who do not have children—these statistics still show that women, even after they are well beyond their reproductive stage, suffered an annual increase in the differential between their own salary and that of their male counterparts. In the case of lower secondary school graduates working in production, an eighteen-year-old female with three years of experience earned 114,000 yen per month in 1987, and a male of the same age and experience earned 118,000 yen. At the age of thirty-five with twenty years of experience, the female earned 180,000 yen and the male 241,000 yen. The differential has shifted from 0.96 to 0.74 (where male wage equals 1.0). In the case of university graduates in clerical work, the differential shifted at the same rate in direct relation to years of service.[38]

Overall, the gender-based wage differential in Japan stood at 56 percent in 1976; however, calculated on the 1988 statistics for average earnings, this figure has actually worsened to 50 percent![39] The dramatic increase in the number of women working part-time is the most obvious explanation for the decrease. By comparison, the 1988 wage differential in Australia was 93.9 percent and 61 percent in the United States.[40] In both of these cases the gap between male and female wages was decreasing annually. That Japanese women were reluctant to reenter the work force as full-time employees and commit themselves to the same level of overtime and stress as their full-time male colleagues for 50 percent of the salary is not surprising. Add to this inequity the poor prospects for promotion in a country where only 0.3 percent of female employees were in positions senior enough to participate actively in management in 1988—a figure that has scarcely fluctuated in the postwar period[41]—and the decision to enter part-time employment, to the extent that this is self-determined, becomes increasingly understandable. While so many profound structural constraints remain, it is problematic to discuss any aspect of women's employment in Japan as representing the preference or desire of female workers.

Much hope was pinned on the 1985 Equal Employment Opportunity Act

38. "Model Wages by Age and Academic Career (1987)," in *Japan Statistical Year Book, 1988.*

39. "Hourly Wage Differential Between Males and Females" and "Average Annual Earnings per Regular Employee (1988)," in *Statistical Handbook of Japan,* 1989.

40. "Hourly Wage Differentials Between Males and Females," in *Facts and Figures of Japan* (1982).

41. "Female Employees by Industry and Management Participation Ratio (1979)," *Facts and Figures of Japan* (1982).

(EEOA) to rectify the inequities surrounding women's employment in Japan. After implementation of the legislation in 1985, its opponents quickly claimed that their worst fears were being realized with the rapid and continuing expansion of the part-time female work force and the overall decline in average earnings for women. Attempts to explain the strength of the trend toward part-time employment for women that has marked the last two decades risk slipping into gross oversimplifications if they do not take into account the complexity of conditions affecting the dominance of this employment pattern. From the 1960s through the 1980s women in part-time employment were better able to fulfill the dual role of mother and wife while also being able to earn supplemental income that both secured a standard of living and kept the household actively participating in the consumer economy. The benefits that accrued to Capital are clear, but to focus only on this aspect ignores the constraints on the self-determination of the female employee. To focus only on the female employee's motivation is to ignore the processes of internalization set in motion through education and the media. Women's work, reproductive and productive, has continued to be located at the interface of the public and private domains and remains fundamental to the androcentric economies (libidinal and monetary) of both.

EDUCATION: ENGENDERING DIFFERENCE

To give a full account of the central determining role that education has played in the status of women in postwar Japan would require a review of the entire history of women's education from the Meiji period to the present.[42] Such a review is simply not possible here. Instead, I offer a brief history of the role of public, popular discourse in the successful institutionalization and legitimization of the concept of "women's education" (an integral function of the construction of the condition of "being-woman"). How is it that in postwar Japan women's education came to be defined not as the acquisition of an external body of knowledge but as knowing the feminine body—the internalization of an external construct?

Kathleen Uno's essay in this volume discusses in some detail the concept of *ryōsai kenbo* (good wife, wise mother), which emerged out of the educational debates of the 1890s. This concept underpinned the gender differentiation that characterized Japanese educational policy and practice throughout the twentieth century. Within this framework women were perceived as having not a right to equal education but an obligation to undertake what was defined as "women's education" in order to satisfactorily fulfill a dual role of wife and mother. In this sense women's education constituted a form of vocational training. The underlying assumption of the concept of women's education was that the natural, and

42. For a brief history in English of Meiji and Taisho women's education, see Robins-Mowry, *Hidden Sun*, 31–54; in Japanese, see Maruoka, *Fujin shisō keiseishi nōto*, vol. 1, and Yoneda Sayoko, *Kindai nihon joseishi* (Tokyo: Shin Nihon Shinsho, 1981), vol. 1.

preferably sole, function of women was that of reproduction and nurturing. There was an implicit contradiction in much of the rhetoric of the public discourse surrounding women's education throughout the century, but particularly in the postwar period. If the nurturing and reproductive function was women's natural role, why did it have to be learned and constantly reinforced over a decade and a half of compulsory education?

In the 1980s Japanese government documents regularly boasted of Japan's high educational standards. It was often said by the late 1980s that more women received postsecondary education than men did. The percentage of female high school graduates continuing on to postsecondary education did in fact exceed the figure for male postsecondary enrollments for the first time in 1989.[43] The percentage of both male and female students increased steadily across the postwar period until the figure for males peaked at 43.3 percent in 1976.[44] From that year the figure for male graduates gradually decreased annually while the figure for females continued to rise. In 1989 the proportion of female high school graduates entering postsecondary institutions reached 36.8 percent in contrast to the figure of 36.6 percent for males.[45] These types of figures were used by the Japanese government as proof of the improvement in access to equal opportunity in education. The media paid particular attention to this shift when it was registered in August 1989; however, the emphasis placed on these figures by the government was clearly intended as a counter to the severe criticism it had weathered on women's issues in the election campaign of that same summer.

Statistics such as these were at best misleading when not broken down to reflect the reality of Japan's dual-stream postsecondary education system. Of the total enrollment of 1,861,306 students in four-year universities in 1988, only 482,844 were women. By contrast, of the 444,808 students enrolled in two-year junior colleges, 404,265 were female. In four-year universities, 47 percent of male students majored in social sciences and 25 percent in engineering. By contrast, 29 percent of female students in junior colleges majored in home economics, 25 percent in humanities, and 20 percent in education.[46]

From the Meiji period onward the percentage of females attending and completing the different levels of schooling was consistently high by world standards; however, the issue was not only one of access to education, but access to equal education. The measure of equality in education should not be comparative years of education but comparative levels and content of completed curriculum. A simple mechanism such as scheduling frequently worked to channel female students into gender-specific courses such as home economics and health and away

43. "Shin gakuritsu demo joshi," *Asahi shinbun,* 4 Aug. 1989. My thanks to Charles Horioka for bringing this article to my attention.

44. "Proportion of Pupils Entering Schools of Higher Levels," in *Statistical Handbook of Japan* (1989).

45. Ibid.

46. "University and Junior College Students by Field of Study (1988)," in *Statistical Handbook of Japan* (1989).

from technology and science subjects. The demarcation between "courses for girls" and "courses for boys" remained clearly drawn, and the positive marking of the latter as serious and career-oriented contrasted strongly with the negative marking of the former. The stability of this pattern of gender-coded courses is clear if one compares the course distribution of male and female university enrollment patterns for the 1950s and 1960s with figures for a similar range of courses in the 1980s.[47] There is almost no difference.

The postwar school system itself did little to relieve the situation in terms of offering positive role models for the female student body. Concentrations of teaching specializations among women closely paralleled concentrations of female students in particular curricula, creating a pattern of gender clustering. Moreover, although 70 percent of teachers at the elementary level in 1981 were female, this figure dropped dramatically to 25 percent at the lower secondary level. Whereas elementary school teaching was considered consistent with the traditional nurturing role of women, the education of secondary students was entrusted to male instructors. In 1981 only 2 percent of school principals were female. Even at the elementary level, where 63.5 percent of teachers were female, 94 percent of the principals were male.[48] Although the classroom education and child-care functions fell within the boundaries of traditional women's roles, the management function of school administration did not.

Another factor that further reinforced gender segregation in education was the private school system in Japan. The vast majority of private schools outside of the Tokyo and Osaka areas were segregated. The limited number of students able to gain entry into public upper secondary schools (50 percent) meant that many students wishing to proceed to the higher level of secondary schooling had no choice but to attend a private, single-sex school.[49] The curriculum in girls' schools was anything but equal, which further reduced the chances of entry into a major four-year university. The Women's Action Group (formally the International Women's Year Action Group) and others, such as the feminists who publish the Equal Opportunity Education series, closely monitored the content of curricula and textbooks through the 1970s and 1980s. Considerable international attention was focused on the so-called textbook scandal during the 1980s. However, the attempt to rewrite the history of World War II was only one aspect of the controversy that has surrounded the government-approved textbooks used in Japanese schools. The repetition of gender stereotyping in the language and images appearing in school texts and other teaching aids was considered particu-

---

47. Enrollment figures for 1950–69 are available in the 1970 "Status of Women Report" in Ichibangase, *Sengo fujin mondaishi*, 310–11; figures for 1988 in "University and College Students by Field of Study (1988)," *Statistical Handbook of Japan* (1989).

48. *Tokyo Educational Statistics Yearbook, 1981*, compiled and published by Tokyo Federation of School Teachers, reproduced in *Women's Statistical Diary*. This diary was purchased through *Agora* but contains no bibliographic information.

49. Interview with Mitsui Mariko, in Buckley, "Broken Silence."

larly disturbing by feminists. The National Teacher's Union commited considerable funds to research on the problem of gender discrimination in the classroom and educational materials. A proliferation of private postsecondary women's colleges over the postwar period was a particular concern to feminist educators, who argued that curriculum content and quality, along with teaching qualifications, were generally unregulated in many of these small, expensive institutions.

Given the overt inequality and gender bias of education in Japan, it is not surprising to find that access to education in the Japanese case produced results quite unlike those in North America or Europe. The usual assumption is that the better educated a woman is, the more likely she is to be employed. In Canada 53.5 percent of women with secondary education participated in the work force as compared with 72.3 percent of university graduates.[50] The opposite trend was true in Japan. The more educated a woman was, the less likely she was to enter full-time employment and the shorter her average periods of stay in the work force.[51] The reason behind this trend appears to have been the differing value attached to education for men and women. For the male each educational achievement was a qualification for future employment, whereas for the female each educational achievement was a potential qualification for a better marriage match. The more economically secure the marriage she made, the less likely a woman was to need to enter or remain in the workplace to supplement family income. The higher the social and economic status of her partner, the more pressure a woman was under to leave full-time employment. Certain specializations were seen as better qualifications for a particular category of future spouse. Pharmacology was popular in the 1980s as a possible entrée to a marriage match with a doctor. Certain women's universities regularly supplied graduating lists to hospitals. One well-known Tokyo women's college was renowned as a source of wives for career diplomats.

Despite the creative use of statistics to suggest otherwise, the reality of postwar Japanese education was that it remained a two-stream, gender-segregated system. The underlying premise of education for females did not fundamentally move beyond the concept of *ryōsai kenbo*. The 1970s and 1980s saw the emergence of an influential genre of popular educational literature devoted to the function of defining the correct code of behavior for young Japanese women and instructing mothers in how to raise good daughters. Two of the better examples of this best-selling genre were Hamao Minoru's *How to Bring Up Girls: A Guide to Raising a Nice Child* and Kawakami Gentarō's *I'd Like to See Their Parents' Faces*.[52] A couple of quotations from these volumes will give some indication of the general tone of these popular educational works. Hamao writes: "Having only one science text-

---

50. P. Phillips and E. Phillips, *Women and Work: Inequality in the Labour Market* (Toronto: Lorimer, 1983), 40.

51. Extensive research has been done in this area by Professor Mary Brinton of the Department of Sociology, University of Chicago.

52. Mack Horton, "Reactionaries on the Shelf: Advice to Japanese Mothers by Gentlemen Amateurs," *Feminist International* (Tokyo) 2 (1980): 28–31, gives a detailed discussion of these works.

book (for example) ignores the logical minds of boys and the daily-life orientation of girls." He suggests that textbooks for girls should be "more practical, with lots of examples related to daily life . . . for example, explaining in a scientific way how the wash gets whiter when you use bleach and how milk curdles when you add orange juice."[53] Kawakami is concerned with the dangers of educating women:

> [Women today] agitate to acquire the knowledge so as to have the same weapons of attack as men. But really, as in the past, it's a losing battle more often than not. If a mother wants her daughter to grow up right, rather than taking into her hands weapons for pressing her own point of view and outargue others, she should look for a treasure she wants to lose least of all. What makes a woman strong is not a job or knowledge for application in the outside world.[54]

Kawakami binds female self-identity to the reproductive body (virginity as treasured object, the property/right of a future husband, the passage to motherhood). Male self-identity is defined by the phallus as the signifier of power. Knowledge and power are conflated into the phallic symbol of "weapons of attack."

Unfortunately, Kawakami and Hamao cannot be ignored as extreme examples. Their books were quite representative of the tone and general content of the genre of guide books to femininity. The durability of the concept of *ryōsai kenbo* was perhaps nowhere more evident than in these contemporary popular educational texts. The body of woman's knowledge remains defined as her own body (cleanliness, hygiene, reproduction), and that body is constructed and contained within the boundaries of her dual role (wife and mother). These works, and many others like them, stacked the "motherhood" and "family" sections of bookstores in the 1980s and frequently sold in excess of a million copies over a series of editions.

Such "authorities" as these carried the discourse on women's education into the popular medium of television talk shows, where such comments as the above became common fare. The reinforcement of the mother's role as guardian of her child's education was not limited to sources clearly related to the educational function but also extended into the realm of representations of gender differentiated roles in the media. For example, in contrast to men, women were seldom ever shown reading or writing in popular television programs of the 1970s and 1980s. The rare exceptions to this rule were scenes of mothers helping their children with homework assignments or engaged in some similar education-related roles. Not surprisingly, women were also portrayed only infrequently as having salaried employment. A strong focus on child health and hygiene in women's magazines during the 1950s and 1960s gave way to an increasing number of articles and special issues dealing with questions of education as the wave of children of the occupation baby boomers began to move through the school system in the 1970s. Feminists were quick to point out the similarities between the public rhetoric of the 1970s and 1980s and that of the Meiji educa-

53. Hamao, *How to Bring Up Girls*, quoted in Horton, "Reactionaries on the Shelf," 30.
54. Kawakami, *I'd Like to See*, quoted in Horton, "Reactionaries on the Shelf," 29.

tional reformists. Once again women's education was being treated by the authorities not as a right but as an obligation that prepared them for their role as nurturer and educator for their children.

The level of mothers' investment in their children's education became so extreme through the 1970s that the expression *kyōiku mama* (education mama) gained wide currency as a derogatory term for mothers who oversaw long hours of cram school and private tutoring to ensure their child's chances of entering an elite educational stream. Daughters, however, were frequently disadvantaged in households with one or more sons to be educated. The energy and money necessary to succeed in the ever more competitive educational environment in Japan led mothers to make certain discriminatory choices. A 1982 government survey recorded that 44.9 percent of mothers felt that they wanted their sons to go on to a four-year university; only 18.6 percent had the same ambition for their daughters. By contrast, 23.3 percent of mothers wanted their daughters to attend two-year colleges, in comparison with a 6.7 percent response in the case of sons.[55] Financial considerations were an important factor in such preferences. The average annual cost of tuition and board for a student attending a national university in 1982 was 970,000 yen, and 1,321,000 yen for a private university.[56] The public discourse on women's education that flowed endlessly from diverse media sources and the negative reinforcement of popular television, film, and comic-book images all combined to foster women's internalization of the secondary and supportive function of women's education.

It is not surprising in this context that feminist groups devoted a great deal of effort to writing and publishing alternative books on female sexuality and mother-daughter relations. Perhaps the most demanding project of this kind was the cooperative translation of *Our Bodies, Ourselves* organized by the Women's Bookstore (Shokado) in Kyoto.[57] These feminist publications acted as one counter to the constant stream of mass-produced educational materials for mothers, wives, and teenage girls. From the earliest years of the second wave of feminism, presses committed to the publication of women's history and resources (e.g., *Domesu*) actively promoted women's research as one means of slowly overcoming the dearth of materials for the teaching of women's issues in schools. The *minikomi* network of publications regularly featured articles dealing with curriculum reform and educational access.[58]

The possibilities for resistance to the gender discrimination in Japanese education remained limited across the postwar period. One feminist remarked on the

55. Prime Minister's Office, "Survey of Attitudes to Education" (Tokyo: Japanese Government Publications, 1982), reproduced in *Women's Statistical Diary*, Group S.R., Tokyo, 1983.

56. "Annual Student Tuition and Living Expenses by Type of Institution," in *Universities and Students*, Ministry of Education Publication 212, 1982.

57. *Karada watashitachi jishin* (Kyoto: Shokado Women's Bookstore, 1988).

58. Collections of *minikomi* publications from across Japan are available at the Shinjuku and Ikebukuro Women's Information Centers.

number of young women who had chosen to operate in small intellectual collectives outside the traditional institutional structures. It was common for such collectives to form around alternative women's publications such as *Agora* (the longest-lived of Japan's feminist journals), *Feminist International* and *Eros* in the 1970s, and more recently *Wonderful Women, Regumi tsūshin* (Newsletter of the Lesbian Cooperative), *Refamu* (Les femmes), *Women's Media, Orange Voice, Women's Cinema Journal,* and others. In various ways, increasing numbers of women and specific interest groups attempted to take up the "weapons of attack" (Kawakami's expression) and to undo the tightly knit structures of gender differentiation encoded into the entire fabric of Japanese education and the related public discourse of women's education. This process of dismantling the discrimination inherent in the structures of gender-segregated education proved to be a slow one as it involved dealing with not only the monolithic institution of the Ministry of Education but also the entire media industry, from women's magazine publishers to the producers of children's television, soap operas, and educational programming. In the 1980s education, as it functioned in the institutions, as popularized in the mass of educational publications, and as constructed in the public imagination, remained a major mechanism for the internalization of the dominant structures of gender discrimination.

THE STATE AND BODY POLITIC(S)

I have thus far argued that the working conditions of women in Japan have represented the desire of Capital at any given historical moment, rather than the desire of individual women workers. The most heated debate in Japanese feminism in the postwar period developed around the issue of the Equal Employment Opportunity Act, which became effective in April of 1986. Many of the feminists on both sides of the debate—those for the removal of the protection clauses for women and those against—drew on the experience of the past to argue for caution in formulating any policy affecting the status of women. Both sides agreed that legislation has seldom been about women's rights and welfare in Japan. Rather, the legislation developed over the last century in relation to women's rights has generally functioned not to liberate women but to restrain them.

During the war years eugenics and labor policy consistently reflected a desire to protect both the reproductive function of young women and the fundamental social organ of the Japanese body politic, the family. By the last year of the war more "realistic" members of government who recognized the possibility of defeat felt that it would be essential to Japan's recovery that the family structure remain intact as a basic unit of social and economic support. These individuals argued strongly against mobilizing mothers into the industrial work force.[59]

59. Barbara Molony, "Women in Wartime Employment," *Feminist International* (Tokyo) 2 (1980): 82. For a more detailed study in Japanese of women's employment during the war years, see Yoneda, *Kindai nihon joseishi,* chaps. 9–10, and Maruoka, *Fujin shisō keiseishi nōto,* vol. 1, chap. 10.

When defeat did come, the family indeed emerged as the primary unit of cooperation and survival in the immediate postwar years of hardship. The array of legislation introduced to deal with the state of emergency—National Assistance Act, Child Welfare Act, Unemployment Benefits Act, and so on—consisted of stopgap measures. Feminists frequently warn against the risk of attributing too much significance to the immediate impact of the constitutional reforms instigated in 1947. They question the usual focus on an immediate quantitative shift in female political representation, for this approach ignores the very unusual context. Although 67 percent of eligible women voted in the election of 10 April 1946 and thirty-nine women were elected to office (8.4 percent of the Lower House membership), over the next decade the success of women candidates fell dramatically. In the 1955 election only nine women candidates won seats in the Lower House.[60] The relevant context for the extraordinary performance of female candidates and the high turnout of female voters in 1946 is the media environment created by both the Japanese women who had fought for women's suffrage (Ichikawa Fusae was the best known of the feminists whose activity spanned the prewar and postwar periods) and by the office of the Supreme Command for the Allied Powers (SCAP).[61]

The intensity of the campaign to educate Japanese women into their new role as voters created a guilt vote. Surveys of women voters in the early postwar period consistently showed that the majority of women voters went to the polls because they believed it was wrong not to do so rather than because they perceived themselves to be exercising a right. By the mid-1970s approximately 95 percent of women voters responded that they voted either because it was their right to do so or because they believed their vote could have a positive effect.[62] Although the reason for voting clearly shifted, there was a corresponding shift in the public perception of women's role in politics over these decades. Whereas a woman's right to vote was fully incorporated within the public memory by the 1970s, other political rights of women, such as the right to run for office, did not gain equal currency. This discrepancy can in part explain the dramatic decline in the number of women elected to office after the initial success of 1945 and the continuation of low levels of representation until the 1989 election, when the next major organized campaign to promote women candidates was mounted. The Japanese feminists I have interviewed who opposed or questioned the EEOA often cited the

60. For detailed account of policies relating to women from defeat through the late 1950s, see Maruoka, *Fujin shisō keiseishi nōto*, vol. 2, chap. 1, and Ichibangase, *Sengo fujin mondaishi*, chap. 3.

61. Ichikawa Fusae's life (1893–1981) spans the twentieth century, and her own activities closely reflect the different stages in the development of feminism in both the prewar and postwar periods. Her decision to work with the authorities in promoting women's cooperation with the war effort was followed by decades of commitment to furthering women's political rights and representation.

62. Robins-Mowry, *Hidden Sun*, describes this phenomenon in her detailed account of SCAP's role in promoting the woman's vote. She does not, however, use the term *guilt vote*. The term was used by a Japanese feminist colleague (*sekinin o kanjita*) in an interview when discussing the same situation. It might also be translated as "vote of obligation."

limited impact of the 1947 constitution as an explanation for their suspicion of legislative reform.

As Japan moved into its period of rapid economic growth, government policies shifted to accommodate new pressures for the creation of an adequate industrial labor force. The 1963 document "Tasks and Measures for Development of Human Resources for Economic Growth" described the need to encourage married women to enter the work force while safeguarding the family structure.[63] The proposal amounted to a significant reversal of the wartime preference for unmarried women as industrial workers. The widespread employment of married women who have completed their reproductive function as a source of low-wage, part-time labor dates from this deliberate policy shift in the early 1960s. Over the 1960s a new employment strategy emerged based on a minimal core of full-time male employees within what, at the time, was presented as a lifetime employment structure, with peak production periods serviced by temporary injections of part-time female workers. The small to medium industries found it economically advantageous, given their often precarious contractual supply relationship with the major corporations, to draw the majority of their workers from the cheaper, "disposable" pool of female part-timers and limited-term employees (women working full-time prior to marriage).[64]

By the mid to late 1960s the first signs of the impact of rapid economic growth on the structure and distribution of households were discernible. Policymakers recognized that the new nuclear unit was not in a position to meet the basic social functions previously performed by the extended family household—for example, welfare and child care—and that the fabric of familial relations was changing substantially. Policies with such homey titles as "Image of the Ideal Japanese" (Central Education Council, 1966) and "Toward Better Family Life" (Family Life Council, 1967) addressed the crisis perceived in the social function of the family.[65] At the same time, the government introduced programs aimed specifically at financing the transfer of the welfare and social security function into the public/consumer domain.

The subtext of these policies was the protection of the family in the wake of Prime Minister Ikeda Hayato's Income Doubling Plan of 1960. The family and welfare related policies of the middle to late 1960s functioned to create the social context for the achievement of the economic goals of the income-doubling plan, which was premised on further developing domestic consumer demand for manufactured goods and overcoming the threat of an acute labor shortage. One mid-1960s response to this situation was Sato's doomed appeal to the women of Japan to have more children. This proved an immediate failure as a long-term solution to the projected labor crisis, for women were already well aware that the child-care support that would allow them to satisfy both policy directions—have

63. Discussed in Fuse, "Japanese Family in Transition," part 2, 11.
64. See Nakamura, *Pāto taimu Q & A.*
65. Fuse, "Japanese Family in Transition," part 2, 11.

more babies and stay in the work force—was not forthcoming. Women continued to have fewer children, but they did extend their total period of participation in the work force by having children later and returning earlier through a reentry pattern as part-timers, a pattern that did offer a short-term stopgap against the labor shortage. Increased individual and household incomes generated higher levels of consumption, which in turn stimulated the domestic economy and industrial growth. Both the national and household "incomes" did in fact more than double over the next decade.

Despite the rhetoric of the social policies of the 1960s, by the mid-1970s it had become apparent that the family was not receiving the support it needed and that the government was not prepared to meet the social security bill now that the full extent of this financial commitment was clearer. The projections for the graying of the Japanese population, increased lobbying by feminists for equal pay for equal work, the continual increase in the number of females entering postsecondary education (delaying labor-force participation), and the rapidly declining birthrate all contributed to a major shift in government policy in the 1970s. The wartime slogan "Reproduce and Flourish" had first been replaced by the "Production First" spirit of the 1960s. Now this slogan in turn was replaced by the catchphrase "Japanese-style Welfare." With Prime Minister Ōhira Masayoshi's declaration of a "new age of culture" in 1980 Japan officially entered a period of neotraditionalism from which it had not emerged by the early 1990s. The concern with identity throughout the 1970s and 1980s remained bound to contemporary constructions of the "roots" of Japanese society. The stated objective of this mass nostalgia was a return to all that was "lost" during the process of modernization. The condition of *nosutarujī* was a wonderful example of history in the making—in a quite literal sense. The media played a major role in the production and marketing of tradition through advertising,[66] historical dramas for television,[67] "epic" movies,[68] the promotion of a "po-mo" (postmodern) chic,[69] endless multivolume pictorial histories and reproductions of first printings of major Japanese authors, and the like. The government's call for a "return" to traditional family values as a fundamental dimension of a new system of Japanese welfare was one more example of the rampant neonostalgia, and the implications of this policy shift were serious for Japanese women.

What were Japanese women to think when Prime Minister Nakasone Yasuhiro appeared on television in the early 1980s in a series of prime-time political

66. For a Japanese feminist analysis of the role of the media, see *Agora: Onna to jōhō*, 25, and Tanaka, *Josei Kaihō*, chap. 4. Marilyn Ivy has written on the "Discover Japan" and "Exotic Japan" advertising campaigns of JNR in "Tradition and Difference in the Japanese Mass Media," *Public Culture Bulletin* 1, no. 1 (Fall 1988).

67. NHK has led the fray in this area with its annual Sunday night epic drama, setting a pattern emulated by the commercial networks.

68. Kurosawa Akira's shift into the epic genre, e.g., in *Kagemusha* and *Ran*, exemplifies this trend.

69. Postmodern chic is exemplified by the designers Issey Miyake, Kawakubo Rei, and Yamamoto Yohji.

advertisements (government policy as commodity) calling for a return to family values? Nakasone, sitting in a "typical" traditional farmhouse surrounded by three generations of family beside the glowing coals of the household hearth, called on all Japanese families to strive to sit down together like this for their evening meal. Nakasone's television appearances were an attempt to gain popular support for the LDP's platform for "Strengthening the Family Base," which was announced as part of Nakasone's Report of the Commission on Administrative Reform—a report that recommended sweeping conservative reforms in almost all aspects of LDP policy. In discussing the proposal for a new Japanese welfare system the report stated: "From now on it will be necessary to develop the special character of our own country's society. We will have to plan to implement a welfare [system] in which an appropriate share is met by a highly efficient government, but which is based on the solidarity of home, neighbourhood, enterprise, and local society, which is in turn founded on the spirit of help and independence of the individual."[70]

Here one begins to get a sense of the reality gap that Japanese women continued to live with throughout the 1980s. The majority of Japanese families no longer lived in houses large enough to accommodate three generations, not to mention a traditional sunken hearth! Family budgets were already stretched, with more and more families resorting to debt as a solution. Nakasone offered no suggestion as to how the family was to take up the financial burden the government was trying to pass on. The government has argued that reincorporating the elderly into the family unit will relieve child-care pressures. Elderly family members can provide child care as long as they remain healthy, but in a country where bed rest is a common treatment of all forms of senile deterioration and where life expectancy is increasing annually, the risk that the wife will be left caring for both children and the elderly is high. The institutionalization of women's welfare function in policy statements in the 1980s implicitly excluded the option of full-time employment for married women.[71]

It can be argued that the proposed Japanese-style welfare system worked in tandem with the EEOA to further the restructuring and relocation (away from the workplace and into the home) of women's work. The most significant change under the new law was the removal of all protection clauses. Under the previous Labor Standards Act women were not allowed to work night shifts or carry excessive weights, and they were entitled to menstruation and maternity leave. The protective measures were all related to the concept of *bosei hogo* (the protection of motherhood). The government took the strategy of challenging feminists with

70. Translated in Sandra Buckley and Vera Mackie, "Women in the New Japanese State," in Gavan McCormack and Yoshio Sugimoto, eds., *Democracy in Contemporary Japan* (Melbourne: Hale and Iremonger, 1985), 184.

71. For a discussion of the issues surrounding the welfare function and women's employment, see the roundtable interview "Bosei o hoshō shi byōdō o susumetai," *Agora: Hirogaru josei kaihō to danjo byōdōhō*, no. 20, and the special issue *Agora: Danjo byōdō to bosei hoshō*, no. 22.

the American example, arguing that if Japanese women wanted equality they should be prepared to forfeit protective clauses, as had American women. Many feminists fought against the new law on the grounds that the comparison with the American situation was a distortion because the overall conditions of employment and the legal history of women's rights were far more advanced in America than in Japan. It was argued that the reforms would lead to a worsening of conditions for factory and part-time workers. It was apparent from early in the government push to approve the new law that it was strongly supported by industry. This support in itself was enough to raise suspicion in the Japanese case. One feminist wrote: "The semi-conductor producing companies are attempting to have the ban on women working the night shift removed. No matter what, these companies intend to be able to use the women—the cheaper labour—on the night shifts too."[72]

That there was a need for reform to the existing Labor Standards Act was accepted by the majority of feminist groups. As early as 1978 the group Watakushitachi no Koyō Byōdōhō o Tsukuru Onnatachi no Kai (Organization for the Formulation of a Women's Equal Opportunity Act) had been established with the specific mandate of lobbying the government for a new act free of discriminatory clauses. This group, like so many other women's organizations formed in the 1970s, gained much of its impetus from the impact of the International Women's Decade. This UN initiative offered Japanese women access to various international forums over the decade to promote reforms in the domestic context.[73] One of the most significant achievements of the Kokusai Fujinnen o Kikakke Toshite Kōdō Suru Onnatachi no Kai (International Women's Year Action Group) was its successful international campaign to pressure the Japanese government into ratifying the Treaty to End All Forms of Sexual Discrimination. Conscious of its international reputation as a newly emerging world power Japan succumbed and signed the treaty in 1980, with a commitment to act on the terms of the treaty before 1985. This date is significant in understanding the speed with which the government moved during 1984 and 1985 in attempting to draft a document that would be acceptable to all the interested parties and be capable of passing through the Diet.

The document that was finally brought to the Diet and passed in April 1986 was considered a major compromise by many feminists. The elimination of all protection clauses was not rejected out of hand by the feminist critics of the act. Rather, they argued that in the absence of any protection and given the existing levels of discriminatory practices in Japan, it was essential that the act include stringent punitive clauses. The version of the act that was finally passed in 1986 included no significant punitive measures. The new act depended on the goodwill of employers, something which feminists argued could not be assumed on the

72. Buckley and Mackie, "Women in the New Japanese State," 177.
73. See *Agora: Onnatachi wa ima kawaru— Copenhagen Kaigi,* no. 23; *Agora: Nairobi ga katarikakeru mono,* special edition 104; and Maruoka, *Fujin shisō keiseishi nōto,* vol. 2, chap. 9.

basis of the past history of discrimination. Almost as soon as the act was passed, employment procedures were being modified to fit the letter of the law without introducing any real change to discriminatory practices.[74] A continued escalation of the part-time employment trend and the rapid insertion of low-wage, part-time female labor into night shifts have validated the initial reservations of those feminists who opposed the act.

Feminist accounts of the success of female candidates in the August 1989 House of Councillors' election emphasize the level of dissatisfaction with the EEOA as a significant factor behind the women's vote. By contrast, media accounts generally focused on what came to be known as "the woman problem"—Prime Minister Uno Sōsuke's relationship with a geisha. Although some women's publications also referred to this issue—which could more accurately have been described as "the man problem"—it was generally presented as only one issue among several. Key concerns were the corruption in government (not only the LDP) exposed in the unfolding saga of the Recruit scandal, the 3 percent consumption tax, which was most directly felt by women in their role of managing household budgets, and a growing sense of disappointment in the apparent ineffectiveness of the EEOA, then in its third year of implementation. The success of 22 out of an outstanding number of 148 female candidates sent a strong message to the legislators that the women's vote could still be mobilized and that it was a powerful force to be reckoned with.

Abortion law was another area of threatened legislative reform directly related to women's work, both productive and reproductive. The campaign against abortion law reform was central to much of the organized political activity of women in the 1970s and 1980s. There were a series of unsuccessful attempts during that period to reform the provision in the abortion law allowing for the termination of pregnancy on economic grounds. Women's groups successfully countered three separate conservative campaigns for the withdrawal of the "economic reasons" clause. The antiabortion law reform coalition saw the proposed reforms as one dimension of a comprehensive ideological push for the curtailment of women's self-determination in both their reproductive and productive labor, yet another redefinition of "being-woman" framed around the shifting priorities of government (privatization of welfare) and industry (reduction of labor costs and fragmentation of labor through increased part-time out-work employment.)[75]

Let us return one last time to the reality gap. A questionnaire issued by the

74. My thanks to Charles Horioka for his helpful comments on the topic of the continued practice of two-stream employment within the structures of *sōgōshoku* and *ippanshoku* since the introduction of the new legislation.

75. There is an extensive literature on the abortion debate in Japanese. Two of the more frequently cited works are *Onna ni wa umenai toki mo aru*, compiled and distributed by the Organization of Women Against War (Tokyo: Gogatsusha, 1983), and *Onna no sei to chūzetsu*, an edited volume compiled and distributed by Shakai Hyōronsha Henshū (Tokyo, 1983). For a summary of the debate and women's reaction to the reform campaigns, see Buckley and Mackie, "Women in the New Japanese State," 178–79.

Japanese prime minister's office sought responses from women to the statement "Husbands work outside the home, wives take care of the household." The Japanese approval rate was 71 percent, as compared with a disapproval rate among American women of 65.1 percent.[76] Given that over half of Japan's adult women are wage workers, it is apparent that there is considerable tension between the ideal and the real. The extent to which Japanese women have internalized the popular projection of the "happy, full-time homemaker" and the ability of the nation-s/State we are calling "postwar Japan" to recuperate or absorb isolated moments of women's resistance can be understood only in the context of all the discursive practices that constitute that s/State. Education, the media, the law, institutional structures (family, schools, courts, hospitals, etc.), employment practices, and many other basic threads of the fabric of daily life have interacted to construct and reconstruct that constantly altered state of "being-woman" at any given moment in Japan's postwar history.

Japanese feminists have concerned themselves increasingly over the last decade with the task of identifying and tracing the complex external structures that transform ideology into the dominant reality. Both at the level of the family (social organ) and the State (body politic), the subjected condition of "being-woman" has been in a constant state of production across postwar history. However, it is essential to both the successful marketing and the internalization of this condition that the modes of production are disappeared. The fallacy that there is a condition of "being-woman" (a fixed ideological construction) obscures the reality of a gender politics within which women are always "becoming-woman" (a fluid cultural and historical inscription). I have attempted here to begin to map, to render visible, the points of intersection of some of the discursive practices that have drawn the boundaries of gender differentiation in postwar Japan.

76. "Survey of International Comparison of Attitudes Towards Gender Differentiation in Work Allocation," Prime Minister's Office, 1982.

CHAPTER FOURTEEN

Contests for the Workplace

Andrew Gordon

The tone of the laboring citizen's voice at work changed dramatically from the contentious early postwar years, through the high growth era, and into the period of "Japan as Number One." No less dramatic was the change in the view from outside the workplace. In the late 1940s American officials feared that a radical labor movement would sabotage their program to revive Japan as the "workshop of Asia." By the late 1970s scholars, journalists, business leaders, and officials in Japan and overseas sang hymns of praise to harmonious labor relations as a central cause of the nation's economic power.

The clash of two distinct versions of workplace culture transformed Japan's labor-management relations in the postwar era. By *workplace culture* I refer to the complex of everyday, "commonsense" assumptions and behavior of managers and workers: What are appropriate arrangements of the work process or levels of pay? Who decides? On what grounds? I place "commonsense" in quotes to stress the contested nature of what one set of participants may feel "goes without saying."

The powerful unions of the early postwar era championed one version of workplace culture. Members of these unions (termed *first unions* in this essay) aspired to shape the work process according to standards independent from the business goals of the enterprise: safety, equality of both opportunity and result for regular male workers, and secure and predictable career paths. They saw the union as the instrument to realize this vision. Nonetheless, they saw the enterprise as the primary arena for their struggle. That is, even powerful first unions organized enterprise units and sought to make the enterprise an institution that would serve their social needs for secure livelihoods, safe and challenging work.

Individual managers and management organizations, as well as the new wave of cooperative *second unions* that emerged in the 1950s, championed a different version of workplace culture. They posited technological innovation, productivity, and profit in a competitive capitalist society as basic objectives. They rejected the *primary* value that more combative unions placed on security and equality of result; managers insisted on freedom to distribute rewards to individuals in accord with their ability and control the workplace to maximize productivity. Yet to achieve these goals, managers cultivated active labor commitment by sharing the fruits of economic gains with cooperative unions and workers who served with ability and loyalty.

Over the long span of forty years this managerial version of workplace culture triumphed decisively, but the struggle was prolonged and varied. In the earliest postwar days workers challenged the very legitimacy of management authority. Well into the 1950s, and beyond in some places, powerful unions persisted or emerged anew. They sought to control work and the distribution of reward while managers, the state, and, increasingly, the broader societal apparatus that molded national ideology—principally the media and the education system—promoted a vision of the enterprise devoted to productivity, in which management would control the workplace and negotiate over granting workers "fair" pieces of a growing pie.

Two sharply opposed historical narratives of this contest have been constructed. One casts the story as the destruction of a workplace culture in which jobs were secure, pay reflected worker need, and employees sought to participate in signifi-cant management decisions. In its place emerged enterprise communities devoted to production first, employees second, using competition and division among workers (regular/temporary, full-time/part-time, men/women), and fear (of low raises, slow promotions, transfers, dismissals) to motivate labor and coerce partici-pation in so-called self-management small-group activities. The second narrative describes the same trajectory in very different terms, as a social miracle unfolding in tandem with the more famous economic one: practical workers and farsighted managers cooperated to overcome divisive polarization and radical unions: they replaced foolhardy confrontation with harmony. This enabled the economy to grow at an extraordinary pace for twenty years and to be resilient and productive through the stagflation of the 1970s and the microelectronic revolution of the 1980s.

Certainly the latter narrative is the dominant one in Western popular and academic discourse and in the official history of major companies. The former narrative has dominated Japanese scholarship for most of the postwar era.[1] Even

---

1. Superior versions of the latter narrative include David Halberstam, *The Reckoning* (New York: William Morrow, 1986), and, as a scholarly venture, Robert Cole, *Strategies for Learning: Small Group Activities in American, Japanese, and Swedish Industry* (Berkeley and Los Angeles: University of California Press, 1989). A superbly executed example of the former narrative is Shimizu Shinzō, ed., *Sengo rōdō kumiai undō shi ron* (Tokyo: Nihon Hyōronsha, 1982). A similar division characterizes English-language Marxist assessments. For a positive view, see Martin Kenney and Richard Florida, "Beyond Mass Production," *Politics and Society* 16, no. 1 (1988): 121–58, which reacts to the negative assessment of

in more nuanced form than these crude sketches, both narratives are too stark to deal effectively with the evidence, but I am basically sympathetic to the first narrative. Creative innovations enabled managerial culture to triumph and win support from workers and transformed unions, but we will end up with a distorted view of history through the lens of the victors if we lose sight of the sacrifices and trade-offs that accompanied the decline of the first-union program.

COMPARATIVE, INTERNATIONAL, AND HISTORICAL CONTEXTS

Japan's postwar history of labor and management is a variant of a process common to all the noncommunist wartime powers: the postwar triumph of the "politics of productivity."[2] Japan's version of this story is not the only one subject to alternative narratives. Historians of Europe have been torn between celebrating the outcome or stressing that men in power tolerated enduring inequality as they exalted productivity and growth.[3] The comparative context turns on the idea that technological advance and increased productivity could serve "as a substitute for harsh questions of allocation." This was a time-honored theme of American social policy and management ideology; business leaders and politicians since the turn of the century had claimed that enhanced productivity would allow the nation to "transcend the class conflicts that arose from scarcity."[4] The men who promoted the managerial culture that triumphed in postwar Japanese factories issued an identical claim. Unions and managers had to replace ideologies of class conflict with new forms of cooperation that would raise productivity and bring prosperity to all citizens.[5]

Japanese managers promoted scientific management as a means to raise productivity as early as the 1920s. Thus, in response to the confrontational postwar unions of the Left they probably would have articulated something like the "politics of productivity" in the 1950s even without American prodding. Yet Japan's was not to be a parallel but separate history. The international similarities would not have been so great, and the drive for productivity in Japan would not have been so powerful, if not for the postwar decision of the United States to extend to the realm of foreign economic policy in both Europe and Japan its

Knuth Dohse, Ulrich Jurgens, and Thomas Malsch, "From 'Fordism' to 'Toyotism'? The Social Organization of the Labor Process in the Japanese Automobile Industry," *Politics and Society* 14, no. 2 (1985): 115–46.

2. Charles Maier, "The Politics of Productivity: Foundations of American International Economic Policy after World War II," in Peter Katzenstein, ed., *Between Power and Plenty: Foreign Economic Policies of the Advanced Industrial States* (Madison: University of Wisconsin Press, 1978).

3. See Maier, "Politics of Productivity," 49, on these alternative perspectives on the European postwar story.

4. Ibid., 29.

5. See Nakamura Seiji, *Nihon seisansei kōjō undō shi* (Tokyo, 1958), 182, for the founding statement, to this effect, of the Japan Productivity Center in 1955.

domestic concern to turn "issues of political economy into questions of output and efficiency."[6]

The American occupation legalized Japan's unions in 1945, encouraged millions of workers to join unions in the next two years, then turned hostile toward the powerful unions of the Left in 1947. This much is well known. Less well known is that after the occupation, in Japan as in Europe, the United States aggressively promoted a movement for industrial productivity for the sake of international prosperity and the domestic stability of these countries. In 1953 American officials disbursing Foreign Operations Administration (FOA) funds began to encourage the Japanese government and business leaders to launch the productivity movement; their exhortation eventually led the government to found the Japan Productivity Center (JPC), a semi-independent institution funded by the two governments. Proclaiming that increased productivity would "expand markets, increase employment, raise real wages and standards of living, and advance the common interests of labor, management and consumers," and bolstered by annual FOA grants of one to two million dollars, the center quickly reached out to factories across the country. In its first two years the center sent fifty-three small groups of managers and union leaders on missions to learn the art of productivity from the American masters, and the pace of exchange increased thereafter. Back home the center promoted the movement with lectures, pamphlets, and a newspaper.[7]

Myriad individual threads of causation ran from American management practice, to foreign policy, through the JPC and other like-minded institutions (such as the Japan Union of Scientists and Engineers) then onto the shop floors of individual factories, where productive innovations took place and a management vision of workplace culture took root. As early as 1958 a Japanese historian of the nascent movement credited the JPC with importing an alphabet soup of cutting-edge American techniques of quality control and production management, helping firms such as Nissan and Toyota to raise worker output dramatically. Over the following two decades Japanese managers and workers transformed American techniques and developed a new generation of acronyms such as JK (*Jishu kanri*, or self-management) and QC circles (Quality Control circles), creating a true national movement of small-group activities.[8]

As American policymakers apparently hoped, the response of Japan's national union federations to the productivity drive after 1955 eventually brought cooperative labor groups into governing coalitions, however informal, and cast dissenting

6. Maier, "Politics of Productivity," 45.

7. On founding and funding of the center, see Nakamura, *Nihon seisansei kōjō undō shi*, 179–83, 192; see also Hyōdō Tsutomu, "Rōdō kumiai undō no hatten," in *Iwanami kōza: Nihon rekishi 23, gendai 2* (Tokyo: Iwanami Shoten, 1977) 113–14.

8. Robert Cole, *Strategies for Learning*, on quality circles. The acronym *QC* stood for "quality control" when it was coined in the United States. In the process of importing the term to Japan, *QC* came to mean "quality circle." This change was not trivial. It reflected the Japanese stress on broad participation versus the original American concern with staff control of quality.

unions as "obstructionist."[9] Echoing international bifurcations among labor federations, the Japanese labor movement split sharply. Sōdōmei, the most conservative federation, cooperated while seeking promises that jobs would be protected and productivity gains shared. Zenrō, composed of the cooperative second unions born of the bitter disputes of the early 1950s, at first took a neutral position. Sōhyō, stronghold of the first unions described in more detail below, opposed the JPC vigorously. But at the enterprise level it appears that labor accepted the movement from the start almost regardless of national affiliation; already in 1957 the Labor Ministry hailed "the birth of a practical, rather than an abstract, response to the productivity movement" at major manufacturers whose unions achieved unprecedented 1956 year-end bonuses with almost no disputes.[10]

America continued to promote unions willing to cooperate in the transformation of workplace culture in the 1960s. The United States encouraged the Japanese in 1964 to form an expanded national federation called Dōmei (Zen Nihon Rōdō Sōdōmei), centered on Zenrō's cooperative second unions. Dōmei came to rival the larger Sōhyō federation.[11] In addition, American and European unions of the International Metalworkers Federation (IMF) in the late 1950s began urging a coalition of Japanese unions in steel, electronics, and shipbuilding, from both Sōhyō and Dōmei, to join the IMF. Eventually (again in 1964) unions representing 540,000 metalworkers founded the Japan Council of the IMF. The Council sought what it called a "free and democratic" movement, in essence a less confrontational relationship with management than that advocated by the left wing of Sōhyō. The secretary of the steel union federation also frankly claimed that "the I.M.F. is so powerful that we may be shut out of world steel markets if we do not join."[12]

But finally, it is crucial to recognize the limit to the impact of the United States. American pressures in the 1950s bolstered the prospects for the minority movement of cooperative second unions and helped these groups build momentum in the 1960s. In part as a result, the balance of power between advocates of opposed versions of workplace culture shifted. But the Americans did not determine the

9. Maier, "Politics of Productivity," 41. See the essay by Garon and Mochizuki in this volume for a fuller analysis.

10. Nakamura, *Nihon seisansei kōjō undō shi,* 255, cites the Labor Ministry's white paper of 1957, 266–67.

11. Hyōdō, "Rōdō kumiai undō no hatten," 129. Dōmei combined the Zenrō and Sōdōmei federations and a "second union" of public employees as well.

12. Hyōdō, "Rōdō kumiai undō no hatten," 131–32. The irony of this visible American hand in the remaking of postwar Japanese labor relations is profound. Nakamura, *Nihon seisansei kōjō undō shi,* 180–81, describes a press conference in 1954 at which the head of an American aid mission, in Japan to promote the productivity movement, confidently dismissed a question about whether a more productive Japan would steal markets from American producers: "With increased productivity, Japan will certainly expand its markets, but expansion will be into the pound regions, not the dollar areas. While deeply rooted fear of Japan still exists in America, Japan's imports from the U.S. last year were $750 million, while exports were just $300 million."

distinctive direction subsequently taken by Japanese managers, who from the 1960s through the 1980s generated the most vigorous movement for industrial productivity in the world and shaped a workplace culture with significant support from employees.

The task of explaining why this movement flowered in Japan must begin with the historical contexts of the prewar and wartime eras. Across decades of turbulent relations with managers from the early 1900s through the 1930s, male Japanese workers articulated a powerful claim to be treated as full members of the enterprise, deserving long-term job security, predictable daily wages, regular pay raises, and "human" treatment as the social equals of managers. State policy during the war was ineffectual, but it reinforced these claims.[13] Japanese workers thus emerged from the war with high expectations of their employers. They demanded egalitarian treatment and a secure place at work. By claiming that the employer was obliged to provide a job and by focusing on the factory and the enterprise as organizing units, workers suggested that the enterprise ought to offer a chance to acquire skills and ought to grant just rewards for effective labor. This historical context of demands and expectations significantly directed the efforts of workers and managers. It initially offered fertile ground to unions that considered the factory a social institution whose primary function was to serve the needs of workers. In later years it gave an opening to managers agile enough to envision a workplace order that retreated from the offer of security but promised to recognize effort and ability.

THE STRUGGLE FOR CITIZENSHIP AND CONTROL OF THE ENTERPRISE, 1945–60

In late 1945 Japanese workers began an intense movement of union organizing and attacks on managerial authority, building on their unrealized prewar aspirations to win full citizenship in the enterprise and the larger society. Union membership rose at an extraordinary pace, from about 5,000 in October 1945 to nearly 5 million by December 1946. Through June 1946 157,000 newly organized men and women engaged in 255 instances of "production control," locking out managers and running "their" enterprises on their own when demands for wages and the "democratization" of the workplace were denied.[14] These workers were challenging fundamental notions of private property and legitimate managerial authority, and given the extraordinary disarray of the "old guard" of business and political leaders in early 1946, a strong case can be made that a revolutionary situation existed *within Japan*.[15]

13. I have analyzed this history at length in *The Evolution of Labor Relations in Japan* (Cambridge: Harvard Council on East Asian Studies, 1985).

14. Joe Moore, *Japanese Workers and the Struggle for Power, 1945–1947* (Madison: University of Wisconsin Press, 1983).

15. Moore, *Japanese Workers*, 156–60.

But the American presence, power, and opposition to any radical movement from below quickly settled the matter; we shall never know how close the workers were to a revolutionary breakthrough, but they were not close enough to resist the Americans. In May 1946 the Supreme Command for Allied Powers (SCAP) condemned production control, and a newly confident conservative cabinet suppressed further takeovers. From roughly fifty production takeovers involving more than thirty thousand workers each month in the spring of 1946, the tactic receded to about twenty-five monthly actions involving five to six thousand in early 1947.[16]

Of greater long-run significance was the labor offensive that began as production control declined. The powerful Sanbetsu union federation, with close ties to the Japan Communist Party, led a drive that culminated in the "October (1946) struggle" of more than one hundred strikes involving 180,000 workers nationwide. Unions in the Japan National Railway (JNR), the electric power industry, and Tōshiba (in the electric machine industry) won major victories. They redefined their terms of employment according to a newly ascendant social logic of labor. This social logic contrasted with the economic logic of capital by claiming a right to guaranteed jobs and living wages. Job security was the focus of the JNR and Tōshiba workers, who forced managers to retract dismissal plans and promise no future dismissals without union consent. Wage security was the focus of the electric power workers (Densan), who won a wage system pegged primarily to objective measures of worker need. In the electric power industry settlement, which served as a model for successful union demands nationwide, age, family size, seniority, and regional costs of living served as the basis for calculating three-fourths of a worker's pay.

More generally, in this early postwar surge of organizing and collective action blue-collar workers gained "citizenship" in the enterprise and a measure of control over it. Workers in companies as diverse as the nation's leading newspapers and steel mills demanded creation of powerful joint labor-management councils. Found in as many as two-thirds of all unionized firms by mid-1946, the councils gave organized workers partial control of the workplace, personnel management, and corporate strategy. Through council deliberations or collective bargaining, workers eliminated many petty and substantive status divisions between white-collar staff and blue-collar workers, which they had found pervasive and repugnant throughout the prewar era. Under union pressure managers did away with separate gates, dining halls, and toilets as well as distinctions in dress and terminology (some companies replaced the terms *worker* and *staff* with the single term *employee*). Workers also gained a new equality in wages and bonuses. Some enterprises replaced a distinction between workers, who were paid by the day, and staff, who were paid by the month, with a common calculation in terms of monthly wages and paid bonuses to all employees as multiples of this monthly amount.

16. Moore, *Japanese Workers*, 104.

Managers accepted some of these changes as inevitable, and the Keizai Dōyūkai, an organization of younger "reform capitalists," spoke of the need to work together with organized labor to reconstruct the economy. But national management federation and individual company leaders viewed with fear and outrage what they considered an intolerable loss of control over this endeavor. In their view the "evil egalitarianism" (*akubyōdō*) imposed by postwar unions had destroyed legitimate, necessary managerial authority, and they resolved to retake the initiative.

The chance to do so was not long in coming. On 31 January 1947 SCAP forbade a threatened general strike aimed at bringing down the conservative Yoshida cabinet, and just eighteen months into the postwar era the labor movement was on the defensive. Two years later, in 1949, reflecting intensified American concern to revive the Japanese economy, the stringent terms of the Dodge line pushed Japanese employers to cut work forces and wage bills. A determined counteroffensive to "retake managerial authority" unfolded.

Showpiece confrontations came once again at Tōshiba and JNR. Companies such as Tōshiba, which dismissed one-fifth of its 22,000 employees after a five-month dispute, refused to bargain with the existing first union or renew its contract while simultaneously identifying a core of cooperative workers willing to lead a second union. The latter repudiated the confrontational first union, accepted some dismissals, restrained wage demands, and supported management efforts at "rationalization." In hundreds of disputes in 1949 and 1950 companies refused to renew the earlier postwar contracts that had granted unions a decision-making voice on management councils. In the new contracts eventually concluded, often with a new union, almost all councils were reduced to advisory bodies. In addition, in 1950 the Yoshida cabinet and private firms, with SCAP backing, carried out the sweeping Red purge and dismissed more than ten thousand allegedly Communist employees.

An extraordinary surge of organizing and radical union actions thus characterized the immediate postwar era. Workers gained citizenship in the enterprise community and won a significant voice in the direction of that community's activity. They lost much ground in the dramatic managerial counterattack of contract disputes in 1949 and 1950, but even after this retreat the struggle over the terms of labor's participation in the enterprise remained sharp.

A number of confrontational unions survived, and others emerged anew in both private and public industries. Many sought to control labor relations at the point of production. Although they generally agreed that some degree of management hierarchy was legitimate, they sought to restrain the pace and extent of "rationalization." In the 1950s such unions dominated in leading coal mines, private rail companies, and the national railways, and for a time they held sway in successful growing companies, briefly among auto and electric power workers, longer among steelmakers and paper and shipbuilding workers.

Among those that for a number of years achieved a measure of autonomy in the workplace were machinists for the JNR and workers in several private rail-ways.[17] At the Hokuriku Railroad in northern Japan the union successfully imple-mented the Sōhyō slogan of "shop floor struggle" in 1952. The union built solidarity with strong shop committees; it also created effective neighborhood or family-centered organizations. Its key tactics were the sit-down strike, work-to-rule slowdowns, and refusal of overtime. It won a contract giving the union a voice in pay raises, hours, pace and order of promotions, and distribution of work assignments. Through the rest of the decade the union codified these favorable "customary" practices by exchanging numerous written agreements with the company in a conscious endeavor to win some authority over production, work speed, transfers, and pay structure. This was a typical example of a workplace dominated by a first union. The union did not deny the legitimacy of the capitalist structure of the enterprise, but it insisted that labor be an equal partner and gained significant control over these critical matters.[18]

At Nissan managers have since portrayed the five-month strike of 1953 as a triumph over a communist union. What particularly upset them, however, was that this union had for several years controlled not only wage decisions but also promotions, work pace, and job assignments. This union, too, was in charge of the shop floor. The union achieved this control under the leadership of an energetic worker and activist, Masuda Tetsuo, by organizing powerful shop committees throughout the Nissan factory. These committees (one member per ten workers in workshops of fifty to one hundred men) became loci of control over work pace, overtime assignments, and even employee transfers.

Unions played a similar, if less extensive, role at Japan's leading paper manu-facturer, Ōji Paper, and the Mitsubishi shipyard at Nagasaki, the nation's larg-est.[19] The Mitsubishi union built a powerful organization out of the esprit of the skilled shipworkers, who exercised "customary" control over actual starting and stopping times. Through the early 1960s the union set the work pace and al-located overtime. Seeking to improve safety at the shipyard, the union in 1962 precipitated a crisis by carrying out a wildcat strike whenever a worker suffered an injury deemed serious.[20]

The most famous case where workers built a powerful union on the base of a local working-class culture occurred at Mitsui's Miike mine in Kyushu. In a successful 113-day strike in 1953 against the dismissal of 5,738 Mitsui miners nationwide, 1,815 of these at Miike, the miners hit on their three-part formula for

17. Kumazawa Makoto, "Soshiki rōdōsha no sengo," *Rōdō mondai*, Feb. 1979, 4–5.

18. Hyōdō Tsutomu, "Shokuba no rōshi kankei to rōdō kumiai," in Shimizu, *Sengo rōdō*, 211–20.

19. For Ōji, see Takeda Makoto, "Minkan dai kigyō ni okeru rōdō kumiai undō no tenkan: Ō seishi dai-ichi kumiai no hōkai," *Ōhara shakai mondai kenkyūjo zasshi*, no. 359 (Oct. 1988): 1–25, and "Kindaishugiteki rōmu seisaku no zasetsu to gendai Nihon-gata keieisha no tōjō: Ō seishi sōgi ni arawareta keieisha ruikei," *Ōhara shakai mondai kenkyūjo zasshi*, no. 366 (May 1989): 19–37.

20. Ueda Makoto, "Kigyō-kan kyōsō to 'shokuba shakai' (3): M zōsen N zōsenjo: 1962–63," in *Ōhara shakai mondai kenkyūjo zasshi*, no. 357 (Aug. 1988): 48–68.

union power: shop floor control, study groups, and community organizing of both wives and local residents. By organizing the miners' wives and residents of this relatively isolated region, the union won crucial local support, and the study groups were important in building solidarity. Also, the union provided welfare benefits and personal care (*sewa*) for its members, who relied on this system rather than on company services. But, as at the Hokuriku Railroad and Nissan, the union's shop, or pit, committees were the locus of control.[21] The committees initiated continual negotiations with worksite supervisors over a wide range of conditions. In the years following the 1953 strike, through the exchange of memoranda and provisional agreements, the union codified these many improvements and secured its position as defender of worker rights at the point of production.

Mine supervisors had customarily wielded great authority in setting output wages and assigning miners to rich or poor coal faces or to lucrative double shifts. The heart of the union drive for control, in the recollection of one activist, was the creation of a less arbitrary, more responsive hierarchy. Union committees won a voice in allocating jobs and overtime, regulating output pay, and, perhaps most important, insuring safety. The deep and leak-prone Miike pits were notoriously dangerous. As the committees gained strength and experience, they brought safety concerns to management attention; typically, if a concern were not addressed immediately, the men at the site would stop work, carrying out what they called an "emergency exit."[22]

The Miike union's offensive between 1953 and 1960 ended long-despised practices of favoritism and arbitrary authority; it reformed the work hierarchy and gave life to the union slogan of "democratization." Neither in theory nor in practice did the union question the legitimacy of managerial authority as other unions had a decade before. Sensitive to outside criticism of its radical tactics, the union took pains to assert in 1957 that "we do not challenge hierarchy, itself. The appropriate supply of labor (to management) is natural, and our goal is not to refuse work orders or loaf."[23] The Miike labor challenge was less a blanket refusal to accept new technology than an attempt to control rationalization and maintain newly achieved work conditions.[24]

In this context the 313-day lockout and strike at Miike in 1960 was a turning point in postwar history. The "social miracle" narrative would dismiss this strike as the dying gasp of an obstructive union in a sunset industry. I see it rather as

---

21. On the wives and residents groups, see Kubo Tokie, "Sōgi o sasaeta shufukai no katsudō," *Rōdō mondai,* Oct. 1980, 34, and Gōshi Yukio, "Arasoi no naka de mesameru rōdōsha," *Rōdō mondai,* Oct. 1980, 26–27. On the study groups, see Shimizu Shinzō, "Miike sōgi shoron," in Shimizu, *Sengo rōdō,* 474–75.

22. Kōno Masayuki, "Shokuba de susumu minshuka tōsō," *Rōdō mondai,* Oct. 1980, 28–29; Uchiyama Mitsuo, "Shokuba tōsō to rōdō kumiai no shutai kyōka," *Rōdō mondai,* Oct. 1980, 89.

23. Uchiyama, "Shokuba tōsō," 91.

24. Kubo, "Sōgi o sasaeta shufukai," 34.

the greatest in a series of defeats for a union-dominated workplace culture. The state's support for managers in these struggles, and the unity and determination of managers nationwide, reflected awareness that a fundamental issue was involved.

One of the first of these clashes came in 1952 with the destruction of the electric power union. Managers resolved to "rationalize" and weaken union control over wages by regaining freedom to vary individual pay in accord with a supervisor's assessment of a worker's ability. The Densan union proved unable to defend the livelihood wage principle it had established in 1946.[25] At Nissan the following year managers concluded that the union had "paralyzed staff functions" and gained intolerable authority. Supported by the new national management federation, Nikkeiren, which feared that the union's committee system would spread, and with special loans from the government's Industrial Bank and the private Fuji Bank, Nissan welcomed a strike over wages as an opportunity to confront and destroy the union. The company succeeded. By late 1953 a second union led by white-collar men had sent its members back to work, and the first union collapsed.[26] Mitsui's hard line at Miike in 1960 thus reflected a managerial consensus that had evolved in the previous decade: firms had to retake control of the workplace before committing major funds to rationalization. Mitsui Mining was able to win broad national support from the government, banks, and other enterprises whose directors recognized the common issue at stake.

A company plan to dismiss 2,000 of roughly 13,000 union members precipitated the 1960 dispute. Mitsui was determined to "rationalize" the mines by strengthening line authority, changing the wage structure, lowering company welfare payments, and ending preferential hiring of worker children. It was also set on dismissing activists and breaking the union. In the spring of 1960 the struggle merged with massive nationwide demonstrations against the U.S.-Japan Security Treaty, and union members showed remarkable discipline and tenacity. They survived for ten months on union allowances of roughly one-third their normal wages. But other mines remained open and temporarily supplied coal to Miike's customers, even if doing so meant shortchanging their own regular customers. Bolstered by this managerial solidarity, the mine company outlasted the union. It finally recognized a second union and forced the strikers to accept its entire rationalization plan.

THE TRIUMPH OF MANAGEMENT CULTURE, 1960–75

These and other bitter disputes dissolved key centers of the first union culture. At such work sites laborers had sought secure jobs and secure pay reflecting age or

25. Kawanishi Hirosuke, "Densan 27-nen sōgi ron," in Shimizu, *Sengo rōdō*, 418–35.

26. Mike Cusumano, *The Japanese Automobile Industry* (Cambridge: Harvard Council on East Asian Studies, 1985), chap. 3, has the best English coverage of the 1953 strike. David Halberstam also presents a dramatic account in *The Reckoning*.

seniority. They had tried to establish a safe, manageable pace of work with only secondary concern for the cost to the enterprise. The ideology of the first unions centered on the belief that the productive needs of management should be subordinate to the social needs of union members. Some managers believed it possible to respect and work with such unions, but most did not. Intense domestic competition in the boom of the late 1950s, and the specter of international competition with the first round of "liberalization" in the early 1960s, greatly boosted the latter group.[27] Their first step was to destroy or weaken the first unions. Often managers achieved this goal by nurturing a second union in the course of a bitter dispute, but they occasionally achieved the same result when a cooperative minority took control of the original union. The next step in the management drive to reshape workplace culture and attract employee support was a general agreement with a second union or defanged first union to grant the workers a negotiated "fair" share of the economic gains accruing from increased productivity in exchange for a freer hand to introduce new technology, redefine jobs, rearrange work, and transfer employees. Managers usually agreed to discuss such matters with the union, but the latter was rarely inclined or able to oppose such plans. This was a substantially weaker managerial commitment to protect particular jobs or overall employment levels than that sought by earlier unions.

Such a settlement emerged in the steel industry in the early 1960s. At major producers such as Nippon Kōkan (NKK), foremen and skilled workers had been central figures in an assertive union in the 1950s, and managers had relied on them to rule the shop floor. NKK wanted to remake the wage and job structure by increasing the weight of merit evaluations in deciding pay raises and by gaining increased freedom to transfer workers. These challenges to the union peaked in the late 1950s, but the work group retained a strong sense of independence, and the union still sought to influence standards for pay increases, promotions, or job definitions. Frequent disputes at NKK and other steelmakers culminated in two intense industrywide strikes in 1957 and 1959 in which management prevailed.[28]

In the 1960s unions and managers in steel reached a historic compromise replicated in major factories throughout Japan, and management objectives clearly dominated the workplace culture. The contrast between NKK union platforms of 1953 and 1965 reveals the shift in union objectives.[29] The union in 1953 called for "shop floor struggle," opposition to the control of monopoly capital and the exploitation of labor, and opposition to "capitalist wage rational-

27. For analysis of the clash between these two types of managers, see Takeda, "Kindai shugi teki rōmu seisaku," 23–37 and Ueda, "Kigyō kan kyōsō," 54–68.

28. Kumazawa Makoto, "Shokuba shakai no sengoshi: Tekkō gyō no rōmu kanri to rōdō kumiai," in Shimizu, *Sengo rōdō*, 98–103; Matsuzaki Tadashi, "Tekkō sōgi: 1957, 1959," in Yamamoto Kiyoshi, ed., *Nihon no rōdō sōgi* (Tokyo: Tokyo University Press, 1991), 161–204.

29. In the steel industry there was no sharp break with the replacement of a first union by a second. The existing unions were gradually transformed through repeated clashes between cooperative and militant factions. See Matsuzaki, "Tekkō sōgi," 53–54.

ization," transfers, and anticipated dismissals. In 1965 the anticapitalist rhetoric was muted. The wage problem was no longer one of structure or basis of calculation but simply the "maintenance of [fair] wage levels." By the early 1960s the union had accepted in principle the practice of interplant transfer and sought only to clarify the transfer procedure and gain some voice in individual cases.[30] It had thus retreated from the effort to control premium levels and the pace of work or to distribute job assignments. The NKK workers accepted a logic of capitalist culture in which significant insecurity in work life was a natural, legitimate element of social "common sense." In this view of work, managers are justified in evaluating ability and effort (while they recognize seniority) in deciding on pay, work assignments, and promotions. As long as company decisions are not wildly unjust, workers accept the process of evaluation and the inequality of outcome.[31] As these policies took root, workers lost the solidarity arising from common treatment in terms of seniority and age. They further lost solidarity as newly introduced technologies transformed the experience of production by deemphasizing group work and requiring less skill. Their status became less secure and more dependent on individual effort and ability than ever before. According to one journalist's report from 1966, many workers at NKK were acutely aware of these losses.[32]

Why did such workers accept the new workplace order rather than revive a surviving first union or create a new one?[33] Creative managerial strategy and the ambivalence of worker values were two key factors. Beginning in the early 1960s managers in Nikkeiren and companies around the country began to place new emphasis on judging a worker's ability when deciding pay raises and promotions.[34] They also began to encourage a wide range of small-group, "self-management" activities, modifying American industrial engineering programs introduced by groups such as the Japan Union of Scientists and Engineers. This strategy worked in part because it satisfied worker expectations that they function as full members of an enterprise, with their efforts justly rewarded.

This reconstruction of workplace culture was a halting process that required determined effort.[35] The managerial drive gained force only after a false start in the 1950s, the push for so-called job wages directly imported from the United States. In this system, pay was determined by a worker's job rather than personal characteristics such as age or seniority. Managers viewed this as a "modern,"

30. Kumazawa, "Shokuba shakai no sengoshi," 108–9.

31. Kumazawa, "Soshiki rōdōsha no sengo," *Rōdō mondai*, Feb. 1979, 6–8.

32. Kumazawa, "Shokuba shakai no sengoshi," 101–2.

33. For an analysis of the problems of the numerous first unions (colloquially termed *zantō*) that persisted as small minorities in the wake of a failed dispute and the unusual case of private railway workers in Hiroshima who did revive their first union, see Yamamoto Kiyoshi and Kawanishi Hirosuke, "Shosū ha kumiai kara tasū ha kumiai e no hatten jōken: Jirei chōsa chūkan hōkoku," *Shakaigaku kenkyū* 40, no. 2 (Aug. 1988): 179–223.

34. Ishida Mitsuo, "Chingin taikei to rōshi kankei," *Nihon rōdō kyōkai zasshi*, Aug. 1985, 10–14.

35. Cole, *Strategies for Learning*, 12.

"rational" form of compensation to replace what they perceived to be "irrational," "inefficient," and inelastic seniority- or age-based pay.[36] Workers resisted job wages for two reasons: first, the reforms detached pay from factors (seniority or age) more likely to reflect an employee's needs; second, to the extent that workers agreed that pay might justly reflect the kind of work they did, they were much more receptive to a policy that rewarded quality of labor expended (effort, attitude, skill) regardless of the job category.[37] Although managers prevailed in virtually all the showdown disputes of the 1950s, they were unable to implement job wages extensively in these years, and around 1960 managers shifted their emphasis away from the notion of job and toward that of ability or merit, broadly defined. The enemy remained the same: wages calculated as entitlements of seniority or age, enforced by unions that hindered corporate efforts to control costs or to motivate workers. But the new attacks on such wages stressed "merit wages," not job pay.[38] One's "job" no longer mattered; one was rewarded for what management called "merit" or "ability" (nōryoku): hard work, loyalty, quickness at learning new skills.

This new approach to pay proved quite popular although merit came to coexist with factors such as seniority, age, and education rather than replace them. Its benefits for management were several, and its appeal to workers was significant. It functioned effectively in an era when technological innovation often made existing jobs obsolete, which in turn made job wages almost as inflexible as rigid seniority pay. It allowed the company to reward loyal men and hold back obstreperous first-union members. If the personnel office carried out its evaluations with care, workers were likely to be far more receptive than they had been to job wages. While workers were giving way on rigid adherence to seniority, they were gaining recognition of their achievements at work. This exchange appealed particularly to younger workers impatient with their slow rise up a seniority ladder. Employees young or old were likely to see such a "merit" wage, perhaps more aptly translated "quality-of-labor wage," as recognition of their "character" or individual worth (jinkaku), a prominent concern of organized workers at least since World War I.[39]

As managers implemented "ability wages" in the 1960s, they spoke with new confidence about their "Japanese style" of management, what we can now see as a new version of workplace culture. It is vital to recognize that by "Japanese style" managers did *not* mean permanent employment and seniority wages. These were

---

36. Ishida, "Chingin taikei to rōshi kankei," 6–7.

37. Ibid., 9.

38. Job wages were called *shokumu kyū*. "Ability" or "merit" pay was *shokunō kyū*. The *nō* is the first syllable of *nōryoku*. By the mid-1960s the overall concept was termed *nōryoku-shugi*, "ability-ism" or "meritocracy." The change in emphasis is clear in the year-to-year evolution of Nikkeiren policy statements analyzed in Ishida, "Chingin taikei to rōshi kankei," 10–14.

39. On *jinkaku*, see Thomas C. Smith, "The Right to Benevolence: Dignity and Japanese Workers, 1890–1920," in *Comparative Studies in Society and History* 26, no. 4 (Oct. 1984): 607–8.

the practices at the heart of the system of labor relations they were attacking.[40] In the managerial view "Japanese-style" workplace culture meant pay based on merit as managers defined it (not job or seniority), a flexible employment structure where transfers were always possible and jobs not always protected, but where devoted employees could find meaning and reward at work as they helped raise productivity and insure the company's prosperity.

Just as they had shifted from American-style job wages to merit wages, managers transformed American models of quality control or industrial engineering when they experimented with small-group workplace activities. Because companies insisted that all workers be involved in these groups, they directly challenged the American conception, rooted in Taylorism, that workers should not be drawn into decisions about work lest they use their considerable knowledge to make their life easier and ignore management goals. Japanese managers believed that with proper controls workers would help them figure out how to increase efficiency.[41]

Early efforts in this direction came in the late 1950s and early 1960s in pioneer industries such as steel. One program that appealed to managers and foreshadowed those to come was called Training Within Industry (TWI). It trained supervisors to encourage the workers themselves to use their ability to reform (*kaizen*) the work process.[42] The first surge of small-group activities came in the mid-1960s, and by 1972 40 percent of firms with more than one hundred employees reported they used some form of small-group activity intended to improve productivity. A second surge came between 1978 and 1984, and by the mid-1980s 60 percent of firms and several million workers were involved in what had become a social movement supported by an infrastructure of publications and regional and national gatherings that transcended the boundaries of the firm.[43]

Managers thus successfully replaced old solidarities with new ones, making company men of all regular male workers and transforming the enterprise culture of the high-growth era. New wage policies both appealed to laborers' desire for recognition of their ability, without entirely repudiating their continued concern for security, and gave managers new flexibility in controlling costs and deploying personnel. Helping legitimize these policies in the minds of workers was a latent belief that competition in the workplace was acceptable. Such a belief, little evident among those who supported the earlier unions, was reinforced by a broader society in which competition was increasingly widespread and accepted as ever larger proportions of the population joined the exam race for admission to high school and college education. The varied array of small-group activities

40. Ishida, "Chingin taikei to rōshi kankei," part 2, *Nihon rōdō kyōkai zasshi*, Sept. 1985, 40.

41. Takeuchi Shizuko, *1960 nendai* (Tokyo: Tabata Shoten, 1982), 134–35.

42. See Nakamura, *Nihon seisansei kōjō undō shi*, 226–28, on productivity gains and 213–23 for the list of quality control and other programs. See also Takeuchi, *1960 nendai*, 117–19.

43. For data on the spread of the movement, see Cole, *Strategies for Learning*, 129. For two descriptions of the "movement" quality to the spread of small-group activities, see Takeuchi, *1960 nendai*, 117–49, and Cole, *Strategies for Learning*, 280–94.

had a similar dual appeal and function. They offered workers an avenue to expand their ability and range of responsibilities and instigated competition among work groups to meet higher productivity goals. This workplace culture, now dominated by management, by no means grew directly out of an earlier "traditional" factory culture. Managers reconstructed it as they overcame the briefly powerful first unions of the 1940s and 1950s, rationalized production, and revived their authority.[44]

In these very years when management transformed the workplaces in private-sector firms, organized workers in the public sector nurtured a variant of the earlier workplace culture. From the mid-1950s through the early 1970s they built powerful organizations in public-sector industries ranging from the national railways and tobacco monopoly to telecommunications and the postal service. These groups probably derived strength from their significant shop floor control as well as from their political ties to the Japan Socialist Party.

For three decades the most important single objective of public-sector employees was to regain the right to strike (the Yoshida government outlawed public-employee strikes in 1949). Ironically, this very restriction forced these unions to seek new bargaining tactics and may have promoted union control in the workplace. For example, the JNR union, Kokurō, pressured management with work-to-rule tactics and small hunger strikes in the early 1950s. Throughout the 1950s Kokurō sought to "democratize" the workplace by gaining a voice in calculating pay raises, restricting efficiency-based wages, and controlling the authority of supervisors. By the mid-1960s various public-sector unions made substantial gains. In 1967 Kokurō forced the railway to create "workplace discussion councils." In the manner of the coal miners in the 1950s the JNR union used these forums to articulate and codify a variety of practices that gave the union control of job assignments and promotions. By the early 1970s this union had reinstated seniority as a major factor in promotions and raises; more generally, public employees had created a workplace culture in which their needs, as defined by the union, were as important as the needs of the enterprise, as defined by management.[45]

The power of these unions reached a peak in the early 1970s, although the broader public turned hostile. When JNR workers used work-to-rule tactics during the 1973 spring offensive, causing rush-hour delays and extraordinary crowding, angry commuters rioted; at twenty-seven stations they beat drivers and smashed trains. During the dramatic inflation of the first oil crisis in 1974, public employees spearheaded the most contentious spring offensive in postwar history, and workers won average raises of 33 percent.[46] A turning point then came in late

---

44. Kumazawa, "Shokuba shakai no sengoshi," 123; Cole, *Strategies for Learning*, 12.

45. Kumazawa Makoto, "Suto ken suto: 1975 nen Nihon," in Shimizu, *Sengo rōdō*, 486–88. See Hyōdō, "Shokuba," 245–58, on public-sector unions from 1949 through 1975.

46. This percentage was well ahead of the annual consumer price inflation rate, which peaked at 25 percent.

1975, when more than one million public-sector workers participated in the "Strike for the Right to Strike."[47]

This "general strike" of public-sector employees failed. The labor movement could not mobilize on a broad front; private railway workers, for example, did not join. The public response was cool, and in contrast to the Miike strike fifteen years earlier, few students rallied in support. After one week the unions called off their strike, having made no significant gains. The long, slow decline of the public-sector unions then began; the government took disciplinary action against roughly one million employees and fired 1,015 leaders of the illegal strike.[48]

This strike was a turning point in postwar history almost comparable to the Miike-Anpo dispute of 1960. The outcome repudiated a union that saw workplace control and activism as the foundations of democracy. The government labeled the right to strike of 1 million employees an infringement on the "human rights" of 120 million citizens, and it criticized the union assertion of power in the workplace as antidemocratic, "minority egoism." The media and the public seemed to accept this interpretation, and the former articulated the ascendant managerial ideology: in contrast to small-business and nonunion workers, employees in public enterprises were privileged, with little ground for complaint; union combativeness was a drag on the national economy, a symptom of the British or, in a new twist, the American disease of nonproductive, failed economies. And in a related popular view, most Japanese apparently saw as entirely reasonable the managerial call for freedom to assess individual merit and diligence and to promote competition within the workplace. From the first union's perspective, the JNR work-to-rule tactic was an emblem of labor's ability to control railway operations, but in the public eye, or at least in the media presentation, it was a sign of lazy workers and a specter of the British disease.[49]

In the aftermath of the strike the government campaigned to destroy the grip of public-sector unions on the workplace. The postal workers resisted longest; not until 1980, with a second union rapidly gaining strength, did the first, Sōhyō union compromise. It accepted a new personnel evaluation system that it had been opposing since 1961. The plan increased management discretion in judging raises, promotions, and transfers, reducing the importance of seniority. The union finally accepted this evaluation plan, hoping to reverse its decline by granting control in the workplace to the postal managers in exchange for protection of overall employment levels and working conditions.[50] This was a compromise similar to that of private-sector manufacturing workers who two decades earlier

47. Unions in eight public enterprises participated: Japan National Railway, Tobacco Monopoly, Postal Service, Nippon Telephone and Telegraph, Government Printing Office, National Mint, Alcohol Sales Office, and the Forestry Division.

48. See Kumazawa, "Suto-ken suto," 491–503, on the course of the strike and reasons for its failure.

49. Kumazawa, "Suto-ken suto," 504–7.

50. On the postal union, see Tsuneshige Saburō, "Yūsei marusei no jittai to zentei no taiō," *Rōdō mondai*, Feb. 1979, 60–64; Tanaka Toshinao, "Rōshi seijōka rosen no ikikata," *Rōdō mondai*, June 1981, 52–56.

conceded control over "rationalization" in exchange for a share of the growing pie.[51]

Throughout the 1970s, facing huge budget deficits, the government wanted to cut the deficits of the postal service and the railway in particular. It criticized obstructive unions for defying plans to "rationalize" and cut costs. In the 1980s the government turned to a new tactic: the campaign for "privatization and administrative reform." In these two policies, among the leading domestic initiatives of the LDP in the 1980s, one government motive was to destroy the last vestiges of the first-union version of workplace culture and regain full control over public-sector workplaces. Thus, a 1982 report of the LDP Committee on National Railway Reconstruction claimed, "The truly most important requirement for JNR reconstruction is the correction of JNR labor-management relations."[52]

This report then called for the transplant to the JNR of the "merit-based management" model of large-scale private enterprises. It insisted that labor and management "cooperate to raise productivity and share the fruits fairly." It criticized union control over raises and promotions as "totally out of step with social common sense." This last criticism is crucial. One way to define culture is to see it as the common sense of a society, attitudes and behavior so broadly accepted that they seem to "go without saying." This document bluntly rejected as nonsense the workplace culture dominated by the JNR union and affirmed the ascendant, "commonsense" managerial culture of the 1980s.[53]

In addition to the privatization of JNR, two other important trends of the years after the oil crisis were the renewed popularity of labor-management discussion councils at the enterprise level and the spread of tripartite consultation at the industry and national level involving union leaders, business leaders, and the government.[54] By the 1980s a degree of consultation and consensus over wage and employment policy emerged among the three groups that was unimaginable from the perspective of the contentious and culturally polarized world of labor of 1960. Labor, led by the private-sector Dōmei federation, agreed with business and government that rationalization, productivity, and international competitiveness were paramount goals. In exchange for keeping its voice low in the workplace, the unions wanted to share the affluence that would result from reaching these goals. Thus, the NKK union platform in 1978 (in sharp contrast to those of 1953 or even 1965) agreed that "a firm base for the enterprise is needed to stabilize livelihoods for the future. However, we need fair, open methods to carry out policies of transfers or reductions. Labor-capital discussion, not bargaining, is the way to achieve this."[55]

51. Kumazawa, "Suto-ken suto," 516.

52. Hyōdō, "Shokuba," 260.

53. Ibid.

54. For a study of these trends, see Daniel M. Fuchs, "Labor Incorporation into the Japanese Political Economy" (senior thesis, Princeton University, 1987).

55. Kumazawa, "Shokuba shakai no sengoshi," 109.

At the national level we can perhaps call this settlement of the 1980s the rise of corporatism *with* labor. Viewed from the workplace, this outcome was possible only because of the cultural consensus reached by management and the second-union movement from the 1950s through the 1970s. By the mid-1980s many surviving elements of the first-union movement within Sōhyō had joined the circle of consensus. In 1987, with the Dōmei philosophy dominant, a new private-sector national labor union federation called Rengō was founded, and in 1989 Rengō expanded to embrace most of Sōhyō's public-sector unions. The greater portion of the two wings of the labor movement were thus united.[56] Rengō showed unexpected political muscle when its eleven candidates swept to victory in the historic 1989 Upper House election. The restrained business response to this massive defeat for the LDP (the stock market hardly blinked) reflected confidence that an "opposition" movement led by Rengō offered no threat to Japan's politics of productivity.

CONCLUSION

How can we explain the triumph of the managerial version of workplace culture? I have thus far identified several causes of the rise of what Japanese critics call the "enterprise society." The American drive to promote productivity and cooperative union-management relations among its strategic allies in the 1950s and 1960s was part of the story. The combined force of American pressure and state hostility toward Japan's first unions created a favorable environment for the management counteroffensive and the second union movement. Yet this pressure cannot explain the staying power of the changed workplace culture that evolved.

Another factor creating a favorable environment for management was the divided character of the work force. Since the 1950s the majority of Japanese workers have been employed in nonunion, small and medium-sized firms offering relatively inferior pay, job security, and benefits. The consequences of a failed strike in a large factory where a first union thrived in the early postwar era were dismissal and reemployment in this sector, and this possibility surely served as a powerful incentive for compromise. Within the large factories millions of women (and some men) designated "temporary employees" in the 1950s and 1960s and "part-time" workers since the 1970s were left outside the circle of *both* visions of workplace culture described here.[57] As such workers received lower pay and less

56. Rengō's full name was Zen Nihon Minkan Rōdō Kumiai Rengōkai. For an account of its founding, see Ohara Shakai Mondai Kenkyūjo, *Nihon rōdō nenkan, 1988* (Tokyo: Rōdō Junpōsha, 1988), 43–71.

57. In 1957, for example, women constituted 39 percent of the work force and just 25 percent of union members; Ohara Shakai Mondai Kenkyūjo, *Nihon rōdō nenkan, 1959* (Tokyo: Tōyō Keizai Shinpōsho, 1959), 141. In 1957 roughly 10 percent of the work force in major factories consisted of temporary workers.

security than regular male employees, they allowed managers to strike more generous bargains with cooperative unions.

The men who led almost all Japanese unions defended these workers with little vigor for two reasons: they recognized that their own relative security would be threatened by a more inclusive movement, and they viewed the women as essentially supplementary wage earners for whom second-class status was reasonable. One irony is that quality circles with high rates of female participation, in contrast to those with all men, appear to have focused more on maintaining the quality of work life than on single-mindedly raising output.[58] If unions had regularly adopted the perspective of such women, they may have been led to defend independent standards of safety and work pace more vigorously.

A third element in the explanation for the ascendance of managerial culture is the conjunction of several factors during the key years in the early 1960s, when ability wages and small-group activities took hold. These factors include a labor shortage and rising turnover, rapid obsolescence of skills, and bitterness in the wake of major disputes. In this environment managers acutely felt a need for strategies to restore morale and gain labor commitment to make productive use of huge investments in new plant and equipment. Quality control circles and the like in some measure compensated for the loss of morale and the decline of the more independent first unions. Supporting such an explanation is the fact that key early innovations in wage policy and small-group activities came in industries such as steel, which faced these problems most acutely.[59]

Yet none of these factors—American foreign policy, divisions of gender and scale, deskilling and new technologies, declining morale—were unique to Japan, but the solutions were distinctive. To further explain the triumph of Japan's particular workplace culture, we must look outside the world of big companies, to the links between the education system and the workplace and the interaction between large and small enterprises. We must return to the value that workers historically placed on winning full membership in the enterprise and respect for their hard work, generating a sense of the enterprise as the focus of all their endeavors, including their efforts to build strong unions.

It is clear, for example, that some of the strongest unions feared that bold actions might harm the enterprise, which they apparently regarded as their social property, and that this fear inhibited their efforts at self-defense. Striking steelworkers in 1957 chose not to "bank" the furnaces (a step short of stopping them entirely). They feared the equipment might have been damaged and recognized that in any case it would have taken two to three weeks to resume normal operations. The union kept furnaces running at 30 percent of capacity and exempted safety personnel from the strike.[60] Likewise, the Miike union left two

---

58. Kumazawa Makota, *Nihon no rōdōsha zō* (Tokyo: Chikuma Shobō, 1981), chap. 5, esp. 131–33.

59. Kumazawa, "Shokuba shakai no sengoshi," 123; Takeuchi, *1960 nendai*, 127, 139–40; Cole, *Strategies for Learning*, 55–61.

60. Although steelworkers around the world have refrained from stopping furnaces completely during strikes, a step that would damage the furnace walls, they have taken the step of "banking" the

thousand "safety personnel" in the mines in 1960 to check that shafts remained structurally sound. According to company documents, their withdrawal would have threatened the literal destruction of the workplace and placed formidable pressure on management to compromise. Apparently, these steelworkers and miners believed they would eventually return to work (with union control intact) and felt overriding responsibility to protect their workplace.[61] The very aspiration to control the enterprise inhibited the effective defense of union control.

Similarly, even those unions willing to subordinate productivity to their independent standards of security or safety could not mobilize effectively by industry nationwide. At Nissan in 1953, in steel in 1957 and 1959, at Miike in 1960, the union, management, and the articulate public all recognized the gravity of what observers called a "general struggle of labor and capital." Yet the steel federation could not prevent some enterprise units from breaking ranks, and neither the Toyota union in 1953 nor other coal mine locals in 1960 offered more than moral support to Nissan or Miike unionists. Institutions of capital were more united and, perhaps, less squeamish about hurting the enterprise. Competitors of Miike and Mitsui supplied Mitsui enterprises with coal during the strike; in 1957 the president of NKK reportedly said that "this is a struggle to destroy the union, even if it means destroying the machinery."[62]

Finally, the ambivalence of workers who sought both security and just reward for their diverse abilities was important. The Mitsubishi union supported seniority-based wages as objective and fair, but union members chafed at the slow pace of promotions. Capable young workers wanted to be able to move ahead.[63] Managers at Mitsubishi and elsewhere could tap such sentiments and create a powerful consensus in support of a changed workplace culture.

No private-sector union since Miike has approached the control and esprit of the miners; Japan's organized workers lost the ensuing battle for the hearts and minds of posterity. Much as the Chichibu rebels of the 1880s were transmitted by establishment history to later generations as outlaws or gamblers, the "conventional morality" (in Irokawa Daikichi's words) of the 1970s and 1980s presented the Miike miners as overzealous radicals out of phase with their times and unreasonable in their demands. In conclusion, we may assess this perspective.

Certainly if the zeal of the Miike miners to control the workplace had prevailed, it would have slowed the increase of productivity. But zeal for rationalization has costs as well. In 1959, at the height of union power, 1 man died in an accident and 3,674 were injured. In 1961, the first year of rationalization under

---

furnaces, which the steel union rejected in this case. The Japanese unions were aware that American steelworkers a year earlier had "banked" their furnaces during a major strike. Matsuzaki, "Tekko sogi," 178–79.

61. Yokoyama Fujio, "Sengo shuyō sutoraiki to Miike sōgi," *Rōdō mondai*, Oct. 1980, 66–67.

62. See Yokoyama, "Sengo shuyō sutoraiki," 69, on Miike; see Matsuzaki, "Tekkō sōgi," 56, for the NKK statement.

63. Ueda Makoto, "Kigyō-kan kyōsō to 'shokuba shakai' (4): M zōsen N zōsenjo: 1962–63," in *Ōhara shakai mondai kenkyūjo zasshi*, no. 359 (Oct. 1988): 45.

the second union, 16 died and 4,230 were injured. In 1962, 15 died and 3,855 were injured.[64] In 1963, Japan's worst mine disaster of the postwar era claimed 458 lives at Miike.[65]

Less dramatic but more widely felt was the persistent gap between national and personal affluence in Japan both during and after the high-growth era. In the 1980s Japanese in the workshops of the enterprise society put in longer hours with fewer vacations than workers anywhere else in the advanced capitalist world.[66] The real buying power of their nominally huge incomes remained low. Although the causes of this gap were complex, the hegemony of a workplace culture in which the needs of the enterprise reign transcendent and beyond reasonable challenge is surely part of the story, dampening current consumption and pursuit of leisure and probably contributing to imbalanced economic relations with the rest of the world.[67]

It is perhaps condescending for an outsider to argue with affluence and suggest that Japan's workers were pushed to make poor choices; yet good or bad, the history of postwar labor-management relations is a story of trade-offs. If workers had sustained institutions with a point of reference independent of the untrammeled pursuit of productivity, then a different sort of democracy, a slower trajectory of growth, and ultimately a more challenging model for the rest of the world could have resulted.

64. The increase in the rate of injury is even greater than the numerical rise, for the size of the work force fell by 10 percent when twelve hundred miners were fired after the strike.

65. Goshi Yukio, "Zen koku no rōdōsha no shien ni sasaerarete," *Rōdō mondai*, Oct. 1980, 43.

66. The average Japanese worker took 9 days paid vacation in 1987, compared to 19 for the Americans and 26 for the French. Total annual work hours were 2,168 in Japan, 1,924 in the United States, and 1,643 in France. See Ōhara, *Nihon rōdō nenkan, 1988*, iii.

67. In yet another ironic turn, sarcastically reported by the Japanese media, American officials in the late 1980s began to publicly urge Japanese to play more and work less to help solve the trade imbalance. See "Friendly New U.S. Line in Trade Talks Strikes Some Japanese as Self-Serving," *Wall Street Journal*, 14 Sept. 1989, A17.

CHAPTER FIFTEEN

Intellectuals and Politics

J. Victor Koschmann

Jean-Paul Sartre delivered three lectures on intellectuals during his visit to Japan in 1965. Published later as a single essay, they suggest a provocative framework for reconsidering the problem of intellectuals and politics in postwar Japanese history. By "intellectuals," Sartre meant highly-trained people who are severely critical of bourgeois society and the role they are assigned in maintaining it. According to Sartre, a person with advanced training is inevitably positioned socially as a "technician of practical knowledge"—someone who employs specialized knowledge and technique on behalf of that society or, more correctly, on behalf of the ruling bourgeoisie. What distinguishes an intellectual from other such technicians is his or her self-consciousness and concern with respect to this social role. That is, for Sartre in the mid-1960s an intellectual was one who recognizes and squarely confronts the contradiction involved in putting "universal" forms of knowledge at the service of the particularistic interests of the ruling class and the state. He or she seeks to use knowledge for humanistic ends and thus speaks out on issues that transcend specialized expertise, strives to adopt the viewpoint of the oppressed majority, and might even strive actively to undermine the established order. At the same time, in terms of Sartre's class analysis, the intellectual inevitably suffers the agonies of what Hegel called "unhappy consciousness": a perpetual inner conflict between what the intellectual is—a petit bourgeois—and what he or she aspires to, which is truth and human emancipation.[1]

In this essay I focus primarily on the political thought and action of Japanese who have tried to behave more or less as intellectuals in the Sartrean sense.

Professor Matsuzawa Hiroaki of Hokkaidō University read an earlier draft and made a number of useful suggestions.

1. Jean-Paul Sartre, "A Plea for Intellectuals," in Sartre, *Between Existentialism and Marxism*, trans. John Matthews (New York: Quill Paperback, Morrow, 1979), 258.

However, as I suggest below, it is possible to argue that Sartre's classical definition of the intellectual is generally appropriate to only the first half or so of Japan's postwar period. In the mid-1960s, precisely in the era when Sartre gave his lectures in Japan, some influential Japanese writers were revising their self-image as intellectuals, turning to a more modest, localized conception of political action.

The topic of intellectuals in relation to politics seems always to beg the difficult question of how much influence they can hope to have on so-called actual events. One factor that should be taken into account in the Japanese case is that postwar cultural and political critics have enjoyed a very large and well-informed readership. Intellectuals have communicated with each other through the so-called comprehensive magazines (*sōgō zasshi*), which are typically monthlies and "usually contain semiacademic articles, reports, interviews, round table discussions, travel accounts, and translations of foreign articles" on political and social topics.[2] Some of the largest, such as *Sekai* (World), *Chūō kōron* (Central review), and, more recently, *Ushio* (Tide) have consistently maintained a circulation of well over one hundred thousand. The weekly *Asahi jānaru* (Asahi journal), which began in 1959 and closed in 1992, was comparable in content to the monthlies and also apparently sold in the hundreds of thousands. Major national newspapers, with circulation in the millions, and television also often contain sophisticated commentary on political, social, and cultural issues. These media encourage academics and critics to address current issues in a broad, nontechnical manner and to communicate with each other and the general populace. They also play a very important role in molding, and to some degree constraining, the range and terms of discourse.

INTELLECTUALS AND THE DEMOCRATIC REVOLUTION, 1945–55

In an essay that he wrote on the occasion of Sartre's visit, Maruyama Masao argued that because of the sectionalism and compartmentalism that have characterized the Japanese intellectual world, the intelligentsia has only rarely produced an independent community of scholars who are free to think in what he calls universalistic terms. He mentions only three such eras: the Meiji Restoration in the late nineteenth century; the 1920s, when intellectuals were "tied together spiritually" by the left-wing movement and its repression; and the early post–World War II period, in which the bond among intellectuals took the form of a "community of contrition." The postwar community formed because of the iconoclastic effect of defeat, the discrediting of institutional loyalties and authority, and a shared sense of the need to articulate the meaning of the wartime experience. Intellectuals were contrite because virtually all felt in one way or another

2. Seki Yoshihiko, "Introduction," *Journal of Social and Political Ideas in Japan* [*JSPIJ*] 1, no. 1 (Apr. 1963): 2.

that they had failed to resist the war, and many were remorseful over various degrees of collaboration with fascism. The most contrite were those who had betrayed the Communist movement in the 1930s through some form of apostasy (*tenkō*), usually under intense police pressure.[3]

Contributing, therefore, to the "community of contrition" was the considerable prestige of Marxism in the early postwar period. This prestige resulted not only from its record as a major vehicle of humanism and social scientific values but also from the exemplary record of resistance against fascism and militarism that certain Communist Party leaders were justified in claiming. Two of these leaders, Tokuda Kyūichi and Shiga Yoshio, were finally released to a hero's welcome on 10 October 1945 after eighteen years in prison. In the "Appeal to the People" that they had composed while incarcerated, they welcomed the Allied forces and expressed support for the Potsdam Declaration as the operative basis for "democratic liberation and world peace." They also called for the democratic formation of a "people's republic government."[4]

On 12 January 1946 another Communist leader, Nosaka Sanzō, returned a hero from China, where he had organized antiwar activities among Japanese prisoners. Nosaka generally supported the program that had been initiated by Tokuda and Shiga but moved even further toward what he called a "lovable Communist Party" (*aisareru kyōsantō*). The resultant party policy, which was made official at the fifth party congress in late February 1946, included commitment to "peaceful and democratic methods," support for labor unions, and a united front among all democratic elements.[5] By the fifth congress the party already had attracted 6,847 members in 399 cells, and its organ paper, *Akahata*, was circulating in 250,000 copies.[6]

Despite its lovable veneer and honeymoon with the Allied Occupation, the Japan Communist Party (JCP) was often narrowly Stalinist, not only politically and philosophically but also in its attitude to culture.[7] This doctrinaire tendency was expressed particularly in the powerful literary movement Shin-Nihon Bun-

---

3. Maruyama Masao, "Kindai Nihon no chishikijin," in Maruyama, *Kōei no ichi kara* (Tokyo: Miraisha, 1982), 73–133. I found very helpful an excellent English translation by Andrew E. Barshay, unpublished.

4. Nihon Kyōsantō Shutsugoku Dōshikai, "Jinmin ni uttau," in *Sengo shisō no shuppatsu,* ed. Hidaka Rokurō, Sengo Nihon shisō taikei 1 (Tokyo: Chikuma Shobō, 1968), 245–46.

5. Nihon Kyōsantō, "Daigokai tōtaikai sengen," in *Kakumei no shisō,* ed. Haniya Yutaka, Sengo Nihon shisō taikei 6 (Tokyo: Chikuma Shobō, 1969), 57–60. See also Joe Moore, *Japanese Workers and the Struggle for Power, 1945–1947* (Madison: University of Wisconsin Press, 1983), 111–19, 122–26.

6. Masumi Junnosuke, *Sengo seiji, 1945–1955* (Tokyo: Tokyo Daigaku Shuppankai, 1983) 1:160.

7. For a critique of Stalin's codification of Marxism, see Leszek Kolakowski, *Main Currents of Marxism,* trans. P. S. Falla (London: Oxford University Press, 1978), 3:91–105. On philosophical Stalinism in early postwar Japanese Marxism, see Ōi Tadashi, *Gendai no yuibutsuron shisō* (Tokyo: Aoki Shoten, 1959), 35–41. For parallel developments in early postwar France, see Mark Poster, *Existential Marxism in Postwar France* (Princeton: Princeton University Press, 1975), 36–42.

gakukai (New Japan Literary Society), which was organized under the party's auspices in early 1946.[8] A leader of this society, Kurahara Korehito, often emphasized the class-based criterion of literary value, objectivist realism, and the importance of strong political control of culture. Nevertheless, a broad segment of the intelligentsia continued to revere and often follow the political lead of the party.

The dominant political conception embraced by the early postwar Left, including the Communists, was democratic revolution. The primary basis for this conception was the Comintern's "1932 Theses," which had prescribed "a bourgeois-democratic revolution with a tendency to grow rapidly into a socialist revolution."[9] In the postwar period the "1932 Theses" were revived as the basis for Communist policy and provided the rationale for the JCP's acceptance of the Occupation.

The strategy of democratic revolution immediately raised the question of agency: who or what would become the revolutionary subject capable of bringing the revolution to completion? Of course, for the time being the Occupation was obviously the major agent of institutional transformation, but the Occupation itself was anxious to push progressive Japanese elements to the fore. In December 1945 Army Chief of Staff Richard K. Sutherland wrote to the Office of the Political Adviser in Occupation headquarters, "Your studies will contribute largely to the determination of the persons who will be permitted to participate in government, in insuring that membership is held only by persons who may be relied upon to further the purposes of the occupation."[10]

This effort to facilitate the emergence of a revolutionary subject was to a large extent exclusionary. Beginning in early 1946 the Occupation authorities initiated a program to purge from public life thousands of Japanese whom Occupation officials believed to have been associated with militarism or ultranationalism. The JCP also began its own purge of writers. The June 1946 issue of the New Japan Literary Society's journal, *Shin-Nihon bungaku* (Literature for a new Japan), published a list of twenty-five Japanese writers who were judged to have contributed to militarism and ultranationalism.[11]

Of course, in the Japanese political arena the process of promoting the subject of democratic revolution was not merely exclusionary. Groups on the Left, including the JCP, generally agreed that some form of united front would be the

8. Kurahara Korehito, "Atarashii bungaku e no shuppatsu" and "Shin-Nihon bungaku no shakaiteki kiso," *Kurahara Korehito hyōron-shū* (Tokyo: Shin Nihon Shuppansha, 1967) 3:3–16; Ara Masato et al., "Bungaku to genjitsu: Kurahara Korehito o kakonde," *Kindai bungaku* 1 (Feb. 1946): 18–30.

9. "Theses on the Situation in Japan and the Tasks of the Communist Party, May 1932," in George M. Beckmann and Okubo Genji, *The Japanese Communist Party 1922–1945* (Stanford: Stanford University Press, 1969), 339.

10. Quoted in Sue Lyn Cowden, "A Brief Concord: General Headquarters and the Japan Communist Party, September 1945–February 1946" (M.A. thesis, Cornell University, 1989), 13.

11. Odagiri Hideo, "Bungaku ni okeru sensō sekinin no tsuikyū," in *Sengo bungaku ronsō*, ed. Usui Yoshimi (Tokyo: Banchō Shobō, 1971), 1:115–17.

most appropriate means of aggregating revolutionary forces, and they advanced a variety of proposals concerning which groups should be included in those forces.[12] For example, in January 1946 Nosaka Sanzō called for a democratic front representing a "new democracy, one in which workers, farmers, the working intellectual class, and small and medium-sized commercial and industrial businessmen will take the leading role."[13]

The question of the subject of democratic revolution was not limited in its relevance to processes of political selectivity and exclusion; it also extended to qualitative issues: what social, existential, and epistemological capacities would qualify an individual or group as a revolutionary subject? This and other questions related to subjectivity and autonomy coalesced in a debate on subjectivity (*shutaisei ronsō*) which occupied many intellectuals between 1946 and 1949.[14] The concept of subjectivity was sufficiently broad—and, according to some critics, sufficiently vague—to allow controversy among participants from a wide range of individual specializations and political viewpoints. It also became the focal point of a political critique not only of feudalism and fascism but also of dogmatism and objectivism in Marxist thought.

For some leftist writers who rebelled against the party's hegemony in culture, the key terms were *individual ego, self-expression,* and *freedom.* Literary figures such as Ara Masato and Hirano Ken, who were affiliated with the journal *Kindai bungaku* (Modern literature), reacted against the party's insistence on the firm primacy of politics over art. They also argued that artists' self-expression (rather than self-denial) should be encouraged: instead of attempting to portray reality objectively from the standpoint of the proletariat, the *Kindai bungaku* critics said, writers should fearlessly express their own worldviews. Indeed, in opposition to the party's insistence on proletarian leadership, these critics intimated that the main subject of Japan's democratic revolution should be the bourgeoisie, particularly "petit bourgeois intellectuals." They tried, therefore, to redress the ambivalent role that historical materialism assigned to intellectuals and the "unhappy consciousness" that role entailed.

Elements of party hegemony were challenged in philosophy as well. Umemoto Katsumi followed Kierkegaard and the neo-Kantians in criticizing what he believed to be a "gap" in historical materialism: its lack of a theory of subjective commitment. Without such a theory Marxism would remain a contemplative science of history without a fully adequate theory of revolutionary action.[15] However, contrary to the egocentric approach of the *Kindai bungaku* critics, Umemoto

12. Yamakawa Hitoshi, "Toward a Democratic Front," *JSPIJ* 3, no. 1 (Apr. 1965): 23.

13. Nozaka Sanzō, "Minshu sensen ni yotte sokoku no kiki o sukue," in Hidaka, *Sengo shisō no shuppatsu,* 247–58.

14. J. Victor Koschmann, "The Debate on Subjectivity in Postwar Japan: Foundations of Modernism as a Political Critique," *Pacific Affairs* 54, no. 4 (Winter 1981–82): 609–31.

15. Umemoto Katsumi, *Yuibutsuron to shutaisei* (Tokyo: Gendai Shichōsha, 1974), and *Katoki no ishiki* (Tokyo: Gendai Shichōsha, 1975), or *Umemoto Katsumi chosakushū,* vol. 1 (Tokyo: San'ichi Shobo, 1977).

emphasized a self-effacing form of partisanship, which he understood in the Lukacsian mode as devotion to the world-historical mission of the proletariat to liberate all humankind.[16]

A third important approach to the problem of what kind of subjectivity was appropriate to an agent of democratic revolution was the ideologically modern emphasis on the classical European bourgeois ethos, or value orientation. Refer-ring to models such as Defoe's *Robinson Crusoe* and Max Weber's *Ancient Judaism,* Ōtsuka Hisao argued in 1946 and 1947 that the Japanese had to overcome their "Asiatic" mentality: "In order that we not conceive of the tiger of democracy as an ordinary housecat, it is first of all necessary to carry out the modernization and democratization of the human subject—that is, to educate the people to fit the modern, democratic human type."[17] Maruyama Masao rested his argument for a modern personality on penetrating studies not only of John Locke but also of such Japanese figures as the Meiji publicist Fukuzawa Yukichi.[18] He sought to show in a series of essays that Fukuzawa's flexible pragmatism, respect for scien-tific method, and emphasis on both individual and national independence were trustworthy guides to the kind of subjectivity that could support the ideals of democratic revolution.[19]

Arguments based on the ideal of subjective autonomy played a key role in the early postwar episteme, contesting deterministic forms of both historical material-ism and liberal behaviorism and highlighting the importance of intentional inter-vention. At the same time, in the early postwar Japanese context demands for subjective participation seemed to make sense only in conjunction with either a historical materialist or liberal humanist metanarrative of progress.[20] Accordingly, when subjectivity was propounded, the effect was paradoxically to reinforce the primacy in discourse of objective, scientistic concepts of class, history, and moder-nity.

The vulnerability of the standpoint of subjective autonomy became vividly apparent in 1948 when, against the background of an increasingly tense interna-

16. Georg Lukacs, *History and Class Consciousness,* trans. Rodney Livingstone (Cambridge: MIT Press, 1971), 149. On Umemoto's concept of *shutaisei,* see J. Victor Koschmann, "Sengo shoki ni okeru hihanteki marukusushugi no unmei: Umemoto Katsumi no shutaiseiron," in *Sengo Nihon no seishinshi: sono saikentō,* ed. Kamishima Jirō, Maeda Ai, and Tetsuo Najita (Tokyo: Iwanami Shoten, 1988), 145–64.

17. Many of these early postwar essays are collected in Ōtsuka Hisao, *Kindaika no ningenteki kiso* (Tokyo: Chikuma Shobō, 1968).

18. Maruyama Masao, "Jon Rokku to kindai seiji genri," in Maruyama, *Senchū to sengo no aida, 1936–1957* (Tokyo: Misuzu Shobō, 1976), 391–420.

19. J. Victor Koschmann, "Maruyama Masao and the Incomplete Project of Modernity," in *Postmodernism and Japan,* ed. Masao Miyoshi and H. D. Harootunian (Durham: Duke University Press, 1989), 123–41.

20. For a critical discussion of the liberal metanarrative of progress that presents history "as a story of liberation—involving the progressive emancipation of man from all kinds of external tutelage or spurious constraints," see Fred R. Dallmayr, *Twilight of Subjectivity: Contributions to a Post-Individualist Theory of Politics* (Amherst: University of Massachusetts Press, 1981), p. 9 and chap. 1.

tional atmosphere and the "reverse course" in Occupation policy, the JCP launched a frontal attack on modernism. By *modernism* it meant not only the arguments advanced by Maruyama and Ōtsuka but also the "revisionist" Marxism represented by Umemoto and the literary individualism of the *Kindai bungaku* group.[21] In parallel with the intensifying cold war the party also began to move away from its early focus on peaceful, democratic revolution toward a more anti-imperialist and nationalist stance.[22] The Cominform's excoriation of the JCP's line on 6 January 1949 greatly reinforced this anti-imperialist tendency and linked it to a much more aggressive revolutionary policy. Then, with the outbreak of war in Korea the Occupation initiated the Red purge and party leaders went underground. By August 1950 the Cominform had told the party to carry out a "general uprising" in Japan.[23]

Related to the party's new nationalism was the debate on national literature (*kokumin bungaku*) initiated by Takeuchi Yoshimi. Takeuchi argued that Japan could achieve an authentic form of modernity only if it ignored extrinsic, European models and developed itself autonomously from within. A national literature that expressed the viewpoints and experiences of the Japanese people and was capable of promoting cultural independence would be the most appropriate vehicle for this autonomous process of modernization.[24]

Also in juxtaposition to the party's rejection of its early postwar policies of democratic revolution, there occurred a movement toward a broader progressive coalition among intellectuals generally sympathetic to the early postwar ideals of peace, democracy, and modernity. This movement represented a milder form of the anti-imperialist nationalism that animated the Communists, but it was also the practical culmination of the early postwar "community of contrition." The major political issue of the time was world peace and, more specifically, the form, terms, and timing of a peace treaty that would bring an end to the Occupation.

The occasion for action was provided by Yoshino Gensaburō, chief editor of *Sekai*, who was instrumental in the republication of a statement on world peace previously issued in July 1948 through UNESCO. Yoshino believed that the statement offered an opportunity for Japanese intellectuals to transcend their differences and reduce world tensions. He proceeded through the agency of sociologist Shimizu Ikutarō to foster the organization of a group that included not only young progressives such as Maruyama Masao but also the conservative philosopher Watsuji Tetsurō and a group of Marxists.[25] The result was the Peace

21. Matsumura Kazuto, "Tetsugaku ni okeru shūseishugi," *Sekai* (July 1948): 23–38.

22. Miyakawa Tōru, Nakamura Yūjirō, Furuta Hikaru, *Kindai Nihon shisō ronsō* (Tokyo: Aoki Shoten, 1963), 221.

23. For details, see Takeshi Igarashi, "Peace-Making and Party Politics: The Formation of the Domestic Foreign-Policy System in Postwar Japan," *Journal of Japanese Studies* 11, no. 2 (1985): 339–43.

24. Takeuchi Yoshimi, "Kindaishugi to minzoku no mondai," *Bungaku*, Sept. 1951, and "Kokumin bungaku no mondaiten," in *Sengo bungaku no shisō*, ed. Takahashi Kazumi, Sengo Nihon shisō taikei 13 (Tokyo: Chikuma Shobō, 1969), 217–27; Miyakawa et al., *Kindai Nihon shisō ronsō*, 220–32.

25. Igarashi, "Peace-Making and Party Politics," 343–44.

Problems Symposium (Heiwa Mondai Danwakai), whose members wrote and published their own statement on world peace in early 1949.

Their discussion focused on the American planning for a separate peace treaty (*tandoku kōwa*), which would include only those former enemies of Japan whose governments would be willing to accept a U.S.-Japan security treaty. Although members were by no means in full accord, they were able to agree on a public statement opposing a separate peace.[26] The statement itself evokes the postwar "community of contrition" by expressing regret that Japanese intellectuals did not more effectively resist the war. It then proceeds to argue for a "complete and overall peace," the pursuit of economic relations with all countries including China, complete neutrality for Japan, and denial of military bases to any country.[27]

Outbreak of the Korean War in June 1950 caused some members to change their minds about the desirability of an overall peace treaty. However, in order to renew the group's commitment to the line it had established, Shimizu pressed for another statement, this one to be drafted by Tsuru Shigeto, Ukai Nobushige, and Maruyama Masao. Maruyama was particularly instrumental in focusing the rationale of the third statement on the irrationality of war in the nuclear age, where "these new super-weapons so increase the scale of destruction that both victory and recovery have become impossible."[28] The statement attracted so much attention it is said to have been responsible for doubling the circulation of the journal *Sekai*.[29]

The symposium failed to achieve its objective of an overall peace. The Korean War effectively disrupted its consensus, and major Japanese newspapers generally rejected its arguments as merely the "idealism of intellectuals."[30] However, the statements do seem to have affected the alignment of political forces, especially on the side of the opposition. The December 1950 statement helped turn the left-wing Socialists toward a policy of neutrality and opposition to foreign bases. It also clearly affected the foreign policy stance of the newly formed labor union federation Sōhyō, especially after members of the symposium "organized lecture programs on peace education with the teachers' union throughout Japan."[31] Sympo-

---

26. The "Statement by Peace Study Group in Japan on the Problems of the Japanese Peace Settlement" was published in *Sekai* (Mar. 1950) and also distributed as an English pamphlet entitled *Three Statements for World Peace* by the editorial staff of *Sekai*; a partial translation appears in *Postwar Japan: 1945 to the Present*, ed. Jon Livingston, Joe Moore, and Felicia Oldfather (New York: Pantheon, 1973), 250–53.

27. Livingston, Moore, and Oldfather, *Postwar Japan*, 253.

28. Heiwa Mondai Danwakai, "Mitabi heiwa ni tsuite," *Sekai*, Dec. 1950, 21–52; Peace Problems Symposium, "On Peace: Our Third Statement," *JSPIJ* 1, no. 1 (Apr. 1963): 14 (this is a summary translation of the Dec. 1950 statement).

29. Seki Yoshihiko, "Notes by the Editor," *JSPIJ* 1, no. 1 (Apr. 1963): 11.

30. Arase Yutaka, "Daiyonpen: Sengo shisō to sono tenkai," in *Kindai Nihon shisōshi kōza*, ed. Ienaga Saburō et al. (Tokyo: Chikuma Shobō, 1969), 1:366.

31. Igarashi, "Peace-Making and Party Politics," 351.

sium statements effectively related international issues to domestic ones in a manner that marked the beginning of the broad coalition among renovationist (*kakushin*) forces that reached its apex in the struggle against renewal of the U.S.-Japan security treaty in 1960. However, the symposium's activities in some ways sharpened differences among intellectuals regarding international and domestic politics. Most noteworthy was a widening split between proponents of the critical modernism and pacifism of the early postwar period—the "progressive men of culture" (*shinpoteki bunkajin*)—and an increasingly vocal group of "realists."

The split between "realism" and critical modernism was clearly illuminated in 1950 in a debate between Maruyama Masao and Hayashi Kentarō on whether or not communism constituted a clear and present threat to Japanese democracy. Propounding the realist argument, Hayashi had argued that democracy was a reality that had to be defended against Communist totalitarianism. Maruyama, by contrast, insisted that Japanese democracy was still an unrealized "fiction" and that cries to defend the actual state of Japanese politics would actually have the effect of strengthening its premodern and undemocratic elements.[32] Hayashi's brand of anti-Communist realism gained momentum in the early 1950s, led in part by defectors from the Peace Problems Symposium who joined conservatives around the journal *Kokoro* (Spirit). A typical debate between idealism and realism on the peace issue occurred in 1952 between Tsuru Shigeto, a leading member of the symposium and coauthor of the third statement on peace, and the neoconservative economist Koizumi Shinzō.[33]

INTELLECTUALS IN THE ERA OF
THE SECURITY TREATY CRISIS, 1955–65

The first decade of postwar consciousness was set off from the second by a clearly articulated sense of historical discontinuity: in February 1956 Nakano Yoshio published an essay called "It Is No Longer 'Postwar'," and in August of the same year *Sekai* ran a special issue entitled "Farewell to the Postwar Era."[34] Moreover, in its 1956 white paper on the economy the government's Economic Planning Agency confirmed that the postwar period was over economically since both GNP and

32. Maruyama Masao, "Aru jiyūshugisha e no tegami," *Sekai*, Sept. 1950, 27–38; Hayashi Kentarō, "Gendai chishikijin no ryōshiki," *Sekai*, Oct. 1950, 97–103.

33. See the summary translations in *JSPIJ* 1, no. 1 (Apr. 1963): 20–24. Koizumi, Takeyama Michio, Fukuda Tsuneari, and others first sought to give positive connotation to the self-designation of *neoconservative* in a 1963 collection of their essays: *Shinhoshushugi*, ed. Hayashi Kentarō, Gendai Nihon shisō taikei 35 (Tokyo: Chikuma Shobō, 1963). Also included in this group were Tanaka Michitarō, Fukuhara Rintarō, and Ikeda Kiyoshi. See Fukuda Tsuneari, "Heiwaron no susumekata ni tsuite no gimon," *Chūō kōron*, Dec. 1954, 18–30, and "Heiwa ka jiyū ka," *Jiyū*, Feb. 1962, 2–15. A summary translation of the latter is in *JSPIJ* 1, no. 1 (Apr. 1963): 54–58.

34. Nakano Yoshio, "Mohaya 'sengo' de wa nai," *Bungei shunjū*, Feb. 1956; reprinted in *Anpo to kōdo seichō*, ed. Yamada Munemutsu, *Dokyumento Shōwa-shi* 7 (Tokyo: Heibonsha, 1975), 24–32. Henshūbu, " 'Sengo' e no ketsubetsu," *Sekai*, Aug. 1956, 8.

national income had rebounded to prewar levels and recovery would now give way to rapid economic growth. Japan was in the midst of the so-called Jinmu boom: investment in plant and equipment expanded rapidly, enterprise profits increased 37.5 percent in 1956, and people began to talk about a consumer revolution. Organized labor also began its spring wage offensives in the mid-1950s.[35]

The important political changes had taken place in 1955, when the fall of the Yoshida cabinet brought an accommodation among conservative political forces, leading to the formation of the Liberal Democratic Party (LDP). The two Socialist parties had buried the hatchet only a month earlier, in October 1955. Japan was now introduced to the idiosyncratic form of the two-party system and also to the perpetual political stand-off between a conservative government and a socialist-oriented opposition that was to prove so durable in later decades. Not long afterward political scientists such as Ishida Takeshi pointed out that the conservative and opposition coalitions relied on a web of newly formed interest groups and organizations that had sprung up throughout Japanese society, and the resulting patterns of pressure-group politics marked a decisive departure from the first decade after the war.[36] In the international realm, summit meetings at Geneva in 1955 encouraged the belief that the cold war was thawing, and a year later Khrushchev's critique of Stalinism and the Hungarian uprising stimulated a prolonged identity crisis among Marxists and laid the foundations for the anti-JCP New Left. In the meantime, the JCP began to turn away from the "left-wing adventurism" that had been precipitated by the Cominform critique of 1950 and increasingly entered the fray of interest-group politics.

In the realm of culture the mid-1950s brought a wave of middlebrow culture typified by the weekly magazines (shūkanshi). Catering to the complacent, "salary-man" life-style produced by economic growth, these weeklies combined entertainment with brief digests of scholarly discourse and practical information. At the same time, the intellectual monthlies had declined since the early 1950s. Moreover, 1954 brought the advent of the first pocket-sized paperback books that, according to Katō Hidetoshi, specialized in "easily-understood, concise presentations of various academic and specialized subjects."[37]

The mid-1950s also saw the publication of a spate of works on Japanese culture and national character.[38] One of the earliest contributions was a group of essays, published in 1950, that sought to refute Ruth Benedict's *The Chrysanthemum and the Sword*. A number of books followed, by psychologist Minami Hiroshi, critic Katō Shūichi, and many others. These works directed attention to what were thought to be the many historical and cultural particularities of Japanese society that the

35. Yutaka Kosai, *The Era of High-Speed Growth*, trans. Jacqueline Kaminski (Tokyo: University of Tokyo Press, 1986), 99–100; Tatsurō Uchino, *Japan's Postwar Economy*, trans. Mark A. Harbison (Tokyo: Kōdansha, 1983), 105.

36. Ishida Takeshi, "Pressure Groups in Japan," *JSPIJ* 2, no. 3 (Dec. 1964): 108–11.

37. Hidetoshi Katō, "Middle-brow Culture," *JSPIJ* 2, no. 1 (Apr. 1964): 71.

38. For a summary, see Ikimatsu Keizō, Sakuta Keiichi, and Furuta Hikaru, *Kindai Nihon shakai shisōshi* (Tokyo: Yūhikaku, 1971) 2:312–17.

earlier "universalism" had ignored or cast in a uniformly negative light. They also directed attention away from the universalist categories that had characterized early postwar thought—such as humanity, the abstract individual, the working class, or the masses—toward distinctions among regions, national cultures, and historical experiences. The category of the nation particularly was greatly reinforced by perceptions of national-cultural peculiarities. One of the most influential essays was by Umesao Tadao, who contested the early postwar dichotomy between Japan and modernity by arguing for distinct but parallel streams of world-historical development.[39]

Studies of Japanese culture were paralleled by the formation in 1957 of the Japan Cultural Forum, less in order to study Japanese culture than to revive and propagate it. The forum included among its members a broad range of rather "liberal" conservatives, such as Takeyama Michio, as well as such Nishida-school ideologues as Nishitani Keiji. Despite their differences, the members were united by a cold-war mentality and the sense that Japan's "unique" cultural heritage was under siege. Their writings in the journal *Jiyū* (Liberty)—which parallels in tone and purpose the English publication *Encounter*—and other cultural activities continued to link an essentialized cultural heritage with economic growth and an image of successful modernization.[40]

The mid-1950s also brought theories of mass society and a wide-ranging debate between advocates of such theories and Marxists of various types. The debate was initiated in 1956 by a special issue of the monthly *Shisō* (Thought). Especially noteworthy were contributions by Matsushita Keiichi, who argued that Japanese society had become fundamentally identical to the mass societies of the United States and Europe and that Marxists would have to revise their paradigm.[41]

The introduction of mass society theory coincided with controversies over de-Stalinization and the JCP's period of left-wing adventurism.[42] It also spearheaded a rapid rise in the importation of American and Western European social theory. Some Marxists responded flexibly, expressing the hope that this new social theory—which in their view could never be comprehensive since it lacked theories of class conflict and imperialism—would nonetheless contribute to positive developments in Marxism.[43]

39. Umesao Tadao, *Bunmei no seitai shikan* (Tokyo: Chūō kōronsha, 1967).

40. See Miyakawa Tōru, "The Japan Cultural Forum: Its Logic and Psychology," *JSPIJ* 2, no. 1 (Apr. 1964): 65–70. This stream of thought parallels the neoconservative opposition to cultural modernism that Jürgen Habermas has criticized in the German and American contexts. See Habermas, "Neoconservative Culture Criticism in the United States and West Germany: An Intellectual Movement in Two Political Cultures," in *Habermas and Modernity*, ed. Richard J. Bernstein (Cambridge: MIT Press, 1985), 78–94.

41. Matsushita Keiichi, *Gendai seiji no jōken* (Tokyo: Chūō kōronsha, 1959).

42. Masao Maruyama, "A Critique of De-Stalinization," in Maruyama, *Thought and Behavior in Modern Japanese Politics* (London: Oxford University Press, 1969), 177–224; Fujita Shōzō, "Gendai kakumei shisō no mondaiten," *Chūō kōron*, Feb. 1957, 213–28.

43. See Ueda Kōichirō, "Taishū shakairon to kiki no mondai," *Shisō*, Oct. 1960, 16–25.

The major focal point of the 1955–65 period—and arguably the major watershed in the postwar political role of intellectuals—was the 1960 struggle against renewal of the U.S.-Japan Security Treaty (Anpo). This struggle was carried out under the organizational umbrella of a "national renovationist movement" (*kakushin kokumin undō*) that took several years to develop and whose antecedents can be traced to the controversy over the peace treaty. Major landmarks in the formation of this umbrella movement include the emergence of nationwide ban-the-bomb activities in the wake of the *Lucky Dragon* incident of 1954, the 1954 movement to protect the constitution from amendments hostile to the pacifism of Article 9, and protests against the teacher rating system announced by the conservative government in December 1956.[44] In 1958 a national council was formed to oppose revision of the Police Duties Law, which would have expanded police prerogatives to search and intervene in anticipation of a crime. The movement included labor unions, women's groups, cultural organizations, and the Socialist Party. It culminated in a general strike by four million workers and a Socialist boycott of Diet sessions that ultimately defeated a government effort to force the revision through.[45]

The 1960 Anpo movement owed its distinctiveness to several ideological and social characteristics. First, despite the revolutionary rhetoric of its Communist and left-wing Socialist elements, the movement was basically conservative in that it sought ultimately to preserve "postwar democracy," protect the constitution, and prevent various forms of reactionary tampering with the postwar democratic order. According to political scientist Takabatake Michitoshi, this conservative orientation was responsible for much of the movement's mass appeal. Second, the movement drew mass support primarily from three social groups that were especially antagonistic toward the prewar regime and had benefited directly from the new constitutional order: young people, women, and urbanites. The movement was also undergirded by strong popular support not only for rapid economic growth but also for individualism and rationalism, consumerism, and the domestic happiness associated with *mai-hōmu* (my home). Takabatake argues that this social base and ideology constrained the movement's activities within certain limits. That is, movement supporters were by and large not prepared to endanger their livelihood or take serious risks on behalf of the cause. They were also vulnerable to co-optation: when the LDP propagated its own ideology of modernist consumerism in the early 1960s, these voters tended to shift their support toward that party. Third, the movement manifested a typical mobilization pattern

---

44. A Japanese fishing vessel, the *Daigo Fukuryū-maru* (*Lucky Dragon 5*), was dusted with radioactive ash by the 1954 Bikini hydrogen bomb test carried out by the United States; the ship's radio operator, Kuboyama, eventually died. For details and commentary, see Tanaka Shinjirō, "Death Ash: Experience of Twenty-Three Japanese Fishermen," *Japan Quarterly* 2, no. 1 (Jan.–Mar. 1955): 36–42; and Stephen Salaff, "Bikini Atoll, 1954," *Bulletin of Concerned Asian Scholars* 10, no. 2 (Apr.–June 1978): 58–59.

45. Masataka Kōsaka, *A History of Postwar Japan* (Tokyo: Kodansha International, 1972), 175–77.

oriented toward participation not by individuals but by all the members of existing groups or institutions, such as unions, workshops, student government associations, and universities. This kind of communalism "imbibed the [wartime] traditions of the Taisei Yokusankai [Imperial Rule Assistance Association] and the Kyōchōkai [Conciliation Society]" and tended to preserve existing hierarchies. It also increased the likelihood that the movement would largely disappear when demonstrators returned to their home, workplace, or school.[46] Of course, the Anpo demonstrations also marked the beginnings of political action by ordinary citizens who sometimes acted outside existing organizational contexts and in some cases joined the loosely constructed Voice of the Voiceless Ones Association (Koenaki Koe no Kai).[47]

When the LDP rammed the revised treaty through a House of Representatives committee on 19 May 1960, the crisis of parliamentary democracy became the main issue and progressives such as Maruyama Masao, Shimizu Ikutarō, Tsurumi Shunsuke, Kuno Osamu, and Takeuchi Yoshimi became the standard bearers of the Anpo movement. They not only joined demonstrations but spoke repeatedly at mass meetings.

Their objective was not socialist revolution but rather an extension of the early postwar ideal of democratic revolution, which would catalyze the formation of a civil society composed of modern citizens (*shimin shakai*). Kuno Osamu characterized this society in terms of adherence to an occupational ethic that cuts across organizational loyalties and demands universal adherence to procedural rules.[48] Kuno also argued that the subject (*shutai*) of antiauthoritarian movements like Anpo was the citizen masses (*shimin taishū*): he agreed with the mass society theorists that one aspect of popular consciousness was passive and apathetic, but he argued that the citizenlike aspect included a tendency to rise up in defense of the peace and freedom of daily life.[49]

Second, some citizen-society theorists attempted to radicalize the Anpo movement by providing it with a more principled political commitment. That is, they held up certain ideals, or fictions, which they hoped would guide the movement toward construction of a more democratic society. For example, Maruyama called for renewed commitment to the democratic idealism of the early postwar:

46. Takabatake Michitoshi, "'Rokujū-nen anpo' no seishinshi," in Kamishima, Maeda, and Najita, *Sengo Nihon no seishinshi*, 74–76. See also Takeshi Ishida, "Progressive Political Parties and Popular Movements," *JSPIJ* 3, no. 1 (Apr. 1965): 116; and Takabatake Michitoshi, "Shūdangurumi undō o kanō ni shita heiwa to minshushugi no jikkan," *Asahi jānaru*, 1 Oct. 1981: 35.

47. See Takabatake Michitoshi, "Citizens' Movements: Organizing the Spontaneous," in J. Victor Koschmann, ed., *Authority and the Individual in Japan: Citizen Protest in Historical Perspective* (Tokyo: University of Tokyo Press, 1978), 189–99.

48. Ibid., 82.

49. Kuno Osamu, "Shiminshugi no seiritsu," *Shisō no kagaku*, July 1960, 9–16; reprinted as "Seijiteki shimin no seiritsu," in *Nichijō no shisō*, ed. Takabatake Michitoshi, Sengo Nihon shisō taikei 14 (Tokyo: Chikuma Shobō, 1970), 273–83.

We are reminded of the phrase, "Remember Pearl Harbor," which served as the motto of the American people throughout the Pacific War. This motto enjoined them not to forget the behavior of Japanese militarism that was symbolized by the attack on Pearl Harbor. If we think of the meaning of May 20 [1960] from this viewpoint I think we are drawn back to August 15 [1945]. The cry, return to the beginning! must mean a return to the moment immediately after defeat; it means return to August 15th! (applause). . . . In the midst of utter ruin, we committed ourselves to the task of building a new Japan, and . . . we should constantly call to mind the feelings we had at that moment.[50]

In view of his earlier criticism of Eurocentric modernization theory, it is to be expected that Takeuchi Yoshimi's position on Anpo should have been somewhat different from those of Tsurumi and Maruyama. In his view the Security Treaty had to be opposed because it interfered with the duty of the Japanese people to atone for their wartime aggression in China and to move toward a restoration of diplomatic relations. Takeuchi not only spoke and wrote against the treaty but also protested government behavior by permanently resigning his faculty position at Tokyo Metropolitan University.[51]

The 1960 Anpo struggle not only represented the culmination of the national renovationist movement and of mass protest against the government but also, according to Takabatake, marked the "apex of social influence for intellectuals" and a "watershed for the role of intellectuals in postwar Japanese society." A major turning point in this regard came after the 10 June 1960 incident at Haneda airport in which student demonstrators surrounded the car transporting Eisenhower's press secretary, James Haggerty. On 17 June Japan's seven major newspapers, which up to that time had opposed the Kishi cabinet, published a joint statement calling for a restoration of order. This action "cast a shadow over the long postwar honeymoon between 'progressive' intellectuals and the media."[52]

Most of the Anpo intellectuals retreated from politics once the Kishi cabinet fell. Shimizu Ikutarō began to turn away from progressive causes altogether. Maruyama returned to more contemplative pursuits, and Takeuchi also fled the public eye except for editing a small magazine devoted to improving Sino-Japanese relations. By contrast, the pragmatist-populists Kuno and Tsurumi, who had embraced a philosophy much more closely attuned to subtle adjustments in popular culture, were able to remain involved in various ways. They associated themselves with the increasingly mundane concerns of the local citizens' and residents' movements, which expanded the new forms of political participation pioneered by the Voice of the Voiceless Ones societies during the Anpo protests. They continued to publish the journal *Shisō no kagaku* and even expanded their activities in the 1960s.[53]

50. Maruyama Masao, "Fukusho no setsu," *Sekai*, Aug. 1960, 370.
51. Takabatake, " 'Rokujū-nen anpo' no seishin-shi," 83–84.
52. Ibid., 70–71.
53. Yamada Munemutsu, *Sengo shisōshi* (Tokyo: San'ichi Shobō, 1976), 315–19.

Another group of intellectuals who had been involved in the Anpo protests continued in the 1960s to press a more radical agenda than either Maruyama or Tsurumi. For them the Anpo protests had served to expose the emptiness of the liberal ideals of postwar democracy. The poet and essayist Yoshimoto Takaaki, for example, argued that the masses had often acted independently of any leadership and their actions had exposed as hypocrites not only the existing left-wing parties (especially the Communists) but also the theorists of civil society and postwar democracy. Arguing against Maruyama, whose postmortem on Anpo had disparaged the tendency of the postwar masses to put private interests first,[54] Yoshimoto argued that "the autonomous attitude of putting self interest before social interest" was itself the "foundation of postwar 'democracy' (bourgeois democracy)," a truer form of democracy than any idealized by Maruyama.[55] He contended that the masses were animated by feelings of alienation that had expanded since the end of the war. In conjunction with his developing concept of the "masses," Yoshimoto was to place the concept of *jiritsu* (autonomy) at the center of his vision of a new ideology for the post-Anpo Left.[56]

Of course, Yoshimoto was by no means the first to orient discourse around a conception of the masses. Shimizu Ikutarō had already argued effectively in the early postwar period that intellectuals should address the "anonymous thought" of the common people.[57] Others, most notably Tsurumi Kazuko, had been active in the circle movement, which encouraged women textile workers, housewives, and others to discuss and write about their wartime experiences, their families, and their own lives. In the process they became more self-aware and capable of coping with the conflicting demands of postwar life.[58]

One of the most important of Yoshimoto's concepts, *taishū no genzō* (the masses' original form of existence), has directly to do with postwar intellectual self-consciousness. According to Yoshimoto, the attempts of postwar intellectuals to enlighten and lead the masses were fundamentally misconceived because the masses naturally tend not to respond outside their own narrow life space.[59] Therefore, rather than preaching to them, the intellectual should try to learn their worldview and explore ways of incorporating it into revolutionary thought. A

54. See Maruyama Masao, "8.15 to 5.19," *Chūō kōron*, Aug. 1960, 44–54.

55. Yoshimoto Takaaki, "Gisei no shūen" (1960), in *Yoshimoto Takaaki zenchosakushū* (Tokyo: Keisō Shobō, 1969) 13:67–68. See also Lawrence Olson, "Intellectuals and 'The People': On Yoshimoto Takaaki," *Journal of Japanese Studies* 4, no. 2 (Summer 1978): 342.

56. Yoshimoto Takaaki, "Jiritsu no shisōteki kyoten" (1965), in *Yoshimoto Takaaki zenchosakushū* 13:240–74.

57. See Matsumoto Sannosuke's discussion in "Introduction," *JSPIJ* 4, no. 2 (Aug. 1966): 2–19.

58. See Kazuko Tsurumi, *Social Change and the Individual: Social Change Before and After World War II* (Princeton: Princeton University Press, 1970), 213–303; Kinoshita Junji and Tsurumi Kazuko, eds., *Haha no rekishi* (Tokyo: Kawade Shobō, 1954); and Kuno Osamu, Tsurumi Shunsuke, and Fujita Shōzō, *Sengo Nihon no shisō* (Tokyo: Keisō Shobō, 1966), 110–47.

59. Yoshimoto Takaaki, "Jōkyō to wa nani ka," in *Yoshimoto Takaaki zenchosakushū* 13:337–408. See also Yoshimoto, "Kyōdō gensōron," *Yoshimoto Takaaki zenchosakushū* 11:5–278.

system of thought like Marxism could be "true" only to the extent that it reso-
nated with anxieties and feelings of oppression that were grounded in the existential situation of the masses themselves. Therefore, Marxism had to be "relativ-
ized" and adapted to the mentality of the masses. This mentality was rooted in
particular experience rather than universal ideals, and Yoshimoto argued that
autonomy had to be based in the community rather than the abstract individual.[60]
Ultimately, he not only sidestepped orthodox categories like class but also called
into question the scientific veracity of historical materialism. His work played a
central role in the left-wing critique of postwar thought that developed in the
1960s.

Yoshimoto's conception of how an intellectual should approach the existence
of the masses was to some extent actualized by Tanikawa Gan, who went to live
among coal miners in rural Kyushu in the role of a *kōsakusha* (facilitator or
fabricator).[61] The need for such "fabricators"—a term that Tanikawa most likely
borrowed from the Chinese revolution—emerged out of the yawning gap perceived by intellectuals in the late 1950s and early 1960s between themselves and
the masses. Thus, Tanikawa can describe his fabricator only in paradoxical, ironic
terms:

> It is the task of the fabricator to fuse the thinking of the lofty but uninfluential
> intellectual with the thinking of the lowly but influential masses; he must coordinate
> these two kinds of thinking within the same dimension. This task naturally leads the
> fabricator into a world of isolation and paradox. He must translate the theories [of
> the intellectuals] into actual feelings [for the masses] and translate into theory the
> feelings [that the masses have developed on the basis] of real-life experiences. At any
> rate, the fabricator is inevitably "caught" between [the intellectuals and the
> masses].[62]

Moreover, as Hidaka points out, Tanikawa's fabricators are "caught not only
between the intellectuals and the masses; they are caught also between the positive
and negative attitudes of the masses." The rural masses are dissatisfied with the
level of their material lives, yet they are quiescent and immersed in traditional
ways. They have an enviable degree of solidarity, but their ethos consists overall
of a "chaotic aggregate of egoism, rudimentary animal instincts, subservience and
sentimentality, the very things that the leaders of the enlightenment movement
had hoped to do away with."[63] As an old man reportedly once told the people's
history (*minshūshi*) researcher, Irokawa Daikichi, "We farmers are hopeless conservatives. We're not waiting to be saved. We're the kind of people who are

60. Sakuta Keiichi, "The Controversy over Community and Autonomy," in Koschmann, *Authority and the Individual*, 240–42.

61. On Tanikawa, see Sakuta, "Controversy," 242–46, and Nakamori Mikata, *Tanikawa Gan: kōsakusha no fuka* (Tokyo: Shichigatsudō, 1983).

62. Rokurō Hidaka, "Intellectuals and the Masses," *JSPIJ* 2, no. 1 (Apr. 1964): 109.

63. Ibid., 110.

content to shut ourselves up in our holes and stay there. But the *buraku* [rural community] is bigger than any of us. That's why we have a *buraku*! Do you understand? You and your friends?"[64]

The disillusionment with postwar democracy and the role of intellectuals as custodians of universal knowledge and enlightenment that was experienced in the wake of Anpo by Yoshimoto, Tanikawa, and many other left-wing activists led to an important change in modus operandi. This change paralleled Sartre's conclusion in the aftermath of May 1968 that one must "suppress himself as an intellectual" and "learn to understand the universal that the masses want, in reality, in the immediate, this very moment."[65] It was also consistent with Michel Foucault's contention that after 1968 "the intellectual discovered that the masses no longer need him to gain knowledge: they know perfectly well, without illusion."[66] The classical intellectual function can no longer be sustained once it is realized that, in relation to power, theory is just a relay among practical actions and therefore can only be "local and regional . . . , not totalizing."[67] Tanikawa's notion of the intellectual as fabricator departs in much the same ways from the universalist, totalizing pretensions of the postwar "progressive men of culture."

Tanikawa and Yoshimoto tried to adapt a revised form of revolutionary Marxism not only to the mentality of disparaged elements of the rural and proletarian masses but also to the realities of nationalism. In this respect, their thought was continuous with that of Takeuchi Yoshimi, and like him they sought to distinguish clearly between nationalism and ultranationalism. According to Yoshimoto, the roots of Japanese nationalism can be traced back to the concept of social life undifferentiated from nature, which was developed in the Tokugawa-period school of *kokugaku* (national studies; nativism).[68] In contrast to this popular nationalism rooted in the cognitive patterns of daily life (*seikatsu shisō*), ultranationalism had been generated primarily by intellectuals: "It was only when popular nationalism lost its emotional substance and took on an abstract air of generality that the nationalism of the intellectuals found an opportunity to crystallize into ultranationalism."[69] Tanikawa also wrote on nationalism in the wake of the Anpo

64. Irokawa Daikichi, "The Survival Struggle of the Japanese Community," in Koschmann, *Authority and the Individual*, 270–71.

65. Jean-Paul Sartre, "A Friend of the People," in Sartre, *Between Existentialism and Marxism*, 293–94.

66. "Intellectuals and Power: A Conversation Between Michel Foucault and Gilles Deleuze," in Foucault, *Language, Counter-Memory, Practice: Selected Essays and Interviews*, ed. Donald F. Bouchard (Ithaca: Cornell University Press, 1977), 207.

67. Ibid., 206–8.

68. Yoshimoto Takaaki, "Nihon no nashonarizumu ni tsuite," *Shisō*, Apr. 1962, 65–74. I have profited from Wesley Sasaki-Uemura, "Neo-Nativism and the Re-Emergence of Nationalist Discourse" (unpublished paper, Cornell University, 1989).

69. Quoted in Sakuta Keiichi, "The Controversy over Community and Autonomy," in Koschmann, *Authority and the Individual*, 241.

struggle, attempting to distinguish between the folk and the nation and arguing that they emerge in tense conflict.[70]

Paralleling the left-wing nationalism of Yoshimoto and Tanikawa was a resurgence of various forms of right-wing nationalism in the early 1960s in conjunction with rapid economic growth. The elections that followed the fall of the Kishi cabinet in July 1960 resulted in a decisive victory for the LDP—much to the dismay of those who thought they saw in the Anpo demonstrations the stirrings of a populist Left—and a new cabinet headed by former Finance Ministry bureaucrat Ikeda Hayato. Ikeda made economic policy the foundation of his administration, and in November 1960 he announced the National Income Doubling Plan. Japan was soon in the midst of the so-called Iwato boom as investment in plant and equipment exploded and the consumer revolution went into full swing. These tendencies soon co-opted for the LDP the desires for modernization and enhancement of private life that had underlain the national renovationist movement and the Anpo demonstrations. They also stimulated nationalistic reassessments of Japanese history and culture, which contrasted markedly with the self-critical thrust of postwar thought. Intellectually, a significant revival of nationalism seems to have taken place in 1963 when the right-wing former Communist Hayashi Fusao took charge of the literary column of *Asahi shinbun*, and *Chūō kōron* began to serialize Hayashi's revisionist history, *Daitōa sensō kōteiron* (Affirmation of the Greater East Asia War).

The willingness of the *Chūō kōron* to publish Hayashi's apology for the Pacific War is significant against the background of one of several cases of ultrarightist violence that occurred in the wake of Anpo. In December 1960 *Chūō kōron* had published a short story by Fukazawa Shichirō in which the imperial couple are beheaded during a dream sequence. Not only ultrarightists but also the Imperial Household Agency condemned the story as disrespectful to the imperial family, and after several threats a rightist youth stormed into the home of Shimanaka Hōji, president of the Chūō Kōron Publishing Company, with the intent of assassinating him. In the company president's absence, the intruder stabbed to death a household maid and seriously wounded Shimanaka's wife. The incident made the company extremely sensitive to right-wing criticism and may be said to have precipitated *Chūō kōron*'s more or less permanent turn toward the Right editorially. Moreover, in 1962 the company canceled publication of the April edition of its magazine *Shisō no kagaku* (Science of thought) because it focused on the emperor system.

The new self-confidence that accompanied high growth rates and levels of consumption was also expressed in increased attention to "modernization" and the possible uses of the Japanese experience as a model for developing economies. Soon after the Anpo demonstrations died down, the Japanese mountain resort of

70. Tanikawa Gan, "Intānashonaru no ne," *Shisō*, Apr. 1961, 740–47.

Hakone provided the site for a preliminary meeting of the Association for Asian Studies' Conference on Modern Japan. Participants included not only such Western Japan specialists as Marius Jansen, John W. Hall, Edwin O. Reischauer, and Ronald Dore but also critical Japanese social scientists such as Tōyama Shigeki, Maruyama Masao, Kawashima Takeyoshi, Katō Shūichi, and Ōuchi Tsutomu. Against the background of the publication earlier the same year of W. W. Rostow's *Stages of Economic Growth: A Non-Communist Manifesto,* John W. Hall introduced to the meeting a "nine-point description of the essential features of modern society."[71] The statement typified the American effort to present modernization as an objectively measurable, universal process of which the United States was the prime example.

Although the Japanese participants were certainly interested in modernization theory, many had serious reservations about the Americans' overly objectivist approach. Maruyama and Kawashima were still closely identified with the kind of "modernism" that had been characteristic of the early postwar period and tended to see modernity less in quantitative economic than qualitative political terms. According to Kawashima, for example, the question of modernization was concerned primarily with "an immediate, practical concern with 'democratizing' Japanese society."[72]

Modernization theory was undoubtedly responsible in part for the resurgence of Japanese nationalism and economic great-power consciousness, especially after Edwin Reischauer returned to Japan the following year as American ambassador. Soon after his arrival he appeared in a *Chūō kōron* discussion with economist Nakayama Ichirō (a leading theorist behind Ikeda's National Income Doubling Plan), in which he suggested that Japan's development could serve as a model for capitalist modernization in Asia.[73] In addition to blunting self-critical postwar views of Japanese society and history and contributing to the spread of great-power mentality, the schematic, unhistorical formulas of American modernization theory helped to discredit the critical view of industrialization that had begun to emerge from the mass society theories of the late 1950s. It also provided an opportunity for renewed emphasis on what were thought to be the essential qualities of Japanese culture.

In January 1965 a committee of leading cultural figures commissioned by the Ministry of Education issued a draft report entitled "Kitaisareru ningenzō" (An image of the ideal Japanese). Written primarily by the wartime fascist thinker

71. John Whitney Hall, "Changing Conceptions of the Modernization of Japan," in *Changing Japanese Attitudes Toward Modernization,* ed. Marius B. Jansen (Princeton: Princeton University Press, 1965), 18. For a telling critique of the Hakone Conference and modernization theory, see John W. Dower, "E. H. Norman, Japan, and the Uses of History," in *Origins of the Modern Japanese State: Selected Writings of E. H. Norman,* ed. John W. Dower (New York: Pantheon, 1975), 3–101.

72. Kano Tsutomu, "Preface to This Issue," *Japan Interpreter* 6, no. 1 (Spring 1970): vi.

73. "Nihon kindaika no rekishiteki hyōka," *Chūō kōron,* Sept. 1961, 84–97.

Kōsaka Masaaki, the report called to mind the state-sponsored ethical orthodoxy that had been propounded in such wartime exhortations as *Kokutai no hongi* (Fundamentals of our national policy, 1937) and *Shinmin no michi* (Way of the subject, 1941).[74] It is especially interesting that the draft linked an ideal of openness to the world with renewed stress on retaining "true Japanese" identity, thus calling attention to growing right-wing defensiveness in the wake of the rapid import liberalization that was carried out under American as well as other foreign pressure between 1960 and 1965.[75]

In sum, the second postwar decade brought intellectuals to a summit of political instrumentality and initiative and then allowed them to be driven back under the combined force of accelerated economic growth, political "realism," a new and cruder variety of cultural essentialism, and imported modernization theory. Postwar thought was eroded somewhat through the influence of mass society theory, nationalism, and economic growth and was subjected to an increasingly effective internal critique based on suspicion regarding the role of the intellectual as a source of enlightenment and leadership. Moreover, its major proponents sometimes struggled unsuccessfully to adapt their paradigms to changing conditions. But it was not overthrown inasmuch as major elements of the early postwar episteme generally remained persuasive well into the 1960s. For many liberal to Left intellectuals, politics continued in the broad sense to be a matter of democratic revolution presaging some sort of socialist transformation, and the terms *modernity, democracy, peace,* and *universalism* retained their force as the major ideals of the national renovationist alliance among the major opposition parties, the Sōhyō labor federation, the peace and antinuclear weapons movements, and other elements. However, once the 1960 protests ended, the low-posture politics of reconciliation and economic growth sponsored by Prime Minister Ikeda tended to undercut the critical force of antiestablishment arguments.

PROTEST AND THEORY
IN THE MANAGEMENT SOCIETY, 1965–75

The continued viability of postwar ideals, in somewhat modified form, was revealed in the emergence of protest against the Vietnam War. In response to the first American bombing raids on North Vietnam in February 1965, the popular writer Oda Makoto and a group of intellectuals that included Tsurumi Shunsuke initiated the Peace in Vietnam Committee, or Beheiren. Beheiren was formed entirely outside the institutional, financial, and ideological channels of the estab-

---

74. These documents are reproduced in Hijikata Kazuo, *"Nihon bunkaron" to tennōsei ideologii* (Tokyo: Shin Nihon Shuppansha, 1983), 177–273. In English, see Robert King Hall, ed., *Kokutai no hongi: Cardinal Principles of the National Entity of Japan,* trans. John Owen Gauntlett (Cambridge: Harvard University Press, 1949).

75. Yamada Munemutsu, *Kiken na shisōka* (Tokyo: Kappa, 1965), 144–45.

lished postwar Left and was to become a model for a variety of citizens' movements that would emerge in the 1960s and 1970s.[76]

In some ways Oda Makoto, the charismatic leader of Beheiren, demonstrated the continued viability of some aspects of the discourse on democratic revolution that had its origins in the early postwar period. In a series of works on democracy Oda often seemed to echo the 1960 sentiments of Maruyama concerning the need to return to the pure spirit of democracy. Yet he remained keenly sensitive to the ways in which a system of "state democracy" could be profoundly inhumane. Indeed, "it was democratic America which began the monstrous evil of the Vietnam War."[77]

Oda is a world traveler who personified the international linkages Beheiren forged with antiwar movements in other countries, particularly the United States. The movement introduced teach-ins, folksinging, and less threatening styles of protest to Japanese politics; it also sponsored some of the largest peaceful demonstrations ever held in Japan, such as the one in Tokyo on 15 June 1969.[78] Despite its numbers, the movement largely resisted the temptation to form large, multipurpose, hierarchically structured organizations of the sort that were typical of the postwar renovationist movement. In an approach that in some ways mirrored the new modesty of radical intellectuals in Europe after May 1968, Oda believed that Beheiren should be "temporary and ad hoc," oriented to a single issue—the Vietnam War—and flexible enough to adapt its tactics to changing situations.[79]

Paralleling the rise of citizens' movements like Beheiren and local residents' movements against environmental pollution was the emergence in political-institutional analysis of theories of overmanagement (*kajō kanri*) and centralized technological manipulation. In the mature form of what Oda called "democratic fascism," parties, elections, and naked coercion seemed less important than bureaucratic control exercised through the sophisticated technology of management society (*kanri shakai*). According to Kitazawa Masakuni:

> The term *kanri shakai* ("managed society") . . . refers to a society administered through highly sophisticated mechanisms for forecasting, planning, and control. Such mechanisms are capable of quantitative analysis of data and compilation of a set of optimum conditions for that society's well-being. . . .
>
> A related phrase, *jōhō shakai* ("information society"), . . . refers not to simple mass

76. On the politics of citizens' movements, see Kurt Steiner, Ellis S. Krauss, and Scott C. Flanagan, eds., *Political Opposition and Local Politics in Japan* (Princeton: Princeton University Press, 1980), 187–313.

77. Oda Makoto, "Making Democracy Our Own," *Japan Interpreter* 6, no. 3 (Autumn 1970): 240–46; Oda, "The Meaning of 'Meaningless Death,' " *JSPIJ* 4, no. 2 (Aug. 1966): 75–85; and Oda, "The Ethics of Peace," in Koschmann, *Authority and the Individual*, 154–70.

78. Thomas R. H. Havens, *Fire Across the Sea: The Vietnam War and Japan, 1965–1975* (Princeton: Princeton University Press, 1987), 63–67.

79. Oda, "Making Democracy Our Own," 250–51. See also Takabatake Michitoshi, "Citizen's Movements: Organizing the Spontaneous," in Koschmann, *Authority and the Individual*, 198.

control or to the image-centered information conveyed by the media, but to quantitative, computerized information that average people need not (or cannot) decipher directly. And because this automatic analysis of quantitative data undergirds the management society, the society itself might well be described as semi-automatic in nature. I say *semi*-automatic because human beings make the final decisions and plan the policies.[80]

Theories of rule by means of management and information problematized the conventional assumption of a political relationship between ruler and ruled. It seemed that the position of the active subject was increasingly being preempted by deceptively neutral technology and automatic processes.

Citizens' movements like Beheiren were not the only political manifestations of resistance against organizational rigidity and managerial forms of control. In 1968, in the wake of African-American struggles in the United States, expansion of the war in Southeast Asia, and the events of May in France, the Japanese radical student movement began to assume the loosely structured, nonsectarian form of the Zenkyōtō (Zengaku Kyōtō Kaigi; universitywide joint struggle councils). The University of Tokyo (Tōdai) Zenkyōtō included prominent veterans of student protest and contributed conceptually as well as actively to the development of radical opposition to structures of overmanagement. In a manner even more pronounced than in Beheiren, the Tōdai Zenkyōtō participants attempted to struggle not only against external enemies but against their own organizational hierarchies, rules, unified ideology, established leadership, and membership boundaries. Rather than an organization, Zenkyōtō was styled as a "perpetual organizing."[81] Zenkyōtō theorists rejected formal or "Potsdam" democracy, with its majority rule, in favor of a free-form style in which a group would take the lead in establishing a situation, such as occupation of a building, and then proceed to debate the merits of the action. The result was interminable discussion, but often after the fact rather than before.

Zenkyōtō participants, many of whom were researchers and interns, were also articulately sensitive to their own role as supports for a repressive system. According to Yamamoto, they recognized that they shared responsibility for the role of the university in strengthening bourgeois society.[82] Therefore, their struggle was as much a self-negation—a struggle against their "imperial university within"— and an effort to establish their own active autonomy (*shutaisei*) as it was a struggle against the university and state.[83] Zenkyōtō's language of *shutaisei* and *jiritsu* connects it ideologically with the early postwar efforts of Umemoto Katsumi and others and, of course, with Yoshimoto's critical interventions of the 1960s. At the same time, the late 1960s student radicals set themselves squarely against "post-

80. Kitazawa Masakuni, "Militarism in the Management Society," in Koschmann, *Authority and the Individual*, 201.
81. Murao Kōichi, "Tōdai Zenkyōtō: Kono kimyō naru 'seitaikei'," *Jōkyō*, Mar. 1969, 32.
82. Yamamoto Yoshitaka, *Chisei no hanran* (Tokyo: Zen'eisha, 1969), 216–17.
83. See the discussion " 'Jiko hitei no shisō' to puroretariāto," *Jōkyō*, June 1969, 51–55.

war democracy" and the older generation of postwar scholars such as Maruyama. Clearly, the intensity of Zenkyōtō's periodic rage revealed the new level of radical frustration occasioned by increasingly pervasive and effective forms of managerial control.

The year 1970 symbolized a turning point for Japanese society in the realm of political economy. In that year the security treaty with the United States was extended automatically without the sort of turmoil that accompanied the 1960 revision, and arrangements had already been made in 1969 for the return of Okinawa to Japanese sovereignty. Osaka's Expo '70, which celebrated Japanese affluence after a decade of accelerated growth, was attended by sixty million people. Then in 1971 the so-called Nixon shocks, which included the dollar float and announcement of the American president's imminent visit to China, rolled over Japan like a tsunami. The American overture to China, especially, disillusioned many Japanese conservatives who had up to that time been among the United States' most stalwart supporters.[84] And when this shock was followed by the first oil shock of 1973, analysts predicted an end to rapid economic growth.

Perhaps it is fitting that the specter of a halt in the upward movement of GNP statistics should have been paralleled by the introduction of structuralism. The most influential Japanese scholar to carry out structuralist analysis was the cultural anthropologist Yamaguchi Masao, whose works on sacred kingship, myth, clowns, and tricksters spanned the 1970s and helped give the era its special intellectual flavor. Yamaguchi built on Edward Shils's concepts of center and periphery and Victor Turner's model of societas and communitas to weave original and thought-provoking studies of Japanese mythology and kingship (*tennō-sei*).[85] Yamaguchi tended to focus on the margin rather than the center, showing the ways in which spaces and entities defined as marginal play an essential role in maintaining the center's vitality. His studies of kingship emphasize the efficacy of the king's capacity to prevent calamity and pollution by carrying out rituals of purification and thus to serve as the symbolic center of the national collective illusion. This conceptualization contributed to overcoming the simple reliance by many postwar historians and others on a unilaterally coercive model of archaic rule. Yamaguchi also studied the tragic cycle from vagabondage to kingship and back to vagabondage, a cycle exemplified in texts as diverse as the Oedipus myth and Thomas Hardy's *Mayor of Casterbridge*.[86] Yamaguchi's influence was accompanied by new interest in non-modern societies, the nonrational aspects of play and ritual, and the carnivalesque world of clown and trickster.

84. J. Victor Koschmann, "Hawks on the Defensive: The Seirankai," *Japan Interpreter* 8, no. 4 (Winter 1974): 467–77.

85. Yamaguchi Masao, *Bunka no ryōgisei* (Tokyo: Iwanami Shoten, 1975); in English, see Yamaguchi Masao, "Kingship, Theatricality, and Marginal Reality in Japan," in *Text and Context: The Social Anthropology of Tradition*, ed. Ravendra K. Jain (Philadelphia: Institute for the Study of Human Issues, 1977), 151–79.

86. Yamaguchi Masao, *Jinruigakuteki shikō* (Tokyo: Serika Shobō, 1971).

Influenced by and to some extent paralleling Yamaguchi's efforts is the provocative work of the anthropologist and feminist Ueno Chizuko, who has produced studies of structuralism and Japanese kingship in addition to several commentaries on women and feminism in Japan. Ueno is one of Japan's best-known feminist writers and attempts in some works to develop a flexibly Marxist analysis of the relation in modern society between capitalism and patriarchy.[87]

In the 1970s philosophers also explored the subject-object ambiguity implicit in the management society by focusing on the body and perception. Ichikawa Hiroshi, for example, followed Maurice Merleau-Ponty in attempting to stitch together the body and mind, which modern thought under the influence of Cartesian dualism had rent asunder.[88] At about the same time, Hiromatsu Wataru pursued a similar problematic from within Marxism, focusing initially on the concept of reification.[89]

The subject-object dualism of modern thought was also challenged by Sakabe Megumi, who focused not on perception but on the self as persona. Avoiding the modern assumption that an essential self-identity is hidden behind social masks, Sakabe located the persona in a surface position where shifting "selves" metamorphose incessantly.[90] Sakabe also criticized modern philosophy in a book on Kant, in which he argues that modern reason is by no means ever complete or self-sufficient but always exists in a tense relationship with unreason. He contends, therefore, that the history of modern thought since Kant is the story of Western philosophy's forgetfulness with respect to this "anxiety of reason."[91] Critiques of modern thought published in the mid-1970s by Ichikawa, Hiromatsu, and Sakabe were among the best of those that helped create an intellectual atmosphere conducive to debates over postmodernity.

POSTMODERN AMBIVALENCE AND NEW ACADEMISM, 1975–88

As a major postindustrial economy Japan has been implicitly associated with postmodernity in the 1980s, and since in the Japanese context modernity has been associated with the postwar, a major question is whether the 1980s produced not only a mood of reaction against postwar modernism but also a new culture that might be called post-postwar. Have significant aspects of Japanese thought and culture finally passed beyond the postwar episteme dominated by the metahistories of class and liberation, the metaphysics of reason and subject-centeredness,

87. See, for example, Ueno Chizuko, *Kōzōshugi no bōken* (Tokyo: Keisō Shobō, 1985); Amino Yoshihiko, Ueno Chizuko, and Miyata Noboru, *Nihon ōkenron* (Tokyo: Shunshusha, 1988); Ueno, "The Position of Japanese Women Reconsidered," *Current Anthropology* 28, no. 4 (Aug.–Oct. 1987): 75–82; and Ueno, *Shihonsei to kaji rōdō* (Tokyo: Kaimeisha, 1985); and Ueno, *Kafuchōsei to shihonsei: Marukusushugi feminizumu no chihei* (Tokyo: Iwanami Shoten, 1990).

88. Ichikawa Hiroshi, *Seishin to shite no shintai* (Tokyo: Keisō Shobō, 1975).

89. See Hiromatsu Wataru, *Shihonron no tetsugaku* (Tokyo: Gendai Hyōronsha, 1975), and *Sekai no kyōdōshukanteki sonzai kōzō* (Tokyo: Keisō Shobō, 1976).

90. Sakabe Megumi, *Kamen no kaishakugaku* (Tokyo: Tōkyō Daigaku Shuppankai, 1976).

91. Sakabe Megumi, *Risei no fuan: Kantō tetsugaku no seisei to kōzō* (Tokyo: Keisō Shobō, 1976).

dualistic tension between value and fact, and committed partisanship in politics? And have intellectuals finally "escaped" the tensions of "unhappy consciousness"?

Again, Yoshimoto's most recent work suggests a certain tendency. In a manner that both draws on and transcends theories of mass society and overmanagement, he now seeks to sever completely the link between the manipulation of signs and political and economic instrumentality. A case in point is his analysis of television commercials. Like Jean Baudrillard,[92] he argues that in their primitive form television commercials were intended to emphasize a product's high quality and low price. In the second stage, however, the attempt was less to highlight quality and price than to associate the product with an attractive image. That is, the product was consumed primarily as a means to possess the image. This trend was extended in ads that sought to enhance the image of the corporate producer rather than of specific products. According to Yoshimoto, however, in their most recent stage some ads have become virtually autonomous from capitalist control since they are intended only to present a beautiful portrait. The image, once merely the means to induce consumption, has now attained its own autonomy in a system of desire for the image itself that is self-contained and irreducible.[93] This system is unconscious and therefore relatively impervious to reasoned analysis or intellectual understanding. It is unintegrated and diffuse, a multiplicity of signs and constantly fluctuating subcultures. Such a worldview suggests the final obsolescence of the postwar logic of tension between subject and object, ideal and reality, essence and appearance.

If Yoshimoto's intentions are still ultimately radical, despite what seem to be the complacent implications of his criticism, the same cannot be said of the neoconservative stream of post-postwar cultural commentary that dominated the media in the 1980s. In 1979 the literary critic Etō Jun began to research diplomatic archives and the records of American occupation censorship to demonstrate that the American interlude had crippled Japan's sovereignty and warped the development of Japanese literature. In 1980 Prime Minister Ōhira Masayoshi commissioned a policy study group that attributed Japan's economic success to traditional cultural values and proclaimed a new "age of culture."[94] Premised on a supposed rejection not only of postwar Japanese thought but also of modern thought and culture in general, this neoconservative discourse again tied "internationalization" to renewed emphasis on the indigenous cultural heritage. Ōhira's successor, Nakasone Yasuhiro, called repeatedly in the 1980s for the formation of an "international state" combined with new efforts to understand Japan's cultural

92. Jean Baudrillard, *Simulacra and Simulations*, trans. Paul Foss, Paul Patton, and Philip Beitchman (New York: Semiotext(e), 1983); and *Jean Baudrillard: Selected Writings*, ed. Mark Poster (Stanford: Stanford University Press, 1988).

93. Yoshimoto Takaaki, *Masu imējiron* (Tokyo: Fukutake Shoten, 1984), 240–41. See also Marilyn Ivy, "Critical Texts, Mass Artifacts: The Consumption of Knowledge in Postmodern Japan," in Miyoshi and Harootunian, *Postmodernism and Japan*, 36–38.

94. See Kenneth B. Pyle, "The Future of Japanese Nationality: An Essay in Contemporary History," *Journal of Japanese Studies* 8, no. 2 (Summer 1982): 223–64; and H. D. Harootunian, "Visible Discourses/Invisible Ideologies," in Miyoshi and Harootunian, *Postmodernism and Japan*, 63–92.

identity. He even proposed that Japan's culture should be exported alongside its commodities.[95] Then in 1984, in a massive effort led by the former bureaucrat Nagatomi Yūichirō to co-opt intellectuals and dominate discourse, the Ministry of Finance recruited hundreds of specialists to study Japan's leading role in the next stage of civilization, "beyond modernity."[96] A central figure in this flurry of neoconservative futurism was the economist Murakami Yasusuke, who coauthored with Satō Seizaburō and Kumon Shunpei the controversial work *Bunmei to shite no ie shakai* (The *ie* society as civilization). In the background was an increasingly variegated defense debate in which Shimizu Ikutarō, now a spokesperson for state-centered nationalism, argued for nuclearization.[97]

It is also significant in relation to the question of postmodernism that a group of intellectuals, including Asada Akira of Kyoto University, Kurimoto Shin'ichirō of Meiji University, and Nakazawa Shin'ichi of the Tokyo University of Foreign Studies, was delineated by the media and dubbed the New Academism. This appellation implied that their work transgresses the established boundaries of academic specialization and affiliation, is light and playful in style in contrast to the high seriousness of faculty seminars and research groups, and appeals because of the authors' personal charm as well as intellectual acumen. It also symbolizes the attention paid to these "new aka," particularly Asada, in the popular media of the mid-1980s and thus suggests that intellectuals, too, are being drawn into and increasingly defined by the realm of mass images and consumption.[98] If true, this development might imply the erosion of the postwar dichotomy between intellectuals and the masses and might even suggest that critical intellectuals of the sort defined by Sartre in the 1960s, or even Foucault in the early 1970s, are an endangered species. One recent writer concludes just that:

> Along with the Left, the group called intellectuals (*chishikijin*) is also little more than a relic of the past. . . . Intellectuals emphasize ethics because they think that people are free and always capable of rational choice. This view, in turn, is supported by the assumption that human beings can understand reality and rationally manage it. But it is characteristic of contemporary society as a gigantic, complex system to charge blindly ahead, laughing off all attempts at analysis and prediction and spurning human control. . . . The assumption on which the very existence of intellectuals was premised—that life is potentially rational and amenable to human control—has collapsed.[99]

95. Nakasone's comment on exporting culture is in Nakasone Yasuhiro, "Minzokushugi to kokusaishugi no shōwa o," *Gekkan jiyū minshu*, Oct. 1987, 64. For a general discussion, see Kenneth B. Pyle, "In Pursuit of a Grand Design: Nakasone Betwixt the Past and the Future," in *The Trade Crisis: How Will Japan Respond?* ed. Kenneth B. Pyle (Seattle: Society for Japanese Studies, 1987), 22–30.

96. Nagatomi Yūichirō, *Kindai o koete*, 2 vols. (Tokyo: Ōkurashō, 1983); cited by Pyle, "In Pursuit," 18. In English, see Yuichiro Nagatomi, *Masayoshi Ohira's Proposal To Evolve the Global Society* (Tokyo: FAIR, 1988).

97. Mike Mochizuki, "Japanese Strategists and the Nuclear Question" (unpublished manuscript).

98. Ivy, "Critical Texts, Mass Artifacts," 21–46.

99. Seki Hirono, "Sayoku no horobikata ni tsuite," *Shisō no kagaku* 134 (Nov. 1990): 4–5.

Nevertheless, the increasing prevalence in Japan of modes of thought and culture that in one way or another contest the logocentric episteme of postwar thought remains controversial, both ideologically and institutionally. For example, in an attack on Japanese appropriations of French postmodernism the Marxist-existentialist writer Takeuchi Yoshirō argues that the implications of this broad stream of thought in Japan are very different from its implications in France. That is, postmodernist thought as advanced by Foucault, Derrida, and Deleuze constitutes an effort at serious self-criticism in the French intellectual context, but its imitation in Japan functions rather as a form of "facile self-congratulation."[100] To make his point, Takeuchi compares Japanese postmodernism to the wartime intellectual pretense of overcoming modernity (*kindai no chōkoku*).[101] In his view, they share the self-satisfied conviction that Japan is better equipped than other nations to transcend the inadequacies of modernity.

> The wartime viewpoint on overcoming modernity and today's post-modern standpoint even originated under similar historical circumstances. . . . In other words, despite the difference between military and economic great-powerism, in both cases the Japanese suddenly converted their inferiority complex into a sense of superiority, and became convinced that they had "nothing more to learn from the West."[102]

He also reacts against the postmodernist critique of subjectivity and self-identity:

> In Japan, the philosophy of human rights became a defense of personal prerogatives, and Western individualism was transformed into selfishness. It is ridiculous, therefore, for postmodern thought—which lacks a mechanism for distinguishing among these—naively to presume to overcome the "modern ego."[103]

Takeuchi's resistance against the neoconservative implications of this kind of postmodernism is fundamentally consistent with the oppositional strategy typical of postwar left-wing thought. That is, he holds up a European counterexample as the basis for political criticism in the Japanese context.

A 1988 incident in academia illuminates some of the ideological ambivalences that surrounded postmodernism and the New Academism. When the historian of social thought Shirozuka Noboru retired in December 1987 from the social science department of the College of Arts and Sciences, University of Tokyo, the

100. Takeuchi Yoshirō, "Posuto-modan ni okeru chi no kansei," *Sekai*, Nov. 1986, 94. Takeuchi might have taken a hint from Maruyama Masao, who, in his 1961 work, *Nihon no shisō* (Tokyo: Iwanami Shinsho, 1961), observes that ideas that in their original European context could properly be understood only as desperate critical responses to hegemonic "tradition" are often extracted from that context and imported piecemeal to Japan, where hegemony is configured differently, and marketed as unproblematical intellectual commodities (14).

101. For other conceptualizations of Japanese postmodernism in comparison with the wartime intellectual vogue for "overcoming modernity," see H. D. Harootunian, "Visible Discourses/Invisible Ideologies," and Naoki Sakai, "Modernity and Its Critique: The Problem of Universalism and Particularism," in Miyoshi and Harootunian, *Postmodernism and Japan*, 63–122.

102. Takeuchi, "Posuto-modan ni okeru chi no kansei," 104

103. Ibid., 112.

department decided to nominate as his replacement the "new aka" scholar Nakazawa Shin'ichi. Nakazawa has studied anthropology and religion, focusing especially on Tibetan Buddhism, but his work ranges widely over contemporary theory. In an unprecedented move the college faculty voted to refuse the department's recommendation, causing a number of scholars who had supported the nomination, including Nishibe Susumu, Murakami Yasusuke, and Kumon Shunpei, to resign from the university faculty.[104] Opponents of the appointment had argued that Nakazawa was inadequately qualified and that his work was unscholarly and even blatantly wrongheaded.[105] But in addition to stimulating epistemological squabbles, the controversy provided yet another occasion for soul-searching by neoconservatives on the contemporary state of higher education and intellectual culture in Japan. It is in the latter context that an essay by Murakami Yasusuke is especially suggestive.

Murakami presents his program for educational reform against the background of a conception of the global rise and fall of civilizations, some aspects of which clearly evoke the wartime discussions on overcoming modernity (i.e., overcoming "the West"). Murakami shares with a variety of so-called postmodernists the insight that modern European thought is premised on a Cartesian worldview. However, according to Murakami, after World War II this intellectual tradition could no longer be upheld in Europe, so the United States "received the torch" and proceeded to build an "advanced mass-consumption society that shattered class barriers and seemed to allow the coexistence of the two fundamentally conflicting ideals of liberty and equality." This achievement "reenergized and prolonged modern Western civilization." Now, however, American mass society has itself become exhausted, just as the "Japanese challenge," an event of "global historical significance," is gaining momentum. Japan is on the ascendant because it has "probably outdone Western Europe and North America in the guarantee of liberties" and has "achieved greater equality than almost any country in the West." Moreover, Japan's success is at least partially the effect of its "non-Western organizational principles."[106]

Is Murakami arguing that Japanese thought and modes of social organization will now "overcome" those of Europe and the United States? Only in part, for he believes the wave of the future to be an intellectual countertendency to Cartesian dualism that is also clearly represented in the European tradition of hermeneutic philosophy. He argues that "[this] approach can provide us with a

104. For an account of the incident in English, see Takashina Shūji, "The Ivory Tower on Trial," *Japan Echo* 15, no. 3 (1988): 68–70; for an account in Japanese which includes documentation by former department head Mita Munesuke and an account by Nakazawa himself, see " 'Nakazawa tōyō' de gekitotsu shita Tōdai kyōju tachi," *Asahi jānaru*, 15 Apr. 1988, 14–20.

105. Takashina, "Ivory Tower on Trial," 69; Sugimoto Taiichirō, "Retorikku de wa naku, gakumon no yūkōsei de shōbu shiyō," *Asahi jānaru*, 3 June 1988, 104–7.

106. Murakami Yasusuke, "The Debt Comes Due for Higher Education," *Japan Echo* 15, no. 3 (Autumn 1988): 78.

meaningful basis for nonspecialized higher education. Although outside the purview of Cartesianism, it has not been completely overlooked by the Western philosophical tradition, and it clearly finds a place within Asian intellectual currents."[107] Thus Asia, led by Japan, is optimally equipped intellectually to assume world leadership by virtue of its non-Cartesian intellectual orientation and organizational style.[108]

What the Nakazawa incident seems to reveal is a broad association among the postmodern stance of some of the New Academics, the neoconservative political program of influential scholars like Murakami, Satō, and Kumon, and certain global conceptions concerning the world-historical ascendancy of Japanese culture. Of course, the incident and the uses to which Murakami puts it do not necessarily warrant any firm conclusions concerning the political character, in Japan or elsewhere, of postmodernism or the New Academism. In Japan, too, some aspects of the work of Karatani Kōjin, Asada Akira, and others suggest the potential for a "postmodernism of resistance" as well as of "reaction."[109] However, at the very least, interventions by Murakami and his associates suggest that in the Japanese context some tendencies associated with postmodernism can easily be yoked to a nationalist agenda designed to promote Japan as a model society.

It appears that in the 1980s prominent Japanese technicians of practical knowledge, including but certainly not limited to Murakami and his neoconservative colleagues, succeeded in liberating themselves from the "unhappy consciousness" that tormented postwar intellectuals and finally achieved that enviable state of "happy consciousness" that Herbert Marcuse defined as "the belief that the real is rational and that the system delivers the goods."[110] These self-satisfied supporters of the status quo have been more successful than the critical intellectuals—of whom there are still many—in seizing the political megaphone provided by the media. In effect, therefore, if 1960 marked the apex of effective intellectual criticism in postwar history—with significant follow-through in the antiwar, citizens', and student movements of the 1960s and early 1970s—then the end of the Shōwa period in 1989 might very well emerge as its nadir.

107. Ibid., 80; my emphasis.

108. Murakami's readers might be confused by the disparity between the supposedly non-Cartesian, "hermeneutic" perspective he espouses and his own typically Cartesian-rationalist analysis and technocratic expository style. See, for example, his deductive, clear and precise, globally inclusive analysis, "The Japanese Model of Political Economy," in *The Political Economy of Japan*, vol. 1, *The Domestic Transformation*, ed. Kozo Yamamura and Yasukichi Yasuba (Stanford: Stanford University Press, 1987), 33–90.

109. The resistance/reaction distinction is from Hal Foster, "Postmodernism: A Preface," in *The Anti-Aesthetic: Essays on Postmodern Culture*, ed. Hal Foster (Port Townsend, Wash.: Bay Press, 1983), xi–xii.

110. Herbert Marcuse, *One-Dimensional Man* (Boston: Beacon, 1964), 84.

CHAPTER SIXTEEN

The Dynamics of Political Opposition

James W. White

Despite the longevity of Liberal Democratic Party (LDP) rule in postwar Japan, the one thing one may say about opposition to the political, economic, and social status quo is that there has been no lack of it, whether by interest groups that wish simply to improve their own position, by partisan groups that wish to wrest power from the LDP, or by radicals who hope to transform the polity completely. The third form of opposition has faded rapidly during the postwar period as public opinion has solidified behind the current political framework. The second, some have suggested, has almost completely atrophied along with the stagnation of the opposition parties and the seemingly eternal hegemony of the LDP and its allies. And although the first form of opposition, more piecemeal and instrumental, has been unceasing and strikingly successful on occasion, it faces both inherent limits and distinctly Japanese obstacles.

The old notion of Japan as a uniquely harmonious society has been superseded by a far more realistic appreciation of the extent and significance of social and political conflict in both public and private arenas.[1] Paradoxically, however, as the old myth of harmony has faded, so have the actual extent and intensity of both radical and partisan conflict in Japan. Indeed, because citizens in a democracy must keep rulers accountable, and in particular must keep the rulers' toes to the

---

1. See, e.g., Kent Calder, *Crisis and Compensation* (Princeton: Princeton University Press, 1989); Yoshio Sugimoto, *Popular Disturbance in Postwar Japan* (Hong Kong: Asian Research Service, 1981); James White, "Protest and Change in Contemporary Japan," in George deVos, ed., *Institutions for Change in Japanese Society* (Berkeley and Los Angeles: University of California Press, 1984). The citations below purposely emphasize English-language sources; for a thorough introduction to Japanese politics in general and opposition in particular, the reader is directed to the currently appearing Tokyo University Press series, Gendai Seijigaku Sōsho (Inoguchi Takashi, general ed.).

fire in a system under the control of a single party for almost forty years, one may worry whether there has been enough opposition in postwar Japan.[2]

In this essay I discuss each of the three major dimensions of political contention mentioned above. The interest-group dimension is dominated by the labor movement and a variety of less institutionalized social movements. The partisan dimension is represented by the parties of the opposition. The radical antiestablishment opposition is composed of a substantial number of small, fragmented groups and is found on both Left and Right.

There has been change in both form and frequency on each dimension since 1945, but they have not changed in tandem. The picture is, rather, kaleidoscopic: some dimensions are crosscutting, some cumulative; some have changed in linear fashion, some cyclically; some have established seemingly irresistible momentum, while others have undergone reverses in salience, intensity, and effectiveness.

Despite this variety, however, there have been three major watersheds in the postwar history of political contention—periods at which Japan could have gone in different directions than it did and after which it became different both from what it had been and what it might otherwise have become—and a single might-have-been: a period of turbulence that appeared briefly to augur momentous change but that passed leaving only a few political aftershocks. The watersheds occurred roughly in 1960, 1970, and 1980 (plus or minus three years); the near miss came in 1988–90. The outcome—what we see for the moment today—is political contention based in a democratic system that is more modern and liberal (but still strongly partisan); more middle-class populist; more solidly (though not thoroughly) institutionalized; and more governmentally decentralized and responsive (albeit still quite *dirigiste*) than it was in 1950, 1960, 1970, or even 1980. And this basis, or context, of conflict is commensurately less authoritarian and traditionalistic, less elitist, and less politicized and ideological than it was.

Nevertheless, political opposition in postwar Japan is complex and ambivalent; so, consequently, is this essay. Opposition per se is essential to democracy in general and has a played a crucial role in postwar Japanese democracy in particular. As noted above, there is good reason to argue that Japan needs more of it; that is, that the powers that be possess altogether too much power. But—as we shall see—some of this opposition is irresponsible and some is but a charade, and even constructive opposition sometimes turns sour. I argue that the relatively institutionalized, elitist, and partisan forms of opposition have often contributed less to the causes of democracy and social justice than have less institutionalized, less structured forms.[3]

2. White, "Protest and Change"; James White, "Accountability and Democracy in Japan," in George Waldner, ed., *Japan in the 1980s* (Atlanta: Southern Center for International Studies, 1982).

3. The same argument is advanced for the United States in Frances Fox Piven and Richard Cloward, *Poor People's Movements* (New York: Random, Vintage, 1979).

In consequence, this essay may seem naively populist, but it is noteworthy that the question that used to figure prominently in studies of Japanese politics— What are the prospects for Japanese democracy?—is seldom asked today. One should also keep in mind that I am comparing contemporary Japan primarily with its own past, not with other contemporary democratic societies, and that the judgment that Japan is a democratic society by no means implies that it is ideally so.[4] As I have argued elsewhere, the ability and will of the Japanese people to oppose their own political elites deserves no little share of the credit for the changes of the recent past.[5] And in light of the impotence in postwar Japan of many of the usual elite-level agents of political accountability—opposition parties, media, judiciary, and so forth—the burden borne by the Japanese people in the prevention of abuse of their democratic system is heavy indeed.

However, one must also acknowledge the relevance of another question often addressed to postwar Japanese politics: is it elitist and relatively closed to dissent, or pluralist and relatively open to opposition and contention by a wide variety of interests? Some observers characterize Japan as under the thumbs of one or more parts of a business/bureaucracy/LDP triumvirate, which has gradually reasserted itself after a burst of reformist energy in the immediate postwar period and today manipulates and controls society in general and political opposition in particular for its own ends.[6] Others—toward whom I lean—see a progressive rooting of democratic institutions and practices and attribute the LDP's continuous rule (1) to its ability to respond to popular and partisan pressures and demands and (2) to the absence on the national level of a viable alternative government in the wings, not to any LDP subversion of democratic institutions or procedures.[7]

In looking at the vagaries of postwar political contention, I have chosen not to cover the postwar years chronologically, touching on changes in each dimension of conflict along the way. Rather, I treat each dimension separately and then combine them into some semblance of a picture of postwar political contention. This picture will seem incomplete to some, although it accounts for the class-based, religious, and ethnic oppositions that loom so large in many industrial democracies. But organized labor, opposition parties, and both moderate and extremist social movements do dominate the arena in which the LDP and its rivals have contended for political power in postwar Japan.

4. Nor, of course, is any other country. For a detailed discussion of the topic, see Ellis Krauss and Takeshi Ishida, eds., *Democracy in Japan* (Pittsburgh: University of Pittsburgh Press, 1989).

5. White, "Accountability and Democracy in Japan."

6. Gavan McCormack and Yoshio Sugimoto, eds., *Democracy in Contemporary Japan* (Armonk, N.Y.: M. E. Sharpe, 1986); Chitoshi Yanaga, *Big Business in Japanese Politics* (New Haven: Yale University Press, 1968); Jon Woronoff, *Japan, The Coming Social Crisis* (Tokyo: Lotus, 1981).

7. Calder, *Crisis and Compensation;* Gerald Curtis, *The Japanese Way of Politics* (New York: Columbia University Press, 1988); T. J. Pempel, *Policy and Politics in Japan* (Philadelphia: Temple University Press, 1982); Michio Muramatsu and Ellis Krauss, in Kozo Yamamura and Yasukichi Yasuba, eds., *The Political Economy of Japan*, Vol. 1, *The Domestic Transformation* (Stanford: Stanford University Press, 1987); and Garon and Mochizuki's essay in this volume.

PARTISAN OPPOSITION

Partisan political forces contend in two principal ways: political parties compete for votes, and agents of political parties compete directly with each other for influence over the policy process and the actions of incumbent officials. Overall, as partisan forces contended in postwar Japan, they consolidated democratic institutions and procedures and depolarized the ideological terrain. As this happened, the electoral strength of the Right decreased and that of the Left increased; the Left then peaked and declined as well (with a number of minor, mostly centrist, parties dividing the Left's losses), while conservatives continued to decline; the conservatives then recovered, while the Left stagnated and the center continued to fragment (figure 16.1). The context of this electoral change was, as noted, multiple:

1. *Institutionalization and consolidation of democracy.* Public acceptance of the main institutional and procedural features of democracy has grown; the courts have gradually expanded their limited function as guardians of democracy against both public and private violations of rights; nondemocratic modes of decision making and articulation have been discredited; and governmental institutions themselves have developed the informal mechanisms not provided by the constitution that enable them to function effectively. An example of this last is the parliamentary boycott. A tactic adopted by the minority opposition to obstruct LDP rule, the boycott performs functions similar to that of the filibuster in the United States: it enables intense minorities to register meaningful resistance without actually contravening majoritarian democratic procedures. Since roughly 1970 the boycott has almost entirely superseded more disruptive tactics with similar ends, such as sit-ins and fistfights in parliament, and constitutes an important aspect of routinization of partisan conflict.[8] The obverse of this tactical evolution may be seen in the LDP's almost complete avoidance, since the mid-1970s, of parliamentary votes rammed through in the face of opposition resistance. However, the contingent nature of this tactical shift, the fragility of informal procedures, and the consequent need for additional agents of opposition may be seen in the LDP's use of the forced vote twice in early 1989 in the face of a surging wave of partisan opposition.

2. *Depolarization.* Over the past two or three decades many issues that once sparked intense partisan conflict in and out of parliament have faded in incendiary potential. This trend progressed faster on the local level, where immediate municipal issues took precedence over abstract ideology and the course of the nation. But nationally, too, the constitution itself, the self-defense forces and the military budget, and the alliance with the United States have come to be taken for granted by more and more Japanese. And the voters themselves have depolarized: many are willing to vote, depending on the candidate and the electoral arena, for parties

8. Iwai Tomoaki, *Rippō katei* (Tokyo: Tōkyō Daigaku Shuppankai, 1988), 131.

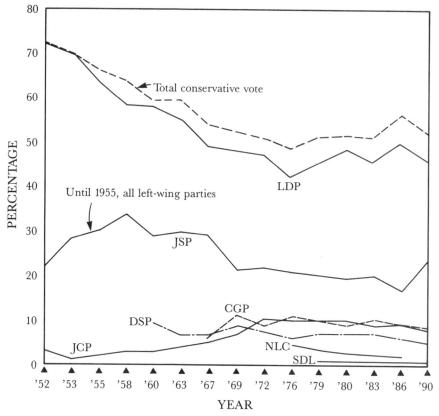

Figure 16.1. Trends in House of Representatives elections, 1952–90.
    Abbreviations:
    LDP   Liberal Democratic Party
    CGP   Clean Government Party
    DSP   Democratic Socialist Party
    SDL   Social Democratic League
    JSP   Japan Socialist Party
    JCP   Japan Communist Party
    NLC   New Liberal Club (dissolved 1986)

NOTES: All curves represent the proportion of the total national vote won by each party.
    The Liberal Democratic curve represents, prior to 1955, the combined vote won by the Liberal and the Democratic parties.
    The area between the LDP curve and the broken curve labeled "Total conservative vote" represents the proportion of the vote won by independent conservative candidates who joined the LDP after winning the election.

of either Left or Right, and multiparty coalitions have become the typical vehicle for gubernatorial and mayoral campaigns.[9]

To some extent Japan was historically free of certain sources of partisan hostility: ethnically homogeneous, religiously tolerant, and interregionally unified since the beginning of modernization, communal factors never became the foundations of major opposition movements. Nor did social class: the timing of Japan's industrial transformation relative to that of the emergence of parties, and the development of the major prewar parties as "catchall" parties rather than representatives of certain classes, muted the early polarization of classes,[10] and postwar affluence has contributed to Japan's position as the industrial democracy in which social class and status are least related to political partisanship.[11] A far more accurate indicator of partisan leanings—union membership—cuts across social class in Japan and subjects both working-class nonunionists and white-collar unionists to the sorts of contrary pulls that reduce the likelihood of intense partisanship.

3. *Moderation.* The centrist trend of the electorate (as fringe positions on political, economic, and diplomatic issues lost their attraction) and progressive embourgeoisement have probably removed socialism irreversibly from among Japan's alternative futures, except perhaps for social democracy à la Germany or France. One can see this trend reflected by the parties of the Left themselves: the Japan Communist Party (JCP) is firmly Eurocommunist, and even the Japan Socialist Party (JSP) was by the 1990s rethinking its more naively extreme and dogmatic policies both domestic and foreign. Such rethinking is probably a requisite for JSP survival; the eclipse of dogmatic socialism is clearly visible in figure 16.1.

Moderation on the Left has been matched by moderation on the Right: over the years the LDP has given up its early intent to revise the constitution and has adopted policies designed to attract voters across the spectrum. Locally, one even sees electoral coalitions in which the LDP and the JSP join hands. Nationally, the LDP has shelved bills calling for, say, greater police powers and greater centralization of government, which revive the specter of prewar autocracy. But one should not equate such tactical moves with unalloyed moderation: within the ranks of the LDP there remain more than a few advocates of constitutional revision, enhanced power for the emperor, rearmament, and greater central authority. Although they do not constitute the party mainstream, they do suggest the salutary role that opposition still has to play.

The above are broad currents; three turning points can be seen along their way. The first, and most significant, is 1959–60: the JSP split, the Democratic

9. Miyake Ichirō, *Seitō shiji no bunseki* (Tokyo: Sōbunsha, 1985).

10. Scott Flanagan, Shinsaku Kohei, Ichiro Miyake, Bradley Richardson, and Joji Watanuki, *The Japanese Voter* (New Haven: Yale University Press, 1991); Scott Flanagan and Bradley Richardson, *Japanese Electoral Behavior* (Beverly Hills: Sage, 1977).

11. Sidney Verba, Norman Nie, and Jae-on Kim, *Participation and Political Equality* (Cambridge: Cambridge University Press, 1978).

Socialist Party emerged, the JSP dropped in the general election, and the Left would never be so strong again. It would never be so rash and provocative either: 1960 saw a nationwide wave of demonstrations and riots opposing the ratification of the U.S.-Japan Security Treaty that shocked and sobered the parties and unions on the Left, the high-handed LDP, and the media. The general consensus seems to have been: never again. And this consensus has stuck: never since 1960 have the major partisan actors gone so far in confrontation, and never have the Japanese people become involved in such numbers in openly confrontational extraparliamentary conflict.

The second turning point is 1969–70, when the JSP suffered its sharpest electoral drop in the postwar period, falling to the roughly 20 percent of the vote that it has marshalled since then. The LDP also continued its slide; the mirror image of the JSP's debacle is thus the fragmentation of the opposition between several parties, a condition that also endures to this day. On the local level, however, where polarization was never so marked, the late 1960s and early 1970s initiated the heyday of opposition mayors and governors who won at the heads of multiparty coalitions.

The third turning point occurred in the last years before 1980. The late 1970s have been described as a period of *hakuchū*, or near parity, between the LDP and the opposition. During this period the LDP held a parliamentary majority of only a few seats and became unprecedentedly careful, moderate, defensive, and responsive in regard to the opposition, to the public, and to democratic norms— especially on the local level, where nonpartisan opposition candidates backed by coalitions of parties and local organizations had wrested control of numerous governorships and mayoralties from the conservatives.[12] The *hakuchū* period ended in 1979 as the LDP recovered to a level near where it is today both locally and nationally. This recovery was partly due to LDP responsiveness to the issues that led to near parity in the first place (in many instances this response involved explicitly co-opting opposition policies), partly to the oil shocks of the 1970s (which put an end to the popular, free-spending practices of some leftist local administrations), partly to shrewd LDP coalitions with centrist parties against leftist candidates for local office, and partly to continued opposition ineptitude and fragmentation.[13]

On the surface the LDP's recovery did not lead to resurgent cockiness or autocratic style: the *hakuchū* years seem to have been a permanent learning experience. And local governments nationwide learned, once they had challenged Tokyo, that they had far greater autonomy than they had realized. Revenue sharing is predominantly nondiscretionary, frustrating Tokyo's desire to whip

---

12. For a study of this phenomenon, see Kurt Steiner, Ellis Krauss, and Scott Flanagan, eds., *Political Opposition and Local Politics in Japan* (Princeton: Princeton University Press, 1980).

13. Both Curtis, *Japanese Way of Politics*, and Calder, *Crisis and Compensation*, contain good descriptions of this process.

recalcitrant local executives into line, and the capacity of local governments to quibble with and delay the implementation of directives from Tokyo has conduced toward far more consultative and reciprocal intergovernmental relations than was previously the case.

However, an alternative interpretation is possible: that is, that the close relationships developed between LDP and opposition during this period have in fact put the opposition parties in thrall to the LDP, which is in a position to pay off them and their constituents with policy in exchange for cooperation and docility.[14] And behind the protection afforded by a facade of partisan opposition, unaccountability ran rampant, only to spill out onto the front pages of the nation's newspapers in the Recruit scandal of 1988–89.

The upshot of these trends and turning points is the situation that pertained at the beginning of the 1990s: on the national level the LDP and its independent, conservative allies controlled roughly half of the popular vote: the JSP took another 20 percent; and the rest of the opposition split the other 30 percent. Locally, coalition campaigns and governments had become typical, as had compromise (either overt or tacit, as seen in the ritualistic resolution of cleavages surrounding parliamentary boycotts) in the Diet and in center-local relationships. Opposition is certainly more energetic and potent on the local than the national level, but the participation of the LDP in many nonpartisan local governments makes one wonder, once again, how to weigh the enhanced participation of the opposition in government against the constraints of exercising power in tandem with the LDP.

The JSP's fade on both levels reflected not simply its own factional squabbling but also the irrelevance of a militantly working-class party in postindustrial society, especially one in which both the rate of unionization and the electoral discipline of union members are waning. The Japanese people are not overwhelmingly conservative—indeed, if the opposition offered a credible alternative government it would win more votes (as has occurred on the local level), and if the LDP were to infuriate enough electors it might lose power without any increase in the intrinsic attractiveness of the opposition—but they are solidly middle-class and jealous of their recently won (and privately possessed) affluence. They want the political stability in which they can enjoy and build on this affluence, and the LDP alone has historically promised this stability.

As the 1980s gave way to the 1990s, however, the ability of the LDP to ensure stable and effective rule was called into question. The Recruit scandal, the imposition of an extraordinarily unpopular sales tax, the inability of the LDP to hide its strains and fissures, and LDP efforts to liberalize agricultural imports shook the confidence of the voters, the business and farm communities, the LDP's own backbenchers, and Japan's trading and diplomatic partners. In the Tokyo prefec-

14. See, e.g., Curtis, *Japanese Way of Politics*.

tural assembly elections of July 1989 the LDP suffered a dramatic defeat, and in a House of Councillors election held the same month an even more crushing blow fell: the LDP's strength dropped from 142 seats (of a total of 252) to 109 as the party won only 27 percent of the vote (versus 39 percent in the previous election) and the opposition took control of the house for the first time ever.[15]

The partisan opposition seemed to have been handed—through no great merit of its own—an unprecedented opportunity to seize power in the general election of February 1990. In the aftermath of the Upper House election, however, the LDP began to backpedal on both the sales tax and the liberalization of imports, and the appointment of a new prime minister restored at least the appearance of competent leadership. At the same time, the opposition in general proved unable to agree on a common program, and the Socialists in particular refused to relinquish unpopular positions on nuclear energy and national defense. The electorate, faced with a choice between stable, albeit corrupt, government under the LDP and instability under some sort of unpredictable opposition coalition, once again opted for the former. In the general election the LDP's margin of victory was reduced from 56 percent of the vote (including conservative independents) and 304 seats in the previous election to 52 percent of the vote and 286 seats. But even this reduction left the LDP with a solid majority. The Socialists rebounded from their dismal showing of 1986, but most of their gains came at the expense not of the LDP but of the other opposition parties.[16] The election was a sobering experience for the Tories, but 1990 is nevertheless a near miss in opposition attempts to end their long rule.

The LDP continued to hand opportunities to the opposition in 1991, and it continued to react disjointedly and incoherently. The Gulf War of 1991 occasioned at first LDP hesitation and then headlong attempts to throw money at the crisis in lieu of constitutionally questionable men or materiel; both left Japan looking irresponsible and indecisive. Ultimately, $13 billion was contributed, but a combination of opposition in the Upper House and divisions within the LDP conspired to prevent any more resolute or belligerent action. After the war ended, the government introduced legislative proposals calling for the provision by Japan of UN peacekeeping forces in future crises, but intraparty disputes gutted these proposals one after another, giving the opposition—despite its own inability to coalesce—the ongoing ability to frustrate whatever bills actually got to the Upper House. As 1992 began, no legislative action had been taken: the opposition was still unable to capitalize on the LDP's international embarrassment and internal disorganization. In 1989–90 it appeared that the LDP had dodged a bullet, but by 1992 it had begun to look as if the LDP had no one to fear at the parliamentary level but itself.

15. The proportion of the vote is that won by the LDP in the national constituency; *Yomiuri shinbun*, 24, 25 July 1989.

16. *Yomiuri shinbun*, 20 Feb. 1990.

THE LABOR OPPOSITION

Closely linked to, but distinct from, the partisan Left is the labor movement, whose opposition to management and to its LDP representatives has been characterized during the postwar period by decline without complete eclipse. Much of its decline is due to the same forces working against the partisan Left: the rapid industrialization and urbanization that brought new recruits into factory and city leveled off during the 1960s, and the secondary sector actually began to shrink as the tertiary sector became paramount. But the developmental trajectory of the unions also followed an autonomous path, from muscle flexing and militance in the early postwar years to confrontation without power in the later 1950s and 1960s to contraction and retreat amid the sharply reduced economic growth and rising unemployment that followed the 1973 oil shock. As the 1990s opened, the labor movement entered a possibly rejuvenating period; paradoxically, however, to the extent that it does rejuvenate itself as an economic and political force, it may lose its oppositionist nature.

Labor unions are not a postwar development in Japan, as pointed out elsewhere in this volume. The postwar movement, however, enjoying the blessings of the Supreme Command for Allied Powers (SCAP) and an infusion of leadership by Marxist activists freed from prison, differed diametrically from the prewar movement in its rights and its objectives: improved wages and working conditions, mitigation of national ties to the capitalist United States, and in the early years militant opposition to conservative rule in toto. The heyday of the labor opposition—described by Andrew Gordon—came early, and the first turning point in its postwar history did also: between the failure of the general strike of 1947 (banned in advance by an occupation regime now fearful of the radical leanings of the movement) and the repression of the May Day Riots of 1952 (a violent protest by some twenty thousand unionists against a proposed antisubversive activities law) the movement lost whatever systemic threat it had previously posed to business and political elites. It was not supine—throughout the 1950s political protest was predominantly a union activity—but it was increasingly economic in its objectives and less and less interested in the seizure of power and transformation of the capitalist system, especially after the collapse of the Miike coal strike in 1960.[17]

But moderation did not lead to the exploitation one might expect: by the 1970s the distribution of income in Japan was among the most egalitarian in the world, and it continues to be so. Why? Can labor win the fruits of growth for its members without opposition? Are Japanese capitalists simply nicer people than those in other countries? There is a paradox here: sharing in the economic pie without strident confrontation and without significant governmental participation by

17. For discussions of the early labor movement in opposition, see Sugimoto, *Popular Disturbance in Postwar Japan;* George Packard, *Protest in Tokyo* (Princeton: Princeton University Press, 1966); and Gordon's essay in this volume.

labor. The paradox might be resolved by working hours: perhaps the workers' large share of the pie is a concession granted by an exploitive managerial elite that imposes the longest working hours of any advanced industrial democracy. But if Japanese work habits were simply management imposed, one would hardly expect to find such habits in noncorporate Japanese, and in Japanese Americans to boot.

Another argument is that of Sheldon Garon and Mike Mochizuki (in this volume): that the agreement of the Sōdōmei unions to the establishment of a productivity center in 1955 marks the inception of a tacit social contract between management and unions. In this view the contract has been continually renegotiated up until the present, with a series of legislative acts recompensing labor for its pliability and diligence. Gordon argues a related position, that the emergence of company-sponsored "second unions" provided management with partners in concert with whom mutually advantageous agreements could be reached.

These arguments also may be rephrased by those who see Japan in a more elitist light: labor's relatively large share of the economic pie is merely hush money for the unions and a soporific for the working class. But both interpretations must consider additional points: first, Japanese business and LDP elites *do* seem to be more egalitarian in their outlook than, say, their American counterparts; and business, labor, and government elites are less polarized regarding their perceptions of their own and each others' power (real and ideal) and their perceptions of what constitutes a "fair" gap between the less well off and the better off.[18] What is social contract and what is normative consensus might be difficult to disentangle here.

Second, inequality of income peaked around 1960, only after Garon and Mochizuki see the emergence of the social contract, and decreased markedly only during the high-growth period of the later 1960s.[19] However, inequality has begun to increase during the 1980s, although the social contract presumably remains in effect.

But whatever labor's (or management's) secret, economic sharing was not built on labor's formal power, as was shown after the second turning point: the oil shock of 1973. The course of labor was subsequently downward in terms of wage raises won, total membership (presently below 30 percent of the eligible work force for the first time since the war), and the ability of unions to mobilize their members behind leftist political candidates. Since the mid-1970s labor's potential for contention has become shallow indeed: continued worker embourgeoisement, privatization of industry in the 1980s (which cut into the membership of Sōhyō, the more militant and public-sector union federation), and the economic worries that surround the internationalization of the Japanese economy all force unions to restrain themselves, and little hope looms on the horizon. The situation is

18. Sidney Verba, *Elites and the Idea of Equality* (Cambridge: Harvard University Press, 1987).
19. Margaret McKean, "Causes and Consequences of Patterns of Economic Distribution in Japan" (unpublished manuscript, Duke University, July 1987).

singularly dire for the JSP, whose leadership, income, and votes emerge predominantly from union ranks.

Nevertheless, two events might, in hindsight, appear as a third turning point in the movement's postwar history: the creation in late 1987 of Rengō, a new labor federation, through merger of the second and third biggest existing federations, and the absorption in 1989 of the largest federation, Sōhyō, by the then-renamed Shin Rengō.[20] Rengō's emergence was not sudden, as Garon and Mochizuki point out, but Shin Rengō now incorporates 65 percent of Japan's organized workers, and as such it could have far more clout than labor previously had vis-à-vis business, government, and—perhaps even more important—the parties of the Left. Shin Rengō explicitly aims at constructing a left-of-center bloc capable of challenging the LDP, and in early 1989 Rengō proposed unified support by all opposition parties of candidates for elective office. In the Upper House election of July 1989 eleven of the twelve candidates put forward by Rengō's political wing were successful. The question remaining, of course, is, What is the implication of Shin Rengō for political opposition? Might it, like the British Trades Union Congress or German Federation of Trade Unions, spearhead and perhaps reinvigorate the partisan Left with what promise to be goals of a more moderate, realistic, and economic thrust than those of Sōhyō and the JSP? Might it bend the JSP itself to its will? Or might its moderate and compromising tendencies draw it into the corporatist embrace of business and the LDP and, in the very process of winning bigger concessions for its members, effectively lead it out of the opposition camp?

COLLECTIVE ACTION: GREAT TRADITION, LITTLE TRADITION

Crosscutting the labor and partisan dimensions of contention is a third, dualistic one, involving relatively uninstitutionalized social groups. One can trace it through centuries of Japanese history, dichotomizing "great" and "little" traditions, or elitist and populist forms, of collective action. Any such dichotomy oversimplifies. All social movements involve mixtures of motives among their participants; social class does not determine conflict style; and even if such a dichotomy is realistic, it is not uniquely Japanese. But there does seem to be a relatively, and distinctively, sharp divide between the forms and goals of two types of political action, one most frequently undertaken by Japanese elites (or elites-to-be, such as students or young military officers) and one most frequently undertaken by the common people. The divide is visible not only in motivations and styles but in actual contentious coalitions: ever since the early Tokugawa period, Japanese popular opposition has been (relative to Western opposition) bereft of elite elements in leadership roles.[21] Even today the common people seem to be

20. Some of Sōhyō's more radical elements refused to join in the merger.

21. For evidence of this in the Tokugawa era, see Aoki Michio, ed., *Ikki* (Tokyo: Tōkyō Daigaku Shuppankai, 1981); for a similar phenomenon visible in the citizens' movements of the 1970s, see

more often the target of scorn (for not furthering adequately the cause of revolution) from intellectuals who, along with other elites, prefer to act in their own distinctive way.[22]

The distinction is this: there is in collective Japanese contention against the status quo a nihilistic, romantic, expressive, millennarian, radical, violent, irrational (by some definitions), value-based, and value-oriented current, in pursuit of abstract or quixotic goals, and its participants are disproportionately social and political elites. Ivan Morris's failed heroes are simply the most convenient examples; the late Tokugawa *shishi*, the right-wing Young Officers of the 1930s, and the postwar radical student Left are of the same ilk.[23] The contrary current, then and now, tends much more toward constructive, realistic, instrumental, moderate, nonviolent, rational (by some definitions) pursuit of concrete, proximate and tangible goals and is far more characteristic of collective contention by the common people. In postwar Japan the most common manifestations of this current have been the environmental, consumer, women's, Korean, and Burakumin movements. This contrast is overdrawn and artificially excludes the middle ground (which I discuss in the following section), but it appears to hold not only for collective opposition but for political phenomena more broadly, at least between the beginning of the Tokugawa era and the present day.[24]

In the postwar period, however, it is possible that the dichotomy has begun to dissolve, at least in the sense that the romantic, nihilistic strain in Japanese political activism has lost its attractiveness to most people. Such activism has not disappeared, but its influence on both policy and the popular mind is practically nil. At the same time that this great tradition is moribund, if not in terminal decline, the populist strain in collective contention has become more salient and more effective than ever before. Postwar Japan is hardly a town meeting, but the common people have more leverage vis-à-vis the government than at any previous time in Japanese history. The process had been gradual, without clear turning points or periods, but it has been consistent and may have become irreversible. Its foundation lies in the progressive rooting of a new constitution, the decisive legitimacy of the ballot box, a plethora of organized interest groups, a democratic educational system, and in the more libertarian, middle-class attitudes that accompany these changes.

Although there have not been sharp turning points in this process, there are

Margaret McKean, *Environmental Protest and Citizen Politics in Japan* (Berkeley and Los Angeles: University of California Press, 1981).

22. Some examples of this intellectual disdain can be found in J. Victor Koschmann, *Authority and the Individual in Japan* (Tokyo: Tokyo University Press, 1978).

23. Ivan Morris, *The Nobility of Failure* (New York: Knopf, 1975); Patricia Steinhoff, "Portrait of a Terrorist," *Asian Survey* 16 (Sept. 1976): 830; John Nathan, *Mishima: A Biography* (Boston: Little, Brown, 1974); Henry Scott-Stokes, *The Life and Death of Yukio Mishima* (New York: Farrar, Straus and Giroux, 1974).

24. Tetsuo Najita, *Japan* (Chicago: University of Chicago Press, 1974). Moreover, it appears that the middle ground is narrower in Japan than in other societies.

milestones along the way. In the late 1940s and 1950s violent protest was almost invariably led by partisan elites or students.[25] A milestone was passed in 1959, when a right-wing radical assassinated Asanuma Inejirō, leader of the JSP. This was the only such incident in the postwar era, and it became the start of— nothing. It was, and remains, a unique tragedy, and it spawned neither copycats nor public sympathy for the assassin. This is not to ignore the continued activities of the radical right: violence has been threatened or visited on targets of the Right a number of times over the years, and the ongoing possibility of such violence casts a chilling shadow of indeterminate length on reporters and union activists. But the universal popular condemnation of such behavior and the fact that Japan today is less plagued by rightist violence than, say, the United States, suggest that the Asanuma assassination was indeed a milestone.

But the real milestones occurred between 1967 and 1973: two great events and two equally great nonevents. First came the wave of contention that swept Japan's universities, and then its cities, in the late 1960s, appearing first as an anti-Vietnam War movement, gathering energy from a plethora of campus issues, and then merging with and eventually being swallowed by the 1969–70 struggle against the renewal of the U.S.-Japan Security Treaty.[26] Its origins lay in the anti-nuclear-weapons movement—which was born in the 1950s but did not become part of the opposition camp until 1961, when conservative elements withdrew—and the 1960 struggle against the treaty. Its real genesis came in 1965, with the creation of the League for Peace in Vietnam (Beheiren), a loose and nonideological movement featuring an internal democracy and structural minimalism that set it apart from the older union- and party-led Left and the citizens' movements of the 1970s.

At first—roughly in 1967—the movement won considerable popular support: large numbers of people signed petitions on Tokyo streets in sympathy with grossly underpaid and overworked medical students or joined demonstrations aimed at preventing Japanese involvement in America's deepening war in Vietnam. But as the movement turned increasingly international, abstract, and violent and proved unable to control its student component, the people (including, reluctantly, Beheiren itself) turned their backs on it. In effect, the people gave the police carte blanche to repress what came to be seen as homicidal radicals, not students with reasonable demands; Vietnam was a concern, but not a crucial issue, to most Japanese. The result was a nonevent: the treaty "struggle" was effectively over by the time of the treaty's renewal in the summer of 1970, and the radical students have not since the early 1970s been able to mount a significant attack on the system, much less generate popular support.

The second milestone was the environmental movement, epitomized by the Big Four pollution lawsuits filed in 1967 and resolved by 1973: these cases were unprecedented examples of common people taking on the giants of Japanese

25. Sugimoto, *Popular Disturbance in Postwar Japan;* Packard, *Protest in Tokyo.*
26. Thomas Havens, *Fire Across the Sea* (Princeton: Princeton University Press, 1987).

business and politics and winning. Some elite elements such as activist lawyers aided these causes, but the nationwide wave of citizens' movements of which these were the crest did not rely crucially on such people: these were truly grass-roots movements, with an efficacy their predecessors never dreamed of.[27] Such movements did, as noted, evince considerable continuity of form, style, and behavior with Beheiren: pragmatism, openness, moderation, egalitarianism, participatory internal democracy, and a focus on limited and realistic objectives quite at odds with more elite forms of opposition.

The third milestone came in 1970 as parliament reflected the upsurge of populist power in the "Pollution Diet," a session in which antipollution laws of unparalleled number, variety, and stringency were passed. One need not claim that the ruling party was acting altruistically or deny that its motives were significantly manipulative to recognize that it made concessions to its plebeian constituents that it has never equaled before or since.

The final milestone was the most flamboyant of all: the ritual samurai-style suicide in 1969 of author Mishima Yukio.[28] He pushed every traditional button, issuing a slate of imperative, selfless goals for the benefit of the nation, calling for popular support against evil elements in government and evil trends abroad in the land, and sacrificing himself for his cause in strictest *seppuku* ritual. And the Japanese people wrote him off as a nut, from the soldiers he tried to rally in a coup (who jeered at him), to the prime minister (who said he must have been insane), to the biographers who attributed his actions to artistic exhaustion or worse. Some on the Right revered him, but for the mass of the people the Asanuma milestone had been passed.

This is not to say that the menace of right-wing terrorism is extinct. The postwar period has seen recurrent outbursts of it, most recently the attempted assassination of the mayor of Nagasaki, who had publicly imputed war responsibility to the emperor. Such events do, by all accounts, have an undocumentable but chilling effect on the expression of certain viewpoints that is antithetical to democratic freedom of expression. But I would assert that the significance for Japanese democracy of right-wing extremism lies elsewhere: every society has its fanatics, and America is not necessarily less democratic for being home to the Ku Klux Klan or Germany for its Baader-Meinhof gang. The relevance of extremism—on either Right or Left—lies first in the government's response: the government's ability to counter such violence without infringing on the basic rights of the people is one true barometer of the democratic quality of society, and Japan here passes the test.[29]

---

27. McKean, *Environmental Protest;* Frank Upham, *Law and Social Change in Postwar Japan* (Cambridge: Harvard University Press, 1987). The parties of the Left tried to join, and to use, the citizens' movement but were for the most part rebuffed.

28. Nathan, *Mishima;* Scott-Stokes, *Life and Death.*

29. The Japanese police do utilize—and the Japanese people accept—methods of investigation and interrogation that go beyond those permissible in America. But so do the police and people of

The second true barometer of democracy is the popular response to extremism: what proportion of the people support the actions of those who would violate or destroy democracy? The Japanese people, if these cases are any indication, have turned their backs on exhibitionistic, dramatic displays of violence by elites on either Left or Right in pursuit of grandiose political or social goals. They have found that in a democracy more modest means can bring fruit, that they can make real gains and force real limitations and sensitivity and responsiveness on their rulers, and they have developed a new repertoire of contentious behavior to which going down gloriously in flames is simply not relevant. This is not to say that collective opposition is dramatically successful, or even predictably so: the most distinctive outcome of Beheiren and the antiwar movement was the emergence of the radical student movement; that of the university movement was the University "Normalization" Act, a law permitting the Minister of Education to close down universities subject to excessive turbulence.

But overall the effect of popular opposition—which includes such movements as those for enhanced rights for women, Burakumin, and Koreans, which have made more piecemeal progress—on the political system seems clear:[30] on the national level, new institutions, policies (including the strictest antipollution laws in the world), and sensitivity to popular concerns; on the local level, more political debate and competition, more confident resistance to edicts from Tokyo (which have brought the nuclearization of the electric power industry to an almost complete halt), more partisan politics, and—again—greater sensitivity to popular concerns. Among the political parties there are new platform planks and new agendas, new relationships and new patterns of coalition that never existed before the 1960s; in the business world as well there is now a realization that there are limits to corporate irresponsibility. And for participants in social movements themselves there are organizational skills, higher levels of politicization, and among Burakumin and Koreans a new sense of identity and efficacy. It is doubtful—given the continuing obstacles to full equality described by Frank Upham and Sandra Buckley—that any of these factors would be present in anything approaching their present extent in the absence of the populist movements of the postwar period.

Are these changes—the eclipse of elitist protest and the enhanced effectiveness of popular—irreversible? One cannot say; certainly in the 1980s the tide of popular protest ebbed from its 1970s high, with some concomitant recentralization of power. But the attitudes that evince little receptiveness to the great tradition are being enculturated year by year, and the upward trend of one tradition and the downward trend of the other will be hard to reverse. The state

---

most of the rest of the world's democracies. One must avoid both an ethnocentric and an idealistic definition of democracy in looking at cases such as these.

30. DeVos, *Institutions;* White, "Protest and Change"; McKean, *Environmental Protest.*

might, of course, hope to reverse the populist current,[31] but there are indications that Japan's political culture has been too much changed for this: disagreement, competition, open conflict, dissent, and democratic practices are more legitimate than ever before, and it is unlikely that women, Burakumin, Koreans, and citizens in general are going to return to previous subservience.

This is not to say that populist social movements are going to be a constant feature of the political landscape. Such movements come and go; they arise in response to specific situations and wax and wane according to the responses of those in power to their causes and to the movements themselves. They can consume whole societies—as occurred in Italy in the 1960s—but they can be short-circuited by shrewd elites, betrayed by inept ones, or swallowed by their more radical elements, as has also happened in Japan.[32] Indeed, the major weakness of the social movement sector in Japanese politics is the absence of effective elite allies. With moribund opposition parties, corporatist unions, incestuously establishmentarian media, and a vacillant judiciary, the people have no one to look to but themselves.

Despite this limitation, protest movements—or at least their populist forms— have served notice to those who rule Japan that they are on a shorter leash than before. Politicization may wax and wane, but it does not vanish, and it needs only a new stimulus, as the events of 1989 showed. Postwar Japan has hardly witnessed the victory of the common people, but they certainly deserve two cheers.

THE SYNERGISM OF TRADITIONS

The comments above should not imply that elites have never managed to act in concert with the common people in Japanese history. Indeed, some of the greatest incidents of insurrection in Japanese history have been precisely those in which elites and masses made common cause upon a middle ground. The Edo-era Shimabara Rebellion, the Freedom and Popular Rights Movement of the mid-Meiji period, the Ashio Copper Mine protest movement, the contention surrounding the Portsmouth Treaty—all combined elite and popular participants and combinations of goals and tactics that severely shook the establishments of the day. And this potential is as present in postwar Japan as prewar.

In the postwar period two massive uprisings of the Japanese people have occurred—one more massive in numbers, one impressive mainly in its duration—plus one "near miss." The first was the anti-treaty (or Anpo) movement of 1959–60, in which the media, all of the opposition parties, labor unions, intellectuals, grassroots organizations, and public opinion united in opposition to ratification of a revised U.S.–Japan Security Treaty.[33] Actually, the movement was a

---

31. Upham, *Law and Social Change*, suggests one way in which state institutions lead in this direction.

32. Sidney Tarrow, "Cycles of Protest and Cycles of Reform: Italy (1965–1979)" (proposal submitted to the National Science Foundation, Mar. 1981).

33. Packard, *Protest in Tokyo*.

hybrid: in its earlier stages it was directed primarily against the treaty itself, which was seen as dragging Japan into a perilous entanglement in America's military adventures in Asia. When the LDP chose to push the treaty through parliament over this opposition, the major thrust of the movement turned against the auto-cratic tactics of the LDP and its leader, Prime Minister Kishi Nobusuke (whose record as a prewar leader and war criminal helped merge the two currents of opposition). Disruptions on the floor of the Diet were matched by massive demon-strations in cities nationwide, which culminated in riots on the grounds of the Diet building itself. The great majority of the opposition was motivated by general antimilitarist and antiautocratic sentiment; not partisan, it profited mightily from its alliance with more articulate, organized and extreme elements of the media, the intelligentsia, and the Left. The partisan Left manipulated the movement to a degree, interpreting it as a massive attack on the LDP; the LDP magnified its scope, too, since certain elements in the LDP were anxious to see Kishi gone and withheld support from him until the domestic situation had gotten completely out of hand; the media also played an inflammatory role.

In fact, however, the movement was overwhelmingly middle-class, nonviolent, and limited in its objectives. It opposed the renewal of the treaty (unsuccessfully), the Kishi government (successfully), and LDP parliamentary high-handedness (also successfully: according to Hans Baerwald's analysis of the Diet, written almost fifteen years later, parliamentary behavior is still being constrained by fears on both Right and Left of a recurrence of such traumatic conflict).[34] George Packard, in his study of the Anpo movement, also attributes it in no little part to the incomplete development of channels of meaningful political dissent in the 1950s. To the extent that violence was subsequently discredited, the media and parties (Right and Left) sobered, nonviolent parliamentary conflict-resolution procedures institutionalized, and dissent responded to short of insurrection, one might evaluate the Anpo movement as successful to no small degree.

The other major contentious upheaval of the postwar period surrounded the construction of the New Tokyo International Airport at Narita.[35] The project, announced in 1966, stimulated immediate opposition among the area farmers, who were threatened with dispossession. They were soon joined by elements of the student Left who provided them with a theoretical interpretation of their situation, organizational expertise, political sophistication, and a repertoire of action beyond the farmers' wildest dreams. The goals of the farmers were to keep their land, whereas those of the radicals were to destroy the oppressive, militaristic capitalist state; a common immediate enemy (the airport) and mutual advantage (the farmers won allies, the radicals won an opportunity to attack the System from a position protected by public sympathy for the farmers) led nevertheless to a solid alliance.

34. Hans Baerwald, *Japan's Parliament* (Cambridge: Cambridge University Press, 1974).
35. David Apter and Nagayo Sawa, *Against the State* (Cambridge: Harvard University Press, 1984).

Opposition to the airport was going full tilt by 1970 and continued until the airport opened in 1978. Thereafter the movement weakened, and in 1983 it split in a dispute between those who wanted to compromise and those who wanted to continue the struggle. The schism appears to have been between the populist and elitist currents of the movement: it was partly caused by the imposition of grand, ideological principles over the practical needs and goals of the farmers and was accompanied by accusations from one side that one ultraradical student faction was trying to take over the movement and, from the other, that certain farmers were about to sell out—literally and figuratively—to the airport authority. At any rate, in the 1980s, with the airport in full operation, the movement gradually lost momentum; at present, though it continues, it is far less visible than the barbed wire and guard towers that it prompted about the perimeter of the airport.

Both the Anpo and Narita struggles have essentially ended, but the potential for such movements has not disappeared. Both of these movements occurred in a context of blended domestic and foreign policy conflict, discord within the LDP, and elite leadership in the service—temporarily—of widely popular goals and tactics. What sorts of issues can generate these coalitions is impossible to predict. The renewal of the Security Treaty in 1970 gave suggestions of becoming one such, but the treaty issue had become a fuzzier target: in contrast to 1960, the Diet was not required to take any action in 1970, and so the treaty was not formally on the parliamentary agenda at all.[36] Second, Prime Minister Satō was far shrewder than Kishi: he avoided arrogant, provocative treatment of both protesters and parliamentary opponents and bought popular goodwill with economic growth and a campaign to win the return of Okinawa from American control. Third, the Vietnam War—the military backdrop of the 1970 movement—was simply not sufficiently crucial to most Japanese to stimulate active opposition to the treaty. Finally, although Beheiren at its inception constituted an elite-popular amalgam with all the promise of its powerful predecessors and did in fact achieve some massive outpourings of popular sentiment, its conscientiously nonviolent and temperate activities were dramatically upstaged by the apocalyptic violence of the student radicals, which alienated the public irrevocably.

As noted, the LDP was a major target in all three of these instances; it blundered egregiously in two of them. For reasons not uniquely Japanese, the potential for revolution is always greatest when a wave of popular dissent breaks against a divided elite. It may thus be that the potential for massive protest movements in Japan is the same as that to be found in all advanced industrial democracies and is no longer the result of a combination of distinctive traditions. The potential for revolution itself is probably nil; mass-elite coalitions are unstable, and a shrewd government can usually concede to part of the movement, co-opt it, or simply outlast it (or, of course, grant its demands). But when elite and

36. In 1970, the government did not have to bring the treaty to a vote unless it wanted to revise or abrogate it, which it did not; see Havens, *Fire Across the Sea*.

mass opposition are in concert *and* the LDP is either disunified, obtuse, or at odds with its customary supporters, then significant change may occur. Such was momentarily the case in 1989; the moment had passed—particularly the LDP's internal crisis—by 1990, but it would be unrealistic not to expect such concatenations of cleavage to recur in the future.

CONCLUSION

Both the forms of political contention, the number and variety of contenders, and the results vis-à-vis government have changed dramatically since 1945; if one begins further back, the change is even starker. More people are involved; opposition is relatively more realistic in its ends and moderate in its means; contention is motivated less by ideology; the national government is more on the defensive in its relationship to local governments in particular and society in general; and traditional, aristocratic, and elitist values are in decline. These changes are due largely to the rooting of the sorts of democratic institutions and practices and to the emergence of the sorts of middle-class social structures and values seen in other societies in which conflict has evolved similarly. Indeed, the decline of political conflict along a Right-Left spectrum and the decay of Marxism are hardly unique to Japan.

The Japanese system is still more state-guided than some because of Japan's uniquely economic definition of national survival, the weakness of the labor movement, and the partisan opposition to which it has long hitched its wagon. And some power may have reverted back into the hands of the elites in Tokyo since 1973 as economic imperatives took on a salience not felt in the high-growth days of the previous decade. Indeed, in the aftermath of the opposition's failure to capitalize on a golden opportunity to upset the LDP in the 1990 general election, one could argue that there is today *no* elite-level opposition to LDP rule in the sense of any powerful, cohesive organization seriously interested in and trying actively to remake the polity overall, to provide a credible alternative to LDP rule, or even to change significantly the thrust of LDP policy. Perhaps the only meaningful political opposition today comes from *within* the LDP and from the populace at large. And, except at the ballot box or in the streets, "the populace" is an abstraction.[37]

37. This essay may sound unduly dismissive regarding the watchdog potential of the media. The media, as Hans Baerwald has noted (*Party Politics in Japan* [Boston: Little, Brown, 1986]), like to see themselves as an opposition force, and their influence is evaluated extremely highly by other elite sectors (Verba, *Elites*). In fact, however, their influence on voters and on the Diet is limited at most (Flanagan et al., *Japanese Voter*), and their open collusion with political leaders to keep certain stories out of the news vitiates this role (see also Richard Halloran, *Japan: Images and Realities* [New York: Knopf, 1969]). The only sector of the media truly willing to speak truth to power is, oddly enough, the frequently sleazy and consistently unprincipled weekly magazines, or *shūkan-shi*, which are not members of the "press clubs" that bind their members to a code of circumspection regarding the particular agencies or leaders they cover.

As noted above, this interpretation may sound naively populist, and it contrasts with other common perspectives on Japanese politics; indeed, some of the other contributors to this volume, who focus more on elite-level power centers, would emphasize the state-centered and co-optive features noted above and question the democratic quality of the system. Some see the Japanese people as authentically thriving and legitimately enjoying the luxury of a well-running economy and society. Low levels of partisan polarization and political contention are simply the consequence of a low level of injustice, exploitation, and need. Perhaps Japan is number one. At the other extreme are those who see Japan as a regimented, managed, manipulated society in which the masses have simply been bought off and either suffer from false consciousness or are deprived by the elites of meaningful opportunities to dissent. A third position sees multiple sources and relations of tension and pressure that are in most instances resolved through mediation, preemptive policy, negotiation, and government concession without going so far as to erupt into overt, disruptive opposition.[38]

This last position is attractive if one perceives the major sources of pressure and tension to be within the LDP or outside of the elite strata altogether. Even the proponents of the statist critique admit that constitutionally and structurally Japan fits any common definition of a democratic nation. The problematic area is that of process and behavior, and in this area, although the fundamental elements of democracy are present, abuses thereof—especially on the elite level—are common. Such abuses may tarnish Japan's democratic *ideals*, but they do not vitiate its *actual* democratic qualities. Democracy requires meaningful elections; if the LDP always wins, one might ask, how can elections be meaningful? The answer is not that elections do not determine who shall rule (a vitiation of democracy) but that no opposition force has presented the Japanese people with the prospect of a competent alternative to LDP rule (an abuse of the responsibility of the opposition in a democracy).

The disturbing aspect of this interpretation is that so much potential abuse is prevented by so little. Within the framework of a functioning democracy, Japan's approximation of democratic ideals is often achieved—in the absence of popular pressure on the LDP—at the suffrance of that party, with few institutional guarantees or elite-level guardians to compel accountability by the ruling government. The sorts of social contracts discussed by Garon and Mochizuki may be widely beneficial, but they are also unilaterally revocable. The techniques of interest expression and conflict resolution through compromise, negotiation, and mediation described by Upham have benefited women and Burakumin, but legally they, too, are built on sand. So, too, with Diet boycotts: unlike the American filibuster, which has de jure power, they enjoy only as much de facto

38. Calder (*Crisis and Compensation*) argues a similar position, holding that the LDP, although unresponsive when electorally secure, becomes extraordinarily responsive and concessionary when it perceives threats to its continued rule. An *absence* of threats to the LDP government thus, curiously but plausibly, seems to constitute the most significant threat to the quality of Japanese democracy.

power as the LDP allows. The constitution, of course, is replete with institutional guarantees—but such guarantees need politicians, parties, courts, and popular movements willing to realize them. The popular sector possesses more power now than before the war, or in the 1950s or 1960s, for that matter, but without elite leadership this sector also remains for the most part an abstraction.[39] Local government is also far stronger than in the past, but it is by definition parochial. In 1989 the partisan opposition led the way, and the LDP was called to account in the House of Councillors election. But by February 1990 this opposition had fallen to bickering, and in the general election the electorate—who could only take the LDP to task by turning the government over to the opposition—chose competence over accountability.

Had the oil shocks of the 1970s not occurred, one might expect that the popular sector's powers would have grown even more than is the case today. However, had the shocks been even more traumatic, it is quite possible that the Japanese people would have relinquished even more of their recently won power to a government then seen as standing between the nation and oblivion and deserving of unquestioning obedience.

The postwar years up until roughly 1960 were ones of learning, a testing and ultimately sobering time for parties, people, media, and movements. From then until the 1980s were years of revelation: the processes of moderation, depolarization, and "middle-classification" became clear as their results emerged one after another, followed by the post-1973 revelation of limits, of vulnerability, of constraint. The 1980s were until the very end, in terms of contention, years of relative stability in interparty competition, in the social movement sector, and in state-society relationships overall. Does this mean some sort of ending? Hardly: economic fluctuations, the tactics of partisan contention, the pursuit of rights and equality by those incompletely empowered, and the intelligence or obtuseness of government in responding to all of the above are unending sources of change in patterns and levels of contention.

As the 1990s opened at least five potential sources of continued political opposition could be discerned. First, and most salient in the headlines between 1988 and 1991, was the crisis of the LDP, a mélange of party corruption, popular revulsion, personal venality, inept tax policy, international embarrassment, and electoral defeat. But the real significance of the Recruit scandal lay in its scope and its revelatory quality: it led to one suicide, sixteen indictments, and the blighting

---

39. This emphasis on legalistic guarantees may sound ethnocentric, and one could of course point out that even in the West, England has come along quite democratically without possessing a written constitution. In rejoinder, I would note that Western-style law is not the only guarantee: the tree of liberty can be watered not only by laws but by the blood of patriots. Moreover, informal democracy (1) has been rooted in England's history for several centuries longer than in Japan's; (2) is crucially dependent on a powerful consensus among elites that the unwritten constitution is to be obeyed (a consensus not visible in Japan); and (3) has not prevented England from maintaining a chillingly repressive Official Secrets Act and an overall level of administrative secrecy quite at odds with some notions of democracy.

of the careers of more than forty individuals in three different political parties, the media, business, academia, and the civil service; indeed, it briefly threatened to topple the LDP.[40] The impression conveyed by the media in mid-1989 was that everyone who was anyone was on the take, and there is no reason to believe that Recruit was alone in filling the trough. The scandal also revealed much: if corruption pervades the elites, then the populace is indeed on its own and cannot rely on any source but itself to curb political abuses. In 1989 the LDP called piously and vigorously for a variety of political reforms but in fact did only the absolute minimum and trusted to the evanescence of public memory.

The significance of the Gulf War was of a good news–bad news nature. The good news for the partisan opposition was that the LDP, and the system it led, might have exhausted their international competence. It is possible that the present Japanese powers that be are simply not capable of satisfying the pressures which intrude from the international arena. The bad news was the revelation that even when the LDP was paralyzed by division, the partisan opposition was unable or unwilling to take advantage of its weakness, much less offer the people a credible alternative vision of government.

But Recruit and the Gulf War were only the most obvious—and most short-lived—incitements to the opposition. Immediately after these causes is the potential decay of the economic egalitarianism that has so clearly characterized postwar Japan, and the key to this decay is the price of land. The gap between the top and bottom economic strata increased slightly during the 1980s, and the gap between popular perceptions of national wealth and personal constraint did also; these gaps were overwhelmingly seen as unfair and also as predominantly caused by the climbing price of land, which rose from an index value of 100 in 1955 to 6,300 in 1988 (13,500 in the major cities). Land loomed ever larger in people's economic self-perceptions and in the egregiously ostentatious well-being of those lucky enough to own some.[41] Together with the reality of dozens of equally undeserving politicians lining their pockets with corporate largesse and with the regressive impact—of which the public is acutely aware—of the 1989 sales tax, this impression may well have lain behind the singularly explosive popular reaction to the Recruit scandal.

The third source of possible opposition is less purely domestic: the interplay of foreign pressures for market opening and the resistance of protected sectors, of which the farmers are most important. This resistance is particularly significant

40. *Japan Times,* 30 May 1989.

41. This summary is based on data taken from OECD, ed., *1987/1988 OECD Economic Surveys: Japan* (Paris: OECD, 1988), 75; Keizai Kōhō Center, ed., *Japan 1989, An International Comparison* (Tokyo: Keizai Kōhō Center, 1989), 87; Keizai Kikaku-chō, ed., *Kokumin seikatsu hakusho* (Tokyo: Keizai Kikaku-chō, 1988), and *Shōwa 63-nendo kokumin seikatsu senkō-do Chōsa* (Tokyo: Keizai Kikaku-chō, 1988); Kokuzei-chō, ed., *Kokuzei-chō tōkei Nenpō sho* (Tokyo: Kokuzei-chō, annual). The same phenomenon is discussed in Toshiaki Tachibanaki, "Japan's New Policy Agenda: Coping with Unequal Asset Distribution," *Journal of Japanese Studies* 15 (Summer 1989): 345. Land prices began to fall in late 1991, but by only a few percent.

because the farm sector has been the LDP's most faithful electoral component and also because, as Charles Horioka points out (in this volume), the diminishing rate of domestic saving creates incentives for the government to liberalize markets and rationalize the distribution system. The LDP's record suggests that it will be able to open Japan's markets gradually and mollify its client groups along the way with subsidies and other concessions. But the fact that it has succeeded in the past is no guarantee that it can continue to do so in the future.

The fourth source of possible opposition has already been discussed: the possible development of the labor movement into a vigorous, united opposition. And the fifth has been touched on also: the ongoing efforts of women, Koreans, and Burakumin to achieve the equality promised under the constitution.[42] In the 1990s these groups will in all likelihood be joined by other non-Japanese groups as increased immigration from Asia creates multiethnic societies in at least Japan's largest cities.

How these various forms of opposition will work themselves out—with or without conflict—one cannot say; it is not even clear that any one of these will continue to be major loci of political opposition in the future. But partisan, popular, and interest group opposition will continue, and freely, thus fulfilling one of the defining characteristics of a democratic society. And should the opposition oust the LDP and replace its hegemony with the alternation of parties in power, it will have moved Japan closer to the democratic ideal.

42. Susan Pharr, *Losing Face: Status Politics in Japan* (Berkeley and Los Angeles: University of California Press, 1990).

Conclusion

Andrew Gordon

DEFINING AND DEMARCATING THE POSTWAR

Two striking continuities define Japan's long postwar experience. Japan's subordinate position in a global system dominated by the United States persisted, despite changes and tensions stemming from the country's surge in economic power, at least until 1990. And for reasons including but not limited to this fact, Japanese have continued to view themselves as living in a "postwar" era, at least until the moment of this writing. At the same time, the essays in this book have shown that postwar Japan can be divided very roughly into three periods corresponding to three different ways of defining the postwar era.

First, the immediate postwar was a distinct epoch ending sometime between 1950 and 1955. These years were marked by economic crisis, political radicalism, and intense social and political confrontation. For masses of people this was a time of deprivation, anger, and hope. People were concerned not with consumption but with avoiding starvation; rates of saving were negative. A popular culture, far less packaged or processed than it would be in later years, flowered, as did a progressive intellectual community of contrition.

The immediate postwar began with an aggressive, radical push by unions and parties of the Left in favor of socialism and against the revival of a capitalist system. It ended with this opposition on the defensive. By the early 1950s surviving elements of the old-guard elites, especially the bureaucrats, dominated the political economy. Yet in this immediate postwar era these elites were divided between vociferous advocates of a return to the prewar status quo and supporters of a strategy of accommodation to consolidate a new conservative hegemony.

The next major era of postwar history stretched from the mid-1950s until the early 1970s. This was the postwar era of high growth, a time of double-digit annual economic expansion dominated by a political belief that growth was the primary national goal, a neat proxy for well-being and success. In the politics of high growth the mainstream of the conservative elite gradually abandoned the reactionary agenda of formal constitutional revision and full-scale rearmament. They instead negotiated social contracts with key potential or actual elements of the opposition. In a parallel trajectory on the shop floors of private-sector corporations, the postwar era of high growth witnessed the triumph of management culture. As conservatives thus consolidated their hegemony at home, the struggle over subordinate independence in Japan's international relations diminished in intensity. This shift was exemplified in the contrast between the dramatic protests against the security treaty in 1960 and the much tamer resistance in 1970.

New forms of social behavior and ideology also characterized the high-growth era. Individual and national rates of savings surged to unprecedented levels, levels of consumption rose sharply, and items of consumption became increasingly Westernized. During these same years a discourse of Japan as a middle-class society with solidly marked gender divisions—the worlds of the professional housewife and the white-collar office worker (*sararīman*)—became increasingly dominant in the face of persistent evidence that attaining the bright new middle-class life was an uncertain struggle demanding sacrifice. Yet throughout these decades Japanese intellectuals persisted in a critical stance. With a gradually flagging confidence that mirrored the changes just noted and differentiated this era from the immediate postwar, most intellectuals nonetheless believed in the possibility and desirability of a progressive version of modernity and sought to expose the flaws of the "managed society." Thus, the high-growth phase of postwar history, from the mid-1950s through the early 1970s, was characterized by the consolidation of various social contracts, bureaucratic political dominance, and the ascendance of a middle-class, corporate (*kigyō*), and managed (*kanri*) society, even as major social and economic divisions, and an important critical tradition, persisted.

Several related changes had been building through the 1960s, and in the early 1970s these changes converged to usher in a third postwar epoch. They included new tensions in the Pax Americana, the rise of an affluent consumer society and new forms of mass culture, the gradual atrophy of the traditional Left, and the surge of citizens' movements questioning the primary emphasis on growth. With the Nixon and oil shocks of the early 1970s these factors converged to inaugurate the late postwar era. Thus, virtually all the essays in this volume identify some point from 1970 to 1975 as a major divide.

This late postwar era is the most difficult to characterize. It is perhaps too recent to constitute an object of historical inquiry. But a number of the essays offer preliminary insight into central, related features of Japan's history of the 1970s and 1980s. The early 1970s marked a turn away from the intense focus by both activists and conservative rulers on the propriety of Japan's anticommunist alliance with the United States. Instead, the elite showed increasing concern with Japan's ability to handle newly intense rivalry within the capitalist order and more variegated, contending interests at home. Yet by the 1980s the demands raised by these interests were so safely within bounds set by the elite that one could hardly characterize much of it as opposition. The response of elites (or "Nipponists," in Koji Taira's rendering) of the late 1960s and early 1970s to the challenges raised on a variety of fronts produced a new synthesis that absorbed or co-opted much of the opposition energy. After the oil shocks, a mobilized, activist opposition of workers, students, and citizens' groups played a less prominent role in politics; if the Sōhyō federation, with its relatively feisty rhetoric of opposition and leadership of the spring offensive, was one emblem of "opposition" of the high-growth postwar epoch, the new Rengō federation of the late 1980s typifies the friendly opposition of the following era.

In addition to such matters of political economy, the end of the high-growth era was marked by changed patterns of consumption and mass culture and change in the consciousness of intellectuals. The dramatic shift in consumption behavior and the Westernization of Japanese tastes reached a plateau in the years after the oil shock. A new generation came of age that had no memory of war or of immediate postwar deprivation. For its members the dramatic material transformation of the previous twenty years was part of a past increasingly taken for granted. The rise of neoconservative thought was part of this change, as was the new debate on the meaning of a "differentiated" consumer. In cultural terms the late postwar has thus been a time when many intellectuals felt the finality of the betrayal of earlier promises, while other dominant institutions articulated a celebratory vision of the recent past coupled with ever-present anxiety over the future.

Although the oil crisis of 1973 thus marked far more than a drop in the rate of economic growth, two features justify conceiving the years from the early 1970s through 1990 as a third era that still remained part of a long sweep of postwar history. Viewed from without, Japan remained an uncomfortable American ally in a continuing "postwar" Asian-Pacific order, while Japanese at home continued to wrestle with two ongoing, central "postwar" issues: the legitimacy of the peace constitution and the role of the imperial institution. In 1989 and 1990 these issues returned to public prominence in the form of debates over the transition to a new emperor and the appropriate limits of legitimate "self-defense" under the peace constitution in a post-cold-war world.

POSTWAR JAPAN IN CONTEXT

Japan's Twentieth-Century Trajectory

Without question, World War II marked the sharpest divide in Japan's twentieth-century history. The mid-nineteenth-century Meiji Restoration and the mid-twentieth-century war and occupation constitute the two revolutionary epochs of Japan's modern history. Yet we have also tried in this book to understand the history of "postwar Japan" as part of a longer process. The statement may not be surprising, but it is worth repeating: the defeat and Occupation did not bring a total rupture with the past. The particular importance of two distinct earlier eras of interwar democracy (1918–32) and wartime mobilization (1932–45) is clear in our analysis. Postwar history was foreshadowed and shaped by the interplay or overlay of developments from these two eras across realms from political economy to culture.

Legacies from the 1930s and the war era shaped the postwar political economy, international and domestic. The 1930s saw the political creation of what Bruce Cumings ironically calls a "natural" economy in which Japan stood as the processing workshop dominating its Asian colonial empire. He shows how this economic structure influenced American policy and Japan's postwar recovery. Similarly, in the debates that shaped economic policy over the postwar years, a bureaucratic vision, with prewar roots, of a "self-sufficient," relatively autarkic path to economic revival contended vigorously with a call for recovery based on interdependence. In addition, Laura E. Hein shows that in dealing with the state, managers and business elites overwhelmingly preferred to protect their "autonomy in a stable environment" rather than demand a free hand to compete in a free, uncertain market. This distinctive mix of concerns for autonomy and for stability had roots in a complex prewar legacy of fear of the "chaotic" competition of the 1920s on the one hand and anger at the oppressive wartime state's interference in business operations on the other.[1] As John W. Dower's earlier work on Yoshida Shigeru demonstrates, there were strong links between the prewar, war, and postwar eras embodied in the "passage-through of the old guard" that wanted to rearm and revise the constitution. The political thought and organization of this old guard clearly was rooted in the imperial order.[2]

The essay on postwar "social contracts" by Sheldon Garon and Mike Mochizuki stresses that their roots lay in negotiations between the state and elements in society reaching back to the turn of the century in the case of small businesses and to the 1920s in the case of labor. In the latter case accommodative bureaucrats and labor movement realists directly carried over their approaches from the interwar era. Gary D. Allinson similarly stresses continuity in bureaucratic politics by contending that a distinctive pattern of authority under what he calls "diffuse elites" characterized the entire era of the 1910s to the 1950s. In the workplace at major companies both the cooperative and the radical streams of the labor movement had roots in prewar years. In addition to these continuities, the workers' demand to be treated as dignified members of "human" society and the firm was a prewar legacy for both the left and right wings of the postwar labor movement.

The 1920s were formative years as well for the postwar histories of intellectuals, mass culture, and popular economic behavior. J. Victor Koschmann situates

1. For further discussion of the multiple wartime legacies in the realm of economic policies, see Nakamura Takafusa, *The Postwar Japanese Economy* (Tokyo: University of Tokyo Press, 1981), chap. 1.

2. John Dower, *Empire and Aftermath: Yoshida Shigeru and the Japanese Experience* (Cambridge: Harvard Council on East Asian Studies, 1980), and "The Useful War," *Daedalus* 119, no. 3 (Summer 1990): 49–70.

the intense intellectual "community of contrition" of the immediate postwar years and the prominence of the Japan Communist Party (JCP) among intellectuals against a backdrop of the flourishing of left-wing thought in the 1920s and the agonized "conversion" of so many left-wing activists before and during the war. Marilyn Ivy finds roots of the commodified postwar industry of mass-consumer culture in the major cities in the 1920s. At the same time, change in the realm of mass culture was pronounced. Charles Yuji Horioka shows that the prewar Japanese were among the poorest savers in industrial nations and did not attain their extraordinary savings rates of the postwar era until the 1950s. This is a little-known (and for many, no doubt, surprising) example of the fact that the war and occupation changed the social and economic, as well as political, contexts.

These three essays on intellectuals, mass culture, and consumption describe a prewar distinction between rural society and an urban world of "modern girls," Marxism, and movies. William W. Kelly's analysis of postwar society picks up this theme. He first stresses that throughout the prewar, wartime, and early postwar eras the nation was consistently divided in its self-images as well as its institutions. He then challenges the common view that the postwar era of high growth witnessed a simple erasure or blurring of such social divisions between city and country life, highly educated elites and simply literate masses, or capitalist and proletarian. He understands the statistical evidence that Japanese became more homogeneous as part of a complex "transposition" in which old differences diminished and new divisions of central and marginal social realms evolved.

As several essays make clear, gender remained a particularly persistent means of differentiating Japanese throughout the postwar eras. Here the longer context of modern Japanese history is critical as well. Kathleen Uno shows that Japanese officials and sympathetic elites formulated a conservative ideal of "good wife, wise mother" in the late nineteenth century that exhibited remarkable staying power throughout the postwar years. Postwar challenges to this ideal were anticipated in the feminist critiques of the 1910s and 1920s. At the same time, many parties to postwar debate on gender issues drew on or transformed concepts of a special role for good wives and wise mothers rather than rejecting them entirely.

Finally, Carol Gluck's analysis of Japan's postwar historical consciousness reveals the intensity of the Japanese sense of historical rupture in 1945, which divided the "two Shōwa eras" of the prewar and postwar in historical imagination. Yet it is striking that the impassioned postwar debate between progressive and official interpreters of the past embodied important continuities with both critical and celebratory historiographic traditions rooted in the earlier twentieth century. These traditions had previously focused mainly on the Meiji Restoration; later they came to include the postwar decades as well.

The Global Context

The global context for postwar Japanese history was a system in which the United States demarcated Japan's "outer limits" in economic and political behavior. This system of American hegemony arguably defined a still lingering postwar era in

Japan's international relations that entered its fifth decade in the late 1980s, although the weight of economic versus strategic tensions within this hegemonic relationship shifted significantly beginning in the 1970s.

Americans set the stage for Japan's domestic politics first by favoring the "peace and democracy" constituencies of the Left and then by promoting the revival of the "old guard" with the reverse course, the Self-Defense Force, and the Security Treaty. But the United States thereafter did not simply concern itself with monitoring or restricting Japan's international behavior; it was "concerned"—either through the intent of its leaders or its structural domination—to shape domestic politics, intellectual discourse, and, indirectly, mass culture. That is, the Americans promoted a technocratic faith in capitalist reconstruction, growth, and technology—at least through the first oil shock—that profoundly influenced the postwar histories of economic strategy, labor-management relations, and the state's social contract with labor. Further, the industry producing mass culture was inextricably linked to the United States as the point of origin for so many of the products consumed by the Japanese.

This cultural subordination was more a reflection of a global system of power than of conscious policy, but Americans intervened more directly in the case of intellectuals. The Americans were agents of political revolution in Japan between 1945 and 1947, and progressive intellectuals hailed them as such. When American policy changed, Japanese progressives condemned the Americans as a reactionary force, especially during the security treaty and Vietnam War protests. But the Americans did not remain passive objects of intellectual criticism. Prominent American scholars sought to reorient the concerns of Japanese intellectuals, calling on them to analyze their history in terms of modernization theory rather than Marxism. Thus, America's political, economic, and cultural ascendance across the postwar decades has influenced matters well outside the realm of international relations.

Despite the broad impact of American hegemony, the global power of the United States has not always shaped Japan's development in a straightforward or intentional fashion. A major theme and conclusion of this volume, discussed further below, is that the landscape of postwar history is littered with the irony of unintended results. This theme is clear in realms as diverse as economic policy and gender relations. In the former, pessimistic economic predictions, from the era of the Dodge Line to that of the oil and yen shocks, were confounded. In the latter, early expectations of dramatic transformation in gender roles were betrayed.

Comparative Perspectives

The role of the United States reminds us that it is not enough to confine our analysis to Japan. We have also examined how problems in contemporary world history unfolded in Japan. We find similarity in many general trends. For example, when Koschmann describes a postwar system of thought dominated by concepts of class, liberation, and the "unhappy consciousness" of the intellectual, he uses an analytic strategy derived from Sartre's observations of postwar European intellectuals, and he suggests that Japanese intellectuals were situated in a similar way in their society. As his analysis turns to the 1970s and 1980s, he regards the decline of a critical intellectual stance in the face of a conservative, self-satisfied worldview as part of a phenomenon that took place across the world of advanced capitalism. At the same time, he argues that the meaning of "post-modern" thought in Japan was distinctive. Thus, in this case and in others our attempts at comparison also reveal areas of significant, ongoing divergence in Japan's experience.

Our explorations of political economy describe trends similar in Japan and in other centers of advanced capitalism. Broadly speaking, the Japanese mode of negotiation between interest groups and the state has been comparable in key particulars to patterns that have evolved elsewhere. Garon and Mochizuki find significant parallels with the Italian case in the pattern of small business and even labor negotiation. Focusing more on the United States as the point of comparison, both Hein and Taira discuss how GNP growth became a politically seductive centerpiece, even amulet, for postwar economic policy in the United States, Japan, and elsewhere. GNP growth achieved this status not simply because of American pressure but because policymakers around the world decided that technology-fueled growth could resolve intractable social conflicts while avoiding the politics of redistribution. Finally, conservative political trends in Japan in the 1970s and 1980s echoed developments in much of Western Europe and North America.

Yet we also find distinctive patterns or unintended results. These include the relatively interventionist set of policy tools fashioned by the state, the long-lived hegemony of the Liberal Democratic Party (LDP), the related prominence of the "Nipponists" vis-à-vis the "people," and the productive dynamism of a workplace culture that had mixed results for individuals but served the aggregate economy handsomely. In sum, the bureaucracy retained an enduring centrality as it dealt with the very significant, often dramatic or explosive protests raised by the political opposition on the Left or by newly mobilized constituencies such as pollution victims. The result by the end of the high-growth era seems to have been a version of democratic practice in which voices for change, however freely expressed, were effectively contained by a bureaucracy that mediated and negotiated but successfully sought to deny individual or group entitlements.

In the realm of mass culture and behavior Japanese consumers followed an expansive course parallel to that of the United States and other Western capitalist societies, though they lagged in absolute level of consumption. Likewise, the United States was not only the dominant influence in the case of mass culture from the 1920s through the 1980s but also the most important comparative case. Yet, whereas mass culture is increasingly manufactured worldwide, Japan stands out as a case where an elite of the LDP, businesses, and bureaucrats have consistently and effectively managed information and culture. A comparative view of the culture industry or the political economy suggests that in the late postwar era of the 1970s and 1980s the Japanese were not simply following capitalist systems elsewhere but, for better or worse, had become pacesetters.

In the institutions and ruling ideas of social life our most salient comparison to North America and Western Europe focuses on the tenacity of both the rhetoric of the middle-class society and of "real" differences among people. Thus, the rhetoric of the "professional housewife" and its poor fit with daily experience had American parallels in the 1950s and 1960s (this parallelism probably helps explain the popularity of a show such as "Father Knows Best" on Japanese television at the time). Here, however, the continued marginal status of a feminist critique is perhaps the most striking divergence since the high-growth era. In Japan of the 1970s and 1980s, unlike the United States, the feminist critique did not permeate the mainstream to the point of provoking a powerful reactionary turn. "Reforms" such as the Equal Employment Opportunities Act were provoked as much by outside pressures from sources such as the United Nations as by the domestic women's movement, and they were not as substantial as those aimed, for example, at Japan's environmental activists.

A global context of American hegemony accounts for much of the "comparability" of Japan's postwar experience with that of advanced capitalist societies of the West. Further, similar processes of technological change, economic growth, the spread of mass higher education, and consumerism have placed postwar Japan in a comparable situation to these societies. Yet the interest of comparative thinking goes well beyond the unsurprising discovery in Japan of these processes. Japan's experience was also comparable in the unraveling of much of the modern paradigm in the 1970s and 1980s. Progressive movements declined and conservatism and traditionalism revived not just in a stubbornly traditionalistic Japan, but all around the world.

Historiographic Contexts

Locating the arguments advanced in this volume in the context of existing perspectives on postwar history is complicated by three facts. First, because historians have been slow to consider the broad sweep of postwar Japan "as history," the context itself is thin. Second, discussions of postwar history among Japanese and in the West constitute two relatively separate streams of inquiry. Third, the essays in this book do not speak in a uniform voice.

Nonetheless, a few observations are possible. In contrast to existing studies, the essays in this volume stress the dialectic and nonlinear quality of postwar history. For example, the negotiation of "social contracts" beginning in the 1950s can be seen as a "synthesis" of the early high-growth era, and Taira points to a new "synthesis" in economic and social policy after 1973.

This interpretation contrasts with one body of existing work that offers a relatively static presentation of "systems" at a given point in time: for example, the system of conservative party rule or the Japanese employment system.[3] In such work, history sometimes slips in the back door as the "background" to a contemporary moment, but no serious attempt is made to understand the dynamics of change. It also contrasts with another influential set of works that describe dramatic change but render it as a postwar history of linear "progress." Such works have depicted Japan as an increasingly homogeneous country that since 1945 was blessed with steady progress from poverty to affluence, weakness to strength, "traditional" to "modern" practices, authoritarianism to democracy.[4] Much of the ethnographic literature suggests that the sharply stratified, immediate postwar society, rooted in the prewar and wartime eras, was transformed into a more egalitarian, homogeneous social order as the result of occupation reforms, economic change, and technological advances linking city and country.

Other recent research has questioned such convergent paradigms of modernization. For example, Chalmers Johnson claims that Japan's twentieth-century experience produced a divergent capitalist political economy marked by the dominance of the bureaucratic state, and Ronald Dore argues that Japan's social structures remained stubbornly divergent from Western trends often assumed to be universal examples of development toward modernity.[5] Recent ethnographic works have analyzed ways in which stratification, division, and opposition have endured in postwar Japan. The essays in this book are relatively close to the spirit of these works. Yet to the extent that studies such as Johnson's or Dore's, while denying convergence, still draw on a linear paradigm that stresses consistent, ongoing differences, our picture differs. We argue that the political or social system was continually reformulated or renegotiated.

This view can be seen in the treatment of two issues of considerable prior debate (discussed further below): the extent of pluralism in Japan's political economy and the extent to which power has been dispersed or shared. Hein's history of policy debates shows that economic policy was far from a simple unfolding of prescient bureaucratic initiatives. Tensions between advocates of sharply opposed policies were enduring and deep, and policy evolved through a process of trial and error. Although our essays differ concerning the effectiveness or depth of movements against the status quo at different times in postwar history, several suggest that those with little formal power, such as small businesses and organized labor,

3. Nathaniel B. Thayer, *How the Conservatives Rule Japan* (Princeton: Princeton University Press, 1969); Chitoshi Yanaga, *Big Business in Japanese Politics* (New Haven: Yale University Press, 1968); Rodney Clark, *The Japanese Company* (New Haven: Yale University Press, 1979). These works generally do not attempt to do more than analyze a system at a given time, and they achieve this objective well. The point is that such studies can offer only a static picture of the postwar era.

4. Ezra F. Vogel, *Japan as Number One: Lessons for America* (Cambridge: Harvard University Press, 1979); Edwin O. Reischauer, *Japan: The Story of a Nation*, 4th ed. (New York: McGraw-Hill, 1990), part 3 ("Postwar Japan").

5. Chalmers Johnson, *MITI and the Japanese Miracle: The Growth of Industrial Policy, 1925–1975* (Stanford: Stanford University Press, 1982); Ronald Dore, *British Factory–Japanese Factory: The Origins of National Diversity in Industrial Relations* (Berkeley and Los Angeles: University of California Press, 1973).

have had significant input. James W. White maintains that relatively less formal opposition movements (antipollution groups) contributed more than did formal groups such as political parties. Allinson argues that negotiation between elites and popular interests became more salient from the early 1970s. Garon and Mochizuki contend that a social contract between these groups and the state began to emerge in fairly clear outline even in the late 1950s.

We also challenge accounts that have too simply equated economic growth over the postwar decades with "success." Taira bluntly criticizes works that identify economic growth with national success and celebrate Japanese history as a narrative of the rise of a virtually unique civilization.[6] Andrew Gordon identifies two sorts of analyses of labor-management relations across the postwar decades, one stressing the social and economic miracle of the productive development of cooperative workplace communities and the other blasting the social disaster of an exploitive regime that denies choice and divides and conquers segments of the work force by pitting them against each other. Although a dynamic, productive economic system evolved across several decades of labor-management interaction, Gordon argues that the result for individual workers was at best mixed.

How have the Japanese themselves understood postwar history? One difference is chronological. At least through the 1980s, most academic historians in Japan still defined "postwar history" as the study of the Occupation era and the 1950s, and they showed particular concern with issues such as the Tokyo trial and the postwar emperor system. A major five-volume publication on "contemporary history" in 1990 reflected this approach. Three volumes focused on the fifteen years from 1945 to 1960. The following thirty years were covered in just two volumes.[7] At the same time, despite such differences in emphasis this series and our book generally agree in the demarcation and definition of periods.

Japanese historians have been sharply divided between those who see the history of the last forty-five years as a betrayal of the progressive promise of the immediate postwar and those who celebrate it as a vindication of the century-long trajectory of Japan's modernization, if not the entire course of Japanese civilization. Positioning themselves as defenders of the dramatic gains of the democratic constitution, the progressive intellectuals have seen the "problem" of postwar history as the evaluation of the present, usually in negative terms, against the early postwar promise. Although the essays in this book are varied, sometimes ambivalent, in their judgments, many share this perspective to a significant degree. If we nonetheless differ, it is probably in focusing on a series of issues emerging from the process of growth itself. Thus, together with a concern for the fading of an

---

6. Murakami Yasusuke, *Bunmei to shite no ie shakai* (Tokyo: Chūō kōron, 1979); an English version is available as "*Ie* Society as a Pattern of Civilization," *Journal of Japanese Studies* 8, no. 1 (Winter 1982): 29–72.

7. Rekishigaku Kenkyūkai, ed., *Nihon dōjidai shi*, 5 vols. (Tokyo: Aoki Shoten, 1990): vol. 1, *Haisen to senryō;* vol. 2, *Senryō seisaku no tenkan to kōwa;* vol. 3, *55-nen taisei to anpo tōsō;* vol. 4, *Kōdō seichō no jidai;* vol. 5, *Tenkanki no sekai to Nihon.*

immediate postwar era of promise, we see postwar Japanese history as one of a number of dynamic variants of the advanced capitalisms of the late twentieth century.

THEMES IN POSTWAR HISTORY

Uncertain Outcomes; Roads Taken and Not Taken

The essays in this book stress the uncertainty, ambivalence, or surprise that people felt about "outcomes" during the postwar era. Japan's rise as an economic superpower looks smooth and certain in retrospect, but many of those who lived through this stretch of history experienced it as an astonishing transformation. Policymakers were unsure of and divided over some fundamental decisions: to promote a coal or an oil-based economy? to stress self-sufficiency and relative autarky or an export orientation and acceptance of interdependence? A variety of outcomes were possible in the immediate postwar era in the interaction of the state with key social interests. Small businesses could have joined forces with labor unions and the opposition parties to oust the LDP, or these groups could have sustained nonaccommodative stances for much longer than they did. The 1950s were thus a time when the *prospect* of an opposition-led mode of interest-group bargaining began to give way to an actual system in which settlements were negotiated within the elite. Yet as late as 1963 a leader of the LDP's right wing lamented that the demographic expansion of the working class was leading inexorably to socialist political rule.[8] To the extent that such views were typical, the political economy of high growth itself was an unexpected "road taken."

Perhaps more numerous and more easily forgotten were the anticipated journeys not taken. Frank Upham shows that the individually based democracy promoted by the American occupation, and adopted as their own vision of "modern" liberation by Japanese scholars such as Maruyama Masao or Kawashima Takeyoshi, proved to be a chimera. Upham, Sandra Buckley, and Uno make it clear that masses of women did not move swiftly into new social and political roles in the high-growth era. Women did redefine the meaning of their roles as wives and mothers to include supplementary wage labor, but any dramatic reordering of gender relations may actually have become a more distant prospect in the late postwar years.

Koschmann is similarly pessimistic as he describes the disillusionment among intellectuals at the failure to achieve liberation through the agency of the working class, the ongoing ambivalence among intellectuals at their inability to play an effective social or political role, and the persistent tension between the Left and the neoconservatives, who gained force over time. Ivy suggests that a popular culture of the immediate postwar years gave way rapidly to a mass culture in which most Japanese participated solely as consumers of sophisticated commodi-

---

8. Ishida Hirohide, "Hoshu seitō no bijiyon," *Chūō kōron* 78, no. 1 (Jan. 1963): 88–97.

ties and rarely if ever as creators. Gordon introduces a theme of lost promise as
he describes the rollback of "the first union movement" and the triumph of a
managerial culture in which employees' interests were submerged into those of
the firm. Taira argues that the conservative elite co-opted various challenges in
a new "synthesis" around the time of the oil crisis.

Although they contrast to most essays in this book, Japan's "official" or conservative versions of postwar history have not simply celebrated the decline of
such alternative visions. These renderings also have been deeply ambivalent about
some fundamental postwar changes. The fear that modernity and the West would
destroy a social order often viewed as the essence of Japaneseness reaches back
at least a century, and the anxiety closet of Japan's postwar conservative elite has
been populated by some frightening and unwelcome companions to the much-
desired economic power. Millions of affluent consumers, and a mass culture that
exalted their life-style, threatened to undermine the work ethic or the acceptance
of hierarchy that helped bring about national wealth.[9] Millions of women in the
work force threatened to undermine enduring gender role divisions and the spirit
of sacrifice for the household collectivity. But the import of our essays is that these
anxieties indeed remained figments of the conservative imagination across the
postwar decades.[10]

Naturally enough, both the authors in this volume and the Japanese who
experienced these changes remain divided in their reading of the "balance sheet"
of postwar history. Whatever our judgments, we conclude that many of the
alternatives that did prevail were sharply contested. Developments that once
looked unlikely or unsure came to seem inevitable only in retrospect. We have
sought to recapture the sense of uncertainty at given moments while analyzing the
forces that foreclosed some options: American power and policy, deeply rooted
traditions of bureaucratic rule, and ideologies of consensus and "proper place."

Conservative Hegemony and the Negotiated Social Order
A second, related conclusion is thus that the result of such contests was a highly
managed Japanese version of democracy. Ivy argues that an "administered" and
commodified mass culture did not serve as an arena for the contention of diverse
popular voices; rather, mass culture quickly became a process of production and
consumption that articulated ruling ideas and reinforced the existing social and
economic order. She rejects the view of some "culture critics" that the 1980s saw
in the emergence of "micromasses" the return to diverse individuals of the
possibility for autonomous activity. Kelly concludes his analysis of social change
in the postwar with the argument that the Japanese social order was effectively

9. Rokurō Hidaka describes the "touchingly foolish" plight of "directors of large firms who are
pressed by their own sons to buy them cars." Such men are disturbed by their sons' consumerism,
although "it is they themselves who have produced the high economic growth that made this possible";
The Price of Affluence (Tokyo: Kodansha, 1984), 30–31.
10. See the essays by Horioka, Upham, Buckley, and Taira.

"co-optive"; that is, its leaders (whether individuals or institutions) have elaborated a powerful ideology of the "inclusive" society precisely because social systems have been necessarily exclusive or differentiated. Koschmann similarly reinforces the picture of the co-optive social order by contending that the prospects for an intellectual challenge to what critics came to call the "managed society" by the 1970s have gradually but consistently receded.

A dialectic interaction between social classes or interests and the state issued in a succession of syntheses from the 1950s through the 1980s. Although these syntheses ultimately confirmed conservative hegemony, they did involve some compromise by the elites. The study of social contracts claimed that negotiation was widespread and effective: "the hegemony of the conservative coalition has been accepted only as long as it seriously negotiates to accommodate the interests of various social organizations." At the same time, Garon and Mochizuki point out that the "contracts" that resulted did serve the "overall objectives of the conservative leadership." Upham offers a closely related vision of intense confrontations and negotiations between the state and Burakumin, pollution victims, and women that were successfully subsumed within a system of bureaucratic dominance. Activists in diverse social groups fought hard for their interests, but the government strategy for social management was to consistently co-opt them via mediated settlements.

Thus, organized societal interests constrained and influenced the elite and its programs but never threatened to dislodge it from power. This is a conclusion of essays that nonetheless differ in their view of the strength of opposition movements. Dower argues that conservatives consistently aspired to reshape the occupation settlement and increase the prominence of the emperor and the military. He also shows that they were considerably constrained by the postwar constitution, by the "peace" constituency led by the political opposition, and by the Ministry of Finance's prominence in economic and overall policy-making. Taira identifies a sharp turning point in the late 1960s and early 1970s, when the conservative government moved swiftly to accommodate popular demands and thereby renew its claim to power. Allinson sees the opposition of the 1960s as relatively less profound than Dower does. He claims rather that the bureaucracy and the LDP became, or were forced to become, increasingly adept at handling the demands of varied interests in the 1970s and 1980s. White also sees the state as effectively co-opting opposition demands in negotiations that steadily became less intense.

Transposition of Difference

We have argued that the concept of Japan as a homogeneous and cohesive middle-class society was a powerful ideological force in postwar history. This concept was supported by many dominant institutions—the mass-culture industry, schools, businesses, and political parties from the LDP through the centrist opposition—and it was articulated over the postwar decades in discourses of culture, class, cohort, and life cycle. We have also concluded that despite the ascendance of the middle-class ideology (and, indeed, stimulating dominant institutions to articulate it), significant groups are only marginally incorporated, and significant divisions have been transposed to new "registers of difference" rather than eliminated. In making this point, Kelly suggests that the transposition of difference was a key mechanism in postwar history for reproducing and managing a conservative social order in a dynamic, changing capitalist economy; the many people in "marginal" roles were vital to the overall functioning of a society that responded by elaborating and perpetuating the rhetoric of "inclusivity."[11]

Such processes can be identified in the household and in the workplace. The rhetoric of the professional housewife as the normative, unproblematic state of the Japanese woman obscured from view the great variety of female lifeways. Ideas of a woman's place shifted as wage work outside the household increasingly was viewed as legitimate, yet the difference in appropriate roles for men and women remained sharp. The mainstream discourse of the "workplace community," which promoted and sustained the ascendance of managerial culture since the 1960s, was likewise an inclusive rhetoric of consensus. Sony's well-known founder, Morita Akio, offered a typical example from the late 1980s, when he claimed that Japan's workplaces (and society more generally) had achieved a happy state of classless, unified community.[12] Yet it was possible to demarcate such a community only by excluding others, by dividing the work force into categories of part-timers and temporaries in large firms as well as millions of employees in smaller enterprises. This conclusion was echoed in discussions of the Equal Employment Opportunities Act. By discouraging job discrimination on the basis of sex, its impact on first glance was "inclusive," as it broke down the wall separating career tracks for men and for women. And, indeed, some women have been able to cross the divide and succeed in formerly male careers. But in overall practice, employers essentially "transposed" the difference by elaborating a new division of the workplace into "comprehensive" (sōgō shoku) and "general" (ippan shoku) job tracks, the former predominantly male, the latter mostly female.

The imagery or ideology of the inclusive harmonious society was amplified in the face of persisting difference. The mass-culture industry across the postwar decades produced a vast array of unifying and standardizing images, resulting in what Ivy calls a "leveling of consciously apprehended class distinctions." This process continued through the 1980s as the culture industry, broadly defined, "managed" the way individuals could imagine their society. In creating a public memory, mainstream historians likewise produced a homogenous version of a Japanese past that left out those on the margins (women, atom bomb victims, Burakumin, Okinawans), who in turn were prompted to write their own separate

---

11. Perhaps an analogous rhetoric on the other side of the Pacific has been that of the melting pot and the American way.

12. Ishihara Shintarō and Morita Akio, "No" to ieru Nippon (Tokyo: Kōbunsha, 1989), 95–101. This book sold more than one million copies in 1989 and 1990.

histories. And the recasting of the ideal of equality as that of homogeneity, rather than equal opportunities for individual expression, was central to a postwar discourse undergirding conservative hegemony and celebrating the arrival of the middle-class society. This notion of Japan as a middle-class society emerged to special prominence in the 1970s just as the inflation and protest in the wake of the oil shock seemed to threaten social cohesiveness.

Finally, Hein identifies a process in which "anxieties over foreign economic pressures . . . recast internal debates over political and economic problems into international ones." Beginning in the 1970s, pressures from abroad over the Mideast conflict, trade liberalization, or capital liberalization deferred domestic political debate just as the emphasis on economic growth had done earlier. In this process, the Japanese have often seen and presented themselves as vulnerable or as victims, clinging to a self-perception of weakness that (at least as applied to the aggregate strength of the nation) struck outsiders by the 1980s as strangely anachronistic. A mechanism of displacement that has persistently transposed Japan from victimizer to victim has been a consistent part of Japanese historical imagination.

THE END OF THE POSTWAR?

The immediate postwar ended in the early 1950s with the economic recovery, prompting the first declarations that the postwar is over. The high-growth era ended in the early 1970s. But did a late postwar era, defined by the persistence of the postwar international system and the "unfinished business" of World War II, both outside and within Japan, finally end with the close of the 1980s? It would be foolhardy for a historian to venture a firm statement on a matter so close to the moment of this writing, but the temptation to answer yes is hard to resist.

When we initiated this project on "postwar Japan as history" in early 1987, many participants shared a sense of an impending ending as we were daily bombarded with the media rhetoric of Japan's emergence not simply to economic respectability (as in the 1960s) or equality (as in the 1970s) but to a position of dominance. The dramatic events of the following four years, but particularly those of 1989–91, reinforced this sense of an ending. The Shōwa era came to a lingering close with the death of Emperor Hirohito in January 1989. For the first time since its founding, the LDP lost control of one house of parliament in July 1989. And in the autumn of 1989, when the European postwar order of forty-four years crumbled in an extraordinary season of popular revolt, pundits and policy-makers in Western capitals joked that "the Cold War is over, and Japan won."[13]

To be sure, in contrast to the fundamental changes in Europe, the basic structures of the East Asian political economy were hardly altered as of 1990.

13. For one example, see a column by James McCartney of the Knight-Ridder newspapers, "World War II Losers Looking More Like Winners Today," in which he attributes this comment to Ezra Vogel; *News and Observer* (Raleigh, N.C.), 11 Apr. 1990, 17A.

Even so there were signs that the European earthquake would have global aftershocks. New and serious moves toward rapprochement took place one after the other in 1990: first the Soviet Union and the South Koreans, then the Japanese and Soviets, and next the Japanese and North Koreans. As the crisis in Iraq unfolded in autumn 1990, all political parties within Japan except the Communists wanted to create a Japanese organization to play an international "peacekeeping" role. Although the place of the military in this entity deeply divided the parties as well as the populace, this attitude still represented an unprecedented consensus in favor of a new international role. Japanese elites, fearful of the vacuum left by the end of the cold war, faced the dilemma of defining such a role while satisfying a politically cynical and still pacifist population.

GLOSSARY

amakudari   Literally "descent from heaven"; the transfer of a national civil servant on retirement to a private-sector position.

Anpo   Abbreviation of Nichibei Anzen Hoshō Jōyaku Hantai Undō, the 1959–60 movement to oppose the revision of the U.S.-Japan Security Treaty.

Asahi shinbun   One of Japan's three major national daily papers.

Asahi soshō   "Asahi suit," a case brought against the Minister of Welfare in 1957 claiming that Japan's public assistance programs were not up to the standards implied by the constitution.

Beheiren   League for Peace in Vietnam, a Japanese antiwar organization of the 1960s.

bosei   Motherhood, nurturing.

bosei hogo   Protection of motherhood.

Boshi Hogo Hō   Pre–World War II Maternal and Infant Protection Law.

bunshū   Fragmented masses.

Burakumin   Japan's outcaste population; also termed *dōwa*.

chōtaishū   Metamasses.

chūryū ishiki   Mainstream consciousness.

chūshō kigyō   Medium and small firms.

danchi   Large apartment complex.

dentō   Tradition.

Dodge line   Anti-inflationary policies of 1949, implemented by Japanese government on advice of Joseph Dodge, economic consultant to SCAP.

dōgyō kumiai   Trade associations.

Dōmei   Major labor federation of cooperative, private-sector unions from 1964 to 1987.

dōwa   Japan's outcaste population; also termed *Burakumin.*

fukushi   Social welfare.

furusato būmu   Faddish boom in nostalgia for one's hometown or home village.

gyōsei-shidō   Administrative guidance; a form of quasi-legal authority that enables ministries of the national government to impose their views on societal interests and entities in the private sector.

hakuchū   Parity, equality; refers to the near parity of the LDP and opposition parties and coalitions in parliament during the late 1970s.

Heisei period   Era of the reign of the Heisei emperor, who acceded to the throne in 1989.

higaisha ishiki   "Victim consciousness" characteristic of much Japanese thinking about the wartime and postwar experience.

ichiokunin sōchūryū   The mass mainstream of 100 million people.

ie   Household; specifically, the early modern and pre–World War II corporate stem household. The *ie* was abolished as a legal entity by the revised Civil Code of 1947.

Income Doubling Plan   Introduced in 1960 by Prime Minister Ikeda; aimed to double national income in ten years.

jimu jikan   Administrative vice minister, the highest career position in the national civil service.

jinsei gojū-nen   Fifty-year life span.

jinsei hachijū-nen   Eighty-year life span.

jishu kanri   Self-management.

jōhō shakai   Information society.

josei wa katei ni   Women's place is in the home.

ka-chō   Section chief, the first significant administrative appointment for civil servants aspiring to *jimu jikan* status; in private corporations, usually the first nonunion, managerial position.

kaku kazoku   The nuclear family.

kanri shakai   Managed society.

katei   Home, household.

kazoku   Family.

Keizai Dōyūkai   A postwar business association of relatively younger, reform-oriented managers.

Kokumin Yūsei Hō   Pre–World War II National Eugenic Law.

kokusaika   Internationalization.

kōreika shakai   Aging society.

kyōiku-mama   Education mother; a mother who exerts considerable energy in educating her child.

kyoku-chō   Bureau chief, the position immediately under *jimu jikan.*

mai-hōmu   "My home"; phrase referring to focus on home and nuclear family as source of value that gained currency during the 1960s.

manga   Comic books.

manshon   Condominium.

masu komi   Mass communications.

masu mejia   Mass media.

Meiji period   Era of the reign of the Meiji emperor, 1868–1912.

Miike   Mitsui Mining Company's principal coal mine in southern Japan; site of a major strike in 1959–60.

mimaikin   Payment as expression of apology, often given to avoid legal action.

Minamata disease   Methyl mercury poisoning caused by industrial wastes released into Minamata Bay by the Chisso Company in the 1950s and 1960s; Japan's first major round of environmental protest was organized in defense of Minamata victims.

minikomi   "Miniature communication"; network of feminist publications and communications developed in the 1960s and 1970s.

mōretsu shain   Workaholic company men.

NHK   Nippon Hōsō Kyōkai (Japan Broadcasting Company); Japan's public broadcasting network.

Nihonjinron   Analyses focused on the uniqueness of the Japanese.

Nikkeiren   Japan Federation of Employers' Associations; business federation with a major focus on labor issues.

Nōkyō   National Association of Agricultural Cooperatives.

nosutarujia   Nostalgia.

raifu kōsu   Life course.

raifu saikuru   Life cycle.

Rengō   Abbreviated title of the National Federation of Labor Unions, established in 1987 as a federation of private-sector unions and expanded in 1989 to include public-sector unions.

ryōsai kenbo   Good wife, wise mother.

Sanbetsu Kaigi   Most radical union federation of 1946–50 era.

Sangyō Hōkokukai   Industrial Patriotic Service Association; wartime labor front organized by the government to mobilize labor for the war.

Sangyō Rōdō Konwakai (Sanrōkon)   Industry and Labor Conference; forum for tripartite (government, business, labor) consultation on wages, founded in 1970.

sansedai kazoku   The three-generation family.

sararīman   Salaried employee of large organization, seen to typify male life-style of postwar middle class.

seppuku   Ritual suicide by samurai warrior; also called *harakiri*.

shimin undō   Citizens' movements.

shin chūkansō shakai   New middle-stratum society.

shin chūkan taishū   New middle class.

shin chūkan taishū shakai   New middle-mass society.

shinjinrui   Literally "alien"; new species or new breed; refers to youth of the late 1980s and 1990s.

shishi   Antiforeign, pro-emperor radical samurai active during the 1860s.

shōchū   Inexpensive traditional wine distilled from potatoes.

shōhi bunka ron   Debates about consumer culture.

shokugyō fujin   Term for working woman that first gained currency in the 1920s.

shōshū   Micromasses.

Shōwa hitoketa   Generation born in the single-digit years of Shōwa (1926–34).

Shōwa period   Era of the reign of the Shōwa emperor, 1926–89.

shufu   Mistress of the house, housewife.

shufu ronsō   "Housewife debate"; controversy of the 1950s on the proper role of women in contemporary society.

shūkanshi   Weekly magazine.

shuntō   Spring labor offensive; a pattern of coordinated wage bargaining by union federations that began in the late 1950s.

shutaisei   Subject, self; key concept for postwar intellectual debate over democracy and individual in Japanese society.

Sōdōmei   General Federation of Labor; largest labor union federation of the prewar era and one element of the "conservative" or "moderate" stream of postwar unionism in the 1940s and 1950s.

Sōhyō   General Council of Trade Unions of Japan; founded 1951 and dissolved in 1989 with formation of the new Rengō federation.

Sōka Gakkai   Largest of the new religions of the postwar era.

Taishō democracy   The era of the late 1910s and 1920s, when democratic institutions and practices reached their zenith in prewar Japan.

Taishō period   Era of the reign of the Taishō emperor, 1912–26.

taishū bunka   Popular culture; occasionally, mass culture.

taishū engeki   Itinerant theatrical performances of the early postwar era.

taishū shakai   Mass society, popular society.

Yūsei Hogo Hō   Eugenic Protection Law of 1948.

Zenrō Kaigi   Union federation founded in 1954, with Sōdōmei support, in opposition to Sōhyō.

CONTRIBUTORS

Gary D. Allinson is the Weedon Professor of Japanese History at the University of Virginia. He is the author of *Japanese Urbanism: Industry and Politics in Kariya, 1872–1972* (1975) and *Suburban Tokyo: A Comparative Study in Political and Social Change* (1979). His latest work, *Political Dynamics in Contemporary Japan* (forthcoming), is an SSRC conference volume, co-edited with Yasunori Sone.

Sandra Buckley is an associate professor in the East Asian studies department at McGill University. Her research interests include postmodernism and contemporary Japanese literature, as well as women in contemporary Japan.

Bruce Cumings is a professor of East Asian and international history at the University of Chicago. He is the author of a two-volume study, *The Origins of the Korean War* (1981, 1990). His current research focuses on the emergence of industrial East Asia during the twentieth century.

John W. Dower is Henry Luce Professor of International Cooperation and Global Stability at the Massachusetts Institute of Technology. His publications include *Empire and Aftermath: Yoshida Shigeru and the Japanese Experience, 1878–1954* (1979) and *War Without Mercy: Race and Power in the Pacific War* (1986). His current research addresses the reconstruction of society and the state in Japan in the wake of World War II.

Sheldon Garon is an associate professor of history at Princeton University. He is the author of *State and Labor in Modern Japan* (1986) and is completing a study of social management in twentieth-century Japan.

Carol Gluck is George Sansom Professor of History at Columbia University. She is the author of *Japan's Modern Myths: Ideology in the Late Meiji Period*, co-editor of *Showa: The Japan of Hirohito*, and is completing a study of twentieth-century Japanese views of modern Japanese history.

Andrew Gordon is a professor of history at Duke University. He is the author of *The Evolution of Labor Relations in Japan* (1985) and *Labor and Imperial Democracy in Prewar Japan* (1991). He is now studying the transformation of labor-management relations in Japan from the 1950s to the 1970s.

Laura E. Hein is an associate professor of history at Northwestern University. She is the author of *Fueling Growth* (1990), a study of energy policy and politics in postwar Japan. Her current research focuses on the social and political context of high-speed economic growth in the 1950s and 1960s.

Charles Yuji Horioka is an associate professor of economics in the Institute of Social and Economic Research, Osaka University. He has published articles on savings, consumption, and housing demand behavior in Japan. He is the author of *Household Saving in Japan: The Importance of Saving for Specific Motives* (forthcoming).

Marilyn Ivy is an assistant professor of anthropology at the University of Washington. Her publications include "Critical Texts, Mass Artifacts: The Consumption of Knowledge in Postmodern Japan" and "Tradition and Difference in the Japanese Media." She is currently completing a book titled *Discourses of the Vanishing: Loss, Phantasm, and the Japanese National-Cultural Imaginary.*

William W. Kelly is a professor of anthropology at Yale University. He is the author of *Deference and Defiance in Nineteenth Century Japan* (1985), a study of popular protest, and of recent articles on contemporary regional society. Topics of current research include Edo firefighting and Japanese professional baseball.

J. Victor Koschmann is an associate professor of history at Cornell University. He is the author of *Mito Ideology: Discourse, Reform, and Insurrection in Late Tokugawa Japan, 1790–1864* (1987) and is completing a book on theories of political subjectivity and the politics of democratic revolution in post–World War II Japan. He is currently involved in a nascent collaborative effort that looks comparatively at Japanese, European, and other fascisms.

Mike Mochizuki is an associate professor of political science and international relations at the University of Southern California. He has written articles on Japanese defense policy and is completing a book titled *Ruling Japan*, a study of the Liberal Democratic Party and postwar Japanese politics.

Koji Taira holds joint appointments as professor in the Department of Economics and the Institute of Labor and Industrial Relations at the University of Illinois. His publications include *Economic Development and the Labor Market in Japan* (1970), *An Outline of Japanese Economic History* (with Sumiya Mikio, 1979), and *Labor Markets: Readings* (in Japanese, 1990). His current research concerns international labor migration, Japan's role in the post–Cold War world order, and Ryukyuan (Loochooan) studies.

Kathleen S. Uno is an assistant professor of history at Temple University. She has published articles on changes in the household division of labor, on children in modern and contemporary Japan, and on work and domestic life of urban lower-class women in the early twentieth century. She is completing *Motherhood, Childhood and the State in Early Twentieth-Century Japan* and researching a new work on the history of Japanese children.

Frank K. Upham is a professor at Boston College Law School. He is the author of *Law and Social Change in Postwar Japan* (1987). He has recently written articles on the Large Scale Retail Stores Law in Japan and is engaged in comparative study of retail regulation in France, Japan, and the United States. He is also interested in changing visions of justice in Japan over the last two centuries.

James W. White is a professor of political science at the University of North Carolina, Chapel Hill. He is the author of *The Soka Gakkai and Mass Society* (1970) and *Migration in Metropolitan Japan* (1982). His current research focuses on peasant protest in Tokugawa Japan.

SELECTED BIBLIOGRAPHY

Adorno, Theodor. "Culture Industry Reconsidered." *New German Critique*, no. 6 (Fall 1975): 12–29.

Allen, G. C. *Short Economic History of Japan*. London: Allen and Unwin, 1972.

Allinson, Gary D. "Japan's Keidanren and Its New Leadership." *Pacific Affairs* 60, no. 3 (Fall 1987): 385–407.

———. "Politics in Contemporary Japan: Pluralist Scholarship in the Conservative Era—A Review Article." *Journal of Asian Studies* 48, no. 2 (May 1989): 324–32.

Anderson, Joseph L., and Donald Richie. *The Japanese Film: Art and Industry*. Princeton: Princeton University Press, 1982.

Apter, David, and Nagayo Sawa. *Against the State*. Cambridge: Harvard University Press, 1984.

Bennett, John W., and Solomon B. Levine. "Industrialization and Social Deprivation: Welfare, Environment, and Post-Industrial Society in Japan." In *Japanese Industrialization and Its Social Consequences*, edited by Hugh Patrick, 439–92. Berkeley and Los Angeles: University of California Press, 1976.

Bernstein, Gail Lee. *Haruko's World*. Stanford: Stanford University Press, 1983.

Bestor, Theodore C. *Neighborhood Tokyo*. Stanford: Stanford University Press, 1989.

Blum, Robert M. *Drawing the Line: The Origin of the American Containment Policy in East Asia*. New York: Norton, 1982.

Borden, William S. *The Pacific Alliance: United States Foreign Economic Policy and Japanese Trade Recovery, 1947–1955*. Madison: University of Wisconsin Press, 1984.

Bronfenbrenner, Martin, and Yasukichi Yasuba. "Economic Welfare." In *The Domestic Transformation*, edited by Kozo Yamamura and Yasukichi Yasuba, 93–136. Vol. 1 of *The Political Economy of Japan*. Stanford: Stanford University Press, 1987.

Buckley, Sandra, and Vera Mackie. "Women and the New Japanese State." In *Democracy in Contemporary Japan*, edited by Gavan McCormack and Yoshio Sugimoto, 173–85. Armonk, N.Y.: M. E. Sharpe, 1986.

Calder, Kent. *Crisis and Compensation: Public Policy and Political Stability in Japan*. Princeton: Princeton University Press, 1988.

Cohen, Theodore. *Remaking Japan: The American Occupation as New Deal.* New York: Free Press, 1987.

Cole, Robert. *Japanese Blue Collar.* Berkeley and Los Angeles: University of California Press, 1971.

Cusumano, Mike. *The Japanese Automobile Industry.* Cambridge: Harvard Council on East Asian Studies, 1985.

Dohse, Knuth, Ulrich Jurgens, and Thoman Malsch. "From 'Fordism' to 'Toyotism'? The Social Organization of the Labor Process in the Japanese Automobile Industry." *Politics and Society* 14, no. 2 (1985): 115–46.

Dore, Ronald P. *British Factory–Japanese Factory: The Origins of National Diversity in Industrial Relations.* Berkeley and Los Angeles: University of California Press, 1973.

———. *Shinohata: Protrait of a Japanese Village.* New York: Pantheon, 1978.

———. *Structural Adjustment in Japan, 1970–1982.* Geneva: International Labor Office, 1986.

Dower, John W. *Empire and Aftermath: Yoshida Shigeru and the Japanese Experience, 1878–1954.* Cambridge: Harvard University Council on East Asian Studies, 1979.

Friedman, David. *The Misunderstood Miracle: Industrial Development and Political Change in Japan.* Ithaca: Cornell University Press, 1988.

Fujioka, Wake. *Women's Movements in Postwar Japan.* Honolulu: East-West Center, 1968.

Fukui, Haruhiro. *Party in Power: The Japanese Liberal-Democrats and Policy-Making.* Berkeley and Los Angeles: University of California Press, 1970.

Garon, Sheldon. *The State and Labor in Modern Japan.* Berkeley and Los Angeles: University of California Press, 1987.

Gleason, Alan H. "The Level of Living in Japan and the United States: A Long-Term International Comparison." *Economic Development and Cultural Change* 37, no. 2 (Jan. 1989): 261–84.

Gordon, Andrew. *The Evolution of Labor Relations in Japan: Heavy Industry, 1853–1955.* Cambridge: Harvard Council on East Asian Studies, 1985.

Halberstam, David. *The Reckoning.* New York: William Morrow, 1986.

Haley, John. "Myth of the Reluctant Litigant." *Journal of Japanese Studies* 4 (1978): 359–90.

Havens, Thomas R. H. *Fire Across the Sea: The Vietnam War and Japan, 1965–1975.* Princeton: Princeton University Press, 1987.

Hayashi, Fumio. "Why Is Japan's Saving Rate So Apparently High?" In *NBER Macroeconomics Annual,* edited by Stanley Fischer, vol. 1, 147–210. Cambridge: MIT Press, 1986.

Hayes, Peter. *American Lake: Militarization and the Nuclear Peril in the Pacific.* London: Zed Books, 1985.

Hein, Laura. *Fueling Growth: The Energy Revolution and Economic Policy in Postwar Japan.* Cambridge: Harvard Council on East Asian Studies Publications, 1990.

Hidaka, Rokurō. *The Price of Affluence: Dilemmas of Contemporary Japan.* New York: Kodansha International, 1984.

Horioka, Charles. "Why Is Japan's Household Savings Rate So High?" *Journal of the Japanese and International Economies* 4, no. 1 (Mar. 1990): 49–92.

Huddle, Norrie, and Michael Reich. *Island of Dreams: Environmental Crisis in Japan.* 2d ed. Cambridge, Mass.: Schenkman Books, 1987.

Imamura, Anne. *Urban Japanese Housewives.* Honolulu: University of Hawaii Press, 1987.

The Industrial Policy of Japan. Paris: Organization for Economic Development, 1972.

Ishida, Takeshi, and Ellis Krauss, eds. *Democracy in Japan*. Pittsburgh: University of Pittsburgh Press, 1989.

Ito, Masami. *Broadcasting in Japan*. London: Routledge and Kegan Paul, 1978.

Johnson, Chalmers. *MITI and the Japanese Miracle: The Growth of Industrial Policy, 1925–1975*. Stanford: Stanford University Press, 1982.

Kasza, Gregory J. *The State and Mass Media in Japan, 1918–1945*. Berkeley and Los Angeles: University of California Press, 1988.

Kawai, Kazuo. *Japan's American Interlude*. Chicago: University of Chicago Press, 1960.

Kenney, Martin, and Richard Florida. "Beyond Mass Production." *Politics and Society* 16, no. 1 (1988): 121–58.

Kogawa, Tetsuo. "New Trends in Japanese Popular Culture." In *The Japanese Trajectory: Modernization and Beyond*, edited by Gavan McCormack and Yoshio Sugimoto, 54–66. Cambridge: Cambridge University Press, 1988.

Koh, B. C. *Japan's Administrative Elite*. Berkeley and Los Angeles: University of California Press, 1989.

Kondo, Dorinne K. *Crafting Selves: Power, Gender, and Discourses of Identity in a Japanese Workplace*. Chicago: University of Chicago Press, 1990.

Kosai, Yutaka. *The Era of High-Speed Growth: Notes on the Postwar Japanese Economy*. Tokyo: Tokyo University Press, 1986.

Koschmann, J. Victor. *Authority and the Individual in Japan: Citizen Protest in Historical Perspective*. Tokyo: University of Tokyo Press, 1978.

———. "The Debate on Subjectivity in Postwar Japan: Foundations of Modernism as a Political Critique." *Pacific Affairs* 54, no. 4 (Winter 1981–82): 609–31.

Kubota, Akira. *Higher Civil Servants in Postwar Japan*. Princeton: Princeton University Press, 1969.

Kusaka, Kimindo. "What Is the Japanese Middle Class?" *Japan Echo* 12 (1985): 40–46.

Lebra, Takie. *Japanese Women: Constraint and Fulfillment*. Honolulu: University of Hawaii Press, 1984.

Lockwood, W. W. *The Economic Development of Japan*. Princeton: Princeton University Press, 1954.

McCormack, Gavan, and Yoshio Sugimoto, eds. *Democracy in Contemporary Japan*. Armonk, N.Y.: M. E. Sharpe, 1986.

McKean, Margaret A. *Environmental Protest and Citizen Politics in Japan*. Berkeley and Los Angeles: University of California Press, 1981.

Mackie, Vera. "Feminist Politics in Japan." *New Left Review*, no. 167 (Jan.–Feb. 1988): 53–71.

Magaziner, Ira, and Thomas M. Hout. *Japanese Industrial Policy*. London: Policy Studies Institute, 1980.

Maier, Charles. "The Politics of Productivity: Foundations of American International Economic Policy after World War II." In *Between Power and Plenty: Foreign Economic Policies of the Advanced Industrial States*, edited by Peter J. Katzenstein. Madison: University of Wisconsin Press, 1978.

Maruyama, Masao. *Thought and Behavior in Modern Japanese Politics*. Edited by Ivan Morris. Expanded ed. London: Oxford University Press, 1969.

Masumi, Junnosuke. *Postwar Politics in Japan, 1945–1955*. Vol. 6 of *Japanese Research Monographs*. Berkeley: Institute of East Asian Studies, University of California, 1985.

Matsui, Yayori. "Protest and the Japanese Woman." *Japan Quarterly* 22, no. 1 (Jan.–Mar. 1975): 32–39.

Minami, Ryoshin. *The Economic Development of Japan: A Quantitative Study.* New York: St. Martin's, 1986.

Miyoshi, Masao, and Harry Harootunian, eds. *Postmodernism and Japan.* Durham: Duke University Press, 1989.

Moore, Joe. *Japanese Workers and the Struggle for Power, 1945–1947.* Madison: University of Wisconsin Press, 1983.

Morris-Suzuki, Tessa. *Beyond Computopia: Information, Automation, and Democracy in Japan.* London and New York: Kegan Paul International, 1988.

Murakami Yasusuke. "The Age of New Middle Mass Politics: The Case of Japan." *Journal of Japanese Studies* 8, no. 1 (1982): 29–72.

Muramatsu, Michio, and Ellis Krauss. "Bureaucrats and Politicians in Policymaking: The Case of Japan." *American Political Science Review* 78, no. 1 (Mar. 1984): 126–46.

Nakamura Takafusa. *The Postwar Japanese Economy: Its Development and Structure.* Tokyo: Tokyo University Press, 1981.

Nathan, John. *Mishima: A Biography.* Boston: Little, Brown, 1974.

Nishibe, Susumu. "A Denunciation of Mass Society and Its Apologists." *Japan Echo* 13, no. 1 (1986): 39–43.

———. "Japan as a Highly Developed Mass Society: An Appraisal." *Journal of Japanese Studies* 8, no. 1 (Winter 1982): 73–96.

Ohkawa, Kazushi, and Miyohei Shinohara, eds. *Patterns of Japanese Economic Development: A Quantitative Appraisal.* New Haven: Yale University Press, 1970.

Okochi, Kazuo, Bernard Karsh, and Solomon B. Levine, eds. *Workers and Employers in Japan: The Japanese Employment Relations System.* Princeton and Tokyo: Princeton University Press and Tokyo University Press, 1974.

Olson, Lawrence. "Intellectuals and 'The People': On Yoshimoto Takaaki." *Journal of Japanese Studies* 4, no. 2 (Summer 1978): 327–57.

Ozawa, Masako. "Consumption in the Age of Stratification." *Japan Echo* 12 (1985): 47–53.

Packard, George R. *Protest in Tokyo: The Security Treaty Crisis of 1960.* Princeton: Princeton University Press, 1966.

Papers Presented at the Fourth International Cultural Conference: Thirty-three Years of Postwar Japan. Fukuoka: Fukuoka UNESCO Association, 1978.

Patrick, Hugh T., ed. *Japanese Industrialization and Its Social Consequences.* Berkeley and Los Angeles: University of California Press, 1976.

Patrick, Hugh T., and Thomas P. Rohlen. "Small-Scale Family Enterprises." In *The Domestic Transformation,* edited by Kozo Yamamura and Yasukichi Yasuba, 331–84. Vol. 1 of *The Political Economy of Japan.* Stanford: Stanford University Press, 1987.

Patrick, Hugh T., and Henry Rosovsky. "The Japanese Economy in Transition." In *Economic Policy and Development: New Perspectives,* edited by Toshio Shishido and Ryuzo Sato, 159–70. Dover, Mass., and London: Auburn House, 1985.

———, eds. *Asia's New Giant.* Washington, D.C.: Brookings Institute, 1976.

Pempel, T. J. *Policy and Politics in Japan: Creative Conservatism.* Philadelphia: Temple University Press, 1982.

———. "The Unbundling of Japan, Inc.: The Changing Dynamics of Japanese Policy Formation." In *The Trade Crisis: How Will Japan Respond?* edited by Kenneth B. Pyle. Seattle: University of Washington Society for Japanese Studies, 1987.

Pempel, T. J., and Tsunekawa Keiichi. "Corporatism Without Labor: The Japanese

Anomaly." In *Trends Toward Corporatist Intermediation,* edited by Phillipe C. Schmitter and Gerhard Lehmbruch, 231–70. Beverly Hills: Sage, 1979.

Plath, David. *Long Engagements: Maturity in Modern Japan.* Stanford: Stanford University Press, 1980.

———, ed. *Work and Lifecourse in Japan.* Albany: SUNY Press, 1983.

Pyle, Kenneth B. "The Future of Japanese Nationality: An Essay in Contemporary History." *Journal of Japanese Studies* 8, no. 2 (Summer 1982): 223–63.

———. "Japan, the World, and the Twenty-first Century." In *The Changing International Context,* edited by Takashi Inoguchi and Daniel I. Okimoto, 446–86. Vol. 2 of *The Political Economy of Japan.* Stanford: Stanford University Press, 1988.

Robins-Mowry, Dorothy. *The Hidden Sun: Women in Modern Japan.* Boulder: Westview Press, 1983.

Rohlen, Thomas. *Japan's High Schools.* Berkeley and Los Angeles: University of California Press, 1983.

Rosovsky, Henry, and Kazushi Ohkawa. "The Indigenous Components in the Modern Japanese Economy." *Economic Development and Cultural Change* 9, no. 3 (Apr. 1961): 476–501.

Rubin, Jay. "From Wholesomeness to Decadence: The Censorship of Literature under the Allied Occupation." *Journal of Japanese Studies* 11, no. 1 (Winter 1985): 71–103.

Sakamoto, Yoshikazu, ed. *Asia: Militarization and Regional Conflict.* Tokyo: United Nations University Press, 1988.

Sato, Kazuo. "Savings and Investment." In *The Domestic Transformation,* edited by Kozo Yamamura and Yasuba Yasukichi, 137–85. Vol. 1 of *The Political Economy of Japan.* Stanford: Stanford University Press, 1987.

Scalapino, Robert, ed. *The Foreign Policy of Modern Japan.* Berkeley and Los Angeles: University of California Press, 1977.

Schaller, Michael. *The American Occupation of Japan: The Origins of the Cold War in Asia.* New York: Oxford University Press, 1985.

Schonberger, Howard. *Aftermath of War: Americans and the Remaking of Japan, 1945–1952.* Kent State: Kent State University Press, 1989.

Shibusawa, Masahide. *Japan and the Asian Pacific Region.* London: Croom Helm, 1984.

Shirai, Taishiro, ed. *Contemporary Industrial Relations in Japan.* Madison: University of Wisconsin Press, 1983.

Smith, Robert J., Jr. *Japanese Society: Tradition, Self, and the Social Order.* New York: Cambridge University Press, 1983.

Steiner, Kurt, Ellis Krauss, and Scott Flanagan, eds. *Political Opposition and Local Politics in Japan.* Princeton: Princeton University Press, 1980.

Steven, Rob. *Classes in Contemporary Japan.* Cambridge: Cambridge University Press, 1983.

Sugimoto, Yoshio. *Popular Disturbance in Postwar Japan.* Hong Kong: Asian Research Service, 1981.

Takahashi, Michiko. "Working Mothers and Families." *Review of Japanese Culture and Society* 3, no. 1 (Dec. 1989): 21–30.

Tomioka, Taeko, Chizuko Ueno, Noriko Mizuta, et al. "Symposium, Women and the Family: Post-Family Alternatives." *Review of Japanese Culture and Society* 3, no. 1 (Dec. 1989): 79–96.

Tsurumi, Shunsuke. *A Cultural History of Postwar Japan.* London and New York: Kegan Paul International, 1984.

Tsurumi, Patricia, ed. *The Other Japan.* Armonk, N.Y.: M. E. Sharpe, 1988.

Uchino, Tatsuro. *Japan's Postwar Economy: An Insider's View of Its History and Its Future.* Tokyo: Kodansha International, 1983.

Ueno, Chizuko. "The Japanese Women's Movement: Counter-Values to Industrialism." In *Modernization and Beyond: The Japanese Trajectory,* edited by Gavan McCormack and Yoshio Sugimoto, 167–85. Cambridge: Cambridge University Press, 1988.

Upham, Frank. *Law and Social Change in Postwar Japan.* Cambridge: Harvard University Press, 1987.

Vogel, Ezra. *Japan's New Middle Class.* Berkeley and Los Angeles: University of California Press, 1963.

Wagatsuma, Hiroshi, and George deVos. *Japan's Invisible Race: Caste in Culture and Personality.* Berkeley and Los Angeles: University of California Press, 1966.

Weinstein, Martin E. *Japan's Postwar Defense Policy.* New York: Columbia University Press, 1971.

Welfield, John. *An Empire in Eclipse: Japan in the Postwar American Alliance System.* London: Athlone Press, 1988.

White, James. "Protest and Change in Contemporary Japan." In *Institutions for Change in Japanese Society,* edited by George deVos, 53–82. Berkeley: Institute of East Asian Studies, University of California, 1984.

Wolferen, Karel van. *The Enigma of Japanese Power.* New York: Knopf, 1989.

Yamamura, Kozo, and Yasukichi Yasuba, eds. *The Domestic Transformation.* Vol. 1 of *The Political Economy of Japan.* Stanford: Stanford University Press, 1987.

Yanaga, Chitoshi. *Big Business in Japanese Politics.* New Haven: Yale University Press, 1968.

INDEX

Compositor:	ComCom
Text:	10/12 Baskerville
Display:	Baskerville
Printer:	Haddon Craftsmen, Inc.
Binder:	Haddon Craftsmen, Inc.